CALIFORNIA
IN-LINE
SKATING

by Liz Miller

Foghorn
Press
BOOKS BUILDING COMMUNITY™

ISBN 0-935701-09-5

51995

9 780935 701098

Publishing Manager
Foghorn Press
555 DeHaro Street, Suite 220
San Francisco, CA 94107

To order individual books, please call Foghorn Press:
1-800-FOGHORN (364-4676) or (415) 241-9550.

Foghorn Press titles are distributed to the book trade by Publishers Group West, based in Emeryville, California. To contact your local sales representative, call 1-800-788-3123.

No liability is assumed with respect to the information or content of this book. No one should participate in the activities described in this book unless they recognize and personally assume the associated risks.

Library of Congress ISSN Data:
June 1996
California In-Line Skating
The Complete Guide to the Best Places to Skate
First Edition
ISSN: 1088-2596

The Color of Commitment

Foghorn Press has always been committed to printing on recycled paper, but up to now, we hadn't taken the final plunge to use 100 percent recycled paper because we were unconvinced of its quality. And until now, those concerns were valid. But the good news is that quality recycled paper is now available. We are thrilled to announce that Foghorn Press books are printed with Soya-based inks on 100 percent recycled paper, which has a 50 percent post-consumer waste content. The only way you'd know we made this change is by looking at the hue of the paper—a small price to pay for environmental integrity. You may even like the color better. We do. And we know the earth does, too.

Printed in the United States of America

Dear Skaters:

The skating tours listed in these pages were carefully researched by expert in-line skater Liz Miller. Every effort was made to be as up-to-date as possible, but, inevitably, things change, especially in one of the fastest-growing sports of the decade. Trailside scenery evolves with the seasons (not to mention with the weather and time of day), paved surfaces erode or are improved, skate shops open and close, city governments decide to curtail skating in crowded areas, neighborhoods alter in character, hangouts start drawing a different crowd—and, happily, new skating paths and in-line clubs continue to crop up.

We hope your experiences on the trails featured in this book are the best each area has to offer. If you discover any information that would be useful for updating the next edition of California In-Line Skating, *please write to the Publishing Manager, Foghorn Press, 555 DeHaro Street, Suite 220, San Francisco, CA 94107.*

—The Editors

Table of Contents

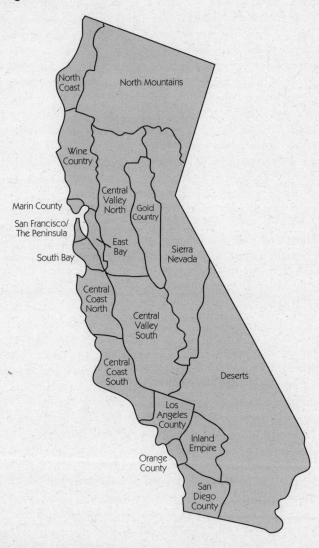

Introduction

A generation ago, Joni Mitchell lamented in song that "they paved paradise and put up a parking lot." How times do change! To the millions of Californians who've discovered in-line skating, this state—with its acres of pavement and celebrated year-round mild climate—is a paradise in itself.

In nearly every community around the state, smooth surfaces suitable for learning to skate, practicing new tricks, or playing roller hockey are conveniently located just a short roll from home. And for skaters who want to explore different routes, meet new people, find the coolest scenes, and train for fitness, speed, or distance, the California boardwalks, bikeways, and river trails can't be beat.

I discovered this for myself not long after that spring day in 1991 when I brought home my first pair of skates and began tottering around the neighborhood. Within minutes, several things became clear: in-line skating is easier than you'd think (in fact, you're gliding along within minutes of those first tentative strokes); it's gentle on the joints, yet also invigorating—even aerobic; and most of all, it feels great, capturing (as few sports do) the pure joy of movement. Like dancing, in-line skating is instinctive and almost effortless, with the capacity to make you feel like a kid again, laughing and excited and eager for more.

Little did I know where such feelings would lead me. A year later, for instance, I quit a very secure job (during a recession) to strike out on my own as an in-line instructor and author of books on the sport. As my agility on skates grew, so did the popularity of in-line skating—metamorphosing from a youth-oriented fad into such myriad subspecialties as hockey, freestyle, downhill, speed, ramp, figure, and street skating, and attracting fitness and recreational skaters of all ages. Created in the early 1980s by Minneapolis hockey players as a way to cross-train on dry land, this sport now attracts hordes of nonathletes who see it as a great way to get exercise and also have fun. In the past three years, the new cuff-activated braking technologies have made the all-important art of stopping both easier and safer, drawing still more devotees. And the trend toward aggressive ramp and street skating has brought a wealth of specialized products and more skating clubs and events than ever before.

California In-Line Skating is your complete guide to finding the most skatable destinations in the state. There are 300 tours to choose from, covering more than 1,140 miles in 18 regions. You'll also find detailed, step-by-step pointers on basic and not-so-basic skating moves; advice on safety, fitness, and skate purchase and maintenance; a glossary of basic skater lingo; and extensive lists of skate shops, rinks, and parks, and local and national clubs. An easy-to-use map system also lets you find a great skate anywhere in the state in less than 10 seconds.

Each tour listing features ratings for scenic beauty, recommended skill level, pavement quality, approximate total mileage, and the kind of skating you're apt to find (i.e., touring, beginners' practice, speed, hockey, fitness training, figure skating or stunts, slaloming, or road skating). Also included are clear directions to the starting point, parking tips, sources for detailed maps of the areas, and the address of the nearest skate shop. Of course, there's also a detailed description of each trip.

Whether you're looking for a workout, downhill thrills, or a relaxed cruise with friends, the ultimate in-line opportunities are all here. But watch out: your life, too, may change irrevocably for the better once you're on wheels. Happy skating!

—Liz Miller

How to Use This Book

You can search for the perfect place to in-line skate in two ways:

1) If you know the name of the tour you'd like to skate or the name of the area or city, look it up in the index beginning on page 450 and turn to the corresponding page.

2) This book is conveniently divided into 18 regions. Find the area you'd like to skate in by checking the California map on page 5 or on the last page of this book. Once you've picked your region (say, San Francisco or the southern Central Coast near San Luis Obispo), look it up in the table of contents. Detailed maps of each region can be found within the skating tour chapters in part two, Great Places to Skate.

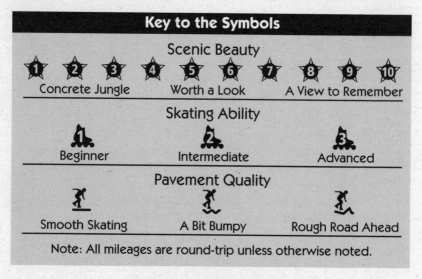

Key to the Symbols

Scenic Beauty

① ② ③ ④ ⑤ ⑥ ⑦ ⑧ ⑨ ⑩

Concrete Jungle   Worth a Look   A View to Remember

Skating Ability

Beginner   Intermediate   Advanced

Pavement Quality

Smooth Skating   A Bit Bumpy   Rough Road Ahead

Note: All mileages are round-trip unless otherwise noted.

What the Ratings Mean

Scenic Beauty

⑩ Each skating tour in this book is designated with a Scenic Beauty rating of 1 through 10. A path that passes through gorgeous natural scenery would rate a 10 whether it's in a national park, a suburban neighborhood, or a city park downtown. A trail that runs through industrial areas or by a concrete culvert might rate only a 3, but it's listed for its other assets, such as length for distance training.

Skating Ability

The ability rating ranges from Level 1 (for beginners) to Level 3 (for advanced), and is based on such conditions as trail width, steepness of inclines, pavement irregularities or stairs, and proximity to passing cars.

When a skating tour has places suited for different levels, the ability rating reflects the highest skill level required. Here are the specific skills each level requires:

Level 1 Basic stroking, large-radius turns, standing in place, and a minimum ability to stop;

Level 2 All of the above, plus swerve, stop within 15 feet at 8 mph, step or jump on or off curbs, negotiate minor obstacles and raised edges or tree roots, and skate across wood-slat bridges;

Level 3 All of the above, plus negotiate rough pavement and stairs, skate next to cars on back roads or in bike lanes, skate up long grades, control speed going downhill, and stop and swerve at high speed.

See the skating instructions in part one, How to Get Rolling, for detailed pointers on mastering these skills.

Pavement Quality

Pavement quality can make a huge difference in the desirability of a particular path—the most preferable being a smooth (not slick) surface unbroken by raised edges or cracks. That quality can deteriorate over time. The more sun and water a stretch of asphalt is exposed to, the more it's apt to have rough patches, which can cause unsettling vibrations. Note: If a trail contains a combination of surfaces, its rating reflects the most predominant type.

Contains smooth surfaces, such as concrete in good repair or fine-grade asphalt.

Contains acceptable surfaces, such as most asphalt trails and some newly paved streets.

Contains rough or rocky surfaces, with cracks or raised slabs caused by tree roots or shifting earth.

Ideal For

In-lining attracts people with a vast variety of interests and skills; there are almost as many forms of skating as there are skaters. So, although the routes described in this book are primarily for touring, the "Ideal for" rating shows what *other* activities they're particularly conducive to, from slaloming to socializing. Here's a rundown:

Beginners Flat, smooth terrain with no cars (can be crowded with rookie skaters on weekends);

Figure/Stunts Large, flat, smoothly paved pads or parking lots (may be used by cars during business hours);

Fitness Longer routes with varied terrain, intersections, and hills;

Hills/Slalom Hills and thrills—bring your rubber-tipped ski poles;

Historic A historically rich area, so plan to slow down and take in the sights;

In-Line Hockey Rink-sized pavement, used regularly by local enthusiasts with sticks and pucks;

Road/Street Routes that require you to skate near automobile traffic, without the benefit of dedicated bike lanes;

Scene A hot spot where skaters congregate to socialize and show off;

Speed Long, fairly flat, uncrowded paths with few intersections;

Touring A great spot for sightseeing at a casual pace.

About Tour Names and Distances

Each skating tour listed has been given a reference number, a name, and the approximate total round-trip mileage. The reference number helps you find it easily on the chapter map; the name of the tour is either the same one listed on local maps or one assigned to reflect its unique traits and layout. Skating times for each tour will vary widely, depending on such factors as route traffic and each skater's abilities and preferred pace.

Get Your Bearings: Where to Find Good Maps

Any detailed city map will help you find your way to the routes described in this book. Particularly handy for in-liners is the California edition of the Thomas Guide map series, available at bookstores, supermarkets, discount warehouses, and map stores around the state.

If you're a member of the California State Automobile Association (CSAA), you can pick up free local and regional maps at the local CSAA office in most towns (or in your own town before you hit the road). Look in the phone book under California State Automobile Association.

Occasionally, a local transportation department or chamber of commerce offers a map showing commuter bike paths. When such maps are available, details on how to obtain them are given in the tour descriptions.

Learning the Basics

Obviously, skaters of all levels should be able to stop and control their speed going downhill. Please take the time to read the Stopping and Speed Control pointers in part one, How to Get Rolling, starting on page 27, which offers crucial tips for making effective use of the in-line heel brake. If you're new to in-line skating, that part of the book will tell you all about getting started, from buying your first skates to conquering your fear of falling to fundamental skating techniques. In addition, a glossary on page 52 defines common in-line lingo and terms. On pages 34 through 45, experienced skaters will find instructions for mastering the more advanced Level 2 and 3 skills cited in this book, so you can tackle the more challenging tours.

Part One
How to Get Rolling

California is a skater's paradise, thanks to the dry pavement and perfect weather that can be found somewhere in the state on just about any day of the year. Although in-line skating is often considered a summer sport (even locals tend to put aside their skates in the wet months), some inland areas can actually get too hot for comfortable cruising; in those regions, winter and spring are the best skating seasons. To skate in colder months (barring ice or snow on the trails), just add an extra layer or two of clothing, wear some thin knit gloves under your wrist guards, and you're on your way. Just like cross-country skiing, you warm up pretty quickly once you get going.

November's rains usher in California's spectacular green season. By December, the brown grasses of late summer give way to lush green hills. As February nears, the bright-yellow mustard blossoms appear, gilding the rolling hills and forming a dappled carpet around the bare-limbed orchards and vineyards across the state. In March the fruit trees blossom, and fields of lavender lupine and orange California poppy burst into bloom. This is prime time for touring the inland areas—before the valley fog and scorching midday heat arrive in late spring and summer.

September's Indian summer brings the balmiest skating weather in the northern coastal areas, from San Francisco to the Oregon border. At the world-famous Southern California beach boardwalks, the climate is ideal pretty much year-round, with cool ocean breezes blowing away the smog, though you may encounter some morning fog in the summer months.

Good Manners: A Code of Skating Behavior

Every year, this popular sport attracts millions of new participants, with hordes of skaters (along with pedestrians and cyclists) filling the most popular boardwalks and bikeways on sunny days. In fact, congestion has become such a problem in some places that city governments have imposed speed limits or banned skating altogether.

You can prevent such restrictions by trying to make sure they're not needed. Learn to stop and maneuver safely in crowds, follow the posted regulations and limits, and skate with utmost courtesy, especially near pedestrians. If you like to skate fast, save it for early-morning or working hours or less-crowded locations.

Better yet, strive to improve your skills each time you skate. Use the lessons in this book to learn the downhill and street-skating techniques that are your passport to all the paved paradise this state has to offer. Then you can don that protective gear, put on the skates, and follow your in-line instincts and inclinations wherever they want to go.

Getting in Gear: Picking Out Skates and Equipment

Pick your skate store carefully, and it could be the start of a long and beneficial relationship. A shop's special services may prove more important than its price tags. Find out if a skate purchase includes free maintenance or discounts on replacement parts. Ask about lessons, clubs, race programs, hockey teams, or the location of local ramps. Check the stock of skating accessories, videos, and books.

A good skate store will have staff who help you get the best boot fit, educate you about safety and gear, and explain the differences among skate models and replacement wheels and bearings. If the skate you want is not in stock or not part of the standard inventory, some shops will special-order them.

Ask if any manufacturers are scheduled to visit locally with their demo van. Often, company representatives show up at in-line events to offer free coaching and supervised use of high-quality skates. It's a terrific learning opportunity for you as well as a promo opportunity for them.

Start By Renting

Anyone unsure if in-line skating is for him or her should rent a pair first. In most major metropolitan areas, rentals are available at specialty skate shops, listed under "Skating" in the yellow pages. In smaller towns or outlying areas, you may have to try outdoor outfitters; skateboard, ski, surf, sailboat, and bike shops; or major sporting-goods stores.

Once you're rolling, it may take an hour or so before any feature of a skate boot starts to bother you. So it's smart to try different models if you can, either on the same day or over several days.

If you like the feel of skating and you've found a rental pair that's comfortable and fits your needs and price range, you're ready to shop for your own pair. And if you don't mind starting with used skates, ask when the rental line will go on sale. Some great deals can be found in the rental bins.

Skate Shopping

First-time buyers usually have no idea how to pick a skate that meets their needs. Too often, their main priority is to spend as little money as possible, in case they don't master the skating skills or their child outgrows the merchandise too soon. Seeking a good deal is the American way, but choosing cost over quality leads to a very disappointing introduction to this sport. Low-end skates are often built of low-quality materials, resulting in insufficient ankle support, less stability, vibrations, and—most dangerous of all—broken buckles or detached wheels.

Unlike higher-quality skates, cheaper models often can't be upgraded with new brakes, better wheels, or faster bearings. Their unwitting new owners, discouraged when they just can't seem to keep up with other skaters or get the hang of the basics, think it's their own lack of skill that's the problem and are tempted to give up. Those who persevere end up spending more money on upgrades (where possible) or, finally, on new, better-quality skates. And children—who usually take to in-line skating almost effortlessly—are likely to wear out a skate's useful life long before they outgrow its size.

Here are some practical tips for purchasing in-line skates for yourself or for kids:

- In-line skates are not toys and should not be purchased at a toy store. Go to a sporting-goods store where you can find a wider selection and qualified sales staff to answer your questions and make suggestions.
- Invest as much as you can afford. For adults, a pair of skates selling for less than $100 will cost more money than a better pair in the long run. Sometimes an extra $10 can make a difference in whether or not you will be able to upgrade a skate's components.
- Set aside enough cash for all the protective gear: helmet, wrist guards, knee and elbow pads. These are usually required if you plan to take lessons, and they're essential both for the safety and the confidence they provide. Pros need 'em, too: when your skills increase, so do the stakes for injury as you progress to faster, more aggressive skating.
- First-timers, especially, need a skate with superior ankle support. Look for a high, molded-plastic cuff and at least one buckle at the top. Skip the laces-only skates, which loosen up and lead to wobbly ankles.
- Check with sales staff to make sure replacement wheels and brakes are available for the skate you choose. If you skate regularly, you'll need to replace the brake two to three times annually and the wheels once or twice a year.
- Try before you buy. If possible, rent first; often, the rental fee can be applied toward purchase. Never buy skates for someone else without the person trying them on; consider a gift certificate instead. The fit should be very snug, but without pressure points.
- Start with three- or four-wheeled skates. Five-wheel models are much more expensive, more difficult to turn, and built for speed.
- The new arm-activated braking technology (such as Rollerblade, Inc.'s ABT, Bauer's Force Multiplier, the GEM brake) is a godsend for new skaters and others who just can't manage to balance on one foot while learning to stop.
- Ladies' models are available from some manufacturers. They usually compensate for the lower position of a woman's calf muscle and her narrower Achilles tendon. If the tag doesn't say Ladies, the skate is unisex. In any case, ask for help in selecting the right size.
- Shop around. Make it a point to visit a couple of skate shops or call around to compare selling prices for the skates you like. With a bit of legwork, you can make sure you're getting the best deal.
- Don't be a cheapskate! Give yourself or your child a fair chance to enjoy this great sport by choosing that first pair of skates with care.

If the Skate Fits ... A Shopper's Checklist

All feet are not created equal. Buying skates is like buying ski boots. They may seem comfortable to stand in, but an hour of vigorous activity may lead to the painful realization that the shell of that particular boot was not designed for your particular foot.

Men's, women's, and junior models are usually available in a good manufacturer's skate line. Some women may find a great fit in a small men's boot (using either the men's or women's boot liner), and men with narrow feet have been known to fit comfortably into women's skates.

When trying on skates, bring along a pair of absorbent socks you plan to skate in. Socks manufactured specifically for athletic activity are best because they are designed to "wick" the sweat away from your foot and prevent blisters.

When you are ready to stand up in a pair of skates for the first time, don't be embarrassed to ask for help if you need it. To stand, first place the skates in a V position (heels together) and hold onto something for balance. After rising, flex your knees a couple of times. Pick up one foot to test your balance. Walk (or roll, if the store has an appropriate place for this) around a bit.

Now run through the following checklist of good fit requirements. You should be satisfied in every area before you buy.

- The boot tongue is not pressing anywhere on your shin or calf.
- There is no pressure on the big and/or baby toes due to the skate's narrow fit.
- There is no crease-type pressure across the tops of the toes when you flex your knees.
- There is no specific pressure point across the top of the arch of either foot.
- The overall fit is very snug, but you can wiggle your toes.
- With straight knees, your toes lightly touch the end of the boot.
- When you bend your knees and press your shin into the tongue, your toes are not touching the end of the boot and your heel does not slide up and away from the sole.

Other nifty features:
- Look for vents in the boot and liners. Breathability slows down the buildup of perspiration as your feet heat up.
- Being lightweight makes any skate more maneuverable and less tiring over long periods. Vents help reduce the weight, too.
- Hinged cuffs improve a skate's ankle support, forward flexibility, and stability. Buckles also improve ankle support, and you will find skates with all combinations of buckles and laces. But while laces keep the fit snug enough for fast-action in-line hockey, during recreational skating they tend to loosen up. Some skaters buy Velcro power straps to add ankle support to skates with only laces.

- Some boot stiffness (determined by the type of plastic and whether laces or buckles are used) is not a bad thing; too much flexibility gives you less ankle support and control.
- Liners are replaceable. These foam-padded boot interiors allow sizing flexibility. For growing children, a slightly large boot shell can accommodate graduated liner sizes as the feet get bigger.
- Insoles provide a preformed arch support and are also replaceable. Some skaters customize the fit by inserting their own arch supports.
- Wheels come in different grades of hardness, widths, and heights. Wheel qualities are suited to the features of the skate on which they are mounted. As for quantity, wheel frames with three wheels are for smaller feet, four wheels are best for recreational, hockey, and artistic skating, and five wheels are built for stability at high speeds.

Helmets and Protective Gear

Wearing a helmet, wrist guards, and elbow and knee pads is the single most effective way to prevent in-line injuries. Of these, your helmet is the most important, because, obviously, if you break your head, it doesn't matter what happens to your wrists, elbows, or knees. (See the Safe Skating section on page 20 for other protective gear pointers.) Here are some tips to keep in mind when choosing a helmet:
- Don't bother with versions lacking the ANSI or SNELL sticker of approval. These don't meet accepted impact safety standards.
- Different competitive skating modes call for different helmet styles; for example, ramp skaters need more head coverage, while speed skaters look for a more aerodynamic shape. Decide what you want to do on your skates and then ask a salesperson for guidance.
- Choose a style of helmet that is comfy and cool. Vented models are light in weight and allow a cooling air flow.
- Shop for a close fit. If your final choice is slightly loose, make sure it comes with lots of removable inserts to customize it for your head. Some helmets have an inflatable inner fit system. To fine-tune the fit for the best protection, spend some time adjusting the chin straps. The helmet should sit snugly enough so that it doesn't shift from front to back or side to side. Adjust it to cover your forehead: it should not slip to the back of your head.
- Any skate shop should have wrist guards and elbow and knee pads for sale. They vary in price by a few dollars a pair, so it doesn't hurt to comparison-shop while you're pricing skates. Sometimes they come prepackaged as a set, but beware: the combo packs sold in many department stores often lack wrist guards.

Suiting Up: Accessories and Clothes

Some shops that sell roller or in-line skates also carry skating clothes and accessories; you can even find matching nylon covers for knee and elbow pads, helmets, and skates. In general, remember that stretchy or loose-fitting clothes are the most comfortable choice. (Jeans, however, are usually *not* comfortable for skating and will bunch up under a knee pad or over a boot.) Bike shorts and spandex tights are good for recreational skating. Baggy T-shirts and even baggier shorts are a favorite uniform among aggressive skaters because it allows them to wear heavy-duty padding underneath while practicing tricks. Speed skaters and hockey players have their own specialized outfits, too, usually available in shops where their gear and skates are sold.

A note to beginners: Don't wear your flashy new outfit until after you've skated a few times. Most skaters lose their balance once or twice during their first skate; it's all part of the learning, so plan for it. Cover up bare arms and legs at first; you can relax this standard as you get more proficient.

Dress kids in bright clothes to make them more visible. Avoid black; it gets too hot on sunny days. Buy your child a white helmet and slap a few awesome decals on it to make it more fun to wear.

On colder days, dress in layers that you can remove as you warm up. If you skate in the sun, make sure you wear sunscreen to prevent sunburn. You'll appreciate a pair of sunglasses as well.

For a longer skate, carry a fanny pack with a small bottle of water. It's surprising how dehydrated you can become; your body is still working hard while you're cooled by the breezes and absorbed in the fun.

Keep your protective gear together in a sport bag. Other items you may want to include:

- sunglasses
- sunscreen and lip balm
- water bottle
- fanny pack
- dry socks and a towel
- ski boot or skate carrier
- windbreaker
- skate maintenance tools
- a spare heel brake
- this book

Skate Maintenance

Take good care of your in-line skates, and the investment will pay dividends for years. You can prevent some wear by storing them properly and keeping them clean. It is easy to replace the brake pad. Periodically rotating your wheels and cleaning your bearings aren't quite so easy, but since these parts are relatively expensive to replace, it's a money-saving step that's worth the hassle.

After Every Skate

Preventive maintenance is as simple as properly storing your boots after each excursion. The boot liners will be warm and moist when you step out of them, and the tongue can easily dry out in an unnatural shape. To prevent that, carefully arrange the tongue in its proper position, then buckle or lace the boot closed to keep it there. Really soaked liners, however, should be removed from the boots to dry.

Periodic Maintenance

When your brake pad is worn down to about half an inch or less, you should replace it. On most skates, this is a simple matter of unscrewing it from the frame and inserting a new heel brake.

You can avoid frequent maintenance if you stay away from puddles, sand, and fine gravel. Technically, skating through some sand or water shouldn't do damage if you give your equipment immediate après-skate attention, but since we humans have a natural tendency to procrastinate, avoiding those conditions is the best protection.

No matter how cautiously you skate, however, you will eventually need to:

- Dry off the wheels and wheel frames (do this immediately after you splash through a puddle);
- Replace worn-out brakes;
- Remove dirt and grime on your wheel bearings after skating outdoors for 15 to 20 hours;
- Replace worn-out wheels (frequent slalom skating will accelerate the wear considerably); and
- Replace slow wheel bearings.

In addition, depending on which model you own, there may be other reasons to sit down with your skates and tools. If you like figure skating, for instance, or enjoy the ski-like feeling of carving short, round turns, you should check to see if your skates allow you to rocker the wheels (for instructions, see page 18). If you want more stability for long forward glides or fast cruising, investigate whether it's possible to extend the wheel base. If you race and need to keep your bearings in top shape, facilitate regular cleaning by converting your sealed bearings to unsealed; ask for pointers at your local skate shop. You can also purchase special bearings with a removable plastic shield.

Rotating the Wheels

Get yourself organized before you disassemble your skates. Make sure you have an area at least three feet by two feet wide where you can lay out a slightly damp cloth or two, your wheel wrench or wrenches, and the removed wheels and their screws.

- Take the skate with the brake and grip it upside down between your thighs, toe end facing out.

- Using the wrenches, remove all four wheels and place them to the side of your working area.
- Scrub each urethane wheel and both bearings with the damp cloth.
- Wipe down the surface of your skating boots, including up inside the wheel frame.
- Make sure the wheel frame is completely dry before reinstalling the wheels (and the brake, if you removed it during the cleaning process).
- In rotating the wheel positions, take two steps to extend their life:
  1) Swap the ones with the most wear (usually at the toe and heel) with those showing less wear (such as the middle wheels).
  2) Flip the wheels over so that the shaved-off (or "coned") edges will face the outside of the foot on each boot. You may also swap wheels between the right and left skate.
- Tighten each wheel screw so that the nut is snug against the wheel frame. Then spin the wheel to make sure there is no undue resistance.

Replacing the Wheels

Depending on how much you skate, your wheels may need to be replaced from one to four times per year. Replace them if they wear off up to the hub, if the writing on the wheel sidewalls is gone, or if rotating no longer fixes the sawed-off look. One set of bearings should last through four or five wheel changes.

When replacing your wheels, you (or your shop) must remove your bearings from the old wheels and install them in the new ones. This is easy. First, remove all wheels and wipe off loose dirt. Wipe the bearings clean as you go. Then do the following for each wheel:

- Grasping it in one hand, use a wrench or other small probe to push the plastic or aluminum spacer in the center of the bearing out the other side, with the bearing ahead of it.
- Flip the wheel over and push out the second bearing.
- Pick up a new wheel and press in a bearing. Flip the wheel and insert the spacer, followed by the second bearing. Reinstall the wheels and you're set to go.

Rockering the Wheels

Some in-line skates allow you to drop the center wheels a fraction of an inch (called rockering) so that the skates arc more sharply for tighter turns. The trade-off is that this reduces the skate's stability for general recreational skating or for skating fast and straight. Warning: If your wheels are badly worn, rockering will feel very unstable. Skaters with worn wheels should postpone their first rockering experiment until the next time they replace the wheels. Here's how to do it:

- Remove the center wheels on your skates to expose the plastic axle guides that are embedded into both screw holes on the sides of the wheel frame.

- Pull out each axle guide, rotate it to the rockered position (usually 180 degrees), and push it back into the side of the frame.
- Reinstall the wheels.

Lengthening the Wheel Base

Some in-line skate frames are set up so you can move the front and rear wheels farther apart, to extend the wheelbase. This longer spread improves stability for recreational skating and provides more stability with speed. (By contrast, a shorter wheel base complements rockered wheels.) Here's how to do it:

- Remove the end wheels of the skate to expose the plastic axle guides embedded into both screw holes on the sides of the wheel frame.
- Pull out each axle guide, rotate it to the lengthened position (usually 180 degrees), and push it back into the side of the frame.
- Reinstall the wheels.

Cleaning the Bearings

Bearings will retain a fast spin much longer than most people realize—contrary to what ads and technical discussions among skaters may suggest. It is not necessary for the recreational skater to be concerned with regular bearing maintenance unless the mechanics of the process are just too fascinating to resist.

You may decide to buy high-performance bearings designed for self-maintenance. Removable shields allow you to easily disassemble and soak them in a solvent that dislodges grit. After soaking, reassemble, relubricate, and reinstall.

Standard sealed wheel bearings can be converted for regular clean-and-lubes to keep them at a like-new performance level by removing one shield. This step is non-reversible, but as long as the exposed side of the bearings face inside, they'll stay clean. If you don't have a tiny, sharp object to pry off the shield (such as an eyeglass screwdriver), you can have the conversion done at your local skate shop.

Preparing for the Elements

When it comes to environmental factors, wet and icy pavements are the only conditions you need to worry about, because you don't want to lose your balance on a slick surface or get your bearings wet. As long as the pavement is dry, though, you can skate outdoors no matter what the weather.

Of course, bright sunny days are the most enticing. In the sun, make sure you add one more protective layer besides your safety gear: use a high SPF sunscreen. A pair of sunglasses and a visor that fits under your helmet are also recommended.

On extremely hot days, take every precaution to prevent dehydration. Drink up before you go out, and carry two bottles of water, one in your gear bag and one in your fanny pack. Once you start enjoying yourself, it's easy to forget that you are perspiring away your body's store of water.

You may not want to skate when it's blustery, but wind can actually enhance your trip, especially if you're interested in a workout. Skating against the wind lets you add extra power to your strokes while working on sprints or speed-skating skills. And when the wind is at your back, the boost makes flat pavement feel like downhill—a situation just right for practicing easy slalom-skating turns. Try to skate into the breeze at the beginning of your trip when you're most energetic; fighting wind resistance all the way back to the car can be brutal when you're tired.

Cold weather alone should not keep you off your wheels. Because in-line skating is such great overall exercise, you can build up lots of body warmth within a few minutes The trick is to prepare for it in the same way joggers or cross-country skiers do: dress in multiple light layers. Depending on the temperature, you may want to wear thermal tights, a turtleneck, a windbreaker, and thermal head and hand coverings under your helmet and gloves. If the wind is blowing enough to make your eyes water, a pair of close-fitting goggle-style sunglasses may help. Wear a fanny pack that's roomy enough to store any removed layers. You'll soon learn how much to wear as you try skating on frosty mornings or below-freezing afternoons.

Safe Skating: From Protective Gear to Rules of the Road

The vast majority of in-line injuries can be prevented by wearing your protective gear. The Consumer Product Safety Commission recommends that, at minimum, everyone should wear a helmet and wrist guards on every skate. Those items, plus knee and elbow pads, are a must for emergency stopping maneuvers, hills, and such aggressive tactics as vertical skating and riding stairs. The baggy shorts you see on stunt skaters often conceal heavily padded briefs with hip and tail-bone protection. Street hockey should be played with all available safety gear; it doesn't take long to find out why.

Wrist Guards

Even the most skilled or cautious skaters can be tripped up by other skaters, cyclists, or pavement debris. Your hands are your first instinctive defense for preventing a head injury during a fall—so make sure you protect them by wearing wrist guards.

If you're reluctant, just imagine how life would be if you were unable to feed and clothe yourself, write, use your computer, or drive. With one or both wrists immobilized in bandages, you'd be dependent on others to perform the most basic daily tasks. Worse, you might not be able to work, meaning no money for skating vacations!

Wrist guards are designed with a slick surface so they will slide easily across the pavement, deflecting some of the impact that could injure your shoulder. In-line instructors can show you how to use them effectively in combination with knee and elbow pads for emergency landings.

Helmets

Helmets play a powerful role in preventing head injuries, which can be the most deadly. Statistics reveal that in-line skating beginners are at a greater risk for injuries to the back of the head because their early strokes are straight-legged, with weight over their heels, resulting in a tendency to fall backward. What's more, experienced skaters push their limits to improve their skills—increasing their need for protection.

Unfortunately, most skaters do not wear helmets. Here are the usual excuses:

"I'll look like a geek in a helmet!"

"I'll lose my sense of freedom."

"Helmets are hot and uncomfortable."

"A helmet would ruin my hair!"

Could funny hair be any worse than never skating (or walking, or thinking) again? Do you refuse to wear a seat belt in your car because it might wrinkle your outfit? As with a seat belt, a helmet could save your life that one time you really need it.

Besides the obvious safety benefits, there are other reasons to slap on a brainpan: to set a good example for friends (and, especially, kids), to improve your ability to compete aggressively without injury (as do free-stylers, hockey players, and speed skaters—definitely not geeks), and best of all, to gain more confidence while learning new skills. Finally, a helmet makes you more noticeable to motorists, who might otherwise expect you to behave like a pedestrian, at pedestrian speeds.

If you're a recreational or fitness skater, a bike helmet will work; if you own one, wear it! If not, pick out a helmet at your local skate shop; for pointers, see page 15.

Wear your helmet correctly. Adjust the chin straps so it fits snugly, covers your forehead, and doesn't shift from front to back or side to side.

Finding Good Lessons

You'll seriously lower your risk of injury if you master all the skating basics *before* exploring the local pavement. Instruction can vary from the quick freebie included in a rental package to store-sponsored lessons to classes offered by a certified in-line instructor. However you start out, you can keep learning at your own pace with an instructional book or video from one of the better skate specialty shops.

A safe learning location is also crucial. Beginners need a traffic-free environment for practicing their first strokes. Ideally, the first few moments on skates should be spent on carpeting or a dry grass. From there, a park with wide, flat sidewalks bordered by grass is best until you get a feel for rolling, turning, and stopping.

For tips on skating basics and a list of certified in-line instructors in your area, call the toll-free number of the In-Line Skating Association's Instructor Certification Program, (800) 56-SKATE, and ask for a free copy of the *Gear Up!* directory.

Adjusting Your Attitude

Attitude is another injury factor—and, alas, can be the hardest to control. More often than not, the skaters least likely to wear protective gear have the greatest tendency to engage in high-risk behavior: "Too cool" to wear a helmet and pads, they're often far too willing to take on hills, stairs, traffic, and other challenges before they're ready. Though people in this category may go on to become tomorrow's roller-hockey stars or Olympic freestylers, they contribute the most to today's in-line injury statistics. According to ongoing emergency-room studies conducted by the National Centers for Disease Control, 15-year-old males account for most of the nation's skating injuries.

Skaters of all ages should be encouraged to emulate those cutting-edge speed, hockey, and ramp skaters who are smart enough to wear the protection that ensures a lifetime of perfecting new skills. It's that kind of pragmatism that defines the true expert's attitude—a realistic readiness to deal with any circumstance that may affect performance. (For ways to develop such mental preparedness along with skating confidence, see Mind Over Matter: Building Confidence on page 26.) Recreational skaters should cop that attitude as well; after all, if you use your head before you start out, there's less chance of ending up with a crack in it. So save your skating trip for some other time if:

- It is foggy or dark outside, or if a rainstorm is brewing;
- You (or drivers in oncoming traffic) will be heading directly into the sun; or
- The pavement is slippery due to recent rain, fog, wet leaves, or sprinklers.

Hill Skills

Obviously, it's also important to choose a route you can handle. Before skating on a steeply sloped trail, make sure you are able to:

- Negotiate sudden encounters with speed bumps, garden hoses, curbs, rough patches, or gravel;
- Slow down and come to a full stop for intersections;
- Stop abruptly or swerve to avoid sudden obstacles;
- Make an emergency exit from a slope onto the road's shoulder;
- Ride your heel brake, drag one skate in a "T"-stop position, or make slalom turns to reduce speed; and
- Remain in control if a car tailgates you and honks.

Rules of the Road

You will find many different versions of the skating code of conduct; no two lists of rules are exactly alike. Yet they all have the same goal: to teach essential trail etiquette and safety habits. Here is the version included in the packaging for all new Rollerblade, Inc., brand skates:

- Always wear your protective gear: helmet, wrist guards, knee and elbow pads.
- Before you skate, take a lesson, or otherwise make sure you learn such in-line basics as speed control, turning, braking, and stopping.
- Stay alert. Always skate in control.
- Stay away from water, oil, debris, sand, and uneven or broken pavement.
- Avoid areas with heavy traffic.
- Observe all traffic regulations.
- Skate on the right side of the path; pass on the left.
- Never allow yourself to be towed by a motorized vehicle or bicycle.
- Avoid wearing headphones or anything that makes it hard to hear.
- Never wear anything that blocks your vision, and never skate at night or anytime when it's hard to see.

Group Conduct

How you skate in a group can greatly affect your safety. When skating with others, keep the following pointers in mind:

- Keep plenty of distance from other skaters so you have enough room to avoid tricky maneuvers or slalom turns;
- Look out for each other by calling warnings about cars or obstacles on the trail; and
- Resist any peer pressure to skate beyond your own control and comfort zones.

Skating Alone

Generally, you can feel safe skating on the trails in this book by day (much of this book was researched on solo trips). However, parts of some trails pass through run-down urban neighborhoods or questionable creekside camping spots. Though such areas are pointed out in the trail descriptions, use caution and common sense: If the trail seems to attract loiterers, for instance, or you see lots of beer or liquor bottles or graffiti, take these as signs that you should not be skating here after sunset. When daylight is waning, don't fool around; skate hard and fast and get a good workout on the way back to your car.

Women in particular should observe certain security measures: skate with a buddy if possible, and never acknowledge or respond to harassing remarks, gestures, or sounds from male strangers, including school-age boys. Be wary of lone male pedestrians in shabby clothing on the trail; acknowledge their presence with a short passing glance, but don't smile or make eye contact. Don't appear unsure of where you are going: look the picture of confidence, skate with authority, and you're less likely to be hassled.

Finally, remember that in certain areas—say, a densely tree-lined inner city path—there's safety in numbers. Besides, skating with a group of friends is fun. Have an experienced skater bring up the rear to assist any stragglers.

Learning to Skate: Essential Steps

Before you start these lessons, make the following preparations. They'll help you make the most of your skating time and fit it into your lifestyle.

Pick your location. If you haven't done it already, find a conveniently located paved area near your home, school, or job where you can go often to practice skating. The surface must be smooth and level, with enough room for you to move about unobstructed. It should be free from traffic (including bikes and pedestrians) and debris. Empty parking lots and unused ball courts are fine choices. At all costs, avoid hills until you've mastered the downhill lessons on page 41.

Join a skating club. One of the fastest ways to learn is to find a group of other skaters to skate with; observation can be a great teacher. Ask about clubs at your local skate shops.

First Time Up: Finding Your Balance

Sitting on a bench or a hard chair with arms will make it easier to stand up in in-line skates for the first time. When trying a pair for purchase or rental, put on the skates and protective gear, place your feet into a V position (heels together), and get up. Then do the following on a stretch of carpet or lawn.

Walk around to get the feel of the sturdy boots and find your balance. If you feel any pressure points in either boot, sit back down and adjust the skate's tongue and the tightness of the laces or buckles. Back on your feet, turn out your toes and practice walking like a duck. This is the proper foot position to use as a foundation for building strong, wide forward glides.

Standing, tip your lower legs to each side. Carefully bend down and touch your knees and then your toes. Notice how your skates angle onto one edge or the other as your lower body compensates for changes in your upper body's position. Observe how mobile you are on in-line skates, and how maintaining your balance is possible in many different positions. Learn to trust the boot construction that has made the sport of in-line skating so popular.

The Ready Position

Learning the proper body position is essential for the beginning in-line skater. Weight distribution is especially important once you start skating faster or down hills; any unexpected event while your balance is compromised is bound to lead to an unwelcome meeting with the pavement. As long as you can calmly and quickly realign yourself into a balanced position, you will be able to skate safely and stay in control. (Actually, the stance you need to adopt—which we'll refer to in these pages as the "ready position"—is exactly the same stance used in tennis and skiing, among other sports.)

You can avoid the typical beginner's balance problems by teaching yourself what the right position feels like—as well as what the *wrong* position feels like and how to correct it immediately. That awareness will give you the confidence you need to enjoy the trails listed in this book.

To master the proper ready position for in-line skating, go to a full-length mirror and look at yourself from different angles. Then follow the pointers on this checklist:
- Your feet are shoulder-width apart.
- Ankles, knees, and hips are flexed.
- Your head is in a natural position.
- Hands and forearms are at waist level and within your peripheral vision.
- When you look down, your knee pads block your view of your toes.
- Your shoulders are directly over your hips, and your hips directly over your ankles.

Next, close your eyes to test your equilibrium and get a sense of the position from within. Take a deep breath. As you exhale, become as relaxed in the upper body as possible. Try to memorize how this feels, noticing the different muscles involved.

Eyes open, once again looking in the mirror, sink down into a more aggressive stance. As your rear end moves back, notice how your shoulders drop slightly forward to maintain the even forward-to-back weight distribution.

Once you become conscious of your body and how to keep it "in line," your skating skills will improve with every hour you're on skates.

Now try arranging your body too far forward and too far back to find out why these positions compromise your ability to skate. When you are too far forward, your body weight is over your toes, you are bent forward at the waist, and your knees are nearly straight. When you are too far back, your body weight is over your back wheels, your shoulders are rotated back, your knees are straight, and you feel you are about to land on your largest unpadded area. And here's another reason why a helmet is crucial: statistics show that falling backward without wearing one causes the most serious injuries among beginning in-line skaters.

Mind Over Matter: Building Confidence

The phrase "expert beginner" may sound odd, but for a skater with the right outlook it's not a contradiction. Unlike many sports that require years of practice, in-line skating is rewarding the very first day you try it. Even the Level 1 skills described in these pages are enough to provide all the fun and fitness benefits in-line skating has to offer.

Your mind is the only obstacle to advancing beyond the forward glide and some minimal turning skills. And once you've learned the basics, your mind is also usually what's behind out-of-control crashes and careless mistakes. It's panic that brings the illusion that the abilities you've already mastered are suddenly not available. The mind is also what leads some skaters to leave caution and protective gear behind, increasing their injury risks.

For many, the fear of falling is the biggest hurdle. Add self-doubt, self-consciousness in front of others, lapses in concentration, or negative thoughts, and you have the physical tension and rigidity that causes awkwardness and, ultimately, loss of control.

You can, however, take charge of many of the elements that affect your learning experience, and the resulting sense of control will erase most of those debilitating thoughts. Here are some factors you can influence:

Variables. When you learn new skating skills, practice them in the same spot. Right now you don't need to be distracted by a new pavement texture or a surprise patch of sand. The less variation you encounter in the beginning, the better you can concentrate on the basics. Besides location, other distracting variables could include first-time adjustments to your skates, such as rockered wheels, a new skating companion, or high winds.

Repetition. Practice new skills often. You will find that in this sport, repetition is not boring. The simple joy of movement will propel you on, whether you're at an indoor rink or in the great outdoors. And focusing on recently learned techniques will provide a foundation for adding more advanced ones later. If possible, skate at least twice a week to keep your learning curve in a strong upward arc.

Observation. You can learn faster by noticing how your skates react to different pressures and angles. Experiment. Play around. Watch and try to copy other skaters. Notice everything and then think about it.

Playfulness. Many skaters have learned the basics and beyond just by getting out on the pavement for hours of play. Once you're comfortable with the rolling feeling, you should make time to go fool around as often as possible.

Music. Try to make music a part of some practice sessions. Tempos and tunes can do wonders to promote spontaneous skating; a strong rhythmic beat will inspire you to perform repetitious drills more fluidly and with less conscious effort. If you're someplace where it won't disturb others, turn up the volume on a radio or tape player. Headphones are often too dangerous to wear unless you're certain you won't encounter *any* vehicles or bicyclists.

How to Use These Lessons

The most important skill any in-line skater needs to learn as soon as possible is how to stop. This ability not only lets you control your speed on hills, but also improves your overall balance for any maneuver you want to attempt. So please make sure you've mastered the skills described in the next section, Stopping and Speed Control, before you skate on any of the trails listed in this book.

The lessons in the next three sections can help you achieve the Level 1, 2, and 3 skills referred to in the trail ratings. You'll also find tips for tackling slalom skating, fitness skating, and simple figure skating and street stunts. To get the most out of the lessons, keep the following in mind:

- Take the time to read, rehearse, and visualize the steps in each lesson before trying them on actual skates. It will start you out on surer footing.
- When you put on your skates to learn something new, skate a few practice laps for five or ten minutes to warm up your muscles and review the skills you've already learned.
- Assume that all new pointers for turning are based on a counter-clockwise direction unless otherwise specified. That seems to be the direction most people favor.
- Remember that everybody favors one leg over the other, and therefore most skills will be easier to learn on one side than the other. So once you've mastered a technique on your good side, work harder on your bad side to balance things out.
- After you learn a new skill, practice it often to improve not only that feat but your balance and confidence, too.

Stopping and Speed Control

It's hard to really relax and enjoy liberated in-line skating until you're sure of your ability to stop. The recent introduction of cuff-activated braking technology has made things much easier for beginners, letting them tackle other basics with more confidence. Cuff-activated brakes are an armlike mechanism mounted on the back of one skate's cuff. As the cuff flexes backward in response to pressure from your calf, it forces the armlike mechanism downward, and the brake at the bottom of the arm begins to drag on the pavement.

What follows are step-by-step lessons for perfecting those cuff-activated and standard-heel-brake stops so you can hit the hills with enthusiasm and aplomb. Remember that all good skating stems from the ability to balance your center of gravity in a relaxed athletic stance, so if necessary, review the basic "ready" position described on page 25. Location also helps: find a short, very gentle slope, bordered by grass, that levels out to flat pavement where you can roll to a stop. Practice the warm-up drills below, then follow the instructions for the kind of brake you use.

Them's the Brakes: Warm-Up Drills

The most important prerequisite to using the in-line heel brake is the ability to simply roll along with one skate advanced half a boot length. Besides its use for stopping, there are other reasons this stance is useful. With one foot advanced, your wheels form a longer, more stable platform, almost like having eight-wheeled skates or skis. So whenever you see a nasty patch of pavement, advance one foot to glide over it more easily.

This position is also a wonderful way to make a sharp swerve or maintain your speed on a corner. In this case you should turn with the advanced skate on the inside; also, it helps to lean your upper body into the curve and to tilt both skates into the turn.

Another good drill for heel braking is to scissor your skates back and forth as you coast along a flat stretch of pavement. Keep your knees bent and maintain even body-weight distribution over both arches as you alternate the leading skate. You'll look like a toy robot, but the payoffs will outnumber the laughs.

Emergency Stops

To reiterate: before you learn to stop properly, you have no business skating near traffic or on trails. That said, these emergency techniques will work for the first-timer moving at slow speeds in a protected environment, such as an empty parking lot.

At slower speeds on level ground, simply relax and roll. The wheels will have enough natural friction to slow you down to an eventual stop.

Head for a patch of lawn or dirt, and step off the pavement. If necessary, take a few running steps on the lawn to maintain your balance.

Only if moving very slowly, roll up to something stationary you can grab. (If you're going too fast, your feet will keep on going without you!)

If in imminent danger, pitch forward and slide on your padded hands and knees.

Cuff-Activated Brakes

Before starting, lower the brake until it almost (but not quite) touches the ground with the skate in a normal upright position.

To engage the brake, roll down the slope in the one-foot-ahead position, and try to press the toe in the brake (front) boot onto the pavement as you push that foot farther ahead. As the toe is pointed and pushed forward, the back of the calf presses the boot cuff, which presses the brake into the pavement, dragging you to a stop.

To reinforce this new skill, practice several complete stops every 10 feet down the slope. Pick a line or crack on the pavement and get a feel for how soon you need to start braking to be able to stop there.

After you gain confidence in your braking and find the brake dragging when you don't want it to, it's time to raise it back up to a level that doesn't hinder your skating.

Please note: really powerful stops require you to learn how to lift your toe so you can burn rubber on a hill. Continue to work on the standard heel brake skills described below as your balance improves; you'll eventually need that more powerful stopping skill as your speeds increase.

Standard Heel Brakes

One-footedness does not often come easily to new skaters, but some degree of independent foot balance is necessary to use the standard heel brake effectively. Here's a drill for attaining it: in an open area, raise one foot slightly off the ground and glide for as long as possible on the other skate. (If you've rockered your wheels, you may feel unstable doing this.) Start taking short marching steps if necessary, then start lengthening the time between steps. As your skill increases, try moving the airborne skate around as you roll.

To practice and get the feel of the braking position off the pavement, assume the readiness stance on a lawn or softer surface, and push the skate with the brake (usually the right foot) straight forward until your ankle bone on that foot is even with the big toe knuckle of the other. Tip up the right toe and press down hard on your heel. If you dare, balance all of your weight on the heel brake and try to lift your left foot. Skaters with solid heel-brake skills can actually stop like this.

After you spend some time practicing this position, roll down your slope in the one-foot-ahead position. Lift the toe of the advanced skate until you feel the rubber drag; let it drag lightly on the pavement and listen to the sound it makes. If necessary, drop your toe to regain balance, then lift and drag. Repeat this step until you can roll several feet while dragging the brake lightly.

Now you're ready to press rubber to road. And that is what is most necessary for effective heel braking: power. Make it smoke! Of course, you need to apply the pressure gradually, in a subtle movement that originates way up in your hip. Gradual pressuring is the hardest trick to learn once you've gotten the other aspects of braking down, but frequent practice will help your body figure out how to apply the increasing pressure.

Braking New Ground

Practice braking a lot! An amazing and wonderful thing about in-line skating is that your body takes notes on everything you try. Your muscles remember the movements that work and toss out the ones that don't. Every time you try any new feat, those muscles respond according to your previous experience, applying the information to your current effort. It may be days, weeks, or months after you first try a new skill or trick, but one day you'll try it yet another time and then, suddenly, you'll have it.

More Stopping Tips

Here are some other tactics that can assist you in stopping with either a cuff-activated or standard heel brake:

- Once you have the rubber dragging in a solid straight line, sit down hard as you shove your braking foot ahead, to finish the stop.
- Make sure your feet are parallel and only five to seven inches apart.
- Try pressing your knees together, and make sure they are both generously bent.
- Imagine that you are squashing a bug with your heel brake. You should be able to stand on that brake one day.
- Plan on a braking distance of no less than 10 feet. The faster you go, the more you'll need.
- Strive to make long, proud black rubber streaks on the pavement.
- Keep shoulders above hips; do not lean forward. The more body mass you place *behind* the brake, the more effectively it stops you.
- If you have trouble keeping your upper body behind the brake, imagine yourself holding onto a tightrope in a tug of war. To hold your ground, you've got to dig in with that heel.
- You can use your brake as a speed regulator. If you're picking up too much momentum on a decline, just brake lightly until you've slowed down enough to feel in control.

Brand-new standard-style brakes are often so thick, you can't raise your toe easily. First-time skaters should consider borrowing a slightly used brake from a friend. This provides better leverage for learning, as it allows you to get the toe up higher and the brake farther ahead of your body mass.

In-line heel brakes really do work, and they are just as important to your safety as your wrist guards or helmet. Practice braking until you feel the freedom and assurance that comes with knowing you are in complete control, thanks to that little piece of rubber. Use it, don't lose it!

Circle Stops

The circle stop evolves out of a hard swerve to one side. It looks rather flashy, but it is quite easy. This drill circles you counterclockwise:

- Roll forward at a slow speed.
- Finish a forward glide on your left foot.
- "Cock" your arms to the right and look left.
- As you shift your weight to start a short glide on your right skate, simultaneously lift the left skate's heel, and swing your shoulders and arms to the left.

- Return your left heel to the pavement and keep your weight evenly balanced between both thighs as you start turning counterclockwise.
- At first, stay in the circle until you stop moving. With practice, you'll be able to shorten it to a half-circle and reverse directions.

"T"-Stops

Skaters who have good one-foot stability are ready to try the "T"-Stop. For many skaters, especially hockey players, this is the preferred stopping method. (Here's a tip: Try it on your "bad" side, too. You may find out that your bad side is really your good side—it has happened!) Be aware that on rough surfaces, this will use up perfectly good wheels in a hurry. A heel brake is cheaper to replace.

- Start coasting on parallel skates at a moderate speed. Be sure to maintain the correct ready position at all times: hands raised and in view, and shoulders, hips, and heels lined up on the same plane, perpendicular to the pavement.
- With all of your weight over one foot, lift and rotate the other a full 90 degrees, placing it behind the front foot's heel.
- Gradually touch all wheels onto the pavement at the same time.
- Move the hip forward over your front foot in a slight lunging movement, to tilt the back skate's wheels more aggressively.
- Gradually lunge deeper to increase the pressure on the dragging wheels.
- As you improve, you can save your wheels somewhat by dragging only the toe wheel, but you will find yourself rotating your wheels often to compensate for the coned wheel profile that results.

Level 1, Beginner Skills:
Standing Up, Basic Turns, and the Forward Glide

These lessons are designed to give you the basic skills for skating all of the trails designated with a Level 1 or beginner's rating in this book. These skills qualify you to skate in public places on flat pavement without endangering yourself or others. If you're just starting out, don't expect to feel comfortable with all of the skills within a day or even a week. It takes a while to get used to these new demands on your strength, agility, and balance.

Don't skate more than two hours your first time out. Most people can expect a little bit of lower leg stiffness for one or two days, until those muscles get accustomed to the new activity.

Review the Ready Position

If you begin to feel out of control or off balance on your skates, you have probably lost the balanced stance of athletic readiness essential to this sport. Check the location of your shoulders, chin, and knees, and the pressure under your feet. You can instantly boost your confidence and control by doing one or all of the following:

- Tuck in your chin or rear end.
- Bend your knees and sink down a few inches.
- Skate more slowly if speed or fear is causing you to tense up.
- Take a deep breath and let your shoulders drop.
- Make sure your feet are directly underneath your hips.
- If coasting, advance one skate slightly forward for better stability.
- Feel the pressure of your body weight just under your arches.

The Forward Fall

It is important to experience some pain-free falls before you begin learning to skate in earnest. Having confidence in your protective gear will greatly enhance the rest of the learning process.

- Stand with skates shoulder-width apart and parallel.
- Bend down and put your hands near your toes.
- Reach forward toward the pavement three feet beyond your toes. As you pitch forward, land on your hands and knees. With wheels under your toes, your feet will roll backward, and your knees will strike the ground. Bang them a couple more times. Doesn't that thick padding feel good? In an emergency situation, you may need to deliberately hit the pavement this way to avoid serious injury. This demonstrates why knee pads and wrist guards are highly necessary in-line gear.
- Get back up and repeat the process until you feel comfortable falling forward and feel you can take full advantage of your protective gear. If you know a fall is coming, always attempt to pitch forward.

Getting Up

To rise from the ground while wearing in-line skates, get on your hands and knees. Lift one knee and place the skate of that foot on the pavement, close to your other knee. Move your weight back so you're upright and sitting on the heel of the other skate. Now, stand straight up. (If you need help, place both hands on the raised knee and push down on it to get an upward boost.)

The Still Position

There are many situations in which you need to be able to anchor your feet and stand still—for instance, when you're chatting with friends, or waiting at an intersection for cars to pass or the light to change.

To stand still, place your feet into a sideways "T" position. Roll the heel of the brakeless boot back until it is touching the arch of the other boot. With knees flexed, wedge your skates tightly together in this position to keep both feet from rolling.

Another option for standing still momentarily is to engage the heel brake. Lift the toe of a skate with a standard brake, or scissors a skate with an arm-activated brake forward until the brake engages.

The Forward Glide

The most important concept to remember about the standard skating stroke is that you must push your skates out to the sides in wide herringbone-like strokes. Do not try to duplicate the movement of walking; that's what gives beginners a tottering gait. A duck-footed push to the side, starting with knees well bent, is the ticket to strong, effective strokes.

- Start from the still position you just learned, with both toes facing out at a 45-degree angle, and the left heel tucked in close to the right arch.
- With knees bent, place your weight on the back (right) skate, tip it slightly onto the inside edge, and push against the inside wheel edges.
- Your front (left) skate will start gliding forward. Allow your right leg to extend and straighten behind you as you transfer your body weight over to the left foot, making sure to keep the toe of that foot pointed out 45 degrees.
- After your weight is fully transferred to the left skate, pick up the right skate and bring it back in close under your body.
- Touch down with the right skate as close as possible to the left foot, with toes angled out 45 degrees to the right.
- Press the pavement with the inside edge of the left skate's wheels to begin a forward glide on the right skate.
- Keep your glides short and sweet for now, as you explore your surroundings and absorb the sensation of this first basic in-line skating skill.

Basic Turning

Turns on in-line skates almost seem to happen by themselves. While practicing your forward glide, you may have effectively changed direction by picking up and putting down your skates as you do when walking. But part of the elegance of skating comes from gliding through smooth turns with both skates on the ground.

Turning is a result of skating on the curved sides of the skate wheels, known as edging. If you have ever skied, you will remember this as the "wedge."

Learn to turn toward whatever is the most comfortable direction first. As soon as it feels good, make turns in the opposite direction.

In an open area such as a parking lot, build up to a moderate speed with a few forward glides.

With both feet parallel and coasting forward, shift most of your weight onto your right skate and twist your head and upper body toward the left. A left turn will be the result.

Repeat, turning to the right by pressing hard on your left foot as you twist your upper body in the opposite direction. As you practice, work toward twisting and pressing with just your lower leg, rather than with your whole body.

This skill is a foundation for the hard swerves and slalom turns of more advanced skating.

Mobility Tips

Work on maintaining a relaxed stance. Take a deep breath now and then and check to make sure your weight is properly balanced and aligned over your feet.

If you are skating laps, reverse directions so you can reinforce your skills equally on both sides. If you have a weak side, do more laps in the direction that lets you work on strengthening it.

To cultivate balance and mobility, practice stooping down to pick up leaves, rocks, or twigs off the pavement. Don't forget to switch hands so the muscles on both sides of your body can get used to this. Continue this session until you feel at ease shifting your weight at different levels.

Level 2, Intermediate Skills: Swerves, Curbs, and Cross-Overs

As an intermediate skater, you should be able to skate on most of the trails described in this book. The most important skill required for many Level 2 and just about all Level 3 trails is your ability to stop at intersections and control your speed on long hills. You must be able to remain in control on blind curves where you are suddenly presented with three pedestrians walking abreast, or when a dog on a leash suddenly cuts you off. More often than not, a trail in a beautiful, natural setting will also have sections that are narrow, crowded, or steep. That's why you should be able to make a controlled stop in 25 feet or less, and reduce your speed when necessary with a "T"-stop or by riding your heel brake.

Find out how far in advance you need to start braking to be able to stop exactly where you want. The best way to do this is to make a mark on the pavement (or choose a line in a parking lot or game court) and approach it at different speeds, always attempting to stop right on that line. The distance will vary, so practice at different speeds to get a good idea of your braking capacity.

While you're doing this exercise, try and shorten those distances. You can add a bit of extra friction to sharpen your stops by "sitting down" on the rubber while you shove hard to push the brake ahead of you just before reaching the line.

Work on using your heel brake as a speed governor. Find a descent with a long, gradual leveling-off at the bottom. Start coasting down from the top, and once you pick up enough speed, engage the heel brake and drag it all the rest of the way down, maintaining a straight path. This is an essential skill for those times when you are picking up too much speed on a narrow or steep incline that's crowded with people and offers no room for slalom turns. On a wide trail where you *can* slalom, it's also the best way to reduce speed gain so you can go back to making those turns.

Swerving

Next to stopping, good maneuverability is the most essential skating skill. The ability to make a hard swerve helps you avoid collisions and gives you more options in tight situations or on crowded trails.

The following instructions will help you swerve to the left, counterclockwise. If that direction seems hard to handle, perhaps your other leg is your strong one; in that case, reverse the directions. Note: this is a parking lot drill. Do *not* do it on a sidewalk where there is no place to go when you swerve to the side.

- On a flat, wide section of the parking lot, give yourself an obstacle to swerve around. Make a mark or place an object such as a full soft-drink can on the pavement.
- Starting from 35 feet away, skate toward the obstacle, building up moderate momentum with some forward glides.
- Just before you get there, turn head and shoulders left, and reach with both arms to the left at the same time, keeping both knees well bent. At the same time, advance the foot nearest the obstacle slightly ahead of the other skate.
- Go back to your starting place and repeat the drill until you can swerve close to your obstacle but clear it with a wide-arced turn. Don't worry if your first tries feel more like lunges than swerves. Eventually you'll feel comfortable in the tilted position this requires.
- Practice until you can do this with both feet shoulder-width apart and both skates tilted, preferably at the same angle. Try to keep your head directly over your object or mark as you turn around it. (This means you'll have to trust centrifugal force to keep you from falling while your feet are angled out to the side.)
- Now learn how to do this on your bad foot, and practice it even more on that side.

Curb Instincts

As your confidence on skates grows, your desire to explore new places will, too. Sooner or later, you will need to be able to step onto and off of a curb, or get up or down a flight of stairs. Here's how:

- To step up onto a curb, either when you're still moving or stopped next to it, simply lift one foot high enough to clear it and step on, pushing off with the other skate from behind. This can be done at any speed, but your balance is better, believe it or not, when you are moving faster than a snail's pace.
- To step down from a curb, come to a complete stop at the edge, and step down as close to it as possible, pressing the first skate back against the edge so it won't be rolling when you bring down the second skate.
- If you aren't at a busy intersection and no cars are in sight, you can simply relax to a moderate speed and roll straight off the curb with

both skates parallel. There's no need to hop or jump: you will drop lightly to the pavement and continue rolling along at the same momentum.

- Practice the hop-over in-line skating drills listed below, and soon you will have the confidence to make a two-footed hop *up* onto most of the curbs in your path.

Hop-Overs

Choose a line or a mark on the pavement to jump over. A crack in the sidewalk is good; so is a painted line of a parking space.

- Start by skating a few forward glides on the way to what may look like your Grand Canyon.
- Go into a coast as you approach your mark or crack, and be sure to keep your knees bent and your weight evenly balanced over both arches. Keep your hands low at your sides.
- To jump high, swing your hands up and forward and pick up both feet at the same time. (Be aware that many obstacles can be cleared with a slight hop and hardly any upper body movement.)
- Continue to skate around and practice jumping, working on good body position throughout the jump and landing.

Urban Obstacles

City terrain is a great recreational obstacle course, full of navigational challenges such as concrete benches, planters, and stairs. But some situations should be approached with care. Here are a few tips for handling a variety of unforeseen elements skaters face every day:

Manhole covers and cattle guards. These are city and country versions of a similar physical hurdle to skaters. You may be willing and able to skate right over heavily textured manhole covers, but don't try it with cattle guards, unless they're only painted renditions of the actual thing. Step or (if you're really a pro) hop over them, and accept the inconvenience as a small price to pay for the privilege of skating everywhere else. Learn to stay on the alert for such obstacles and enjoy the challenge of dealing with them.

Slick spots, wet leaves, and puddles. In-line wheel traction will disappear on slick surfaces. If you get caught in the rain or find yourself skating across a large patch of oil or water, take short, light strokes and keep your weight directly over your feet. If you cannot avoid skating across a puddle, ride on one skate so you'll only have to wipe dry four out of eight wheels to prevent rusted bearings.

Wooden bridges. In some cases, the planks of wooden bridges don't match up well or are full of knotholes, or the bridge is arched. Again, take short, powerful strokes and keep your weight centered. On the downhill part of an arch, just relax and roll if the cracks between planks are smooth enough to allow it.

Crossover Turns

Crossovers let you continue stroking as you turn: the outside skate crosses over the inside one to take you in the new direction. The crossover turn is not required to skate on the Level 2 trails in this book. However, an intermediate in-line skater *should* be able to round a bend in the trail with fluidity and grace, and the crossover is one way to accomplish that.

Pre-Crossover Drills

For new skaters, crossovers can be difficult to learn, because they require you to lean your weight outside the center axis of your body onto the outside edge of your skate. When you complete a crossover turn, at first it feels as though you are catching yourself just before a fall. This is scary enough on your good side, but it's even trickier on your weak leg. Here is a preliminary drill to help you get the feel of crossovers (you may only need to do this for your weak side):

On the grass or perfectly flat pavement where there is nothing obstructing your path to your left, stand in a solid ready position with knees well flexed. Pick up your right skate, pass it across and in front of the left skate, and place it back down on the pavement. As you do so, let the left skate rock over onto its side, but don't worry, because your in-line skate cuff will give you all the ankle support you need. Now pick up the left skate and move it to the left so that both feet are again parallel and below your hips and shoulders. Continue this sideways stepping until you run out of pavement or lawn, then repeat, coming back in the other direction.

Now find a spot on your practice pavement where there is the tiniest slope. It should be invisible to the naked eye, but you know it's there because it is easier to skate in one direction than the other. Stand with your skates perpendicular to the subtle incline. Repeat the side-stepping drill, stepping sideways down the slope, but this time, imagine that you are stepping around a big circle with its center behind you. Angle around its perimeter until your skates begin to roll between crossovers. This should trick you into your first crossover turns. Repeat several times in both directions.

Forward Crossovers

Crossovers are used for turning corners while maintaining or gaining speed. These turns are easier to learn if your practice spot has a large painted circle, such as a dodge-ball circle on a school playground. If you do not have such a spot, place an object on the pavement that you can skate around.

This drill uses a counterclockwise circular move (toward the left), which is easier if you are right-footed. Lefties should reverse the directional instructions. Make sure you practice more on your awkward side so you can keep both sides of your body equally trained.

- Start by skating a few forward glides and try to build up some speed as you go.
- Begin skating around the edges of your circle at least 10 feet away from the center or from your marker, keeping both knees well bent.
- Get low as you glide on the left skate; turn your upper body and lean in toward the center of the circle. Your weight is transferred to the outside of the left skate's wheels, just as it was in the pre-crossovers drill.
- As you skate the circle, place your right foot on the pavement directly in front of the left. Gradually try to cross the right skate farther over the left skate as you continue circling and lean your upper body into the center. Congratulations—these are your first crossovers!
- To improve your technique: Keeping knees well bent, continue to look toward the center of your circle. Retrieve your left skate (which is heading away from the center) and place it on the pavement directly under your body. It will automatically tilt toward the center of the circle to receive pressure along the outside edges of the wheels.
- Continue to skate around the perimeter of your circle with both skates tipped toward the center.
- Repeat the crossover turn in laps, making progressively smaller circles. Practice counterclockwise until you have the mechanics down.
- Change directions and make clockwise circles and laps. Spend more time rehearsing the direction that feels most awkward to you.

Figure Eights

You can strengthen both directions of your crossover turns by skating in big figure eights. At a schoolyard, look for side-by-side painted circles. If none are available, place two objects that won't blow away on the pavement about 25 feet apart.

- Begin skating a counterclockwise lap around one of the circles with forward glides.
- Once your body position is stable, turn your head toward the center of your first circle (to your left) and start making crossover turns.
- As you complete a lap around the first circle and approach the second, make one or two straight forward glides and turn your head to the right to look at the second circle's center.
- Tilt your upper body into the circle and begin clockwise crossover turns.
- Continue repeating the figure eight to practice crossovers in both directions.

Alternating Crossovers

In the alternating crossovers drill, you simply alternate forward glides with crossover turns. This is a rhythmic and fun movement that you can use for exercise, climbing hills, or as a variation of the regular forward glide. It requires a wide swath of pavement and is not suitable for sidewalks. Make it a point to first rehearse these motions without skates.

- Start out from the left edge of a wide paved area, in a right-footed forward glide.
- Cross over with the left skate and place it on the pavement in front of the right skate.
- Angle farther to the right with another forward glide on the right skate. By now you should be a good 15 feet to the right of where you started.
- Now push off on the left skate in a forward glide angling back to the left side of the road.
- Cross over the left skate with the right skate.
- Make a second forward glide on the left skate.
- Angle back toward the right side of the road with a right forward glide, and continue the sequence as long as you have the room. Your rhythm is: right-glide, crossover, right-glide; left-glide, crossover, left-glide.

Level 3, Advanced Skills:
Stairs, Roads, and Downhill Thrills

Once you've mastered the Level 1 and 2 skating skills, you have a solid grounding in the fundamentals: you can handle basic gliding, turning, and stopping, are able to manage your speed, and can skate on most sidewalks, pathways, and park trails. Now you're ready to tackle Level 3—techniques that open the door to a much wider variety of skating situations.

Mastering Stairs

Accomplished street skaters can do some amazing stunts with stairs, including riding them forward, backward, or with knees pointing both fore and aft. They see stairs as something to roll down or jump over, possibly with a 360-degree rotation thrown in, and stairway railings as something to either "grind" on the wheel frame or ride down on the skates' inside or outside soles. Such stunts are not described here. For skating on the Level 3 trails in this book, you just need to be able to get up and down the steps.

At first, this is easier to learn if you're facing up the stairs. As your balance improves, you will be able to go down them, facing forward.

Whether you're going up or down, reach for the railing. Step onto the first stair in front of you, and push your skate back up against it to prevent rolling. Using the rail for balance, reach with your other foot for the next step, keeping your weight centered and your skates stabilized against the back of each step.

Road Warriors

With enough experience under your belt, you'll be ready to enjoy the benefits of road skating. Many skaters take to the street to avoid the boardwalk crowds, liven up their commute, or explore a smooth country road; some even organize after-hours group skates downtown. Some veteran street skaters in New York City have made skating in traffic an art form.

To skate some of the trips in this book, you will need to take to the street occasionally. Usually, they are streets with light traffic, or with wide, marked bike lanes that are clean enough to accommodate in-lines. (Since skating near cars can be risky, most of the tours are on dedicated bike paths.) Remember that you are no longer a pedestrian when skating on the street, and are required to obey the same laws bicyclists do. Here are some other general safety tips for skating on California roads:

Traffic direction. Skate in the direction of the traffic.

Skating on the shoulder. The area on the other side of the white line (away from the cars) can be narrow, gravel-strewn, and basically unfriendly to in-line wheels. If it's a narrow shoulder, you'll barely have enough room to stroke, which means you may end up stroking across the line, so watch out for the foot closest to traffic. Keep your ears tuned and stop stroking when a car approaches. And unless you're moving at least as fast as the cars, do *not* swoop into their lane when you slalom the downhills on a narrow shoulder. On shoulders of country roads, watch out for intersections with driveways; they are often strewn with gravel.

Automobile awareness. Stay alert to all that is happening around you. This means everything within your peripheral vision as well as in the direction you happen to be looking. Don't wear your portable headphones near traffic; you need to be able to hear just as well as you can see. If you're skating in a fairly large and speedy group, you may get away with slaloms across the width of a lane on downhills, but don't depend on it. (In some places, using the car lanes is not even legal.) It's better to have a team of friendly bicyclists escort your group in such a situation, both in front and in back. Once you have made the choice to occupy a lane normally reserved for automobiles, hold your ground; don't be intimidated into going faster than your abilities allow. If you hear a car horn honking angrily behind you, you aren't skating fast enough to be in its lane.

Night Moves

Every year with the return of Daylight Saving Time, die-hard urban skaters across California resume the guided week-night group skates that grow more popular with each passing year. Usually, group skates are loosely organized eight-to-20-mile affairs, with participants responsible for their own safety and behavior, but helmets are typically required.

Afterwards, many skaters often head to a local night spot for beverages and snacks.

Before you attend a group skate, make sure you have solid speed control and stopping abilities. Take a friend along, too, because if you're at the back of the pack and take a spill, it's possible nobody will be around to help. General rules are: stick with the group, and bring along some money and an ID.

For nighttime skating, wear white or attach reflective patches to your clothing. It's also smart to wear one of the flashing lights or head lamps that can be fastened to a helmet or belt; look for them at your local skate shop. Wear all of the protective gear.

Downhill Knowhow

Anybody can crouch into a tucked position and roll straight down a hill. But it is very easy to reach "terminal velocity" and go out of control while descending an incline that's long or steep. By learning how to make slalom turns, you can enjoy speed yet retain control. Once you can make these turns and use the heel brake as a speed governor, you can skate just about anywhere.

Slalom turns allow you to press your urethane wheels hard against the pavement and effectively reduce your downhill speed, using friction. This is an advanced skill that takes some time and effort to learn, even for expert snow skiers already familiar with the mechanics. The following lessons take you gradually through a series of skills that will build up your slalom abilities. The first drills should be performed on a flat surface, preferably at a schoolyard or an empty parking lot where you have lots of pavement to work with.

The Hourglass

This movement is good for overall mobility and as preparation for future slalom-skating drills:

- Start from a slow forward roll, with knees slightly bent and feet at shoulder width.
- With your weight evenly distributed on both feet, push them out to the sides, sinking slightly to add more flex to your knees and more power to your push.
- Next, tilt your knees and skates inward, and pull with your inner thigh muscles to bring your feet back together. As you do, begin to rise so you can pull your feet back together more easily.
- Rotate your knees back out when your feet are close, and push your feet back out to the wide position.
- Continue the in-and-out movement of your feet so that your skates make repeated hourglass figures on the pavement. With repeated practice, you should be able to maintain momentum doing hourglasses while going up a slight slope in the pavement.

One-Footed Hourglasses

Once you've learned how to maintain your momentum with hour-glasses, you're ready to tackle the one-footed version. Place a soft-drink can or other object on the pavement where you have room to skate around it in a circle. Perform the hourglass movement, but with only the outer foot stroking, while the inside foot simply glides around the circle, supporting most of your weight. Rotate your shoulders so that they are always facing the object in the center of your circle, and keep your eyes fixed on it, while you pump the outside foot out and in, carving arcs on the pavement. After you get the hang of it, reverse directions to work on your other foot.

Linked Turns

With linked turns, your skates snake around in a series of arcs on flat terrain, so that you're basically achieving just a lazy forward glide, or a sequence of alternating one-footed hourglasses. Both skates remain in constant contact with the pavement, covering a lot more of it than you would just rolling forward over the same stretch. This extra friction boosts your ability to slow down, which translates directly into slalom-skating speed control on the slopes.

- Start by building up some momentum with a series of strong forward glides.
- With feet shoulder-width apart, begin coasting with knees bent and upper body relaxed in your best ready position.
- To turn to the left, twist your right skate so the toe points to the left, a movement not unlike the one-footed hourglass drill. Your left skate will also begin to turn left as you transfer most of your body weight onto the "carving" right skate.
- At the end of the arc (your skates are pointing across your direction of travel instead of toward it), begin to twist and pressure your left foot to repeat in the opposite direction.
- Repeat until you attain a rhythmic alternating stroke. Add forward glides as often as necessary to maintain momentum while you link as many turns as possible.

Linked turns are precursors to slalom skating turns. On a windy day, you can rehearse for slalom skating on the safety of flat terrain. Find a stretch of pavement that forces you to skate directly into or away from a steady wind. You'll get a workout on the "uphill" stretch skating into the wind, while you can pretend to ski on the "downhill" tailwind stretch.

Your First Hill

Learn to slalom skate on a consistent, gentle slope with smooth pave-ment that's at least 10 feet wide. At the bottom, you want a long, flat stretch to serve as a run-out. If the pavement is bordered by lawn, so much the better.

Test your hill. Roll forward for five or 10 feet and then terminate the roll with a heel-brake stop. If you cannot stop that way, this hill is too steep for you to learn to slalom.

If the only slope you can find is too intimidating or steep, walk or drive to the bottom, skate partway up, and start from there to give yourself a shorter hill. As you get more capable and confident, skate back up a bit farther for each run. Soon, you'll find you can start at the top.

Four Linked Turns and a Stop

With deliberate one-foot-at-a-time pressure, linked turns become slalom-skating turns. For this first run, you are going to stop after every four turns to make sure you can stay in control of your speed; you need to be able to halt or slow down the minute you feel things getting out of hand.

- With knees bent and your weight evenly balanced, slowly start coasting forward.
- Begin a linked turn on the right skate. As it begins its arc, your weight will be transferred to its inside wheel edges.
- Use the muscles below your right knee to tilt and slightly twist the right skate around its arc, applying firm pressure to the inside wheel edges. The more pressure you apply, the better braking action you will get.
- Following the movement of your turning lower body, bring your right arm across your body for added stability.
- At the moment the right or downhill skate reaches the bottom of its arc, shift your weight to the uphill skate to send it downhill around its own arc. The right skate now rolls in a parallel position, relatively unweighted.
- Make a total of four slalom turns, then use your heel brake to stop or slow down so that you retain absolute control.
- Repeat the exercise, making four to six turns and then checking your speed with the heel brake, until you can make it safely all the way down the hill.

Advanced Slalom Skating: Handle Those Hills!

In-line skating is so complementary to skiing that the World Cup and professional ski teams skate for cross-training in the dry months. Recreational skiers, too, improve their skills whenever they skate "carved" turns down hills; similarly, practicing this move will give nonskiers an advantage if they ever take up snow skiing.

Slalom skating requires good independent footwork. Before you risk skating down a hill, you must be very comfortable using your heel brake and making linked turns and one-footed glides. You must also be able to maintain the balanced ready position.

Lower Body Control

As your lower leg tilts around to arc into a slalom turn, you can govern your speed and improve your balance by taking advantage of the centrifugal force that builds up under the wheels. This drill teaches you a more aggressive slalom turn that provides better speed control.

- Begin to skate down your hill, and at the bottom of each turn, increase pressure on the downhill skate by bending your knees and flexing your hip joints while bearing down on your arches. This causes your body to dip slightly, as though you are starting to sit down.
- Rise up again just as you transfer your weight onto the other, edging skate, initiating a new turn.
- Finish each turn with a small dip and start the next one with a rise. Make sure you do not bend at the waist to do this—you still need to maintain your ready position.
- Continue down the slope, practicing a rhythmic down-up movement with each turn.

Upper Body Control

Your arms help you make strong, complete turns as well as provide stability and rhythm. When the arms are properly placed, they affect the position of the upper body, which influences the pressured edging that controls your speed. To practice upper body control:

- Begin slalom-skating down a slope, making controlled turns.
- Starting a right-footed turn toward the left, use your right hand to point down the hill and across the sidewalk to the place on the pavement where you want to dip at the start of your next turn.
- At the moment you start rising from that dip to transfer your weight to the left skate, use your left arm to point at the site of your next dip and rise.

Hand Placement

This next drill demonstrates the proper hand and arm positions for skating short and long slalom turns. In both cases, you must keep your hands just a few inches apart from each other and in full view, directly in front of your chest:

- Raise both hands and position them as though you're gripping the steering wheel of a car.
- Start down the hill making short, tight turns. For these smaller turns, your hands (placed on the invisible steering wheel) will always follow a straight path square to the bottom of the hill as your lower body sweeps smoothly from side to side.
- Now make the biggest turns you can manage. For these turns, your hands and upper body will rotate from side to side as you round each curve. Still, your shoulders and hands should remain lined up with your lower body, helping you complete each turn.

Short Turns

On steeper hills, you'll need to shorten your turns to maintain appropriate speed control. The more turns you can make to press those edges into the pavement, the less velocity you will build. Shorter turns will also make for better skating agility. To practice them, try using the following guidelines:

- Start down a hill, making frequent short turns using the dip and rise movement. Keep your shoulders facing straight down the hill, and relax your lower back so that your hips and feet swing freely from side to side.
- When your feet curve around in front of you, make a deliberate punch on the heel of the arcing skate to finish the end of each turn with extra pressure. Your body will advance to a position over your feet.
- Start the next turn by pressing the toe or first two wheels of the new edging skate into the pavement, asserting control from the very start.
- During the arc, rock the pressure back so that you can add the finishing punch from the back two wheels of the skate. (If you really get into short radius turns, you may want to rocker your wheels as described in the Skate Maintenance section on page 16.)

Skating With Ski Poles

Poling is a skill that is very ski-specific, but for skiers who cross-train with skates, it promotes an element of confidence and security on steeper hills. For this purpose, the poles are fitted with rubber-covered tips, available at most quality in-line skate shops. Here are some of the basics of the poling procedure:

- Grip them lightly, with pressure only at the fingertips.
- Your hands must always be in view, and no more than two feet apart. Don't let them trail behind you.
- Use the ski pole to mark your rhythm. Tap it on the pavement directly in front of you the moment you start the rising part of the dip-and-rise movement.
- Do not jab the pole out in front of you; just flick it out, by swiveling your wrist.
- Practice poling with the upper-body and hand-placement drills described in the previous lessons. This will help you properly initiate and complete your turns, maintain proper arm placement, and more effectively use those poles as a tool to improve timing and balance.

Fitness Skating: The Ultimate Workout

We've all heard that sustained aerobic exercise can bolster overall health and even add years to your life. What's more, by adding 25 minutes of such activity to your regular routine, you can actually turn your body into a fat-burning machine. It's a self-perpetuating process: As your muscles get firmer and denser, you get stronger and stronger, building ever more muscle mass. And the more mass you gain, the more calories you burn, even when you're asleep!

In-line skating is an easy, spontaneous way to get such a workout, since it doesn't require a lot of preparation or bulky equipment. Just keep your skates and gear in the trunk of the car, and grab a quick workout whenever the opportunity strikes.

A Running Comparison

Recent studies have even proved that in-line skating can deliver the same aerobic and calorie-burning benefits as running, as long as you keep the pace above 10 miles per hour. A serious half-hour skate can burn up to 450 calories an hour; even a recreational session can burn about 285.

Unlike jogging, however, in-line skating is relatively kind to your joints. The movements have the fluidity of swimming: Skaters glide smoothly and rhythmically along without any jarring footfalls. That's a particular plus for frail-boned older people and lifelong athletes with sensitive joints. And because skating is weight-bearing, there's also the potential benefit of building up bone mass—a special concern for women, who face increased risk of osteoporosis in midlife.

Roller Aerobics

You're ready for in-line exercise as soon as you've learned some form of stopping. (Make sure to wear your helmet and other protective gear, and remember that locations conducive to aerobic skating attract lots of other skaters as well as pedestrians and bikes.) Once you're rolling, you'll often find yourself in aerobic training mode even when you're just having fun or trying to learn new tricks. When you sustain that energy on a long trail, the fun doesn't stop and the exercise benefits are guaranteed. And sustained aerobics is not a problem, since you probably won't be satisfied with just 15 or 20 minutes on skates. Even if you're tired, it could be hard to make yourself stop and rest after two hours!

The Feel-Good Effect

As anyone who's tried it knows, 15 or 20 minutes of aerobic exercise can put you in a great mood. Some scientists have chalked that up to body chemicals called endorphins, which are often released through long, gentle muscular activity (the term is derived from medical words that mean "in the body morphine"). Whatever the cause, the mood elevation that comes from aerobic exercise such as skating is the world's best stress-reduction therapy. It's a bit like the high you feel after that second cup of coffee or glass of wine, without the negative effects. As you skate along, you'll gradually find yourself feeling benevolent, inclined to animated conversations with skating partners or clowning around. If you're alone, you may find yourself inventing creative solutions to problems at work, or perhaps even cooking up a get-rich-quick scheme.

Take advantage of the high. Bring along a note pad and jot down your thoughts. When you get home, take action on your plans—don't let the fruits of your in-line inspiration slip away.

Where to Work Out

For most skaters, a scenic paved path is a good spot for an aerobic workout if there are only a few gently sloping hills. Actually, any stretch of road or wide sidewalk will do, as long as there's little or no traffic and you can keep moving for at least 25 minutes without getting bored with the scenery.

The Warm-Up

To prepare for a workout, start skating slowly and maintain a moderate pace for four or five minutes to get your blood circulating. Some people also like to stretch beforehand—but actually that's of dubious benefit when the muscles are cold; some people prefer to stretch afterwards when the muscles are more elastic.

Your feet need to warm up, too, since they take a few moments to reach full circulation. If the blood headed their way can't get past the tight boot cuff, the muscles will let you know. Your arches may start burning during the first five minutes; if that happens, stop and loosen your boots.

The Cardiovascular Skate

Ideally, you should stroke along with long, rhythmic forward glides. To maximize the effect of each stroke and gain power to skate up a hill, push directly out to the side, but swing your arms from front to back.

There is an informal-but-accepted way to determine if you're skating at an aerobic training rate: you should be slightly breathless, but still able to carry on a conversation or recite something quietly to yourself while maintaining your fastest comfortable speed. To increase aerobic benefits, make your strokes vigorous, and swing your arms to involve your upper body. Try to maintain a speed of at least 10 miles per hour. Speedometers, available for mounting on in-line skates, can clock your current and maximum speed as well as miles covered, both cumulatively and for individual trips. Look for them in the ads in skating magazines.

If your back can tolerate the speed-skating "tuck" position, you may want to use it to make your body more aerodynamically efficient. But be careful: it could take several months of conditioning to build a pain-free tolerance to this position.

The Cool-Down

When you're ready to call it a day after a hard skating workout, don't just jerk to a stop and kick off your skates; ease into it. Take an extra five or 10 minutes to skate slowly or play around and practice some skills or stunts. And when you do sit down to take off your skates, take a minute to stretch; this is a good time to do it, while your muscles are warm.

Stretch your hips, quadriceps, and lower back. Do not bounce; instead, concentrate on deep breathing. With each exhalation, the muscle being stretched will lengthen on its own.

Back on your feet, it may take another half hour to feel completely refreshed (and to stop shuffling your feet when you walk!).

Nifty New Stunts: Figure and Street Skating

This book is not the place (and I'm not the person) to teach the sophisticated figure skating seen on television. However, one of the joys of recreational in-line skating is simply fooling around in the wide-open spaces of parking lots, pushing your ability and agility to new levels. Here are some simple stunts and drills that can improve your overall balance and grace on skates. Practice them in any location designated as ideal for figure-skating in the tours listed in part two, Great Places to Skate.

On One Foot

Although your skater's equilibrium will automatically improve with time, you can hurry it along by practicing one-footed skating as often as possible. Improved one-footed balance will also enhance your ability to learn other skating feats.

- Start by skating a few forward glides and building up some speed. Then, hold each forward glide as long as possible, balancing your weight on the gliding foot.
- Try leaning forward to lift the other skate out and up behind you. If you feel stable enough, try to emulate the soaring arabesque of professional figure skaters.
- Make sure you alternate feet, and strive for the longest glides you can manage. If your glides are short and jerky, check your body position and reestablish your ready position before lifting a skate.

The Kneel

This is an easy stunt that builds confidence and mobility. You should be aware of which leg is your strongest by now; these instructions are written for those with a stronger right leg (if yours is the left, reverse them):

- Build up enough speed to start coasting.
- Pick up your right heel and allow your right toe-wheel to bear about a third of your body weight as it rolls close behind your left heel.
- When you can roll along with your right skate upright and stable, slowly sink straight down into a kneel, lowering the right knee close to the pavement.
- As you kneel, balance your weight equally across the right toe wheel and all four of the left skate's wheels.
- To get up, press the pavement with your right toe wheel as you rise straight up (if you need some extra oomph to supplement your leg strength) and push down with your hands on your left knee.

Scissor Handiness

Here's a stunt to impress your friends. To do it, you must have only one heel brake attached. If the motions feel too awkward, or if you have your heel brake attached to the left skate, use your left foot instead of your right in the following instructions:

- Begin coasting at a moderate pace on a smooth, flat area with your feet shoulder-width apart.
- Pick up your right heel and allow your right toe wheel to bear about a third of your body weight as it rolls close behind your left heel.
- Shift your weight back slightly, and then push your left skate ahead of you, lifting the toe so that you are only rolling on its back wheel. At the same moment you initiate this tricky maneuver, it may help to throw your hands up to lighten the load on your feet for a second.
- Now you are rolling forward on the right toe wheel and the left heel wheel in a scissors-like position. See how far you can spread your skates apart and how low you can get to the ground (this may depend more on flexibility than skill).

The Tip-Toe Roll

Once you've got a feel for the scissors, you're ready to try rolling on both toe wheels at the same time. This looks pretty flashy going forward, and it's also very impressive when you can do it backwards.

- Begin coasting at a moderate pace on a smooth, flat area with your feet shoulder-width apart.
- Pick up your right heel and allow your right toe wheel to bear about a third of your body weight as it rolls close behind your left heel.
- Now lift the left skate's heel as high as possible. It helps to sink down so you can bend your knees more to raise both heels high off the pavement.

Skating Backward

It should take no more than three or four sessions of dedicated effort to learn to skate backward, which results in fluid linked backward turns. But don't be discouraged if you can't get the hang of backward skating right away; just remember that once you get the feel of it, it will soon be quite easy.

- Give yourself an advantage when you are first learning to skate backward by finding the drainage area of a parking lot where the pavement has a very gentle pitch.
- Start by standing with your back to a very slight slope. Make backward hourglasses by sinking down as you push your skates outward, then rising as you pull them back in with the inner thigh muscles. Continue until you can make as many hourglasses as you wish without grinding to a stop.

- Now, when your feet are in the pigeon-toed position of the hourglass, press against the inside edge of the right skate while you look over your right shoulder behind you. Your hips should rotate 45 degrees toward the right, but most of your weight will be over the left foot while the right foot swipes out to the side.
- Next, veer to the left by turning to look backward over your left shoulder as you press against the inside edge of the left skate's wheels. Make sure you keep both skates in constant contact with the ground. (At first, use exaggerated upper body rotation and movements of the hips from side to side to switch pressure from one foot to the other.) Try to manage the same movement while looking over just one shoulder.
- Continue until you can generate enough momentum for a short glide between alternating strokes.
- As you begin to gain control of your backward strokes, try to lower the main muscle movement down to knee level and reduce the wagging of your hips.

Forward-to-Reverse Turns

You can switch from forward to backward skating with a half circle followed by a backward glide. This is the same movement as the one in circle stops (see page 30), except that your legs stay closer beneath your body, the circle is smaller, and you continue skating backward after the turn. (Well, it's almost the same.)

The following instructions assume you have a stronger right leg; you will turn counterclockwise. If your left leg is stronger, swap the directions and turn clockwise.

- Start skating with forward glides until you gain enough momentum to feel stable, yet are not inhibited by your speed.
- Switch to a coast with the left foot advanced.
- When you feel ready, cock your arms to the right just as you did for the circle stop drill (see page 30).
- In one swift, slightly rising motion, swing your arms and rotate your hips counterclockwise, initiating the circle.
- As your hips rotate backward, your left knee turns out. Lift the left heel for just half a second to pivot it around backward. After the left skate reaches the reversed direction, shift your weight from the right skate to the inside edges of the left skate.
- Complete the transition by pushing off the left skate's inside edge into a series of backward glides.

Backward-to-Forward Turns

Now you need to learn how to transition smoothly from backward to forward motion. This is much easier than you might think.

- Start by rolling slowly backward in a good body position. (A slight slope helps.)
- Turn your head and shoulders to the right to look over your shoulder in the direction you're headed. In response, your weight transfers to your left skate and it automatically begins to arc slightly outward, turning you part of the way around.
- With your right foot already halfway around, all that's left is to pick it up and rotate the toe the rest of the way around so it is lined up in your direction of travel.
- Put your skate on the ground and step onto it, pushing off the left foot into a forward glide on your right skate.

Jump Turns

Here's how to make hot-looking forward-to-backward and backward-to-forward turns by rotating 180 degrees in mid-air. On the lawn or carpet, wearing your skates, practice jumping up and turning halfway around before landing. You do not need to jump very high, and you may find you prefer one direction over the other.

After you feel confident enough, try some jump turns on the pavement, starting from a complete standstill. After more practice, try it while gliding very slowly forward as well as backward. To improve your stability, practice a sequence of jump turns centered over painted parking lot lines, alternating forward-to-backward with backward-to-forward turns. It's easier if you keep your eyes on the far end of the painted line as you turn toward it.

For smoother jump turns, keep the jump low and the rotation subtle. To do a smooth forward-to-backward jump turn, pick up just your heels and pivot around quickly on the front wheels. To smooth out your backward-to-forward turns, lift your toes slightly and pivot on the heel wheels.

Backward Crossovers

Backward crossovers are most useful for in-line hockey and figure skating. This skill does not come easily to most skaters, but fortunately, it is not necessary for having fun or for touring any trails in this book. But this is another skill that delivers better overall balance and agility once you've mastered it.

This drill is best performed on the edge of a large painted-on circle, such as those found in schoolyards:
- Start skating with backward hourglasses in the counterclockwise direction to build up some momentum. (Your right skate should be on the inside of the circle.)
- Go into a coast with both feet close together, and rotate your shoulders slightly toward the center of the circle. Sink down to bend your knees deeply and improve your balance.

- Still leaning into the center of the circle, transfer your weight to the outside of the right skate's wheels and pick up your left foot.
- Use your inner thigh muscles to pull the right skate underneath your body and away from the center of the circle. As you do so, the left skate will automatically cross in front of the right. As soon as it does, place it on the pavement, while allowing the right skate to continue its roll away from the center.
- At the end of the right skate's stroke, pick it up and replace it under your hip near the painted-on line.
- Continue passing the left skate toward the center of the circle, while the right skate rolls out and away from the center on the outside edges of the wheels.
- It is easier for some people to learn backward crossovers on a long straight stretch of pavement rather than trying to skate in a circle, by alternating crossovers with a pair of forward glides.

The Circle Spread

Spend some time working on expanding your circle stops into full 360-degree turns. Once both skates are in the turned-out position, a wide, knees-out squat makes this possible:

- Start by initiating a turn on the right skate's inside edge. This will make you turn to the left, counterclockwise.
- Pivot the left skate's heel around so you are skating heel to heel on both the inside edges.
- Keep both feet wide apart and squat deeply so that you make a big circle until the momentum dies.
- If your joints are mobile enough, try this: do the circle spread, except that in step two, try to put your left skate down on its outside edge. Adjust your balance and skate forward in a straight line instead of in a circle. Your knees will be bent at nearly 90 degrees to maintain this position.

Skate Speak: A Glossary of In-Lining Terms

To the uninitiated, in-line skaters sometimes seem to be speaking their own language. The following list defines the sport's most common terms, many of which are used throughout the book.

Aggressive skating. This has become the accepted term to describe two groups of extreme skaters: those who skate on nearly vertical ramps called half-pipes to perform aerial or edge tricks, and those who jump or grind with different parts of their skates against surfaces found in urban terrain (or in similar conditions), such as stairs, railings, and curbs. This discipline has its own quirky and quite large selection of colorful in-line skating terms, some taken from the world of skateboarding, to describe its amazing feats.

Black diamond hills. Taken from skiing, this term describes a steep hill that requires the skater to have expert downhill and stopping skills.

Carved turn. Another ski term, used here to describe an edged turn in which pressure from the skate's tilted wheels creates friction, which helps control a skater's speed. This is basically a more athletic version of a linked turn.

Curb waxing. Street skaters, like skateboarders, actually wax the edges of curbs and concrete planters so that the frames of their skates will slide more easily across them (it's called curb grinding). The greasy discoloration it leaves behind is often the cause of much strife between the skaters and their communities.

Grinding. Several grinding tricks challenge aggressive skaters, who use different parts of their skates to slide across surfaces of all kinds. Grinding can be tough on skates, but it seems to be addictive, especially with young male skaters. One version involves leaping onto a curb, handrailing, or planter edge and slipping sideways on the skate's wheel frame until loss of speed requires the skater to jump back off. Special skate features (or modifications) are necessary for this skill. The center two wheels are usually smaller than the outer two and are mounted on the frame wide enough apart to allow more room for the curb or railing to fit. Usually, the wheel frames are also outfitted with a plastic or metal grind plate, depending on the skater's preferred grinding surface. "Soul" grinds are performed forward or backward by sliding on the boot's inner or outer sole (and, yes, that is how they spell it). These are usually performed on hand rails.

Linked turns. Skating is particularly like skiing when turns are linked in a series of rhythmic "S" turns, usually on a downhill. The skates never leave the pavement, but instead swing from side to side where they are tipped onto their edges to apply enough pressure and friction on the skating surface to control speed.

Ramps, ramp skating, vertical skating. Full half-pipes and other ramps of various sizes are used by skaters to gain the height needed to perform aerial stunts.

Stair jumping. Dedicated aggressive skaters have been known to not only clear flights of 20 or more stairs, but to actually spin 180 to 360 degrees before landing at the bottom in a lunge position and skating safely away. Locations ideal for budding stair jumpers are noted throughout this book.

Stair riding. Another skill that seems impossible to non-skaters (and many skaters, too) is stair riding. Some say it's easier to learn backwards, but this trick basically consists of rolling down a flight of stairs with skates slightly staggered fore and aft, and with very loose legs to absorb the bouncing.

Tuck position. The tuck position is a low crouch that adds a burst of speed. It's also used by speed and fitness skaters when traveling long distances to reduce the wind drag. In the tuck position, the upper body is held parallel to the ground with arms either folded behind the back or swinging from forward to back (not side to side). Knees are bent at close to 90 degrees to generate a longer range of motion for each stroke, which is pushed out to the side. At first, skating any distance in the tuck causes a sore back, but with diligent practice, the muscles eventually adapt.

Part Two
Great Places to Skate

Almost every community abounds in paved playlands. Newcomers to in-line skating are often amazed to find themselves looking at local streets, parks, and sidewalks from an all-new perspective. Once your eyes are peeled for pavement, they'll discover all sorts of places with just the right terrain for your favorite style of skating. Here are a few examples:

Paved bike paths, striped lanes, designated routes. When they extend out into rural areas, well-maintained paved bike paths are a prime spot for in-line touring. In some cases you can get a map of a town's paved bike-path system through the chamber of commerce or the local visitor's bureau. On these maps, the Class One bike paths—dedicated paved trails with no automobile traffic—are what you're looking for. Ask for suggestions from the staff of a local skate shop (during off-peak hours, that is; forget asking on weekends, when they'll be busy selling or renting skates).

In addition, look in libraries and bookstores for books that list premium bike routes. Use such books only as a starting point, however, because roads and paths that are great for street bikes often have narrow shoulders, gravel, and other conditions dangerous to skaters. Also check hiking guides for trails marked wheelchair accessible. Sometimes these are packed dirt, but if they're paved smoothly, they can be good for skating.

Bike lanes, usually designated Class Two on bicycle commuter maps, are great for experienced skaters. Remember that when skating on public roads, you share the same rights—and the same responsibilities—as bicyclists. Stay to the right when possible, but if you're descending a hill at the same speed as the traffic, you're legally entitled to take enough lane space to react safely to unforeseen situations. Use directional hand signals to make your intentions clear to motorists or to indicate whether they should pass you on the left.

When skating on the street, beware of "right hooks," in which an overtaking motorist suddenly cuts across your path to make a right turn—which could very well result in a collision. Your helmet and other protective gear, in addition to shielding you against falls, *should* serve as a red flag to remind such drivers that you're moving much faster than pedestrian speeds, but don't count on it: if you anticipate a possible right hook, slow down and let the vehicle pass you, so *you* can maneuver around *it* rather than vice versa. (Beware: legal restrictions for leaving the bike lane and entering the roadway can vary from city to city and may even be different for skaters than for bicyclists, so learn the score to avoid a citation.)

After-hours schoolyards. Schoolyards are everywhere! And after hours and all summer long, school parking lots and paved playgrounds offer a variety of surfaces to challenge and inspire skaters of all ages. With a good mix of terrain, you can learn how to ride and jump short flights of stairs, make slalom turns, conquer curbs, and perform all manner of show-off tricks.

Business park sidewalks and parking lots. As with schools, you need to time your visits for the off-hours. Often these areas contain vast parking lots and wide sidewalks bordered by manicured lawns. Streets in business park complexes can be virtually deserted on weekends, and for this reason, they're sometimes used for workouts or speed-skating events.

New neighborhoods. Time was, you had to look for pricey neighborhoods to find fine-grade street pavement, wide concrete sidewalks, and a neighborhood park with drinking fountains and perhaps a basketball or volleyball court. Today, many new housing developments offer these amenities, and it's not unusual to find a paved multiuse path linking them all, much to the delight of local bikers, runners, strollers, and skaters.

Foothill neighborhoods. Slalom skaters, this tip's for you! Some communities have ritzy hillside neighborhoods with wide streets and very little traffic; there, expert ski-skaters can practice downhill slalom turns and get an uphill aerobic workout while taking in spectacular views of valley, bay, or sea. Residents don't seem to mind, especially when they see seriously attired skaters practicing equally serious moves. When you slalom by with a pair of rubber-tipped ski poles, it adds a whole new flavor to a neighborhood.

Have Wheels, Will Travel: Expanding Your Options

Also remember to bring along your skates on any trip, whether it's for business or pleasure, domestic or overseas. When flying, pack your protective gear and helmet in your luggage (for weekends a backpack works great), but consider taking your skates on board as a carry-on. Besides saving suitcase room, it's a great conversation starter. Here are some more ideas for on-the-road rolling:

Urban downtowns, day or night. City ordinances vary for downtown skating, so ask at a local shop first. Parking structures are another skating favorite, but save these for night when there's less traffic and less chance of being asked to leave by security guards. Be respectful of city property; if you aren't, you risk depriving us all of the privilege to skate the urban landscapes.

Campgrounds. Take along your skates on all car-camping trips so you can explore the paved roads winding through the entire campground. Watch out for kids, cars, and debris on the road.

Unfinished housing or business developments. Look on the outskirts of growing towns, where streets and wide, landscaped sidewalks are created in preparation for new businesses or homes. You're often rewarded with wide-open views of the countryside in a quiet, traffic-free setting. Brand-new pavement ices the cake.

Bikeways and city parks. Parks built along canals, rivers, and creeks, sometimes called linear parks, are great places to look for paved, landscaped touring paths. Man-made and natural lakes in and around town are often encircled by concrete sidewalks or bike paths—a paved loop in a beautiful natural setting.

Unused tennis, basketball, and volleyball courts. If nobody else is there and no restriction on skating is posted, grab some court time yourself on some of the most prime outdoor surfaces you'll find anywhere. These are perfect locations for beginners to take their first roll or to practice figure skating and stunts. In some cities, such a court may be set aside for in-line hockey practice.

Roller-hockey arenas, indoor roller rinks, skateboard parks. A mere sampling of California's skating facilities is listed in the Resource Guide on page 444. Outside the state, check the yellow pages under Roller or Skate, or call a local skate shop.

Low-traffic rural roads. As long as you have skates and skills, you can explore any scenic country road that has great pavement and few cars. Rolling quietly past the sights, sounds, and smells lets you fully experience the beauty of the countryside.

Ready to roll? The chapters that follow present you with detailed, specific descriptions of 300 routes just waiting to be skated in every corner of the state. Have fun!

North Mountains

3 Great Places to Skate

North Mountains

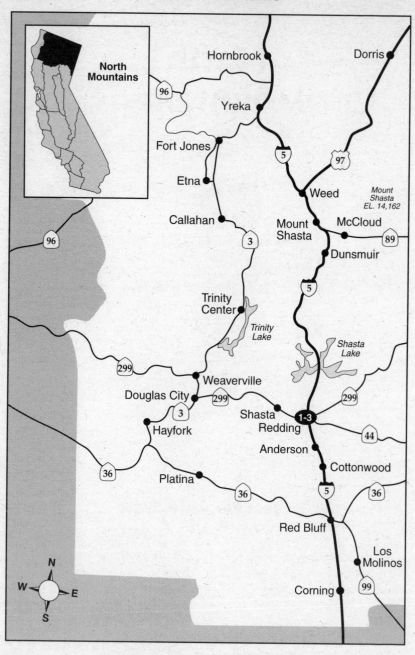

Skating Regions Beyond the North Mountains

South .... Central Valley North, p. 201   West .... North Coast, p. 65

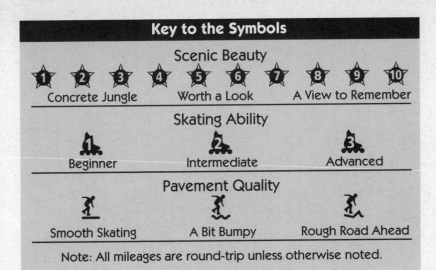

Key to the Symbols

Scenic Beauty

1 2 3 4 5 6 7 8 9 10

Concrete Jungle   Worth a Look   A View to Remember

Skating Ability

Beginner   Intermediate   Advanced

Pavement Quality

Smooth Skating   A Bit Bumpy   Rough Road Ahead

Note: All mileages are round-trip unless otherwise noted.

This geographically rich region is filled with mountains and volcanoes, glaciers and waterfalls, canyons and national forests (including Shasta-Trinity, Lassen, Klamath, Six Rivers, Mendocino, and Modoc National Forests)—terrain that makes it a little difficult for a sport like in-line skating to gain a foothold, so to speak.

The most populated areas are in the northern Sacramento Valley, and without a doubt, the best skating spot in the region is at the spectacular Sacramento River Trail in Redding. The scenery, hills, and extra-wide, extra-smooth pavement make this long loop on both banks one of the top places to skate in northern California.

---

1. Sacramento River Trail   8.25 miles

Reference: **A bikeway near downtown Redding; see number ❶ on page 60.**

Ideal for: Beginners—Fitness—Hills/Slalom—Touring

Directions: From Interstate 5 in Redding, take the Highway 299/Downtown Redding exit and cross the bridge over the river. Turn right at the light for North Market/State Highway 273 and turn left onto Riverside Drive two blocks up. Follow Riverside three blocks west above the river bank. Just before the road veers right to cross the river, enter a parking lot for the Sacramento River Trail straight ahead. The trail begins at the far end of this upper lot. Alternatively, you can go right to continue across the bridge and park at the Senior Citizens Center on the other side of the river to the left. The trail is on both banks.

Local shop: Board Mart, 1261 Market Street, Redding, CA 96001; (916) 243-2323. Other contact: Terry Hanson, City of Redding Planning Department, 760 Park Vies, Redding, CA 96001; (916) 225-4030.

Tour notes: Besides gorgeous scenery and perfect pavement, there's a treat for everyone who skates the Sacramento River Trail: the ultra smooth asphalt is an unusual 12 feet wide so that twosomes can actually skate side-by-side. Beginners will find an ideal lawn-bordered location for first strokes in Caldwell Park on the north bank, and intermediates can safely enjoy the entire loop by skating in the clockwise direction. Following the trail counterclockwise results in more demanding hills with sharp curves at the bottom—the expert's choice. Finally, the loop plus the new north shore extension to the east results in a serious 8.25-mile fitness workout. Best of all, because of Redding's out-of-the-way location, visitors are likely to skate along the Sacramento River Trail for long stretches without seeing another soul, even on a beautiful weekend morning!

A large, worn map is posted at the entrance to the trail. Its weathered condition is the only indicator that the south section of the path is in its second decade. It's amazing that the asphalt has held up so well. Taking the clockwise route, start down a wide service road through a shady corridor of tall trees and dense brush. In the summertime, you can eat your fill of the wild Himalayan blackberries that flourish here and elsewhere on the river's banks. Within a quarter of a mile, the fine, 12-foot-wide bike path takes over, and most of the signs of development are left behind.

As you continue west on a relatively flat route, the foothills of the Trinity Alps are framed by the trees and walls of the wide river banks. Emerging from the forested corridor into a more open area, you can see the scars left on the far river bank by hydraulic gold mining years ago. (A series of interpretive plaques along the trail serve to educate users on the history and natural surroundings of the river.) As you near the pedestrian bridge that takes you across the river to the more hilly north side, signs warn, "Rollerbladers, Use Caution." The bridge is made of smooth concrete and has protective barriers on either side, but it dips down in the middle and then arcs back up, adding a swooping slope and a touch of speed to your ride across the river.

Now the fun (and work) begins. After touring a while with a totally different but still beautiful perspective of the Sacramento River, you'll reach a steep little hump near the mile 3.5 marker, followed by two more climbs. Fast descents bring you to mile 4.0 with an elevated heartbeat—is it the aerobic effort or the thrill? (You just skated the section that is truly thrilling in the opposite direction.)

The trail seems to end in a neighborhood cul-de-sac. Skate a few yards up the street and enter the continuing asphalt trail on the right, just beyond the Buckhorn River Ranch sign. Pass through a grove of oaks to a landscaped section of trail with iron gates. Just after the iron ends, the trail branches. To return to the other side of the river to your car, go left (away from the river) and cross the parking lot to the entrance road into the Senior Citizens Center. Turn right onto the street and right again to cross the bridge. Don't forget to stop and admire the breathtaking views up and down river. (Cars are not allowed to cross the bridge in this direction, so relax and enjoy.) This completes a six-mile loop.

To continue skating on the north bank, turn right at the aforementioned trail branch and follow the trail to the edge of the river, under the bridge and past some concrete bleachers next to the park. Here you'll find a grassy lawn at the edge of the wide concrete trail, a great spot for beginners to get rolling for the first time. At the far side of the park, a boat launch parking lot interrupts the trail, but just keep heading east and up the service road with the bike lane, which takes you to another grass-bordered park. Watch out for a 20-foot section of very rough pavement behind the swimming pool. After you pass under Highway 273, a return back to an asphalt surface signals the start of the newest trail extension. It features the splashing sound of a low dam spillway, two sunny meadows, a smooth, new asphalt parking lot with trail access, a sudden curving descent to a jungle-like pond full of lounging turtles, and a concrete bridge over a creek.

When you have explored it all, turn and head back to the branch in the trail behind the Senior Citizens Center. Cross the bridge to return to your car.

---

2. The College Circuit   5 miles 🟡⭐ 🛼 🎿

Reference: **A roll around two colleges in northeast Redding; see number ❷ on page 60.**

Ideal for: Hills/Slalom—Road/Street

Directions: From combined Interstate 5/Highway 299 in Redding, take the 299 East exit leading to Shasta College. Exit half a mile up at Hawley Road and turn right onto College View Drive. Ascend the hill on the street bordered by flags, and park in the parking lot of Bethel College to play on the entrance road hill, the first description below. Back on College View, go east until you see the gated entrance to Simpson College. Turn right and park on the campus for more exploration described below.

Local shop: Board Mart, 1261 Market Street, Redding, CA 96001; (916) 243-2323.

Tour notes: Two educational institutions on College View Drive make for great skating, thanks to their hilltop locations and smooth-as-silk new pavement. (The older Shasta College campus located farther up

Highway 299 has terrible pavement and parking lots covered with Bott's Dots.)

Follow the first set of directions to drive up the hill to Bethel College if you're a speed or slalom enthusiast. Driving up will help you get a feel for the day's traffic and tell you if this hill is within your range of abilities. If not, the Bethel College parking lot offers much gentler pitches on good pavement.

Be sure to check out Simpson College next, half a mile to the east on College View Drive. Its entrance road is also smoothly paved and inviting. Simpson College—new and still growing—is located up on a mesa with gentle slopes. At the south edge of the campus, more good pavement can be found in the nearby housing development called The Vineyard.

3. Mary Lake Loop .5 miles

Reference: **On the western outskirts of Redding; see number ❸ on page 60.**

Ideal for: Fitness—Touring

Directions: From Interstate 5 in Redding, take the Highway 299/Downtown Redding exit, and head west through and beyond downtown almost three miles to Buenaventura Boulevard. Turn left and then take the first right, which is Lakeside Drive. Follow Lakeside as it climbs a ridge, and just after passing Ridge Drive on the right, you'll come upon the lake. Park at the curb.

Local shop: Board Mart, 1261 Market Street, Redding, CA 96001; (916) 243-2323.

Tour notes: Mary Lake is a good spot for a few aerobic laps or for building up the skills needed to skate on Redding's Sacramento River Trail (see page 61). The Mary Lake hills are smaller and fewer in number, but the path still has one good descent with a blind curve at the bottom, a tamer version of what the River Trail delivers.

Although the trail-side markers read .25, .75, and 1, this trail is actually only half a mile long, leading you to assume that the marker posts are measuring kilometers. The little neighborhood park where Mary Lake is situated is barely developed. On the neighborhood side of the lake, wild grass is trimmed down to lawn height, and one or two picnic tables are a short distance from the water. Marshy foliage, some trees, and wild berry vines border the asphalt path. On the side of the lake that's away from the neighborhood, the vegetation remains in its more natural state. In season, you can snack on fresh, wild berries just around the corner from the south end of the lake. After you've gotten your fill of the loop or the berries (whichever comes first), skate around the neighborhood to enjoy the smooth and much wider pavement on its hilly streets.

North Coast

10 Great Places to Skate

North Coast

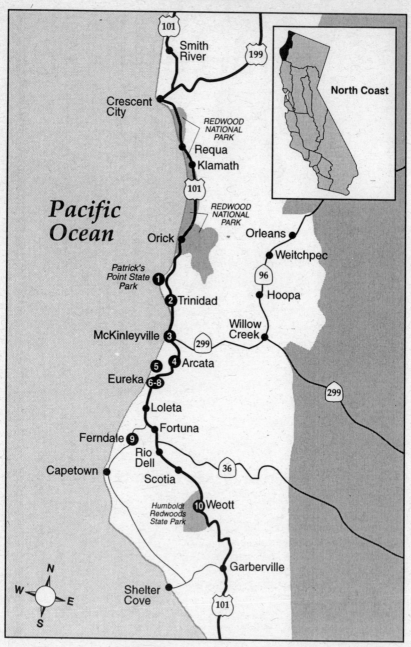

Skating Regions Beyond the North Coast

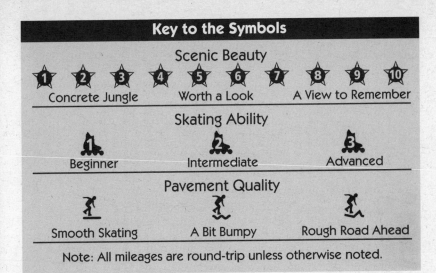

Key to the Symbols

Scenic Beauty

1 **2** **3** **4** **5** **6** **7** **8** **9** **10**

Concrete Jungle   Worth a Look   A View to Remember

Skating Ability

Beginner   Intermediate   Advanced

Pavement Quality

Smooth Skating   A Bit Bumpy   Rough Road Ahead

Note: All mileages are round-trip unless otherwise noted.

In the northern reaches of California, a little skill and a pair of inlines can take you through a forest of giant redwoods, down Main Street in a quaint seaport village, and along a path strewn with pine needles. Fine skating opportunities can be found throughout the North Coast region, which stretches for more than 200 miles along the rugged shore of the Pacific Ocean and reaches inland to the majestic Six Rivers and Mendocino National Forests.

Way up in Humboldt County, you can skate in and around the coastal towns of Arcata, Ferndale, and Trinidad. Crescent City, 20 miles from the Oregon border, even has its own in-line hockey rink at the fairgrounds. Although there are fewer dedicated bicycle paths and lanes this far north, the historic flavor preserved in many of the Victorian-era buildings and the relaxed character of the towns deliver a truly special California skating experience.

1. Patrick's Point State Park   5 miles

Reference: **On the Pacific coast north of Trinidad; see number ❶ on page 66.**

Ideal for: Touring

Directions: Fifteen miles north of Trinidad on U.S. 101, take the Patrick's Point State Park exit. Follow Patrick's Point Drive half a mile south of the exit and park on the wide gravel shoulder outside the park's entrance to avoid the $5 day use fee. Pick up the park's map at the entrance kiosk.

Map: Patrick's Point State Park Map and Guide, 4150 Patrick's Point Drive, Trinidad, CA 95570.

Local shop: New Outdoor Store, 876 G Street, Arcata, CA 95521-6216; (707) 822-0321. Other contact: Patrick's Point State Park, 4150 Patrick's Point Drive, Trinidad, CA 95570; (707) 677-3570.

Tour notes: Save your visit to Patrick's Point for a fog-free spring or fall afternoon when you can better appreciate the spectacular views and beautiful scenery. You definitely don't want to skate on the roads until the sun has been shining brightly for a few hours; otherwise you may be dealing with a surface that's treacherously slick with moisture.

Starting from outside the entrance of the park on Patrick's Point Drive, skate into the park on the smooth and down-pitched slope past the entrance kiosk. (Stop here to pick up a map from the friendly staff.) Still gently flowing downhill, the road enters a stand of trees—mostly spruce, hemlock, pine, fir, and red alder. As you curve to the right, you'll come upon a wide meadow filled with bright wildflowers and thick grasses in the spring and early summer. At the far side of the meadow, a handsome rock formation stands guard like a medieval castle. When you reach an intersection, ignore the invitation to branch off to the left. The road and parking lot in that direction have the worst pavement at Patrick's Point, although you can hike down to the park's namesake rock formation from there.

Follow the signs pointing to campsites 86 through 123. Several lookout points offer great views over the lagoon. If you walk through the trees to reach the cliff side, watch out for poison oak, especially in spring when it's still colored camouflage green. As you enjoy the vistas from here, you can't help but envy the campers who were lucky to nab sites 98 through 101 (available first-come, first-served). Just around the corner from the rest rooms, a long flight of stairs leads down to Agate Beach.

The road circles around the campsites and then past a branch to the Yurok village, finally bringing you back to the meadow. Skate back up the hill and through the trees. Just before you reach the entrance kiosk, go right at the sign for campsites 1 through 85. Here you'll find mostly smooth pavement and green hills that roll through the forest toward the south end of the park. Traffic lessens on the road beyond the two campground entrances. Halfway down, you'll hit a very rough patch of asphalt, but it's fairly short. Skate to the end of the road at the edge of the cliff and enjoy the view from the sunny meadow. If you packed along your hiking shoes, you can climb down the cliff to the seashore.

2. Touring Trinidad 2 miles 🟊 🐾 🏊

Reference: **In the seaside town of Trinidad; see number ❷ on page 66.**

Ideal for: Hills/Slalom—Touring

Directions: From U.S. 101 fifteen miles north of Arcata, take the Trinidad exit west, which puts you on Main Street. Bypass the little shopping mall area close to the freeway and continue west until Main terminates at the intersection with Trinity Street. Turn left on Trinity and left again when you reach Edwards Street, which runs alongside the cliff. Park on the shoulder next to the cliff.

Local shop: New Outdoor Store, 876 G Street, Arcata, CA 95521-6216; (707) 822-0321.

Tour notes: As a skating tourist in the quaint seaport village of Trinidad, you can cover more ground and see more sights than you can on foot. It seems like less effort, too, as long as you don't skate down (and back up) the steep hill to the beach.

Start your Trinidad tour on scenic Edwards Street, skating east up the street along the cliff. Test the fine pavement on one or two of the streets that lead north back up to Main Street, and check out the tourist shops along the way. If you enjoy taking a turn now and then through shopping center parking lots, by all means do a little trick practice if you spot one that's empty enough. Return to Edwards via Main and Trinity, the way you drove in. Buy some fresh salmon at one of the seafood shops, or inspect the old lighthouse and its gigantic fog bell preserved for posterity atop the cliff overlooking the harbor.

Expert down-hillers will want to take the steep descent down Edwards to the gravel parking lot near the wide beach next to the marina. Climbing back up the hill with a decidedly anaerobic effort, you'll appreciate the always fresh and cool ocean breeze.

3. Hammond Trail 4.4 miles 🟊 🐾 🏄

Reference: **A rail-trail running along the west side of McKinleyville; see number ❸ on page 66.**

Ideal for: Touring

Directions: From U.S. 101 five miles north of Arcata in McKinleyville, take the Murray Road exit heading west. Murray comes to a dead end at a Coastal Access point, but here the Hammond Trail is still gravel. Turn left (south) on Kelly Avenue and follow it one block to where Knox Cove Court turns right. Knox Cove ends in a cul-de-sac surrounded by four large stone homes that look like modern-day castles. Park in the cul-de-sac. The trail crosses Knox Cove.

Map: Call the Humboldt County Business and Parks Department at the number below to ask if there is an updated version of the out-of-print Humboldt County Coastal Access Guide.

Local shop: New Outdoor Store, 876 G Street, Arcata, CA 95521-6216; (707) 822-0321. Other contact: Karen Suiker, Humboldt County Business and Parks Manager, 1106 Second Street, Eureka, CA 95501; (707) 445-7652.

Tour notes: The Hammond Trail is a Coastal Access route designed for equestrians, bicyclists, and hikers. So far, 2.2 miles of this old railroad line have been paved, but only one of those miles can really be called a "trail." Although Humboldt County's green hills and redwood forests offer a nice change from the urban trails so common further south, the main disappointment of the Hammond Trail is that you never really get a view of the Pacific.

For folks who feel compelled to skate the entire length of every trail (you know who you are), exit the north side of the cul-de-sac and skate the uppermost half-block of the Hammond Trail to satisfy your curiosity. Someday, when funding is finally attained, the gravel trail that continues on up the coast from here will be paved. Turn around and return to the cul-de-sac.

To skate the main part of the trail, head south from the cul-de-sac on the dedicated eight-foot-wide asphalt bike path. Here, the trail does deliver some of its scenic potential as you pass through a corridor of sandy banks lined with tall trees, dense ferns, and wild berry vines. Half a mile from Knox Cove, you'll cross a very nice little concrete bridge over Widow White Creek. Continuing south, the trail passes next to Hiller Park and across Hiller Road. Another half mile of trees and vines brings you to the end of the dedicated path. Here Fischer Road, a narrow lane serving a few homes nearby, takes over as the Hammond Trail.

If you're game for some adventure alongside a cow pasture, continue south on Fischer another half mile to where it drops down a hill between two fenced fields full of cattle. The Hammond Trail Bridge dominates this pastoral scene, but save some attention for the road. Besides its fairly rough surface, a wide puddle of pungent mud (cow manure, no doubt) tends to pool at the bottom of the dip. Make your way past it and skate over the bridge.

Bicyclists commute between McKinleyville and Arcata on the roads that continue south. A dedicated skater with soft wheels might be able to do the same. Traffic is usually light but the pavement is pretty rough.

4. Urban Arcata

5 miles ⭐⑧ 🏃 🏄

Reference: **Downtown Arcata; see number ❹ on page 66.**

Ideal for: Hills/Slalom—Touring

Directions: Approaching Arcata on U.S. 101, exit at Samoa Boulevard (nine miles north of Eureka) and head west on Samoa. Turn right on G Street and proceed four blocks to Eighth Street. The Arcata Plaza occupies the block on the left at G and Eighth. Park on a side street.

Local shop: New Outdoor Store, 876 G Street, Arcata, CA 95521-6216; (707) 822-0321.

Tour notes: Arcata is a small town with a decidedly rustic and slightly retro character. It's home to Humboldt State University, and many of the students look as if they're from the 1960s, with their long hair and tie-dyed T-shirts. The town has only one or two stoplights and a similar number of cutesy tourist attractions. Since the village is so compact, you can tour downtown, the college, and the east-side hills in one afternoon.

Starting in the tiny square at the center of town, you may be forced to compete with skateboarders on the pavement in the middle of the plaza. Sidewalks radiate out to each of its corners and encircle the grassy block. The plaza is too small to stay for long, so follow G Street north to 11th Street and turn right to cross over the highway. Just beyond the overpass, D Street slopes down on the right to a cul-de-sac. This street's fine pavement, great views of the town and coast to the west, and lack of traffic have made it a favorite hill for local skaters. You'll see an asphalt trail leading further south from the cul-de-sac, but it's only a short connector path that's better suited to bikes and foot traffic.

Dedicated slalom skaters will find one or two other streets in the hilly neighborhood with suitable surfaces and terrain for fun linked turning. In-liners with good uphill skills should make the climb up B Street to reach the campus of Humboldt State. From B, turn left onto Laurel Drive to find sidewalks on the right that allow you to enter the relatively flat heart of the campus. Alternatively, from B at 14th Street, you can cross back to the west side of the highway to cruise Arcata neighborhoods that date back to the town's beginnings as a lumber town in the late 19th century. Follow the smooth pavement of 14th and 15th Streets, where several stately Victorian homes still stand in all their original glory. Use I or J Streets to descend the hill with the least amount of traffic on the return to the plaza.

5. Arcata Marsh Interpretive Center

.25 miles

Reference: **The marshes on the south edge of Arcata; see number ❺ on page 66.**

Ideal for: Beginners—Figure/Stunts

Directions: From U.S. 101 in Eureka, take the Samoa exit (Highway 255) heading west. Turn left on I Street and drive to the end. The parking lot at the interpretive center building is your skating rink.

Local shop: New Outdoor Store, 876 G Street, Arcata, CA 95521-6216; (707) 822-0321.

Tour notes: It's no wonder that the Arcata Marsh is known locally as one of the nicest places around to skate. The parking lot has some of the smoothest pavement you'll find in these parts, and it's located right next to 154 acres of restored marshland on the northern edge of Arcata Bay. At the side closest to the interpretive center, an asphalt path lures you into the habitat of more than 200 bird species. Even though the trail branches off into the brush, appearing to promise a variety of tours through the marshland, the pavement ends abruptly within a few yards no matter which of the paths you choose. If you can survive being deprived of a rolling marshland tour or a bird-watching expedition, you'll find the empty parking lot as smooth as butter and roomy enough even for the most awkward attempts at backward crossovers.

6. Woodley Island

1 mile

Reference: **A refuge area and fishing marina just north of Eureka; see number ❻ on page 66.**

Ideal for: Figure/Stunts—Historic—Touring

Directions: As you enter Eureka on U.S. 101, the northbound lane becomes Fifth Street and the southbound lane becomes Fourth Street, both one-way avenues through town. From either, turn at R Street/Highway 255 near the northwest corner of town and proceed north across the channel to Woodley Island. Take the Woodley Island Marina exit to get onto the island's Startare Drive. Follow Startare to the last parking lot and park near the Fisherman's Memorial.

Local shop: New Outdoor Store, 876 G Street, Arcata, CA 95521-6216; (707) 822-0321.

Tour notes: Woodley Island is another one of those great little spots in Humboldt County that may be small, but thanks to a variety of charms, is well worth a tour. Starting from the westernmost end of the island, take a moment to read some of the names on the Fisherman's Memorial, dedicated by Arcata widows who lost men at sea. It's likely that there will be a few dried flowers at its base or a photograph of a loved one newly missing. Just offshore stands an oversized bronze statue of a fisherman with a net.

Skating east, follow the Don Clausen Embarcadero, a clean asphalt trail at the waterfront, complete with old-fashioned lampposts and benches. You may see harbor seals at play or the occasional large white egret flying by. Regularly spaced displays provide interpretive descriptions of the variety of vessels moored here and the catch in which they specialize.

The fine asphalt trail terminates at the east end parking lot, offering that bit of random play that's so good for grown-ups. Even better pavement can be found across Startare in the parking lot in front of the NOAA (National Oceanographic and Atmospheric Administration) building. If the generator is running, though, the noise will make a long visit undesirable. Skate back to where you started by taking to the street pavement of Startare, or returning to the Embarcadero to enjoy the smoother asphalt of the path.

---

7. Embarcadero and Old Town   4 miles

Reference: **On the waterfront and through Old Town Eureka; see number ❼ on page 66.**

Ideal for: Hills/Slalom—Historic—Road/Street—Touring

Directions: As you enter Eureka on U.S. 101, the northbound lane becomes Fifth Street and the southbound lane becomes Fourth Street, both one-way avenues through town. Turn north on L Street and follow it up to the waterfront area. Turn left after crossing Second Street to park in the lot across from the Eureka Recreation Center building. If this parking lot is empty enough, you'll notice the roller hockey lines painted on the pavement.

Local shop: New Outdoor Store, 876 G Street, Arcata, CA 95521-6216; (707) 822-0321.

Tour notes: A tour of Eureka on in-lines is a good way to get a feel for the history of Humboldt County itself. Eureka was founded in the spring of 1850 after gold in the Trinity region brought wagon loads of miners north. They soon discovered another valuable resource in even greater abundance: lumber. Located on the Humboldt Bay, Eureka became an important port for fishing and whaling vessels as well as those that brought in supplies for the miners and lumbermen. Today you can skate on the Eureka waterfront, through Old Town, and past beautifully restored Victorian homes, all within close proximity to the bay and one another.

Start your tour on the short Eureka waterfront path (only a third of a mile), down at the water's edge. The eight-foot-wide asphalt trail begins next to the small amphitheater at the east end of the parking area and passes under Highway 255 at the boat launching ramp.

The highly textured surface on the ramp keeps boats from slipping away, but it's too rude for words from a skater's point of view. Beyond the boat ramp, the waterfront trail continues only a few more yards before terminating at a small gravel parking lot.

Return to the Eureka Recreation Center building and skate on its waterfront side. A concrete sidewalk imprinted with a wood-grain texture leads to a bay-front viewing platform. If you cross the parking lot on the other side, another short stretch of asphalt and sidewalk (take your pick) takes you a block further to a disappointingly early end.

Eureka's waterfront skating may be short, but that leaves you with lots of energy for skating up to the Carson Mansion and touring the improved sidewalks of Old Town. From the Second Street entrance to the waterfront parking lot, turn east on Second and skate up the short hill to beautiful Carson Mansion, raised in 1885 by lumber magnate William Carson. (He had it built by mill workers during a slow period in the industry to keep them busy.) Today it's a private club that's not open to the public, but the spectacular exterior and grounds are the showpiece of the town.

The fancy Second Street sidewalk running from the mansion to downtown passes some homes that can only be described as shacks—they're old, all right, but definitely not preserved. Fortunately, most of the buildings are in better repair once you reach the business district, where there are signs that the Old Town improvements are still a work in progress. The centerpiece of Old Town is the plaza's brick gazebo with its inviting spiral ramp. Watch the pigeons scatter when you roll back down!

---

8. Sequoia Park   1.5 miles ⑨ 🛹 🛼

Reference: **A park on the southern edge of Eureka; see number ⑧ on page 66.**

Ideal for: Hills/Slalom—Touring

Directions: From U.S. 101 entering Eureka about a mile up from where the freeway ends, turn right onto Harris Street, a one-way street heading west. After 2.25 miles, turn right on W Street and pull into the Sequoia Park entrance on the right.

Local shop: New Outdoor Store, 876 G Street, Arcata, CA 95521-6216; (707) 822-0321.

Tour notes: Sequoia Park is a fantastic little ecosystem still standing within the city limits of Eureka. The forest primeval momentarily surrounds you as you skate among the gigantic redwoods and dense fern undergrowth in the park's 54 acres. Besides its incredible beauty, Sequoia Park offers one of the most thrilling skates around. Half of the three-quarter mile loop is flat and covered with pine needles, but the other half consists of steep hills with surprise lumps in the pavement.

Starting from the park's W Street parking lot, take the short tour to the right (north) that follows a narrow asphalt service road (as a skating path, it's actually quite wide) winding through the shade of the tall trees. Here the pine needles lie in a brown carpet that often hides the pavement, but they're not so thick as to prevent stroking and gliding. You'll emerge into the daylight at T and Glatt Streets. To the left you can see Glatt's "Wrong Way-Do Not Enter" sign where the trail re-enters the forest to drop steeply into the dark. You don't want to enter here either, because in this direction, the hill is too steep for a safe descent on in-lines, and meeting a car coming uphill could be deadly. Turn around and return to the W Street parking lot.

Expert skaters who can control a steep descent around a hairpin turn can visit the duck pond from here. Enter the trees on the service road that heads west into the dark forest from the parking lot. Soon the trail curves to the right and then dips down, down (watch out for the log-sized raised ridge in the road), around a hard left hairpin turn, and down some more to a little flat spot next to a concrete pool where you can feed the ducks. Now it's time to pay your dues. Are you ready to climb? Remember, short, wide strokes work best, and don't stop or you'll lose your momentum. You'll emerge from the forest at Glatt and T Streets again. Once your heart resumes a more or less normal rate, enjoy the soothing roll through the forest back to the main park area.

And why not do it all over again!

---

9. Victorian Ferndale   3 miles 🌟 🐾 🏊

Reference: **South of Eureka in the village of Ferndale; see number ❾ on page 66.**

Ideal for: Historic—Touring

Directions: Twenty miles south of Eureka on U.S. 101, take the Ferndale/Fernbridge exit. Follow the frontage road next to the freeway to the bridge. Turn west to cross the bridge over the Eel River and proceed on Highway 211 for four miles to the town of Ferndale. Park near Main Street in a parking lot or on a side street.

Local shop: New Outdoor Store, 876 G Street, Arcata, CA 95521-6216; (707) 822-0321.

Tour notes: You won't find long bike paths or major flights of stairs in the village of Ferndale. But you will find plenty of old-fashioned charm, making this small town the perfect place to take it down a notch and enjoy being an in-line tourist for awhile. Founded in 1854 by Danish immigrants, Ferndale's street's are lined with well-kept Victorian homes and stores—many of them more than a hundred years old.

Flat Main Street and its wide sidewalks have the best skating surfaces, although side streets are passable, too. The downtown shop proprietors are friendly and welcome customers who roll in to, say, order an ice-cream cone.

After you've done the town, skate to the south end of Main Street and turn left just before the last house. This places you on the smooth pavement of the parking lot at Fireman's Park, a dandy spot to shoot a puck or practice tricks. Public rest rooms and a drinking fountain can be found at the east end of the park on the other side of the baseball diamond.

---

10. Avenue of the Giants   6 miles

Reference: Parallel to U.S. 101 in Humboldt Redwoods State Park, Weott; see number ⑩ on page 66.

Ideal for: Road/Street—Touring

Directions: From U.S. 101 45 miles south of Eureka, take the Weott exit and go west to reach the Avenue of the Giants (also known as Highway 254), parallel to Highway 101. To skate near Miranda and Phillipsville, take the exit 10 miles south of Weott between the two towns. Park on the shoulder near the downtown areas to skate the nearby section of the Avenue.

Local shop: Skate City Roller Center, 2146 South State Street, Ukiah, CA 95482; (707) 468-8600.

Tour notes: The Avenue of the Giants is a 33-mile-long road that hugs the banks of the Eel River and passes through the dramatic forest scenery of Humboldt Redwoods State Park. Experienced road skaters will find the two-lane passage through towering redwood groves irresistible.

While much of the Avenue's pavement is very rough, it's smooth enough for skating just outside of Weott and near the towns of Miranda and Phillipsville, ten miles south of Weott. The forest is at its most beautiful on sunny days, but this also means that motorists may not see you in the shadows when the glare of the sun flickers through the tree tops across filmy windshields. The curvy lane has no paved shoulders, so it's also very important to hug your side of the road. Listen for traffic and skate with care. In Weott, the best pavement is found by skating to the north of town. For both Miranda and Phillipsville, the smoothest pavement extends at least one mile to the south.

Wine Country

5 Great Places to Skate

Wine Country

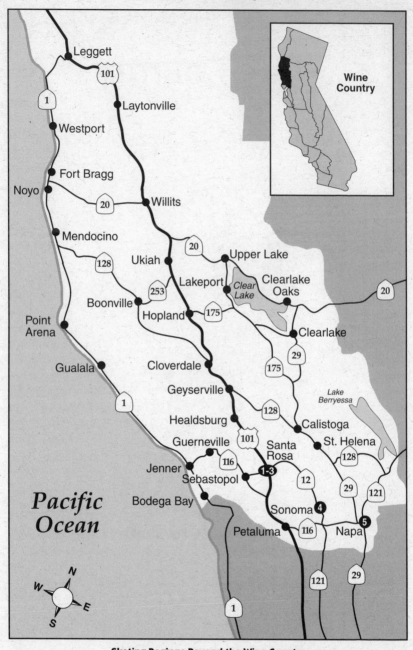

Skating Regions Beyond the Wine Country

North .... North Coast, p. 65
East .... Central Valley North, p. 201
South .... Marin County, p. 105; and
S.F. Bay Area: East Bay, p. 157

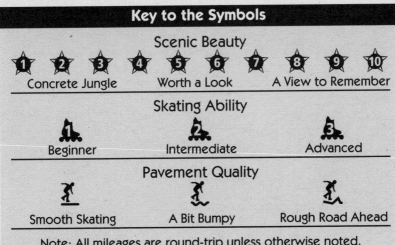

Key to the Symbols

Scenic Beauty

1 2 3 4 5 6 7 8 9 10

Concrete Jungle   Worth a Look   A View to Remember

Skating Ability

1   2   3

Beginner   Intermediate   Advanced

Pavement Quality

Smooth Skating   A Bit Bumpy   Rough Road Ahead

Note: All mileages are round-trip unless otherwise noted.

Napa and Sonoma Counties are renowned for their premier wines. But within the warm Wine Country valleys, one of the state's most diverse in-line communities is growing as vigorously as the region's grape vines do each spring.

Santa Rosa is prime roller hockey territory, but the city also attracts aggressive skaters from miles around, thanks to its own in-line skate park. The city is also the west coast site of Camp Roller-blade, where hundreds of skaters converge each summer (see page 436). Heading up the team of expert instructors is camp director and Santa Rosa native Jill Schulz, who is also a nationally known figure-skating choreographer. In addition, Santa Rosa's In-Line Club organizes frequent outings throughout the area for recreational skaters, including the occasional trip south to San Francisco.

In the town of Sonoma, the Historic Vineyard Trail passes right through one of the oldest vineyards in the state. A few miles to the east, Napa County's Silverado Trail (it's really a scenic, winding road) is the site of a popular 27-mile in-line marathon open to professional and recreational skaters.

---

1. Sonoma County Bike Trail   6 miles 8 1

Reference: A rail-trail connecting Sebastapol to Santa Rosa; see number ❶ on page 78.

Ideal for: Beginners—Touring

Directions: From U.S. 101 just south of Santa Rosa, take Highway 12 heading east. Proceed three miles, passing the stoplight at Fulton

---

Road. Turn left (south) at the next street, Merced Avenue. Park immediately on the gravel shoulder at the edge of the eucalyptus trees. The trail starts to the west from here.

Map: California State Automobile Association (AAA) North Bay Counties map, Russian River Area.

Local shop: Sonoma Outfitters, 145 Third Street, Santa Rosa, CA 95401; (707) 528-1920. Other contact: Philip Sales, Sonoma County Regional Parks, 410 Fiscal Drive, Santa Rosa, CA 95403; (707) 527-2041.

Tour notes: This wide, flat, three-mile stretch of good asphalt takes bicyclists, skaters, and equestrians from the rural countryside outside of Santa Rosa to the town of Sebastapol. One young local described it as "pretty boring," but precious few skating tours pass by a working dairy farm or require a pause while a tractor topped with smiling children crosses the trail.

Near the beginning of the trail, the noise from nearby Highway 12 is difficult to ignore, in spite of beautiful, open panoramas to the south. But you'll leave the traffic far behind after passing by the dairy farm. In late winter and early spring, yellow mustard blossoms brighten the marshy field to the south, and benches are provided if you want to sit for a spell and enjoy the scenery. After crossing the wooden bridge, skate through a lightly wooded area and, all too soon, you'll reach the edge of Sebastapol.

Plans exist for extending the asphalt on this old railroad bed to stretch for 10 miles, all the way up to Forestville. But for now, the trail disappears into a parking lot across Highway 116, so turn back when you reach Sebastapol.

2. Spring Lake 6.5 miles 🎱 🐾 🛼

Reference: **A lake on the east side of Santa Rosa; see number ❷ on page 78.**

Ideal for: Touring

Directions: From U.S. 101 in Santa Rosa, continue north past Highway 12 (the Sebastapol Freeway) and take the Third Street exit at the Santa Rosa Plaza Mall. Turn right and you'll be on Third Street. Four blocks east, Third becomes Montgomery Drive, which you'll follow for 2.5 more miles. To park at Howarth Park, turn right onto Summerfield Road. The first left is the entrance to Howarth Park. It gets crowded here, but parking is free. (The trail description starts from the Spring Lake parking lot, described below.)

To park at Spring Lake, continue on Montgomery another four miles through a densely forested area. The road will suddenly open up again near a newer neighborhood with the Spring Lake levee above on the right. Turn right at the Annadel Spring Lake Park signs. Turn right again on Voletti Street a short way down, and proceed to the

Spring Lake Park entrance. There's a $3 fee per car to park here, but a swimming beach and showers make it worth it.

Map: California State Automobile Association (AAA) North Bay Counties.

Local shop: Sonoma Outfitters, 145 Third Street, Santa Rosa, CA 95401; (707) 528-1920.

Tour notes: Rather than a day of wine tasting, why not enjoy Sonoma County the way many Santa Rosans do? Take a couple of laps on the bike path around Spring Lake on a warm summer morning, and then rinse off in the lake and laze around near your picnic table.

Skating at Spring Lake is fun and full of variety, thanks to the curves that dip and rise around the lake's convoluted western edge, a straight, forthright border on the north, and a gently meandering southern shore. You'll share the trail with parents pushing strollers, street and mountain bikes, and a few other skaters. Because it does get so crowded, be careful with speed, and watch out for chance meetings around the blind curves.

Starting in the clockwise direction from the Spring Lake parking lot (toward the south), the eight-foot-wide path is easy enough to follow, with a dividing line painted down the middle. Take the low road, ignoring the path leading to the upper road, which is gravel. Several yards after rounding the southwest corner of the lake, the trail disappears into a parking lot. Skate toward the west and up the slope. Turn right when you come to the top of the rise to follow the road north as it passes through a campsite, where the trail levels out. In the middle of the open area on the knoll, the trail resumes to the left. A side trail takes you to Howarth Park, which isn't much more than a parking lot from this trail's perspective, but it's worth it just to get some more pavement under your wheels. From the intersection with the Howarth Park side trail, the path continues north, up a hill, and across the top of a levee. Near the far end of the levee, drop down the slope of the levee wall to your right to continue the loop back around to the Spring Lake parking lot.

3. Santa Rosa Junior College   1 mile ⚐ 🐜 🏃

Reference: In the city of Santa Rosa; see number ❸ on page 78.

Ideal for: Beginners—Touring

Directions: From U.S. 101 heading north in Santa Rosa, take the Steele Lane exit east, and turn right on Mendocino Avenue. The college campus is two blocks away at the intersection with Elliott Avenue.

Local shop: Sonoma Outfitters, 145 Third Street, Santa Rosa, CA 95401; (707) 528-1920.

Tour notes: Located just a short roll north of downtown Santa Rosa, skaters come to Santa Rosa Junior College on weekends to enjoy the plentiful pavement and wide open spaces this campus offers. Decorative pebbles embedded in the pavement may cause some wheel vibrations, especially at slower speeds. Stairs are few and far between, but there are many streets and parking lots, making this an ideal playground in a very skater-friendly town. Beginners will enjoy the flat terrain and lack of automobile traffic, and more advanced skaters can extend the in-lining fun by cruising south to Santa Rosa's vibrant downtown area.

---

4. Historic Vineyard Trail 5 miles 🎱 🐾 🏄

Reference: **A converted rail-trail in the city of Sonoma; see number ❹ on page 78.**

Ideal for: Beginners—Historic—Scene—Touring

Directions: Around the north end of San Francisco Bay, where it's known as San Pablo Bay, Highway 37 runs east-west between U.S. 101 on the west and Interstate 80 on the east. From Highway 37 at Sears Point, take Highway 121 north. After seven miles, you'll pass the right turnoff to the combined Highways 12 and 121. Stay on 121 and continue to where the signs indicate you're on Arnold Drive, approaching Sonoma from the southwest. Arnold veers off to the north (left) just past Olive Avenue, but you should take Petaluma Avenue by veering slightly to the right to meet the Sonoma Highway (Highway 12) at the west edge of Sonoma. Go straight to follow Highway 12 (named West Napa Street here) through town and beyond the plaza. Turn left on Fourth Street and park in the Sebastiani Vineyards lot at Fourth and Lovell Streets. (If you brought a picnic, park at the northeast corner of the lot, near the picnic tables on Lovell Street at the edge of the vineyard).

You can also start skating at the trail's west end, from Maxwell Farms Regional Park (but if you plan on wine tasting at Sebastiani before going back to your car, this would be ill-advised). To reach the park from the Sonoma Highway/Petaluma intersection, turn north and drive half a mile to Verano Avenue. Turn left and follow the lane to the parking lot. Rest rooms are located on the far side of the park.

Local shop: Sonoma Outfitters, 145 Third Street, Santa Rosa, CA 95401; (707) 528-1920. Other contact: Patricia Wagner, City of Sonoma, #1 The Plaza, Sonoma, CA 95476; (707) 938-3743.

Tour notes: This converted railroad line starts at a grand brick archway with a plaque describing the history and current use of the Sebastiani Vineyards, one of the oldest vineyards in California. The perspective gained from the short history lesson enhances your appreciation of the gnarled old grapevines as you begin skating right through the middle of the vineyard.

The trail's next point of interest is a park located on the site of an old train station. Just a couple of blocks south of here is Mission San

---

Francisco de Solano and a plaza full of delightful opportunities for exploration and eating. On the north side of the trail is a vast lawn, Arnold Field. For the next half mile, the route passes through Sonoma State Historic Park. Turn right on the tree-lined lane in the middle of the park's open area to visit the grounds of the General Vallejo Home. From here on, the trail meets several street crossings, but they're in low-traffic neighborhoods. If you're lucky, the basketball court with excellent pavement next to the trail will be free for some mobility and stunt practice.

The trail seems to end at the Sonoma Highway, but if you look to the left side of the park across the street, there it awaits. The highway is too busy for "jay-rolling," so skate left one block and cross at the stoplight. Now you can skate the loop around Maxwell Farms Regional Park. Picnic tables, a children's playground, rest rooms, drinking fountains, and a large lawn can be found here, as well as a big loop encircling the playing field. Since both sides of the trail are bordered by lawn, this is a good spot for beginners to practice slalom turns or heel braking skills on gentle slopes.

After returning to the Sebastiani Vineyards, if you still feel energetic, continue skating east on Lovell Street. The pavement isn't the finest, but street signs point the way to more vineyards on the outskirts of town. In the off-season or on weekdays, traffic is light enough for safe exploration.

5. Silverado Trail   27 miles one-way

Reference: **A tour through Napa County's Wine Country near the city of Napa; see number ❺ on page 78.**

Ideal for: Fitness—Hills/Slalom—Speed—Touring

Directions: From Highway 29 heading north, pass by the town of Napa and exit right on Trancas Street, which becomes rural after you drive a few blocks east. At the intersection of the Silverado Trail, turn left and park off the right side of the road on one of the gravel pullouts, or drive as far north as you wish to park further up the trail.

Local shop: C C Skates, 930 Coombs Street, Napa, CA 94559; (707) 253-2738. Other contact: David Miles, in-line marathon promoter, President of the California Outdoor Rollerskating Association; (415) 752-1967.

Tour notes: In the Napa Valley, you can skate past vineyards and wineries along the Silverado Trail on smooth asphalt with mostly wide shoulders. The beauty of the region is a year-round spectacle. In springtime, the vineyards exhibit row after row of twisted trunks with freshly pruned vines outstretched like arms, awaiting the next crop of grapes. Under each, the dark bark is offset by the unabashed yellow blossoms of wild mustard. As the season progresses, the rolling green hillsides surrounding the valley turn California gold, and the vines themselves decorate the valley floor in emerald grids. In autumn, they take on the colors of fall in all their glory.

To avoid the heavy weekend automobile traffic on the Silverado Trail, it's best to start your tour early in the day. Pay attention near driveways, where gravel is left by the treads of farm equipment going about the wine-making business. Traffic and midday heat are less of a problem in winter and spring, although you may encounter some muddy patches after a rain.

Few people will want to skate the entire 27-mile length of the Silverado Trail in one day, although it's the site of a popular Bay Area in-race held several times every year. For shorter trips, park on the shoulder near one of the cross roads, such as Oakville Cross Road. There are only a few rolling hills at the lower end of the Silverado Trail, where the shoulders stay wide and clear. However, the northern portion of the trail between Howell Mountain and White Cottage Roads gets slightly twisty with narrower shoulders (the width varies from one to three feet). You might want to scout your route by car first.

Slalom skaters will enjoy the parking lot at the Mumm Winery between Oakville Cross Road and Conn Creek Road. The driveway has a sloping hill that curves down to a smooth parking lot, faintly marked by the herringbone tracks of other skaters who couldn't resist the allure of gravity.

After you explore the Silverado Trail, drive across Oakville Crossing to Highway 29. At the Oakville Market, a gourmet grocery store and deli located one block north of this intersection, you can purchase a wonderful variety of snacks or sandwiches. Less than a mile north of Oakville is the Mondavi Winery, where wine tasting and public toilets are available. Picnic facilities can be found at Conn Creek Winery (12.5 miles north of Trancas Street on the Silverado Trail).

Gold Country

16 Great Places to Skate

Gold Country

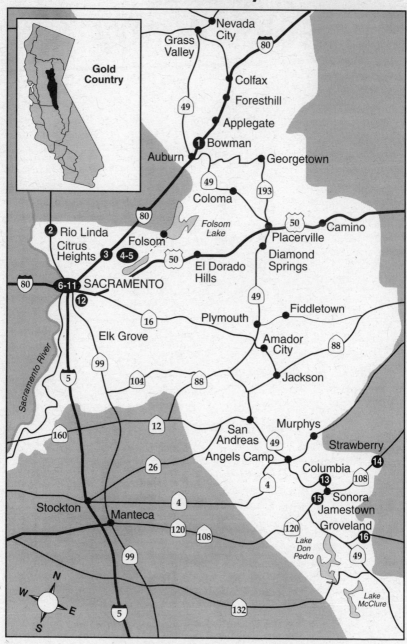

Skating Regions Beyond the Gold Country

North .... North Mountains, p. 59   South .... Central Valley South, p. 225
East .... Sierra Nevada, p. 243   West .... Central Valley North, p. 201

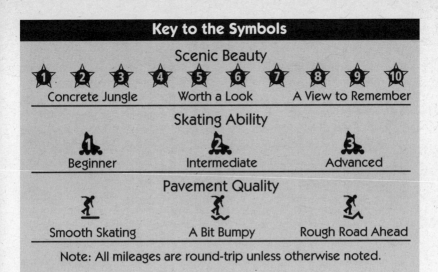

Key to the Symbols

Scenic Beauty

① ② ③ ④ ⑤ ⑥ ⑦ ⑧ ⑨ ⑩

Concrete Jungle   Worth a Look   A View to Remember

Skating Ability

Beginner   Intermediate   Advanced

Pavement Quality

Smooth Skating   A Bit Bumpy   Rough Road Ahead

Note: All mileages are round-trip unless otherwise noted.

California's Gold Country spans the length of Highway 49—the Gold Country Highway—which connects the counties of Sacramento, Nevada, Placer, El Dorado, Amador, Calaveras, Tuolumne, Mariposa, and Madera. This region steeped in the history of the gold rush days offers a gold mine of hill skating for adept downhill skaters, plus a fair share of flat trails for beginners.

The city of Sacramento is the center of urban skating activity in these parts. In-liners can take to the streets and sidewalks around the state capitol building and the downtown area any time, or join weekly evening outings for a guided tour.

Closer to the foothills near Roseville, Citrus Heights, and Folsom, skaters are blessed with access to one of the longest and most scenic trails in northern California, the eastern section of the 32-mile-long Jedediah Smith National Recreation Trail. Efforts are in progress to open up the downtown Sacramento end as well, which is still the domain of bicyclists.

Now that it's no longer an active military base, Mather Air Force Base, located just southeast of Sacramento, is also a prime place to skate during the cool days of early springtime. Here a bike path and nearly empty streets are bordered by grassy meadows with a view of the Sierra to the east.

Farther south, the hills that brought on the gold rush make for some thrilling rides on seldom-traveled back roads. Hill-skating enthusiasts should definitely visit the Sonora and Groveland areas.

1. Sierra Sunrise Building

1 mile

Reference: **Just off Interstate 80 in the Sierra foothills town of Bowman; see number ❶ on page 86.**

Ideal for: Figure/Stunts—Hills/Slalom—Touring

Directions: On Interstate 80 just east of Auburn, take the Bowman exit and go south one block toward the canyon to the intersection with the frontage road at the south side of the freeway. Turn right and then take the first driveway left into the parking lot of the Sierra Sunrise Building; the street address, 13620, is displayed on a big sign out by the road. Park at the east end of the lot near the dumpster.

Local shop: Sierra Skate, 365 Nevada Street, Auburn, CA 95603; (916) 823-2763.

Tour notes: Don't miss making a stop to play at the Sierra Sunrise Building if you're passing through the Auburn area on a weekend. The pavement around the building is ideal for practicing slalom turns, stunts, or figure skating. (During weekday business hours, skating here isn't a safe or appealing option.) As an added bonus, the overlook at this attractive building's large parking lot offers one of the most spectacular views around. Here the upper side of the deep canyon carved by the North Fork of the American River drops steeply away from the back of the property, delivering a grand vista of the mountaintops stretching far to the east and south.

Still relatively new, the Sierra Sunrise Building has pristine pavement, including both gentle slopes and flat areas. Even though the site is quite close to the interstate, it's at a lower level, so the noise from the busy freeway is dulled. A ramp from the upper parking lot to the lower one challenges beginning daredevils to roll down and off the step at the bottom. At the west end of the lot, you can slalom all the way down to what looks like the edge of the world, but railings are there to stop you from flying off into the canyon.

More skilled skaters will want to test their slalom turns on Sierra Sunrise Street bordering the west side of the building's parking lots. The street ends another block down in a patch of gravel and thorny bushes on private property, so make sure you can stop before rolling into that rude bail-out net.

Here's a food tip: If you love great burgers, you can't beat the freshly made hamburgers, milkshakes, and potato wedges cooked up just a block west at Ikeda's on the frontage road.

2. Sacramento Northern Bike Trail

16 miles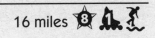

Reference: A rail-trail between Sacramento and Rio Linda; see number ❷ on page 86.

Ideal for: Fitness—Speed—Touring

Directions: From Interstate 80 due north of downtown Sacramento, take the Marysville Boulevard/Rio Linda exit. (This is also the Del Paso Heights and Rio Linda Road exit.) Go north 3.5 miles on Marysville Boulevard and then, half a mile after it crosses Elkhorn Boulevard, make a right onto M Street. Five blocks east, turn right again onto Seventh Street. Park next to the tiny Rio Linda Depot.

Local shop: The Shop, 306 North Sunrise Avenue, Roseville, CA 95661; (916) 773-2020. Other contact: Kim Yee, Bikeway Coordinator, Transportation Division, 1023 J Street, Sacramento, CA 95814; (916) 264-5145.

Tour notes: The best part of the Sacramento Northern Bike Trail is at the beginning, where it passes through a shady tree-lined lane and out to the rural countryside. Grassy fields border either side, and the route offers grand 360-degree views of the fields backed by distant mountains. The trail is a must-skate in the spring, but loses its appeal later in the year, when the central valley heat dries out the grasses. But even in cooler seasons, make sure to fill up a water bottle at the Rio Linda Depot water fountain to carry along with you. Most of the trail has very little shade, and there's no other place to find a free drink.

For the first two miles, the trail traverses the fields all by itself, away from automobile traffic except where it crosses a couple of streets. It then follows alongside Rio Linda Boulevard before passing under Interstate 80.

Just beyond the freeway, you must cross over to the well-tended greenbelt island in a tidy but decaying neighborhood. The signs on the grass next to the trail say "Stay Fit, Stay Safe: Exercise with a Friend." The further south you skate, the more you might consider this advice; the next neighborhood is even older and shabbier, and the greenbelt is replaced by a raised path. After passing through the south end of the second neighborhood, an unattractive industrial area appears to the left. Up ahead, you'll skate over a railroad crossing and then climb up the bank of the American River levee. Just a mile further on, the trail connects with the Jedediah Smith National Recreation Trail (see pages 90 and 92). This trail is a very popular asphalt bike path that runs through the American River Parkway to Old Sacramento, but at this point, it's officially off limits to in-line skaters. You'll risk a $75 fine if you skate here, and remember, you still have to skate all the way back to Rio Linda.

3. American River Canyon Drive

1.75 miles 🏅 🛼 ⛷

Reference: Two miles west of Folsom Lake in the town of Citrus Heights; see number ❸ on page 86.

Ideal for: Hills/Slalom—Touring

Directions: From Interstate 80 just west of Citrus Heights, exit at Antelope Road heading east and follow it for two miles to Sunrise Boulevard. Turn right on Sunrise, and then turn left onto Oak Avenue two blocks down. Follow Oak east for about five miles as it heads out into foothills country. Take American River Canyon Drive North (left) up a hill and park on the street below the waterfall at the housing development entrance.

Local shop: The Shop, 306 North Sunrise Avenue, Roseville, CA 95661; (916) 773-2020.

Tour notes: Bring your rubber-tipped ski poles to this irresistible housing development loop, where the streets and bike lanes are wide, the pavement is perfect, and the homes are pretty. The neighborhood is right on the edge of Gold Country, and you'll have a lofty view of the Sacramento Valley to the west as you skate. The new sidewalks alongside the loop road are too narrow for skating. But nobody parks their cars on the street, thanks to all the three-car garages, so your path to a great skate is wide open.

Unlike many of the new housing developments that are springing up all over the state, this one isn't surrounded by big walls that shut out strangers and invite graffiti artists. Another nice touch is that native trees were left in place when the homes were built, adding a mature, natural look not usually seen in neighborhoods as new as this one.

The longest downhill run is on the southeast curve of the loop going clockwise. If you skate the loop counterclockwise, you'll descend a shorter, steeper hill coming around the northeast curve. For beginners who aren't yet ready to attack the hills, a flat neighborhood park with a short stretch of concrete sidewalk can be found on the west side of the development.

4. Jedediah Smith National Recreation Trail West

8 miles 🏅 🛼 ⛷

Reference: At the Folsom Lake State Recreation Area outside of Sacramento; see number ❹ on page 86.

Ideal for: Fitness—Hills/Slalom—Touring

Directions: From U.S. 50 going east away from downtown Sacramento, exit at Hazel Avenue heading north. Pass Gold Country Boulevard, cross the American River on the bridge, and continue up to Sunset

Street, 2.5 miles from U.S. 50. Turn right and follow Sunset until you reach its intersection with Main Street. The access path to the trail is just east of this intersection. Look for curbside parking if nothing else is available near the access path. From here you'll join the main trail about 1.5 miles beyond the bridge at Hazel Avenue between mile markers 24 and 25.

Rough-and-ready skaters can choose a second, more challenging trail entrance near marker 22. To reach it, turn left at Gold Country Boulevard just before the bridge over the American River. Take the first right to enter the fish hatchery, where parking is free, although the lot is paved with gravel and dirt. Park close to the entrance driveway, because the trail crosses it at Gold Country Boulevard. The trail description starts at this parking location.

Map: The Folsom Lake State Recreation Area newsletter, with a map and other information, is available at the paid entrance kiosks.

Local shop: The Shop, 306 North Sunrise Avenue, Roseville, CA 95661; (916) 773-2020. Other contact: Folsom Lake State Recreation Area; 7806 Folsom-Auburn Road, Folsom, CA 95630; (916) 988-0205.

Tour notes: The Jedediah Smith National Recreation Trail is indisputably the best skate near the city of Sacramento, taking a scenic route along the bank of the American River. Unfortunately, to the west of Hazel Avenue, the trail is off-limits to skaters. However, the best and wildest part of the river is to the east, following the north shore of Lake Natoma. Along this section, the trail is fairly flat, with only one hill that will challenge intermediate skaters.

Beautiful weekends bring out lots of pedestrians and packs of fast-moving cyclists. In addition to the crowds, beware of mountain lions (several signs along the trail are posted with this warning, anyway). In the summer, the trail can be sunny and hot, so carry a large water bottle and wear your sunglasses and a high SPF sunscreen.

Starting at the fish hatchery, skate back up to Hazel Avenue. Turn left to head north across the bridge, taking advantage of the protection from the heavy, fast-moving traffic offered by the Arthur L. Kiefer Pathway. At the other end of the bridge, walk sideways down the steep gravel and grass slope (hold onto the wire fence so you won't slip) to the paved path that picks up under the bridge. Now you can start skating for real on the 10-foot-wide path with its yellow dividing line.

You must first pass the Nimbus Spillway and Dam before getting into more natural scenery. But from here on, the view just keeps getting better and better. Look across Lake Natoma and you're likely to see crew or waterskiing teams from Sacramento State University's Aquatic Center competing on the water. The trail veers away from the lake near mile 24 (each mile is painted on the pavement in big white numbers). Between the trees, you'll see piles of rounded rocks nearby on the left. These are the tailings left behind by the placer mining efforts of the forty-niners in the days of the gold rush. Just around the corner is the intersection with the access path from Main Street and Sunset Avenue, the location described under "Directions" on page 90, where beginning skaters should park.

The wide open area of the Mississippi Bar narrows somewhat at mile 26, and a wonderful, long hill where you can see the trail and approaching traffic far ahead descends down to lake level from here. This is a great spot to practice slaloms or enjoy a little speed, as long as you can get it back together if you meet a large bicycle club just around the corner. The trail flattens out again as it follows the narrow strip below the cliffs that drop straight down to the water's edge. Watch out for mud slides here in the winter and spring.

The trail stays relatively flat for the next mile, still far from the sights and sounds of urban life. Turn back when you reach the little meadow at the group camping area at Negro Bar, where this description ends. (See the Jedediah Smith National Recreation Trail East below for a continuation of this trail in reverse.)

---

5. Jedediah Smith National Recreation Trail East

12 miles 🌟 ⛹ 🏄

Reference: **At the Folsom Lake State Recreation Area outside of Sacramento; see number ❺ on page 86.**

Ideal for: Fitness—Hills/Slalom—Touring

Directions: From U.S. 50 going east away from downtown Sacramento, exit at Hazel Avenue heading north. Pass Gold Country Boulevard, cross the American River on the bridge, and continue to Oak Avenue. Turn right and follow Oak to Folsom Auburn Road, where you'll turn left. After about 1.5 miles, you'll pass the stoplight at the first entrance to Folsom Dam. Proceed one more mile and turn right at the Beals Point entrance.

To reach Oak Avenue from Interstate 80, take the Douglas exit east (it's also called the Folsom Lake exit) and follow it to Folsom-Auburn Road. Turn right and proceed south one mile to the Beals Point entrance on the left.

There is a day use fee of $6 to enter the Folsom Lake State Recreation Area at Beals Point, but for your money, you'll receive a map and enjoy the clean facilities available for swimming, camping, and picnicking. Beals Point has a smooth and easy loop around its perimeter that beginners and kids will enjoy. The Jedediah Smith National Recreation Trail is just up the hill from the entrance road.

Map: The Folsom Lake State Recreation Area newsletter, with a map and other information, is available at the paid entrance kiosks.

Local shop: Play It Again Sports, 1016 Riley Street, Folsom, CA 95630-3269; (916) 983-6376. Other contact: Folsom Lake State Recreation Area, 7806 Folsom-Auburn Road, Folsom, CA 95630; (916) 988-0205.

Tour notes: As you glide on in-lines through the Gold Country hills on the Jedediah Smith National Recreation Trail, the silence is broken only by the sound of birds warbling in the trees and squirrels rustling the grass (plus the hum of bicyclists and other skaters, of course). Following the banks of the American River, this trail, also known locally as the American River Bikeway, has much to offer the experienced hill skater. But be forewarned: it comes with its share of challenges, too.

On weekends and in good weather, the Jedediah Smith Trail is one of the most popular bicycling destinations in Sacramento County. Put a large amount of traffic on a trail full of blind corners with hills that encourage high speeds and you've got one radical skate. Make sure you're wearing all of your protective gear before starting out. As a matter of fact, on this trail, wearing a helmet and padding seems to engender a bit more respect from the serious bicyclists.

Begin skating at the north edge of the little path around Beals Point, a deceptively tame warm-up loop. Around the corner, you'll find the intersection with the Jedediah Smith Trail, a smooth path paved in asphalt and divided by a yellow line. Turn right to skate on the top of the levee to the absolute end of the trail at mile 32, where the asphalt is replaced by a gravel road. This termination point is a great spot to enjoy a view of Folsom Lake.

Turn around and get prepared for some hills. Immediately after the trail crosses the Beals Point entrance road, the first long descent adds speed to the wheels, taking you down past the rocky banks of the Folsom Dam, where the scenery is temporarily overtaken by the water works. Over the meadow and through the bridge, you'll see the first of two caution signs for the upcoming grades. A speed limit of 15 miles per hour is advised in painted letters on the path.

Now the long descents begin in earnest. While negotiating the many blind curves, it's very important to pay attention to controlling speeds that can get up to or beyond 20 miles per hour. Some skaters will find it desirable to brake to a stop now and then, not only to regain control, but to appreciate the beautiful riverside scenery of natural grasses and oaks. An entrance road at Negro Bar marks the end of the hairy hills section. Ahead, one long uphill and a series of flats and gentler slopes continue all the way to Nimbus Dam, described in the Jedediah Smith National Recreation Trail West (see page 90). If you decide to continue on, don't skate beyond Hazel Avenue at the far side of the dam four miles ahead, unless you're

---

ready to fork over $75 for a citation. (Skaters are only allowed on the state park section of the trail, not the county park section that begins past the dam.)

6. State Capitol Skate   5 miles 🌟 👤 🏄

Reference: **Downtown Sacramento; see number ❻ on page 86.**

Ideal for: Beginners—Historic—Road/Street—Touring

Directions: Entering Sacramento from the west on Interstate (Business) 80, follow the Downtown Sacramento signs to exit at Highway 106, which doubles as 16th Street. Turn left when you reach 16th and proceed north nine blocks to O Street. Turn left again and look for curbside parking (free on Sundays), or turn right at 15th Street to get to the parking lot at N Street. The state capitol is bordered by Ninth Street on the west and 15th on the south, by L Street on the north and N on the south.

Entering downtown from the north on Interstate 5, take the J Street exit and start looking for curbside parking at Eighth Street.

Finally, coming from the east on Interstate (Business) 80, follow the signs to Highway 160 and Downtown Sacramento. You'll emerge downtown at 12th Street.

Local shop: Alpine West, 1021 R Street, Sacramento, CA 95814-6519; (916) 441-1627.

Tour notes: Ignore the faded signs painted on the pavement around the grounds of the state capitol depicting a skate, a skateboard, and a bicycle within a "busters" circle. Those old ordinances are no longer enforced, so you're free to skate around the capitol and on the sidewalks and streets of downtown Sacramento. (In fact, touring the capitol park on skates is easier and more fun than walking because you can roll from site to site, reading the placards.)

Metal maps are placed strategically throughout the gardens on the east side of the capitol building so you can get an idea of what it is you're seeing. Weekends and evenings are the best times to visit on skates; there's less traffic and you're more likely to be able to park for free. Although you can skate on the state government grounds, you'll be asked to leave the steps of the capitol building. Never fear, there are lots of other steps around the capitol mall area that are well suited for riding or jumping, and even some easier ones for people just learning these skills. Wherever you skate, keep your eyes open for raised cracks between the aging slabs of concrete sidewalks.

7. Monday Night Skate   8 miles 🎯 🕴️ 🏄

Reference: **Downtown Sacramento; see number
    ❼ on page 86.**

Ideal for: Beginners—Touring

Directions: Entering Sacramento from the west on Interstate (Business)
    80, follow the Downtown Sacramento signs to exit at Highway 106,
    which doubles as 16th Street. Turn left when you reach 16th and
    proceed north nine blocks to O Street. Turn left again and look for
    curbside parking, or turn right at 15th Street to get to the parking lot
    at N Street across from the state capitol.

Local shop: Alpine West, 1021 R Street, Sacramento, CA 95814-6519;
    (916) 441-1627. Mari Tonin, IISA Certified Instructor, (916) 446-9223.

Tour notes: On Monday evenings during daylight saving time from
    spring to fall, you can participate in an organized tour of downtown
    Sacramento, including the state capitol area. Participants meet at 7:00
    P.M. at the parking lot on 15th and N Streets. Beginners are welcome,
    and for the first hour, they receive free tips from a certified in-line
    skating instructor on in-line basics and slalom skating. The city tour
    starts at 8 P.M. and covers five to eight miles of easy-paced urban
    terrain. Contact Mari Tonin at (916) 446-9223 for more information.

8. Wednesday Night Skate   15 miles 🎯 🕴️ 🏄

Reference: **Near the state capitol in downtown Sacramento;
    see number ❽ on page 86.**

Ideal for: Historic—Road/Street—Touring

Directions: From the Interstate (Business) 80 loop in downtown Sacra-
    mento, exit at N Street and jog one block north to reach the asym-
    metrical intersection of Alhambra Boulevard and Folsom Boulevard
    (which becomes Capital Avenue going west toward the state capitol).
    The tour leaves from the parking lot of Andiamo Restaurant at 3145
    Folsom Boulevard near the corner of the intersection with Folsom.

Local shop: Alpine West, 1021 R Street, Sacramento, CA 95814-6519;
    (916) 441-1627. Other contact: Dennis McIntire, Wednesday Night
    Skate group leader, (916) 444-2241.

Tour notes: Sacramento's Wednesday Night Skate is for experienced in-
    liners capable of skating 15 to 17 miles over a variety of terrain and
    pavements. The route varies from week to week, but always leaves
    promptly at 6:30 P.M. from the parking lot of Andiamo Restaurant.
    Plan on arriving 15 minutes before the scheduled start time. (If
    you're from out of town, it's a good idea to call ahead and confirm
    the meeting time.)
    Wednesday night in-liners need to be able to skate safely at a fast
    pace while dealing with cars, pedestrians, and other skaters. The size

of the group at the beginning of the 1995 season (and this was a wet spring) was up to 36—a number that's sure to grow as word continues to spread among enthusiastic skaters about the tours. Contact Dennis McIntire at (916) 444-2241 for more details.

9. Sacramento State University 3 miles

Reference: **East of downtown Sacramento; see number ❾ on page 86.**

Ideal for: Beginners—Road/Street—Touring

Directions: From U.S. 50 east of downtown Sacramento, the Sacramento State University exit is at Howe Avenue and Power Inn Road. Turn west at College Town Road, immediately after you get off the freeway (exiting U.S. 50 coming from the east, proceed straight ahead). Follow College Town to the southern border of the campus and stop at the information kiosk to check out the campus map posted on the window. You can park on campus for $1.75 (all quarters) at any lot that has a self-service coin drop box. Look for the bright yellow metal boxes mounted on poles in the lots.

Local shop: Surf & Skate, 2100 Arden Way, Sacramento, CA 95825; (916) 927-2005.

Tour notes: Skaters are welcome on the shady Sacramento State University campus, which has enough asphalt and concrete to make for a fun weekend roll. Favorite spots for in-liners include the ramped sidewalk that leads up to the front entrance of the library, or the stairs of the neighboring building (great for skaters with jumping skills). The concrete benches in the library area add another aspect to stunt skating practice. Cruising around by the Physical Education area on the north end of the campus is a fun roll, but in some places, the pavement is in poor condition or the brick tiling makes skates vibrate uncomfortably. Grassy lawns and wide asphalt stretches in the middle of campus encourage beginners to take their first strokes in a relatively safe environment. During times of low use (try weekends, evenings, and spring or summer breaks), the huge parking lots are great for figure skating or just fooling around.

10. William Land Park 3 miles

Reference: **South section of Sacramento; see number ❿ on page 86.**

Ideal for: Beginners—Road/Street—Touring

Directions: From Interstate 5 south of downtown Sacramento, take the Sutterville Road exit and head east. Turn left just a couple of blocks away on South Land Park Drive, then left again at the first street to park close to the sidewalk.

Local shop: Play It Again Sports, 3176 Arden Way, Sacramento, CA 95825-3700; (916) 971-1269. Other contact: County of Sacramento Department of Parks and Recreation, 3701 Branch Center Road, Sacramento, CA 95827; (916) 366-2072.

Tour notes: William Land Park is an oasis of shade in the Sacramento Valley, remaining relatively cool even as the rest of the valley bakes during the summer. The park covers several blocks, bordered by Freeport Boulevard, Sutterville Road, and Riverside Boulevard. While the streets winding through its grassy acres get a fair bit of automobile traffic, the wide concrete sidewalk next to South Land Park Drive is a fine spot for beginners. This stretch is quite flat, but probably no more than half a mile long. You can extend your rather limited tour of the park by exploring the streets and sidewalks of the attractive—and shady—neighborhood to the north.

11. Folsom South Recreational Trail

14 miles

Reference: **Southeast area of Sacramento; see number ⑪ on page 86.**
Ideal for: Fitness—Speed—Touring
Directions: From U.S. 50, take the Sunrise Boulevard exit heading south. After less than two miles, look for the stoplight for Sun Center (west) and Sunrise Gold (east). A quarter of a mile after this light, you'll see yellow gates across the trail on the right side of Sunrise. Pull in and park in front of the gates, next to the trail's entrance.

Local shop: Play It Again Sports, 3176 Arden Way, Sacramento, CA 95825-3700; (916) 971-1269. Other contact: County of Sacramento Department of Parks and Recreation, 3701 Branch Center Road, Sacramento, CA 95827; (916) 366-2072.

Tour notes: The Folsom South Recreational Trail runs alongside the Folsom South Canal for 14 miles, cutting a sunny swath through treeless fields south of Sacramento and connecting the Nimbus Dam with Sloughhouse Road. Don't expect great scenery: the wide bike path runs low next to the canal rather than up on the levee, so there's no view—and not much of a breeze, either. But this helps keep away the crowds, leaving the trail for dedicated speedskaters interested in serious distance or endurance workouts. Feel free to go as fast as your wheels will travel!

Be sure to bring water, since you're certain to get thirsty and there are no amenities along the way. The posted sign at the gate says that trespassing and loitering are prohibited by law, but this trail is recommended in "Rolling Right Along," a pamphlet about skating locations distributed by park rangers and Sacramento County.

12. Mather Air Force Base

6 miles ⑧ 🅐 🅘

Reference: At the southeast outskirts of Sacramento; see number ⑫ on page 86.

Ideal for: Beginners—Touring

Directions: From U.S. 50, take the Sunrise Boulevard exit heading south. After three miles, turn right at the stoplight for Douglas Road and drive past the empty guard kiosk after crossing the bridge over the canal. Just after you drive by Mather Lake, turn left onto Eagles Nest Road and drive past the golf course. Just beyond the driving range, you'll see an unmarked road on the right that is blocked off to automobile traffic. This is Woodring Road; park in front of the barricades.

Local shop: The Shop, 306 North Sunrise Avenue, Roseville, CA 95661; (916) 773-2020.

Tour notes: On sunny spring days, in-line it to Mather Air Force Base, where you can skate alongside grassy, green fields abloom with wildflowers and in view of the white-capped Sierra Nevada mountains. (In mid-summer, you'll wonder how this drab brown scenery could possibly rate an eight.) When I last took a spring roll here, I crossed paths with few cars and even fewer bicyclists or skaters—but plenty of large jackrabbits and buzzards. Since its closing as a military base in 1993, Mather has remained relatively undiscovered by the local skating community, offering the adventurous explorer miles and miles of deserted streets. There's even a clean asphalt bike path winding through the fields on base. But the recreational potential of this location is no secret to planners in Sacramento, and the city already has big ideas for its future. Try to visit soon while you still might have most of the place to yourself.

Scenic Eagles Nest Road is fair game for skating, but the pavement is quite rough. Instead, start by skating up Woodring Road into the residential ghost town. The homes, streets, and sidewalks are all still in good repair, though it's kind of eerie to skate without any signs of cars or people. Thigh-high grass grows in the front yards, yet healthy rose bushes next to the picture windows are still producing lovely blossoms. After cruising a few streets like this, it's a bit disconcerting to come around a corner and see lawns that are mowed. (The caretakers of Mather must have a rotating mowing schedule to keep the weeds at bay.)

Turn right at Mather Boulevard to skate by the Youth Center on the left side of the street. Out in back, you'll find the smooth pavement of enclosed tennis, basketball, and volleyball courts, although tufts of grass are now poking up from many cracks. The sign warning that "toy wheeled vehicles" (meaning skates and skateboards) are prohibited on the courts seems rather absurd in the ghost town context. Who's going to enforce it?

A gem of a bike lane picks up at the edge of the housing development and follows Mather for four miles, curving around the broad, grassy fields to gradually reach the heart of the base at the north side. Most of the small side roads the bike lane crosses are spattered with gravel, but the path itself is quite acceptably paved, and is much better than the road it parallels. Unfortunately, two miles up from the housing development, a deep 30-foot-wide culvert washout makes it difficult to continue on this route. Skate the mile back to where Mather and Douglas Road intersect, turn left to follow Douglas a quarter of a mile, and then turn right onto Eagles Nest to return to Woodring.

---

13. College Loop   6 miles ⭐7 🐾 🏊

Reference: **A country road just north of Sonora in the town of Columbia; see number ⑬ on page 86.**

Ideal for: Fitness—Historic—Road/Street

Directions: From Highway 99 in Manteca, take Highway 120 east to Oakdale, where it makes a 90-degree turn in the middle of town to join Highway 108. At the Yosemite Junction, the two highways split and 108 becomes the Sonora Pass Highway. Follow it about 4.5 miles beyond the Yosemite Junction and, just after passing through Jamestown, exit to the north onto Highway 49. Closer to the town of Sonora, 49 becomes Stockton Street. Turn left onto Washington Street where Stockton dead ends in central Sonora (you're still on Highway 49). Proceed 2.5 miles north to the intersection with Parrotts Ferry Road (County Route E18) and follow it into the old west-style town of Columbia, where it assumes the unlikely (in this case) name of Broadway. Turn right to follow Yankee Hill Road two blocks east to the parking lot on the left just before Columbia Street, in the heart of Columbia.

Map: For a free map of Tuolumne County, call or stop by the First American Title Company at 71 Shepherd Street, Sonora, CA 95370; (209) 532-3156.

Local shop: Sierra Cyclery, 55 South Washington Street, Sonora, CA 95370; (209) 532-3654.

Tour notes: This loop skate on country back roads is best done early on a weekend morning when traffic is low and the lack of a paved shoulder isn't as much of a safety issue. Experienced road skaters will enjoy the challenge offered by the hills, but do be extra careful, since folks going about their business out here aren't necessarily on the lookout for in-liners. Thick stands of trees create some blind curves, so be sure to listen for the sound of approaching cars; also keep your eyes on the road for a few cracked patches of pavement.

Starting from the small old-west town of Columbia, skate east on Yankee Hill Road, which passes by a couple of small ranches on the way out of town and then enters a forest that shades the road. A hairpin turn signals the start of Sawmill Flat Road. Watch out for gravel near driveways as you head south toward the entrance of Columbia Community College, about a mile from the start of the path. For the next mile after that, you'll dip down and then climb a hill up to a more level stretch of road with few curves. Turn right when you reach Parrotts Ferry Road and follow it north to return to the town of Columbia, a mile and a half away.

14. Old Strawberry Road

6 miles

Reference: **Along the south fork of the Tuolumne River in Strawberry; see number ⑭ on page 86.**

Ideal for: Fitness—Hills/Slalom

Directions: From Highway 99 in Manteca, take Highway 120 east to Oakdale, where the highway makes a 90-degree turn in the middle of town to join Highway 108. At the Yosemite Junction, the two roads split again. Continue going straight and 108 will become the Sonora Pass Highway. Proceed 32 miles beyond the Yosemite Junction to the town of Cold Springs. A mile beyond central Cold Springs, you'll see the Old Strawberry Road exit on the left. Turn here and drive the road's entire three miles. (You might want to take this opportunity to weigh the hills you pass against your abilities.) Park in the residential area beyond the bridge half a mile before the road rejoins Highway 108.

Map: For a free map of Tuolumne County, call or stop by First American Title Company at 71 Shepherd Street, Sonora, CA 95370; (209) 532-3156.

Local shop: Sierra Cyclery, 55 South Washington Street, Sonora, CA 95370; (209) 532-3654.

Tour notes: If you happen to be 1) passing by on Highway 108 with your skate gear; 2) fit enough to climb relentless uphills; and 3) skilled enough to survive long curving downhills on variable pavement, you'll absolutely love Old Strawberry Road, a favorite route for local bicyclists.

Located in the higher Sierra foothills, Strawberry is well-known as the site of an annual bluegrass festival. It's also situated just eight miles northwest of the Emigrant Wilderness and 10 miles northeast of the Yosemite National Park boundary. You know the elevation is high (just below 6,000 feet) when you see the stakes used to guide snowplows on either side of the road. These should also remind you to watch out for sand on the road's surface, left over from winter and spring ice-control efforts.

Start out by crossing the bridge over the south fork of the Stanislaus River and rounding the curve to begin the long climb. Scan the pavement along the way for rough patches and slippery spring run-off—you'll need to plan ahead for your descent. Follow the narrow, winding road past the sparsely populated outskirts of Strawberry, through shady pine forests, and gradually up the hill. After a long climb, you'll reach the Sonora Pass Highway. Take a well-deserved breather before enjoying your thrilling descent down three miles of back-country roads.

15. Algerine and Murphy Roads   14 miles 🎱 👟 🏊

Reference: **Country roads north of Lake Don Pedro in Jamestown; see number ⓯ on page 86.**

Ideal for: Hills/Slalom—Touring

Directions: From Highway 99 in Manteca, take Highway 120 east to Oakdale, where it makes a 90-degree turn to the east and joins Highway 108. At the Yosemite Junction, the two highways split and 108 becomes the Sonora Pass Highway. Follow 108 about four miles beyond the Yosemite Junction and turn right onto Bell Mooney Road. One mile up, you'll find the beginning of Algerine Road. Turn right and follow it to the junction leading off to Groveland and Moccasin at Jacksonville Road, where the traffic thins out dramatically. Find a strip of shoulder where you can park.

Map: For a free map of Tuolumne County, call or stop by First American Title Company at 71 Shepherd Street, Sonora, CA 95370; (209) 532-3156.

Local shop: Sierra Cyclery, 55 South Washington Street, Sonora, CA 95370; (209) 532-3654.

Tour notes: Algerine Road is truly a find for skaters in the mood for exploring. The pavement is smooth and the grassy Sierra foothills are still gently rolling, not yet the rugged granite slabs found a few miles further east. The occasional lone oak cools the road as you skate past a few homes. Along the way, you'll encounter some relatively gentle hills and cross a one-lane bridge over the creek where cows often stop to enjoy a slurp of water.

A series of sharp curves follows the bridge, and you'll climb to the top of a hill where a curious yellow sign warns "Residential Area." It turns out that a small farm straddles the road, with its dusty corral on one side and several other ranch structures on the other. Down the slope, and four miles from where you started, you'll meet Twist Road. Turn left onto Twist and proceed three quarters of a mile through a big meadow to reach Murphy Road on the right. The pavement on Murphy looks much worse than it feels, and you can continue on through more gentle curves, meadows, and hills for another three miles until you reach Old Wards Ferry Road, where you should turn around and skate the seven miles back the way you came.

16. East Ferretti Road
6 miles

Reference: **A rural road parallel to Highway 120 outside of Groveland; see number ⑯ on page 86.**

Ideal for: Hills/Slalom—Touring

Directions: From Highway 99, take Highway 120 east, following the signs to Yosemite National Park. After climbing the grade beyond Lake Don Pedro, you'll pass through Big Oak Flat and Groveland. Five miles east of Groveland, Highway 120 straightens out in one of the few passing areas between Groveland and Yosemite Valley. Just past Smith Station (a store where you can even get a cup of espresso), turn left onto Ferretti Road. Don't be intimidated by the cattle guard and narrow asphalt as you climb the hilly first three miles. When you reach Yosemite Vista Estates (a planned retirement community, according to the sign), you'll know it, because the pavement suddenly sports a double yellow center line and white-bordered shoulders. Park just off the right shoulder in front of the big sign that points the way to Pine Mountain and the airport.

Map: For a free map of Tuolumne County, call or stop by First American Title Company at 71 Shepherd Street, Sonora, CA 95370; (209) 532-3156.

Local shop: Oakdale Sports, 1275 East F Street, Oakdale, CA 95361-4140; (209) 847-0648.

Tour notes: The light traffic, plus the exhilaration of skating up and down the grassy Sierra foothills, is what makes Ferretti Road such a wonderful skating site. Even at 6 P.M. on a workday, automobiles are so scarce at the road's east end that you can hardly believe it's rush hour, a definite plus for a road with no shoulders. (The speed limit is set at 35 miles per hour, but the few cars that do pass move much faster, so be sure to look and listen.)

Starting from your parking spot on the shoulder of the road, skate to the west to climb the first small hump, passing a boat-repair shop—the only commercial building you'll see—and stepping around a cattle guard. Continue over the first couple of gentle hills through grassy pastures, where small groups of cows and horses graze peacefully. If you really look, you may be lucky enough to spot a deer, too.

On the other side of the pastures, you'll encounter your first long climb, passing a shady grove of trees. The road descends right after the "School Bus Stop" sign, only to climb again. Ferretti's broad curves and fine asphalt surface make fast cornering easy on the descents. Each hill delights with a pretty scene, sometimes of grassy fields, and other times of a small ranch or trees. As you near Clements

Road, Ferretti hugs the side of a hill, gradually descending. When you see Elderberry Road on the right, turn back. Here the traffic picks up as residents enter and exit the gated communities near Pine Mountain Lake (we plebeians never even get a glimpse of the lake).

Marin County

9 Great Places to Skate

Marin County

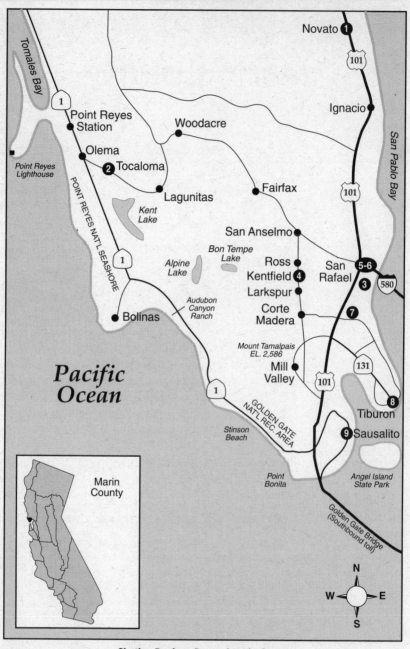

Novato ①

Ignacio

Tomales Bay

Point Reyes Station

Woodacre

Olema

② Tocaloma

Point Reyes Lighthouse

POINT REYES NAT'L SEASHORE

Lagunitas

Kent Lake

Fairfax

San Pablo Bay

San Anselmo

Bon Tempe Lake

Alpine Lake

Ross

Kentfield ④

San Rafael ⑤-⑥

③

580

Larkspur

Audubon Canyon Ranch

Corte Madera

⑦

Bolinas

Mount Tamalpais EL. 2,586

Mill Valley

131

101

⑧ Tiburon

Pacific Ocean

GOLDEN GATE NAT'L REC. AREA

Stinson Beach

⑨ Sausalito

Angel Island State Park

Point Bonita

Golden Gate Bridge (Southbound toll)

Marin County

N
W — E
S

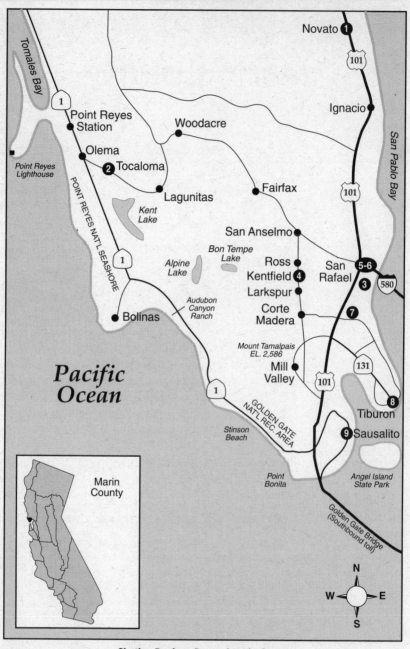

Skating Regions Beyond Marin County

North .... Wine Country, p. 77   South ...... San Francisco/The Peninsula, p. 117
East .... S.F. Bay Area: East Bay, p. 157

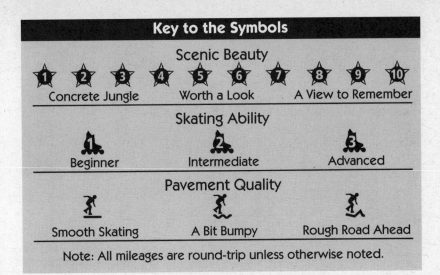

Key to the Symbols

Scenic Beauty

① **②** **③** **④** **⑤** **⑥** **⑦** **⑧** **⑨** **⑩**

Concrete Jungle   Worth a Look   A View to Remember

Skating Ability

1. Beginner   **2.** Intermediate   **3.** Advanced

Pavement Quality

Smooth Skating   A Bit Bumpy   Rough Road Ahead

Note: All mileages are round-trip unless otherwise noted.

Just over the Golden Gate Bridge from San Francisco and nestled between the Pacific Ocean and San Pablo Bay, the hilly terrain of Marin County is a breathtaking place to skate—in more ways than one. But despite the hills, in-liners will find plenty of trails suitable for all skill levels, especially around the flat areas of San Rafael.

Thanks to a well-established network of bike trails, Marin has long been a mecca for bicyclists, so expect to share many of the trails with wheels of a different kind. In comparison with other regions in the state, the pavement on these trails is generally a bit rough, thus not always ideal for skating. But the scenery—where dense forests cover the coastal hills—more than makes up for a few vibrations underfoot.

The most scenic and remote skate in Marin County is the Sir Francis Drake Bikeway connecting Tocaloma to Samuel P. Taylor State Park. Even beginners can enjoy this mostly flat trail through grassy meadows and a redwood forest—and it's less than an hour's drive from San Francisco.

---

1. Stafford Lake Park   6 miles ⑦ 🛼 🛹

Reference: **A park northwest of Novato; see number ❶ on page 106.**

Ideal for: Touring

Directions: From U.S. 101 heading north from San Rafael or south from Petaluma, take the Atherton Avenue/Marin Drive exit and follow Marin Drive west and then south. To park for free, turn left when you

---

reach Novato Boulevard, and then after a block and a half, turn left again to park at the Miwok Indian Museum. To park at Stafford Lake (and do this trip in reverse), turn right on Novato Boulevard and drive 2.5 miles west to the entrance of Stafford Lake Park on the left. You'll need four quarters to pay for parking.

Local shop: Demo Ski, 509 B Francisco Boulevard, San Rafael, CA 94901; (415) 454-3500.

Tour notes: Are you ready for some adventure skating? Choose an absolutely gorgeous spring day to skate the trail connecting Novato to Stafford Lake and adventure is just what you'll get. The rural country setting and peaceful presence of cud-chewing Holsteins will make up for the poor quality of the trail's surface.

By parking at the small Miwok Indian Museum, you can indulge yourself in the lot's perfectly smooth asphalt before starting out. Is it really that bad? Forewarned is forearmed: the trail surface is rough and generally in ill repair. Near the reservoir, cracks and shifting asphalt are marked with traffic cones, which makes the trail that much narrower. You can hear nearby traffic, and the trail is often covered with debris from the trees overhead and the nearby road. (One 10-yard stretch near the entrance to a quarry is so littered with gravel that you'll need to walk through it.) Because it isn't very wide, the section of trail up the side of the reservoir takes a bit of effort to get up and much skill to get down.

Are you still with me, adventurers? For those of you who are willing to put up with such inconveniences, the Stafford Lake Park Trail offers the kind of scenery you don't usually find in urban areas.

Start skating at Novato Boulevard, turning right as you leave the Miwok Indian Museum and returning to the intersection at Marin Drive. Cross to the south side of Novato Boulevard at the intersection and continue heading west as Novato Boulevard becomes Hicks Valley Road. Just past some horse pastures, you'll reach a pleasant section bordered by fields.

A short time after you pick your way across the gravel patch near the quarry, the trail dips down toward Novato Creek, a nice spot far enough away from traffic to feel like you're really communing with nature. Just after the trail goes back up to rejoin Hicks Valley Road, you'll begin the short-strokes climb up the side of the reservoir. A view to the southwest of sparkling water backed by rolling hills greets you when you arrive at the top. Stafford Lake Park is a great spot to rest and picnic, with a water fountain and children's play yard, cool grass for soothing tired toes, and rest rooms.

After gazing across the rippling lake and watching the geese and ducks for half an hour, the trip back will somehow seem better. But first you must successfully negotiate that hill where the trail descends from the top of the reservoir next to the road. The slope spits you out at an intersection where cars approaching at a hard angle on your right can't see you at the stop sign. You absolutely must be prepared to stop here before crossing and negotiating your way between the trail posts just beyond the intersection. Back at the Miwok museum, reward yourself for the rough pavement with another loop on the perfect asphalt in the small park.

---

2. Sir Francis Drake Bikeway 6 miles 🔟 🏔 ⛷

Reference: **A rail-trail near west Sir Francis Drake Boulevard starting in Tocaloma; see number ❷ on page 106.**

Ideal for: Beginners—Touring

Directions: From U.S. 101 heading north from San Francisco or south from San Rafael, exit at Sir Francis Drake Boulevard and get ready to enjoy 15-plus miles of Marin County before even reaching the trail. After passing the town of Jewell, you'll see Platform Bridge Road. Just after this intersection to the right, you'll cross a concrete bridge. Look on the other side of the bridge on the right side of the road for the sign that says Bike Path. Turn right here, into the trees, and turn left to park on the old roadbed shoulder. The bike path begins back at the bridge underpass.

Local shop: Demo Ski, 509 B Francisco Boulevard, San Rafael, CA 94901; (415) 454-3500. Other contact: Lanny Waggoner, State Park Ranger, Samuel P. Taylor State Park, P.O. Box 251, Lagunitas, CA 94938; (415) 488-9897.

Tour notes: Looking for the ideal nature skate? The Sir Francis Drake Bikeway ranks right up there with the best of them. What could be better than rolling on a clean, paved surface surrounded all the while by a wealth of natural beauty? The scenery is constantly changing along this three-mile trail, from the dappled shade of tall redwoods, to open grassland, to stands of eucalyptus trees. The only hill is a dip under the bridge as you enter the trail from the parking area, so even beginners can enjoy the privilege of skating this near-perfect trail. Built on an old rail line, the Sir Francis Drake Bikeway—which is also known as the Cross Marin Trail—follows alongside Lagunitas Creek back toward Jewell and then on into Samuel P. Taylor State Park. As for asphalt quality, you'll probably encounter some debris under the trees, and there are some rutted areas embedded in the asphalt that look worse than they feel. Rest rooms are available at the campgrounds, but not food, so pack a picnic. Make sure you stay to the right of the trail to make room for serious bicyclists heading to or from San Francisco.

---

3. Larkspur to Kentfield Trail

4 miles 🟊 ⛸ 🧍

Reference: A rail-trail in Larkspur; see number
❸ on page 106.

Ideal for: Beginners—Figure/Stunts—Touring

Directions: From U.S. 101 heading north from San Francisco or south from San Rafael, exit at Sir Francis Drake Boulevard to the east. Drive past the entrance to the ferry landing and beyond the tall statue of Don Quixote. Half a mile away from the freeway, you'll see a small parking lot on the right just after the statue. The sign says City of Larkspur Remillard Park, but all you can see is a gravel lot with a drinking fountain. Park here.

Local shop: Demo Ski, 509 B Francisco Boulevard, San Rafael, CA 94901; (415) 454-3500. Other contact: Ron Miska, County Department of Parks and Open Spaces, Marin Civic Center, Room 417, San Rafael, CA 94903; (415) 499-6387.

Tour notes: As you begin skating west on the trail next to Sir Francis Drake Boulevard, Don Quixote stares intently to the east above you, his silvery armored vest gleaming in bright contrast to the rust red of his limbs. His gaze makes you want to check over your shoulder to see what draws his attention. Skate across the ferry parking lot entrance; just beyond it you'll see some old-west storefronts, marked by a slightly hilarious 15-foot-high papier maché cactus. The pavement between the two facing rows of buildings stops short of the end of the storefronts, but you can skate in far enough to discover the Mexican food and antiques offered in this quaint setting. Back on the trail, you'll skate under another artifact, the old railroad trestle, with the ramps of U.S. 101 just beyond in all their modern efficiency. After you skate a zig and a zag over a bridge and pass under the freeway, you'll finally reach Corte Madera Creek. Now you can relax and enjoy the view of Mount Tamalpais (or Mount Tam, as the locals call it) looming off to the southwest. The asphalt trail is wide and smooth from here on, curving past a clean and modest office park (building 300 has a wonderful parking lot) and elegant condominiums. Wide concrete sidewalks beckon to the right, and there seems to be no reason to resist exploring the condo grounds. Can the residents possibly appreciate what they've got here? Only if they skate! The creekside trail terminates all too soon at a cul de sac on South Eliseo Street. Turn around here to complete the four-mile roundtrip. Experts skaters with the skill and leg power to take them up and over the short but steep hump in the middle of South Eliseo can continue on the low-traffic street to Creekside Park for another quarter of a mile, where the Kentfield to Ross Trail (see page 111) begins just across Bon Air Road. (There is a crosswalk at the intersection of Bon

Air and South Eliseo.) Climb the nasty patch of pavement on the hill with hard and short strokes, maximizing their effectiveness with toes pointed out.

4. Kentfield to Ross Trail   4 miles

Reference: **Alongside Corte Madera Creek in Kentfield; see number ❹ on page 106.**

Ideal for: Figure/Stunts—Touring

Directions: From U.S. 101 heading north from San Francisco or south from San Rafael, exit at Sir Francis Drake Boulevard and go west, following the signs to Marin General Hospital. Turn left onto Bon Air Road and park in the lot across the street from the hospital, where you'll find Creekside Park.

Local shop: Demo Ski, 509 B Francisco Boulevard, San Rafael, CA 94901; (415) 454-3500.

Tour notes: Skate south and cross over the pretty arching wooden bridge from Creekside Park to access the Kentfield to Ross Trail. Turn right to follow the creek west. Although the pavement is rough enough to give you a vibrating foot massage here, the natural beauty surrounding Corte Madera Creek very nearly makes up for it. Soon the pavement quality improves, though the trail is interrupted at times by wooden bridges across the creek and a couple of street intersections. The farther west you travel, the closer to the creek the trail becomes. When you cross College Avenue to the College of Marin, the trail leaves the side of the creek and seems to disappear into the college parking lot. Keep a westerly course as you skate behind and around a couple of buildings. Sure enough, the trail resumes at the far side of the parking lot next to the creek. The trail is now so narrow and close to the bank that a fence has been installed to prevent passers- and rollers-by from falling into the water below. Diehard explorers can continue on rough pavement for another three-quarters of a mile to the trail's end at Ross Common. But you might have more fun turning around here and skating back to play on the smooth pavement of the wide-open college parking lot.

5. Marin Civic Center Bike Path   1.5 miles

Reference: **On the San Pedro peninsula northeast of San Rafael; see number ❺ on page 106.**

Ideal for: Historic—Touring

Directions: From U.S. 101 heading north from central San Rafael or south from Novato, exit at North San Pedro Road and take the first left to reach the county offices, where parking can be found along most of the streets on the Civic Center grounds.

Local shop: Demo Ski, 509 B Francisco Boulevard, San Rafael, CA 94901; (415) 454-3500. Other contact: Ron Miska, County Department of Parks and Open Spaces, Marin Civic Center, Room 417, San Rafael, CA 94903; (415) 499-6387.

Tour notes: On a beautiful day, you may be able forgive the poor condition of the pavement around the lake as you visit Marin County's government seat. The path is pretty awful near the pond, and it may be covered with debris, but you should consider a short skate trip here anyway if only to see the work of famous architect Frank Lloyd Wright, who designed the Marin Civic Center building. The bike path doesn't completely encircle the pond, but there's more to explore on the grounds and parking lots of the civic center. This location offers an excellent opportunity to get a bit of fresh air and exercise while you critique Wright's design. As you picnic at the lakeside, the local seagulls are happy to put on an air show, and ducks and geese go about life on the surface of their pond (with the help of children who feed them bread crumbs). The surrounding hills make lovely scenery, and they also serve as a sound buffer against the highway's roar.

6. Loch Lomond/Peacock Gap Neighborhoods

4 miles

Reference: West shoreline of the San Rafael Bay in San Rafael; see number ❻ on page 106.

Ideal for: Fitness—Hills/Slalom—Touring

Directions: Heading north on U.S. 101 from San Francisco, take the Central San Rafael exit and turn right onto Second Street. A block later, merge onto Third Street heading east. Third very soon becomes San Pedro Road. Follow San Pedro for four miles as it curves around the peninsula. Just as the road starts climbing toward the Peacock Gap Golf and Country Club, you'll see the entrance to the Loch Lomond neighborhood on the left. Park on the street. Heading south on U.S. 101 from Novato, take the Central San Rafael exit and turn left (east) onto Fourth Street, following it under the freeway. When Fourth dead-ends at the high school, go one block south to get onto Third Street, and follow the directions above to San Pedro Road and the skating location.

Local shop: Demo Ski, 509 B Francisco Boulevard, San Rafael, CA 94901; (415) 454-3500.

Tour notes: In many towns up and down California, some of the best recreational and hill skating around can be found in upscale or newer neighborhoods. That's the case here. Wide streets, little traffic, and rolling hills make this one of those ideal skating locations. The homes are attractive and well maintained, and residents are used to seeing skaters since the neighborhood is well known among local in-line enthusiasts. Do your best to control your speed here, which you'll want to do anyway since the terrain is hilly.

From some locations on a clear day, the view of the bay can be stunning, so stop and take some time to enjoy it. You can get a little higher for a better view by skating back out to San Pedro Road and up to the next development, Peacock Gap.

---

7. Paradise Trail   2 miles 🅐 🐾 🏄

Reference: **On the Tiburon peninsula east of Corte Madera; see number ❼ on page 106.**

Ideal for: Beginners—Fitness—Road/Street—Touring

Directions: From U.S. 101 going north from San Francisco or south from San Rafael, take the Tamalpais/Paradise Drive exit to Corte Madera and head east toward the San Francisco Bay. Turn left at Redwood Highway, which veers north; Paradise Drive runs south. A short distance up Redwood Highway, you can park on a gravel pad right next to the trail.

Local shop: Demo Ski, 509 B Francisco Boulevard, San Rafael, CA 94901; (415) 454-3500.

Tour notes: From this corner of the Tiburon peninsula, you can see the Richmond Bridge crossing the San Francisco Bay to the north—just one more of those spectacular views that can be easy to miss and hard to appreciate on a bad-weather day. This may be one of the shorter locations to skate, but it's a good spot for beginners and doesn't seem to attract the hoards you'll find in other Marin County locations. You'll be slightly exposed to the sun and the wind as you skate along this totally flat, treeless, wide open stretch of pavement, near enough to the bay that only seaside scrub is between you and the water. Bay breezes will usually keep you cool on the sunniest of days, but as always when spending the day outside, coat yourself in a high SPF sunscreen before you start your skate.

The trail heading north is close to the noisy freeway, while the trail south toward San Clemente and Paradise Drives has a few trees and is more protected from sand blowing from the bay.

At the southern termination of the dedicated path, road skating experts can make an 8.5-mile loop encircling the entire Tiburon peninsula. Some serious Bay Area skaters make this a regular workout routine, but they're skilled enough to successfully handle steep hills, blind curves, and an absolute absence of paved shoulders while confidently maneuvering on sometimes wet pavement. It's safer if you can convince two crews of bicyclists to both lead and follow your group of skaters to help control automobile traffic. (Trestle Glen Drive, about four miles west of U.S. 101, is the connecting road that you take to return from the south side of the peninsula to the north.)

---

8. Tiburon Linear Park Trail 5 miles

Reference: **A rail-trail between Blackie's Pasture and Belvedere in Tiburon; see number ❽ on page 106.**

Ideal for: Scene—Touring

Directions: Heading south from San Rafael or north from San Francisco on U.S. 101, exit at Tiburon/Mill Valley (the Tiburon Boulevard/Highway 131/East Blithedale Avenue exit) and head east. Follow Tiburon Boulevard about 1.5 miles and turn right when you see the sign for Blackie's Pasture Road to park in the large dirt lot (some pasture!). Try to avoid raising dust as you drive to the far west end of the lot where the trail begins. Walk, don't roll, to preserve your wheel bearings between car and asphalt.

Local shop: Demo Ski, 509 B Francisco Boulevard, San Rafael, CA 94901; (415) 454-3500. Other contact: Ron Miska, County Department of Parks and Open Spaces, Marin Civic Center, Room 417, San Rafael, CA 94903; (415) 499-6387.

Tour notes: It's hard to think of this trail as a railroad line, since there's no remaining trace of it. But the Tiburon Linear Park Trail was once part of the north bay terminus for barges carrying railroad cars across the bay for Northwestern Pacific Railroad. Now it's one of the most popular destinations for Bay Area skaters, offering excellent views across the shimmering waters of Richardson Bay.

Begin by skating up a short hill and continuing southeast above the McKegney Green soccer fields on the right, which are closed to soccer after 1 P.M. on Sundays so that others can enjoy them, too. Continue through the Max H. Grefe Wildlife Sanctuary, a series of small ponds maintained by the Richardson Bay Sanitary District, complete with mud flats. The trail gradually moves closer to Tiburon Boulevard after this, with a semi-blind street crossing. After you cross a second street, the trail splits into a bike path parallel to the pedestrian sidewalk. Both paths continue east to enter the shopping area of Tiburon. Here, the trail intersects a traffic circle. On the east side of the traffic circle, you can continue skating next to the water on a truly fine concrete surface. This section is lighted for night skating and still off-limits to bicycles. Who could ask for more?

9. Richardson Bay Bike Path 5 miles

Reference: **A rail-trail connecting Mill Valley to Sausalito; see number ❾ on page 106.**

Ideal for: Road/Street—Touring

Directions: Heading south on U.S. 101 from San Rafael or north from San Francisco, exit at Tiburon/Mill Valley (it's also called the Tiburon Boulevard/Highway 131/East Blithedale Avenue exit) and head west.

Turn left at Roque Moraes and follow the road as it curves to the southeast to meet Hamilton Drive. Turn right on Hamilton and park across from the fire station at Bay Front Park.

Local shop: Demo Ski, 509 B Francisco Boulevard, San Rafael, CA 94901; (415) 454-3500. Other contact: Ron Miska, County Department of Parks and Open Spaces, Marin Civic Center, Room 417, San Rafael, CA 94903; (415) 499-6387.

Tour notes: The Richardson Bay marshes and the views of the hills to the south and west sure are pretty, but this is no trail for a first-time skater, even though it's as flat as can be. On fair-weather weekends, it's crowded with walkers, joggers, and serious cyclists, but the main problem is that the pavement is extremely coarse at the trail's northern end. If you go less than five miles per hour, you feel like you're riding a jackhammer. Softer wheels (with a hardness or durometer rating in the low 70s) help absorb some of the vibrations, but a fast pace can also make it tolerable enough to enjoy the scenery. Just be sure you don't collide with anyone! (Full protective gear would be well-advised here.)

To reach the main trail, head west from the parking lot on the rough pavement. Cross the first of three wooden bridges you'll encounter on this trip and turn left to join the trail, heading southeast through the park along the edge of a marsh. (You can continue west here if you're interested in a diversion on the grounds of the shoreline condominiums in that direction).

As you approach the freeway, you'll cross two more wooden bridges, also easier to skate when you keep your speed up. It's somewhat noisy under and alongside the Shoreline Highway, but you'll be partly compensated by smoother pavement from here on. The dedicated trail ends at Gate Road in Sausalito, next to the Harbor Center Shopping Center. Street skating in the harbor area beckons, for those who are ready for more adventure.

San Francisco/
The Peninsula

20 Great Places to Skate

San Francisco/The Peninsula

Skating Regions Beyond San Francisco/The Peninsula

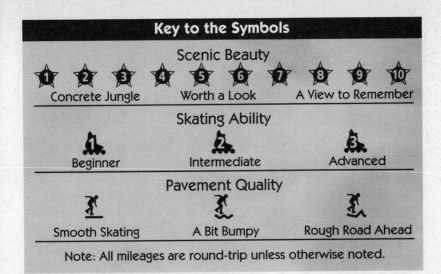

Key to the Symbols

Scenic Beauty

1 2 3 4 5 6 7 8 9 10

Concrete Jungle   Worth a Look   A View to Remember

Skating Ability

Beginner   Intermediate   Advanced

Pavement Quality

Smooth Skating   A Bit Bumpy   Rough Road Ahead

Note: All mileages are round-trip unless otherwise noted.

Views, views, and more views bring skaters to the city of San Francisco, where trails along the Embarcadero and Ocean Beach offer glimpses of everything from the Golden Gate and Bay Bridges to Alcatraz Island and the windswept Pacific coast. But the city's inlining hub is Golden Gate Park. Every Sunday, a section of this 1,017-acre green oasis closes to traffic so skaters can slalom, stair ride, and just plain fool around in safety.

San Francisco itself sports a very active skating community dedicated to recreational skating as well as roller hockey and speed skating. Several local shops sponsor and promote a host of skating events, while the California Outdoor Rollerskating Association (C.O.R.A.) puts on the infamous Midnight Rollers Friday Night Skate (see page 120), plus other year-round events for roller and in-line skaters of all skill levels. If you're planning an extended visit to San Francisco, be sure to contact C.O.R.A. for a list of upcoming events. See the Resource Guide on page 432 for information on C.O.R.A. and other local events.

South of San Francisco, the rolling coastal hills continue down the Peninsula to the Dumbarton Bridge. Over on the coast, Half Moon Bay offers skating alongside the Pacific, while San Francisco Bay's western shore is almost totally lined with paved trails. Inland, local favorites are the Sawyer Camp Trail and Canada Road, located right on top of the San Andreas Fault.

1. Treasure Island

2 miles ⭐9 🛼🏄

Reference: **An island at the center of the Bay Bridge connecting San Francisco/Oakland; see number ❶ on page 118.**

Ideal for: Beginners—Fitness—Historic—Road/Street—Touring

Directions: Take Interstate 80 across the Bay Bridge from San Francisco or Oakland (there's a $1 toll from the Oakland side). At the center of the bridge, take the Treasure Island exit (coming from Oakland, the exit is to the left.) Follow the signs to the Exposition museum. Pass through the main gate and park at the museum (on your right) or anywhere nearby. The island is also served by AC Transit buses.

Local shop: Golden Gate Park Skates and Bikes, 3038 Fulton Street, San Francisco, CA 94118; (415) 668-1117.

Tour notes: Though Treasure Island is an active naval base, it's open to the public, which is great news for skaters: the island's streets deliver rare, mid-bay views of San Francisco, the Oakland and Berkeley Hills, and the San Francisco Bay. The island itself was created from mud flats for the 1939-40 Golden Gate International Exposition, and many of the buildings you see today were built for the Exposition.

Automobile traffic is very light, so you can skate pretty much wherever you please without worry. Pavement quality varies from excellent to fair. Rest rooms and water are available at the Exposition museum, which is open from 10 A.M. to 3:30 P.M. Picnic tables are positioned along the east and west sides of the island. If you do bring along a picnic lunch, pack a sweater or windbreaker, too; it's often cold and windy here, even during the summer.

2. Midnight Rollers Friday Night Skate

12.5 miles ⭐6 🛼🏄

Reference: **Through the streets of downtown San Francisco; see number ❷ on page 118.**

Ideal for: Road/Street—Scene—Touring

Directions: Entering San Francisco from the east on Interstate 80 over the Bay Bridge, prepare to take Main Street, the first exit when you reach solid ground. The off-ramp makes a hard counterclockwise loop to cross back under Interstate 80; stay to the right. Turn right at Harrison Street, the first intersection, which leads directly to the Embarcadero. Park in the public lot between Justin Herman Plaza and the Ferry Building clock tower.

Entering the city from the Golden Gate Bridge on U.S. 101, take the Lombard Street/Downtown exit. After a few blocks, veer to the left onto Lombard, following it for 12 blocks. At Van Ness Avenue, turn left (north) and drive two blocks; then turn right onto Bay Street. Follow Bay another dozen or so blocks until you reach the

Embarcadero, where you should turn right and continue to the public parking lot.

Finally, entering the city from the south, follow U.S. 101 to the 101/Interstate 80 interchange and stay right, following the signs for the Bay Bridge. Exit at Third Street, turn left to go under the freeway, and then turn right onto Harrison Street, which takes you to the Embarcadero and the public parking lot.

To avoid the task of driving and parking in this city altogether, take advantage of Bay Area Rapid Transit (BART) from an outlying community, where parking at the BART stations is free and, on weekends, easy to find. Get off BART at the Embarcadero station, put on your skates, and head toward the bay on Market Street. You'll enter the Embarcadero at Justin Herman Plaza, a fun place to warm up. Ferries and numerous city buses also serve this area, and the CalTrans train station is only a few blocks from the south end of the trip.

Local shop: Skate Pro Sports, 2549 Irving Street, San Francisco, CA 94122; (415) 752-8776.

Tour notes: Guided by members of the California Outdoor Rollerskating Association (C.O.R.A.), the Midnight Rollers meet in the parking lot across from the Ferry Building on the Embarcadero at 8 P.M. on Friday nights, departing at 8:30 P.M. This skate has taken on a life of its own, according to organizer and local skating events promoter, David Miles. Many regulars see it as a way to forget the stress of the workweek. At times, the number of participants has reached more than 400. For a preview of part of the route, see The Embarcadero/South Beach on page 123 and The Embarcadero/Fisherman's Wharf on page 124.

Choose a clear, dry night for your first skate with the Midnight Rollers. Make sure you have the skills to climb the two steep hills (one on very rough pavement) and are able to ride your heel brake through a long downhill tunnel on a pedestrian path only three feet wide and paved with textured iron. You should be in good enough physical condition to skate the full 12-mile loop without dropping back. If that happens, you may lose the route and won't have the group to protect you from traffic. If you do find yourself in over your head, simply skate back the way you came rather than trying to keep up.

In spite of the numbers, the group skate is surprisingly orderly. Starting with the first checkpoint at the end of Pier 39, where an organizer checks the night's head count, short breaks are taken every two or three miles so stragglers can catch up. Later, when the skating is actually on city streets with traffic, it becomes important to stay with a large group for more protection from cars. Cab drivers are notoriously intolerant of the weekly traffic disruption, but most other drivers are pretty patient.

When group skating, keep in mind that ultimately, only you are responsible for your own safety. Don't depend on somebody in charge to be watching out for skaters at the back of the pack. Bring your I.D. and money for a taxi just to be safe.

---

3. Monday Night Skate
10 miles 🌟**9** 🏃⚡

Reference: **San Francisco; see number ❸ on page 118.**

Ideal for: Fitness —Hills/Slalom—Road/Street

Directions: From south of San Francisco, take U.S. 101 north to Fell Street in the city. After two blocks on Fell, turn right (north) onto Fillmore Street and stay on Fillmore up and down the many hills until you reach Pixley Street, three blocks before Lombard Street. Park on the street, and be sure to set your emergency brake! Skaters meet at Nuvo Colours at 3108 Fillmore Street.

Local shop: Nuvo Colours, 3108 Fillmore Street, San Francisco, CA 94123; (415) 771-6886.

Tour notes: Athletic skaters looking for the best, most challenging urban and hill skating tour San Francisco has to offer won't want to miss the Monday Night Skate, which has gained a reputation as one of the most demanding city skates anywhere. The challenge is inherent in San Francisco's hilly geography. Although parts of most routes pass through the smooth pavement in the Marina and Embarcadero areas, the group inevitably takes to the hills. A favorite location is the Presidio, a converted army base with steep slopes and spectacular urban scenery (see the Presidio on page 128).

Depending on the weather and time of year, the size of the group ranges from 10 to 40 skaters. A few diehards continue to meet year-round; in a city known for its fog and damp conditions, even wet pavement doesn't stop them. As the long days of summer begin to wane, the routes get more challenging, the idea being that by then, the core group of 10 to 20 regulars has reached peak physical condition. As aggressive as they are, however, these skaters make it a point to look out for each other, keeping tabs on folks at the back and those who crash.

To join the Monday Night Skate, meet at Nuvo Colours at 7:30 P.M. (Nuvo employees participate and sometimes lead the tour, but skaters are responsible for their own safety.) Wear the appropriate gear, be prepared for all types of pavement, and make sure you've polished up your best hill skating skills.

4. The Embarcadero/ South Beach

Reference: **The southern section of San Francisco's waterfront; see number ❹ on page 118.**

Ideal for: Fitness—Hills/Slalom—Historic—Road/Street—Scene—Touring

Directions: See the directions for the Midnight Rollers Friday Night Skate on page 120 for directions into San Francisco from the Bay Bridge, the Golden Gate Bridge, or areas south of the city, plus information on public transportation. Once you reach the Embarcadero, park anywhere you can.

Local shop: Golden Gate Park Skates and Bikes, 3038 Fulton Street, San Francisco, CA 94118; (415) 668-1117.

Tour notes: Skate on the edge of the San Francisco Bay along the newly refurbished Embarcadero to see great views of the bay, the Bay Bridge, Yerba Buena and Treasure Islands, and the East Bay hills. The sidewalk promenade that runs along the bay seems to have been designed with skaters in mind. Stretching for four picturesque miles from Fisherman's Wharf at the north end to Fourth Street near China Basin at the south, its wide concrete surface is prime for polyurethane wheels. Be sure to enjoy the water and city views from the plaza near the Ferry Building before you start skating.

This tour explores the south end of the Embarcadero, which is often sunny when the rest of the city is blanketed with fog. The scenery for the first half mile is dominated by the mighty Bay Bridge, spanning the waters from the city to Treasure Island and the East Bay. Unfortunately, this stretch of the Embarcadero can get crowded during weekday lunch and rush hours, so try to skate it on weekends or during off hours. Turn back where Berry Street meets Fourth.

If you're up for extending this four-mile trip, an excellent diversion awaits adventurous and proficient skaters a few blocks away from the water's edge. Cross to the inland side of the Embarcadero and skate down Brannan Street. Turn right on Center Place to reach South Park and start exploring the area known locally as South of Market. You can go as far out as 11th Street, a mile way from the Embarcadero, and skate the streets from either side of Interstate 80 from Market to Berry Streets. On weekends or when traffic has died down after work hours, you can skate to your heart's content. Return to the Ferry Building by way of the Embarcadero.

From here, why not check out the fountain in Justin Herman Plaza across the street at the intersection with Market Street? You'll find a fun hill and stairs near the Alcoa Building just north of the plaza, and the plaza itself has a variety of concrete walks.

5. The Embarcadero/ Fisherman's Wharf

12 miles 🎖️ 🏃 🏄

Reference: **The northern section of San Francisco's waterfront; see number ❺ on page 118.**

Ideal for: Fitness—Hills/Slalom—Historic—Road/Street—Scene— Touring

Directions: See the directions for the Midnight Rollers Friday Night Skate on page 120 for directions into San Francisco from the Bay Bridge, the Golden Gate Bridge, or areas south of the city, plus information on public transportation. Once you reach the Embarcadero, park anywhere you can.

Local shop: Nuvo Colours, 3108 Fillmore Street, San Francisco, CA 94123; (415) 771-6886.

Tour notes: This tour of the Embarcadero passes by working piers, through prime tourist country around Pier 39, alongside Fisherman's Wharf and Aquatic Park, and up to historic Fort Mason. If that isn't enough for you, there are unlimited options for side trips to other interesting spots. If you want to avoid the crowds, save skating here for early fall, after tourist season has peaked. And be sure to get an early morning start if you want to see the "real" Fisherman's Wharf at work.

Start at Justin Herman Plaza or the Ferry Building at the foot of Market Street. Skate north on the smooth new concrete walkway of the Promenade along the bay side of The Embarcadero, which is a working port facility. Make sure to take a detour onto Pier 39, where you can follow another concrete walkway all around the pier. Sea lions can often be seen sunning themselves in the marina near the end of the pier.

Continue through Fisherman's Wharf, past all the touristy shops and restaurants, to Jefferson Street and the Aquatic Park. The Aquatic Park Pier on the west end of the park is definitely worth a look. This route continues past the pier and up a short, steep road that leads into Fort Mason. Although this road is closed to cars, the horrendous pavement on the first third of the climb may turn you off. But if you know you can get back down safely, get up the hill, one way or another; the little park on the north side has great pavement and superb views. The park is dedicated to Congressman Phil Burton, who worked to make the Golden Gate National Recreation Area a reality. The south end of the park is just a parking lot away from the Marina Green (see page 125), if you want to hook up with that trail.

On your return to the Embarcadero, be very careful when going back down the steep hill out of Fort Mason. Walking is probably a good choice for most skaters; the pavement is so rough it can dislodge the grip of your heel brake.

---

6. Marina Green

8 miles

Reference: The north shore of the bay in San Francisco; see number ❻ on page 118.

Ideal for: Beginners—Fitness—Scene—Touring

Directions: From U.S. 101 heading into San Francisco on the Golden Gate Bridge, take the Marina Boulevard exit, driving east toward Fort Mason. From south of San Francisco, take U.S. 101 north to Fell Street. After skating for two blocks on Fell, turn right (north) onto Fillmore Street and stay on it up and down all the hills until you reach Marina Boulevard. Parking lots are available off Marina Boulevard at Fort Mason, Marina Green, Crissy Field, and near the St. Francis Yacht Club.

Map: For a free map, contact the Golden Gate National Recreation Area at the address below.

Local shop: Achilles' Wheels, 2271 Chestnut Street, San Francisco, CA 94123-2637; (415) 567-8400. Other contact: Golden Gate National Recreation Area, Fort Mason, Building 201, San Francisco, CA 94123; (415) 556-0560.

Tour notes: Perfectly smooth red concrete and spectacular scenery make this loop near the San Francisco Bay shoreline a memorable tour. The pavement encircles the grassy Marina Green, where kites threaten to impale unsuspecting lawn loungers. It can get crowded quickly, especially on weekends, but the view of the bay, Alcatraz, and the Golden Gate Bridge make it worthwhile.

Take a detour up to the yacht club parking lot for a less crowded place to practice slaloms and heel-toe rolls. More adventuresome skaters will get bored after half an hour's play here and want to skate west through the rough parking lot of Crissy Field to Fort Point at the southern end of the Golden Gate Bridge. (There's a trail closer to shore, but it's paved with clay.)

Another fine detour (frequented by the Midnight Rollers) is just across the street from the far end of the green. The sidewalks around the Palace of Fine Arts offer a short but fun skate, and you can practice artistic skills and tricks under the grand dome. Fort Mason, located just east of the Marina Green, is a skater-friendly area to explore, too. The little park on the west side of Fort Mason has some fine, moderately sloped sidewalks to play on, plus rest rooms and water (see page 124). Trendy Chestnut Street, a few blocks south of the marina, is the place to take a break on sunny weekends, when locals hang out on the sidewalk sipping espresso drinks from the slew of coffee shops on the street.

7. Golden Gate Park   2.5 miles 🟡 🛼 🏃

Reference: In the heart of San Francisco; see number
   ❼ on page 118.

Ideal for: Beginners—Figure/Stunts—Fitness—Hills/Slalom—
   Historic—In-Line Hockey—Scene—Touring

Directions: Entering San Francisco from the south on Interstate 280,
   take the exit marked Highway 1 North (which is also 19th Avenue).
   After driving five miles through city block after city block, you'll pass
   Lincoln Way, Golden Gate Park's southern border; continue through
   the park until you meet Fulton Street. Turn right on Fulton, where
   parking is free and close to the skating, as long as you arrive by 10 A.M.
   Leave your car at the west end of the park (or carry your skates) if you
   can't ride your heel brake down the narrow sidewalk from the east end
   of Fulton.

   Entering the city from the Golden Gate Bridge on U.S. 101, take
   the 19th Avenue/Golden Gate Park exit after crossing the bridge and
   head south through the Presidio, now named, appropriately enough,
   Park Presidio Boulevard. After you emerge from the tunnel, continue
   south on Park Presidio for seven more blocks until you reach Fulton.
   Turn left and park as explained above.

   From Interstate 80 and the Bay Bridge, follow the signs for U.S.
   101 north and the Golden Gate Bridge. Turn left (west) at Fell Street,
   and follow it until you meet Stanyan Street, which is the eastern
   border of the park. Turn right onto Stanyan and go up a hill. The first
   left at the top of the rise is Fulton.

Local shop: Skates on Haight, 1818 Haight Street, San Francisco, CA
   94117; (415) 752-8375. Other contact: Golden Gate National Recreation Area, Fort Mason, Building 201, San Francisco, CA 94123;
   (415) 556-0560.

Tour notes: Golden Gate Park is the place to skate in the Bay Area on
   Sundays. Year round, hundreds of in-line and quad (roller) skaters
   congregate from 10 A.M. until dark, frolicking without fear of traffic
   on 2.5 miles of wide, barricaded streets at the park's east end. There's
   enough room and variety of terrain for skaters of all skill levels to
   have fun. No other Bay Area skating location can compare with the
   scene you'll find here.

   The skating activity takes place up and down the length of John F.
   Kennedy Drive. Two levels of slalom runs are set up on Conservatory
   Drive, and a lip of asphalt on the shoulder nearby attracts trick jump-
   ers as well. A roller hockey game is almost always in progress where
   East Middle Drive meets John F. Kennedy Drive. Off Tea Garden
   Drive, two sets of stairs near the Music Concourse offer intermediate
   and advanced stair riding and jumping opportunities.

Near the Seventh Street entrance to the park, a grassy slope makes perfect seating for spectators to watch artistic skaters, first-timers on rental skates, and general show-offs who share a rink-like rectangle of smooth pavement. A boom box provides a variety of tunes that are great for dancing. When asked, the experts here are generous about sharing their tips. Keep a lunch in your car, and when you get hungry, bring it here for a picnic. A water fountain is located nearby.

Throughout the barricaded area, the San Francisco Skate Patrol watches for unsafe behavior or injured skaters.

8. Lake Merced   4.5 miles

Reference: **On the southwestern border of San Francisco; see number ❽ on page 118.**

Ideal for: Fitness—Hills/Slalom—Speed—Touring

Directions: Lake Merced is located in the southwestern corner of San Francisco, accessible from city streets that connect with Highway 35 on the west side of town. Free parking can be found around the lake, though the best lot is located at the intersection of Sunset Avenue and Park Merced Boulevard. Another lot is at Brotherhood Way. The lake is also served by Muni buses.

Local shop: Nuvo Colours, 3108 Fillmore Street, San Francisco, CA 94123; (415) 771-6886.

Tour notes: The Lake Merced Trail circumnavigates the large reservoir of the same name just inland from the shoreline sand dunes of southwestern San Francisco. Blessed with wide, smooth pavement, the route passes through pleasant half-urban, half-park surroundings, enhanced by trees and lawns.

The trail's 4.5-mile length makes it an ideal place for fitness training and fast laps. While many stretches are suitable for beginners, you really should have intermediate skills before attempting the full loop. There are several moderate hills on the way around, just steep enough for some fun slalom turns or breezy cruising. The best hill is on the east side between Font Boulevard and Brotherhood Way.

9. Ocean Beach   6 miles

Reference: **The shore of the Pacific Ocean in San Francisco; see number ❾ on page 118.**

Ideal for: Beginners—Fitness—Historic—Touring

Directions: Entering the city on U.S. 101 from over the Golden Gate Bridge, take the 19th Avenue/Golden Gate Park exit. After emerging from the tunnel, cross four city blocks and turn right (west) on Geary Boulevard. Veer right onto Point Lobos Avenue when you reach 40th Street. Point Lobos meets the shore in eight more blocks. The road turns south down a steep hill. Park at the bottom of the hill on the street, now called the Great Highway. To start from the south end, take Sloat Boulevard west to the Great Highway. Cross the Great Highway and park at the beach parking lot. The trail begins north of Sloat, on the east side of the highway.

Local shop: Golden Gate Park Skates and Bikes, 3038 Fulton Street, San Francisco, CA 94118; (415) 668-1117.

Tour notes: Wild, windblown, and foggy most of the time, Ocean Beach is a far cry from its warm, sun-drenched Southern California counterparts. But it's the place to be on one of those hot Indian Summer days in the fall, when the rest of the city is wilting under the heat.

From the bottom of the Point Lobos hill, start by skating south on the Esplanade (the pavement is a bit uneven), which takes you past the western end of Golden Gate Park and a couple of windmills. At Lincoln Way, the southern border of the park, cross to the other side of the street. Here begins two miles of a well-maintained, but rough-surfaced, asphalt trail, which ends at Sloat Boulevard and the San Francisco Zoo (no skating allowed).

You can also start this trip at the zoo and skate north. More adventurous skaters will want to skate up the hill at the north end of the Esplanade to the Cliff House, a popular, if touristy, restaurant with a fine view of the ocean and the southern end of San Francisco. Make sure you have good downhill or braking skills for the skate back before attempting the climb. Watch out for the pedestrians on your descent. They're more likely to be looking at the view than at you.

If you're game for more, you can find good street skating with light traffic and moderate slopes in the residential areas to the east of the Great Highway and south of Golden Gate Park.

---

10. The Presidio
4 miles ⑨ 🛼 🏃

Reference: **Near the Golden Gate Bridge in San Francisco; see number ⑩ on page 118.**

Ideal for: Fitness—Hills/Slalom—Historic—Road/Street—Touring

Directions: Entering the city on U.S. 101 from the Golden Gate Bridge, just after the toll plaza, turn right onto Merchant Road, which meets Lincoln Boulevard within a quarter of a mile. Go south on Lincoln for about a half mile to Kobbe Avenue. Turn left and park at the old warehouse near the corner of Harrison Boulevard. From the southern part of San Francisco, take 25th Avenue to Lincoln. Turn right and follow Lincoln about a mile to Kobbe. Turn right and park as described above. This area is also served by Muni buses.

Local shop: Achilles' Wheels, 2271 Chestnut Street, San Francisco, CA 94123; (415) 567-8400.

Tour notes: Some of the most spectacular urban scenery in the world is found in San Francisco's Presidio, and since the army departed in

1994, it has become a great place to skate. The Presidio was first occupied by the Spanish in the 1700s and was later acquired by the U.S. Army when California became one of the United States. By a fortuitous quirk of fate, the property at either end of the Golden Gate Bridge has since been protected from urban development because of its military importance. Only recently has the army moved out, leaving the base behind to be converted to a park.

Pick a fair-weather day to visit; this area is often windy and cold, although it's a little more protected than other places on the west side of San Francisco. Nicely paved streets wind through the pine and eucalyptus forests and almost deserted housing areas, offering fabulous views of the Pacific, the Golden Gate Bridge, and the Marin Headlands. You could spend hours skating all of the roads here, and as long as you avoid Lincoln and Arguello Boulevards, which are the main through streets, you'll encounter little automobile traffic. If you really want to explore, bring along a city map so you can find your way back to where you started.

Unfortunately for lower-level skaters, the Presidio has a fair share of hills. A sweet spot for hard-core down-hillers is Pershing Drive, off Lincoln Boulevard, near the southwest corner of the Presidio. Hill skaters also won't want to miss the slope on Kobbe Avenue and the view point at the north end of Washington Boulevard. Washington is also a good spot for intermediates to improve their downhill skills. Some short, steep drops can be found in a nearly deserted housing area, and the National Cemetery has great pavement and nice hills.

San Francisco's best beach, Baker Beach, is located off Lincoln Boulevard if you want to take a break after your workout. Be forewarned: clothing is optional at the northern end of the beach.

---

11. Candlestick Point State Recreation Area

3 miles ⑦ 🧍🏃

Reference: **Near the San Francisco Bay just south of San Francisco; see number ⑪ on page 118.**

Ideal for: Beginners—Historic—Touring

Directions: From U.S. 101 heading north, take the first Candlestick Park exit and follow Harney Road to Candlestick Park. Turn right on Jamestown Avenue Extension. The entrance to the recreation area parking lot is about a quarter of a mile farther up on the right. From U.S. 101 heading south, take the Candlestick Park/Beatty Avenue exit. Follow the signs to Candlestick Park, looping around to the right on Alana Way to go back under the freeway. Follow Harney Way to Candlestick Park, where you'll turn right on Jamestown Avenue Extension, about a quarter of a mile from the entrance to the recreation area parking lot.

Local shop: Skates off Haight, 384 Oyster Point Boulevard, South San Francisco, CA 94080; (415) 873-0200.

Tour notes: Candlestick Point State Recreation Area is a small state-run park that sits in the shadow of Candlestick Park, where the San Francisco Giants and 49ers play. The park trails are short and quirky in character, but perfectly suited for beginners. Dress in layers for this excursion: like many areas near the bay, it can be uncomfortably cold and windy.

The recreation area has a maze of nicely paved trails that are fun for folks on wheels looking for an adventure at the edge of the bay. Some of the trails seem to beckon you into the distance only to end abruptly. One trail ends at a strange Stonehengelike structure built from broken chunks of concrete. Another trail is gated by sculpted concrete walls that seem to promise grandness to come, but it never materializes.

You'll also find nicely maintained picnic areas, grassy play areas, plenty of rest rooms and water fountains, and even a small beach. Of course, you should avoid this area during Giants and 49ers home games, when the traffic is dreadful.

---

12. Sierra Point Public Trail   2 miles 🌀 🐾 🏄

Reference: Near the San Francisco Bay in Brisbane; see number ⑫ on page 118.

Ideal for: Beginners—Touring

Directions: From U.S. 101 heading north from the south bay, exit at Sierra Point Parkway. Turn right onto the parkway and take the first left on Marina Boulevard. From U.S. 101 heading south from downtown San Francisco, exit at Sierra Point Parkway (south of Candlestick Park). Turn left onto the parkway and follow it south for about a mile. Pass back under the freeway and take the first left, Marina Boulevard. Park in the Good Guys parking lot.

Local shop: Skates off Haight, 384 Oyster Point Boulevard, South San Francisco, CA 94080; (415) 873-0200.

Tour notes: While not a major destination for skating in the Bay Area, the Sierra Point Public Trail is worth checking out if you happen to be nearby with your skates handy. This short paved trail on the north and east shore of Sierra Point passes by the Brisbane Marina. Although the trail is rough in spots, there are good views of Candlestick Point, Hunters Point (the big structure is a dry dock), and the East Bay hills. You'll also find several office parking lots to play in nearby, plus rest rooms and water at the marina.

13. The City of the Dead   3 miles 🌴 👟 🏃

Reference: **Central Colma; see number ⓭ on page 118.**

Ideal for: Fitness—Hills/Slalom—Historic

Directions: From Interstate 280 heading south from downtown San Francisco, take the Serramonte Boulevard exit, turning left onto Serramonte. In less than a mile, you'll come to El Camino Real. Turn right to get to your destination, the Cypress Lawn Cemetery. From Interstate 280 heading north from the south bay, exit onto Hickey Boulevard and follow it west less than a mile to El Camino Real. Turn left onto El Camino Real and look for Cypress Lawn about half a mile up, on both sides of the road. Park on the shoulder.

Local shop: Skates off Haight, 384 Oyster Point Boulevard, South San Francisco, CA 94080; (415) 873-0200.

Tour notes: Colma's claim to fame is its dead, not living, residents. Cemeteries line both sides of El Camino Real, and it may seem like a bizarre place to skate, but several of these cemeteries are also beautiful parks. Cypress Lawn is the best, thanks to the smooth pavement that winds its way past monuments and mausoleums, all surrounded by well-tended grounds. You won't find many flat spots, and in fact, some of the roads get pretty steep. This translates into great fun for slalom skaters but trouble for beginners.

Olivet Memorial Park is a better choice for those who aren't ready for the Cypress hills. You'll find it at Hillside Boulevard and Olivet Parkway. The pavement is not quite as good, but the hills are less steep. Although it looks tempting, avoid Woodlawn Cemetery, where the pavement is quite bad.

Note: If you do choose to skate at Colma or any of the other cemeteries, please respect those who are visiting for more serious reasons.

14. Bayside Park/   7 miles 🌴 👟 🏃
Airport Hotel District

Reference: **South of San Francisco International Airport in Burlingame; see number ⓮ on page 118.**

Ideal for: Beginners—Fitness—In-Line Hockey—Touring

Directions: From U.S. 101 heading north from the south bay, exit at Anza Boulevard and park at the Days Inn or the Doubletree Hotel. Both have "Public Shore" parking near the lagoon. From U.S. 101 going south from downtown San Francisco, exit at Broadway. Follow the signs to Bayshore Highway, looping back over the freeway to the northeast. Turn right on Bayshore and left on Airport Boulevard. Continue on to Anza and park as described above.

Local shop: Skates off Haight, 384 Oyster Point Boulevard, South San Francisco, CA 94080; (415) 873-0200.

Tour notes: Despite the fact that the San Francisco International Airport hotel area is heavily developed, the intrepid skater will find some peaceful spots and spectacular vistas by following the edge of the bay and exploring the nearby lagoons. A bonus for airplane lovers, the shoreline parallels the normal flight approach to the airport.

Starting near the Doubletree Hotel just north of Anza Boulevard, follow the trail next to Anza west toward U.S. 101. It soon loops under the Anza Boulevard bridge and heads south along the edge of the lagoon. Enjoy the marshy scenery for approximately half a mile until the trail veers sharply left toward the bay. (A footbridge goes straight to cross the slough here, but it was closed at press time) The remainder of the trail is in need of repaving on the approach to its termination at Airport Boulevard. From this point, you can turn right to continue south on the edge of Airport Boulevard to reach Coyote Point County Recreational Area. Turn around here and return to the lagoon, following it until you reach the Anza Boulevard bridge. Before you head back under the bridge, go left and skate on it to cross the lagoon heading toward U.S. 101. On the other side of the lagoon, the Sanchez Creek Marsh has a short nature trail that passes between the freeway and the lagoon, offering a tiny wildlife haven from all the development in the area. Return to the Doubletree Hotel by following the trail back across the lagoon and under Anza Boulevard.

To explore the Bayside Park Trail, cross Airport Boulevard to the bay side and continue skating northwest until you reach Bayside Park. This is a perfect spot for beginners; the pavement is new and smooth and there are some great bay views. On the north side of the park, the dedicated trail curves to the west and then ends too soon at Bayshore Boulevard.

If you're eager to continue on, turn right and follow the terrible sidewalk next to Bayshore. Be careful on the rough, narrow surface, and watch for obstacles such as manhole covers and frequent driveways. Just north of the One Bay Plaza building, an almost hidden "Public Shore" sign points the way to a trail on the right that leads back to the shore. Skate next to the San Francisco Bay on varying pavement textures to pass by hotels and restaurants until you finally reach a pretty little park (with a water fountain) just south of the roar of the airport.

One last diversion awaits on your return to the Doubletree. Just past the Crown Sterling Suites on the east side of Airport Boulevard, a short trail extension leads south to a loop around the pretty Anza Lagoon, where rest rooms and water are available.

One final note: A pickup hockey game starts at noon most Sundays in a parking lot between the two lagoons. Look for the players behind the Airport Corporate Center at 533 Airport Boulevard.

15. Sawyer Camp Trail

12 miles ⭐️**8** 🥾**3** 🏃

Reference: **Alongside Crystal Springs Reservoir outside of San Mateo; see number ⑮ on page 118.**

Ideal for: Fitness—Hills/Slalom—Historic—Touring

Directions: West of San Mateo at the interchange of Interstate 280 and Highway 92, exit onto 92 and follow the signs toward Half Moon Bay. You'll drive north for a short stretch next to Crystal Springs Reservoir before 92 turns once again toward the ocean. Rather than following 92 west, turn right on Skyline Boulevard (Highway 35) to continue north alongside the reservoir for two more miles. Park on the gravel pullout about two miles up, just above the Crystal Springs trail entrance sign.

Map: For a free trail map, contact San Mateo County Parks at the address below.

Local shop: Nuvo Colours, 1600 South El Camino Real, San Mateo, CA 94402; (415) 571-1537. Other contact: San Mateo County Parks, 590 Hamilton Street, Redwood City, CA 94063; (415) 363-4020.

Tour notes: The Crystal Springs Reservoir sparkles to the west at the beginning of the Sawyer Camp Trail, known officially as the Sawyer Camp County Historic Trail. The long, dedicated bike path winds along the banks of the reservoir and through tunnels made by shady groves of trees. It can get very hot during the summer in this protected valley, and as the day heats up, take care to avoid the tarred repairs striping the asphalt, because they become soft and grabby.

The wide, hilly trail is very popular with Bay Area families on weekends, forcing you to compete with many other wheeled users equipped with everything from tricycles to baby strollers to mountain and street bikes. After a tour up the east side of the reservoir, the trail crosses to the base of some foothills on the west. There's a water fountain after about two miles, plus a chance to see the biggest bay laurel tree around. But it's better to stick to the pavement if you want to avoid the abundant poison oak. This is a good place for beginners to turn back.

A long cruise north passes through trees and then begins to wind up the side of a hill to reach the south end of San Andreas Lake. Take a rest in the shade before taking on the final, even steeper climb up ahead, rising about 400 feet. Don't waste your effort on the climb unless you can take its steep, winding curves coming back down without losing control. Use your best speed-control skills on the mostly downhill return trip, because even if you don't find yourself flailing in the poison oak, you could still get a speeding ticket. The posted five mile-per-hour limit is enforced by rangers with radar on the big hill and in congested areas.

16. Canada Road

7.6 miles

Reference: **In the coastal foothills west of the town of San Mateo; see number ⑯ on page 118.**

Ideal for: Beginners—Fitness—Hills/Slalom—Historic—Speed—Touring

Directions: From Interstate 280 near Redwood City, take the Edgewood Road exit. Go west about half a mile to Canada Road and park near its intersection with Edgewood. To start from the north end of Canada Road, leave Interstate 280 on Highway 92 West. Just beyond the interchange, you'll see Canada Road heading south on your left. Park your car at the designated parking area at Canada Road.

Local shop: Nuvo Colours, 1600 South El Camino Real, San Mateo, CA 94402; (415) 571-1537. Other contact: San Mateo County Parks, 590 Hamilton Street, Redwood City, CA 94063; (415) 363-4020.

Tour notes: Imagine skating on a smooth, wide, two-lane highway for more than seven miles through beautiful, undeveloped scenery— without a car in sight. What you're envisioning is "Bicycle Sunday" on Canada Road. Every first, second, and fourth Sunday from March to October, Canada Road is closed to motor vehicle traffic from 9 A.M. to 4 P.M., and is open to bicyclists, walkers, runners, and skaters. The pavement is top quality, smooth from shoulder to shoulder. And since the road is closed, you can play on its entire width. (Should you come here on an off weekend, the shoulders are still wide enough for skating, but the cars do move fast.)

Although you can start at either end of the trail, it's best to begin skating at the less crowded southern end (Edgewood Road). That way, the prevailing winds will be against you on the way out and behind you for the return. There are flat areas near both ends that are suitable for beginners.

Skate north from the Edgewood parking area, where the road drops a bit and then flattens out. You may catch a glimpse of the old Filoli Mansion to the west. About a mile and a half north, you'll see the Pulgas Water Temple, also on the west side of the road. Its gate is closed on weekends, but you can easily skate around it. The Temple is the terminus of the Hetch Hetchy Aqueduct that brings water from Yosemite National Park to San Francisco to make Anchor Steam Beer. This is a great spot for a picnic, and appropriately enough, drinking water is available.

Just after the Water Temple, you will encounter the longest climb of this skating trip. As you ascend, just keep thinking about how much fun it will be to skate back down. Nearing the north end of Canada Road, you'll be rewarded with views of the Upper Crystal Springs Reservoir. The infamous San Andreas Fault traces the length of this man-made lake.

Skate within your abilities on the return trip: Although the hills aren't terribly steep, some are long. Good braking skills are a must for lower-level skaters to control speed. For more advanced skaters, these hills are great for practicing slalom turns or speed training.

17. Foster City Shoreline Trail   8 miles

Reference: On the west shore of the San Francisco Bay in Foster City; see number **17** on page 118.

Ideal for: Beginners—Touring

Directions: Heading either east or west on Highway 92 in Foster City, take the Foster City exit. Once on Foster City Boulevard, follow it to the north until it dead-ends at Third Avenue. Park alongside the street. The Shoreline Trail is up on the levee between your parking spot and the San Francisco Bay.

Local shop: Foster City Cyclery and Sport, 999 B Edgewater Boulevard, Foster City, CA 94404; (415) 349-2010.

Tour notes: Spend a morning exploring this unusual section of San Francisco Bay's shoreline on curves of excellent pavement. Come early before the inevitable winds come up; otherwise, you may get more of a workout than you bargained for.

Start off by skating northwest on the levee overlooking the bay. If you did choose a windy day, when you reach Coyote Point, you'll see some of the best boardsailers in the area making good use of their favorite natural resource. On your return, if you're enjoying the wind at your back too much to stop at your car, continue south and under the highway to follow Beach Park Boulevard (see the Foster City Loop below). But remember, you'll still have to battle the head winds on your return up the bay.

18. Foster City Loop   12 miles

Reference: A circumnavigation of the bay side town of Foster City; see number **18** on page 118.

Ideal for: Touring

Directions: From U.S. 101 in San Mateo, take the Hillsdale Boulevard exit. Turn south on Edgewater and follow it to the end, where you can look for a place to park. From the San Mateo Bridge (Highway 92) take the Edgewater exit and repeat the above directions.

Local shop: Foster City Cyclery and Sport, 999 B Edgewater Boulevard, Foster City, CA 94404; (415) 349-2010.

Tour notes: Just about anywhere you skate in Foster City is clean and scenic, with premium touring along its many waterways. In these parts, it's best to skate in the morning before the wind comes up.

The Foster City Loop takes you on a clockwise route along a canal-side bike trail. (Reverse the direction if the winds are blowing south to north.) From the end of Edgewater Boulevard, skate to the right (southwest) along the Belmont Slough. Soon you will cross to the Marina Lagoon Trail, which takes you past upscale condominiums and then under the San Mateo Bridge. Skate on Fashion Island Boulevard, and turn left onto Mariner's Island Boulevard to reach East Third Avenue. At Third, you can regain the levee bike path and skate closer to the water.

Continuing your loop at Third Avenue, the path goes to Little Coyote Point and then passes under Highway 92 (watch for arrows marking the way). The trail curves along the bay next to Beach Park Boulevard and through the Belmont Slough. Continue on until you reach your starting point at Edgewater. If you're still fresh, explore the neighborhood streets, where good pavement and light automobile traffic ensure a fun jaunt.

19. Half Moon Bay Beach Trail   6 miles

Reference: **On the Pacific coast in Half Moon Bay; see number ⑲ on page 118.**

Ideal for: Touring

Directions: From U.S. 101 in San Mateo, take Highway 92 heading west. Pass the 280 interchange and follow the signs to Half Moon Bay on the now two-lane highway. Continue west through the hills and turn left again where 92 ends in a "T" intersection with Highway 1/ Cabrillo Highway. Take the first right (Kelly Avenue) and follow it to the Francis Beach entrance gate. Avoid the $4 parking fee by parking outside the gate and skating down the road to the trail. To park at the middle section of the trail, turn right at Highway 1 and take the Venice State Beach access road two miles up.

Local shop: Nuvo Colours, 1600 South El Camino Real, San Mateo, CA 94402; (415) 571-1537.

Tour notes: Half Moon Bay's fog-weary residents know they can bank on autumn to be the prime time of the year to get out and celebrate. That's one reason why the famous pumpkin festival has become so popular. Fall is also the best time of year to skate the Half Moon Bay Beach Trail.

Explore this little-known path within a few hundred feet of the ocean in good weather to best enjoy the scenery. Low sand dunes extend between the trail and the beach, and at some points, they're low enough to offer a glimpse of the Pacific Ocean to the west. At its northern extreme, the trail ends at Mirimar Beach, after passing through Francis, Dunes, Venice, and Roosevelt Beaches.

The right attitude for this trail is to come with high expectations for the beach, and not the skating. Frankly, the pavement of the beach parking lots and entrance roads are better than the old asphalt on the trail itself. Still, a visit here does have a certain appeal, since there are so few on-beach trails in the upper half of the state. The beach trail is worth at least one trip for that fact alone.

---

20. Bayfront Trail/ Dumbarton Bridge

18 miles 🏆 🛼 🧍

Reference: **Near the San Francisco Bay in Menlo Park; see number ⑳ on page 118.**

Ideal for: Fitness—Touring

Directions: From U.S. 101 in Menlo Park, take the Marsh Road exit and proceed one block northeast to park at Bayfront Park.

Local shop: Nuvo Colours, 1600 South El Camino Real, San Mateo, CA 94402; (415) 571-1537.

Tour notes: The Dumbarton is the only bridge you can skate on that crosses the San Francisco Bay. If you have the skills, it's worth a once-only trip on a clear day just to stop at the top of the bridge and enjoy the view. A good starting point is Bayfront Park, a former landfill on the edge of the bay that has been converted into an attractive park. For the purposes of touring, skating within the park is limited to a half mile of paved roads. (The trails that head up into the landfill-created hills are paved, but unfortunately, they're covered with loose gravel, and the surface is too slippery for skating.)

The Bayfront Trail starts at the entrance to the park and extends southeast along Bayfront Expressway. It can be quite windy out here, and the return is usually against the wind, so plan accordingly. The first mile or so of the trail has a fairly rough surface, though the quality does improve further on. Just before it reaches Willow Road a mile and a half from the Bayfront Park entrance, the trail makes a sharp left to follow the edge of the bay around the Sun Microsystems "campus." Skate around Sun (and its tempting parking lots) to University Avenue.

Strong skaters ready for a mile-long climb and narrow return descent can continue to the Dumbarton Bridge by crossing Bayfront Expressway at the University Avenue stoplight. The trail continues east toward the bay and is almost totally flat until you reach the bridge, where it climbs fairly steeply to the top of the arc. Here you'll be skating on a path separated from the roadway by a low barrier. This may be unnerving for lower-level skaters, since the bridge traffic is fast, close, and noisy.

From the center of the bridge on a clear day, you can see most of the Bay Area shoreline communities, including Foster City, Oakland, San Francisco, and Palo Alto. Just to the south is an old railroad bridge (unused) and the suspended pipeline of the Hetch Hetchy Aqueduct, which brings water from the Sierra Nevada. If you're ready

---

for more adventure, you can continue skating all the way to the East Bay (see the Wildlife Refuge/Dumbarton Bridge tour on page 190), or return the way you came. Be very careful to control your speed when descending the bridge. Since there's no room to make slalom turns, a thick brake pad and good heel braking skills are a must.

San Francisco Bay Area: South Bay

13 Great Places to Skate

San Francisco Bay Area: South Bay

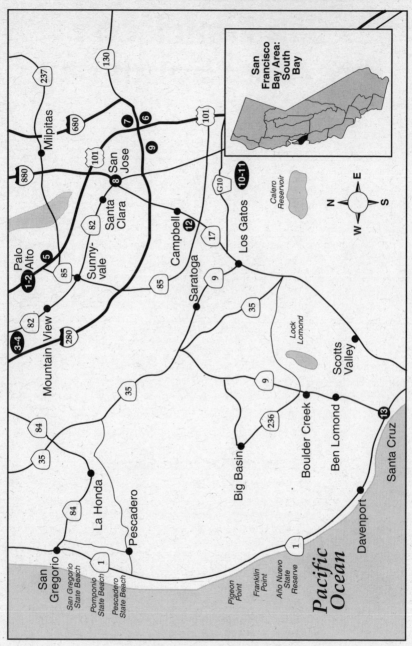

Skating Regions Beyond the South Bay

North ...... San Francisco/The Peninsula, p. 117   South .... Central Coast North, p. 273
East .... S.F. Bay Area: East Bay, p. 157

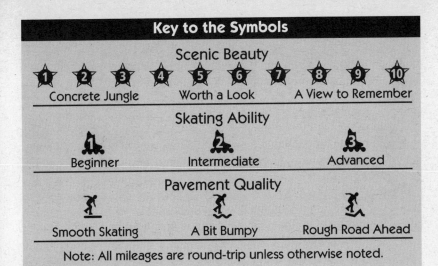

Key to the Symbols

Scenic Beauty

⭐1 ⭐2 ⭐3 ⭐4 ⭐5 ⭐6 ⭐7 ⭐8 ⭐9 ⭐10

Concrete Jungle　　Worth a Look　　A View to Remember

Skating Ability

Beginner　　　Intermediate　　　Advanced

Pavement Quality

Smooth Skating　　A Bit Bumpy　　Rough Road Ahead

Note: All mileages are round-trip unless otherwise noted.

The South Bay, home of the Silicon Valley, has the kind of land-scape in-line skaters learn to love: Office park after office park, with some of the best concrete sidewalks and smoothest parking lots you'll find anywhere, not to mention dedicated bike paths for lunchtime workouts. But then again, the area has plenty to please nature lovers, too. One trail in south San Jose starts at the end of a street with the high-tech name of Silicon Valley Boulevard and offers access to the more back-to-nature street called Coyote Creek Parkway. When fully connected, this will be one of the longest skating trails in northern California. (Unfortunately, due to the heavy rains of recent winters, paving the final connection of the trail is on hold because of the corridor's non-recreational use as a flood control area.)

The local in-line scene is centered south of San Jose along the Los Gatos Creek Trail, where day after day, in-line experts and tottering beginners compete for their share of pavement with joggers, strollers, and bicyclists. Fine skating can also be found along the wetlands trails on the southwest shores of the San Francisco Bay and on the cliffside Natural Bridges State Park Trail in Santa Cruz.

1. Cornelius Bol Park Bike Path   5 miles ⭐ 🚴 🏊

Reference: A rail-trail and bike path in south Palo Alto; see number ❶ on page 140.

Ideal for: Fitness—Hills/Slalom—Touring

Directions: From U.S. 101 outside of Palo Alto, take the Embarcadero/ Oregon Expressway exit. Follow the signs to the Oregon Expressway, heading west. After passing under the Alma Street overpass, turn left onto El Camino Real and then right on Matadero Avenue. Continue to where Matadero terminates at Cornelius Bol Park, and park on the small gravel area next to this neighborhood park.

Local shop: Palo Alto Sport Shop, 526 Waverly Street, Palo Alto, CA 94301-8555; (415) 328-8555. Other contact: Julie Bonderant, County Trails and Pathways Committee, 298 Garden Hill Drive, Los Gatos, CA 95030; (408) 358-3741.

Tour notes: The Cornelius Bol Park Bike Path is a favorite not only for residents of the nearby neighborhood, but for employees of the Lockheed, Hewlett Packard, and Syntex Labs, all located nearby in their Silicon Valley office parks.

Starting from tiny Cornelius Bol Park, the trail follows a canal between the office parks and Henry M. Gunn High School, until it reaches the major intersections of Miranda Avenue and Foothill Expressway at Arastradero Road. At press time, the original trail at Bol Park was closed due to a flood-control canal project. Bright orange signs marked the detour on Laguna Avenue and Ilima Way through the neighborhood. At McGreagor Way and Paradise Avenue, the trail picks up on a new (temporary bypass) section of gently sloping asphalt that dips and winds through the high school playing fields, bordered on both sides by chain-link fences.

Take the crosswalks over Miranda and Foothill to get to the north shoulder of Arastradero, where a wide concrete sidewalk beckons invitingly. From here on, no bicycles are allowed. On your left, the wooded hillside offers a decidedly rural scene, belying the high-tech goings-on in the area. On the right, the Syntex buildings and parking lots are set back from the road, made almost unnoticeable by landscaped strips next to the street, with many leafy trees for shade. Keep a sharp eye out for cars during business hours as you cross two Syntex driveways. Two street intersections are served by stoplights.

After you cross Deer Creek Road, the trail becomes rural on both sides, and you'll actually pass a horse stable on the left. The scenery is very pretty, with grassy hills rising up on all sides—and a long hill of your own to slalom back on. This bit of pure nature must seem far, far away from the stacked-up in-baskets and voice-mail calls awaiting the return of the lucky people who can take their lunch breaks here. Conveniently, a drinking fountain marks the trail's end at Arastradero.

After you return to Cornelius Bol Park (a breeze, since it's generally downhill) you'll find another short section of the trail at the north end of Bol Park where Matadero Avenue meets it. The setting here is mostly ivy-covered chain-link fencing and the backs of buildings bordering a wide corridor with varied asphalt. The trail emerges and terminates less than a mile up at Hanover Street. If you want to skate a few more blocks, turn right and cross a driveway to get to the excellent 10-foot-wide concrete sidewalk that curves around Hanover Street and meets Page Mill Road.

Local bicycle and running enthusiasts turn this into a seven-mile loop. To follow their route, after the water fountain at Arastradero, continue further west on the road's shoulder to where it passes over Interstate 280. Turn right when you reach Page Mill Road on the other side and pass back under the freeway heading east. Cross to the north side of Page Mill after just a quarter of a mile to skate on one mile of Old Page Mill Road in very light traffic. Turn right onto Porter Drive at the end of Old Page Mill (Porter curves around to become Hanover Street), and then turn left after the Lockheed employee parking lot to follow the Bol Park Bike Path back to the park.

2. Baylands Trail   6 miles 🟢 🧍 🏃

Reference: **East San Francisco Bay's Baylands Nature Preserve area in Palo Alto; see number ❷ on page 140.**

Ideal for: Beginners—Fitness—Touring

Directions: From U.S. 101 (the Bayshore Freeway) going north in Palo Alto, take the Embarcadero East exit and turn toward the bay. Driving south, take the Embarcadero/Oregon Expressway exit and follow the signs to East Embarcadero. Turn right at Faber Place, the second street after the stoplight. (You'll be entering an office park.) Park in the cul-de-sac at the end of the street, right next to the trail's entrance.

Local shop: Palo Alto Sport Shop, 526 Waverly Street, Palo Alto, CA 94301-8555; (415) 328-8555.

Tour notes: The Baylands Trail has loads of potential, especially if the San Francisco Bay Trail project is ever completed (see Trail Advocates on page 435 in the Resource Guide). When that happens, this section will become part of the paved route that will someday fully encircle the bay. It already connects with Mountain View's Shoreline Park to the south. The territory around the Baylands Trail offers great bayland views, with both saltwater and freshwater marshes and the wildlife they support, including ducks, terns, and flocks of white pelicans.

Starting at the end of Faber Place, enter the Baylands Trail heading south. At first, you must put up with the roar of traffic on U.S. 101, but the scenery to the east is of marshland, high grasses, a pond, and birds, seemingly deaf to the noise. This section of the trail would be perfect if only there was a time warp, taking you back to pre-automobile days. About three-quarters of a mile up, the trail emerges onto the shoulder of East Bayshore Frontage Road. Office buildings and their driveways soon appear on the left and then, two and a half miles from the Faber Place entrance, you'll cross a second wooden bridge and make a 90-degree turn inland.

As you leave the buildings behind, the asphalt deteriorates somewhat, but the natural beauty of the scenery and the diminishing traffic noise make up for it. After half a mile, a trail intersection is marked with the sign, "Welcome to Shoreline at Mountain View." The south leg of this six-mile round-trip ends here, but if you want to connect with Shoreline Park (see page 146), turn left at the welcome sign and then take the first right and go another half a mile to a fork in the trail. Take the left fork and ascend the slight rise to follow what becomes a gravelly service road for another half mile. Watch for a wooden trail marker post on a rise to your right. Just beyond the marker, take a hard right to skate up to it. Go south and you'll see the gray wooden fence next to Shoreline Lake, with a steep, narrow, gravel-spattered slope leading down to the good pavement of the Shoreline Trail. You may elect to sidestep down this mess.

Back at Faber Place, more diversions await to keep you in your skates, if you're not tired. First, you can explore the three-quarter-mile section of the Baylands Trail on the north side of Embarcadero. To get there, skate back up Faber and turn left toward the freeway to return to the stoplight. Cross Embarcadero to skate up Geng Road, following the signs for the Athletic Center (a couple of baseball diamonds and unlocked rest rooms). You'll see the trail rising up to a levee at the end of the athletic center parking lot. At first it's rather overgrown, with large bushes closing in from the sides, but soon your view will open up to reveal the municipal golf course on the right and, to the left, a creek that has been left in its natural state. Just as you start to feel you're really going to enjoy the scenery, the trail comes to a rust-red iron bridge at the end of the golf course. Don't bother crossing unless you want to examine the graffiti on the side of the utility building where the trail terminates.

Return to Embarcadero, and, if you're still eager for more, skate on the bike lane past the office buildings on the right and the golf course and airport on the left. Turn left at the intersection where a big wooden sign announces that you're entering the Baylands Nature Preserve Center. You'll be skating on the street here, but there's a bike lane on the shoulder. The speed bumps are flat in the bike lane. (They're also fun to jump over or launch off.) The scenery is open and natural all around. Follow the road to its end, about a mile from your parking spot on Faber.

3. Stanford Wednesday Night Skate

7 miles

Reference: **Starting on the Stanford University campus in Palo Alto; see number ❸ on page 140.**

Ideal for: Road/Street—Touring

Directions: From U.S. 101 north of Palo Alto, take the University Avenue exit and follow it west for 2.5 miles until it reaches the Stanford University Oval, a grassy area encircled by the campus driveway called Palm Drive. Parking can be found along the Oval or on Sierra Street.

Local shop: Nuvo Colours, 162 University Avenue, Palo Alto, CA 94301; (415) 326-6886.

Tour notes: Join an informal group skate through the Stanford University campus and surrounding neighborhoods that takes place every Wednesday evening. Participants meet at the western end of University Avenue at the Oval's circular parking lot at 7:30 P.M. and follow the same seven-mile course every week, which offers a mix of challenging urban terrain suitable for skills ranging from mid-level to stair thrasher. The route hits some favorite campus play areas as well as some nearby streets. Staff from the local in-line specialty shop, Nuvo Colours in San Mateo, are usually present.

4. Stanford University Campus

4 miles

Reference: **On the Stanford University campus in Palo Alto; see number ❹ on page 140.**

Ideal for: Historic—Road/Street—Scene—Touring

Directions: From U.S. 101 north of Palo Alto, take the University Avenue exit and follow it west for 2.5 miles until it reaches the Stanford University Oval. Parking can be found along the Oval or on Sierra Street.

Local shop: Nuvo Colours, 162 University Avenue, Palo Alto, CA 94301; (415) 326-6886.

Tour notes: Pack a picnic and spend a weekend afternoon of play at the Stanford University campus, which attracts skaters of all levels. The terrain offers a multitude of stairs for hard-core jumpers and riders, wide and almost glassy concrete walkways for smooth cruising, and a gentle asphalt slope on the north side that's perfect for a long series of slalom turns. And on weekends, you can enjoy even more slalom practice in the top levels of the parking garage. Try circumnavigating the University Oval and take a roll around the Main Quad. The Quad itself is paved with a cobblestone style of bricks, but the big circular planters make a fun place to show off your toe-rolls. Guided tours and night skates on the campus are offered by Nuvo Colours, a local in-line specialty shop (see page 438).

5. Shoreline Park   7 miles 🏅 👫 🏊

Reference: **A park on the southwest shore of the San Francisco Bay in Mountain View; see number ❺ on page 140.**

Ideal for: Touring

Directions: South of Palo Alto on U.S. 101, take the Shoreline Boulevard exit and head east. Turn left to drive through the gated park entrance located at the far side of the Shoreline Amphitheater. Beyond the amphitheater grounds, the road curves toward the west to the Sailing Center, a Victorian mansion, a restaurant, the golf course, and free parking.

Local shop: Courtesy Sports, 4856 El Camino Real, Los Altos, CA 94022; (415) 968-7970.

Trail notes: Surrounding the rolling hills of what used to be the Mountain View landfill are the marshy wetlands of the southern San Francisco Bay. Mountain View's Shoreline Park is situated right next to these saltwater and freshwater ponds, which are protected to preserve the environment for the wildlife living in and around them. As you skate, you'll comes across lots of interpretive signs about the wetlands, including one on the burrowing owl habitat here. Starting from the golf course parking lot, cross the road you entered on and take the paved path up a rise that serves as a creekside levee to Permanente Creek, leading toward the bay. Turn right at the trail intersection near a wooden bridge to take Stevens Creek Trail. Continue to skate toward Moffett Field Naval Air Station, which presents a decidedly unnatural view to the south with its great humpbacked hangars.

When you reach the Moffett gates, turn right to slalom (or ride your brake) down the incline to the cul-de-sac at the end of Crittenden Lane, a low-traffic street near office parks in the Shoreline area. Follow Crittenden back out to Shoreline Boulevard and turn right to skate (still on the street) back to the beginning of the loop.

Another half-mile stretch of good pavement starts from the parking lot at the Club House (a pro shop) and heads off to the north, circling around the north side of Shoreline Lake. When you run out of good pavement at the gray fence, look next to the fence to see where the gravel-strewn trail leads up the hill. This is the access route to the Baylands Trail (see page 143). To make the connection, duckwalk or sidestep up the dirt beside the narrow, rough path and you'll find a trail angling off to the right next to a marker post. It leads down to a gravelly road, where you must turn left to make your way west and north to the small park service building half a mile away. The Baylands Trail is just a few strokes from here.

6. Cunningham Park Lake Loop   4 miles 🌟 🧍 🏃

Reference: **A water park in southeast San Jose; see number 6 on page 140.**

Ideal for: Beginners—Figure/Stunts—Touring

Directions: Heading south along the east side of downtown San Jose on U.S. 101, take the Tully Road exit just beyond the Interstate 280 interchange and head east. Follow busy Tully for 1.5 miles. Just beyond its intersection with Capitol Expressway, turn left into the entrance of Cunningham Park, which is also the site of the Raging Waters theme park. There is a $2 fee for parking from mid-June through Labor Day (but it's free during off-season weekdays.) Turn left after the kiosk to park in the Marina Lot just ahead.

Local shop: Go Skate Surf & Sports, 2306 L Almaden Road, San Jose, CA 95125; (408) 978-6487.

Tour notes: Lake Cunningham Park is a great location for an all-day family outing. Although swimming is not allowed here, fishing, picnicking, sunbathing on the beach, boating (rentals are available), and water slides are all activities you can add to your romp on skates to make a day of it. The sound of small planes taking off and landing at the nearby Reid-Hillview Airport actually creates a pleasant drone in the background on a lazy day, punctuated by the quack-quack of ducks or the clack-clack of a toddler's first try on roller skates.

The smooth pavement throughout the park is in excellent condition, both on the dedicated bike paths and on the wide park roads (occasionally, local in-line races are held here). When you arrive, pick up a free map of the park at the Marina snack bar so you can check out the location of the bike paths and parking lots to plan your day. After exploring the path along the lakeshore and the parcourse loop around Big Meadow, head over to Parking Lot E. If it's a slow day or during the off-season, this lot is large enough and far enough out of the way to be nearly empty, making it a perfect spot for figure-skating practice or in-line kite flying.

7. Penitencia Creek Trail   4 miles 🌟 🧍 🏃

Reference: **A creekside trail in east San Jose; see number 7 on page 140.**

Ideal for: Touring

Directions: From Interstate 680 in San Jose, take the Berryessa Road exit, heading east. After four stoplights, pull into the parking lot at the Berryessa Community Center/Penitencia Creek Park on the right.

Local shop: Inline Sports, 19998 Homestead Road, Cupertino, CA
   95014; (408) 252-5233. Other contact: Penitencia Creek County
   Park, c/o Ed Levin County Park, 3100 Calaveras Road, Milpitas,
   CA 95035; (408) 262-6980.

Tour notes: Skate east San Jose's Penitencia Creek Trail in the springtime to see the sycamores, oaks, and cottonwoods at their finest.
   During the summer, this in-line tour is best taken while the sun is low
   on either horizon.

   From the parking lot at Penitencia Creek County Park, cross or
   circle around the big lawn on one of the paths to reach the far southwest corner of the park. Across Penitencia Creek Road, you'll see the
   wide asphalt trail with its yellow dividing line emerging at Viceroy
   Way. Cross the street and skate through the grasses heading west
   toward the freeway. At busy Capitol Avenue, a crosswalk and stoplights enable you to cross safely. Turn left at what seems like a dead
   end to cross the bridge over the creek. At the far side of the bridge,
   you'll find the trail again, almost hidden on the right.

   Eucalyptus trees line Penitencia Creek as you continue south,
   following it under the multiple lanes of Interstate 680. A few blocks
   further on, the trail enters a residential area and terminates on Moss-
   dale Way, just across Jackson Avenue from Penitencia Creek County
   Park. One block south of here, a crosswalk gives you access to the
   park's wide concrete paths, worth exploring before you head back.
   On your return to Penitencia Creek Park, end your skate with a loop
   around its wide-open spaces.

---

8. Sports Arena Parking Lot   2 miles 🌟 🏂 🏃

Reference: In downtown San Jose; see number ❽ on page 140.

Ideal for: Beginners—Figure/Stunts—Fitness

Directions: From Interstate 880 between downtown San Jose and the
   airport, exit onto The Alameda, going south. Veer left at the "Y" in
   the road to stay on The Alameda where Race Street continues south.
   Six or seven short blocks east, just beyond the railroad crossing, you'll
   find the San Jose Sports Arena on the left. Park wherever you wish.

Local shop: Inline Sports, 19998 Homestead Road, Cupertino, CA
   95014; (408) 252-5233.

Tour notes: The San Jose Sports Arena is home to the Sharks (the ice
   hockey team), the Rhinos (the roller hockey team), and a parking lot
   that's large enough to accommodate thousands of loyal fans during
   games. Translation: when there's no event in progress, skaters can play
   on the vast expanse of excellent concrete. Since the lot is slightly
   sloped, you can practice slalom skating as well as tricks. Feel free to
   skate all the way around the arena itself or venture east towards downtown on Santa Clara Street (which was The Alameda to the west).

9. Coyote Creek Parkway   15.5 miles 🌟 🛼 🏃

Reference: A long creekside trail starting in south San Jose;
  see number ❾ on page 140.

Ideal for: Fitness—Speed—Touring

Directions: At the southeastern end of San Jose on U.S. 101, take the
  Bernal Road/Silicon Valley Boulevard exit. Turn left at the bottom of
  the off-ramp and drive half a mile east to where Silicon Valley Boulevard meets Coyote Creek. Turn left again at Eden Park Plaza and
  park on the shoulder nearest the trees by the creek. The trail crosses
  Silicon Valley Boulevard on the west side of the creek.

Map: The Coyote Hellyer County Park map is available at the park
  ranger station or from the Santa Clara County Parks and Recreation
  Department (see below).

Local shop: Go Skate Surf & Sports, 2306 L Almaden Road, San Jose,
  CA 95125; (408) 978-6487. Other contact: Santa Clara County Parks
  and Recreation Department, 298 Garden Hill Drive, Los Gatos, CA
  95030; (408) 358-3741.

Tour notes: One of the greatest charms of the Coyote Creek Parkway is
  that you're likely to see more wildlife than people, especially in the
  cooler early morning hours. The banks of the creek attract wood
  ducks, egrets, and great blue herons. Another plus is that there are
  only three very minor intersections on the nearly eight-mile route
  described here. Like so many other inland trails in California, the
  Coyote Creek Parkway is at its prettiest when the rains of winter have
  turned the surrounding fields and hills a fresh green. But even in the
  summertime, the acres of dry grasses bordering this countryside tour
  are sprinkled with yellow mustard blossoms and the occasional California Golden Poppy. Water-seeking big leaf maples, cottonwoods,
  sycamores, and willow trees mark the path of the creek after the trail
  leaves its side.

  Start skating south on the eight-foot-wide asphalt trail next to the
  trees hiding Coyote Creek. The pavement is smooth, but for the first
  mile and a half, be on the alert for a few raised cracks, especially the
  pair lurking in the shade just before you pass under the first freeway
  ramp. After the upscale neighborhood begins on your right, the trail
  meets Metcalf Park, which has a playground, picnic tables, and the
  necessary plumbing, if not shade. This is your last chance for water,
  so if you plan to make the full 15.5-mile round-trip, top off your
  water bottle before continuing.

  Now the newest pavement begins, and from here south, it remains
  smooth and in excellent repair. South of the park, the path continues
  away from the housing development and past a gravel pad where
  alternate trail access parking is available. Two-tenths of a mile farther,

keep your speed up to more easily cross the iron-framed bridge with its loose wood slats.

Cross Metcalf Road (very light traffic) and pass the PG&E substation on the left. The willows are close to the trail here, and you can hear Monterey Road behind them, but traffic noise becomes less noticeable the further south you go. After another mile and a half near the creek, the trail seems to end at Coyote Ranch Road. Turn left and skate a block east on the low-traffic street to get to the south leg of Coyote Ranch Road, to your right. Step around the gate if necessary and skate on the smoothly paved road for another block. The trail resumes where the road crosses the culvert next to the Schutzhund Dog Club. A series of fun curves takes you on a lively swoop down to cross the dry creek bed and back up a low hill. A straighter swoop back across the creek is repeated half a mile away after you pass behind the farm with old equipment rusting near the trail. (During wet winters, this trail is closed when the crossings are under water.)

The trail continues on good pavement, with a long stretch that's great for practicing your speedskating strokes. Pass through sunny fields without worrying about pedestrians, who rarely stroll out here, though you'll see cyclists and other skaters. Go by the Riverside Golf Course on the left and soon you'll come upon shady Sycamore Rest Area, with its picnic tables and emergency call box. Around the next corner, the trail crosses Riverside Drive to continue south, passing not too near a few rural backyards and the creek. Another iron bridge takes you across Coyote Creek toward the broad fields next to the Ogier Quarry. Enjoy the fine asphalt as you skate around the edge of the quarry and climb a gradual hill to the Eucalyptus Rest Area (this hill is a real treat on the trip back). At press time, half a mile farther on, the paved path became gravel at the entrance road to the Model Aircraft Skyway Park. Park rangers say the remaining gravel stretch is supposed to be paved to meet with Anderson Lake County Park's trail, which would extend the parkway another two miles. Unfortunately, two years of unusually heavy rains have filled Anderson Dam, and the paving can't be completed until the flood gates can remain closed long enough for the trail to dry out. During the summer of 1995, a washed out bridge at Anderson Park prevented skaters from accessing this section from the south.

After returning to your starting point at Silicon Valley Boulevard, you can skate north for four more miles to Coyote Hellyer County Park. The pavement in this direction is older and quite hazardous because of the many raised cracks where tree roots have pushed up the asphalt into ridges across the trail.

10. Alamitos Creek Trail

9 miles 🏅 👫 🛼

Reference: A creek in a residential area in south San Jose; see number ❿ on page 140.

Ideal for: Touring

Directions: From U.S. 101 on the southern edge of San Jose, exit toward the west at Highway 85, also known as the West Valley Freeway. After approximately five miles, take the Almaden Expressway, heading south. Go left on Camden Avenue after about 2.5 miles, and follow Camden as it curves around to the south alongside Alamitos Creek. As you proceed south, you'll see the Almaden Lake Trail (see page 152) at the roadside, but this trail terminates in gravel. The Alamitos Creek Trail picks up as you pass Shearwater Drive on the right, and just two blocks farther is Carra Belle Park, also on the right. You should find ample curbside parking on Villagewood Way, which marks the southern border of the park. The paved bike path is just across Camden Avenue.

Local shop: Gremic Skates & Hockey, 15349 Los Gatos Boulevard, Los Gatos, CA 95032; (408) 358-1169.

Tour notes: South San Jose residents enjoy strolling, biking, and skating on the Alamitos Creek Trail, which keeps getting longer as new homes are built ever further south alongside this pretty creek. Lucky for residents, the newer neighborhoods are being designed with the recognition that people need a place to walk their dogs, take an after dinner stroll, or get a serious workout.

The Alamitos Creek Trail picks up just a few blocks south of the Almaden Lake Trail (see page 152), and it's only a matter of time before the gravel connection between them is paved as well. For now, you can skate out and back from all three legs of the trail or stick to the best two legs.

Starting at Carra Belle Park, skate the least interesting stretch first, going back toward the north next to Camden Avenue. The trail here is closer to the street than it is to the creek, so your view is dominated by the nice-looking neighborhood. Turn around at Shearwater Drive and return to your starting point, continuing on to the bridge at the intersection of Camden Avenue and Royalwood Way. Cross Royalwood and skate left over the short bridge and then immediately right to follow the trail that begins on the east side of the creek. (You can also continue on the trail on the west side of the creek after you cross the street, but this has some pretty rough pavement and would only be enjoyable at high speed or with soft wheels to absorb the vibrations.)

The creekside trail is quite pretty, and it's much closer to the water and shady trees than the first section. You'll find quite a few raised cracks caused by the roots of the trees growing right next to the trail, so keep alert and be prepared to hop over them. The trail dips down for the underpass of Almaden Expressway, finally terminating at Harry Street. Return to Royalwood, and instead of crossing the bridge back to Camden Avenue, stay on the east side of the creek. After you cross Camden, turn right to follow the bike path that runs next to the street. This is not quite as scenic as the creekside trail, but is has a better surface. It also terminates at Harry.

11. Almaden Lake Trail

4 miles ⑦

Reference: **On the southern edge of San Jose; see number ⑪ on page 140.**

Ideal for: Beginners—Touring

Directions: Heading south on U.S. 101 in south San Jose, take the West Valley Freeway exit (Highway 85) and proceed west. After six miles, you'll come to the Almaden Expressway, just before the Almaden Plaza Mall, visible across the intersection on your left. Exit south onto Almaden Expressway and drive 1.75 miles south to the Coleman Road stoplight. Almaden Lake Park can be seen diagonally across the intersection to your left. Just after the intersection, you can turn left into the parking lot. There is a $3 fee for parking between May and September, but free parking can be found in a gravel area on the left further down Almaden Expressway. According to the San Jose Regional Parks office, it can be pretty hard to find parking here during the finest weather days. If this is true in your case, continue south on Almaden Expressway to Camden Avenue and park near the Alamitos Creek Trail (see page 151).

Map: A free map of Almaden Lake itself (but not the portion of the trail outside of the park) is available from San Jose Regional Parks at the address below.

Local shop: Gremic Skates & Hockey, 15349 Los Gatos Boulevard, Los Gatos, CA 95032; (408) 358-1169. Other contact: San Jose Regional Parks, 6099 Winfield Boulevard, San Jose, CA 95120; (408) 277-2757.

Tour notes: The Almaden Lake Trail is a fantastic place to skate, and the best part of all is that it's still relatively unknown to people outside of San Jose (until this book gets into enough hands). The park was once a privately owned rock quarry, and the lake was progressively created by the excavation process. Transformed into a 65-acre park in 1982, Almaden Lake now offers swimming, fishing, and paddle boating, among other activities.

Starting your skate from the south end of the Almaden Lake parking lot, you'll encounter the only hill on the trail. Beginners can simply walk down the short slope on the lawn, but it's a pretty safe spot to let 'em roll, with the grass bordering both sides.

Just beyond the entrance to the park, you'll skate past the sandy swimmers' beach, watched over by lifeguards between Memorial Day and Labor Day. After the trail veers around toward the southern shoreline, you'll skate in a shady area that soon leads you to the bridge over Alamitos Creek. Cross the wooden bridge with care; it's built in a sloping arc and you'll need to stay in control to make the hard right turn on the other side. It's highly likely that you'll have a sudden meeting with other trail users approaching the intersection from the south. From here, you'll leave the lake and skate on perfect pavement that meanders through trees at the creek's edge. At some places, the neighborhood homes and streets are far enough from the trail to be forgotten, and this continues for two miles, with one more bridge to cross.

A separate dirt path paralleling the pavement helps reduce traffic from mountain bikers and joggers. Your trail is 10 feet wide—so wide, in fact, that in most cases you won't feel the need to call out "On your left!" as you approach pedestrians or slower rollers from behind. But it's wise to call out anyway; when the trail is crowded, there's a higher likelihood that somebody might cross your path. At the time this book went to press, the pavement ended (although a gravel path continued) at Graystone Lane.

For intermediate skaters ready for a longer trip, skate left on Graystone Lane, across the bridge and over the creek. Turn left on the other side of the creek to skate through a relatively new housing development at the base of the low foothills. Here you'll find two or three medium-grade slopes on fine pavement with little traffic. When you're done playing on these hills, you can get back on the trail right next to the residential street. You'll find it by watching for people passing by through the trees. Walk across the grass to join the trail.

12. Los Gatos Creek Trail   13 miles 🎱 🐱 🏃

Reference: **Alongside Los Gatos Creek between Campbell and Los Gatos; see number ⑫ on page 140.**

Ideal for: Fitness—Hills/Slalom—Scene—Touring

Directions: From Highway 17 in Campbell, take the Hamilton Avenue exit and head east, crossing above the freeway to Bascom Avenue. Turn right (south) onto Bascom, and just after the Pruneyard Shopping Center, turn right again onto Campbell Avenue. You must cross back under the freeway and over the creek. Immediately after the bridge, look for the driveway to Campbell Park on the left, at unmarked Gilman Avenue. Turn in and park in the lot.

Local shop: Gremic Skates & Hockey, 15349 Los Gatos Boulevard, Los Gatos, CA 95032; (408) 358-1169. Other contact: Vasona Lake County Park, 298 Garden Hill Drive, Los Gatos, CA 95030; (408) 356-2729.

Tour notes: Except for the stretch near Campbell Park, the Los Gatos Creek Trail is no place for beginners or skaters who haven't yet learned good, solid heel braking skills. But for those who can negotiate hills and crowds, this is a dynamite skating trail, truly a classic. And because of that, it has become the most popular in-line spot in the south San Francisco Bay area.

With its varied scenery and long length, the trail attracts everyone from serious cyclists in sleek lycra, to packs of mountain bikers, to fitness walkers, to parents pushing baby strollers. A 15 mile per hour speed limit is enforced by rangers on bikes. As long as you keep alert and mind your best trail manners, you should be able to relax and skate without any collisions. Just make sure you warn folks that you're about to pass as you approach from behind in crowded conditions.

The view of Los Gatos Creek is sometimes blocked by fences and trees, but it's wide open in other spots, such as through Los Gatos Creek Park and next to Vasona Lake. It's easy to relate to the joie de vivre displayed by the quacking and honking ducks and geese who inhabit these waters.

To start your excursion south from Campbell Park on the west side of the creek, look for the trail close to the creek's bank just beyond the paved circle below the parking lot. The path inclines quite steeply near the first dam, as it does for all three dams it passes. At Lark Avenue, there's even a special sign just for skaters that says "Skaters Slow." That's because coming from the opposite direction, the trail rounds a very sharp curve, dips down into the shadows of overhanging trees, and then abruptly swerves once more. This setup causes several accidents a year, so an Emergency Call box is right next to the warning sign. (There are three such boxes on this trail.)

At the bottom of at least two sloping underpasses, the flow of traffic is blocked by gates that force you to slow down to a near stop so you can zig-zag through them in single file. The one at the southwest crossing of Lark is almost too steep for skating because it also has the same gate setup at the top, and it takes some fancy footwork to get your heel brake in place in time to avoid crashing into the gate at the bottom of the drop. (I admit it; I landed on my "best asset," and so did the expert-looking cyclist negotiating the gates in front of me.) The only way to avoid this nasty underpass is to cross the creek up on Lark itself, roll two blocks down to the crosswalk at Canada Court, and then skate back up to the east side trail. (Yes, you'll see jay-walkers and -rollers here.)

After the last hill climb, you'll arrive at pretty Vasona Lake County Park. After rounding the south end of the lake, you'll realize that this is a good time to take that competitive spirit down a notch or two. Go ahead and relax as you explore the many pathways of the park. The trail ends at Blossom Hill Road on the southern border of the park. (To start your trip from this end, park for free south of Blossom Hill, up the first road on the left.)

On your return to Campbell Park, if you're ready for more, skate up the asphalt ramp to the sidewalk on Campbell Avenue, cross the creek, and access the northbound trail. Though not very long, this stretch is quite pretty and well landscaped. At the time of this writing, it terminated at Leigh Avenue, but plans are to extend the trail north to connect it with the currently very short Guadalupe Expressway Trail.

---

13. Natural Bridges State Park Trail

5.5 miles

Reference: **On the cliffs over the Pacific Ocean in Santa Cruz; see number ⓭ on page 140.**

Ideal for: Beginners—Scene—Touring

Directions: Approaching Santa Cruz from the north on Highway 17, follow the signs to Highway 1 North. Don't follow the big green signs pointing the way down Ocean Avenue to the beach, wharf, and boardwalk. Instead, stay to the right to go under the Ocean Avenue overpass and merge onto Mission Street. After 1.25 miles, turn left at Swift Street and follow it all the way to the seaside cliffs. Turn right onto West Cliff Drive and park in the small lot just up the street on your left. You can also pay $6 to park (plus $1 for your dog) at the Natural Bridges State Beach parking lot seven blocks north of Swift. If you arrive late, look for parking on side streets. The residents are quite tolerant of this.

Local shop: Go Skate Surf & Sports, 601 Beach Street, Santa Cruz, CA 95060; (408) 425-8578.

Tour notes: The cliff-side trail in Santa Cruz is rich with the ocean sights, sounds and smells that create a truly memorable visit. On a clear day, you can admire the Monterey Peninsula across the bay as you skate along on the mostly smooth, eight-foot-wide asphalt path. The route snakes along the edge of the rocky cliff, thirty feet above the crashing waves. Occasionally, a lone cypress tree is perched on an outcropping nearby, adding drama to the scene. For most of the way, iceplant with purple blossoms clings to the rocks, and a low log fence prevents you from accidentally slipping down the cliff. Two long but fairly gentle hills will challenge beginning skaters, and on warm, sunny days, the weekend crowds will be a challenge for anybody.

Well-kept homes with decks that overlook the sea occupy the left side of the trail near where it begins at Natural Bridges State Beach. About a mile and three-quarters down the trail, you'll pass the Lighthouse Field State Beach on the inland side of the street (with more parking, rest rooms, and a drinking fountain). The trail then passes by the tiny Surfer Museum on a little grassy outcropping of the cliff. Appropriately enough, swarms of surfers can be seen on the water just around the corner, and even more around the next corner, where a set of steep stairs takes them down to Cowell Beach. From here, the view of the Santa Cruz Municipal Pier is at its best. That briny smell on the breeze is kelp drying on the sand below you. The asphalt path comes to an end at Bay Street, just before a steep drop down a narrow sidewalk to the intersection at the end of the pier. Skating is not permitted on the boardwalk or downtown, so don't bother with this sidewalk.

Before turning back, satisfy your lust for downhills with a loop around the parking lot slope on your right. Ramp skaters will want to visit Derby Skate Park, located back near Natural Bridges State Beach. Four blocks north of Swift Street, take Sacramento Street to where it ends at Woodland Street. The park is hidden away behind the houses lining Woodland. Turn left and enter it at the corner.

San Francisco
Bay Area: East Bay

39 Great Places to Skate

San Francisco Bay Area: East Bay

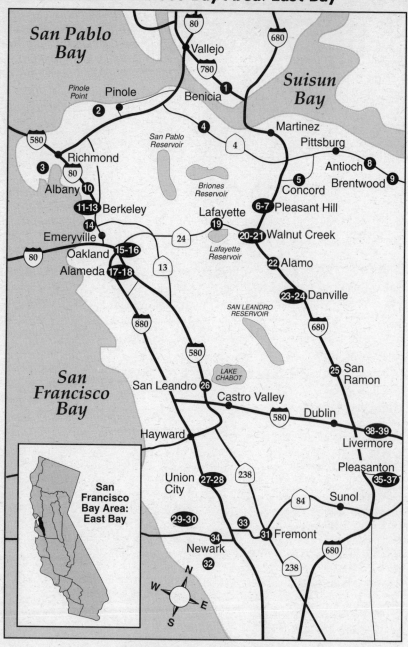

Skating Regions Beyond the East Bay

North .... Wine Country, p. 77
East .... Central Valley North, p. 201
South .... Central Valley South, p. 225
West .... San Francisco/The Peninsula, p. 117

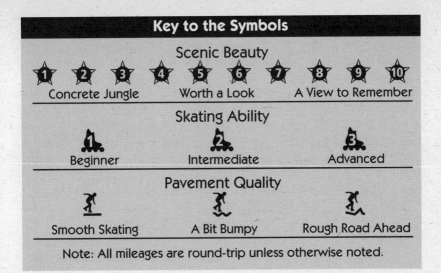

Key to the Symbols

Scenic Beauty

1 **2** **3** **4** **5** **6** **7** **8** **9** **10**

Concrete Jungle   Worth a Look   A View to Remember

Skating Ability

Beginner   Intermediate   Advanced

Pavement Quality

Smooth Skating   A Bit Bumpy   Rough Road Ahead

Note: All mileages are round-trip unless otherwise noted.

Thanks to an extensive canal system and a couple of converted railway beds connecting its towns, Contra Costa County is an ideal in-line skating destination in the East Bay. You could even skate several 20-mile days in a row here without seeing the same trail twice. Many of the trails are in the valleys nestled under the western base of Mount Diablo, which can be seen in the distance from most of the places described in this chapter. Views from the top of Mount Diablo on a very clear day (you can drive up) extend all the way across the central valley to the peaks of the Sierra Nevada.

Closer to the shores of the San Francisco Bay, towns such as Berkeley, Richmond, and others overlooking the Carquinez Strait make it possible to skate within view of the water, the bay bridges, and even the dramatic San Francisco and Oakland skylines. Expect breezy and cool weather near the bay—even in the summer.

Alameda County makes up the other half of this region, with several choice skating locations not far from the Interstate 880 and 580 corridors. The Alameda Creek Trail, connecting the village of Niles with the southern edge of the bay, offers a prime opportunity to skate nonstop for seven miles without hitting a single intersection.

1. Dillon Point
6 miles 🌟 👟 🛼

Reference: **Along the shore of the Carquinez Strait in north Benicia; see number ➊ on page 158.**

Ideal for: Fitness—Hills/Slalom—Road/Street—Touring

Directions: Going north on Interstate 680, cross the Benicia-Martinez Bridge and immediately get onto Interstate 780 northwest. Take the Military West exit. Just west of the freeway overpass, turn right and park in the free lot outside the Benicia State Recreation Area.

Local shop: Surf & Skate, 655 Contra Costa Boulevard, Pleasant Hill, CA 94523-1514; (510) 798-4400. Other contact: Benicia State Recreation Area, (707) 648-1911.

Tour notes: Benicia's Dillon Point offers a fine view of the Carquinez Strait to the south from a wide, lightly traveled road. To reach the Benicia State Recreation Area entrance, skate on the divided two-lane bike path (bikes on one side, pedestrians on the other) that runs north along the bay as a connecting trail, a nice tour in itself. Cars *are* allowed on the road to Dillon Point, but traffic is light except on the most gorgeous weekend days, when it's best to arrive early for safe skating.

   Skate on the road next to the bay, past several picnic areas and around to Dillon Point. There are a few marshy areas, so watch out for streams of water crossing the road in winter and early spring. You'll also be skating up and down some hills, but with the wide street, you'll have lots of room for slaloms, and for most of the way, the shoulders are grassy if you need to bail out. Once you reach Dillon Point, you'll be rewarded with a commanding view of the Carquinez Strait.

   Return to the parking lot the way you came, and if you want to continue exploring Benicia, skate south to the sidewalk and follow it along West K Street down to Ninth Street Park at Commodor Jones Point. Or, if you like practicing your jumps, visit Benicia's mini skate park at the intersection of West K and West Seventh Streets.

2. Point Pinole Trail
6 miles 🌟 👟 🛼

Reference: **Bordering the San Francisco Bay near Richmond; see number ➋ on page 158.**

Ideal for: Hills/Slalom—Touring

Directions: Take Interstate 80 north of Richmond and San Pablo to the Hilltop Drive exit. Follow Hilltop to San Pablo Avenue and turn right. Turn left onto the Richmond Parkway, and turn right again after about 1.5 miles at the "T" intersection onto Giant Highway. Cross the railroad tracks and take a left to enter the park. There's a fee for parking and dogs when the kiosk is attended.

Map: For a free trail map, call the East Bay Regional Parks District at
(510) 562-PARK (7275) and ask for the Point Pinole Regional Shoreline brochure.

Local shop: Karim Cyclery, 2801 Telegraph Avenue, Berkeley, CA
94705-1118; (510) 841-2181. Other contact: East Bay Regional Parks
District, 2950 Peralta Oaks Court, P.O. Box 5381, Oakland, CA
94605-0381; (510) 635-0138, ext. 2203.

Tour notes: What a find! This wide, smooth trail passes through inland
grasslands and takes you by stands of stately blue gum eucalyptus
trees, open meadows, and richly populated marshes. After the first
hill, you'll come to a level area with barbecue pits, picnic tables, and a
children's playground. Beyond the picnic area are salt marshes, wildflowers in native and non-native grasses, and the ever-present terns,
gulls, and hawks.

   To best enjoy the vast views of the San Pablo Bay, skate out to the
fishing pier at the end of the trail. (No fishing license is required.) It's
obvious from the tired gait of the anglers you pass on the way back to
your car that skates make the long return hike much easier. On the
way to the pier, one long hill (about a third of a mile long) is the
perfect pitch for linking slalom turn after slalom turn, but not so
steep that a fast descent in the tuck position is unreasonable, as long
as nobody is on the trail ahead of you (and your skills are up to it).
Toilets and water fountains can be found at each end of the trail.

---

3. Miller/Knox Shoreline   .75 miles 🎿 ⛵ 🏊

Reference: **Bordering the San Francisco Bay near Richmond;
see number ❸ on page 158.**

Ideal for: Beginners—Figure/Stunts—Touring

Directions: From Interstate 80 in Albany, take the Interstate 580 exit
north, heading toward the Richmond-San Rafael Bridge. About 1.5
miles before the toll plaza, take the Garrard exit and turn left, heading west under the freeway. Go through the tunnel, after which
Garrard becomes Dornan Drive. On the west side of the tunnel,
you'll find Miller/Knox Shoreline Park on your right. Take the first
driveway and park in the first lot. (The second lot is usually closed.)

Map: For a free trail map, call the East Bay Regional Parks District at
(510) 562-PARK (7275) and ask for the Miller/Knox Shoreline area
brochure.

Local shop: Karim Cyclery, 2801 Telegraph Avenue, Berkeley, CA
94705-1118; (510) 841-2181. Other contact: East Bay Regional Parks
District, 2950 Peralta Oaks Court, P.O. Box 5381, Oakland, CA
94605-0381; (510) 635-0138, ext. 2203.

Tour notes: Breezy Miller/Knox Shoreline will delight both novice and
advanced skaters. Though it's not well-known as a skating destination

in the Bay Area, it's a perfect spot for beginners to get rolling—and not because of the sidewalk that loops around the pond or the spectacular views across the bay. What attracts skaters is the large concrete pad the size of an indoor skating rink—or maybe even two. The pad is located between the pretty Miller/Knox Shoreline Park and a closed-off asphalt parking lot that also has excellent pavement for skating.

As for touring, an asphalt trail encircles the small pond where mallard duck families congregate. The paving is rough next to the parking lots, but it's in better condition on the loop itself, which is just big enough for lap work.

Experienced skaters (or those interested in practicing heel brake skills) can head up the short hill at the east end of the park. At the top of the hill, a sidewalk leads to Keller Beach close to the entrance to the tunnel. The pavement down the steep driveway to Keller is very rough, making it difficult to maintain a grip with the heel brake. Also beware of the nasty lip at the bottom of the driveway. But persevere and you'll be treated to some magnificent views across the bay from the two concrete overlooks at the edge of the park.

---

4. Carquinez Scenic Drive
10 miles ⑧ 🏔️3 🚶

Reference: **Overlooking the Sacramento River near Martinez; see number ❹ on page 158.**

Ideal for: Fitness—Hills/Slalom—Historic—Touring

Directions: From Interstate 680 in Martinez, take the Martinez exit (Highway 4), heading west. After three miles, exit on Alhambra Avenue, heading north. Two miles up, cross Main Street, turn left onto Escobar Street, and take it one block to Talbert Street. Turn right and continue north. Talbert makes a 90-degree curve to the right and becomes Carquinez Scenic Drive. Go another mile to avoid the first long hill, and park in a gravel pull-out overlooking the Carquinez Strait.

Local shop: Surf & Skate, 655 Contra Costa Boulevard, Pleasant Hill, CA 94523-1514; (510) 798-4400. Other contact: East Bay Regional Parks District, 2950 Peralta Oaks Court, P.O. Box 5381, Oakland, CA 94605-0381; (510) 635-0138, ext. 2203.

Tour notes: Diehard adventure skaters in great shape who love hills and can handle 45 minutes of buzzing feet won't want to miss this trail—and you might just miss it if you don't skate it soon. This closed road is in the process of eroding its way down to the sea 150 feet below.

The Carquinez Strait Regional Shoreline borders the historic gateway between the San Francisco Bay and California's Central Valley, where steamships once carried passengers and cargo along the Sacramento River. Start skating east above the shore from the gravel pull-out, but be sure to stop now and then to enjoy the views of ships, piers, and the Martinez Toll Bridge from the nearly abandoned two-lane road. Unfortunately, your attention while in motion must remain on the path ahead; the surface is quite rough and cracked, and in some spots, it's slipping down toward the ocean.

The entire length of the trail is made up of long hills and curves winding alongside tree- and shrub-covered cliffs above the water. Step around the barrier gate that blocks automobile traffic about two and a half miles from the parking area. From here you'll climb up to what's left of the road after a washout closed it in the mid-1980s: a 30-foot stretch of sinking, cracked-off pavement followed by a total washout. The only thing between you and the drop-off to the ocean is a narrow, 20-foot-long patch of packed dirt connected to where the road is mostly intact again. Trees with rotted roots from one-too-many wet winters have toppled onto the road at one point (you can skate around them), and bushes are encroaching from the sides.

Another gate marks the far side of the washout. Ironically, the pavement between the two gates is smoother than the rest of the road. Continue the last mile to the Port Costa Materials Inc. gravel plant. Here you'll hit a mess of dirt and gravel under the conveyor belt, used to haul gravel to the plant. The trail extends only a few more yards, and the dirt isn't worth crossing, so now is the time to turn around and head back.

---

5. Port Chicago Highway   4 miles 🟦 🐾 🏃

Reference: **In the northern part of Concord; see number ❺ on page 158.**

Ideal for: Fitness—Hills/Slalom

Directions: From Interstate 680 in Pleasant Hill, take the Willow Pass Road exit, heading northeast. After two miles, turn left at East Street, proceed three blocks, and then turn right at Bonafacio Street. A block away, you'll pass under the BART (Bay Area Rapid Transit) tracks and over Port Chicago Highway. The sidewalk trail parallels the east side of the highway.

Map: For a copy of the Bicycle Transportation Map of the East Bay: Map 2, East of the Hills, send $1 to the East Bay Bicycle Coalition, P.O. Box 1736, Oakland, CA 94604. No phone orders are accepted.

Local shop: Any Mountain Ltd., 1975 Diamond Boulevard, Concord, CA 94520; (510) 674-0174.

Tour notes: An eight-foot-wide concrete bike path runs alongside the Port Chicago Highway next to a BART (Bay Area Rapid Transit) line that was installed in 1995. It connects neighborhoods starting just north of Willow Pass Road with the BART station at the north end of Concord. If you don't mind skating in a landscaped concrete corridor or within earshot of the highway and the occasional passing train, you'll find the Port Chicago Highway trail a very acceptable spot for an in-line workout.

The trail makes a gradual climb all the way from Bonafacio Street up to its termination at the North Concord/Martinez BART station. If you get tired, benches shaded by arbors that sport pink blossoms in the spring are provided in strategic locations. Happily for the skaters of the world, what goes up must come down, and that means you can enjoy the gradual descent all the way back to the start of the path.

6. Contra Costa Canal East   13 miles 🎱🔣🏃

Reference: **A connecting trail between Concord and Pleasant Hill; see number ❻ on page 158.**

Ideal for: Fitness—Hills/Slalom—Speed—Touring

Directions: From Interstate 680 in Pleasant Hill, take the Geary Road/ Treat Boulevard exit, turning east to get onto Treat Boulevard. At the stoplight surrounded by tall office buildings, take the first right, which is Oak Road. This intersection is just after you pass under the BART (Bay Area Rapid Transit) tracks. (The Pleasant Hill BART station is one block north of the Treat Boulevard intersection with Oak Road.) Park along the curb on the first block of Oak or on one of the side streets. If possible, park on the east side of Oak so you won't have to cross the street to access the canal and trail just a few yards further down the block.

Map: For a free trail map, call the East Bay Regional Parks District at (510) 562-PARK (7275) and ask for the Contra Costa Canal Regional Trail brochure.

Local shop: Sunrise Mountain Sports, 490 Ygnacio Valley Road, Walnut Creek, CA 94596; (510) 932-8779. Other contact: East Bay Regional Parks District, 2950 Peralta Oaks Court, P.O. Box 5381, Oakland, CA 94605-0381; (510) 635-0138, ext. 2203.

Tour notes: The eastern portion of the Contra Costa Canal Trail has a great variety of scenery, with everything from mallards floating in the culvert between shady ivy-covered backyard fences to wide-open views of the hills on both sides of the Diablo Valley. Mount Diablo is a spectacular sight at the end of this trail on Willow Pass Road.

To start, skate to the east from the Oak Road trail access point. Just a block or two up the trail, you'll cross the four-way intersection with a disjointed 1.3 mile-long section of the Iron Horse Trail, which will someday be connected with its 12.5 mile western portion that starts a mile south (see page 165). The first half mile of the Contra Costa Canal Trail to the east passes through a mature, well-tended neighborhood with shade trees and backyard fences supporting foliage that varies from home to home.

At the open area near Heather Farm City Park, a bulletin board maintained by the East Bay Regional Parks District is posted with the Contra Costa Canal Trail map, great for a quick orientation if you don't have your own map. Continuing on from the park, you'll cross two major intersections with stoplights and crosswalks before the trail leaves the urban noise and traffic behind. Street names are conveniently painted on the pavement at the intersections.

Turn left after crossing the rather imposing Ygnacio Canal. (A right turn takes you up the steep slope to the Ygnacio Canal Trail, described on page 179, which loops back around to Heather Farm City Park.) From here, the pavement on the trail changes from good to excellent as you climb very gently to the north. After three intersections, you must cross busy, four-lane Treat Boulevard, which has no pedestrian crossing at the trail, although the meridian divider is open for those who dare to jay-roll across. The alternative is to skate the awful and narrow sidewalk up Treat to Navaronne Way and wait forever for the light to change. Once across Treat, the wide asphalt downslope back to the canal lures you to skate too fast for the hard right back onto the trail. Watch out! You'll have to jump a wooden fence if you make too wide a turn.

Negotiate Treat successfully, and the scenery will be your real treat. The view includes the hills far across Diablo Valley to the west and the rolling hills of the Lime Ridge Open Space to the east. A mobile home park nearby is somehow appealing with its rows and rows of ridiculously tall palm trees. The big view lasts as the trail passes behind a new neighborhood, and then you enter a shady little forest to cross the wooden bridge before Cowell Street. Unfortunately, the scenery then becomes comparatively plain as the trail travels through an older neighborhood with very little shade. The original Contra Costa Canal Trail sign is an interesting landmark at one intersection, giving you a bit more perspective on the history of the county's pavement projects.

---

7. Contra Costa Canal West   14.5 miles

Reference: **A connecting trail between Pacheco and Pleasant Hill; see number ❼ on page 158.**

Ideal for: Fitness—Hills/Slalom—Touring

Directions: From Interstate 680 in Pleasant Hill, take the Geary Road/ Treat Boulevard exit, turning east onto Treat. At the stoplight surrounded by tall office buildings—just after you pass under the BART (Bay Area Rapid Transit) tracks—take the first right onto Oak Road. (The Pleasant Hill BART station is one block north.) Park along the curb on Oak or on one of the side streets. The canal and trail are just a few yards further down the block.

Map: For a free trail map, call the East Bay Regional Parks District at (510) 562-PARK (7275) and ask for the Contra Costa Canal Regional Trail brochure.

Local shop: Sunrise Mountain Sports, 490 Ygnacio Valley Road, Walnut Creek, CA 94596; (510) 932-8779. Other contact: East Bay Regional Parks District, 2950 Peralta Oaks Court, P.O. Box 5381, Oakland, CA 94605-0381; (510) 635-0138, ext. 2203.

Tour notes: Bay Area residents who live and work in the heart of the Diablo Valley are lucky to be near a large and well-maintained network of canal trails. The best of them is the Contra Costa Canal Trail, a 14-plus-mile stretch of pathway used by Pacheco, Pleasant Hill, Walnut Creek, and Concord residents for human-powered commuting and exercising in the fresh air.

Reserve your judgment on this western section of the canal during the first half mile leading away from Pleasant Hill. The start of the trail passes under the BART tracks and Interstate 680 in a tube-like tunnel and then right through a couple of auto body shop yards. After that, the picture becomes much prettier as you skate alongside a non-imposing (and sometimes non-existent) waterway. You'll have to cross many neighborhood intersections, constantly interrupting what would otherwise be a much nicer roll, but fortunately, many of them are small enough to coast through after a quick glance up and down the street.

As with all of the Contra Costa County trails, the pavement is in good repair and clean except for the occasional leaves and debris from nearby trees. Water is available at Las Juntas Park about three miles up the trail. Soon after the park, you'll reach Taylor Boulevard, a major four-lane street with a meridian divider. You can't see the trail from the south side of the street, but it picks up again behind a low hill just across the street. Skate left up the sidewalk to cross at the stoplight and re-enter the trail back down Taylor. As you near Diablo Valley College, the terrain becomes rather hilly (prepare to use your heel brake), but the skyline view from higher up reveals distant hills behind an urban silhouette. These grades are great for slalom practice in both directions when you have the pavement all to yourself. The trail comes to an end in the town of Pacheco at Center Avenue, but word has it that it eventually will continue to Highway 4, and, possibly, all the way to Suisun Bay.

8. Delta de Anza Regional Trail 10.5 miles 🌟 🐾 🏊

Reference: **Along the southern border of Antioch; see number 8 on page 158.**

Ideal for: Fitness—Hills/Slalom—Touring

Directions: Heading south on Interstate 680 after crossing the Benicia-Martinez Bridge, exit onto Highway 4 East. Approaching from the south on Interstate 680 in Pleasant Hill, take the Highway 242 exit toward Concord and Pittsburg, and follow it northeast and then east as it merges onto Highway 4 after 2.5 miles. Follow Highway 4 approximately 10 miles to Antioch. Take the Hillcrest Avenue exit and follow Hillcrest south about 1.25 miles until you see Wild Horse Road on the left. It's marked by a sculpture of wild horses on the hillside, but watch for the 7-11 store and you can't go wrong. Before turning onto Wild Horse, look to the right from the stoplight and you will see the trail entrance. Park in Hillcrest Plaza near the convenience store.

Map: To order the Bicycle Transportation Map of the East Bay (Map 2, East of the Hills), send $1 to: East Bay Bicycle Coalition, P.O. Box 1736, Oakland, CA 94604 (no phone orders).

Local shop: Champs Sports, County East Mall, Antioch, CA 94509; (510) 706-9553. Other contact: East Bay Regional Parks District, 2950 Peralta Oaks Court, P.O. Box 5381, Oakland, CA 94605-0381; (510) 635-0138, ext. 2203.

Tour notes: The Delta de Anza Regional Trail is truly an excellent find. It's just far enough away from the heavily populated areas near the San Francisco Bay to be pretty much unknown. Until 1995, "Rough Pavement" signs posted at the trail entrances kept most people away. But a repaving project completed in the summer of 1995 has turned this section of the ubiquitous Contra Costa Canal into a prime spring destination skate. What's more, a proposed extension to the east is shown on the East Bay Bicycle Coalition's maps. This would extend the canal trail 1.3 miles east over a ridge to connect with the 2.25 miles of paved trail in Oakley (of which only one mile is currently open to the public). In short, there's a lot of potential here.

If you plan to skate this full 10.5-mile round-trip in the summer, make sure to carry something to drink, because these hills heat up, and the only water fountain is at Antioch Community Park three miles up the trail.

Start skating on the west side of Hillcrest Avenue, on an eight-foot-wide asphalt trail that flows down a gentle hill next to the canal on your left. The landscaping along Hillcrest is extensive, so even in the hot season, there's green scenery, if not shade. A couple of intersections lead off to residential areas up the hill on your left, but cross traffic is light. Leaving Hillcrest, the canal and trail climb up a low ridge and curve to the west. At press time, the trail dumped out onto a sidewalk on Wildflower Drive. Follow the sidewalk west to the stoplight at Deer Valley Road, cross Deer Valley, and turn south on the sidewalk until you regain the canal trail a block away.

The Contra Costa Canal now stretches out to the west, bisecting a pretty valley bordered by low hills (with homes on them—you can't have everything). Mount Diablo dominates the view ahead. The new asphalt sections are on again-off again from this point. The older sections of paving aren't rough, but remaining tar patches can be slick or grabby. A couple of streets cross the canal on bridges that make short but fun hills on the trail. At Lone Tree Way, stop and check the trailside kiosk for free brochures on the Contra Costa Canal Trail. Beyond the busy crosswalk at Lone Tree, the canal side is free of urban scenery for half a mile, until it rounds a corner to meet James Donlon Boulevard. Cross the boulevard and skate another half mile to the entrance of Antioch Community Park on your left. The sidewalks in the park are pebbled, which makes skating less fun, but it's a nice spot to get water and take a break.

When you're refreshed, continue on your westward trek along the newest asphalt of the Delta de Anza Regional Trail as it weaves along the valley behind two more Antioch neighborhoods. The trail terminates at Somersville Road, so turn around here and skate back the way you came.

9. Marsh Creek Trail   10.5 miles

Reference: **Connecting the towns of Oakley and Brentwood; see number ❾ on page 158.**

Ideal for: Fitness—Touring

Directions: Coming from the north on Interstate 680 after crossing the Benicia-Martinez Bridge, exit onto Highway 4 East. Approaching from the south on Interstate 680 in Pleasant Hill, take the Highway 242 exit toward Concord and Pittsburg, and follow it northeast and then east as it merges onto Highway 4 after 2.5 miles. Once on Highway 4, follow it east approximately 12 miles. Just after the freeway makes a 90-degree curve to the north, look for the Brentwood/Stockton Highway 4 exit. This also happens to be Main Street, Oakley. Follow Main and the Highway 4 signs two miles east through town until you reach the stoplight at the intersection with Cypress Road. Turn left, cross the canal, and park on the small gravel pad at the levee trail's entrance.

Map: For a free trail map, call the East Bay Regional Parks District at (510) 562-PARK (7275) and ask for the Marsh Creek Trail brochure.

Local shop: Champs Sports, County East Mall, Antioch, CA 94509; (510) 706-9553. Other contact: East Bay Regional Parks District,

2950 Peralta Oaks Court, P.O. Box 5381, Oakland, CA 94605-0381; (510) 635-0138, ext. 2203.

Tour notes: From its plain, treeless start near the Amtrak line and a shabby convenience store, the Marsh Creek Trail takes you south on a delightful tour of what remains of the bucolic Oakley and Brentwood farm country. Cornfields and fruit trees still grow near the banks of Marsh Creek, which is now a levee-banked canal. Leaving the old days behind, the two agricultural towns have since expanded to welcome retirees or commuters who work throughout the greater Bay Area.

Don't judge the Marsh Creek Trail by the first tenth of a mile. For some odd reason, the pavement at the start is extremely rough. But once beyond it, you'll be skating on prime asphalt, thanks to some of the newest paving done by the East Bay Regional Parks District. Mount Diablo shows off its familiar profile to the west, and more distant ridges ring the horizon. There are still several citrus, plum, and other fruit trees growing next to the creek, plus a couple of rustling cornfields in the summer. All of these sights combine to paint a peaceful pastoral scene, with the sounds of trickling water, chirping birds, and the occasional farm engine as audio accompaniment.

The trail's entire length doesn't pass through peaceful farm country, however. One section (not too long) has a very high chain-link and barbed-wire fence at its edge. You'll pass by some housing developments and must also cross several intersections. At press time, a death-defying crossing at Highway 4 was necessary to continue to the end of the trail. But in July of 1996, the city of Brentwood is scheduled to add a safer diversion that includes two bridges across the creek and a signal crossing at Grant Street. Until then, the approach to Highway 4 may still require climbing over a barricade to continue next to Marsh Creek on private property for about a tenth of a mile. Wait for a lull in the highway traffic before very carefully crossing to where the trail resumes on the other side.

South of Highway 4, the final leg of the trail passes through the booming town of Brentwood, where recent development has resulted in widened roads with sidewalks and bike lanes and a brand new park with tiny saplings for shade trees. You'll find the park and its smooth concrete sidewalks just across the bridge that marks the trail's termination. Watch for the wide expansion cracks at each end of the bridge.

10. Golden Gate Fields

2 miles 🌟6 🛼🐦

Reference: **Bordering the San Francisco Bay near Albany; see number ⑩ on page 158.**

Ideal for: Beginners—Speed—Touring

Directions: From Interstate 580/80 going east outside of Albany, take the Albany exit and go under the freeway to the racetracks on the west. Take Buchanan Street to the parking lot.

Local shop: Karim Cyclery, 2801 Telegraph Avenue, Berkeley, CA 94705-1118; (510) 841-2181.

Tour notes: Golden Gate Fields has a gigantic parking lot just begging for in-line activities. It's not the best spot for fooling around, since the pavement is rather rough and covered with debris, but that doesn't stop wild-haired windsailors from tearing across the pavement on tricked-up skateboards with sails. On the northeast side near the bay, there's a small, newly paved section where speedskaters have painted an oval track for workouts.

11. Nimitz Trail

8 miles 🌟10 🛼🐦

Reference: **In the hills above Berkeley; see number ⑪ on page 158.**

Ideal for: Fitness—Hills/Slalom—Touring

Directions: Approaching from the San Ramon Valley, get onto Highway 24 from Interstate 680 in Walnut Creek. Take the Orinda exit and follow Camino Pablo northwest for about two miles. Take a left onto Wildcat Canyon Road and follow it up to Inspiration Point on the right, where you'll park. From the west, take Interstate 80 north to Albany and exit on Buchanan Street. After jogging south for a block on San Pablo Avenue, continue east on Marin Avenue as it enters Berkeley and, past Arlington Circle, begins to ascend the hills. Turn right when you reach Grizzly Peak Boulevard, and follow Grizzly about a mile southwest to Shasta Road, where a big sign points the way to Tilden Regional Park. Turn left and wind your way down the hill, where you'll merge toward the right onto Wildcat Canyon Road. Pass the Botanic Gardens and the intersection with South Park Drive (often closed in winter for newt migrations) and follow the road uphill to the Inspiration Point parking area on your left.

Map: For a free trail map, call the East Bay Regional Parks District at (510) 562-PARK (7275) and ask for the Tilden Regional Park area brochure.

Local shop: Karim Cyclery, 2801 Telegraph Avenue, Berkeley, CA 94705-1118; (510) 841-2181. Other contact: East Bay Regional Parks District, 2950 Peralta Oaks Court, P.O. Box 5381, Oakland, CA 94605-0381; (510) 635-0138, ext. 2203.

Tour notes: Believe me, the Nimitz Trail is worth every minute of the drive up into the hills. On a clear day, you'll be able to see the San Pablo Reservoir, Mount Diablo, and the San Francisco Bay all the way to the delta. Combine this vista with pastoral scenery at the trail side, rolling hills, and wide, mostly smooth pavement, and you've got a first-rate skate destination.

Since you're sharing the only paved section of the East Bay Skyline National Trail with hikers, bikers, and horseback riders, there's quite a bit of traffic for the first two miles, especially on a clear, dry day. (Mileage markers keep you posted on your distance from the trail's start.) Beyond mile two, truly daring skaters keep up their speed on the downhills and jump the wide cattle guards, making a thrilling addition to the skate. (Please don't try this the first time without checking one out to make sure it's within your leaping abilities.) Most skaters, however, will want to step around the cattle guards through the gates. Watch out for dogs on leashes and the occasional cow pie. If it's not too windy or foggy, pack a sweater and lunch so you can chew your own cud awhile at the pavement's end. Make sure to bring along something to drink, since there's no water fountain at Inspiration Point.

---

12. Berkeley Marina   4 miles 🕗 🐾 🚶

Reference: **Bordering the San Francisco Bay near Berkeley; see number ⓬ on page 158.**

Ideal for: Beginners—Fitness—Hills/Slalom—Scene—Touring

Directions: From Interstate 80 around Berkeley, take the University Avenue exit and head east toward the Marina. Take the first right (Marina Boulevard) and follow the road around the bend. Park on the shoulder of Spinnaker Way or, if there's still room, in the small lot where Spinnaker terminates. Berkeley city buses 51 A and M will drop you off at the end of the pier on Sewall Drive.

Local shop: Karim Cyclery, 2801 Telegraph Avenue, Berkeley, CA 94705-1118; (510) 841-2181.

Tour notes: The Berkeley Marina is a favorite destination among Bay Area skaters. The scene may not be as "happening" as the one you'll find at Golden Gate Park in San Francisco, but it's still worth a visit on a weekend when you're here with skates at hand (or should I say at foot). At the park's northeast border, the sign says Cesar E. Chavez Park, but at the parking lot it's called North Waterfront Park.

The Berkeley Marina Perimeter Trail, an eight-foot-wide path of smooth asphalt, circles the old converted landfill that is now the park. A few gentle slopes traversing the rolling grass mounds are paved, making them excellent for intermediate-level slalom turn practice. Across the bay to the north, the Richmond towers reflect the hazy sunlight, and from the northwest side of the parking lot, the Bay Bridge can occasionally be picked out against the glare of the light afternoon fog.

This breezy park attracts people with kites and kids, and there are ample picnic tables, drinking fountains, and barbecue grills for relaxing on warm days. If you're up for more skating (in traffic), explore to the south along Seawall Drive in front of the amazingly long pier where skating is prohibited, and in the parking lots across from coincidentally named Skates Restaurant (no relation to in-lines).

---

13. Ohlone Greenway
7.5 miles

Reference: **A rail-trail following the BART route connecting El Cerrito to Berkeley; see number ⑬ on page 158.**

Ideal for: Beginners—Fitness—Touring

Directions: From Interstate 80 (also known as Interstate 580 through this area) around Berkeley, take the University Avenue exit heading into North Berkeley to the east. Three blocks past San Pablo Avenue, turn left onto Acton Street. Follow Acton four blocks until you reach the North Berkeley BART (Bay Area Rapid Transit) station. Park in the BART lot or on Acton close to the barricades at the northwest corner of the BART parking lot. The trail starts just behind the barrier.

Local shop: Karim Cyclery, 2801 Telegraph Avenue, Berkeley, CA 94705-1118; (510) 841-2181. Other contact: Joe Witherell, Community Services, 10890 San Pablo Avenue, El Cerrito, CA 95430; (510) 215-4322.

Tour notes: Whether you're commuting to work, looking for a quick lunch workout, or just getting your first feel for in-lines, the Ohlone Greenway is a good downtown route for all three because the pavement is smooth and there are no hills.

Skate north to follow this bike trail that passes under the BART tracks between stations in North Berkeley, El Cerrito Plaza, and El Cerrito Del Norte. The trains going by on the tracks above you can be noisy, but they pass quickly and run less frequently on weekends. On the first section of the trail in Berkeley, where you'll hit most of the street intersections, you won't get lost as long as you follow the green "Bike Route" signs. (Make sure you know how to stop at intersections before attempting the entire tour.)

Once you enter Albany, the trail's character changes for the better. Here the route is enhanced by a park with grass, trees, flowers, and a separate path for pedestrians. There's even a par course for those who want to get fit as they stroll or roll. The tiny but well-maintained older homes across the way add a sweet charm to the scene.

The Emporium shopping center signals your entry into El Cerrito, near the trail's halfway mark. Shrubs are in a more wild state here, and weeds grow around the bases of trees planted for landscaping. The backyard fences on your right may detract from the scenery, but the pavement remains smooth. Shortly after skating past the El Cerrito Del Norte BART station, a sign marks the end of the trail at the intersection of Key Boulevard.

---

14. Emeryville Marina   4 miles ⭐8 🐾 🛼

Reference: **Bordering the San Francisco Bay near Emeryville; see number ⑭ on page 158.**

Ideal for: Beginners—Touring

Directions: From Interstate 80 just north of the Bay Bridge turnoff, take the Powell Street exit at Emeryville and turn west toward the bay, following the street as it curves around to the north. Parking is available in the lot at the end of the street near the marina.

Local shop: Karim Cyclery, 2801 Telegraph Avenue, Berkeley, CA 94705-1118; (510) 841-2181.

Tour notes: The bike path pavement is unusually smooth at the Emeryville Marina, making for an excellent, if short, cruise along the east shore of the San Francisco Bay. It's flat enough for all skating levels to enjoy, but be sure to bring along a windbreaker. Like most bay-side locations, the wind can really whip up here.

Follow the marina-side trail to the Harbor Department and back, and then go around the picnic area to get to the trail along the bay that goes all the way back to Interstate 80. When you reach your car again, skate out on the pier, located close to the parking lot at the far corner of the little picnic area. A quick skate to the end of the pier's easily traversed wood planks will give you a closer look at the boats in the marina.

---

15. Tunnel Road   4 miles ⭐6 🐾 🛼

Reference: **The east hills of Oakland; see number ⑮ on page 158.**

Ideal for: Hills/Slalom—Road/Street—Touring

Directions: From Interstate 80 (also known as Interstate 580 through this area) around Berkeley, take the Ashby Avenue exit and head south past the Claremont Hotel. Go left at the stoplight and follow the signs pointing to Highway 24. At the top of the hill, make a left on Caldecott Lane and park on the shoulder near the "H" intersection where Hiller Drive becomes Tunnel Road, a block up from Caldecott. From the south, take Interstate 580 north and exit to Highway 13 (Warren Freeway). Follow the signs to Oakland and Berkeley, until you pass under Highway 24. At the stop sign, turn right and you're on Caldecott. Park near Hiller Drive.

Map: For the Bicycle Commute Map of the East Bay, send $1 to: East Bay Bicycle Coalition, P.O. Box 1736, Oakland, CA 94604.

Local shop: Karim Cyclery, 2801 Telegraph Avenue, Berkeley, CA
94705-1118; (510) 841-2181.

Tour notes: Experienced skaters in great condition will enjoy Tunnel
Road, a two-lane street open to automobile traffic. It's a steep climb
even for those in good shape, but offers a screaming descent as the
reward. At the bottom, you can admire the far-reaching views of
Oakland, Berkeley, and the San Francisco Bay.

On the way up, watch the pavement so you can plan ahead for the
trip down, especially the long pitted area covering the last ten yards at
the bottom. Even skaters competent in using their heel brake at high
speeds will find that the narrow shoulders, multitude of curves, occasional wet patches, and debris from the ongoing 1991 fire reconstruc-
tion make this evenly pitched descent highly challenging. However,
with this road's constant use for training by local cyclists and skaters,
you can feel welcome here as one of the elite.

---

16. Lake Merrit   3.5 miles ⭐ 🛼🏊

Reference: **Downtown Oakland; see number
🔟 on page 158.**

Ideal for: Beginners—Figure/Stunts—Fitness—Hills/Slalom—
Historic—Road/Street—Touring

Directions: From Interstate 880 going north in Oakland, take the Oak
Street exit and turn right. From Oak turn left onto Lakeside Drive,
then right onto Grand Avenue. Park on Grand or pay $2 to park in
Lakeside Park on Bellevue.There are three BART stations within
rolling distance of the lake: Lake Merrit, 12th Street, and 19th Street.

Local shop: Karim Cyclery, 2801 Telegraph Avenue, Berkeley, CA
94705-1118; (510) 841-2181.

Tour notes: Lake Merrit offers skaters of all levels a wide variety of
activities, from riding stairs to slaloming to just rolling along. Starting from Grand Avenue, more competent skaters can easily circumnavigate this lovely urban lake reflecting nearby modern high rises
on its blue surface, while novices can stick to the wide sidewalks on
the south shore. Glittering nighttime lighting makes it possible to
enjoy Lake Merrit after dark as long as you watch out for frequent
variations in pavement width and quality. During the day, the sidewalks on the Lakeshore Avenue stretch can be crowded with strolling
residents.

At the west end of the lake, skaters who like the challenge of riding
stairs or enjoy an open area for working on new skills can take the
tunnel to get to the Kaiser Convention Center Auditorium and its
parking lot. Slalom skaters will appreciate the short asphalt slope near
the historic Victorian Camron-Stanford House, rolling a short way
down to a finely paved parking lot at the water's edge. Watch for two

narrow and poorly paved (but short) connections in the trail along the Lakeside Drive stretch.

Near Grand Avenue at Bellevue Avenue, there's more pavement to explore in the parking lots near the Lakeside Garden Center and the Natural Science Center. Just below the big gazebo, a circle of fine, smooth concrete offers a place for beginners to get rolling safely the first time out.

The pavement quality is quite rough on the lakeside trail facing the skyscrapers, so if you want to bypass it, follow Grand Avenue's sidewalk or take the sloped service road behind the Children's Fairy Land.

17. Crown Memorial State Beach

5 miles ⭐ 🦀 🚶

Reference: The island beachfront of Alameda; see number **⑰** on page 158.

Ideal for: Fitness—Historic—Touring

Directions: From Interstate 980 in downtown Oakland, exit at 11th/12th Streets, go through several traffic lights, and make a left onto Fifth Street just beyond the 880 underpass. This will take you to Broadway and the Oakland/Alameda Tube. From the south, exit Interstate 880 at Broadway. Turn left on Broadway and left again into the Oakland/ Alameda Tube. Once through the Tube, you'll be on Webster Street, which you should follow to its dead end at Central Avenue. Go right onto Central and then left on McKay Avenue to the Crab Cove entrance. There's a parking fee during peak hours.

Map: For a free trail map, call the East Bay Regional Parks District at (510) 562-PARK (7275) and ask for the Crown Memorial State Beach brochure.

Local shop: Willows Skate & Surf, 1431 Park Street, Alameda, CA 94501; (510) 523-5566. Other contact: East Bay Regional Parks District, 2950 Peralta Oaks Court, P.O. Box 5381, Oakland, CA 94605-0381; (510) 635-0138, ext. 2203.

Tour notes: Crown Memorial State Beach reigned as the "Coney Island of the West" from the late 1800s until World War II. Neptune Beach, as it was known then, was the hot spot for concerts, prize fights, carnivals, and baseball games. Now the beach, with its sand dunes and shoreline trail, is a gem of a different, quieter kind.

Just for fun, start by taking a short but sweet skate north from the Crab Cove parking lot on lawn-bordered pavement, past a nicely tended condo complex. This section ends at Central Avenue, where you'll turn around and head south on the coastline. As you pass Crown Memorial State Beach, note the designated swimming and wading areas in case you want to take a dip later. Signs say no alcoholic beverages are permitted at Crown Beach, but beer and wine are okay at the picnic areas. The Sand Castle picnic area has bathrooms, parking lots, and, for just a short (but seemingly endless) stretch, some of the worst pavement around. (It's scheduled for repaving before July of 1996.) You may want to walk on the lawn, if it's dry, until you reach the better asphalt several yards down from the snack bar. The pavement is very good from here on as the trail borders Shore Line Drive, and water fountains and toilets are abundant.

Near the southern end of Shore Line, you'll see the Elsie Roemer Bird Sanctuary at the end of the Marsh Overlook. The asphalt ends when Shore Line jogs inland. History buffs can finish the day by visiting the Crab Cove Visitors Center at the north end of the trail, where the story of Alameda Beach is told.

---

18. Bay Farm Island Loop
6 miles 🌀 🐜 🏃

Reference: **Between Oakland International Airport and the island of Alameda; see number ⓲ on page 158.**

Ideal for: Beginners—Fitness—Touring

Directions: From Interstate Highway 880 in south Oakland, exit at Hegenberger Road and follow the signs directing you west toward Oakland International Airport. Just after passing the Oakland Airport Hilton, turn right on Doolittle Drive (a sign before the intersection says "Alameda"). Follow Doolittle as it curves around the east and then north border of the island. When you reach the stoplight for Harbor Bay Parkway, turn left into the business park. Pass South Loop and North Loop Roads as you check out the scenery and pavement on your way up to the Harbor Bay Maritime ferry harbor, where you can park your car. This point is also accessible by ferry from San Francisco's Ferry Building. You'll see the asphalt trail next to the rest rooms.

Local shop: Willows Skate & Surf, 1431 Park Street, Alameda, CA 94501; (510) 523-5566.

Tour notes: Bay Farm Island is the place to be on a sunny weekend to enjoy the unparalleled views of the Oakland and San Francisco skylines across the bay and the pavement in and around the nearby office park. But just so you know what you're getting yourself into, sections of this loop tour will have you lurching, and in one short stretch, the pavement rises like mini volcanoes in the middle of the trail. Most of the path is just fine, however, and the views from the shore make the bumps worthwhile.

Start your trip by skating north from the ferry harbor parking lot to pass through Shoreline Park. The best views across the bay are from this section of the trail. On a clear day, you can see Mount Tamalpais behind the San Francisco skyline, and further east, the Oakland cityscape rises in the distance beyond the shores of Crown

Memorial State Beach. It's too bad the pavement is so terrible here. The rough stuff reaches its worst near the swimming pool at the recreation center just before you reach the bridge to Alameda. A separate, rather narrow bridge takes you under the drawbridge and to much smoother skating. Follow the trail alongside a grassy, undeveloped hill, the now-closed Doolittle Landfill, and past the Model Airplane Field located at the intersection of Doolittle Drive and Harbor Bay Parkway. Cross Doolittle to follow the asphalt bike path next to Harbor Bay Parkway, the same road you drove in on. Behind the wire fence on the right is the Alameda Municipal Golf Course. Watch out for the little volcano-shaped mounds at this point. The pavement on the street here is much smoother than the asphalt, and since Harbor Bay Parkway is a four-lane road, feel free to take to the street if traffic is light enough.

A quarter mile up from the Doolittle intersection, a water fountain splashes invitingly in the shade on your left, and picnic tables under the trees increase the temptation to stop for a rest. Explore the parking lots and paved areas of businesses on both sides of the main road and on South Loop Road, where you're likely to encounter bicyclists working out in colorful skin suits and helmets. If you want, you can follow North Loop Road all the way back to the marina, but more bayside skating on the best pavement of the loop awaits if you continue heading west on the trail on the south side of Harbor Bay Parkway. When you reach the shore, look for the wide concrete sidewalk next to the water. Less adventurous skaters come here to glide up and down this short, smooth stretch. If the wind is blowing off the bay, you'll appreciate the undemanding surface all the more. When the sidewalk ends, return to the asphalt trail just behind it to make your way north back to the ferry dock.

---

19. Lafayette–Moraga Trail   15.2 miles

Reference: **A rail-trail traversing the inland hills south of Lafayette; see number ⑲ on page 158.**

Ideal for: Beginners—Fitness—Hills/Slalom—Touring

Directions: From Highway 24 at Lafayette, exit at Pleasant Hill Road. Head south on Pleasant Hill, and at the intersection with Olympic Boulevard, park in the staging area at the south side.

Map: For a free trail map, call the East Bay Regional Parks District at (510) 562-PARK (7275) and ask for the Lafayette-Moraga Trail area brochure.

Local shop: Nuvo Colours, 1602 North Main Street, Walnut Creek, CA 94596-4609; (510) 938-6886. Other contact: Steve Fiala, Trails Coordinator, East Bay Regional Parks District, 2950 Peralta Oaks Court, P.O. Box 5381, Oakland, CA 94605-0381; (510) 635-0135.

Tour notes: The Lafayette-Moraga rail-trail was one of the first in California to be converted for recreational use by hikers, equestrians, and bicyclists, and now it's a prime spot for in-liners, too. Skating the full 15-plus-mile round-trip is a real joy for experienced skaters in good physical condition, but beginners who can stop for the intersections on the flat neighborhood section in Lafayette will also enjoy it. The original trail passing through the pretty foothills was once used by mule trains carrying redwood up to Oakland. Later, steam trains replaced the mules. For the first three miles, the trail is flat, but it does pass through several minor intersections where you'll need to slow down and watch for cars.

The intersections become few and far between the further south of Lafayette you go. At about four miles, the trail begins to get hilly, with slopes ranging from four to nine degrees for the rest of the trip. Skate past St. Mary's College on the left, which is an especially beautiful site on a bright California winter day, with its old-style buildings in clean white contrast against the grassy hills and Mount Diablo as the backdrop. Perhaps to encourage you to pause and enjoy this view, picnic tables have been provided at a small rest stop across from the college.

After the rest stop, another long uphill stretch takes you to the Moraga Commons, where the trail cuts along the left side of a park. Just across the next intersection, you'll reach Old Town Moraga—not exactly quaint in its current state, with a shopping center just across the street. You'll have to navigate through this part of town without a trail or even markers to guide you. But if you're ready for more hill skating, follow the decrepit sidewalk alongside School Street. Watch for Country Club Drive about three blocks down, where you'll need to jog right (west) for about half a block before picking up the southbound trail again.

South of downtown Moraga, the trail becomes more rural and hilly. The trail map shows the last long climb as a nine degree slope. At the top of this hill, the paved path ends next to Canyon Road. Unfortunately, skating back down that same hill doesn't invite relaxed slaloms or descent in the tuck position because there are multiple tar patches and a blind corner at the bottom.

One stretch of pavement half-way back to the beginning of the trail is smooth enough to encourage some fast skating. Just watch out for the sloped wooden footbridge with raised knotholes. It's difficult to get any kind of stroke because of the knotholes and the narrow width, so approach it with some speed so you can coast up it.

20. Nuvo Tuesday Night Skate   12 miles

Reference: On a rail-trail and in neighborhoods south of Walnut
   Creek; see number ⑳ on page 158.

Ideal for: Touring

Directions: From Interstate 680 in Walnut Creek, take the Main Street
   exit. If approaching from the north, follow Main south through town
   to the 1600 block. Nuvo Colours is at 1602 North Main Street, on
   the southeast corner. Approaching Walnut Creek from the south,
   follow Main north to the same corner. Park at the Broadway Plaza
   shopping center on Newell Avenue and Broadway a block east, and
   then check in at Nuvo Colours.

Local shop: Nuvo Colours, 1602 North Main Street, Walnut Creek,
   CA 94596-4609; (510) 938-6886.

Tour notes: Join the friendly folks who meet for guided skating tours at
   Nuvo Colors, an in-line specialty shop in downtown Walnut Creek.
   Throughout most of the year, the shop has a standing Tuesday night
   skate that departs at 7:45 P.M. The trips are tailored to match the skills
   of the skaters who participate, so make sure and mention your prefer-
   ences before departure. The trail of choice is often the nearby Iron
   Horse Regional Trail (see pages 182 and 183). An evening roll
   through the San Ramon Valley on this trail can be truly blissful in
   early spring, especially after a hard day at work.

   With a more advanced group of skaters, the Nuvo tour is likely to
head southeast into the hilly neighborhood streets in and around
Alamo, the next town south of Walnut Creek. Bring along your street
smarts and stopping skills. If you're a skier, look for those low-traffic
side streets that are so great for practicing slalom turns.

   After returning to Nuvo Colours, the group often heads for a local
cantina or nightclub to trade skating stories over a beer and snacks.

21. Ygnacio Canal Trail   6 miles

Reference: Traversing the outskirts of Walnut Creek;
   see number ㉑ on page 158.

Ideal for: Hills/Slalom—Touring

Directions: Traveling north on Interstate 680 in Walnut Creek, stay in
   the right lane through the Highway 24 interchange and exit at
   Ygnacio Valley Road. Go straight to pass under the BART tracks.
   Continue heading east for about a mile until you see John Muir
   Medical Center on the right. The trail starts in a patch of lawn
   immediately afterwards, also on the right. Turn right onto the next
   street, San Carlos Drive, and continue four blocks south to the entrance of tiny San Miguel Neighborhood Park, again on your right.
   Park here and pick up the trail across the lawn. You'll also see the

beginning of the Briones to Mount Diablo Trail heading up the slope from here.

Map: The Iron Horse Regional Trail map, which shows the Ygnacio Canal Trail, is available from the East Bay Regional Parks District, 2950 Peralta Oaks Court, P.O. Box 5381, Oakland, CA 94605; (510) 635-0135, ext. 2200.

Local shop: Sunrise Mountain Sports, 490 Ygnacio Valley Road, Walnut Creek, CA 94596; (510) 932-8779.

Tour notes: The varying terrain of the Ygnacio Canal Trail starts by following a small culvert through a corridor between Walnut Creek backyards. The fences on either side of this little canal are covered with lovely, mature foliage of all kinds, giving it a garden feel. Mallard ducks happily float here in post-storm runoff, but during the warmer months, the canal can often be quite dry.

In many places, the name of the street you're approaching is painted on the pavement at the intersection, a nice, reassuring touch for out-of-towners. You'll hit some rough patches between Meander and La Loma Streets, and stormy weather often leaves behind tree debris, but for the most part, the asphalt is very nice. Be careful when you cross the busy Walnut Avenue intersection: a pedestrian cross-walk offers some protection as long as you stop and look both ways before crossing.

Charming Arbolado Park is located at the street of the same name. New pavement makes for smooth skating, and the terrain is more country than town, with grassy hills rising behind the park to the east. A gradual incline begins at the golf course just around the corner from the park. The scenery is not particularly pretty near the wire fence behind the golf course, and a nasty pitted stretch mars the pavement leading up to a tunnel under Ygnacio Valley Road.

But once you skate through the tunnel, you're richly rewarded with grand views of the western hills above urban Concord. As you climb further up the trail and around one last bend, the path suddenly makes a steep, short drop with a hard right turn at the bottom to meet the Contra Costa Canal East Trail (see page 164). Unless you're an expert at fast cornering and braking and are fond of skating steep uphills, you're better off turning back here rather than dropping down that last tenth of a mile.

---

22. Stone Valley Road   4 miles 🌟 🐾 🛼

Reference: **Entering the hills south of Alamo; see number ㉒ on page 158.**

Ideal for: Fitness—Road/Street—Touring

Directions: From Interstate 680 in Alamo, take the Stone Valley Road exit, heading east. Drive 2.25 miles to Glenwood Court, where you'll

---

see a small park on the right. Pull in and park in the lot here. You'll be skating to the west.

Local shop: Nuvo Colours, 1602 North Main Street, Walnut Creek, CA 94596-4609; (510) 938-6886.

Tour notes: Even though the Stone Valley Road bike path must compete with numerous better-paved and better-connected trails throughout the San Ramon Valley, this location offers a pleasant in-line tour through pretty Stone Valley.

Starting from the park at Glenwood Court, skate west on the trail at the south side of Stone Valley Road, back toward the freeway. A hill on good eight-foot-wide asphalt makes for a thrilling start. The dedicated path disappears for a short stretch between Cortaderia Court and Roundhill Drive, forcing you to skate on the bike lane until the path resumes on the north side of Stone Valley. For the most part, this path/sidewalk combination remains in fairly good repair, although it can be dirty in places and sometimes grass grows in the cracks. You'll skate past homes alongside the road, mostly hidden by trees or shrub-covered fences. Just after you pass some neighborhood tennis courts, the wide sidewalk is replaced by a narrower one covered with grit and debris. It's time to turn back.

If you want to add another hill to this jaunt, when you get back to the park, cross to the north side of Stone Valley Road and take the sidewalk down and back from Green Valley Road, which is the next block to the east.

---

23. Blackhawk Road Trail   7 miles ⑧ 🏃 🎿

Reference: **In the San Ramon Valley near Danville; see number ㉓ on page 158.**

Ideal for: **Fitness—Hills/Slalom—Touring**

Directions: **From Interstate 680 in San Ramon, take the Crow Canyon exit heading east. Follow Crow Canyon Boulevard about four miles to Blackhawk Plaza, just across Camino Tassajara. You can park in or near the plaza.**

Local shop: Any Mountain Ltd., 490 Market Place, San Ramon, CA 94583; (510) 275-1010.

Tour notes: Miles of prime concrete sidewalk parallel Blackhawk Road, passing by the newly developed, upscale neighborhoods and golf courses outside of east Danville. Two significant hills add a thrill to this trail—one near the beginning and then a steeper one at about 1.7 miles. Since the sidewalk isn't wide enough to allow you to slow down with slalom turns, make sure that your braking skills and brake pad are in good shape. If you aren't into hills, start about a mile further east up Blackhawk Road (park at the entrance to the Blackhawk Country Club), and skate to the base of the second hill.

Starting at the Blackhawk Road entrance to the Blackhawk Plaza, head uphill towards the east. The trail rolls through park-like surroundings with views of the Mount Diablo foothills and occasional glimpses of the mountain itself. It ends just short of the entrance road to Mount Diablo State Park. The last few hundred yards are apparently not maintained and are littered with vegetation debris. A couple of notes: it can be quite warm in the San Ramon Valley on summer afternoons, and there are no bathroom facilities or water fountains along the trail.

After your skate, be sure to stroll around Blackhawk Plaza, which is home to a series of fountains and waterfalls and a number of fine eateries. Two outstanding museums adjoin the plaza: the Behring Auto Museum and the UC Berkeley Museum of Art, Science, and Culture. Both are well worth a visit.

---

24. Iron Horse Regional Trail North

11 miles 🟊 🐎 🏃

Reference: A rail-trail traversing the San Ramon Valley through Danville; see number ② on page 158.

Ideal for: Fitness—Touring

Directions: From Interstate 680 just north of Danville, take the Rudgear Road exit and park at either the Park and Ride lot (on the east side of the freeway) or the gravel pad at the trailhead (south side).

Map: Pick up a free trail map in Danville at the trailside sign or contact the East Bay Regional Parks District at the address below and ask for the Iron Horse Regional Trail brochure.

Local shop: Any Mountain Ltd., 490 Market Place, San Ramon, CA 94583; (510) 275-1010. Other contact: East Bay Regional Parks District, 2950 Peralta Oaks Court, P.O. Box 5381, Oakland, CA 94605-0381; (510) 635-0138, ext. 2203.

Tour notes: The Iron Horse Trail is a lovely spot to be in the spring when the foothills are green and the wildflowers are abloom in shades of gold and lavender. Once an important part of the San Ramon Valley's farming and ranching community, today this converted section of the Southern Pacific Railroad serves skaters, hikers, equestrians, and bicyclists. When the planned northern extensions of the trail are complete in a couple of years, it will connect to the Contra Costa Canal trail system and eventually stretch all the way to the Suisun Bay in Martinez.

From the Park and Ride lot on the north side of Rudgear Road, you can continue north only about a mile to Newell Avenue at Miguel Drive, but by late 1996, you'll be able to continue as far as Ygnacio Valley Road. You may elect to skip this section of the trail, where you'll mostly be skating between a fence and a high brick wall close to the backs of a row of apartments. The trees here can leave the trail quite messy for skating, although their shade helps keep the temperature cool on hot summer days. The dedicated path soon terminates at a busy downtown intersection.

To take the more pleasant journey heading south, go west on Rudgear, skating under the freeway and taking the crosswalk over to Danville Boulevard. You'll leave the sounds of traffic behind as the trail curves south toward downtown Danville. The fine asphalt path with a gentle slope runs along the edge of the valley's western hills, passing some open meadows and even corralled ponies in backyards. Though the trail is well maintained and clean, at times you may find yourself skating across soft pine needles; most of the trail is cooled by the shade of the tall trees.

Closer to Danville, the trail crosses several not-too-busy streets, but the interruptions can be annoying, since for safety's sake you really do need to slow or stop to check for oncoming cars. The path ends at Prospect Street in the small, friendly town of Danville, but the trail continues across the street next to a wood fence. For more skating, follow the signs at the south end of the parking lot on the other side of Prospect to cross Railroad Avenue and then, a block over, San Ramon Valley Boulevard, working your way south and east to where the Iron Horse Regional Trail resumes about five blocks away. (See the next listing.)

25. Iron Horse Regional Trail South   15 miles

Reference: **Parallel to Interstate Highway 680 in San Ramon; see number ㉕ on page 158.**

Ideal for: Beginners—Fitness—Touring

Directions: From Interstate 680 just north of Dublin, exit at Alcosta Boulevard heading east. Follow Alcosta for 1.5 miles as it veers around to the north. Turn left at Pine Valley Road and park near Walt Disney Elementary School. The pavement for the Iron Horse Trail starts just west of the school on the north side of Pine Valley. From here, you can skate north non-stop through Alamo.

Map: Pick up a free trail map in Danville at the trailside sign or contact the East Bay Regional Parks District at the address below and ask for the Iron Horse Regional Trail brochure.

Local shop: Any Mountain Ltd., 490 Market Place, San Ramon, CA 94583; (510) 275-1010. Other contact: East Bay Regional Parks District, 2950 Peralta Oaks Court, P.O. Box 5381, Oakland, CA 94605-0381; (510) 635-0138, ext. 2203.

Tour notes: The south section of the Iron Horse Trail is a great workout skate, especially in the spring when the weather is still cool and the wildflowers are putting on a show or in the golden glow of a late fall afternoon. There's no water and almost no shade along this stretch of the extensive trail, so if you come in midsummer, plan to skate during the early or late hours to avoid the midday heat. The first two miles of the trail are straight, with no hills and just a few low-traffic intersections, until you hit Bollinger Canyon Road. An easy-to-reach diversion from this intersection is just to the right at San Ramon Community Park. There you'll find lawns and lots of concrete in mint condition, as well as drinking fountains and rest rooms. After the Bollinger crossing, the trail is paved with wide concrete slabs as it passes behind the Bishop Ranch office parks.

For the next two miles, several intersections interrupt the path. Just beyond Sycamore Valley Road, the trail turns northwest to cross under the freeway and enter Danville. Then it disappears for a third of a mile on city sidewalks (but signs point the way). Turn right on the sidewalk of San Ramon Valley Boulevard, and a few blocks up, cross to the west at its intersection with Railroad Avenue. Follow Railroad as it curves around to the north, where you'll see the next Iron Horse Trail sign across from a parking lot. Pick up the trail again on the west border of the parking lot near a wood fence. (This lot is a convenient starting place if you want to skate the route in reverse, and you can also pick up the north section of the trail here. See page 182 for more information.)

---

26. Lake Chabot   8 miles

Reference: **Eastern edge of San Leandro; see number ㉖ on page 158.**

Ideal for: Fitness—Hills/Slalom—Touring

Directions: From Interstate 580 in San Leandro, take the Fairmont Drive exit and follow it east to Lake Chabot Road. The entrance to Anthony Chabot Regional Park is just across Lake Chabot Road. Park in the parking lot. If you want to save yourself the fee, leave your car on the street near the parking lot entrance and skate in.

Map: For a free trail map, call the East Bay Regional Parks District at (510) 562-PARK (7275) and ask for the Lake Chabot brochure.

Local shop: Sports Mart, 1933 Davis Street, San Leandro, CA 94577; (510) 632-6100.

Tour notes: Nestled in the foothills just east of San Leandro, pleasant Lake Chabot has a hilly, paved trail that follows the shoreline of the reservoir. Though it's popular with hikers, mountain bikers, anglers, and boaters, skaters are only just beginning to discover it, probably because the terrain requires strong speed-control skills. Due to the lack of flat terrain, this route is not recommended for beginners.

You can access the trail below the parking lot. Start skating to the left (northwest) and head down the hill, passing the marina and cafe. The trail continues along the southwest shore of the lake, soon rising fairly steeply. The surface quality varies, and it can be dirty in spots.

There are several ups and downs as the trail follows the lakeshore to the dam. You can continue beyond the dam for a short distance, but the path soon narrows and then drops steeply into the canyon. Skating beyond this point is not recommended.

Return to the marina the way you came, being careful on the steeper sections. Pass by the marina and the parking lot where you left your car and continue around the southeast end of the lake toward the east side. Here, the hills are generally less steep, but even so, there are several thrilling drops leading to sharp turns where side canyons meet the lake. Follow the trail until the pavement ends.

---

27. Union City Trail West   2.6 miles ⑥ 🧍 🏊

Reference: **A flood-control trail alongside the creeks of Union City; see number ㉗ on page 158.**

Ideal for: Beginners—Touring

Directions: From Interstate 880 at the northernmost edge of Fremont, take the Alvarado-Niles Road exit. At the top of the ramp, turn west to cross the freeway. Turn right at Dyer Street and then left at Ratekin Street to enter the housing development. Take the first left at Courthouse Avenue and drive to the end of the street to park in the cul-de-sac next to the trail that runs through Sugar Mill Landing, a little neighborhood park.

Local shop: Tri-City Sporting Goods, 40900 Grimmer Boulevard, Fremont, CA 94538; (510) 651-9600.

Tour notes: This unassuming but very pretty creekside trail remains virtually unknown as a skating location in the San Francisco Bay area. Even though I live in Union City, it took me four years of skating around these parts to discover it. (You might have a trail just waiting to be "found" in your community, too.)

Starting from the east end of the trail at Sugar Mill Landing, you'll pass under some handsome but messy-eucalyptus trees while the path edges closer to Alameda Creek on its south side. Half a mile from the trail's start, step around the low iron gate that protects you from the railroad tracks. You'll have to tread gingerly to cross the rocky shoulders of the railroad bed and then step over the iron rails. But on the other side of the tracks, the pavement suddenly becomes top quality in both smoothness and repair, and now you can see the clover growing in the wide creek bed below to your left. On the right you'll pass two housing developments. The second, Meridian Court, is new and upscale and has a green iron fence running next to the trail. The residents have their own entrance from a small park where they can access the trail, but the gate is locked to keep outsiders away.

Just beyond Meridian Court, the trail passes over an iron bridge with wide wooden planks, crossing to the levee on the south side of the canal. Just around the corner from here, you're forced to decide whether to jay-roll across four-lane Whipple Avenue and its grassy meridian strip, or skate up to the stoplight a block away at the entrance to Meridian Court. Make your decision according to the amount of traffic on the road and the level of your crossing skills.

Now begins the prettiest section of this trail, as it extends toward the San Francisco Bay in open fields a quarter of a mile behind a couple of small office parks. Down in the mud of the creek bed, sandpipers search for their meals, and across the fields as you round the last bend, you can see the hills that rise above the far side of the San Francisco Bay. The trail comes to an end at the bridge where Union City Boulevard crosses the creek.

28. Union City Trail East   12.8 miles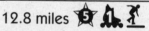

Reference: **A cross-town path in Union City; see number ㉘ on page 158.**

Ideal for: Touring

Directions: From Interstate 880 in Union City, exit at Alavardo-Niles Road and go east three blocks to Hop Ranch Road. Turn right and park at the Cesar Chavez Middle School or on the street near the point where Hop Ranch curves to the south and becomes Marsh Hawk Road.

Local shop: Tri-City Sporting Goods, 40900 Grimmer Boulevard, Fremont, CA 94538; (510) 651-9600.

Tour notes: Here's another little-known creekside trail with two big plusses: excellent skating pavement and very little company. Start near the corner of Hop Ranch Road and Marsh Hawk Road at Hop Ranch Park (officially named William Cann Memorial Park), and skate east. The trail heads straight from Hop Ranch Road into the park. After a short passage along the back border of the park, it climbs up onto the Alameda Creek levee. The better known and more traveled Alameda Creek Trail is just across the creek on the other levee (see page 192). After about a quarter of a mile, a canal branch called Dry Creek veers left toward Alvarado-Niles Road. A couple of blocks later on this levee, you'll meet the sidewalk bordering the south side of Alvarado-Niles Road. Directly across the street where the canal passes under Alvarado-Niles, you can see the Dry Creek levee trail continuing north. (To skate the rest of the Dry Creek levee, cross at the stoplight a block to your left. Cruise the canal bank 0.8 miles past industrial plants to the trail's end between 13th and Lewis Streets.)

Continuing on the intended route, at Alvarado-Niles Road, skate to the right to cross the canal and enter the Dry Creek bike path on its opposite bank, heading back toward the south. Here the pavement is generally good, although you might find some tree root cracks and debris. This trail follows Dry Creek back to Alameda Creek. After another short stretch along Alameda Creek, the path turns away again to follow another creek alongside residential backyards, passing the Union City Civic Center, crossing a residential street or two, and then ending at busy Decoto Road. Throughout this section, the pavement is new and excellent.

After returning to Hop Ranch Park, explore the trail to the northwest. The path takes you behind Cesar Chavez Middle School (note the paved courts and play areas). From the far side of the school yard, the trail heads to the left, passing over some low-traffic residential streets, across a small foot bridge, through shady creekside areas, and under Interstate 880 before ending at San Andreas Drive and Park a mile from the start. The section under the Interstate can be muddy during rainy season.

For those with good navigational skills, more skating can be found on the Union City Trail West (see page 185). To connect with it, follow the marked bike route on residential streets: take San Andreas Drive north to Santa Maria Street and turn right. Cross the street so you can turn left on San Luis Court, which terminates at a small neighborhood park. Cross to the other side of the park to reach San Carlos Way, and follow it one block to the intersection with Dyer Street. Turn right on Dyer and skate north one block to the intersection with Alavardo-Niles Boulevard. You need to cross both Dyer and Alvarado-Niles. The trail starts across the intersection behind the Union City activities sign.

29. Ardenwood Office Park   2.25 miles 🌀 👤 🏃

Reference: **Near the west end of the Dumbarton Bridge in Union City; see number ㉙ on page 158.**

Ideal for: Beginners—Figure/Stunts—Fitness—Touring

Directions: From Interstate 880 in Fremont, follow the signs to exit at Highway 84 (also Decoto Road), which crosses the San Francisco Bay on the Dumbarton Bridge connecting Fremont with Palo Alto and U.S. 101. After half a mile on Highway 84, take the Ardenwood Boulevard exit and turn right for Ardenwood. After two stoplights, you'll see the Mylex building on the left, and just beyond the parking lot, a volleyball and fenced tennis court. Make a U-turn at the next intersection (Commerce Drive) and either park in the tiny lot in front of Linear Park or pull into the parking lot next to Mylex. Skate north on the sidewalk.

Local shop: Tri-City Sporting Goods, 40900 Grimmer Boulevard, Fremont, CA 94538; (510) 651-9600.

Tour notes: The Ardenwood business park has more than two miles of wonderful eight-foot-wide concrete sidewalks, grounds landscaped with lawn and trees, and easy access to lots of fun places to play. But what makes this an exceptional place to skate is the north end of the office park, where you'll find plenty of sidewalks but very few buildings—all right at the edge of scenic Coyote Hills Regional Park on the San Francisco Bay.

To start your tour from the Mylex parking lot, skate on a narrow sidewalk up Ardenwood Boulevard back to Commerce Drive. (Across Ardenwood on your right, behind the baseball diamond, the double-wide basketball court with spectacular concrete is a must-skate if it's not in use.) Stay on the west side of Ardenwood to cross Commerce and continue one more block to the stoplight where Ardenwood meets Paseo Padre Parkway. This is a relatively busy access road that connects Fremont to Highway 84. Another trip tip: before turning left onto Paseo Padre's wide sidewalks, look diagonally across the intersection to see where another wide sidewalk continues over a hump to the north. That hump is the Alameda Creek overpass (see the Alameda Creek Trail on page 192). It's also where I learned to skate downhills, and underneath the hump is where the troll under the bridge taught me an early lesson about speed control. (Ouch!)

As you skate west up Paseo Padre, you're treated to fine views of the Coyote Hills across the fields. After half a mile, you'll cross the north end of Commerce Street, paved with more wide concrete. Continue another half mile to Kaiser Drive, which is roughly paved and bordered by narrow landscaped sidewalks. This part of the office park is still free of buildings, so every street and sidewalk beckons. There are no cars or people around, save the occasional golfer practicing his or her putting on the grass. Paseo Padre's sidewalk ends just before Highway 84.

Heading back, Kaiser Drive will take you to Ardenwood Boulevard, where a jewel of a parking lot awaits at the big orange Kelly building. On weekends, the place is deserted, and the smooth pavement is perfect for figure skating, beginner slaloms, laps around the building, or just learning how to get rolling. Besides Kaiser and Commerce Streets, another return option is available. Skating back on Paseo Padre, look for the asphalt trail that branches off the sidewalk and into the weeds. The pavement on this little nature path is pretty rough, but it follows a creek through Linear Park all the way back to the tennis and volleyball courts on Ardenwood Boulevard.

30. Coyote Hills Regional Park

3.5 miles

Reference: **Bordering the San Francisco Bay near Fremont; see number ③ on page 158.**

Ideal for: Fitness—Hills/Slalom—Historic—Touring

Directions: From Highway 84 westbound in Fremont, take the Paseo Padre Parkway exit, turn right (north), and drive to Patterson Ranch Road. Turn left and continue to the parking area. From Highway 84 eastbound on the Peninsula, cross the Dumbarton Bridge and take the Thornton Avenue exit. Turn left, where the road becomes Paseo Padre Parkway, and continue north to Patterson Ranch Road. Turn left here and continue to the parking area. There is a $3 parking fee from Wednesday through Sunday.

Map: For a free trail map, call the East Bay Regional Parks District at (510) 562-PARK (7275) and ask for the Coyote Hills Regional Park brochure.

Local shop: Tri-City Sporting Goods, 40900 Grimmer Boulevard, Fremont, CA 94538; (510) 651-9600. Other contact: East Bay Regional Parks District, 2950 Peralta Oaks Court, P.O. Box 5381, Oakland, CA 94605-0381; (510) 635-0138, ext. 2203.

Tour notes: On a clear day, the Coyote Hills Regional Park loop offers excellent views across the San Francisco Bay. Besides the silhouette of the city itself, you can pick out bay-bordering towns stretching from Oakland to San Jose.

On the marshy inland side of the loop, you'll skate past a wildlife sanctuary with a rich Native American history and an assortment of waterfowl, deer, and yes, even coyotes. Downhill enthusiasts should skate the trail counterclockwise, starting at the parking lot on the inland side. Skate clockwise to focus on an aerobic workout and a different version of the same hills. Enjoy the views, but stay to the right of the trail, and remain alert for cyclists and pedestrians around the trail's many curves. The asphalt surface is about eight feet wide and drops off steeply on the bay side, so make sure you skate in control on the downslopes. Just south of the picnic area parking lot, the steepest slope of the loop is next to a campsite named Dairy Glen. It offers prime slalom practice, but watch out for the blind curve at the bottom. The long Alameda Creek Trail (see page 192) starts at the far northern tip of this loop, accessed by a short, rough path that drops steeply to the levee on the south side of Alameda Creek.

31. Lake Elizabeth Loop
1.5 miles 🟍 👤 🏃

Reference: **Near downtown Fremont; see number ③❶ on page 158.**

Ideal for: Beginners—Touring

Directions: From Interstate 880 in Fremont, take the Stevenson Boulevard exit and head east for four miles. Turn right at the intersection with Paseo Padre Parkway. Drive alongside Fremont Central Park and past the first left into the park. Turn left after you see the sign for the Community Center and park next to the sandlot, where a wide sidewalk awaits.

Local shop: Tri-City Sporting Goods, 40900 Grimmer Boulevard, Fremont, CA 94538; (510) 651-9600.

Tour notes: Lake Elizabeth is the best bet for beginning skaters who live in Fremont and the neighboring communities of Newark and Union City. The west side of the park has eight-foot wide concrete sidewalks bordered by dense lawn. There are also some very slight slopes where novices can get the feel for using their heel brake without gaining too much speed. Once they've got the hang of starting, turning, and stopping, most first timers will feel confident enough to embark on the Lake Elizabeth Loop, where more experienced skaters can get a good workout doing laps. On the south side of the lake, there's an arching wooden bridge to cross that most beginners can negotiate successfully. Just after the bridge, a branch of the concrete sidewalk leads off to the right toward a children's sandlot, but it gets pretty sandy, making for slippery skating. Sticking to the trail, proceed around to the lake's southern tip, where the surface becomes asphalt. It's not as nice as the concrete, but still quite serviceable. The east side of the lake is exposed and sunny, but Fremont gets enough bay breeze to remain cool on most summer days. After you round the north tip of Lake Elizabeth and start heading down the west shore, you'll suddenly encounter an unexplained section of terrible, narrow asphalt that is barely navigable. It's a very short stretch, so if the lawn is dry, walk on the grass. Otherwise, keep up your speed and good luck. After this nasty patch, go right to cross the parking lot to the sidewalk on the edge of the lawn. You'll pass the concession stand and return by the gazebo to the parking lot where you started.

32. Wildlife Refuge/ Dumbarton Bridge
14.8 miles 🟍 👤 🏃

Reference: **Near the Dumbarton Bridge in Fremont; see number ③❷ on page 158.**

Ideal for: Hills/Slalom—Touring

Directions: From Interstate 880 in the city of Fremont, take the Highway 84 West/Dumbarton Bridge exit. Leave Highway 84 at the Thornton

Boulevard exit before reaching the toll plaza. Go left (south) about a quarter of a mile to Marshlands Road. This is the entrance to the San Francisco Bay Wildlife Refuge. Turn right and park at the visitors center. From eastbound Highway 84, exit at Thornton Boulevard after crossing the Dumbarton Bridge. Turn right and proceed to Marshlands Road and the wildlife refuge, as described above.

Local shop: Tri-City Sporting Goods, 40900 Grimmer Boulevard, Fremont, CA 94538; (510) 651-9600.

Tour notes: The Dumbarton Bridge is the only bridge crossing the San Francisco Bay that can be skated, and on a clear day, the view from the top is great. You can see from one end of the bay to the other, including San Jose, Oakland, San Francisco, and even Marin.

To cross the bridge, start at the San Francisco Bay Wildlife Refuge Visitors Center, where there are exhibits about local flora and fauna, along with historical information about the original Native American residents and early settlers. Follow the bicycle lane on lightly traveled Marshlands Road toward the San Francisco Bay. The pavement is rough but skatable. Starting on a moderate downslope, the road becomes flat as it approaches the bridge. Since 1993, from April to September, Marshlands Road has been closed to vehicular traffic to protect nesting shore birds. During nesting time, the entire road can be used for skating.

After 2.5 miles, the path veers right and climbs to the bridge across the bay waters. If you continue on Marshlands Road an additional third of a mile, you'll reach the fishing pier, which is actually part of the old bridge. The center section of the old bridge was once a drawbridge, and today the warning bell for that drawbridge is mounted on a monument near the foot of the pier. Unfortunately, the pier itself has a gravel surface and is unsuitable for skating.

Back at the bridge crossing access, be prepared for a fairly steep, 0.9-mile climb up and across on a path separated from traffic by a low barrier. Traffic here is close, fast, and loud. Return the way you came, being careful to control your speed on the descent. You can also continue on down the west side of the bridge toward Menlo Park.

Note: There is often a strong wind blowing off the bay, especially on spring and summer afternoons. This invariably means that one direction of the tour is likely to be against the wind. Confidence next to six lanes of fast-moving cars and a firm grip on the heel brake are also necessary to enjoy the bridge part of this route.

33. Alameda Creek Trail

24 miles 🎱 🛼 🏃

Reference: **Alongside Alameda Creek in Fremont/Niles;
    see number ㉝ on page 158.**

Ideal for: Fitness—Speed—Touring

Directions: From Interstate 680 in Fremont, take the Mission Boulevard
    exit and drive west to Highway 84/Niles Canyon Road. Turn right
    onto Niles Canyon Road and then make another immediate right
    onto Old Canyon Road. The creekside staging area (a large gravel
    pad) is down a slope on the left after you cross a bridge; park here. To
    park at the Coyote Hills end of the trail, from Highway 84 westbound
    in Fremont, take the Paseo Padre Parkway exit just before the Dum-
    barton Bridge toll plaza, turn right (north), and drive to Patterson
    Ranch Road. Turn left and continue to the parking area. From High-
    way 84 coming eastbound from the Peninsula, cross the Dumbarton
    Bridge and take the Thornton Avenue exit. Turn left to reach Paseo
    Padre Parkway, and continue north to Patterson Ranch Road. Turn
    left onto Patterson and continue to the parking area. There is a $3
    parking fee from Wednesday through Sunday.

Map: For a free trail map, call the East Bay Regional Parks District at
    (510) 562-PARK (7275) and ask for a copy of the Alameda Creek
    Trail brochure.

Local shop: Tri-City Sporting Goods, 40900 Grimmer Boulevard, Fre-
    mont, CA 94538; (510) 651-9600. Other contact: East Bay Regional
    Parks District, 2950 Peralta Oaks Court, P.O. Box 5381, Oakland, CA
    94605-0381; (510) 635-0138, ext. 2203.

Tour notes: The Alameda Creek Trail is a long, luxurious skate that
    includes great scenery, lots of wildlife, and a glimpse of south San
    Francisco Bay as a reward at the end. And it's pretty hard to beat all
    those miles of skating with absolutely no intersections!

Make sure to start out early in the morning before the inevitable
head-wind off the bay kicks up. It's generally best to begin from the
Niles Canyon Road end of the trail, so that the wind will be to the
rear for the return trip. Take the paved trail on the south side of
Alameda Creek, where you'll cruise on the eight-foot-wide asphalt
trail that winds through a wide, sunny flood-control basin past Shinn
Pond, some quarries and, near the bay, the protected marshes and
Indian shell mounds of Coyote Hills Regional Park. At times, quiet
neighborhoods line the south side of the canal, some with access
paths and grassy or shady little parks nearby where you can take a
rest. Ever present to the right, Alameda Creek eventually becomes
just a tidal trickle within the wide confines of the flood control canal.
If you're lucky, you'll spot some of the egrets, terns, and jackrabbits
that make their homes here.

The Alameda Creek Trail is flat except for the occasional drop for underpasses, where you'll need to stay to the right and be on the alert for fast-moving cyclists. When the path comes to the edge of the bay, a short, steep climb to the left connects to the Coyote Hills Regional Park Loop (see page 189). Heading back toward Niles, it's likely you'll enjoy a tailwind strong enough for practicing slalom turns.

---

34. Lakeshore Park/ Newark Lake

1.25 miles 🟊**6** 🔥 🏃

Reference: **A residential area in the town of Newark; see number ❸❹ on page 158.**

Ideal for: Beginners—Touring

Directions: On Interstate 880 in Fremont, take the Thornton exit and head west. Turn right onto Cedar Boulevard, pass two stoplights, and then turn right onto Lake Boulevard and follow it to the grassy area next to the lake, where you can park at the curb on the street.

Local shop: Tri-City Sporting Goods, 40900 Grimmer Boulevard, Fremont, CA 94538; (510) 651-9600.

Tour notes: Newark Lake—a small, relatively unknown neighborhood lake in a pretty setting—is a great location for beginning skaters to practice their basics and for fitness buffs to skate a few laps without becoming too bored with the scenery. Other than the big ducks and geese who think they own the place, the loop around the lake is used by a few neighborhood walkers and parents pushing strollers. Trees and grass surround the water, and since the lake is close to the bay, it rarely gets hot enough to need the shade, thanks to cool bay breezes.

---

35. Sports and Recreation Park Paths

1.5 miles 🟊**7** 🔥 🏃

Reference: **Near downtown Pleasanton; see number ❸❺ on page 158.**

Ideal for: Beginners—Fitness—Touring

Directions: From Interstate 680 in Pleasanton, take the Bernal Avenue exit (follow the signs to the fairgrounds) heading east. Turn left at Valley Avenue and proceed north to the Hopyard Road intersection. Turn left onto Hopyard and take the first right, Parkside Drive. Pass the first lot to turn in at the second parking lot driveway on the right. The sidewalk path is at the edge of the parking area.

Local shop: Nor Ski, 4855 Hopyard Road, Pleasanton, CA 94588-3224; (510) 460-0222. Other contact: City of Pleasanton Department of Parks and Community, 200 Old Bernal Avenue, Pleasanton, CA 94566; (510) 484-8291.

Tour notes: Pleasanton's Sports and Recreation Park is the ideal spot to learn how to get rolling on in-lines. Actually, the city built the park to accommodate up to twelve soccer games and at least 10 baseball games all at once, but a mile of sidewalk with irresistible concrete encircles the fields. The large rectangle of lawn and trees was built less than ten years ago and has been maintained with great civic care. The trees are tall and plentiful, and in the summer when the midday temperatures climb up into the hundreds, their shade is not only welcome but necessary.

Besides the shade and a very "pleasanton" atmosphere, the eight-foot-wide concrete sidewalks draw beginning skaters because of their forgiving lawn-bordered edges and very gentle curves and slopes. First-timers struggling to get used to the rolling feeling will welcome a relaxing break on the lawn.

Three sidewalks divide the elongated park to connect the north border (with parking lots and Parkside Drive) with the south border. Starting at the second parking lot from the west entrance, the sidewalk loop skirts the westernmost park border along Hopyard Road to turn east and follow along the back of a canal next to a housing development. This is the long stretch, and it's great skating. Take detours up and down the side trails cutting between sports fields back to the other side, or make it a fitness skate and go for a mile-long loop. Three-quarters of the way around the park perimeter from where you started, the sidewalk ends at a set of rest rooms just beyond the one and only basketball court near the east end of the park. It's not clear why the city wouldn't just build in one contiguous loop, unless this was an attempt to control sidewalk traffic passing between the busy central parking lots and the playing fields. Accomplished skaters can simply skate in the parking lots to make the loop connection two or three lots farther on. Since the pavement isn't as fine in the parking lots and there could be cars to deal with, beginners should skate back by returning to the far side of the park on one of the cross trails.

---

36. Bernal Boulevard Path   5.5 miles

Reference: Along the southern border of Pleasanton; see number **36** on page 158.

Ideal for: Touring

Directions: From Interstate 680 in Pleasanton, take the Bernal Avenue exit (follow the signs to the fairgrounds) heading east. Park one block up at Bernal Plaza, the little shopping center on the left at the corner of Bernal and Valley Avenues. The trail starts on the south side of Bernal Avenue at the Valley Avenue stoplight.

Map: For a copy of the Bicycle Transportation Map of the East Bay: Map 2, East of the Hills, send $1 to: the East Bay Bicycle Coalition, P.O. Box 1736, Oakland, CA 94604 (no phone orders).

Local shop: Nor Ski, 4855 Hopyard Road, Pleasanton, CA 94588-3224; (510) 460-0222.

Tour notes: The city of Pleasanton really makes it easy to commute on skates. The town is small enough so that no distance is unreasonable, and the combination of wide, landscaped sidewalks and designated bicycle lanes makes it that much easier—unless you happen to be climbing the considerable hill at the east end of Bernal Avenue, where your stamina and uphill stroke efficiency will be taxed.

Hills are not a problem at Bernal's west end, however, and this street on the southern border of the Pleasanton city limits even has its own dedicated bike path, but with a price. Cross Bernal at the Valley Avenue crosswalk to enter the chain-link fence corridor. If it wasn't for this rude wall, the rural view to the south would be much more satisfying. The wide grain field changes from a rich, velvety green blanket in winter and spring to row after row of rectangular golden hay bales in the summer. A tractor may be parked nearby, and in the distance, mounds of low hills dotted with oak trees complete the bucolic scene.

Half a mile to the east, you'll emerge from the chain link fence to follow the trail, now concrete, under some railroad tracks. Since the path bows out under the tracks, it's impossible to see if someone is approaching from the opposite direction, so even though this is a fun little downhill, be sure to leave some room to your left for a chance meeting. After you swoop up the other side, the sidewalk turns to the right at the Case Avenue stoplight and passes next to Pleasanton Middle School. The basketball courts here are easy to reach and have become a regular site for the recreation department's roller-hockey games.

Beyond the school at the end of Case Street, an asphalt trail ventures out into the middle of another grain field, promising a real nature roll. But the promise is all too short. After you round the first bend, the trail makes an "S" turn to cross over a small canal and then passes between an empty city lot and a lumber company to terminate at Sunol Boulevard. Turn around here. When you get back to Valley Boulevard at Bernal Avenue, skate one block down Bernal toward the freeway and cross to the sidewalk beginning at Koll Center Drive. This landscaped concrete pathway makes its way through shade trees up to the noisy freeway before curving to the north around the outside edge of the Bernal Corporate Park, eventually turning away toward the east at the northern border. Once the sidewalk runs out, make your way back to Koll Center Parkway, the street that circles around the center of the office park. This way, you can finish your excursion on the parking lots prized by local skaters for having the smoothest pavement around.

37. Stanley Boulevard Bike Path   8 miles ⭐🏊

Reference: A bike path connecting Livermore with Pleasanton; see number **37** on page 158.

Ideal for: Fitness

Directions: From Interstate 680 in Pleasanton, take the Bernal Avenue exit (follow the signs to the fairgrounds) heading east. Just past the Main Street intersection, turn left on First Street and follow First for six blocks, where it merges into Stanley Boulevard. Parking is possible to the left on Stanley's curb. However, the sidewalk path starts on the east side of Stanley after the First Street merge.

Map: For a copy of the Bicycle Transportation Map of the East Bay: Map 2, East of the Hills, send $1 to the East Bay Bicycle Coalition, P.O. Box 1736, Oakland, CA 94604 (no phone orders).

Local shop: Nor Ski, 4855 Hopyard Road, Pleasanton, CA 94588-3224; (510) 460-0222.

Tour notes: Pleasanton's many bike lanes, wide, landscaped sidewalks, and streets in good repair invite in-line commuting, and the dedicated bike path along Stanley Boulevard makes it just as easy to commute to Livermore. The best part is that there are very few street crossings to interrupt your progress, and none of those have stoplights.

Unfortunately, this bike path parallels both the Western Pacific and Southern Pacific Railroads, just across Stanley Boulevard. As you might guess, the railroad side of Stanley is pretty unappealing, especially when unconnected railroad cars sit in wait on the tracks. Because of this, consider the Stanley Boulevard Bike Path ideal only for commuting or getting a great workout, not for enjoying a roll through the countryside.

Tidy, path-side landscaping disappears once you leave the Pleasanton city limits heading east. Even though you're entering the countryside for the next three and a half miles, there are no trees nearby to shade this corridor. Your best hope for attractive scenery is to admire the grassy ridge of hills to the south, looking over the chain link fence at your side. You'll pass some public water slides less than a mile outside Pleasanton's city limits; on a very hot day, cars are lined up in the bike lane on the street next to your trail, waiting to make the turnoff. The eight-foot-wide path alternates between concrete and asphalt, and it can be gritty in places, so watch your step.

Isabel Avenue signals your arrival at the Livermore city limits. Shade awaits one block up at Murdell Lane. You have three choices for skating the last quarter mile up the low hill here: you can use the debris-strewn sidewalk, skate on the bike lane that is almost half gutter, or cross to the better bike lane on the north side of Stanley Boulevard. This trip ends at Arroyo Mocho Creek, where the trail passes behind the gas station on the corner of Stanley and Murietta Boulevards. See the Cross Livermore Trail below to continue heading east along a much prettier creekside path.

38. Cross Livermore Trail 8 miles 🟊⑦ 🚶🏃

Reference: **Alongside Arroyo Mocho Creek in Livermore; see number ⑱ on page 158.**

Ideal for: Fitness—Touring

Directions: Approaching from the south on Interstate 680, exit at Highway 84, the Livermore exit. This road is named East Vallecitos Road up to the Livermore city limits, where it becomes Holmes Street. (North of downtown it becomes First Street all the way up to Interstate 580.) Turn left at Murietta Boulevard (it's College Avenue on the right). Make a U turn two blocks up at Stanley Boulevard and drive through the ARCO station and out into the small dirt staging area in the back to park in a stand of eucalyptus trees. From Interstate 580, exit at North Livermore Avenue heading south. Turn right onto First Street and follow it as it veers south and becomes Holmes Street. Make an immediate right onto Murietta and follow it to the Stanley intersection, where you'll make your U turn to pass through the ARCO station.

Map: The Livermore Area Recreation and Parks District's Parks and Facilities map is available at the parking lot.

Local shop: Sunrise Mountain Sports, 2290 First Street, Livermore, CA 94550; (510) 447-8330. Other contact: Livermore Area Recreation and Parks District; (510) 373-5700.

Tour notes: The Cross Livermore Trail is exactly what its name implies, but in spite of the fact that it's a convenient way for residents to do some human-powered commuting across town to their places of work, a good portion of the trail-side scenery is entirely natural and even has great views. What a way to start the day!

The path runs through several mature stands of stately eucalyptus trees, and some of the grassy open spaces on the south side offer spectacular views of the Ohlone Wilderness, miles to the south. When I skated this trail, a rare blanket of snow was still faintly visible on those peaks the day after a winter storm had caused flooding. Unfortunately, the high waters of Arroyo Mocho Creek also made it necessary to wade across the overflowing culvert with skates in hand. Though the trail is generally pretty flat, there are two underpasses that require good control or braking skills.

Starting at the ARCO station staging area (it doesn't look like a park, but a map labels it as Oak Knoll Pioneer Memorial Park), skate to the east next to Arroyo Mocho Creek, passing the high school on a stretch of trail that is unshaded and likely to be hot on a summer day.

The area after the school is Mocho Park, but here, too, there is no development indicating it as such. After crossing Holmes Street, you'll enter Madeiros Parkway on the left and Sunset Park on the right. A dip under Arroyo Street takes you to the Robertson Equestrian Center, offering the best view of the Ohlone Wilderness. From here, the trail jogs sharply north to cross South Livermore Avenue (a crosswalk is provided).

On the other side of South Livermore, you'll pass signs for the Concannon and Retzleff Vineyards next to their grape-producing vines. (The Wente Brothers Sparkling Cellars tasting room is also quite close to downtown, just four miles south on Arroyo Road.) Now the scenery opens up on the north side of the trail as you pass Sunken Gardens Park. All too soon, the path enters a residential area. The trail system is quite civilized as it passes the homes on Findlay Way. There are three—count 'em, three—paths provided here: the sidewalk, the asphalt bike path, and a gravel path, all running parallel to Findlay Street for half a mile. At Madison Avenue, you'll jog left and then right to skate along the west and then north borders of Almond Park. The dedicated bike path terminates here, although the city maps show the bike route continuing on city streets, first up Almond Avenue and then to the right along East Avenue.

39. Sycamore Grove Park   4.5 miles 🔟 🛼 🧍

Reference: **South of Livermore; see number ③ on page 158.**
Ideal for: Fitness—Hills/Slalom—Scene—Touring
Directions: Approaching Livermore from the south on Interstate 680, exit at Highway 84, the Livermore exit. Turn right onto Holmes Street, which very soon becomes Wetmore Road after a 90-degree turn east. Just around that bend lies the Sycamore Grove Park entrance. From Interstate 580, exit at North Livermore Avenue south and turn right at First Street. Turn left onto Arroyo Road to head south. Just past the entrance to the Veterans Hospital is Veteran's Park, the east end of the trail. The parking fee is $2 at either end. Consider parking free at the Wente Brothers Sparkling Cellars if you'd like to taste their champagne (free) afterwards.
Map: The Livermore Area Recreation and Parks District's Parks and Facilities map is available at either parking lot.
Local shop: Sunrise Mountain Sports, 2290 First Street, Livermore, CA 94550; (510) 447-8330. Other contact: Livermore Area Recreation and Parks District; (510) 373-5700.
Tour notes: The trail at Sycamore Grove Park is a gorgeous roll through the countryside, far from the sights and sounds of civilization. It's at its greenest on midwinter days, thanks to the bordering fields of wild grasses. In the springtime, delicate pink blossoms sprout along the

branches of the trees in the almond orchards. Besides the equestrians who ride just off the paved trail, chances are you'll see such wildlife as squirrels and deer. Pastures stretch to the base of the hills on the south, and most of the north side of the trail follows a creek. Benches are supplied here and there, and bathroom facilities are available near the parking lots at either end of the trail.

Beginning skaters and those unable to control their speed will enjoy the Sycamore Grove end best, once they get across the dreadful 10-foot section of pitted cement crossing the dry stream bed. Starting at Veteran's Park at the east end, you must negotiate two or three short semi-steep hills with blind curves. Stay well to the right of the trail and be prepared for a sudden meeting with groups of bicyclists who unthinkingly occupy its entire width.

Central Valley North

22 Great Places to Skate

Central Valley North

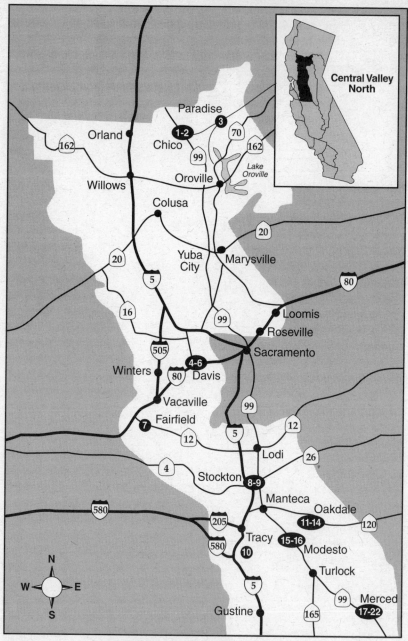

Central Valley North

Paradise
3
1-2
70
Orland
Chico
162
99
162
Lake Oroville
Willows
Oroville
Colusa
20
20
Yuba City
Marysville
5
80
16
99
Loomis
505
Roseville
Winters
4-6
Sacramento
80
Davis
Vacaville
99
Fairfield
7
12
12
5
Lodi
26
4
Stockton
8-9
580
Manteca
Oakdale
205
11-14
120
580
15-16
Tracy
10
Modesto
5
Turlock
99
Merced
Gustine
165
17-22

N
W — E
S

Skating Regions Beyond the Central Valley North

North .... North Mountains, p. 59   South .... Central Valley South, p. 225
East .... Gold Country, p. 85   West .... S.F. Bay Area: East Bay, p. 157

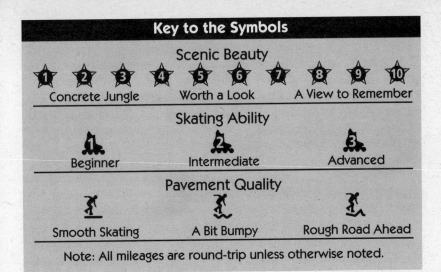

Key to the Symbols

Scenic Beauty

1 2 3 4 5 6 7 8 9 10

Concrete Jungle   Worth a Look   A View to Remember

Skating Ability

1   2   3

Beginner   Intermediate   Advanced

Pavement Quality

Smooth Skating   A Bit Bumpy   Rough Road Ahead

Note: All mileages are round-trip unless otherwise noted.

The best in-line season in the Central Valley is early spring, not only because of the scenery but the weather as well. As long as the sun is out and the pavement is dry, you can comfortably skate all day in April; starting in May, however, midday skating is no longer an option, unless you carry lots of water and are fond of dry, relentless heat. Yet despite the arid climate, a skater in these parts is rarely far from the water, as most paved paths are built along rivers that flow down from the mountains or near natural or landscaped creeks.

When cruising in the foothills on the eastern perimeters of the valley, be sure to visit the towns of Paradise and Oakdale. Above Sacramento, in the fertile flatland of the Sacramento Valley, the farming-and-college towns of Chico and Davis are each served by a well-used network of bike routes that seem tailor-made for in-line touring and training. South of Sacramento is the expansive San Joaquin Valley, where in spring the Modesto orchards are frothy with pink blossoms and the fields and foothills outside of Merced are a deep green.

1. Bidwell One-Mile Park

5 miles

Reference: **A park in the heart of Chico; see number ❶ on page 202.**

Ideal for: Touring

Directions: From State Highway 99 in Chico, exit at Eighth Street, the main downtown exit, and follow the one-way street seven blocks southwest. Turn right when you reach Cypress Street and follow it another four blocks north until you see the gated entrance to Bidwell Park at Woodland Avenue. Turn right to enter, and park in the lots serving the picnic and swimming area on the southern riverbank.

Local shop: Chico In-Line Sports, 336 Broadway, Chico, CA 95926; (916) 894-7528.

Tour notes: Bidwell One-Mile Park is where the first Robin Hood movie was filmed, and when you see the tangle of dense underbrush and tall, vine-covered trees that almost completely hide Big Chico Creek, you'll understand why: it's a jungle out here! Most of the place remains robustly untamed, with a timeless charm that might have you identifying with one of Sherwood Forest's merry men (or women).

Pedestrians, cyclists, and skaters are welcome to traverse either of Big Chico Creek's level banks on shady roads that wind through the forest for about two and a half miles each. Car traffic is scant enough on these one-way lanes to make them safe for skating, and numerous signs and painted skater icons (a figure doing what looks like a heel-toe roll) warn motorists to drive with care.

Start your tour on the sidewalk beyond the rest rooms at the far end of the parking lot near the swimming area. Don't let this first bit of smooth (almost-slick) green surface get your hopes up; all too soon it delivers you to a rough asphalt trail passing under Highway 99. The path takes you to Woodland Avenue, the first portion of the southern creek bank's one-way street. Woodland curves through the dense forest and passes under Highway 99, where it becomes South Park Drive. Soon you'll find yourself passing small picnic areas that were literally carved out of the underbrush. This section of road is off-limits to cars for a nice stretch all the way to Cedar Grove Road, about three-quarters of a mile from where you started. Just beyond where cars *are* allowed, you'll see a bridge over the river that provides access to North Park Drive, one of three such crossings along the way; these can be used to take shortcuts if you don't want to skate the entire loop described here. Continuing east on South Park, you pass fenced-off backyards on the right, and breaks in the foliage offering creek access (over dirt and leaves) on the left.

South Park Drive ends where it meets Centennial Avenue. Stick to the now-dedicated trail as it follows Big Chico Creek on another section of fine green sidewalk (interrupted by wood drainage slats). At Manzanita Avenue, go left to cross the bridge over the creek. (It's possible to continue skating east on the other side of Manzanita Avenue on a quarter-mile trail that leads upstream to Five Mile Park, but it's hardly worth the effort, even when you add on the service road and a one-block section of a newly paved residential street on the far side of the park.)

After crossing the bridge to the north side of the creek, skate west for a quarter-mile on a third section of green sidewalk to meet up with North Park Drive, another shady lane on the banks of Chico Creek. This street is also disappointingly rough compared to the green sidewalk you just left, but the surrounding natural beauty helps compensate. Make your way back up the long, tree-lined corridor near shady picnic sites till you reach a parking lot that serves the swimming area from the north creek bank. At the far end of the lot, skate a block down Vallombrosa Way to reach the bridge that crosses back to the south side of the creek, to the area where you parked.

2. Airport Connection   9 miles 🟊 🏃 💺 🎿

Reference: **Connecting the Municipal Airport with downtown Chico; see number ❷ on page 202.**

Ideal for: Touring

Directions: From State Highway 99 north of downtown Chico, exit north on Cohasset Road (to the south it's Mangrove Avenue) and proceed 1.5 miles to East Eaton Road. Turn left and park on the shoulder. You'll see the trail at the intersection, running north and south.

Local shop: Chico In-Line Sports, 336 Broadway, Chico, CA 95926; (916) 894-7528.

Tour notes: Starting at East Eaton Road, you can piece together a well-paved and varied tour of northern Chico. Start by skating north on the path that connects to the Chico Municipal Airport. The prime pavement crosses Sycamore Creek and proceeds one mile through open fields, up to the semi-industrial area surrounding the airport, to its termination at Marauder Street. In the surrounding blocks, several streets with aviation-related names and good pavement invite exploration during low-traffic periods. To continue this tour, return to where you started at the East Eaton intersection, go east to cross Cohasset, and skate on East Eaton Street in the bike lane. After one long block, a housing development appears on the left; cross to the trail that starts here, passing behind the homes. This is a slightly marshy area with beautiful vistas of the hills to the east across broad, grassy fields. The asphalt nature trail ends after only a third of a mile, at East Lassen Avenue. Skate west on wide East Lassen to return to and cross

Cohasset, on the south side of East Lassen. A block or so beyond the intersection, you'll meet the Airport Connection trail a block south of where you started.

For the last leg of this trip, skate south on a narrow but attractive corridor between backyards. Streetlights make this a viable commute route for Chico's residents even during the short days of winter. The trail makes its way through neighborhoods and across a few streets to the Lindo Channel. Cross the bridge over the channel; on the other side, the fine asphalt of the dedicated trail terminates in front of the Chico Nut building at the north end of Chico's Esplanade. You can skate one mile south on either of the two frontage roads next to the Esplanade to reach downtown, the college, and the Bidwell Mansion.

---

3. Paradise Memorial Trailway   8 miles 🎱 🏂 🏃

Reference: A rail-trail running through the town of Paradise; see number ❸ on page 202.

Ideal for: Fitness—Hills/Slalom—Speed—Touring

Directions: Approaching the town of Paradise from the south on State Highway 99, exit at State Highway 70 heading north. Two miles up, take Clark Road (State Highway 191) north and follow it 15 miles into Paradise. You'll find the east end of the paved trail just a few yards before Clark meets Skyway, the main east-west street in town. You will start at the other end, however, so turn left onto Skyway. (To park here and do the downhill direction first instead of last, ask the owner of the air conditioning and heating shop next to the trail if you can park on the property.) About 3.5 miles to the west on Skyway, turn left onto Fir Street, and drive down to where it ends, next to the Paradise Irrigation District corporate yard. Park on the shoulder of one of the streets near the trail entrance sign.

Approaching from Chico, head south on State Highway 99 and take the Skyway exit heading east. After about 10 miles and 2,000 vertical feet of climbing, you'll enter the town of Paradise. Drive through town on Skyway until you reach Fir Street on your right. Turn onto Fir and park near the trail sign by the Paradise Irrigation District corporate yard.

Local shop: Chico In-Line Sports, 336 Broadway, CA 95926; (916) 894-7528. Other contact: Al McGreehan, Town Planning Director, 5555 Skyway, Paradise, CA 95969; (916) 872-6284.

Tour notes: It seems too good to be true, but the name Paradise really does apply to this trail that runs through the small town of the same name. Located at about 2,000 feet in the foothills south of the California Cascade Range, the town is a great destination for skaters seeking to escape the hotter climates of the Sacramento River Valley. The newest section of the Trailway was added during the summer of 1995, making the longest continuous section about four miles long. South of Fir Street, a gravel section extends west to Foster Street, where another half mile of asphalt is in place. Once that connection is paved, the skatable trail will be a total of five miles long.

Starting at the Fir Street entrance, the smooth eight-foot-wide asphalt trail passes by the sign dedicating the Paradise Memorial Trailway "to all of the persons who lived, worked, and died to make Paradise a better place to live." The path takes you through a quiet corridor of shady pines and brightly colored wildflowers. Occasionally you catch a glimpse of the backyards of modest homes, but for the most part the scenery and sounds are natural. You'll cross five or six intersections along the way where side streets connect with Skyway; some are equipped with rustic benches, though it's not as if there's any traffic to sit and wait for out here. At a couple of the intersections a low hill blocks your view of oncoming traffic, so listen first and then cross quickly. After Rocky Street, the newest section of trail begins on pavement that was installed as recently as 1995, stretching up to Clark Street. Beyond Clark, the trail continues for another third of a mile, terminating at Pentz Road.

The Paradise Memorial Trailway makes a gradual incline in the Fir-to-Pentz direction. In most places the gentle grade is so easy it's hardly noticeable. And of course, the payoff comes when you turn back, rolling down smooth pavement through a forested landscape for four now-effortless miles.

4. Russell Boulevard Bike Trail   10 miles 🌀 👥 🚶

Reference: **Along the northern boundary of UC Davis; see number ❹ on page 202.**

Ideal for: Fitness—Speed—Touring

Directions: From Interstate 80, just outside of Davis, exit north onto State Highway 113. Take the Russell Boulevard exit and turn left at the end of the off-ramp. Look for curbside parking on Russell or on the side streets, Arthur or Eisenhower. You will see the bike path on the south side of Russell.

Local shop: Sportlife, 514 Third Street, Davis, CA 95616; (916) 758-6000.

Tour notes: The Russell Boulevard Bike Trail sets a standard for in-line touring that's hard to beat. It's a paved, very smooth dedicated path with light traffic, which means you can safely enjoy fast cruising right out in the middle of gorgeous Sacramento Valley farm country.

The trail starts at the UC Davis campus, heading west out of town along Russell Boulevard, the university's northern boundary. For the first two miles the wide asphalt trail is bordered on the south by the wire fence of the University Airport. You will pass through a shady residential area just beyond the Davis city limits, then emerge into the sunny farmland, finally leaving the wire fence behind. The trail is narrower here, only about five feet wide, but it's still separate from the roadway and in great condition. From here on, you have an unobstructed view of the country with its corrals of grazing horses and sheep. At one point the trail takes a short jog to the north of Russell, but puts you back on the south side within a quarter of a mile.

You'll probably hate to see the trail end at the intersection with Road 95a, but at least you get to re-do it on the return trip. If you're not too tired after you get back to Davis, continue to the campus to explore its winding paths and the Putah Creek trail bordering its southern edge.

---

5. UC Davis Campus   5 miles ⑦

Reference: On the grounds of UC Davis; see number ❺ on page 202.

Ideal for: Road/Street—Touring

Directions: From Interstate 80, exit at Richard Boulevard and take the first left after you pass under the freeway. This is First Street. Look for curb parking on the right while you're still off campus.

Local shop: Sportlife, 514 Third Street, Davis, CA 95616; (916) 758-6000.

Tour notes: In-line skaters are not hassled on the UCD campus, which has more than accommodated bike commuters for years. You may find yourself competing with cyclists for pavement if classes are in session, but even then you can still find enough of your own space. There are also several areas where cars are prohibited, which makes the skating that much better. The campus pavement varies in quality, from fine concrete to asphalt to a pebbled conglomerate.

To get your bearings, look for one of the campus maps posted at major campus intersections (a good one's at A Street and Hutchinson, just a block down from First Street). As soon as you're on campus, try to work your way south to one of the asphalt trails on either side of Putah Creek. Watch out for raised cracks there, and stay in control when the trail becomes steep and narrow where it passes under Old Davis Road. The creekside trails are generally hilly.

At the west end of the creek, the trail loops around a pond, then resumes on the creek's north bank. Make a circle around the gazebo on the hill before heading back to the main campus area. The trail leaves the creek for a short way at the north shore; take the wooden bridge to the south to stay near the water. There's another diversionary route farther south next to Old Davis Road, passing under the freeway, but the pavement is full of debris and is better left to cyclists.

6. Davis Covell Greenbelt

5 miles 🟊 🐜 ⛸

Reference: **Northern Davis; see number ❻ on page 202.**

Ideal for: Beginners—Touring

Directions: From Interstate 80, exit at Richard Boulevard and follow it under the freeway and across First Street, where it becomes E Street. Before Seventh Street, go one block to the right and then north on F Street, which takes you to the Community Park. Continue to the north end of the park and turn left onto Covell Boulevard. Take the first left to park in the lot close to the pedestrian overpass above Covell. Skate over the overpass to get to the greenbelt path.

Local shop: Sportlife, 514 Third Street, Davis, CA 95616; (916) 758-6000.

Tour notes: Created for local residents, the beautiful Davis Covell Greenbelt is well thought out; anybody can skate, stroll, or bicycle on this parklike loop through the grass-bordered neighborhoods.

You enter the area just on the other side of the overpass from the parking lot. The greenbelt is marked by numbered signs throughout; the first section is in Covell Park, where the low, grassy hills are wide enough to accommodate kite-flying, sandlot structures for kids, and games of Frisbee, as well as beginning skaters. Continuing north, you'll notice streetlights and signs naming the nearby cul-de-sacs that are the neighborhoods' greenbelt access. These signs are more than just a nice touch: the farther you go, the more you see the need for them as navigational aids. It would be very easy to get lost in here, especially at night.

Make it a point to skate out onto the wooden boardwalks that bring you closer to the marshy area north of Covell Park. You'll be standing among ducks and marsh grasses, and on a clear spring day you may even be able to make out the snowy Sierras in the distance. The path continues north toward new, grand homes that are still pitifully unshaded by the saplings in the newer greenbelt section. The trail is obviously intended to continue farther north as more homes are built, but for now you must circle around the lawn back to the older trail. Here you'll follow a row of trees bordering a playing field on your right till you reach the west side of the park. When you see the little playground there, head south toward Covell to continue skating the western part of the greenbelt.

Unfortunately, here most of the greenbelt's 10-foot-wide asphalt is in poor condition, with lots of raised cracks. In particular, one pitted section of the western part of the loop is horrendously bad for skating; try to keep your speed up to decrease the vibration. When you see a fork in the path near the Barcelona Avenue sign, stay to the left unless you feel like visiting an apartment complex. The trail now veers east to take you back to Covell Park. Heading back to your car, if you're willing to trade bad pavement and great scenery for perfect concrete next to a noisy road, you can extend your tour by turning right after re-crossing the Covell overpass to skate the sidewalk along the southern edge of Covell Boulevard.

7. Fairfield to Solano College   8 miles ⭐ 🏃 🎿

Reference: **Along Interstate Highway 80 in Fairfield; see number ❼ on page 202.**

Ideal for: Beginners—Fitness—Touring

Directions: From Interstate 80, take the Travis Boulevard East exit. Pass the first stoplight and turn left at the next light, into the Solano Mall parking lot. Turn right immediately to park behind the Firestone building next to Travis. The grassy linear park with its many rose-bushes awaits just across Travis at the Solano Mall stoplight.

Local shop: Sportlife, 514 Third Street, Davis, CA 95616; (916) 758-6000. Other contact: Fairfield Community Services Department, 1000 Webster Street, Fairfield, CA 94533; (707) 428-7431.

Tour notes: The path between Fairfield and Solano College is a great spot for a workout or commuting between the mall and class. Starting in Fairfield in a garden of rosebushes, a path of 10-foot-wide coral-colored sidewalk meanders peacefully along a wide corridor, landscaped with a variety of trees, grasses, and shrubs. It's in immaculate condition, possibly because local community groups adopt portions of it to maintain.

Along the trail's first mile and a half, before it passes under Interstate 80, are two sandlot playgrounds with picnic tables, plus streetlights to permit skating at night. There are also rest stops with benches and drinking fountains, and exercise stations dot the sides every few yards for those who like to stop and follow instructions to do a set of pushups or high kicks. The terrain includes some very gentle hills, and since the path is bordered by lawn, it's a good place for beginners to practice slalom turns or heel-brake stops.

Two or three intersections interrupt the trail in the first section. And take care: the last one becomes a ramp for the freeway one block up, so cars are moving pretty fast. Next, after passing through the tunnel under Interstate 80, you'll negotiate a stoplight and two crosswalks to get over the north-side freeway ramps. Just around the corner, the rosy sidewalk gives way to asphalt of equal quality if not color.

Although Fairfield did a wonderful job of landscaping, that can't hide the fact that this section parallels the busy, noisy freeway for nearly two miles. Still, trees have been planted that will someday provide shade, and a scattering of benches, trash cans, and drinking fountains add a very user-friendly touch. Aluminum fencing protects you on both sides while affording glimpses of the gorgeous wide-open farm country (including vineyards) to the north. To the south, an interesting view of the Anheuser Busch brewery is framed between the freeway and an overpass; the Cadenasso Winery and an orchard are on your right.

After crossing a wooden bridge, the trail turns sharply north and runs into the Solano Community College athletic fields. Skating is discouraged but not prohibited on the campus, which is sunny, flat, and full of wide sidewalks.

---

8. Brookside Area   4 miles 🌟6 👥 🛹

Reference: **A housing development just north of the Calaveras River in Stockton; see number ❽ on page 202.**

Ideal for: Beginners—Touring

Directions: From Interstate 5, take the March Lane exit and head west for several blocks, until you reach the brand-spanking-new Brookside Business Park. You'll know you're there because you see infant-sized trees and three or four very stylish multistory office buildings. Turn left onto Brookside Avenue, go a quarter-mile, and make a U-turn in the driveway of the ritzy gated community. You can park in front of the open area on the east side of the street, where a bike path winds away toward town.

Local shop: Sundance Sports, 3201 West Benjamin Holt Drive, Stockton, CA 95219; (209) 477-3754.

Tour notes: This tour is an exploration of perfect, flat pavement in Stockton's newer well-heeled neighborhoods. Start by crossing Brookside Avenue to the two-skaters-wide concrete sidewalk (notice the abundance of in-line tracks here) and head north to skate back to the Brookside Avenue intersection. Here's where you can start exploring, either in the neighborhoods straight ahead or to the left, approaching the country club. The only off-limits areas are the business-park parking lots, protected by a fleet of friendly security guards. As you cross March Lane, the wide, grass-bordered sidewalks continue north, and the residential streets up that way are also wide and pristinely paved. Returning to the Brookside Avenue/March Lane intersection, head west past the million-dollar homes and the country club, toward the marina. The roomy sidewalks end just before the marina, but the development plans call for paving a connection from here to the Calaveras River Levee Bike Path (see the next listing) that ends half a mile to the southeast.

---

9. Calaveras River Levee Bike Path

12 miles

Reference: **Along the north shore of the Calaveras River in Stockton; see number ❾ on page 202.**

Ideal for: Fitness—Hills/Slalom—Touring

Directions: From Interstate 5, take the March Street exit and head west for several blocks, until you reach the brand-spanking-new Brookside Business Park. You'll know you're there when you see infant-sized trees and three or four very stylish multistory business buildings. Turn left onto Brookside Avenue and make a U-turn a quarter-mile down in the driveway of the ritzy gated community so you can park in front of the open area on the east side of the street, where a bike path winds away toward town.

Local shop: Sundance Sports, 3201 West Benjamin Holt Drive, Stockton, CA 95219; (209) 477-3754.

Tour notes: This trip is better for fitness training than for touring, though the tule vegetation and wildlife of the Calaveras River have more scenic appeal than many other rivers that have been put to use as flood-control canals. To reach the levee bike path, cross Brookside Avenue to the double-wide sidewalk and head one block south. The concrete sidewalk terminates at an asphalt bike path that slopes up to the levee, accessing three miles of wide pavement that's in good condition. The path actually gets wider at the underpasses, where it becomes rather steep, dipping close to the riverbed and then back up again. If you happen to be skating during or after an especially heavy rainy season, watch out for a layer of mud or dried silt in those dips.

The river trail starts near a nice residential area, with the riverbed growing grassier and the bulrushes more profuse as you proceed east. The section of bike path that runs through University of the Pacific is kept clean by college volunteers. Half a mile beyond Pershing Avenue, the riverside standards of living drop considerably, and soon the trail surface and all structures nearby are thoroughly decorated in colorful graffiti. (Because this area can be unsafe at night, the local skate shop warns skaters to avoid the levee after dark.) Finally, just past the last small shacklike homes, the paved levee trail terminates. If you're hungry when you get back to your car, take the adjacent winding bike path to the corner fast-food establishments a mile away to the east (through an easement between fenced backyards). The path does continue into town, but is too mottled and full of holes to be skated safely.

10. Tracy Bike Path

6 miles

Reference: A bike path south of downtown of Tracy; see number **10** on page 202.

Ideal for: Beginners—Fitness—Touring

Directions: Approaching Tracy from the west, Interstate 580 splits off to the south and Interstate 205 continues east. Take the south (580) fork and exit at 11th Street (this is business Interstate 205), then proceed east to Corral Hollow Road at the Gateway Plaza shopping center. Turn right onto Corral Hollow and take the first right, Krohn (which looks almost like a private driveway) to park at Plasencia Fields a quarter-mile down the lane.

Approaching from the east on Interstate 205, exit at Tracy Boulevard and turn right onto 11th Street. Follow it west through town until you reach Gateway Plaza shopping center at Corral Hollow. Turn left and make the immediate right onto Krohn.

Local shop: Pacific Underground, 894 11th Street, Tracy, CA 95376; (209) 836-9460.

Tour notes: Tracy serves as one big bedroom community for many who work in the San Francisco Bay Area. They come here for affordable real estate, and developers reward them with new, well-planned housing developments and wide-open streets bordered by sidewalks, all perfect for miles and miles of carefree skating.

This town is firmly located in the hot Central Valley, and residents plan their outdoor lives accordingly—recreating at any time of day in winter and spring, but confining summer skating to morning, late afternoon, or evening to avoid the intense midday heat. Though the terrain is mostly flat, gently rolling hills have been built into some of the bike paths, enhancing the fun factor.

The first mile of this round-trip route is a bit convoluted and includes several street crossings, but staying on the trail is easy enough. Starting at Plasencia Fields, skate back down Krohn and turn right onto the beginning of the trail that runs next to Corral Hollow. At Cypress one block up, cross Corral Hollow and continue on the asphalt path (a concrete pedestrian sidewalk runs parallel) a couple of blocks to Ceciliani Park; you'll see it across the street. Cross Cypress and follow the northern border of the park and adjoining schoolyard to Schulte, where the trail takes a turn to the south. Cross Schulte at the Sycamore Parkway stoplight, the last major crossing. Starting here, the bike path parallels the sidewalk for two more miles of dependably smooth, well-maintained asphalt, with only minor street crossings. (Try to avoid skating across the scored bike ramps at each curb—the deep cuts into the asphalt cause considerable vibration.)

At this writing, the trail ends just before Windham Street at a little park that boasts some fine picnic facilities. And while "No In-Lines" signs are posted at the fenced-in tennis courts, the basketball courts, gazebo, and parking lots are actually better for skate play, anyway. If you don't mind street skating, you can make this into a loop trip: head east on Windham to Tracy Boulevard, turn left, and take another left at 11th Street to return to Corral Hollow. You'll go right past the local in-line shop, Pacific Underground.

---

11. Woodward Reservoir   3 miles 🔴 🛼 🛹

Reference: Northwest of the town of Oakdale; see number
⑪ on page 202.

Ideal for: Hills/Slalom—Road/Street—Touring

Directions: Take State Highway 120 east from State Highway 99, following the signs to Oakdale. Just west of town, turn left onto rural Route J14, also known as 26-Mile Road. Proceed north for four miles to the entrance of Woodward Reservoir Regional Park, and pay the $6 day-use fee at the kiosk (an envelope is left here for this purpose in the off-season). The road curves around to the left to follow the lakeshore for a quarter-mile, then comes to a four-way intersection where a big sign points the way to the lake's attractions. Turn left to go to the marina and park up by the marina store, where the best pavement begins.

Map: Modesto and Stanislaus County; Compass Maps, Inc., P.O. Box 4369, Modesto, CA 95352.

Local shop: Oakdale Sports, 1275 East F Street, Oakdale, CA 95361-4140; (209) 847-0648.

Tour notes: Skating is good at Woodward Reservoir in early spring or early on weekend mornings. Summer weekends, however, can be pretty crowded: up to 10,000 people come here for swimming, boating, fishing, go-carting, and in-season duck hunting.

There are no paved bike paths, so if you do come on a busy weekend, you'll be sharing the street and parking lots with cars and trucks pulling trailers loaded down with water-sports vehicles. Yet despite the background noise of Jet Skis and motorboats, you'll get some sunny vistas of water and grassy shores to the north.

Your first view once leaving the marina, though, may be the odd sight of a long row of Holsteins trying to eat with their heads sticking out between the bars of a feeder apparatus, like inmates at some kind of bovine prison. The pavement is great for 1.3 miles, starting at the marina store parking lot; the lot itself is also fun—large, sloped, and perfect for slalom practice when empty. Skate past the first set of campgrounds and continue east on the new asphalt that curves around the lakeshore all the way to the RV Pump Station. Undeveloped camping and rough roads are beyond this point; if you'd like to add another seven miles to your trip, skate out of the park the same way you entered, and cruise the wide shoulders of 26-Mile Road (see page 216).

12. Orange Blossom Road   4 miles

Reference: **A country road northeast of Oakdale; see number**
⑫ on page 202.

Ideal for: Fitness—Hills/Slalom—Road/Street—Touring

Directions: Take State Highway 120 east from State Highway 99 into the town of Oakdale. Turn left at the downtown intersection with State Highway 108 and go four miles to make a left at Orange Blossom Road. Proceed about a mile and a half to the intersection with Rodden Road, and look for parking on the shoulder.

Map: Modesto and Stanislaus County; Compass Maps, Inc., P.O. Box 4369, Modesto, CA 95352.

Local shop: Oakdale Sports, 1275 East F Street, Oakdale, CA 95361-4140; (209) 847-0648.

Tour notes: Orange Blossom Road is a very pretty rural route with grassy hills and shady curves. The rolling grades will entice roadwise in-liners who don't mind skating without benefit of paved shoulders. Early on a spring weekday is the optimal time to encounter the least traffic and the best scenery. This road is sometimes used to bypass Highway 120 on busy weekends, so avoid skating here when local traffic is heavy anywhere else. In any case, always keep your ears tuned for approaching cars, which seem to appear out of nowhere (and whose drivers may not see you) over the curves and hills.

The best pavement on Orange Blossom Road is for the first two miles; after that it ranges from smooth to very rough, but when traffic isn't bad you can enjoy some wonderful scenery all the way to the quaint little corner town of Knight's Ferry, six miles up the road.

13. Oak and Fox Hollow Estates   8 miles

Reference: **Northern outskirts of Oakdale; see number**
⑬ on page 202.

Ideal for: Hills/Slalom—Road/Street—Touring

Directions: Take State Highway 120 east from State Highway 99. Just as you enter the outskirts of Oakdale, you'll come to the first stoplight at Rodden and River Roads. Turn left onto Rodden, and pay attention to the street signs to stay on that road. First, it curves northward to meet Gibbers Road; turn right here. Soon, Rodden makes another turn to the north, and half a mile later meets 26-Mile Road: turn right again. Immediately after that, turn right to enter North Oaks Drive. Cruise around and check out the skating territory before choosing a place to park on the shoulder.

Map: Modesto and Stanislaus County; Compass Maps, Inc., P.O. Box 4369, Modesto, CA 95352.

Local shop: Oakdale Sports, 1275 East F Street, Oakdale, CA 95361-4140; (209) 847-0648.

Tour notes: If you love carving turns, you'll want to check out the long, sloped driveways to be found in these two high-rent neighborhoods of Oak and Fox Hollow. The driveway pavement here tends to be concrete, making it pretty irresistible for slalom practice.

Below the driveways leading up to the first set of estates where you parked, the shady streets are all named with some form of the word Oak: Oak Creek, Oak Drive, River Oaks, Oak View, etc. You'll find about two miles of streets and as many driveways as you can handle.

If you don't wear yourself out here, follow Oak View Drive north to skate back down to Rodden Road. Follow Rodden for half a mile and look for the big ranch entrance sign on the left that says Persimmon Hills. Turn right across the street onto Red Fox, and explore a newer, less shaded set of hilltop homes still in the making, with foxy street names such as Silver Fox and Gray Fox. The driveways are shorter here, but the street pavement is agreeably smooth.

---

14. 26-Mile Road
7 miles ⭐ 🅱 🎿

Reference: **Northwest of the town of Oakdale; see number ⑭ on page 202.**

Ideal for: Fitness—Hills/Slalom—Road/Street

Directions: Take State Highway 120 east from State Highway 99, following the signs to Oakdale. Just west of town, turn left onto rural Route J14, also known as 26-Mile Road. Proceed north to just beyond the slight bend to the right; a few yards away you'll see yellow warning stakes on both sides of a low bridge where the road crosses a ditch. Continue up another three miles until you see Dorsey Road on the right. Make a U-turn to park on the shoulder of 26-Mile Road across from Dorsey.

Map: Modesto and Stanislaus County; Compass Maps, Inc., P.O. Box 4369, Modesto, CA 95352.

Local shop: Oakdale Sports, 1275 East F Street, Oakdale, CA 95361-4140; (209) 847-0648.

Tour notes: Come enjoy the wide pastures and rural scenery of 26-Mile Road in the spring, before the renowned valley heat has taken its toll on the Sierra foothills' wildflowers and grasses. This is also the best time to avoid skating next to a steady stream of motorists pulling boats, Jet Skis, and camper trailers on their way out to Woodward Reservoir. But you should still be comfortable skating on roads next to traffic, because there's no dedicated bike lane here. On the plus side, you're able to see pretty much the whole road, which is quite straight.

Begin by skating south down 26-Mile Road. The pavement quality on the two-foot-wide shoulder is excellent, with just one long but gentle hump that requires you to add that extra push to your strokes. Make sure to watch for approaching vehicles as your roadside stride ventures over the white line. At the top of the hump you can see farmland all around, mostly pastures full of cattle. As you pass, the grazing animals look up; the more alert ones stare at you and chew their cuds even more thoughtfully, pondering this rolling apparition. Continue skating until you reach the end of the good pavement at a low bridge where the road crosses a ditch, then return to your car.

If you have very soft wheels or an iron will, you can add another two miles to your trip by skating up Dorsey Road and back. The rough pavement will have your feet tingling, but more rolling hills and farmland make for a visually pleasing payoff. Alternatively, skate up to Woodward Reservoir (neatly avoiding the $6 parking fee) and explore the marina parking lot and new asphalt road described on page 214.

15. Hetch Hetchy Bike Trail 2.8 miles

Reference: A bike path in northern Modesto; see number **15** on page 202.

Ideal for: Touring

Directions: From U.S. 99 north of downtown Modesto, take the Standiford Exit east. Immediately turn right on Sisk Road and park in one of the shopping center lots on the first block. You'll see the power lines overhead and the start of the trail across the street.

Local shop: Valley Sporting Goods, 1700 McHenry Avenue #D50, Modesto, CA 95350; (209) 523-5681.

Tour notes: Thus far, the Hetch Hetchy Bike Trail is not much more than a promise—a short stretch of asphalt so new that the nearby trees are still saplings. The nicely paved trail curves about under the Hetch Hetchy project power lines, through an apartment complex, and behind homes in a clean, fairly nice section of Modesto. Miniature stop signs mark the intersections, some of them with major streets, so make sure you have good stopping skills, and look both ways before you cross. Extended another mile or two, this trail could be a major asset to the city.

16. Dry Creek Bike Trail 4 miles

Reference: A creekside trail in the city of Modesto; see number **16** on page 202.

Ideal for: Beginners—Touring

Directions: From State Highway 99, exit at U.S. 132 (L Street). Turn right on 9th, left on D, and right at Yosemite Boulevard (you're still on Highway 132). After 1.5 miles heading east, turn left onto Phoenix Avenue. Follow Phoenix until it dead-ends at Edgebrook. Across Edgebrook, take the unnamed street dipping down toward the creek, into the La Loma Park parking lot.

Local shop: Valley Sporting Goods, 1700 McHenry Avenue #D50, Modesto, CA 95350; (209) 523-5681.

Tour notes: This popular bike path has excellent pavement and winds through a wide, mostly natural creekside area, with bathrooms located at both ends of the trail. La Loma Park has clean sidewalks and a basketball court for in-line activity and general fooling around. The beautiful natural and enhanced landscape of Dry Creek also draws local joggers, walkers, and bicyclists, along with a large population of magpies and ground squirrels. At the downtown end of the trail, the vegetation becomes a bit denser and wilder just before Moose Park. Moose Park itself has its own brand of wildness—it's a local homeless peoples' hangout best avoided after dark. Some local skaters venture beyond here for a bit of street skating, but it's officially against the law to skate in downtown Modesto or on school property.

---

17. Yosemite Lake

1 mile

Reference: A lake and park just north of Merced; see number on page 202.

Ideal for: Beginners—Figure/Stunts—In-Line Hockey

Directions: From State Highway 99, exit north on Interstate 59 (J Street). Across the railroad tracks, turn right on 16th Street, and three blocks down, turn left onto G Street. Follow G north about a mile to Yosemite Avenue, where you must turn right, and proceed another mile to the intersection with Lake Road on your left. Follow Lake Road north for another mile to Lake Yosemite County Park. Turn right just inside the entrance and park in the first lot you find.

Map: For a free map of the Merced Bike Routes, contact the Merced Conference and Visitors Bureau at the address below.

Local shop: McNamara's Sports, 3144 North G Street, Merced, CA 95340; (209) 722-3593. Other contact: Merced Conference and Visitors Bureau, 690 West 16th Street, Merced, CA 95340; (209) 384-3333.

Tour notes: Yosemite Lake has two very fine parking lots near the baseball field along the southeast border of the park. During off-season or off hours, these long, crescent-shaped asphalt pads are just the right size for anything from practicing backward crossovers to playing roller hockey. When empty, they're an ideal place for first-time skaters.

The wide-open scenery makes skating here a very *un*-urban experience, a real plus if you're from the city. Fields of dense, wild grasses stretch on and on to the south, bending in waves with the breeze. But that's not even the best part: when you stop frolicking long enough to gaze off toward the east, you can see the deep-purple ranges of the Sierra Nevada, their snowcapped peaks still startlingly white in the cooler climes of spring. The roads through the rest of the Yosemite Lake area vary in quality, with none coming close to the ideal smoothness of these two lots.

18. West Olive Avenue 1.5 miles

Reference: **A downtown mall boulevard in Merced; see number ⑱ on page 202.**

Ideal for: Road/Street—Touring

Directions: From State Highway 99, take the V street off-ramp and turn northeast onto V Street. Cross the railroad tracks and turn left onto 16th Street, which soon veers right to become the Snelling Highway, or State Highway 59. Go up half a mile, turn right onto West Olive Avenue, and turn left to park at the southwest corner of the Merced Mall. The wide sidewalk trail borders Olive Avenue, heading east.

Local shop: McNamara's Sports, 3144 North G Street, Merced, CA 95340; (209) 722-3593.

Tour notes: If you like to go mall-hopping on wheels, West Olive Avenue is your kind of skate, with wide concrete sidewalks extending for ten blocks between R and G Streets. This is your standard strip—a busy street where residents tend to the busy-ness of living. Unlike other Central Valley towns, though, Merced has only one such strip, so the community still has a friendly, small-town feeling. West Olive Avenue may lack the beauty of Merced's creekside trails, but it's become a favorite in-line commute route for younger residents, connecting North Merced High to the Merced Mall, and linking comfortably wide R, M, and G Streets with the dedicated bike lanes of the North Merced neighborhoods.

19. Lake Road Trail 5 miles

Reference: **A bike path connecting Yosemite Lake with Merced; see number ⑲ on page 202.**

Ideal for: Fitness—Touring

Directions: From State Highway 99, exit north on Interstate Highway 59 (J Street). Across the railroad tracks, turn right on 16th Street, and three blocks down, turn right onto G Street. Follow G north for about a mile to Yosemite Avenue, where you must turn right, and proceed for another mile to the intersection with Lake Road. Turn left and follow Lake Road north for another mile; you'll be able to see the trail on the right. After you enter Lake Yosemite County Park, take the first right and park in the first lot. The trail is by the park entrance. (You may be able to skip paying the entrance fee by parking on the road shoulder near the entrance instead.)

Map: For a free map of the Merced Bike Routes, contact the Merced Conference and Visitors Bureau at the address below.

Local shop: McNamara's Sports, 3144 North G Street, Merced, CA 95340; (209) 722-3593. Other contact: Merced Conference and Visitors Bureau, 690 West 16th Street, Merced, CA 95340; (209) 384-3333.

Tour notes: If you're feeling adventurous and strong, you're ready for the Lake Road trail, a stretch of country asphalt that's seen better days. But the view from here is worth the extra effort, because fields of the Central Valley's agricultural wealth stretch for what seems like forever to the north and south, and the Sierra Nevada peaks make a dramatic and jagged horizon to the east.

The connecting trail leading out of Yosemite to the Lake Road trail is truly awful, with grass growing from the raised cracks; you're better off walking on the lawn from the south parking lot. Two gravel driveways to Lake Road litter the trail with tiny pebbles in the first mile, which also necessitates a bit of roller-hiking, but the pavement quality improves greatly within a quarter-mile of leaving the park. The only other problem is the messy debris that collects under the stand of eucalyptus trees near the trail's end at Yosemite Avenue; watch out for twigs, bark, and acorns! And a final warning to you hardy adventurers: Lake Road may *look* flat, but you'll notice a gradual increase in your heart rate with the trail's gradual rise. You can definitely get a great cardiovascular workout on this skate.

20. Black Rascal Creek Trail   7.5 miles 🌀 🚴 🏃

Reference: **A city bike route on a creek in Merced; see number ❷⓿ on page 202.**

Ideal for: Touring

Directions: From State Highway 99, take the V Street off-ramp and turn northeast onto V Street. Cross the railroad tracks and turn left onto 16th Street, which soon veers right to become the Snelling Highway, or State Highway 59. Go up half a mile and turn right onto West Olive Avenue. Take the first left, Loughborough Drive, and follow it as it curves around toward the right. Take a left at Bismark Drive and park a block and a half up where it dead-ends at an embankment next to Black Rascal Creek on the edge of Fahrens Park. From here you can also skate the Bear Creek and the Fahrens Creek Trails, described in the next two listings.

Local shop: McNamara's Sports, 3144 North G Street, Merced, CA 95340; (209) 722-3593.

Tour notes: For skaters of all abilities, this trail is a real find: a stretch of perfect pavement following a tule-filled creek with a string of tidy neighborhood parks along the banks. In fact, there's parkland at each end and just about everywhere in between, so consider bringing a picnic, or at least a drink and a snack, so you can savor the scenery that much longer.

Although the Black Rascal Creek Trail crosses the pretty town of Merced less than a mile north of a main commercial street, skating here feels rural, and open fields still border some stretches. Other sections are edged by emerald lawns and graced with eucalyptus, pine, aspen, and sycamore trees.

From the end of Bismark Drive, begin skating east along the south side of Black Rascal Creek. After skating through a forest of eucalyptus, you'll cross a wooden bridge over the creek; on the other side, you'll come to the intersection that leads to the Fahrens Creek Trail. Turn right to follow Black Rascal Creek through Santa Fe Strip Park to the east. The 10-foot-wide path starts out as asphalt, then switches back and forth between concrete and a quality of asphalt so fine you can't feel the difference. Some nicely designed underpasses where the trail crosses R, M, and G Streets let you skate for at least two and a half miles without any need to stop. In the section between M and G Streets, the trail borders a narrow easement between the creek and some apartment buildings and is in rather poor repair until it reaches the border of North Merced High School. Look east from this open terrain to see the peaks of the High Sierra.

After the G Street underpass, you enter the clean and attractive northeast Merced neighborhoods. Here you'll cross two streets without benefit of crosswalks (but very little traffic) before entering Black Rascal Creek Park. Just as this park seems to be coming to an end, take the bridge on the right to return to the south side of the creek, and continue on the last stretch to Rahilly Park. The trail crosses to the far end of the park and dead-ends at Parsons Avenue. Cross the wooden bridge to the park on the north side of the creek so you can relax and get a drink of water. Such a great skate!

21. Fahrens Creek Trail 3 miles 🌀 🛼 🚶

Reference: **A creekside trail northwest of downtown Merced; see number ㉑ on page 202.**

Ideal for: Touring

Directions: From State Highway 99, take the V Street off-ramp and turn northeast onto V Street. Cross the railroad tracks and turn left onto 16th Street, which soon veers right to become the Snelling Highway, or State Highway 59. Go up half a mile and turn right onto West Olive Avenue. Take the first left, Loughborough Drive, and follow it as it curves around from north to east. Take a left at Bismark Drive and park a block and a half up where it dead-ends at an embankment next to Black Rascal Creek, on the edge of Fahrens Creek Park. From here you can also skate the Black Rascal Creek and Bear Creek trails (see the previous and the next listing).

Local shop: McNamara's Sports, 3144 North G Street, Merced, CA 95340; (209) 722-3593.

Tour notes: It may be close to Merced's northern neighborhoods, but the Fahrens Creek Trail has the look and feel of a nature walk. Follow the first part of the Black Rascal Creek Trail heading east (see the previous listing) until you cross the first wooden bridge that leads to the north side of the creek, bringing you to an intersection. Turn left here to follow the Fahrens Creek Trail.

Immediately, you'll appreciate this trail's wild streak as it heads through a field of chest-high weeds toward a dense-looking but narrow forest of eucalyptus trees. On a very windy day, the gangling branches of these tall trees imported from Australia thrash themselves furiously, making an uproar you may never forget and hurling bark and twigs down to snag between your wheels. Even so, the trail is quite glorious, especially when fields are still green. Follow its winding route along Fahrens Creek at the northwest border of Merced. A field of wild mustard flourishes to the north, gilding the terrain with bright yellow in spring.

There are no roads nearby to intrude with the rude sounds of passing autos, and the houses to your right are almost hidden by the trees crowded into the creek bed. Every once in awhile, a bridge leads off into the neighborhoods, and one steep dip takes you into the dark of an underpass that makes you want to whip off your sunglasses, just in case. Here and there, peppercorn-like tree droppings rough up your ride, but, for the most part, this is a great trip that reaches its end at the city limits all too soon.

---

22. Bear Creek Trail

6.5 miles

Reference: A creekside trail in Merced; see number **㉒** on page 202.

Ideal for: Touring

Directions: From State Highway 99, take the V Street off-ramp and turn northeast onto V Street. Cross the railroad tracks and turn left onto 16th Street, which soon veers right to become the Snelling Highway, or State Highway 59. Go up half a mile and turn right onto West Olive Avenue. Turn right again at the Walmart and park as far south as you can. Two short asphalt strips connect the parking lot to the trail, which is between you and the raised railroad tracks.

Local shop: McNamara's Sports, 3144 North G Street, Merced, CA 95340; (209) 722-3593.

Tour notes: While nowhere as new or as manicured as nearby Black Rascal Creek Trail to the north, the Bear Creek Trail has been serving

---

Merced residents well since 1976. It does show some cracks and signs of wear, but not as much as you'd expect from two decades of fond use, and if you try, you'll find you can skate right across a grassy two-inch crack with no problem.

Start skating to the east, parallel to the railroad tracks. (You can also hook up with the Black Rascal Creek and Fahrens Creek Trails from here by skating west and crossing West Olive Avenue on the trail that leads to Fahrens Creek Park just half a mile to the north. See the previous two listings for more details.) The Southern Pacific Railroad isn't exactly lovely company, and a large dirt lot spreads to your left as you begin, but you'll be right next to the creek as soon as you cross narrow Mistwood Drive and the bridge just beyond. A very tall wood fence at first makes skating a bit crowded next to the wide bed of Bear Creek, and equally tall trees block part of the view from the banks.

Half a mile down this odd corridor, though, you finally reach Applegate Zoo and Park, complete with the Kiwanis Kiddies Carnival. Now the asphalt becomes as wide as a street (in fact, for about 100 feet it *is* a street that runs one-way, so stay alert). For a short stretch you follow the tracks of the tiny kiddie railway, which soon curves back into the park. Picnic tables, drinking fountains, and rest rooms are available, as well as the much-needed shade trees that make Central Valley life tolerable in the summer heat. Five blocks past Mercy Hospital, you must negotiate the steep, curved underpass of G Street, marked by raised yellow traffic dots, no less. Stay on your own side; there's a blind corner here, and you wouldn't want to collide with a cyclist and have to go back to the hospital.

After the underpass, the trail scenery becomes consistent, with relatively undeveloped creek to your left and attractive neighborhoods on the right. The trail comes to a sudden end at McKee Road, but a wide bike lane beckons on the bridge where McKee crosses Bear Creek. Go ahead and cross to the north side; the trail continues along a slightly hilly route all the way back to G Street. Cross on the sidewalk of another bridge back to the trail on the south side of the water. Take a hairpin left after you cross, to get to the access trail that swoops back down the G Street underpass. Warning: if it's a terribly windy day, you'll find the last stretch of skating, between the railroad and the dusty field before Walmart, to be quite brutal, with a head wind that cuts your stroke strength in half and sends pebbles in a stinging spray against your face.

Central Valley South

13 Great Places to Skate

Central Valley South

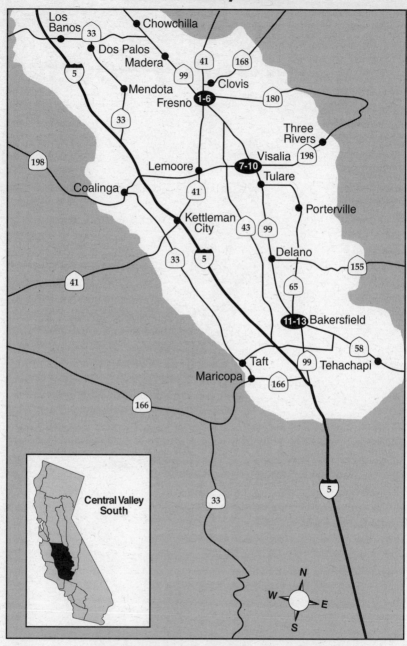

Skating Regions Beyond the Central Valley South

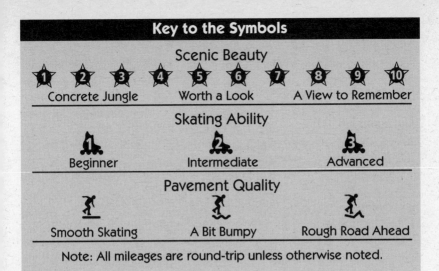

Key to the Symbols

Scenic Beauty

1 2 3 4 5 6 7 8 9 10

Concrete Jungle   Worth a Look   A View to Remember

Skating Ability

1   2   3

Beginner   Intermediate   Advanced

Pavement Quality

Smooth Skating   A Bit Bumpy   Rough Road Ahead

Note: All mileages are round-trip unless otherwise noted.

Highway 99 bisects the southern portion of California's San Joaquin Valley, passing through Madera, Fresno, Tulare, and Kern Counties. Radiating outward from hubs in the cities of Fresno, Visalia, and Bakersfield, the number of in-line skaters is steadily growing, despite the often stiflingly hot summer climate.

Smooth pavement proliferates in the newer city parks on the edge of Fresno's expanding city limits, and some fine road skating can be found just northeast of town. At the southern end of the valley, Bakersfield is sprucing up its popular Kern River Bike Path.

But for those who can visit in early spring, the prize of the region is St. John's River Parkway in Visalia. Here the still-creamy pavement, quiet riverbank location, and up-close vistas of the snow-frosted high Sierra peaks add up to an absolutely unforgettable skate.

1. Woodward Lake   3 miles 5 1

Reference: **A gated lakefront community on the northeast outskirts of Fresno; see number ❶ on page 226.**

Ideal for: Beginners—Fitness

Directions: From State Highway 99, take the Pinedale/Herndon Avenue exit and head east on Herndon. Seven and a half miles out, just before you reach the intersection with State Highway 41 (you can see it a block away), take a left on Blackstone Avenue. One mile north, Blackstone curves right to pass under Highway 41; at that point it becomes Friant Road. Proceed about 2.5 miles on Friant to the

Woodward Lake housing development on the right, which is marked by big entrance gates. Turn in onto Lakewood Drive, and follow it one block to cross Westshore Drive and park in the Yacht Club parking lot and dock.

Local shop: Herb Bauer Sporting Goods, 6264 North Blackstone Avenue, Fresno, CA 93710; (209) 435-8600.

Tour notes: Here's a great workout loop that lets even beginners stretch their muscles. The Woodward Lake loop road (Westlake Drive on the west side of the lake and Eastlake on the east side) circles within a relatively new housing development, offering a choice between a marked bike path on the shoulder of the road, or one of two wide concrete sidewalks. If your curb skills are good enough, choose the inside sidewalk. (You'll want to avoid the bike path, because it's split down the middle to allow a gutter next to the curb, leaving you with only two feet of asphalt for curbside stroking.) The outside sidewalk is interrupted with heavily textured iron manhole covers that are too large to jump.

Overall, this could be a much better skating location, good for touring as well as fitness, if you weren't skating between high solid walls for most of the loop and could see the lake itself. As it is, only in four very brief sections—three of them enclosed in the iron bars of a 10-foot-high fence—can you glimpse the water and some property along the shore.

If you feel you need more than 2.2 miles to get your workout, slip into a few of the streets whose names end with "Circle" as you go along. Each of these small loops-within-the-loop adds another third of a mile to your distance. There are at least three gated (and closed up tight) communities inside the main loop, and you can be sure most of those homes have waterfront access; you can see their wide sundecks and private docks through those stretches of iron fence.

After you've burned enough calories for the day, take a rest on the dock at the end of the Yacht Club parking lot and watch the mallards rush over, expecting to be fed. They put on quite a show if you reach into a bag as though for food. Sit there long enough, and they're likely to jump up on the dock to preen and ruffle their feathers like a hungry troupe of street performers.

2. Keith Tice Memorial Park .75 miles ⑥ 🧍 🏃

Reference: A park in northeastern Fresno; see number ❷ on page 226.

Ideal for: Beginners

Directions: From State Highway 99, take the Pinedale/Herndon Avenue exit and head east on Herndon. Seven and a half miles out, just before you reach the intersection with State Highway 41 (you can see it a block away), take a left on Blackstone Avenue. One mile north, Blackstone curves to the right to pass under Highway 41; at that point it becomes Friant Road. Proceed about 1.5 miles on Friant to Shepherd Road and turn right. Turn right again about a mile to the east, onto Millbrook. One long block down on the right, wide Cedar Street marks the northern border of the park. Turn right and make a U-turn to park on the curb next to the park on Cedar.

Local shop: Herb Bauer Sporting Goods, 6264 North Blackstone Avenue, Fresno, CA 93710; (209) 435-8600.

Tour notes: Beginning in-liners, rent some skates and bring them to Keith Tice Memorial Park. You'd think it was designed with you in mind; it's a great spot for those first tentative strokes. The very smooth concrete sidewalks are eight feet wide and bordered by cushiony green grass. Practice rolling right off the sidewalk and making a running or rolling grass stop. And, even if you have to do it deliberately (because you never *plan* to do it by accident), make a test fall forward on your padded hands and knees. That will build up a little trust in your gear and inject a little confidence into your skating.

The loop of this sidewalk circles near the perimeter of the park, making a "rink" about three-quarters of a mile in length. You'll see several workout stations next to the path along the way. Ignore them; you have enough on your plate for now. Another section of sidewalk will bring you closer to the kiddie sandlot in the middle of the park, but stay away, because the sand can be quite slippery, as well as bad news for your bearings. The small park is clean and well maintained, with picnic tables; just across the street you can see West Clovis High School, which is officially off-limits to skaters, though you'll see 'em there anyway. If you're here after school hours and can cross Millbrook Street safely, do it and explore this campus's vast parking lot and expanses of concrete. If you're asked to leave, just be very polite and go.

---

3. Cal State University, Fresno   3 miles 🏆 🐾 🏃

Reference: **Bordering the town of Clovis in eastern Fresno; see number ❸ on page 226.**

Ideal for: Touring

Directions: From State Highway 99, take the Pinedale/Herndon Avenue exit and head east for eight miles on Herndon until you pass under State Highway 41. About 1.75 miles after that junction, turn right on Cedar Avenue and proceed south to Bieden Field on the right, home of the Cal State Fresno Bulldogs. As long as there isn't a game in progress, curbside parking should be available on Barstow Street or San Jose Street, bordering the north and south edges of the arena, respectively. Parking on campus is prohibited without a permit, and

---

violators risk being towed. The sports-field access to the campus is across Cedar and north a short way up the sidewalk, through the fence entryway.

Local shop: Herb Bauer Sporting Goods, 6264 North Blackstone Avenue, Fresno, CA 93710; (209) 435-8600. Other contact: John Lewis, Athletic Manager, Herb Bauer Sporting Goods, 6264 North Blackstone Avenue, Fresno, CA 93710; (209) 435-8600.

Tour notes: Crisscrossed with a network of wide, flat concrete paths, Fresno's Cal State University is beautiful in the evening light, especially the walkways and buildings of the southwest corner of campus, which are surrounded by lawn and shade trees. The campus is ideally laid out for in-line commuting between classes (excluding those held near the farmland north of campus). Cruise around the library, the student union building, the cafeteria, and up the wide avenue to the big fountain. It's easy to put five miles on your skates if you add the circle around Bullfrog Stadium, though the scenery isn't that great out this way, and two or three severely pitted driveways interrupt the smooth concrete sidewalk. In general, the asphalt roads on campus are very rough and worth avoiding. There are only a couple of short man-made slopes, and the ramps on either side of the cafeteria probably get pretty crowded when it's open. You'll find a better, less-crowded hill near the dumpsters behind the Extended Education building on Cedar, near the Maple Street campus entrance. Hundreds of heel brake marks can be detected at the bottom of this short hill, curving right up to the loading dock doors—a sure sign that someone besides you has been having a lot of fun here.

---

4. Friant Road   20 miles 🐢 🛼 🏊

Reference: A connecting road between Millerton Lake and Fresno; see number ❹ on page 226.

Ideal for: Fitness—Road/Street—Touring

Directions: From State Highway 99, take the Pinedale/Herndon Avenue exit and head east on Herndon. Go 7.5 miles and, just before you reach the intersection with State Highway 41 (you can see the overpass a block away), take a left on Blackstone Avenue. One mile north, Blackstone curves to the right to pass under Highway 41 and at that point becomes Friant Road. Go 10 miles north until you can see the dam of Millerton Lake. A sign marks the turnoff for Lost Lake Recreation Area on the left. Park off the shoulder of Friant Road to avoid paying the $5 fee at Lost Lake (charged only at peak season).

Local shop: Herb Bauer Sporting Goods, 6264 North Blackstone Avenue, Fresno, CA 93710; (209) 435-8600. Other contact: John Lewis, Athletic Manager, Herb Bauer Sporting Goods, 6264 North Blackstone Avenue, Fresno, CA 93710; (209) 435-8600.

Tour notes: Experienced distance and road skaters will want to check out this long roll from Fresno to Lost Lake at the base of Millerton Lake Dam. It's also a favorite route for cyclists, thanks to the bike lanes painted on both shoulders for the entire 10-mile length.

Without cars on the road, this would be a truly epic skate. Be warned, however, that motorists (and on weekdays, heavy-duty semis) scream down this relatively straight two-lane road at 60 to 70 miles per hour. You have enough room to make wide strokes, but be sure to skate in the direction of the traffic on your side of the road to protect your face from flying pebbles.

Leaving Lost Lake, the road back toward Fresno remains flat for two miles, with low plateaus rising to your left, and fields, gullies, and more flat-topped hills on the right. The rural setting comes complete with grazing cattle, cactus, a windmill, vineyards, and hilltop homes. The asphalt is clean and in good repair, but when you come upon the newly paved section of Friant Road, with slightly wider shoulders, you can't help but grin with glee and stroke a bit wider. It only lasts a mile and a half, until the Willow Road turnoff.

At Willow, you've just passed RMC Lonestar, an asphalt company. You don't know whether to love 'em or hate 'em, because this outfit is one of the major reasons for the terrifying trucks on the road, but could also be responsible for the great surface you're skating on. Not far beyond Willow, the steepest hill of the trip awaits. If you're in fairly good shape it's a piece of cake, especially if the wind is at your back.

Half a mile after the road flattens out again, you approach the new country club on the south side of Friant Road, with baby palm trees lining an inviting access road; that nice pavement is worth a quick roll. From here on, Friant becomes four lanes, and the newest housing developments begin to appear on the left. The bike lane to the left of the road seems to be cleaner in this section than the right-hand shoulder, but it will be easier to take a break in Woodward Park just ahead if you stay on the right-hand side.

In-lining is not allowed within Woodward Park (though bicycling is), but you *can* legally skate a two-mile strip of asphalt between the park and Friant Road—reportedly the first section of a San Joaquin River multiuse pathway planned for the Fresno area. On your trip back, you may want to check out Friant View Lane or the Lost Lake loop, skate tours described in the next two listings.

5. Lost Lake Park

3 miles

Reference: **On the San Joaquin River, 10 miles north of Fresno; see number ❺ on page 226.**

Ideal for: Road/Street—Touring

Directions: From State Highway 99, take the Pinedale/Herndon Avenue exit and head east on Herndon. Go 7.5 miles and, just before you reach the intersection with State Highway 41 (you can see it a block away), take a left on Blackstone Avenue. One mile north, Blackstone curves to the right to pass under Highway 41 and at that point becomes Friant Road. Proceed 10 miles north until you see the dam of Millerton Lake. A sign marks the turnoff for Lost Lake Recreation Area on the left. In the off-season you can drive in and park for free; if the kiosk is attended, you can avoid paying the $5 entrance fee if you turn around, park on the shoulder of Friant Road, and skate in on the wide, perfect pavement of the park's half-mile access road.

Local shop: Herb Bauer Sporting Goods, 6264 North Blackstone Avenue, Fresno, CA 93710; (209) 435-8600.

Tour notes: The namesake lake is truly lost here, unless the name is meant to describe the San Joaquin River in the wake of the rain-soaked winter of 1994-95. After that deluge, the river ran so wide through Lost Lake Recreation Area that by April, several picnic tables were still immersed up to their benches and a section of park road was submerged under three feet of water. But normally you should be able to skate a full loop around the park all year round.

Start skating west on the high road by the entrance kiosk. This road connects to the lower river road in the shady picnic area, and it's wide and paved with top-quality asphalt for its entire length. On a busy midseason day, the high section is apt to have cars parked on the shoulder and a lot of foot and automobile traffic. But in the cool and unpredictable weather of early spring, you can have it all to yourself.

To the south, the view is wide open, revealing low hills that are oddly flat on top, perhaps due to some long-ago volcanic lava flows. Wild grasses by the road hold at least three kinds of prickly stickers that are sure to lodge into the stockings of children and the ears and noses of pets during summertime. Squirrels scamper onto the road and then dart quickly back into the grass before you roll by. At the west end of the upper road, a picnic area and shade trees have been added fairly recently. Ignore the left fork where the road makes a "Y" just after the picnic area—the pavement is too rough for skating. Instead, turn right and follow the road down into the shade next to the river's edge, to where it heads back in the opposite direction. Again, on a busy day you need to stay alert for children, cars, and all of the other action happening in the heart of the park.

At the far east end, the park road dissipates into a parking lot, but you can keep skating by taking a loop through the small campsite area, if you like checking out how folks "rough it" in these parts. Exit the campground near the check-in hut to get back to the high road and return to the entrance kiosk. Add another very sunny mile, if you aren't tired yet, by skating out to Friant Road and back. Unfortunately, this is the only paved "trail" of any kind next to the San Joaquin River in the entire Fresno area. The city hasn't yet built a path on the riverbanks, but plans are in the making for a very long multiuse pathway that will someday stretch all the way from Lost Lake to State Highway 99, a good 20 miles. Land acquisition is still in the talking phase, though, and that path will probably materialize "later than sooner," as one local put it.

6. Friant View Lane   3 miles 🔅 🏃

Reference: **A rural area north of Fresno; see number ❻ on page 226.**

Ideal for: Hills/Slalom—Touring

Directions: From State Highway 99, take the Pinedale/Herndon Avenue exit and head east on Herndon. Go 7.5 miles and, just before you reach the intersection with State Highway 41 (you can see the overpass a block away), take a left on Blackstone Avenue. One mile north, Blackstone curves to the right to pass under Highway 41 and at that point becomes Friant Road. Proceed about 4.5 miles north, until you reach the bottom of the long hill. Turn right at the sign for Friant View Lane and park on the shoulder near the row of mailboxes.

Local shop: Herb Bauer Sporting Goods, 6264 North Blackstone Avenue, Fresno, CA 93710; (209) 435-8600. Other contact: John Lewis, Athletic Manager, Herb Bauer Sporting Goods, 6264 North Blackstone Avenue, Fresno, CA 93710; (209) 435-8600.

Tour notes: Here is one of those "secret spots" that will delight the touring slalom skater. Picturesque Friant View Lane curves invitingly up the side of a low mesa, bordered on both sides by wooden fences. It takes some effort to reach the top, but before you even leave your car, you can see that this is a perfect spot to indulge in carving rhythmic, carefree slalom turns. The little lane is not marked as a private road, but it is basically the access road for no more than 10 homes that overlook the newly installed country club golf course to the south.

Once you reach the top of the mesa, the road flattens out and splits in two directions toward private driveways. The pavement is delightful and the scenery pristine. On a weekday during work hours, this place is totally traffic-free and serenely quiet. Besides your wheels stroking the pavement, the only other sounds you are likely to hear are hissing sprinklers, the chirping of birds, or the bark of a backyard dog.

After you finish exploring the lane, you're ready to play on the hill going back down. There's a blind curve as Friant View Lane leaves the top of the mesa to descend to Friant Road. Either start lower down where you can see around the bend, or send a skate partner to the curve to watch for oncoming cars. (Even if you haven't seen a single car since you arrived, Murphy's Law dictates that one will show up the minute you start making wide slalom turns down the hill.)

7. Country Club and County Center

5 miles 🌀 🐾 ⛸

Reference: **A tour of downtown Visalia; see number ➐ on page 226.**

Ideal for: Historic—Road/Street—Touring

Directions: From State Highway 99, exit to the east on the Mineral King Highway, State Highway 198. After five miles, take the West Main Street exit going north. West Main turns quickly to the right to parallel Highway 198, separated from the highway by narrow West Main Park and its protected oak trees. Park across from West Main Park in the large Elks Lodge lot, close to Main Street.

Local shop: Valley Sports, 2333 South Mooney Boulevard, Visalia, CA 93277; (209) 636-7050.

Tour notes: Just because they live near the heart of the agriculturally rich Central Valley doesn't mean residents here don't know how to live as well as folks in more urban parts of the state. Just south of the attractive country club golf course, a mature and elegant neighborhood near Mill Creek demonstrates the local talent for creating an oasis amongst the fields.

From the Elks Lodge parking lot, skate to your left, heading east on the narrow sidewalk bordering Main Street. When you reach the left turn onto wide Mill Creek, cross to the bike lane painted on the far side to start your tour of this fine neighborhood. Follow the bike lane past finely manicured lawns and landscaping that reflects the alpine scenery of the nearby Sierra. Mill Creek ends at Demaree Road half a mile up. Demaree is bordered by wide sidewalks, but the traffic noise and view-obstructing stucco walls make it strictly a fitness tour; for more interesting scenery, turn back via Mill Creek instead. Along the way, take the first left on Hyde, where super-black, super-smooth asphalt irresistibly beckons. Just a warning, though: there are no sidewalks or marked bike lanes here, so you'll be street skating, sharing the right-of-way with cars. But in the middle of a weekday there's hardly a moving vehicle (or person) in sight.

Hyde takes you past more expensive homes and delightful shady yards, meeting up with Hillsdale a few blocks away. Hillsdale takes you back to Mill Creek if you turn to the right. Turn left and it becomes Keogh, which terminates at the intersection with Border

Links. Go left here to explore Border Links en route back to Hyde. You won't get lost as long as you remember that Hillsdale, Hyde, and Keogh all return to Mill Creek when you're skating toward the west.

After exploring the country club neighborhood, return on Mill Creek to Main Street. If you're still feeling adventurous, turn left to take a quick tour around the grounds of the Tulare County Civic Center. You'll have to skate on the shoulder of Main Street after the sidewalk ends at Ranch Street. Although there's no crosswalk or light, with care you can safely cross Main Street at Sunset. Concrete sidewalks run throughout the complex, and the main building's breezeway is the only place posted as off-limits to skaters.

8. St. John's River Parkway   4 miles 🔟 ♿ 🏃

Reference: **A riverside trail in northeast Visalia; see number ❽ on page 226.**

Ideal for: Road/Street—Touring

Directions: From State Highway 99, exit to the east on the Mineral King Highway, State Highway 198. Exit at Ben Maddox Way and loop around so that you're heading north. Continue for 1.5 miles and turn right at well-marked St. John's Parkway. Take the first left, Gowdy, and follow it around a slight curve that leads to a dead-end with a big yellow END sign posted on the wooden fence. Through the gated opening you'll see an asphalt path leading up to the riverbank. Park at the curb.

Local shop: Valley Sports, 2333 South Mooney Boulevard, Visalia, CA 93277; (209) 636-7050.

Tour notes: On a blue-sky spring afternoon, this trail is the jewel of the entire Central Valley. Skating toward the east, you'll be smitten by the breathtaking view of the snowcapped Sierra, whose foothills begin rising just half an hour's drive away. The relatively new asphalt of the St. John's River multiuse pathway is in perfect condition and is a generous 10 feet wide; the only hills along its two-mile length are the access paths from the street. If plans to lengthen the trail another mile come through, there will be an extension from the east end, starting with an underpass for McAuluff Street, and landscaping will beautify the wide riverbank between the levee and the water's edge. At this writing, the stretch of trail west of this trip's starting point consisted of a mere quarter-mile of pavement from the Gowdy Street access—hardly worth skating when there's such a grand view in the other direction. Still, there's also talk of extending the trail farther west, so it's worth a look-see.

Skating toward the east, a low dam near Gowdy Street generates the music of falling water. If you can tear your eyes from the glorious mountain view, you'll see the river and a few creekside trees and shrubs to your left—sometimes near, sometimes a bit farther away from the raised levee bank. On the right, the street named St. John's Parkway flows almost as wide and calm as its namesake, connecting the homes of the Visalia's newer northeast neighborhoods. Traffic noise is not a problem, as this isn't a major artery for the town. Passing above the north end of Lover's Lane, you'll see a small dedicated parking lot for the trail, with a rather steep access ramp. Just beyond are the oddly named Wutchumna Ditch and the sports fields of the new Golden West High School. The St. John's River Parkway trail terminates at the eastern edge of the high school on McAuluff Street.

9. Plaza Park Bike Lane   4 miles 🌟 **6** 🔼 〜

Reference: **A bike lane in west Visalia; see number ❾ on page 226.**

Ideal for: Fitness—Road/Street

Directions: From State Highway 99, exit to the east on the Mineral King Highway, State Highway 198. Take the first right turn, Plaza Drive, following the signs to Plaza Park, next to Visalia Municipal Airport. Park in the provided lot. You will be skating on the marked bike lane of Plaza Drive.

Local shop: Valley Sports, 2333 South Mooney Boulevard, Visalia, CA 93277; (209) 636-7050.

Tour notes: This is a fitness skate for the road-ready in-liner, best done in the cooler morning and evening hours. Your tradeoff for unobstructed views of California's produce business is the absence of shade trees most of the way. Begin skating to the right on wide Plaza Drive at the small park's parking lot. Plaza Drive circles to the south past the park and rodeo grounds, then west to meet up with Hangars Way, which leads back toward the airport. (The airport is not exactly bustling with traffic, and you may not see or hear a plane at all.) Plaza Drive turns left here, and now you have a broad view of several Central Valley agricultural enterprises to the south and west, with a shady golf course across the street on your left. Continue down Plaza Drive as it curves gradually east. An orchard replaces the golf course across the street, and as you reach its far side at Shirk Road, the painted bike lane comes to an end. For skaters who like to explore the smooth pavement of new neighborhoods, cross to the north side of Plaza Drive before you cross Shirk, and continue on the sidewalk along Walnut Street to the entrance of the Savannah Heights housing development, a block up on the left. As this neighborhood grows, the bike lane may be extended to Walnut Street.

10. Mill Creek Garden Park 5 miles ⬡**6** 🏃**2** 🚶**1**

Reference: A neighborhood park in Visalia; see number ❿ on page 226.

Ideal for: Touring

Directions: From State Highway 99, exit to the east on the Mineral King Highway, State Highway 198. Exit at Ben Maddox Way and follow the exit loop to Ben Maddox Way north. Just after you cross the freeway, take an immediate right onto Mineral King Avenue. Follow Mineral King for four blocks east, paralleling Highway 99, and turn left at Lovers Lane. One block up, you'll cross Mill Creek and see the sign for Mill Creek Garden Park on the right. Turn right here, and park in the small lot on the right, marked by the sign "Allergy Free Demonstration Garden." The trail begins at the end of this lot.

Local shop: Valley Sports, 2333 South Mooney Boulevard, Visalia, CA 93277; (209) 636-7050.

Tour notes: The loop around Mill Creek Garden Park is less than half a mile long, but this park is situated near other Visalia skating attractions, and hence makes a good spot for embarking on a morning tour and winding it up with a picnic in the shade. Warm up by skating the loop around this lovely park once or twice. Watch out for some raised roots near the creek. The sidewalk bordering Mill Creek Parkway is just wide enough for medium-length in-line stroking. Cross to the north side of Mill Creek Parkway to follow Lovers Lane. A nicely landscaped concrete sidewalk makes Lovers Lane an attractive if noisy place to skate, and it passes some big, smooth parking lots on the way to Houston Avenue.

Use the crosswalk at Houston to continue up Lovers Lane. Three new schools are on your right, and so far, skating is still permitted on these campuses when school's out. Just before Lovers Lane dead-ends in a small parking lot at the base of the levee (see the description of St. John's River Parkway in the previous listing) you'll cross an access road that passes through the north part of Golden West High School.

To continue your skate on the St. John's River trail, go through the Lovers Lane lot and up the access path. If you want to take a longer route up to the river trail, turn right to skate through the high school campus to McAuluff Street. If you're visiting on a weekend, dally awhile in the large school parking lot to the right on McAuluff. To get to the levee trail entrance from here, turn left and skate uphill on the sidewalk.

On your return to Mill Creek Garden Park are some additional pavement and scenery worth exploring, to the east on Mill Creek Parkway. If this is still not a through street (as was the case at this writing), you'll be delighted to find that there's little or no traffic to speak of. It may be only a couple of blocks long, but the pavement is new and smooth on the north side of the wide, divided street, which is adjacent to some nice neighborhoods just waiting to be toured.

11. Seven Oaks   3 miles ⭐🔟🏃

Reference: Southwest neighborhood of Bakersfield; see number ⓫ on page 226.

Ideal for: Fitness

Directions: On State Highway 99 approaching Bakersfield from the north, go past the junction with State Highway 204. One mile south of the junction, take the exit for Rosedale Highway (State Highway 178) and 24th Street, and turn left to pass under Highway 99 and cross the Kern River. Turn right onto Oak Street just after the bridge, and follow Oak for just under a mile. Turn right at California, and follow it about 2.75 miles, first to the west and then, after a very gradual curve, to the south. When you see Patriots Park on your left, get ready to turn right at the next intersection, onto Ming Avenue. Follow Ming to the west for three miles, where very grand gates announce that you are entering the Seven Oaks area. Seven Oaks Country Club and Golf Course are to the left, and more homes are to the right. Park at a curb where your car doesn't look too out of place, and get out and explore.

Local shop: Action Sports, 8200 Stockdale Highway, Bakersfield, CA 93311; (805) 833-4000.

Tour notes: The Central Valley's towns just keep on growing, and there's no physical boundary to stop the spread. Cruise to your heart's content as you check out the Seven Oaks area, where you'll find the newest and best housing developments of Bakersfield.

From your valley vantage point, a clear day reveals mountains rising from the floor of the San Joaquin Valley on three sides: to the east, the Greenhorn Mountains (a southwest line of the Sierra Nevada range); to the south, the Tehachepi Mountains (Los Angeles is just 100 miles beyond that narrow ridge, over which passes the infamous Grapevine of Interstate 5); and to the west, the Temblor Range, the first of a series of ridges between Bakersfield and the Pacific.

This development makes a great workout location for skaters drawn to the new pavement and wide walkways found near the better housing developments being built these days. At Seven Oaks, you'll be skating amid great big houses, tiny new trees, and eight-foot-wide, landscaped concrete sidewalks that connect the entire string of elegant west-side neighborhoods.

12. Kern River Bike Path West   5 miles ⭐7 🐾 🏃

Reference: **Alongside the Kern River in Bakersfield;
see number ⑫ on page 226.**

Ideal for: Beginners—Fitness—Touring

Directions: On State Highway 99 approaching Bakersfield from the
north, go past the junction with State Highway 204. One mile south
of the junction, take the exit for Rosedale Highway (State Highway
178) and 24th Street, and turn left to pass under 99 and cross the
Kern River. (You can look down from the 24th Street bridge to see
the Kern River trail.) Turn right just after the bridge onto Oak Street,
which marks the east border of small Bakersfield Beach Park, and take
the first right after that, 21st Street, to leave your car in the shade of
the park. The Beach Park access ramp up to the river trail is at the far
side of the park toward the river. (If you can't find a curb space in the
park, go back to 21st Street and turn right to park in the sunny dirt
lot next to the river, and carry your skates up the bank of the levee.)

Local shop: Action Sports, 8200 Stockdale Highway, Bakersfield, CA
93311; (805) 833-4000.

Tour notes: The Kern River Bike Path has so much potential that when
you talk to the locals they'll tell you it's already 18 miles long. That
may be in the *plans*, but the painted distance markers put the actual
length at 7.5 miles, and a round-trip (both ends described in this
chapter) only brings your total mileage to 15 miles at the time of this
writing. Word has it that someday the trail will follow the river all the
way from California State University at Bakersfield—situated about
3.5 miles west of Bakersfield Beach Park—to Lake Ming, 10 miles
upriver from town. Whatever the eventual distance, the city of Bakersfield clearly recognizes what a wonderful community resource it has
here: New landscaping in progress includes plans for thousands more
trees, along with a campground near the newer section at the west end.

This 2.5-mile tour explores the trail's western section. Just after
leaving Bakersfield Beach Park, you'll dip under State Highway 99
(watch out for oncoming trail traffic around the blind curve). After
skating under the graffiti-decorated railroad trestle (how did they
reach those places!?), you see the new campground next to the river
on your right. Beyond the campground, on your left, you can see
Truxton Avenue and its row of modern business-park buildings. At
Commercial Drive, a small park offers a drinking fountain, benches,
and an inviting lawn. The paved trail to this park is on the far end,
close to Truxton Avenue.

Proceeding west, the contrast in sights and scenery becomes very
dramatic: modern multistory buildings line Truxton on the left, in
tidy new business parks. But look across the river to the right, and

there's the nitty-gritty reality of oil refineries stretching toward the distant northwest horizon. It's a spectacle totally unlike your usual urban landscape, and the pastel greens, pinks, blues and yellows of the massive tanks, interspersed with the tall spikes of metal towers and electrical power lines, are eerily beautiful in their own way.

A bit farther on, you'll find a cute little rest stop just for trail users, complete with bench, shade, water, and its own on- and off-ramp. The scenery to the south between the trail and Truxton is now marked by frequent signs that warn, "Stay Out and Stay Alive!" The big water-filled depression down the steep bank is labeled a Ground-water Recharge Basin, and signs warn that the water is unsafe for recreation or drinking. After passing the recharge areas, this skate becomes more of a workout than a tour, most suitable for commuting between the university and town. Here the asphalt path comes within three feet of Truxton's fast and noisy traffic. According to the painted distance markers, you're only a mile from the west end, and with so much natural scenery waiting for you to the east, it's a good idea to turn back now.

---

13. Kern River Bike Path East   8 miles

Reference: **Along the Kern River in northeast Bakersfield; see number ❸ on page 226.**

Ideal for: Fitness—Touring

Directions: On State Highway 99 approaching Bakersfield from the north, go past the junction with State Highway 204. One mile south of the junction, take the exit for Rosedale Highway (State Highway 178) and 24th Street, turn left to pass under Highway 99, and cross the Kern River. (You can look down from the 24th Street bridge to see the Kern River trail.) Turn right just after the bridge onto Oak Street, which marks the eastern border of small Bakersfield Beach Park, and take the first right after that (21st Street) to leave your car in the shade of the park. The Beach Park access ramp up to the river trail is at the far side of the park toward the river. (If you can't find a curb space in the park, go back to 21st Street, turn right to park in the sunny dirt lot next to the river, and carry your skates up the bank of the levee.

Local shop: Action Sports, 8200 Stockdale Highway, Bakersfield, CA 93311; (805) 833-4000.

Tour notes: Skate alongside the mighty Kern River toward its source— the same river that slices north to south from the base of Mount Whitney through the highest of the High Sierra. By contrast, here the river winds past the flat farmlands and oil refineries of the southern San Joaquin Valley.

As you skate away from Bakersfield Beach Park, you'll see the sandy "beach" on the riverbank, where it drops steeply down from the trail. Swimming is permitted, though lifeguards are not evident. This trail is obviously the best spot in town for all kinds of competitive activities: various start and finish lines and distance markers are painted on the asphalt, possibly adding to the local confusion about the trail's length, which is claimed by some to be up to 18 miles long, but currently includes only 7.5 miles of actual pavement end to end.

Just beyond the park area, the chain-link fence on the right does a good job of adding an industrial flavor, so it's best to direct your attention to the left, to the variations of the river itself. This section of the Kern River Bike Path has been around a while, and its surroundings have been left in a more natural state than the eastern part of the trail, except, of course, for the omnipresent dams and canals. Landscaping is supposedly in the works, but there hasn't been a beautification project here yet.

The asphalt path is in quite good condition for most of the four miles heading east from Beach Park. However, just before you cross under the railroad tracks, you'll find a .10-mile stretch of very coarse pavement. Consider turning back here, because after the painted six-mile marker, rough asphalt makes the last mile and a half quite unpleasant. These bad patches seem to have gotten so much sun that the tar has evaporated from between the pebbles that make up the asphalt; where the underpasses create shade, the trail improves.

For those continuing on: after a long, seemingly unnecessary curve to the southeast, a hairpin turn swerves the trail around to the north, running parallel to Manor Street. You'll see a blocked-off tunnel under Manor with no trail leading to it, possibly indicating plans to extend the trail beneath that street and toward the high mesa hills on the other side.

The path finally terminates at a staging area at the intersection of Manor and Georgia. A drinking fountain would be very welcome by the time you arrive, but there's no plumbing here as of yet—nor even, for that matter, a smidgen of shade or grass, or a bench where a weary skater might rest.

Sierra Nevada

24 Great Places to Skate

Sierra Nevada

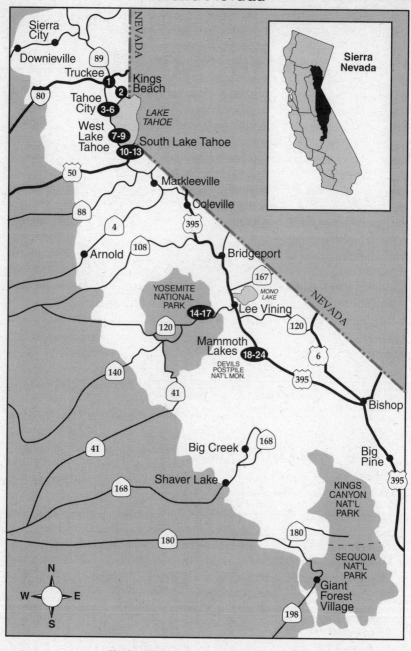

Skating Regions Beyond the Sierra Nevada

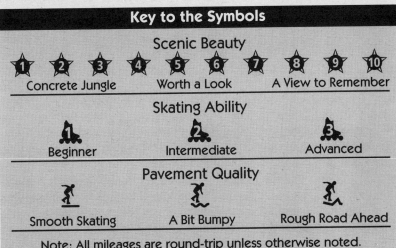

It's no surprise that the Sierra Nevada region—defined by the immense Sierra Nevada and dominated by Mount Whitney, the highest peak in the continental United States—poses something of a challenge to would-be skaters; gentle paved slopes aren't exactly plentiful in such dramatic terrain. But in-liners of all abilities, have no fear: what you *can* find in abundance are the byways and trails of two unforgettable valleys and a world-class lake. In fact, at Tahoe, Yosemite, or Mammoth, you can spend a full day skating amid some of the most gorgeous landscape in the state.

In crowded Yosemite Valley, skating is actually the best way to get around, thanks to eight miles of bike paths, and the scenery is incredible at every turn. For navigating, make sure to accept the free map at the entrance gate to use in tandem with the directions in this book. Parking is at a premium here, so even though most of the skating trails begin from public lots, you may need to leave the car at your campsite and use the free shuttle system to get to the starting point.

In the Mammoth Lakes area, road skating is much more the order of the day. Car traffic is usually light enough so that the Mammoth locals, many of them expert skiers, are now actually spoiled by the option of skating road-width slaloms at will.

All around Lake Tahoe, skating opportunities abound: bike paths stretch for miles along the shimmering water. On the western shore, quiet roads lead to sloped, tree-filled mountain canyons. North of the lake, enjoy scenic rolls on the banks of the Truckee River or through the grassy meadows of Squaw Valley.

1. Martis Creek Lake Road

3 miles ⭐8 🛼 🏃

Reference: In the Martis Valley north of Lake Tahoe, outside Truckee; see number ❶ on page 244.

Ideal for: Beginners—Fitness—Road/Street—Touring

Directions: From Interstate 80, take the Truckee exit. Drive through downtown and turn right at the sign for State Highway 267 and Kings Beach. Approximately four miles south of town, turn left at the small sign for Martis Creek Lake Recreation Area. Proceed about half a mile to where the road curves around to the north. Just around the bend, park on the left shoulder.

Local shop: Dave's Summer Sports, 10200 Donner Pass Road, Truckee, CA 96160; (916) 582-0900.

Tour notes: From Martis Creek Lake Road, a broad panorama shows off the Northstar Ski Area to the south across the tumbleweed flats of Martis Valley. Because Martis Lake is small compared to Lake Tahoe a few miles away, it pales as a recreation destination; the benefit to skaters, however, is that car traffic on the Lake Road is usually pretty light. But there is one annoying drawback: for some reason the pavement, while smooth enough, is broken up into short sections connected by raised tar seams—causing jolt after jolt as you skate over them. Skate a few laps on the flat part of the road to get a workout or perfect your speed-skating technique. Because it's so straight, you can easily see the infrequent car approaching.

When you're ready to increase your workout a notch, explore the campground just over the hill, next to the small lake formed by Martis Creek Dam. Follow the road north to climb the hill; at the top, turn right onto the consistently smooth asphalt to take a loop through the new campsites. Playful skaters should have fun using the two speed humps (a wider version of speed bumps) for attempts at flight.

2. North Tahoe Regional Park Bike Path

2.5 miles ⭐9 🛼 🏃

Reference: In Tahoe Vista, north of Kings Beach; see number ❷ on page 244.

Ideal for: Hills/Slalom—Touring

Directions: From North Lake Boulevard in Kings Beach, take the Truckee exit going north on State Highway 267. Drive .7 miles to Pinedrop Lane and turn left. Proceed less than a quarter mile and you'll see the trail's beginning on the right side of the road. Park on the gravel shoulder across the street. (Official parking is at the west end of the trail, accessed by following the North Tahoe Regional Park signs from Highway 89 at National Avenue in Tahoe Vista, but there's a short downhill hike across rubble to get to the trail.)

Map: Recreation Map of Lake Tahoe, Tom Harrison Cartography, 2 Falmouth Cove, San Rafael, CA 94901-4465; (415) 456-7940.

Local shop: Porter's Ski & Sport, 501 North Lake Boulevard, Tahoe City, CA 96145; (916) 583-2314.

Tour notes: The unpretentious bike path running through North Tahoe Regional Park is a nature skater's dream come true. It's rare to find such untouched scenery on skates; in fact, this paved path winds through the kind of pine-forest scenery that normally only hikers or backpackers get to appreciate.

The pavement on the trail next to Pinedrop Lane is old and beaten, and its cracks, sharp curves, and sudden dips are a challenge even to experienced skaters. Since cars pass infrequently, it is safe to start out on the much better pavement of Pinedrop Lane. Climb the hill on the street next to the trail heading west. A Bike Trail marker sign is positioned within sight of the street where the trail leaves the roadside to enter the forest. This is where you leave the street to take the path.

Now the pavement is smooth and surprisingly clean as the trail makes a delightful tour through the loose growth of pine trees. There is no sight or sound of urban development here, just the trail and the forest, which continues on both sides for nearly a mile.

Lest you think this pretty scenery will prove too tame, two surprise dips and curves add an element of thrill, reminding you that yes, indeed, you are in the mountains. After the second wild dip, the last quarter mile once again becomes docile enough for beginners, passing a sunny meadow dotted with smaller trees. Look to the south to catch brief glimpses of the great lake and the mountain ridges behind it. The path ends in a pile of rubble at the base of the parking lot serving the ball park at North Tahoe Regional Park.

This trail is short enough that you might want to skate it two or three times until you learn when to exercise tight control and when to just let 'em roll. If you do that, make sure to watch out for others on the trail, and try to maintain some respect for the quiet of the forest as you surrender to the urge to yell, "Yeehaw!"

---

3. Squaw Valley Trails   3 miles

Reference: Near the Squaw Valley meadow north of Tahoe City; see number ❸ on page 244.

Ideal for: Hills/Slalom—Touring

Directions: From Interstate 80 near Truckee, exit south on State Highway 89 and continue south for seven miles. Turn right at the entrance to Squaw Valley USA on the right side of the road. Follow the main road toward the ski area as far as the Squaw Valley Property Realty Sales lot. Park here; the trail begins across the street.

Map: Recreation Map of Lake Tahoe, Tom Harrison Cartography, 2 Falmouth Cove, San Rafael, CA 94901-4465; (415) 456-7940.

Local shop: Porter's Ski & Sport, 120 North Lake Boulevard, Tahoe City, CA 96145; (916) 583-0293.

Tour notes: Skate in the Squaw Valley meadow not so much for the paved bike trails, but the fabulous view—across a marshy meadow that runs down the center of the valley like some green royal carpet leading to the throne. Dominating the ridge at the valley's west end is majestic KT-22, an 8,070-foot-high mountain that has turned boys into men and, a few times, into ski-video stars.

The trail on the north edge of the Squaw Valley meadow is one mile long. Skate from its start near the Realty Sales lot; after passing the horse stables, you gain a view to the southeast across the lush grasses and wildflowers, which the presence of a golf course renders only slightly less pristine. A zig-zagging log fence borders the meadow for the rest of the mile, and slight slopes add some fun before you roll to the end of the path across from Victor Road. As you start back, your view of the meadow is best of all, displaying the famous Squaw Valley mountains in a wide tableau. Patches of snow on the northern faces pick up the sunlight to add even more dramatic allure.

If you want a wide, smooth area to practice tricks or figure skating, one repaved area of the ski area parking lot may still be in relatively good condition. From Squaw Valley Road, go left to cross the bridge beyond the Realty Sales lot and turn right off the parking lot road to approach the smoothest pavement. You'll know it when you see it. If you don't see it, winter conditions got to it before you did.

A second trail is located along the road to the Squaw Creek Inn, on the south side of the meadow and the east end of the valley. To find it, follow Squaw Valley Road about a quarter of a mile from Highway 89, and turn in at the Resort at Squaw Creek sign, onto Squaw Creek Road. Take an immediate left to pull into the condo parking lot, and park near the path that crosses the driveway. Skate west on the trail, climbing uphill most of the way. The path, only half a mile long, is not well maintained and may have gravel patches or rough, cracked sections left by the ravages of winter; it would actually be a better skate in the downhill direction—if not for the luscious view of the ski area peaks you have while skating up.

---

4. Alpine Meadows Road   6 miles 🎱 🐾 🏃

Reference: **A ski area access road near north Tahoe City; see number ❹ on page 244.**

Ideal for: Fitness—Hills/Slalom—Road/Street

Directions: From Interstate 80 near Truckee, exit south on State Highway 89 and continue south for seven miles. One mile past the entrance

---

to Squaw Valley USA, the Alpine Meadows sign on the right marks the beginning of Alpine Meadows Road. Pull to the right side of 89 and park on the gravel shoulder next to the bike path near the intersection with Alpine Meadows Road.

Map: Recreation Map of Lake Tahoe, Tom Harrison Cartography, 2 Falmouth Cove, San Rafael, CA 94901-4465; (415) 456-7940.

Local shop: Porter's Ski & Sport, 120 North Lake Boulevard, Tahoe City, CA 96145; (916) 583-0293.

Tour notes: Appropriately enough, Alpine Meadows Road is a favorite Tahoe skiers' cross-training location. Even though it gets plowed and sanded all winter long, the pavement surface is surprisingly smooth, and the off-season car traffic is fairly low. These are important considerations in a place where an 800-foot descent over three miles can easily build skating speeds of up to 40 miles an hour. If you aren't in excellent condition, consider having a friend drop you off at the ski area parking lot on top, because tired legs will limit your speed-control capabilities on the way down. In any case, you should be prepared to handle fast skating and be comfortable sharing the road with cars without benefit of a bike lane.

Start up Alpine Meadows Road by crossing the bridge next to the River Ranch. Climb the first steep section as you pass the little shopping center and condominiums near the intersection with Highway 89. Now the road is relatively flat, winding gradually up past a stable and the maintenance yard. Cross the narrow bridge to begin the second hard climb. From here on, most of the scenery is alpine forests with homes scattered among the trees. The hillside on the right is an active wintertime avalanche zone, but during summer a trailhead allows hikers to enjoy the pine forest and rocky slopes. Just beyond the trail head, the final climb awaits, with a snaking turn thrown in.

On the way back down, the three steeper sections of road will require good technique, along with judicious application of the heel brake. Make sure to keep tight control on the hill down the snaking turn, where you won't be able to see oncoming traffic. The remainder of the descent is manageable with consistent slalom turns and a rest stop or two.

5. Truckee River Bike Trail   7 miles

Reference: Along the Truckee River north of Tahoe City; see number **5** on page 244.

Ideal for: Fitness—Hills/Slalom—Scene—Speed—Touring

Directions: From Interstate 80, exit south on State Highway 89 and proceed to Tahoe City, 12 miles south. Turn right at the stoplight to stay on 89. Less than a quarter mile down, turn right at the sign marked Truckee River Recreation Trail and Public Access. A parking lot is available one-tenth of a mile into the trees. The trail passes near the north end of the lot, close to the bridge over the Truckee River.

Map: Recreation Map of Lake Tahoe, Tom Harrison Cartography, 2 Falmouth Cove, San Rafael, CA 94901-4465; (415) 456-7940.

Local shop: Porter's Ski & Sport, 120 North Lake Boulevard, Tahoe City, CA 96145; (916) 583-0293. Other contact: Tahoe City Parks and Recreation Department, P.O. Box 33, Tahoe City, CA 95730; (916) 583-3796.

Tour notes: The Truckee River Bike Trail is a really fun and hilly trail through beautiful mountain scenery. One of its best assets is that over the entire length, there's only one street intersection to interrupt the flow downstream. The fine pavement on this route attracts so many skaters, you'll swear they make up at least half of the trail population. In any case, on a sunny summer's day you can expect to share this trip with many other fun- and fitness-seekers, including fast-moving bicyclists and slow-moving strollers.

With so many people on the path, you really must mind your best trail manners. For safety's sake, it's important to stick to the right side of the trail (a yellow line down the middle reminds you) and announce your intention to pass when approaching others from behind. Since the pavement is no more than eight feet wide, skaters with wide-stroking speed-skating skills will need to coast to give bicyclists room to pass. Make it a point to step off the trail whenever you pause to admire the river or wait for a friend to catch up.

From the bridge at the Public Access parking lot, turn left onto the trail running beside Highway 89. Be patient as you pass an industrial area and lumberyard; soon the scenery starts to improve, and after a thick patch of riverside brush, the Truckee River finally comes into view. Skating near the mossy-green waters of the canyon, you can almost forget the noise of the traffic on Highway 89 a few feet away; the trail's lower siting, five to ten feet below the highway's, helps block the sound. The narrow intersections you cross for the next mile are merely driveways to the riverbank homes, requiring just a glance to be sure the way is clear. You might notice a gradual descent as you follow the river north; even if you don't, you'll surely feel the gradual ascent on the way back, especially if there's a head wind.

In fact, the trail's slight hilliness is what makes it so much fun. The steepest up-and-down is the hump just south of the River Ranch parking lot; when you skate such steep and narrow sections, try to wait until there's no traffic going either way. Heading north down the hill that dumps you into the River Ranch parking lot, be prepared to make a sudden stop to avoid cars entering and leaving. North of there, cross Alpine Meadows Road (described in the previous listing) and follow the newest section of trail another half mile, past a tiny riverside park, where there's a rest room and picnic tables. The trail ends under the bridge where Highway 89 crosses over the Truckee River. Don't bother climbing the final few steep yards beyond the hairpin turn to another gravel parking area; just turn around and head back to where you started.

If you're in no hurry to get back to your car, the most happening scene is lunch at the River Ranch Inn. An outdoor grill is set up on a riverside patio to supply burgers, smoothies, and beer to tired bodies that need to recover from exercise. No need to remove helmet or skates here; the staff is used to serving come-as-you-are patrons.

6. North Lake Boulevard Bike Path

4.6 miles

Reference: **Along the north shore of Lake Tahoe in Tahoe City; see number ⑥ on page 244.**

Ideal for: Touring

Directions: From Interstate 80, exit south on State Highway 89 and proceed to Tahoe City 12 miles south. North Lake Boulevard starts at the stoplight. Drive through town and park in the Safeway shopping center at the east end of the lot. The dedicated bike path starts on the south side of Highway 89.

Map: Recreation Map of Lake Tahoe, Tom Harrison Cartography, 2 Falmouth Cove, San Rafael, CA 94901-4465; (415) 456-7940.

Local shop: Alpenglow, 415 North Lake Boulevard, Tahoe City, CA 96145; (916) 583-6917.

Tour notes: The North Lake Boulevard Bike Path runs right next to the main road of north Lake Tahoe, connecting the east end of Tahoe City to Dollar Hill. The trail makes a great commute route while also serving as a recreational trail for bicyclists, joggers, equestrians, folks going fishing and, of course, in-line skaters. Unfortunately, for most of its length it doesn't offer much of a view of the lake.

If you're looking to expand your tour to include a picnic or some serious lounging on the beach, though, the trail does offer access to Tahoe State Park, Burton Creek State Park, Skylandia Park, Pomin Park, and Lake Forest Beach. Be prepared to stop for cars when crossing the streets that lead to the lake shore from the boulevard.

At the beginning of the dedicated asphalt trail, the pavement runs west from the Safeway parking lot, on the south side of North Lake Boulevard. A detour onto the frontage road (with no dedicated path) lasts about a quarter mile; watch out for rough asphalt and patches of gravel here. Back on the dedicated path a mile from the Safeway, you reach the Star Harbor housing development, with Lake Tahoe visible across the meadow in front. Half a mile farther on, skate next to the grassy area locals have dubbed "Ghetto Meadow" (home to ski area employees on a budget), a name that belies the pretty scenery you see from the trail. A quarter mile up from here, the path begins its steep .7-mile climb up Dollar Point. At the top, the dedicated bike path ends.

---

7. Blackwood Canyon

5 miles

Reference: **A canyon in West Lake Tahoe; see number
❼ on page 244.**

Ideal for: Beginners—Road/Street—Touring

Directions: From Interstate 80, exit south on State Highway 89 and proceed to Tahoe City 12 miles south. Turn right at the stoplight to stay on 89. Another three miles to the south, look for the Kaspian National Forest and Bicycle Camping sign, then turn west onto Barker Pass Road. Now you're in Blackwood Canyon. You can park on the gravel next to Highway 89 or up next to the rest rooms in the free parking lot that serves the nearby bike-in campgrounds.

Map: Recreation Map of Lake Tahoe, Tom Harrison Cartography, 2 Falmouth Cove, San Rafael, CA 94901-4465; (415) 456-7940.

Local shop: Cycle Paths Mountain Bikes, 1785 West Lake Boulevard, Tahoe City, CA 96145; (916) 581-1171.

Tour notes: Skate through beautiful Blackwood Canyon on deliciously smooth pavement that has never felt the blade of a snowplow. Although Blackwood Canyon Road isn't particularly wide as far as roads go, the traffic is so light that the whole road is your trail—what a luxury! The few cars that do pass are usually driving no more than 35 miles an hour, and local drivers are used to sharing this popular spot with skaters and bicyclists.

This tour begins at the gate near the bicycle campgrounds. There's a very gradual ascent as you enter the canyon, with one quarter-mile stretch that requires a little extra effort. As you skate away from the Highway 89 traffic noise, it's soon replaced by the sounds of buzzing beetles, chirping birds, and water flowing into Blackwood Creek. The pine forests that fill the canyon are populated by tiny squirrels that scamper across the road as you pass, darting into pockets of purple and yellow wildflowers. Although most of the road is bordered by woods, look left to catch glimpses of meadows filled with the golden blossoms of mule ears.

The good pavement terminates at the concrete bridge that crosses Blackwood Creek. Stop and enjoy the view to the west of the infamous Pacific Crest, rising in snow-dappled glory at the far end of the canyon. From here, Blackwood Canyon Road continues up the side of the canyon, but is too steep, narrow, and poorly maintained for skating (fallen branches and rock slides are left right where they landed).

On the way back, the gentle hills are fine for practicing wide slaloms. Level 1 skaters will be able to coast pretty safely here as long as there are no obstacles (as in oncoming cars or other people). For beginners, Blackwood Canyon is also an excellent place to work on those all-important heel-brake skills.

8. West Shore Bike Path — 10 miles 🌟 🚴 🏃

Reference: **Along the shore of West Lake Tahoe; see number ❽ on page 244.**

Ideal for: Fitness—Hills/Slalom—Road/Street—Scene—Touring

Directions: From Interstate 80, exit south on State Highway 89 and proceed to Tahoe City 12 miles south. Turn right at the stoplight on the edge of town to stay on the highway. Less than a quarter mile down, turn right at the sign marked Truckee River Recreation Trail and Public Access. There's a parking lot located .10 mile into the trees; the trail passes near the north end of the lot, close to the bridge over the Truckee River.

Map: Recreation Map of Lake Tahoe, Tom Harrison Cartography, 2 Falmouth Cove, San Rafael, CA 94901-4465; (415) 456-7940.

Local shop: Cycle Paths Mountain Bikes, 1785 West Lake Boulevard, Tahoe City, CA 96145; (916) 581-1171.

Tour notes: Tahoe's West Shore trail is a long and thrilling roll that solid intermediate skaters can enjoy from end to end. The divided, smoothly paved asphalt path passes through tall pine forests and right along a beach at the edge of the lake. However, this hilly route does have a few drawbacks. As you might expect in such a gorgeous setting, traffic on the path becomes increasingly crowded with bicyclists, joggers, and pedestrians toward midday on weekends, so get an early start. Besides negotiating many hills, stay alert for cars, especially in the business districts, where the trail is often replaced by driveways and parking lots. There are four busy highway crossings along the route; none have stoplights, and one doesn't even have a crosswalk.

Starting from the Truckee River Recreation Trail parking lot, access the trail on the west side of the lot and follow it through the trees, back toward the Highway 89 roadside. Go right at the three-way trail intersection. (A left takes you to the parking lot entrance road and just beyond, to the trail's northern end across from the Truckee River Bank.) The trail climbs a long and fairly gentle hill leading up to Grant Road and then passes through the business district. In front of Corpus Christi Catholic Church, where the trail passes through the parking lot, the devout tend to park on top of your pavement on Sundays. A mile from the start, the trail crosses to the east side of Highway 89 at Timberland Lane. Be very careful crossing here, because fast-moving cars appear suddenly from around the corner on either side.

On the lake side of the road, the trail makes a fast descent to merge onto a residential street. Slalom skaters will love this widely paved, fairly steep hill where few cars pass. Follow the bike route signs posted next to the sometimes roughly paved street until you reach the small park on the lake shore to the left. Next to the rest rooms, the dedicated bike path picks up once again, taking you back to Highway 89. A cruise through the trees brings you to the next highway crossing a quarter of a mile south. Across the highway, a short, steep climb introduces you to a nice roll through more pines for half a mile, followed by an even steeper drop down to the next highway crossing, where the trail returns to the highway's shore side. Here is where the most recently repaved section of trail begins.

Another quarter of a mile south, the trail meets the beach and follows Lake Tahoe's western shore for nearly a mile. The rocky beach makes an ideal spot for a short rest or a lazy picnic, offering views of the docks, bikini-clad sunbathers, boaters, and the silhouettes of the Nevada mountains far to the east. After a wet winter, a cloak of white may still cover the shoulders of Freel Peak.

Just before the trail once again veers away from shore, you can look across the highway to find Blackwood Canyon, another excellent skating location (see the previous listing). At the gates of the ritzy community that was once the Kaiser family estate, the trail crosses one last time to the west side of Highway 89, and soon you regain your view of Lake Tahoe. The dedicated path gives way to a roadside bike lane at Cherry Street.

---

9. Sugar Pine Point Trail
4 miles

Reference: **Connecting Meeks and McKinney Bays at West Lake Tahoe; see number ❾ on page 244.**

Ideal for: Touring

Directions: From Interstate 80, exit south on State Highway 89 and proceed to Tahoe City 12 miles south. Turn right at the stoplight to stay on 89 and continue south another nine miles to Meeks Bay. The trail crosses Highway 89 just before the Meeks Bay State Park entrance. You can park for free on the shoulder near the trail crossing, or pay $5 to park in the state park's lot. The southern termination of the trail is just a few yards away from the park's entrance kiosk.

Map: Recreation Map of Lake Tahoe, Tom Harrison Cartography, 2 Falmouth Cove, San Rafael, CA 94901-4465; (415) 456-7940.

Local shop: Cycle Paths Mountain Bikes, 1785 West Lake Boulevard, Tahoe City, CA 96145; (916) 581-1171.

Tour notes: The Lake Tahoe western shore trail at Sugar Pine Point starts just south of the Ehrlman mansion, in a forest belonging to the Edwin L. Z'Berg Natural Preserve. As of the summer of 1995, the eight-foot-wide asphalt path was newly resurfaced and a joy to skate. Be forewarned, though, that the scenery it passes is restricted to inland towns and forests along Highway 89, and not the lake views one might expect.

The trail starts with a descent from Sugar Pine Point State Park near the Ehrlman mansion. After a mile, it enters the town of Tahoma, where it crosses to the west side of Highway 89. Here, as it passes through town, the trail is broken up to accommodate business driveways, parking lots, and intersections with residential streets. On busy summer weekends, stick to your own side of the yellow line, because this trail—like others in the Tahoe area—can get very busy. The dedicated bike path ends shortly after it crosses McKinney Creek.

---

10. Pat Lowe Memorial Bike Trail 1.5 miles ⑥ 🏕 🏃

Reference: **In the town of Meyers, just outside South Lake Tahoe; see number ⑩ on page 244.**

Ideal for: Beginners—Touring

Directions: From U.S. 50 in Meyers at the south end of Lake Tahoe, turn south onto State Highway 89. Take the first left onto Pomo Street and park on the north shoulder right at this corner, where you'll see the trail's beginning. To park slightly farther up the trail, stay on U.S. 50 and turn right on Navajo Road, where you can park on the gravel shoulder, just behind the visitor center parking lot (parking at the center itself is limited to 15 minutes).

Map: Recreation Map of Lake Tahoe, Tom Harrison Cartography, 2 Falmouth Cove, San Rafael, CA 94901-4465; (415) 456-7940.

Local shop: Vertical Sports Limited, 2318 South Lake Tahoe Boulevard #4, South Lake Tahoe, CA 96150; (916) 542-1411.

Tour notes: For most of its length, the Pat Lowe Memorial Bike Trail borders Highway 89. To appreciate the beauty of the mountain scenery that surrounds you, make it a point to look beyond the highway: admire the peaks of the range to the west, or peer into the forest on the south side of the trail.

Bordering both sides of U.S. 50, the Pat Lowe trail is a good spot for beginning skaters to hone their skills before exploring the more advanced Tahoe-area trails; this smoothly paved, eight-foot-wide asphalt is as flat a path as you'll see in these mountainous parts. From the start at Pomo Street, the trail makes a right turn to parallel U.S. 50, then passes behind the visitor center and continues next to several rather unattractive roadside businesses. Within the first quarter mile, a nearly neon two-dimensional sculpture of a cliff-jumping skier is mounted in an open area amoung the trees just off to your right, standing in bright contrast to the muted colors of the surrounding pines. Cross Apache Street and then pass the Wedding Paradise

---

Chapel, where you might see a ceremony in progress in the gardens; the grass of a nearby golf course adds a rich backdrop of green.

Soon after the trail enters the edge of a pine forest, it comes to an end at Pioneer Trail, which is decidedly *not* a trail. However, this street does have a bike lane on both shoulders. Although the pavement is pretty rough, an ambitious and fit skater could follow Pioneer Trail for five and a half miles up the long, almost constant hill to the bike path on Al Tahoe Boulevard, described in the College Bike Path Route (see the next listing).

Backtracking on the Pat Lowe Memorial Bike Trail, you can cross to the trail to the north side of U.S. 50 from the parking lot driveway near the Century 21 real estate office, providing the traffic is light enough. There's no crosswalk over the busy highway, so cross at your own risk. The trail's north section is just as close to the highway's edge as the south section was, so don't be too distracted by the gorgeous ridge to the west; there's constant traffic to and from the gas station, the Indian fur shop, and the home supply store. Cross back to the south section of trail at the U.S. 50/Highway 89 intersection, again with no crosswalk or stoplight to protect you. (Beginners should stick to one side of U.S. 50.)

---

11. College Bike Path   4 miles

Reference: A bike path in South Lake Tahoe; see number ❶ on page 244.

Ideal for: Hills/Slalom—Touring

Directions: From U.S. 50 in South Lake Tahoe, take Al Tahoe Boulevard heading southeast. Turn right at the entrance to Lake Tahoe Community College and follow the signs to park in the lots on the south side of the campus.

Map: Recreation Map of Lake Tahoe, Tom Harrison Cartography, 2 Falmouth Cove, San Rafael, CA 94901-4465; (415) 456-7940.

Local shop: Vertical Sports Limited, 2318 South Lake Tahoe Boulevard #4, South Lake Tahoe, CA 96150; (916) 542-1411.

Tour notes: If you're willing to turn your back on the namesake attraction in these parts, the best east-facing scene in South Lake Tahoe is the spectacular view of snowcapped Freel Peak framed by a pine forest that's rooted in a bed of bright lavender lupines. Al Tahoe Boulevard's roadside bike path connects the bike lanes on Pioneer Trail with nearby South Lake Tahoe Community College, a campus situated in such beautiful natural scenery that there's absolutely no need for man-made landscaping. A series of smooth asphalt trails serves pedestrians and wheeled folks on the campus grounds. As an added attraction, in-line hockey enthusiasts meet every Sunday afternoon at a parking lot that was seemingly designed for their favorite summer sport. You can see hockey lines painted on the blacktop, and the faint, tell-tale arcing streaks left by in-line wheels on the pavement.

Follow the path at the northern border of the parking lots, or skate on the smoothly paved street past the modest administration buildings (not an area worth exploring, as the tiled concrete has big cracks) and back out to Al Tahoe Boulevard. Turn right onto the dedicated bike path that leads east, and follow next to the zigzagging wooden fence. From here on there's forest on your right and lots of trees in the neighborhoods across the street on your left. On the Al Tahoe bike path, you'll skate across some pretty wide (but not raised) cracks in the otherwise-good asphalt. Keep your skates perpendicular to the cracks and you'll roll right over without even noticing them. A couple of fairly long, not-too-steep hills adds to the fun. At the top of the best hill, you can stop and rest on the fence across from the landscaped Marjory Anne Johnson Springmeyer Conservancy sign. The last quarter mile is flanked by trees, with filtered sunlight dappling the carpet of lavender lupines below. The path ends at the street called Pioneer Trail. On the way back, turn left onto the first college entrance trail, a quarter mile east of the one you started out on. That path takes you across the eastern edge of the campus through the pine forest, before returning you to the parking lot area.

---

12. El Dorado Trail   4 miles

Reference: **Near the shores of South Lake Tahoe; see number ⑫ on page 244.**

Ideal for: Beginners—Fitness—Touring

Directions: From U.S. 50 in the El Dorado area of South Lake Tahoe, turn toward the lake at the Lakeview Avenue stoplight. Park wherever you can find a spot, in a lot or on a street nearby. On weekends, you may have to go a block or two south of El Dorado Park to find a shoulder on neighborhood streets.

Map: Recreation Map of Lake Tahoe, Tom Harrison Cartography, 2 Falmouth Cove, San Rafael, CA 94901-4465; (415) 456-7940.

Local shop: Lakeview Sports, 3131 Highway 50, South Lake Tahoe, CA, 96150; (916) 544-1083.

Tour notes: On a sunny summer day, vistas across Lake Tahoe are spectacular from small El Dorado Park at South Lake Tahoe Recreation Area. A plush lawn borders the trail here, and the straight trunks of tall pines frame the view in individual snapshots as you roll by. Near the beach, the bright-colored umbrellas of snack vendors by the picnic tables add a festive note; it's a pity that traffic noise from nearby Lake Tahoe Boulevard never lets up.

Skate north to the end of the El Dorado Trail a quarter of a mile away. The rest of this trip basically extends your skate with a loop through the campgrounds, followed by an excursion south to the edge of the Tahoe Keys housing development.

At the north end of El Dorado Park, cross Lake Tahoe Boulevard at the Rufus Allen Boulevard stoplight to enter the city campground, a prime vacation spot if ever there was one. Go straight to follow Rufus Allen on the northern edge of the campground. When the path ends at the public works yard, take to the street for just a few feet. Turn right up the driveway (on terribly rough, dirty pavement) to the recreation area swimming pool, then go left behind the pool building to skate on better asphalt, around to where the bike path resumes in the forest to the south. The path curves first west and then north, with two or three options for returning to busy Lake Tahoe Boulevard. When you reach Lakeview Avenue, cross back over to El Dorado Park. The total campground loop is no more than three quarters of a mile long.

If you don't mind losing your view of Lake Tahoe, you can put some real mileage on your wheels by continuing south. Start out next to U.S. 50, following the bike route signs that take you to the frontage road, Harrison Avenue. The path is patchy here: sometimes it's a street and sometimes a bike path. Watch for stop signs. After crossing Los Angeles Boulevard, the path becomes a wide, landscaped asphalt trail for a couple of blocks, crosses the rough wooden bridge near the Edgewood neighborhood, then veers away from Lake Tahoe Boulevard near the pretty, marshy meadow surrounding Trout Creek. Watch for the low section of trail behind the lumberyard; it may be under water during the spring thaw. If it's too wet, return to the shoulder of Highway 50 to walk around the lumberyard on the dirt.

South of Trout Creek, the trail enters a neighborhood in the forest, where you do a bit of street skating among the homes (in very low traffic). Keep your eyes open for the Bike Route signs and watch for some large cracks in the pavement. At the end of Ponderosa Street, you'll enter the south section of Truckee Marsh, a lovely wet meadow traversed by the Upper Truckee River. But to earn that view, you must first cross the river on a very long, rough wooden bridge; try to keep up your speed and it'll feel smoother. Skate through one more neighborhood, and soon the trail ends at the bike lane that runs up and down Tahoe Keys Boulevard.

---

13. Camp Richardson Trail   4.5 miles 🎱 🛼 🏃

Reference: **Near Camp Richardson Resort, in South Lake Tahoe; see number ⓭ on page 244.**

Ideal for: Hills/Slalom—Historic—Touring

Directions: At the south end of Lake Tahoe, follow State Highway 89 west from the U.S. 50 intersection for approximately 1.5 miles. Look for the National Forest Lands/Lake Tahoe Basin sign on the right side of the road. About .2 mile after this sign, park on the gravel shoulder of Highway 89, where you'll see the trail's beginning at the edge of the trees.

Map: Recreation Map of Lake Tahoe, Tom Harrison Cartography, 2 Falmouth Cove, San Rafael, CA 94901-4465; (415) 456-7940.

Local shop: Lakeview Sports, 3131 Highway 50, South Lake Tahoe, CA, 96150; (916) 544-1083.

Tour notes: In the middle of a long, hot summer, come to the high country near Lake Tahoe to enjoy spring all over again. The green season is still in full bloom up at 6,000 feet in July. Wildflowers in wide variety display their colors beneath the pines and in small meadows next to the Camp Richardson Trail.

Enter the trail where it veers into the trees next to Highway 89. The eight-foot-wide asphalt path is smooth, but in a few places near the highway it's scattered with piles of gravel, a remnant of winter attempts at ice control. Cracks up to two inches wide look more threatening then they feel—just roll straight across.

Half a mile from the start, the trail passes the Pope Beach entrance, where the pavement takes a temporary turn for the worse. Pass the Camp Richardson Resort entrance and its general store. Note the ice cream parlor across the highway.

Following the trail's westward route, make sure to enjoy the great view of Mount Tallac through the trees ahead. Though the trail generally parallels Highway 89, in places it does get far enough away to escape the traffic noise. As the trail curves northwest, it dips into meadows and passes tall grasses in the shade of the loosely spaced pines flanking the road. The path crosses only one bridge, but it's a bridge to beat all others, with smooth concrete spanning the outlet of Fallen Leaf Lake.

On the return trip, turn left at the Baldwin Park entrance road to pass through historic old estates that have been converted for public use. A wide asphalt path can be found at the east edge of the parking lot. Skate through the shady grounds of the Baldwin House, past several old structures and a blacksmith shop, and enjoy glimpses of Lake Tahoe between the buildings and trees. At Valhalla House on the far side of the Baldwin estate, the path veers back up to rejoin the Camp Richardson Trail.

Have you ever tried dancing on in-lines? On weekend afternoons, it's party time at Richardson Resort. Skate past the entrance kiosk (and over some rough pavement) to the bar at the end of the street. Opportunities for fun include a live band and beer on the deck overlooking the lake. This is the place to be, on skates or not.

14. Upper Pines Loop   2.25 miles 🌟 🏔 🏊

Reference: **In Yosemite National Park, a loop at the northeast end of Yosemite Valley; see number ⑭ on page 244.**

Ideal for: Road/Street—Touring

Directions: From Groveland, follow Highway 120 (Tioga Pass Road) east to the entrance of Yosemite National Park. Pay the $5 entrance fee (good for the next five days at any National Park, as long as you save your receipt). At the Crane Flat area, continue straight ahead to bypass the Tioga Pass turnoff and continue another 10 miles to the Yosemite Valley via New Big Oak Flat Road. Pass through the valley floor for another five miles on the one-way road that passes Housekeeping Camp and Curry Village. Just past Curry Village, go straight at the four-way intersection to park in the Curry Village lot on the right. Your route starts on the bike path that runs along the street you just drove in on, heading east.

Local shop: Oakdale Sports, 1275 East F Street, Oakdale, CA 95361-4140; (209) 847-0648.

Tour notes: The Upper Pines loop is a wide, slightly sloped road where cars are excluded, but bicycles, shuttle buses, and skaters are allowed. As you leave Curry Village behind, you'll pass through one of those fantastic Yosemite meadows that offers views of sheer granite walls graced with splashing, thundering cascades of snow melt. The road curves east into the trees, passing an intersection near Upper Pines campground. Continue straight ahead into the woods. (If you want, you can follow a nearby bike lane through the trees instead, but why bother when there's that wonderful wide road?)

Half a mile beyond the intersection, you come to the Happy Isles Nature Center, located at the trailhead for the Vernal and Nevada Falls and Half Dome hikes. If you have a skate carrier, sturdy shoes, and a day pack, it's entirely feasible, and even desirable, to skate to the trailhead, swap skate gear for shoes, and hike up to Vernal Falls and back (less than four miles round-trip) before continuing around the loop. The wide asphalt sidewalk from the road up to the Nature Center is smooth and, in between shuttle buses, empty enough for some short but fun "roll-bys." There are two possible paths for this purpose; the one on the south side (behind the busy rest rooms) is less crowded and has just enough slope to allow you to pick up some speed. Stay alert near the merging bike path on the left as you approach the loop road.

Leaving Happy Isles, go right to continue around the loop. Half a mile up the forested road and around a bend, you'll come to the intersection with the Mirror Lake Road route (see the next listing). Stay to the left to skate past the stables and across the bridge on the only section of road open to cars; that returns you to the Upper Pines intersection described above. Turn right there to return to the Curry Village parking lot.

---

15. Mirror Lake Road 5.5 miles ⑩ 🚴 🛼

Reference: **In Yosemite National Park, a lake in Yosemite Valley; see number ⑮ on page 244.**

Ideal for: Fitness—Hills/Slalom—Touring

Directions: From Groveland, follow Highway 120 (Tioga Pass Road) east to the entrance of Yosemite National Park. Pay the $5 entrance fee (good for the next five days at any National Park, as long as you save your receipt). At Crane Flat, continue straight ahead to bypass the Tioga Pass turnoff and continue another 10 miles to the Yosemite Valley via New Big Oak Flat Road. Go through the valley floor for another five miles on the one-way road that passes Housekeeping Camp and Curry Village. Just past Curry Village, go straight at the four-way intersection to park in the Curry Village lot just beyond on the right. The bike path starts at the bridge back at the four-way intersection, and heads west.

Map: The "Yosemite Guide Newsletter" and a map are handed out for free at all entrance kiosks.

Local shop: Oakdale Sports, 1275 East F Street, Oakdale, CA 95361-4140; (209) 847-0648.

Tour notes: Mirror Lake Road is the best skate in Yosemite Valley for working up an aerobic (and possibly anaerobic) heart rate. The climb to Mirror Lake can make you breathless, and if it doesn't, the view of Half Dome on the way up is sure to do the trick. But if you don't know how to control your speed on long downhills, don't skate here: your crash and burn could be the one to make this spot off-limits to the rest of us.

Starting from the Curry Village parking lot where you parked (it's dirt, so you might want to carry your skates to the bike path), cross the one-way street and follow the bike path across Stoneman's Bridge heading west. You'll see the Upper River campgrounds on your right, and just a few yards through the trees beyond the entrance, you'll come to a three-way trail intersection. Instead of the left turn to Yosemite Village and Falls (see the next listing), take the right turn toward Mirror Lake.

Soon you'll cross two bridges over a 180-degree curve in the Merced River; the trail widens out to street width as you cross, so there's plenty of room to practice a few tricks, with low stone walls to keep you from rolling off into the water. The trail continues on through the trees, in some places 10 feet wide.

A dip to the right, followed by a sharp turn to the left, brings you out onto the wide road leading up the Mirror Lake Road hill. No cars are allowed here except for those carrying disabled visitors, so there's lots of room to make the wide strokes you'll need to ascend the remaining half mile. Watch out for loose gravel on the surface, but make sure you look up to enjoy the view and to check the trees for tame, grazing deer. The first half of the hill is the steepest; as the road curves toward the left, the grade relaxes a little, and once you get to the top, so can you. Rest on the rocks overlooking Mirror Lake with its reflections of Half Dome and Cloud's Rest. There's a small half-gravel, half-asphalt parking lot just around the corner where you can cruise around a bit before heading back down. If you want to slalom back, wait for an uncrowded interval to make sure there's plenty of room, and don't forget to watch for the gravel patches. Otherwise, ride near the edge of the road with your heel brake dragging or at the ready. And just so you know, visitors from other countries (there are many here) don't behave predictably near skaters.

16. Yosemite Falls to Curry Village

3 miles

Reference: **In Yosemite National Park, a connecting trail in the Yosemite Valley; see number ⑯ on page 244.**

Ideal for: Beginners—Historic—Touring

Directions: From Groveland, follow Highway 120 (Tioga Pass Road) east to the entrance of Yosemite National Park. Pay the $5 entrance fee (good for the next five days at any National Park, as long as you save your receipt). At Crane Flat, continue straight ahead to bypass the Tioga Pass turnoff and continue another 10 miles to the Yosemite Valley via New Big Oak Flat Road. Go through the valley floor for another five miles on the one-way road that passes Housekeeping Camp and Curry Village. Just past Curry Village, go straight at the four-way intersection to park in the Curry Village lot just beyond on the right. The bike path starts at the bridge back at the four-way intersection, and heads west.

Local shop: Oakdale Sports, 1275 East F Street, Oakdale, CA 95361-4140; (209) 847-0648. Other contact: U.S. Department of the Interior, National Park Service, P.O. Box 577, Yosemite, CA 95389.

Tour notes: This Yosemite route is one of the most remarkably beautiful skating trails you'll ever see, bar none. And part of the beauty is the fact that even beginning skaters can successfully make their way from one end of the central Yosemite Valley to the other, as long as they know how to stop for intersections.

As you skate along in either direction, you can admire a changing view of the immense granite walls rising straight up on both sides of the valley. Through the groves of trees on the valley floor, you glimpse the famous Half Dome, El Capitan, and Yosemite Falls, the tallest waterfall in North America.

Depending on where you park or camp, you can access this trail from any number of points, but this description starts near Curry Village, at the intersection where one-way Southside Drive, which runs east, meets Northside Drive, which crosses the Merced River to return to the other end of the park. Starting from the Curry Village parking lot where you parked, cross the one-way street and follow the bike path across Stoneman's Bridge heading west. Follow the trail past the Upper and Lower River campgrounds. Just past Upper River's entrance road, you meet up with the Mirror Lake bike path (see the previous listing) at a triangle intersection meant to encourage compliance with the yield and stop signs. Make sure to comply, especially during peak times when trail users are at their densest (in both senses of the word). Take the left fork.

Now the trail enters its first open meadow, where you get one more great view of Yosemite Falls; the Awahnee Hotel is hidden in the trees at the base of the cliffs across the way. As the trail nears the visitor center and Yosemite Village, trees hide those buildings as well, but driveways and streets give them away. The busiest intersection is at the road leading in to Yosemite Village; cross here and gently climb as you enjoy another spectacular view of Yosemite Falls, perfectly framed by the trees on either side of the path.

As you near the visitor center, the trail merges with the wide pedestrian way, and you can skate pretty much wherever you want. Some areas are big enough to practice stunts or sloped enough to string together a series of ski turns to impress the crowds.

Continuing, you cross a few more intersections, then enter another luscious meadow that opens up the scenery. This time, you can also see the massive granite walls across the valley before entering a pine forest that guards the base of Yosemite Falls. The trail then comes to a busy bus parking lot next to the walkway that leads to the bottom of the thundering waterfall. If it's not too crowded, you can skate up the walkway, which takes you through a corridor of trees directly under the falls. It's a perfect photo opportunity, as so many people around you will demonstrate. They may not see you as they snap pictures or smile for the camera, so be extra-careful here. The walkway ends at the path leading up to the base of the falls; that path is crowded, steep, wet, and rough enough to dislodge the grip of your heel brake, so don't try skating it.

17. Swinging Bridge Loop   1.75 miles

Reference: **In Yosemite National Park, a tour of the southwest end of Yosemite Valley; see number ⑰ on page 244.**

Ideal for: Beginners—Touring

Directions: From Groveland, follow Highway 120 (Tioga Pass Road) east to the entrance of Yosemite National Park. Pay the $5 entrance fee (good for the next five days at any national park, as long as you save your receipt). At Crane Flat, continue straight ahead to bypass the Tioga Pass turnoff and go another 10 miles to the Yosemite Valley via New Big Oak Flat Road. Pass through the valley floor until just past the chapel. Turn left to cross a bridge over the Merced River heading toward Yosemite Village; when you reach the village, turn left onto the one-way road that heads back toward the park entrance. Park in one of the Yosemite Falls lots. The bike path starts at the west end of the parking lots, heading toward the meadows through the series of small huts in the Yosemite Lodge/Sunnyside Walk-In Campground.

Local shop: Oakdale Sports, 1275 East F Street, Oakdale, CA 95361-4140; (209) 847-0648.

Tour notes: Bear with me (pardon the Yosemite pun) as you pass through a non-scenic section of Yosemite Valley. Farther on, after the sandy trip past the green wooden walk-in huts and around the rather barren employee housing, the scenery once again meets Yosemite standards.

Pass the sand test, and you earn a beautiful vista of a grassy meadow, the glistening Merced River, and the unmistakable profile of Cathedral Rocks across the valley, framed by tall pines. Down the meadow you roll, until you reach the swinging bridge over the river. Fortunately, it doesn't swing noticeably. Across the river, the trail passes a picnic area in the trees and curves up the meadow, running close to Southside Drive and its camera-snapping crowds. On a busy day, rather than fighting your way through the tourist throngs, you might as well join 'em: take a moment to sit on the low wooden fence to admire the view of Yosemite Falls. Past the chapel, the trail veers back across the meadow toward the village; once it meets the road, cross to the other side to return to your starting point on the paved bike path.

---

18. Minaret Road   8 miles

Reference: **A ski area access road in Mammoth Lakes; see number ⑱ on page 244.**

Ideal for: Fitness—Hills/Slalom—Road/Street

Directions: From U.S. 395, exit at the Mammoth Lakes junction, State Highway 203 heading west. About 3.75 miles from the junction, Highway 203 takes a right at the second stoplight in town to turn up Minaret Road, leading to the ski area. Turn left and go just a block or

---

two up this street to park in the Footloose Ski Shop parking lot. Stop in and say hi before you skate up the hill.

Local shop: Footloose Ski Shop, 6175 Minaret Road, Mammoth Lakes, CA 93546; (619) 934-2400.

Tour notes: How many times do you get a chance to skate on a state highway? Minaret Road, otherwise known as State Highway 203, is strictly for strong and experienced skaters who are fit enough to climb for four miles and skilled enough to skate back down in the traffic lane.

Starting at Footloose Ski Shop, you can skate in the bike lane all the way up Minaret Road to the Mammoth Mountain ski area. It gets pretty curvy and narrow-shouldered in a couple of sections, so stay close to the edge of the pavement and keep your ears open so you won't be surprised by cars. After three quarters of a mile, you'll pass the Mammoth Scenic Loop, an emergency access road from Upper Mammoth Lakes to U.S. 395. This is a possible alternate skate, but the 4.5-mile-long Scenic Loop has no shoulders, fairly rough pavement, low traffic, and a gradual climb; weigh its pros and cons against your own skating skills to decide if you'd enjoy it.

The scenery is mostly forest on both sides of Minaret Road, with an occasional glimpse through the trees of mountain peaks to the south. Another mile up, the shoulder becomes wider where parking is allowed on busy ski days. As you near the ski area, these wide shoulders expand here and there into parking lots, which in early spring may be strewn with gravel left over from the wintertime practice of sanding icy roads. During the last two miles, the road rolls up and down on its journey to the Mammoth Main Lodge. At the lodge area, rest up so you'll be ready to enjoy the fast ride back down to town. If you're a dedicated hill skater or ski cross trainer, see if you can hitch a ride back up for another run or two.

19. The Ghetto
2.5 miles 🌀 🔙 🛼

Reference: **A residential area in the town of Mammoth Lakes; see number ⑲ on page 244.**

Ideal for: Beginners—Fitness

Directions: From U.S. 395, exit at the Mammoth Lakes junction, State Highway 203 heading west. Take Center Street, the second left just beyond the Old Mammoth Road stoplight, and immediately turn right to get onto Main Street South, the frontage road beside busy Highway 203. Park in the business parking lot near the intersection with Manzanita, the first street to the left, or near any of the intersections with the next three streets that run north-south to connect Main Street South with Meridian.

Local shop: Footloose Ski Shop, 6175 Minaret Road, Mammoth Lakes, CA 93546; (619) 934-2400.

Tour notes: This downtown Mammoth Lakes neighborhood is a good place for checking out the resident youth culture while skating a few laps to get an aerobic workout. A recent repaving project left some prime in-line surfaces in what locals call the ghetto, a forested enclave of small, older A-frames whose residents range from ski or snowboard addicts to serious athletes to folks just trying to make a living in one of California's biggest playlands.

As with most of the roads in Mammoth Lakes, there are no painted bike paths here, but traffic is generally scant enough that you can skate in the street without any problems. Smooth pavement runs up and down four half-mile-long, north-south streets: Joaquin, Lupin, Mono, and Manzanita, with Dorrance Drive crossing them east-west at the midway point. The southern border is wide Meridian Road, and at the north end is Main Street South, a low-traffic and equally fine frontage road, with a gradual westward incline that parallels the rise of Highway 203 nearby.

---

20. Meridian Trail/ Main Path Loop

3.25 miles 🔟 🏃

Reference: A loop on the southeast outskirts of Mammoth Lakes; see number ⑳ on page 244.

Ideal for: Figure/Stunts—Hills/Slalom—Touring

Directions: From U.S. 395, exit at the Mammoth Lakes junction, which is State Highway 203 heading west. About three miles up, just after you pass the U.S. Forest Service and Visitor Center on the right, turn left at the first stoplight onto Old Mammoth Road. Drive four blocks to cross Meridian Boulevard at the second light, the mall corner. A block and a half farther on, just after crossing Chateau Road, you'll see the parking lot and jungle gyms of Mammoth Creek Park on the left. Turn in and park here. You'll find toilets and a drinking fountain; the trail starts on the south side of the parking lot. (Though small, this lot has prime-quality pavement and is great for play.)

Local shop: Footloose Ski Shop, 6175 Minaret Road, Mammoth Lakes, CA 93546; (619) 934-2400.

Tour notes: The alpine views from the southern section of this loop are so beautiful that in spite of the drab, developed, and dirt-strewn Meridian Trail section, the trip still earns a solid "must-skate" rating of 10—for those with the skills to handle it, that is. Words truly are inadequate to express the impact of the Sierras seen from this close; their dramatic beauty, a product of nature's most powerful geologic forces, will make even the jaded feel privileged to admire their steep granite slopes.

Starting from the parking lot of Mammoth Creek Park, skate down a short slope toward the bank of Mammoth Creek, and turn left at the

"T" intersection with the Main Path Loop. (At this writing, the pavement to the right was only a quarter mile long and terminated at the shoulder of Old Mammoth Road. However, it looked as though the town had plans to extend that section, perhaps to the condominiums farther up the street.) The Main Path dips in an underpass under Old Mammoth Road, and then rises to traverse the north bank of Mammoth Creek heading east. On the left, a gravel road is near enough to cause an irritating dust cloud whenever a car passes by. Fortunately, traffic here is fairly low, and you cross the road a quarter of a mile up (on the only section of the road that's paved) and leave it behind.

Little markers depicting cross-country skiers are mounted high on metal stakes beside the trail, to point the way when the path is buried under winter snow. Stop and turn around after climbing the first hill to admire the view of Mammoth Mountain and, behind it, the peaks of the Minarets and 13,000-foot-high (give or take a hundred feet) Mount Ritter and Banner Peak. Just a bit farther up, over the hump, you can skate out to a vista point, furnished with benches and a railing so you can really relax and enjoy the 365-degree view of desert valleys backed by truly mammoth peaks.

Beyond the vista point, the trail curves toward the north and through some trees, with a rather long descent. If it feels too narrow for your slalom abilities, ride your heel brake to retain speed control. Just after a hard swerve to the right, the trail rises to meet Meridian Boulevard at Commerce Drive. This is the official end of the Main Path, so there's no pedestrian crosswalk to join up with the Meridian Trail. To get there, cross Meridian Boulevard to Commerce Drive, and just a few yards up Commerce, go left at the entrance sign for the start of Meridian Trail. The pavement connecting the street with the trail rises abruptly at the curb and climbs steeply before making a sharp curve to the right. This is important to know if you plan on doing the loop in the opposite, clockwise direction, because you'd be moving pretty fast when you roll onto Commerce Drive.

The Meridian Trail scenery starts out industrial, then borders the elementary and high schools closer to downtown. Making up for the restricted eight-foot width of the bike path, the elementary school driveway offers wide, smooth pavement to practice hill skating. The game courts on the west side of the school are big enough for carefree stunt practice or figure skating.

Just up the trail (and up another hill), the high school has basketball courts a yard away from the trail. Between the volleyball courts and the auto shop, the dirt and gravel covering the trail was so thick during one recent visit that skating was impossible. This may have been a temporary result of spring melting, though, and the trouble zone was only about 30 feet long. The trail ends at the corner of

Sierra Park Road. Cross Meridian quickly at this corner, because it's on a rise and oncoming drivers can't see you until the last minute. Once in the shopping center parking lot, stay alert as you make your way toward the west side to skate south along Old Mammoth Road, which has no shoulders or bike lanes. A string of parking lot pavement extends almost all the way back to your car, leaving only half a block where you must skate on Old Mammoth Road. A short access trail returns you to the Main Path Loop, where you can skate back under Old Mammoth Road to return to Mammoth Creek Park.

---

21. Ranch Road   3 miles 🎱 👤 🛼

Reference: **South of downtown Mammoth Lakes; see number ㉑ on page 244.**

Ideal for: Hills/Slalom—Touring

Directions: From U.S. 395, exit at the Mammoth Lakes junction, State Highway 203 heading west. About three miles up, turn left onto Old Mammoth Road at the first stoplight, and drive the four blocks through town. Cross Meridian Boulevard at the second light, the mall corner. The street veers west to pass Snowcreek Golf Course after crossing the creek, and soon after, you'll see Ranch Road on the left. Turn down the slight slope and park in the paved lot just a block down, on the right side of the road.

Local shop: Footloose Ski Shop, 6175 Minaret Road, Mammoth Lakes, CA 93546; (619) 934-2400.

Tour notes: It may be short, but Ranch Road is a great place to get into hill skating. Surrounded by this area's wealth of natural beauty, you can really enjoy a repetitive workout while improving your speed control, braking skills, and slalom turns.

To get the full mileage and an additional hill out of this one, start by skating back up to the stop sign where Ranch Road meets Old Mammoth Road. Coming back down Ranch Road, you'll be able to do lots of slalom turns due to the gentle slope and lack of traffic, and what better way to cross-train on a day off from skiing? Half a mile from the starting point, the road forks off into two half-mile streets, both of them cul-de-sacs. Take the high road on the right to stay on steeper, curvier Ranch Road, with its expensive-looking homes (the main plus is the joy of skating back down once you've climbed it). Take the lower lefthand fork to skate up easier, better-paved Woodcrest Trail, with its unobstructed Sierra views to the east.

22. Fairway Drive
1.5 miles ⭐🔟 🛼 🎿

Reference: **In the town of Mammoth Lakes; see number**
㉒ on page 244.

Ideal for: Beginners

Directions: From U.S. 395, exit at the Mammoth Lakes junction, State
Highway 203 heading west. About three miles up, turn left onto Old
Mammoth Road at the first stoplight, and drive the four blocks
through town. Cross Meridian Boulevard at the second light, the mall
corner. After crossing the creek, the street veers toward the west to
pass Snowcreek Golf Course, and soon after, you'll see Fairway Drive
on the left. Turn in and park just after the landscaping ends, on the
east shoulder where the pavement is wide enough to accommodate
two or three cars.

Local shop: Footloose Ski Shop, 6175 Minaret Road, Mammoth Lakes,
CA 93546; (619) 934-2400.

Tour notes: Beginning skaters, do you feel tense, awkward, unable to
make an effective stroke? Here's a great location for a first or early
skating experience. Fairway Drive is very flat, very smooth, and very
pretty. And although it's a public road leading out to the Snowcreek
condos, most of the time traffic is usually minimal.

Take your eyes off the pavement when you skate here, and instead
gaze up at the mountains in the distance all around. The mesmerizing
beauty of those grand formations is bound to help you relax. The lush
greens of Snowcreek Golf Course run along the road's western border, making up for the drab desert scrub that's so prevalent in these
parts. There's a driving range just across Old Mammoth Road—just
one more reason to make sure you wear your helmet.

23. Lake Mary Loop
3.75 miles ⭐9️⃣ 🛼3️⃣ 🎿

Reference: **A loop just south of the town of Mammoth Lakes;**
see number ㉓ on page 244.

Ideal for: Fitness—Hills/Slalom—Road/Street—Touring

Directions: From U.S. 395, exit at the Mammoth Lakes junction, State
Highway 203 heading west. At the second stoplight in the town of
Mammoth Lakes, about 3.75 miles up from the junction, the road
becomes Lake Mary Road. (Highway 203 takes a right turn here and
becomes Minaret Road, heading toward the ski area.) Go straight on
Lake Mary Road and proceed another three miles past Twin Lakes,
taking the high road on the left at the "Y" intersection, until you
reach a bend where Lake Mary Road makes a 180-degree turn back
toward the west. Right in the middle of this bend, turn left onto
Crystal Crag Drive, and park at the campground parking lot. Crystal
Crag Drive is the Lake Mary Loop.

Local shop: Footloose Ski Shop, 6175 Minaret Road, Mammoth Lakes, CA 93546; (619) 934-2400.

Tour notes: The Lake Mary Loop is one of the most popular places to skate in the Mammoth Lakes area, no surprise given its many blessings. To name a few: it's only about two and a half miles south of downtown Mammoth Lakes, it's surrounded by the gorgeous lakeside scenery and pine forests of Mammoth Lakes Basin, traffic is usually low enough to allow worry-free road skating, and the pavement is unplowed in winter, meaning it's protected by a layer of snow during the year's most brutal weather. It seems quite fitting that the Tamarack Cross-Country Ski Center, located just up the road at Twin Lakes, should have the Lake Mary Loop marked on its trail maps; in fact, Tamarack skiers who love to skate are directed to special lanes of the Loop where they can hone skills that translate directly to the pavement later in the year.

There's one fairly steep hill on the loop, so bring along your slalom abilities or heel-braking skills. After you return to your car, you might be tempted to explore Lake Mary Road farther to the west. Don't bother; the pavement is poor and the tar patches so grabby in summer heat that skating actually becomes dangerous.

24. Benton Crossing Road   26 miles ⑨ ⚡3 🏃1

Reference: Long Valley, just north of the Owens Valley outside Mammoth Lakes; see number ㉔ on page 244.

Ideal for: Fitness—Hills/Slalom—Speed—Touring

Directions: Benton Crossing Road is a turnoff from U.S. 395, about 5.5 miles southeast of the Mammoth Lakes junction, State Highway 203. Look for the sign for Whitmore; you can't miss it if you also look for the pea-green A-frame church right next to the highway. Turn north and park at the church. (For a shorter trip on the newest pavement, or if you're a novice on in-lines, drive 6.5 miles more to cross the Owens River and park on the shoulder just around the bend past Brown's Campground.)

Local shop: Footloose Ski Shop, 6175 Minaret Road, Mammoth Lakes, CA 93546; (619) 934-2400.

Tour notes: Just ten minutes' drive from popular Mammoth Mountain ski area, Benton Crossing Road is the number-one year-round favorite in-line skating destination for expert locals and visitors alike. Yes, you read it right: you really can bring your skates along on a Mammoth ski trip. At a 7,000-foot altitude, Benton Crossing Road is regularly plowed all winter long, but unlike most California roads, it's never sanded to reduce icy conditions. So as long as the pavement is dry and not icy, you can skate.

No matter what time of year you visit the area called the Long Valley, you'll be richly rewarded, because the scenery is truly spectacular. In winter you'll skate between snow banks that can rise up to 12 feet high on each side. On a cold, clear day, you stand a good chance of meeting up with cyclists and joggers, as well as snowshoers and cross-country skiers (who often reward themselves afterwards by going off-road to one of the many natural hot springs scattered across the valley).

In the longer days of spring, there's more daylight to admire the craggy snow-capped peaks towering over the perimeter of Long Valley. Mammoth Mountain dominates the view of the Sierras to the west and south, the Glass Mountain range is close by to the north, and the White Mountains decorate the eastern horizon. After a particularly wet winter, the high peaks will still wear their brilliant white crowns for several months.

On Benton Crossing, you skate for the first six and a half miles on a perfectly straight road that rises gradually—except for one long hill—as you proceed northeast. You'll meet the occasional car going to or from Lake Crowley, but one of the best aspects of skating this road is its low automobile traffic. You must cross three cattle guards (the first one is right at the green church) as you climb, so take note, because you'll need to deal with them at higher speeds on the way back down.

After you round the corner to cross the bridge over the Owens River, you'll find a 1.6-mile-long section of newer, prime-quality pavement. This is a good spot for a lap-style workout on flatter terrain (beginners like to drive to this point and skate, to get a feeling for rolling on a smooth surface). This stretch is followed farther up by some pretty rough old pavement that's still worth skating if you have the desire to continue on. Here, too, the road is very straight with a gradual rise, as it heads southeast for four miles. At the top of a low hill, the road curves downward toward Lake Crowley, where a very short but smoother stretch of improved pavement gives way, all too soon, to rough stuff. Turn back at the next cattle guard.

Central Coast North

6 Great Places to Skate

Central Coast North

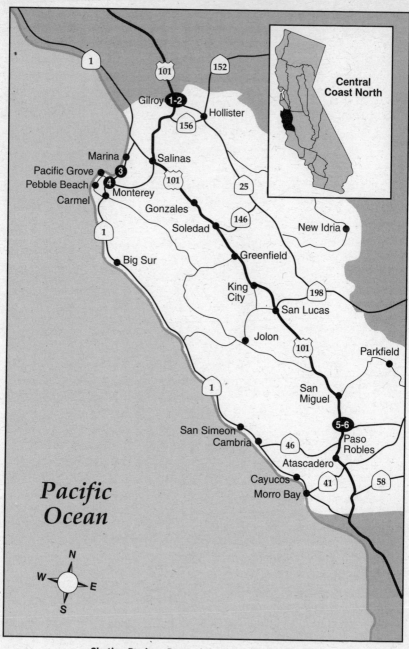

Central Coast North

Pacific Ocean

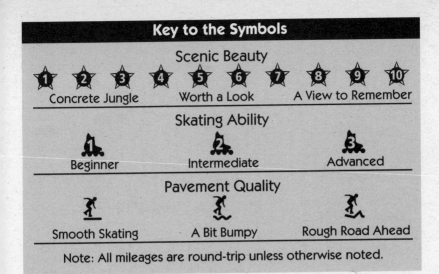

Key to the Symbols

Scenic Beauty

1	2	3	4	5	6	7	8	9	10

Concrete Jungle   Worth a Look   A View to Remember

Skating Ability

1 Beginner   **2** Intermediate   **3** Advanced

Pavement Quality

Smooth Skating   A Bit Bumpy   Rough Road Ahead

Note: All mileages are round-trip unless otherwise noted.

California's golden hills are at their loveliest in the waning light of a clear Central Coast evening. And skating here is most popular in the more populated areas near the coast and bordering mountain ranges.

Although Monterey has several scenic beach routes for recreational rolls, there's also a dedicated aggressive skating scene. Team Adventures of Pacific Grove, a very active group that competes on the aggressive skating circuit, travels around Northern California to perform demos at various in-line events, with tryouts once a year to bring in new talent.

In the farming communities of the Salinas River valley floor, in-lining has yet to overtake skateboarding. To the south in Paso Robles, however, roller hockey has taken off in a big way, with teams practicing and competing at the fairgrounds arena. Equally gung-ho leagues have formed across the hills in coastal Morro Bay.

1. Gavilan College   3 miles

Reference: **Southwestern hills of Gilroy; see number ❶ on page 274.**

Ideal for: Road/Street—Touring

Directions: Traveling either north or south on U.S. 101 in south Gilroy, take the Gavilan College exit to the west. This is Castro Valley Road, which is not a ramp exit but a simple "T" intersection at 101. Half a mile up the road, turn right at the stop sign onto Santa Theresa Boulevard, then left at the Gavilan College entrance sign. Park where you think you can get away with it without a sticker.

Local shop: Play It Again Sports, 220 East 10th Street, Gilroy, CA 95020; (408) 847-7678.

Tour notes: In hot garlic country, it's nice to have shade when you take to the pavement. Gavilan College officially "frowns on" in-lining (as officials themselves put it), but no one asks skaters to leave. You can play it safe on the sidewalks and roads or explore more challenging campus terrain. Because the college is at the base of some low hills, there are quite a few stairs and slopes. The downside: many sidewalks are made of a pebbled composite that causes wheel vibration.

---

2. Uvas Creek Levee

4 miles 🎱 🛼 🚣

Reference: A creekside trail in south Gilroy; see number ❷ on page 274.

Ideal for: Beginners—Touring

Directions: From U.S. 101, exit at Pacheco Pass Road/10th Street and head west to get onto 10th. Follow 10th across Monterey Highway. Soon after you enter the residential area, the street veers down toward the levee. At the base of the levee (where the trail awaits), a right turn transforms 10th into Uvas Park Drive. Follow this to the intersection with Miller Avenue, turn left, go down the dip, and take the first left into the lot at Christmas Hill Park. Park close to Miller.

Local shop: Play It Again Sports, 220 East 10th Street, Gilroy, CA 95020; (408) 847-7678.

Tour notes: Uvas Creek Levee is another tour that's truly spectacular in the spring, with a wealth of natural scenery and great views of the coastal hills. Of course, as the summer heat dries out the grasses of the surrounding slopes and fields, those bright yellows and lush greens are inevitably singed to duller golds and browns. But since the most comfortable summer skating is in early morning or evening when the sun is low, you're often apt to find a landscape bathed in lovely golden light.

Join the trail near the middle by skating to the right out of the parking lot, on the shoulder of Miller, and scooting up from the dip. Gliding along on the wide, zebra-striped pavement where the raised levee parallels the tree-filled creek bed, you may be impressed by all the work that went into tar-patching the trail's many longitudinal cracks. But also be aware that on very warm days, that tar will soften and become grabby, causing sudden and alarming slow-downs. A playing field and school are up ahead on the left, and just after you see an overpass at the creek, the trail comes to an end.

Back at Miller Avenue, cross to the western half of the trail. This is the really spectacular section—hence saved for last. The farther west you skate, the more expansive the creekside scenery to your left, with vast vistas of low, rolling hills leading up to a coastal mountain range. This panorama is hard to match, and you'll rightly want to pause with the squirrels and savor the view. The town of Gilroy would do well to extend this trail; in fact, when it ends after only a mile, you'll be tempted to skate on the street that beckons up ahead below the levee, wide and traffic-free. Don't, unless you enjoy obnoxiously rough pavement. Christmas Hill Park is a fine place for a picnic after the skate.

3. Marina Seaside Trail   10 miles

Reference: **Between scenic Highway 1 and the Pacific Ocean near Sand City; see number ❸ on page 274.**

Ideal for: Fitness—Speed—Touring

Directions: From U.S. 101 just north of Salinas, take the State Highway 156 exit, heading west toward Monterey. Continue past the Castroville/Salinas exit about four miles, and drive across the Salinas River. About half a mile after the river, exit onto Del Monte Road and follow it another mile and a half as it parallels the freeway to take you to the outskirts of the town of Marina. Turn left on Cosky to park at the curb near the intersection with Del Monte. You will see the trail starting a block to the south, on the west side of Del Monte.

Local shop: Adventures by the Sea, Inc., 299 Cannery Row, Monterey, CA 93940; (408) 372-1807.

Tour notes: Although this is known as a seaside trail, the sea is mostly hidden by sand dunes. For the skater with a portable radio, though, this is the perfect spot for a long workout on a not-too-windy day. The Marina Trail is mercifully uninterrupted by intersections for its entire five-mile stretch; most of its length is tucked between the railroad tracks and a stretch of Highway 1 that connects Sand City with the small town of Marina via the Fort Ord Military Reservation. There's no getting around the fact that the freeway and its noise pretty much dominate the experience once the trail leaves Del Monte to cross to the west side of the road. Yet despite those man-made intrusions, you get some beautiful views of the dunes.

4. Monterey Peninsula   17.2 miles
Recreational Trail

Reference: **A coastal rail-trail passing through Monterey; see number ❹ on page 274.**

Ideal for: Scene—Touring

Directions: From U.S. 101 just north of Salinas, take the State Highway 156 exit, heading west. At Castroville, State Highway 1 takes over its rightful job as coast highway as you begin to approach the sea. In the small town of Seaside, exit at Canyon Del Rey Boulevard. Turn left to pass under the freeway, then make a right onto Roberts Avenue to park at Roberts Lake. Skate back out to Del Rey and down the sidewalk to where the trail starts, next to the Seaside sea horse sculpture.

Local shop: Adventures by the Sea, Inc., 299 Cannery Row, Monterey, CA 93940; (408) 372-1807. Other contact: City of Monterey Recreation and Community Services Department; (408) 646-3866.

Tour notes: Monterey's converted rail-trail runs the full length of its coastal city limits and beyond, from Seaside to Pacific Grove. Along the way, the trail spans a lively mix of urban, historic, industrial, marina, and beach scenes. The city is still improving this beloved avenue; as of this writing, for instance, lighting was being extended to the southern section so that the entire trail can be lit at night.

The scenery is a bit industrial starting from the southern end, as you pass the Del Monte Gardens Skating Arena across the street. Soon you enter an imposing eucalyptus forest; watch out for acorns on the trail. Emerging from the trees, you skate next to some back fences for a short way and then, suddenly, you're right between a grassy lawn and the beach. You can see right over the dunes to the ocean; in fact, it's so close you may feel like taking off your skates for a quick run down to the water.

Suddenly, the trail makes a hard turn away from the beach, and you must skate on a pathway that's unpleasantly close to busy Del Monte Road. This culture shock won't last long, because you soon cross the entrance to Fisherman's Wharf and the Monterey Harbor parking lots. You may think you've lost the trail at Washington Street, but just turn right to go around the boat on the corner (named Francesca) and you'll see the trail behind it.

In the Embarcadero area, the trail is superbly smooth and wide as it enters Monterey State Historic Park. Here you'll find a wide red-brick area with a fountain; this is the Custom House Plaza, used by the city for events of all kinds. Some nights, residents sneak in a pick-up roller-hockey "event" at the plaza (the steps and walls make a natural enclosure for the puck). Skaters are welcome in this area "as long as they keep their wheels on the ground," the ranger says. That means no jumping stairs or grinding curbs and rails. But the sidewalks leading away from the trail and plaza are off-limits, and a 10-mile-per-hour speed limit is enforced to protect pedestrians from fast folks on wheels.

After a relatively open section that really does tempt you to skate fast, the trail passes through the Cannery Row area, a block up from the street John Steinbeck made famous as well as the Monterey Aquarium, among other attractions. A short way after entering the Pacific Grove city limits at David Avenue, the trail returns to the shore, following the low seaside cliffs. This very pretty stretch follows the aptly named Ocean View Boulevard, past Andy Jacobsen Park and Berwick Park, and finally comes to an end just before Lovers Point.

5. River Road
13 miles ⭐ 👟 ⛸

Reference: **Along the Salinas River in Paso Robles;**
   see number ❺ on page 274.
Ideal for: Fitness—Historic—Speed—Touring
Directions: Four miles north of Paso Robles and just south of San
   Miguel, turn off U.S. 101 at Wellsonia Road (at the Doll House
   Museum), heading east. Follow Wellsonia to North River Road,
   which runs parallel to the highway. Park on the shoulder here.
Local shop: Sunstorm Skatery, 811 13th Street, Paso Robles, CA 93446;
   (805) 237-8766.
Tour notes: Pastured cows, working farms, no traffic, and good pavement make for a pleasant rural cruise along the banks of the Salinas
   River, in spite of the audible freeway traffic to the west. This is a skate
   best done on a sunny midwinter day when all is green and cool. The
   13-mile round trip is long enough for a great workout if that's your
   pleasure. Start by skating south and continue for about 3.5 miles,
   enjoying the countryside and a few short hills. Then the good pavement ends abruptly. If you're still fresh after returning to your car,
   skate the three miles north to Estrella Road. You'll know it's time to
   turn back when the good pavement suddenly becomes severely pitted.
   After skating, California history buffs will want to drive up to Estrella
   Road, take it across the river to the sleepy town of San Miguel, and
   explore the old Mission San Miguel Archangel. Wine tasting can be
   found off San Marcos Road just across U.S. 101 from here (described
   in the next listing) or to the south off 101 (exit onto State Highway 46
   and look for the Eberly and Estrella Brothers wineries along the first
   10-mile stretch).

6. San Marcos Road
10 miles ⭐ 👟 ⛸

Reference: **Near the vineyards northwest of Paso Robles;**
   see number ❻ on page 274.
Ideal for: Hills/Slalom—Road/Street—Touring
Directions: From U.S. 101, take the San Marcos Road exit. You can
   park on the roadside or at Caparone Winery, about 1.5 miles up the
   road on the right.
Local shop: Sunstorm Skatery, 811 13th Street, Paso Robles, CA 93446;
   (805) 237-8766.
Tour notes: San Marcos Road is delightful for a winter or springtime roll
   in Central Coast wine country. The fine-grade asphalt passes through
   a beautiful pastoral setting of gently rolling hills, white fences, and
   quiet farms. The road, which connects Highway 101 to Nacimiento
   Lake Drive, was never intended for bikes, so there are no paved
   shoulders or painted lines, but traffic is scant enough so that's not a

problem. Note: summers often get hotter than 100 degrees Fahrenheit and the heat can be draining even with an early-morning start, so bring something to drink.

After the skate, stop in for some wine tasting at the unpretentious Caparone Winery on the north side of the road. The vintner specializes in unfiltered red wines. He, his son, or their one employee will serve you delicious samples, sometimes right from the barrel.

Central Coast South

27 Great Places to Skate

Central Coast South

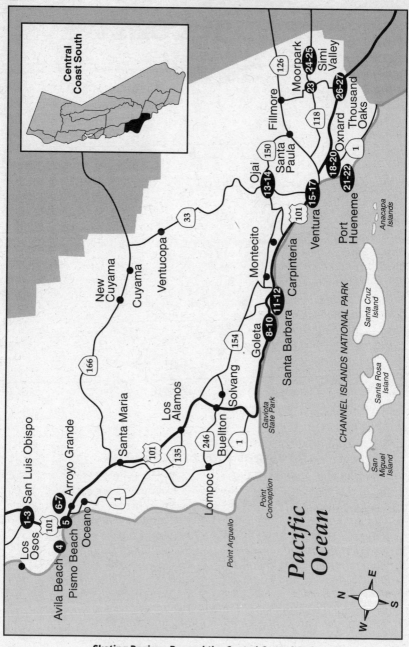

Skating Regions Beyond the Central Coast South

North .... Central Coast North, p. 273   South .... Los Angeles County, p. 311
East .... Central Valley South, p. 225

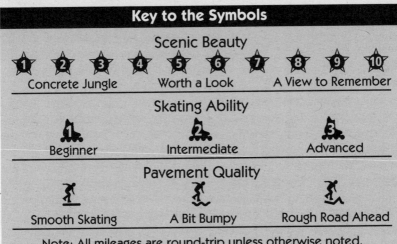

Key to the Symbols

Scenic Beauty

1 2 3 4 5 6 7 8 9 10

Concrete Jungle · Worth a Look · A View to Remember

Skating Ability

1 · 2 · 3

Beginner · Intermediate · Advanced

Pavement Quality

Smooth Skating · A Bit Bumpy · Rough Road Ahead

Note: All mileages are round-trip unless otherwise noted.

Easygoing San Luis Obispo—a college town with enviable weather, hills, and a centralized downtown area—could be an ideal in-line community. But because downtown skating is in violation of city ordinances, local enthusiasts have had to map out some scenic but demanding road skates outside of town. If you're into endurance or speed training, the 10-mile trip from "SLO-Town" (as locals call it) to Avila Beach offers the well-earned rewards of sun, sand, and sea.

Then again, if a quiet roll through a valley filled with oaks and past a windmill and cud-chewing bovines is more your style, head to the hills east of the historic village of Arroyo Grande (my hometown).

Down the coast in Santa Barbara and Ventura Counties, the picturesque marinas and seaside routes in Goleta, Santa Barbara, Ventura, and Oxnard attract a devoted in-line crowd. Just inland from Ventura, rugged Pine Mountain towers over the gorgeous Ojai Valley Trail, a not-to-be-missed skating tour for all levels. Farther south, the foothills of the Santa Susana Mountains have gentle slopes that spice up the skating in the Thousand Oaks and Simi Valley areas.

1. Santa Rosa Park .5 miles 🟊6 🛼 🏃

Reference: **On the west side of San Luis Obispo; see number ❶ on page 282.**

Ideal for: Beginners—In-Line Hockey

Directions: From U.S. 101 in San Luis Obispo, take the Santa Rosa exit and turn west. Three blocks up, turn right at a short driveway entrance to small Santa Rosa Park, conveniently located just before the hospital. Park near the basketball court.

Local shop: Copeland's Sports, 1144 Chorro Street, San Luis Obispo, CA 93401; (805) 543-3663.

Tour notes: Tiny Santa Rosa Park is not exactly a destination skate, but its basketball court is the practice location used by the local roller hockey league. And when roller hockey is not in progress, beginning skaters come here to practice on the smooth concrete. Afterwards, hungry or thirsty folks can refresh themselves at one of the fast-food places on the way back toward the freeway.

2. French Park .5 miles 🟊7 🛼 🏃

Reference: **On the eastern outskirts of San Luis Obispo; see number ❷ on page 282.**

Ideal for: Beginners—Hills/Slalom—Touring

Directions: From U.S. 101 at the south end of San Luis Obispo, take the Marsh Street exit, which heads north toward downtown. Four blocks up, turn east onto Broad Street (State Highway 227). After almost two miles you'll see the sign for Tank Farm Road. Turn left toward the housing development, then right onto Poinsettia. French Park is a couple of blocks up, on the corner of Fuller and Poinsettia. Park on the street.

Local shop: Copeland's Sports, 1144 Chorro Street, San Luis Obispo, CA 93401; (805) 543-3663.

Tour notes: This small, relatively new park is set on a knoll with a 365-degree view of the surrounding hills, crisply outlined against blue skies that know no smog. The property includes enclosed tennis courts and a basketball court popular with neighborhood skaters and skateboarders alike. The dense lawn edging the smooth concrete sidewalks that criss-cross the knoll make this a great place to learn slalom turns. When balls and players are absent, first-time skaters can learn to glide safely on the perfect concrete of the basketball court.

3. Perfumo Canyon Road 5 miles 🟊7 🛼 🏃

Reference: **A rural road south of San Luis Obispo; see number ❸ on page 282.**

Ideal for: Fitness—Hills/Slalom—Road/Street—Touring

Directions: From U.S. 101 just south of San Luis Obispo, take the Los Osos Valley Road exit, heading west. Follow the road beyond Madonna Road until you see a schoolyard on the right. Just opposite, on the left, is the small sign for Perfumo Canyon Road, which leads south from a housing development. Follow the road to the base of the hill, beyond the marked bike path (on pitted asphalt), to where the pavement becomes smooth enough for skating. Park on the roadside (it's a tight squeeze).

Local shop: Copeland's Sports, 1144 Chorro Street, San Luis Obispo, CA 93401; (805) 543-3663.

Tour notes: The pavement of this curvy, lightly trafficked road eventually dissipates to gravel, but what there is of it is in quite good repair, making this a good workout hill for experienced skaters. The tree-lined road creeps up a rather narrow canyon and gains quite a bit of vertical rise en route. Unfortunately, the climb does not culminate in much of a view, due to the dense forest. Keep your ears open for approaching cars because there's no paved shoulder and plenty of blind corners. And speed demons, beware on the curvy trip back down! If you don't bring along your best braking skills, you may find yourself hugging a patch of prickly pear by the road.

4. Avila Beach to San Luis Obispo

20 miles 🌀 🏃 🏄

Reference: The central coast of San Luis Obispo County in Avila Beach; see number ❹ on page 282.

Ideal for: Fitness—Speed—Touring

Directions: About two miles northwest of downtown Pismo Beach, U.S. 101 leaves the Pacific Ocean at the coastal hills to head inland. Traveling either north or south, take the Avila State Beach exit there. You'll pass the old developed hot springs plunge on the right, and half a mile farther on, the Sycamore Hot Springs on the left, either of which you may want to visit for a muscle-relaxing soak after a hard skate. San Luis Bay Drive continues past a golf course and curves behind some low hills; as you emerge from behind the hills, the small town (and beach) of Avila Beach comes into view. Park in the big public lot at the end of town.

Local shop: Central Coast Surfboards, 986 Monterey Street, San Luis Obispo, CA 93401; (805) 541-1129.

Tour notes: Experienced road skaters who don't mind freeway noise will enjoy this round-trip excursion from Avila Beach. It's a favorite with the local in-shape in-liners. Starting at the Avila parking lot, follow San Luis Bay Drive back to the Avila Mineral Springs public pool. There are no shoulders on this windy road, so keep a close watch for cars. Just before the swimming pool, turn left onto Ontario Road.

Speed-skating races are sometimes held on Ontario, which is closed to cars for the first mile due to bridge problems. Ontario makes a gradual incline alongside the freeway, then becomes somewhat level for several miles. About one mile from the San Luis Obispo city limits, it passes under 101 and becomes Higuera Street on the east side. This route ends at the housing developments near Los Osos Valley Road, because skating is not allowed within San Luis Obispo city limits. Back in Avila, the main beachfront street can be a sandy roll, but it's a fantastic beach on a sunny summer day, and quite the scene with the local college crowd. After your long tour, rinse off in the showers at the public rest rooms and pick up a snack and a drink from one of the many seaside shops.

5. Urban Shell Beach   4 miles

Reference: **In the coastal town of Shell Beach, part of Pismo Beach; see number ❺ on page 282.**

Ideal for: Hills/Slalom—Touring

Directions: From U.S. 101, take the Mattie Road/Shell Beach exit to get to the Shell Beach frontage road. Head east for half a mile and park along the curb or on a side street at the west end of town.

Local shop: Power Play In Line, 200 Traffic Way, Arroyo Grande, CA 93420-3335; (805) 473-0282.

Tour notes: Considered part of Pismo Beach, Shell Beach is a quiet town between U.S. 101 and the Pacific. Many of the residential streets leading down to the cliffs are smooth and have little traffic; however, sidewalks were obviously not part of early city planning. Newer single-family homes, painted in seafoam pastels, are gradually replacing the older, much more modest houses built by the town's early residents, so each street offers its own interesting interpretation of seaside living. The grandest homes tend to be at street's end, along the rocky cliffs that rise 50 feet from the protected little beaches below. Near the east end of town, several streets lead to a cliffside frontage road, where concrete stairs lead to the surf and sand. West of downtown, next to the school on the frontage road, is Terrace Avenue, a particularly fine street for slalom practice. The ball courts and concrete ramps of the little school itself also make for a fun skating playground in the summers and after-hours.

6. Ranchita Estates   6 miles

Reference: **The countryside near Lopez Lake east of Arroyo Grande; see number ❻ on page 282.**

Ideal for: Hills/Slalom—Touring

Directions: From U.S. 101, take the Grand Avenue exit in Arroyo Grande and head east, passing through downtown. Veer right at

Branch Street to go around Crown Hill, then turn right onto Huasna Road, which becomes Lopez Drive a mile down. Just before the Lopez Lake entrance station (another nine miles away), take a right onto Pozo Road. Continue across the cattle guard and follow the road another mile to the entrance sign at Ranchita Estates. Turn left and park near the sales office.

Local shop: Power Play In Line, 200 Traffic Way, Arroyo Grande, CA 93420-3335; (805) 473-0282.

Tour notes: The friendly atmosphere of old Arroyo Grande (my hometown) is enhanced by the western-style storefronts and antique shops that line Grand Avenue, the main street. Just a short drive away, you'll find a skater's paradise. Located in the hills beyond the Lopez Lake Recreation Area east of town, Ranchita Estates is beautiful in the cool green of California's midwinter. At press time, the local real-estate market was in a slump, and the housing development consisted of only three or four homes served by curbed streets meandering among oaks, with most lots occupied only by numbered signs.

Skating up and down the wide asphalt streets, you may see a herd of deer grazing on a hill. Right next to the streets, cows watch humans rolling by on wheeled shoes with alert interest, ready to lumber away when startled. Keep your eyes peeled, don't make any sudden moves or approach mothers with calves, and you should be okay. Only four or five houses have been built on two or three of the streets, and the other roads, save for the occasional cow pie or patch of gravel, remain in good repair. You will find three or four gently rolling hills steep enough for uninhibited schussing and wide enough for exciting slaloms.

---

7. Pozo Road
8 miles 🔟 🐾 🛼

Reference: **The countryside near Lopez Lake east of Arroyo Grande; see number ❼ on page 282.**

Ideal for: Hills/Slalom—Touring

Directions: From U.S. 101, take the Grand Avenue exit in Arroyo Grande and head east, passing through downtown. Veer right at Branch Street to go around Crown Hill, and then turn right onto Huasna Road, which becomes Lopez Drive a mile down. Just before the Lopez Lake entrance station (another nine miles), take a right onto Pozo Road. Continue across the cattle guard, and follow the road another mile to the entrance sign to Ranchita Estates. Turn left and park near the sales office.

Local shop: Power Play In Line, 200 Traffic Way, Arroyo Grande, CA 93420-3335; (805) 473-0282.

Tour notes: Just outside the Ranchita Estates gate, Pozo Road continues up a pretty valley. There is no marked or paved shoulder, but car traffic is scarce because the road turns to rough gravel on top of the

---

hill. Climbing through the valley, however, the road is paved, straight, wide, and clean, passing a barn and a tule-filled pond populated by ducks and egrets. A windmill makes it all the more picturesque.

Skating here is a refreshing change from congested urban areas. In this canyon you'll hear only the peaceful warbling of birds, the occasional lowing of a cow, and the roll of your wheels over the smooth pavement. If you're up for the climb, the hill at the end of the valley is a truly fantastic spot for downhill slalom turns, with a long, flat run-out at the bottom. Start with a test run from lower down to make sure you can handle the speed.

8. UCSB Campus   4 miles

Reference: **University of California at Santa Barbara, in Goleta; see number ⑧ on page 282.**

Ideal for: Beginners—Road/Street—Touring

Directions: Five miles north of Santa Barbara on U.S. 101/State Highway 1, take the State Highway 217/UCSB exit and follow this short highway all the way to the campus. Park in one of the lots on campus.

Map: The Official Bike Map of Santa Barbara, Goleta, Montecito, Summerland, and Carpenteria; available free by calling (805) 568-3232.

Local shop: A Skater's Paradise, 537 State Street, Santa Barbara, CA 93101; (805) 962-2526.

Tour notes: You'll find plenty of lawn-bordered, 12-foot-wide (and double-wide), smooth, concrete pathways on this campus. Street skaters will delight in the profusion of stairs, ramps, and curbs. At the shoreline edge of campus near Lagoon Road is a stunning view of the Pacific—it's hard not to envy the students who get to see this every day!

The most obvious place to skate is a well-marked bike path that runs through and around the main campus area, sometimes with a meridian strip between lanes. Where pedestrian walkways cross the path, 18-inch knobby strips border either side, so sidewalk skaters will want to jump over these rude obstacles.

The large, central section of campus is also paved, but stay attentive to the surface; there are a few raised edges that might trip you. You'll also notice telltale shiny edges on concrete tree planters that have obviously seen a lot of grinding action. Nearby, wide, shaded sidewalks cross the lawn to connect campus buildings.

If you're a daring soul, take the connection trail next to Lagoon Road, down the steep hill to Goleta County Beach, where you can have a picnic or hook up with the Atascadero or Maria Ygnacia Creek trails. (See the tour descriptions in the next two listings.) The descent is very rough and steeply pitched, with a few cracks to add to the thrill; beginners and skaters without a heel brake will want to carry their skates down.

9. Atascadero Creek Trail 7.5 miles 🌀 🐾 🛼

Reference: **A creekside trail in the town of Goleta; see number
   ❾ on page 282.**

Ideal for: Beginners—Fitness—Touring

Directions: Five miles north of Santa Barbara on U.S. 101/State Highway 1, take the State Highway 217/UCSB exit and follow this short
   highway toward the ocean. Take the Sandspit Road off-ramp, turn left
   on Moffett Road, and follow it back under the highway. Take a right
   onto Sandspit to cross a bridge into Goleta Beach County Park. Turn
   right as you enter the park and right again into the first parking lot.
   The inland side of the lot is right by the trail.

Map: The Official Bike Map of Santa Barbara, Goleta, Montecito,
   Summerland, and Carpenteria; available free by calling (805) 568-3232.

Local shop: A Skater's Paradise, 537 State Street, Santa Barbara, CA
   93101; (805) 962-2526.

Tour notes: An early-morning skate on this trail rewards you with memorable views of the inland mountains emerging from the rising fog. The
   surface is smooth, eight-foot-wide asphalt, and the border of street
   lamps and newly planted seedlings suggest an attentive maintenance
   policy that will likely serve this community well for years to come.
   One of the nicer touches is the separate and parallel gravel path used
   by equestrians, joggers, and mountain-bikers, leaving the pavement
   less crowded for faster folks on wheels. But on Saturday mornings,
   watch out for the swift, silent approach of street cyclists, who train in
   packs on this trail.

   Exit the Goleta Beach County Park on Sandspit Road to skate back
   across the ocean inlet that creates the sandspit. The trail turns right on
   the other side to parallel Maria Ygnacia Creek as it veers inland away
   from the inlet. For the first mile, the trail passes through a fairly open,
   natural marshy area. To your left are the often misty peaks of Los
   Padres National Forest; beyond the creek to the right is the ocean,
   hidden by low trees at the beginnings of a ridge.

   A few yards after crossing the first wood-slat bridge, you'll see the
   two-mile marker painted on the pavement (measured from Goleta
   Beach) and a fork in the trail. Take the right fork to follow Atascadero
   Creek. (The left fork is described in the following listing for Maria
   Ygnacia Creek.) For the rest of the route, the Atascadero Creek Trail
   passes alongside a housing development with a fairly low wall that
   remains untouched by graffiti. Don't waste your time exploring the
   next left fork in the trail; it's just a short connection path leading to the
   neighborhood termination of Turnpike Road.

   After another wooden bridge, the trail offers a brief peek into the
   Hidden Oaks Country Club, where members practice their golf

strokes behind the chain-link fence. Farther on, Atascadero Creek remains in sight, a small canal next to the trail. You'll make your only street crossing at Puente; soon after, with one last little bridge, the trail comes to an end at Arroyo Road.

10. Maria Ygnacia Creek   6 miles

Reference: **A creekside trail in the town of Goleta; see number ❿ on page 282.**

Ideal for: Touring

Directions: Five miles north of Santa Barbara on U.S. 101/State Highway 1, take the State Highway 217/UCSB exit and follow this short highway toward the ocean. Take the Sandspit Road off-ramp, turn left on Moffett Road, and follow it back under the highway. Take a right onto Sandspit to cross a bridge into Goleta Beach County Park. Turn right as you enter the park and right again into the first parking lot. The inland side of the lot is right by the trail.

Map: The Official Bike Map of Santa Barbara, Goleta, Montecito, Summerland, and Carpenteria; available free by calling (805) 568-3232.

Local shop: A Skater's Paradise, 537 State Street, Santa Barbara, CA 93101; (805) 962-2526.

Tour notes: Ready for an adventure? The skate-rattling pavement where this route branches off from the smooth Atascadero Creek Trail should weed out all but the hardiest in-liners. But the payoff for skating two miles on rough pavement comes at the northern end near the banks of Maria Ygnacia Creek, when you roll through a tunnel of magnificent, mature eucalyptus that momentarily hides any trace of civilization. You'll also enjoy the route's two fast freeway underpasses, where excellent concrete makes up for the roughness elsewhere.

Start this trip from Goleta Beach County Park. Take Sandspit Road back across the sandspit bridge and turn right. The Maria Ygnacia Creek Trail starts next to the sandspit inlet, which gradually veers off into the trees. For the first two miles, you'll be following the Atascadero Creek Trail (see the previous listing). Take the left fork to follow Maria Ygnacia Creek.

The first mile after the fork has some truly awful pavement (especially compared to what you just left), but the neighborhood nearby is quiet and pretty, with good shade trees. After the first underpass, Hollister Avenue, the trail begins a slight climb next to shady oaks and pines at the creek's edge. A short way upstream, it crosses the water to pass alongside an oddly detached lawn bordered by a picket fence. Just around the corner is the U.S. 101 underpass, a fun ride that stretches under the wide freeway for a tenth of a mile. On the other side of that underpass, you'll reach a fork in the trail at a bridge. The right fork, which runs along noisy 101, is nothing more than a neighborhood connection trail. Go left to cross the bridge, and ignore another useless right fork as you begin to climb a low hill.

Finally, the reward! The passage through the mature stand of eucalyptus, though all too brief, is on decent asphalt, allowing you to fully savor the splendor. At the end of the stand, the trail ascends a steep little hill to emerge at another quiet neighborhood. To continue to the absolute end, cross University Drive and skate on a narrow (five-foot-wide) asphalt path for two more blocks, to Pintura Drive. You'll know you're at the end because the sign posted there says, "No horses on sidewalk." Fine by me!

---

11. Shoreline Park   1.5 miles

Reference: **Perched on the cliffs above the Pacific Ocean in Santa Barbara; see number ⓫ on page 282.**

Ideal for: Hills/Slalom—Touring

Directions: From U.S. 101 North in Santa Barbara, take the Carrillo Street/Downtown exit, and turn left at the end of the off-ramp to take West Carrillo Street to the beach. From U.S. 101 South, the exit reads only "Carrillo" and requires a right turn to get onto West Carrillo Street. After Carrillo crosses Cliff Drive a few blocks down, it becomes Shoreline Drive. Follow Shoreline as it curves to the left near the coast, taking you to Shoreline Beach Park and its parking lots.

Map: The Official Bike Map of Santa Barbara, Goleta, Montecito, Summerland, and Carpenteria; available free by calling (805) 568-3232.

Local shop: Skates on State, 324 State Street, Santa Barbara, CA 93101; (805) 963-9008.

Tour notes: It may be small, and it may not be the first place you'll want to skate when you arrive in Santa Barbara, but pretty little Shoreline Park is a really fun roll! Two features make this true: first, everybody else is busy bumping into each other down at the Shoreline Trail, leaving the sidewalks here relatively free. Better yet, the cliffside park is sloped consistently from north end to south, making the lawn-bordered eight-foot-wide sidewalks fantastic forums for hill skating, slalom-turn practice, or even, heaven forbid, learning to use your heel brake for speed control. High on the cliffs above the Pacific, Shoreline Park also makes a dynamic spot for snapping some prime panoramic photos of the Santa Barbara Yacht Club and Harbor, with the long shore stretching into the distance below.

From anyplace in the parking lot, the Shoreline Park sidewalk is just across the lawn. As you skate up the hill, there will be people picnicking and enjoying the view, but for the most part they stay on the grass or benches or at picnic tables. There are no blind curves or other obstacles as you come back down the hill, so you can keep watch on the path ahead. At the end of the park, the cliff turns inland, as does

---

the chain-link fence keeping you from skating right off the edge. A paved vista point gives you extra space to make a big turn to the left.

If you want to skate the Santa Barbara Shoreline Trail (see the next listing) from the south end of Shoreline Park, a connection is possible, if hairy. A narrow sidewalk next to Shoreline Drive descends steeply down to Leadbetter Beach. It's best to ride your heel brake down, because you'll want to be ready for the uphill mountain biker or spaced-out kid carrying a surfboard in your path. And then there are the two monstrous, raised eruptions in the sidewalk about two-thirds of the way down. Be prepared to jump twice within about five feet! If you feel comfortable skating in a bike lane that's half gutter, you can step off the sidewalk as necessary. A hard right-angle turn toward the water marks your arrival at sea-level Leadbetter Beach.

---

12. Shoreline Trail   6.5 miles 🌀 🚶 🏃

Reference: **Along the Pacific Ocean in Santa Barbara; see number ⑫ on page 282.**

Ideal for: Beginners—Scene—Touring

Directions: From U.S. 101/State Highway 1 in Santa Barbara, exit at Castillo Street and head toward the sea. Turn right on Shoreline Drive and follow it to the pay parking lots at Leadbetter Beach. (Note: There's free parking near the end of the trail at Los Patos, and at the curb by the nearby beach, for those who arrive early enough.)

Map: The Official Bike Map of Santa Barbara, Goleta, Montecito, Summerland, and Carpenteria; available free by calling (805) 568-3232.

Local shop: Skates on State, 324 State Street, Santa Barbara, CA 93101; (805) 963-9008.

Tour notes: Skated end to end, Santa Barbara's popular Shoreline Trail delivers a rich array of scenery, from bikinied beaches at one end to the marshy secluded bird sanctuary at the other. The coastal mountain range rises close to shore, displaying Montecito's ritzy hillside homes. The Shoreline Trail is wide, clean, and almost totally flat, hence irresistible to skaters of all levels. In summer, even weekdays bring throngs of tourists, pedestrians, and cyclists; come prepared to deal with the clueless.

Starting from Leadbetter Beach, warm up on the concrete pad near the rest rooms and telephones just below the Santa Barbara Yacht Club and restaurant (notice the waxed curbs—sure signs of skateboard and in-line grinding activity). The trail connects Leadbetter Beach and the Yacht Harbor to West Beach, then travels the coastline next to East Beach.

Take the 10-foot-wide sidewalk at the edge of the Leadbetter Beach parking lot past the little restaurant of the Yacht Club. Continue south as painted lines show the way through the parking lots that service the marina of Santa Barbara Yacht Harbor. A separated divided asphalt bike path starts at Harbor Way, supplementing the concrete pedestrian way that runs next to the Naval Reserve Center, eventually taking you across one last parking lot, where it crosses to the asphalt bike path on the left. Suddenly, as you enter the concrete boardwalk trail at Ambassador Park, skaters seem to be everywhere. And although a wide pedestrian way is on the left, that doesn't prevent the unwheeled from sharing your side of the Shoreline Trail.

The view ahead starts with Stearns Wharf extending onto the aqua-blue sea. Beyond, the rows of statuesque palm trees are backed by the purple silhouettes of the coastal range, the highest being Rincon Mountain. At the end of the wharf, a fountain featuring life-sized, bronze dolphins makes a nice spot to stop and take in the view while you get a feel for the Shoreline Trail scene.

Continuing from the far side of the pier, the path enters the vicinity of East Beach and the adjacent Chase Palm Park. Across the park to your left, the scenery opens up, with a great view of the hills above Montecito. If the crowds on the trail tempt you to cross the lawn and skate on the sidewalk bordering East Cabrillo, think twice, because the cement in such bad disrepair it's actually dangerous; though there are fewer moving obstacles, you must constantly weave and hop over the ruts, raised cracks, and sloppy asphalt patches to avoid a major crash.

Near the end of Chase Palm Park, the trail crosses East Cabrillo at Milpas Street and continues on a bikeway with painted lines and the frequent posted admonition to use it "with courtesy and caution." But on a busy day that's sort of a moot request, given the sheer volume of pedestrians, skaters, tykes on bikes, families pedaling buggies, mountain bikers, and recumbent cyclists all vying for space. The now-asphalt path along East Cabrillo is landscaped with low shrubs and shaded by a row of trees as it passes a line of apartment buildings. After half a mile and another street crossing or two (watch out beginners—one is sloped), the dwellings end. Now a marshy pond appears close to the trail on the inland side: the Andree Clark Bird Refuge. As the trail skirts its perimeter, you can admire a picturesque hillside view of the Montecito Country Club. The trail comes to an end at Los Patos, near the freeway at the far side of the pond.

13. Ojai Valley Trail North   9 miles 🎖️ 🐾 🏄

Reference: **A trail on the banks of the Ventura River starting in Ojai; see number ⓭ on page 282.**

Ideal for: Hills/Slalom—Touring

Directions: From U.S. 101, exit at the Ojai Freeway, State Highway 33, and proceed 11 miles north (it may seem like you're going east as you head away from the ocean, but it's really north) to the Ojai city limits.

A mile and a half after you pass the big intersection where Highway 33 heads off to the left as the Maricopa Highway, look to the right, for Montgomery and then for Fox Street. Turn right on Fox to park at the curb near the Ojai Valley Racquet Club. You'll see the trail across the street from the racquet club entrance sign.

Map: Ojai Valley Trail Map, posted on trailside signs and at a kiosk on Willey Street.

Local shop: Dave's Skateboards, 2098 East Main Street, Ventura, CA 93001-3543; (805) 656-7207. Other contact: Andrew Oshita, GSA/ Recreation Services, 800 South Victoria Avenue, Ventura, CA 93009; (805) 654-3945.

Tour notes: If you have friends willing to pick you up at the end of this route in Foster County Park in Casitas Springs, and you're not too proud to skate the entire 8.8-mile length of the Ojai Valley Trail in the downhill direction only, go for it! (See the next listing for the second half of this trail.) Otherwise, use the directions that follow to skate a shorter route on the northern half of the trail, down to Barbara Street in south Mira Monte. Whichever route you choose, you'll be delighted with the Ojai Trail: it's well marked and maintained, with gorgeous mountain views, wonderfully smooth pavement, and a gentle grade that is very doable in both directions. Unfortunately, most of the northern section is also within earshot of the highway.

Start skating west on the shady, 10-foot-wide asphalt path leading away from the Racquet Club. There are a few neighborhood street crossings along this section; check for cars before rolling through. Soon, to the left, the Ojai Valley Country Club Golf Course appears through the trees, in all its green and grassy glory. Before long, you're standing at the only stoplight on the trip, waiting impatiently to cross to where the path resumes at the other side of the highway.

As the trail leaves the town of Ojai behind, it curves south through some trees, then west next to a wide, grassy meadow. About two miles from Fox Street is a shaded wood-and-stone bench, donated by the Rotary Club, where you can admire the panorama of the mountainous Los Padres National Forest to the north. Wait long enough and you might also get the chance to watch a red-tailed hawk ride the updrafts over the sunny meadow.

Resuming your roll, continue beyond the intersection where State Highway 150 merges into 33. If you check out the wood trail map posted there, you can determine exactly where you are and how far you've gone; similar maps are posted every couple of miles along the entire length of the trail. At Willey Street, another mile to the south, is a kiosk-on-a-stick with free color maps of the Ojai Valley Trail (built as a project by a local Eagle Scout). Two blocks away, the wooden map posted at Barbara Street marks the end of this tour.

14. Ojai Valley Trail South

8 miles

Reference: A trail on the banks of the Ventura River, starting in Casitas Springs; see number **14** on page 282.

Ideal for: Touring

Directions: From U.S. 101, exit at State Highway 33 and proceed north (it may seem like you're going east as you head away from the ocean, but it's really north). Exit at the Casitas Vista off-ramp and loop under the freeway. Turn right before the bridge at the entrance to Foster County Park and follow the park road about a quarter-mile to where the pavement jogs up to the barrier at the end of the trail. Park on the dirt next to the trail entrance.

Map: Ojai Valley Trail Map, posted on trailside signs and at a kiosk on Willey Street.

Local shop: Dave's Skateboards, 2098 East Main Street, Ventura, CA 93001-3543; (805) 656-7207. Other contact: Andrew Oshita, GSA/Recreation Services, 800 South Victoria Avenue, Ventura, CA 93009; (805) 654-3945.

Tour notes: The Ojai Valley Trail is so great that even if you have the stamina to continue up the north half and skate the entire 17.6-mile round-trip, you'll still hate to see it end. (This tour covers the scenic southern half of the trail.) It's a cruise with views in both directions, and the incline going north is so gentle you hardly notice you're climbing, though you get ample proof of the climb when you average an effortless 10 miles per hour on the way back down. Eucalyptus trees, oaks, and willows provide enough shade to keep the inland route cool. And even though it would be impossible to lose your way on the well-marked trail, excellent wooden maps with the current mileage are posted at intersections every few miles. You'll share your bucolic tour with half-tame cottontails, friendly corralled horses, and lazily circling red-tailed hawks. And you'll meet very few if any skaters.

Starting out from Foster County Park, skate the first quarter-mile next to a stand of eucalyptus near Highway 33. (Warning: during the wet season, stroking across the blanket of leaves and silt here will be very slippery.) The route continues behind a ridge that separates it from the sights and sounds of the highway, and that's where the best part starts. Beyond the ridge you're rewarded with a wide-open country view of the valley formed by the Ventura River, with oak-covered hills backed by higher ridges on the horizon—a classic California vista in grand scale. The river itself is not a dominant presence in the dog days of summer; except for the bordering levees, you can hardly tell it's there.

As you proceed north, signs of development are limited to a few modest homes with paddocks in back. You might recognize the odor of a penned-up billy goat or fresh horse droppings. If you hadn't noticed it before, along the left side of the trail is a post fence separating an equestrian path from the pavement.

The homes get more numerous on the gradual ascent to the tiny village of Oak View, and by the time you reach the spectacular valley view at the intersection with Santa Ana Boulevard, you wonder why the homes aren't million-dollar models. And then you smile for these residents, because the scenery here is light-years better than is often found in much pricier communities.

After the Santa Ana intersection, the trail gradually returns to the west shoulder of Highway 33, and by the time you reach Barbara Street it has entered the south end of Mira Monte, a quiet little town at the junction of Highways 150 and 33. Although the tour ends here, you might want to skate two blocks farther up the trail to pick up a free color trail map at the little box posted on Willey Street by an Eagle Scout. (See the previous listing for more trail details.)

For the absolute best experience of the Ojai Valley Trail, get your body in good enough shape to skate the entire round-trip starting from Foster County Park. Go on a weekday and get started by 9 A.M. to avoid the crowds and intense heat, and bring your ski poles and some food and drinks.

---

15. Surfer's Point Bike Path   3 miles 🌀 🏊 🏃

Reference: **A shoreline trail on the Pacific coast in Ventura; see number ⓕ on page 282.**

Ideal for: Touring

Directions: Approaching Ventura from the west on U.S. 101, take the Main Street exit and follow it up to California Street. Turn right on California and follow it over the freeway; on the other side, look for the public parking lots on the right in an area known as Paseo de Playa. Approaching Ventura from the east, take the California Street exit and turn toward the beach at the end of the off-ramp. Cross the freeway to reach the parking lots at Paseo de Playa.

Map: Bikeways Map, A Guide to Biking in Ventura County; published by the Ventura County Transportation Commission; (805) 642-1591.

Local shop: Sport Chalet, 1885 East Ventura Boulevard, Oxnard, CA 93030-1823; (805) 485-5222.

Tour notes: With an ideal location near the Pacific shore in an attractive part of town, Surfer's Point Bike Path has tremendous potential as a skate destination. Unfortunately, the pavement quality—even on the wide and beautifully designed Promenade—just does not live up to the scenery.

Explore the area near the Holiday Inn before you start skating the promenade. The hotel's large plaza has a sloped surface and some steps worth jumping. The uphill view of mural-decorated California Street on the other side of the freeway is unique and memorable, even if the mural's vaguely aquatic subject matter is not.

Out on the promenade, first head west, skating up the coast on the bumpy paved surface (it's a combination of concrete and rock that rattles even the highest-priced skates). This 30-foot-wide and otherwise very attractive thoroughfare is decorated with benches, tree planters, and a low wall that separates it from the beach without blocking the view. A short way up from the Holiday Inn plaza, a narrow lawn follows the promenade on the inland side, and the wide beach begins to narrow, until you're almost at the rocky edge by the time the wide promenade ends at Surfer's Point. The bike path continues up the coast all the way to Santa Barbara, but the pavement and demanding terrain aren't really skater-friendly.

Skating south from the Holiday Inn plaza, the promenade ends abruptly after passing under the Ventura Pier, returning to a more humble and roughly paved asphalt bike path. Now about eight feet wide, the trail follows the relatively undeveloped shores of Buenaventura State Beach; to the left are Harbor Boulevard and the freeway. Soon you come to the giant Buenaventura Beach parking lot; here, a snack bar and rental concession are on the ocean side of where the Surfer's Point Bike Path continues south, at the edge of the lot.

You might want to end your trip here and join the other skaters and cyclists on the empty edge of the lot. If you do plan on skating to the end of the line, consider avoiding the bike path, because it's even bumpier up ahead; if traffic is low enough and your skills are up to it, use Harbor Boulevard instead. (There is no bike lane, so skate at your own risk.) The Surfer's Point Bike Path officially ends near the park headquarters on San Pedro Street a block away.

---

16. Marina Park   5.5 miles

Reference: **A park on the Pacific Ocean in Ventura; see number 16 on page 282.**

Ideal for: Beginners—Road/Street—Touring

Directions: From U.S. 101, exit on Seaward Avenue and head toward the ocean. Turn left on Pierpont Boulevard and follow it to its termination at Marina Park, where you will find free parking at the northern edge of the Ventura Harbor.

Map: Bikeways Map, A Guide to Biking in Ventura County, published by the Ventura County Transportation Commission; (805) 642-1591.

Local shop: Sport Chalet, 1885 East Ventura Boulevard, Oxnard, CA 93030-1823; (805) 485-5222.

Tour notes: The greatest charm of pretty Marina Park is that it's located right at the mouth of Ventura Harbor in the Pierpont Bay area of

---

Ventura. From its sidewalks near the water's edge, you get some terrific views of the channel and harbor. Beginners will find the park's palm-dotted lawns a comfort when learning to skate on the smooth, six-foot-wide sidewalks.

Near the children's sand lot (and a unique cable swing attached to a concrete rendition of a shipwreck) the sidewalk snakes up toward the rocky spit that forms the north border of the harbor channel. Don't try to skate there unless the walkway has been recently vacuumed, because summer crowds tend to track sand across it an inch deep. If it *is* skatable, this little trail offers the best view of the mouth of the harbor and the marina. You can also see Harbor Village across the way (where skating on the lively promenade is not allowed).

After enjoying the harbor view, street-ready skaters can continue up the bike lane on Pierpont Boulevard all the way to San Buenaventura State Beach. On the way, make a left turn at Seaward Avenue to check out the young crowd's hangout near the cul-de-sac where Seaward meets the beach. At San Pedro Street, Pierpont meets the gate for the southernmost parking lot of San Buenaventura State Beach. If traffic is light enough entering the lot, don't bother skating on the rough trail to the left of the entrance: If you've skated on the street this far, you've earned the right to the smooth pavement on the road curving toward the freeway on the lot's inland side. There is no bike lane.

At the north end of the vast beach parking lot, a beach concession rents skates, four-wheel buggies, and the newfangled, odd-looking recumbent tricycles. There's usually enough parking to attract scores of these wheeled recreationists, who find the pavement here preferable to the rough stuff on the trail continuing north. (See the Surfer's Point Bike Path description in the previous listing.)

---

17. County Government Center   8 miles

Reference: **In the town of Ventura;
   see number ⑰ on page 282.**
Ideal for: Touring
Directions: From U.S. 101, the Ventura Freeway, take the Montalvo/ Government Center exit, Victoria Avenue. Proceed to the second stop light, at Telephone Road, and turn right. Take the first entrance driveway into the Government Center parking lot and park close to the Telephone Road sidewalk. Skating is only allowed outside of the center property; this route circles the government grounds, on a bike path along bordering streets.
Map: Bikeways Map, A Guide to Biking in Ventura County, published by the Ventura County Transportation Commission; (805) 642-1591.
Local shop: Sport Chalet, 100 North La Cienega Boulevard, Los Angeles, CA 90048-1938; (310) 657-3210.

Tour notes: Eucalyptus trees, dense ivy, and wide lawns enhance the grounds of the attractive Ventura County Government Center in Ventura's Montalvo district. A network of linking, dedicated bike routes delivers four miles of skating on the bordering streets of Victoria Avenue, Webster Street, Telephone Road, and Kimbell Road. In addition, nearly all of the neighboring streets have wide concrete sidewalks, and diversions abound, branching off in all directions; the creative skater can pick up a lot of mileage in these parts.

Heed the signs, however, and do *not* skate on the off-limits government property. A big No Skating sign is posted near the Telephone Road entrance just east of its intersection with Victoria Avenue. Although that means you'll have to resist the parking lots and sidewalks of the grounds themselves, there's lots to enjoy on the shaded route of the designated bike paths that encircle the complex.

If you're still raring to go after completing the Government Center loop, skate east on Telephone Road, where those aforementioned diversions await. Starting out from the south edge of the Center, you'll skate east past Victoria Avenue, Hill Road, and Johnson Drive, all tempting you to leave Telephone and explore. Each offers a short route on a bike path or bike lanes, perfect for burning off a few extra calories while seeing the sights.

Back on Telephone, after you pass Johnson, keep a lookout to the right for Antelope Drive, where a roughly paved little creekside canal path extends south for just a few blocks. You should skate here only if you enjoy the tickle of vibrating feet. Telephone Road's designated bike lane ends one and a half miles beyond the Government Center, but other, streetside bike lanes extend the possibilities for another two miles before ending at Placid Avenue, two blocks before Montgomery Avenue.

Turn right to skate south on Montgomery's wide sidewalks for another three quarters of a mile. Cross Bristol Road and continue two blocks into the neighborhood to access another mile-long dedicated bike path that runs next to the Santa Clara River at the edge of town. By the time you've explored that and every other branching path along the way, you'll have had a decidedly satisfying skate.

---

18. Oxnard State Beach Park 4 miles 9 🏌 ⛸

Reference: **On the Pacific Ocean west of Oxnard;**
 see number ⑱ on page 282.
Ideal for: Beginners—Touring
Directions: From U.S. 101 in Oxnard, take the Victoria Avenue South exit. Proceed about five miles south to Channel Island Boulevard and follow it to the Harbor Boulevard intersection. Turn right, proceed one block on Harbor Boulevard, and then make a left on Mandalay

---

Beach Road. Park at the curb or in the free public lot; you're at the south end of Oxnard State Beach Park.

Map: Bikeways Map, A Guide to Biking in Ventura County, published by the Ventura County Transportation Commission; (805) 642-1591.

Local shop: Sports Mart, 230 North Rose Avenue, Oxnard, CA 93030; (805) 988-5000.

Tour notes: Spend an afternoon or early summer's evening playing at Oxnard State Beach Park, a beginner's paradise featuring palm trees, vast lawns, and wonderfully broad concrete walkways (one section of the palm-lined path is at least 15 feet wide). When there aren't too many other people competing for pavement, this is an excellent site for dancing to a boom box or showing off a few tricks. It may be less crowded in the morning, though chances are it will be damp and foggy as well.

This oceanfront park boasts outstanding landscaping and design. It's situated a few hundred yards off the beach, with tantalizing glimpses of the ocean beyond a low sand dune that partially blocks the constant offshore breeze. The sidewalk meanders through the beachfront lawns and on both sides of an attractive dwelling complex. At the park's south end where Sunset and Mandalay Beach Road meet is a smoothly paved parking lot that, when empty, is another good site to practice artistic skating or brush up on stunts.

After exploring Oxnard State Beach Park, experienced street skaters might want to follow Mandalay Beach Road for another mile north if traffic is light enough. This sandy street route leads past beach houses of various interesting designs; while there are no bike lanes and the surface isn't the best, it's worth exploring if the sun is out, just to take a look. (There are some sidewalks, but they're generally too sandy for skating.) Mandalay Beach Road ends where it meets Fifth Street, just over the low dunes from Mandalay State Beach. Note: If there's no parking near Oxnard State Beach Park, you can park at the curb near this intersection and take the adventurous route in.

---

19. River Ridge
4.5 miles

Reference: Next to agricultural fields and a country club in Oxnard; see number **19** on page 282.

Ideal for: Fitness—Scene—Touring

Directions: From U.S. 101 in Oxnard, take the Victoria Avenue South exit. Proceed 2.5 miles through the farmland to Doris Avenue; turn left and proceed to the intersection with Patterson Road, where the avenue widens. Continue driving straight but look to the left, and you'll see the trail entrance. To park, drive far enough up Doris to make a U-turn and park at the curb.

Map: Bikeways Map, A Guide to Biking in Ventura County, published by the Ventura County Transportation Commission; (805) 642-1591.

Local shop: Sports Mart, 230 North Rose Avenue, Oxnard, CA 93030; (805) 988-5000.

Tour notes: The River Ridge bike path is a tidy little landscaped lane that runs flush up against the rich agricultural fields bordering northwestern Oxnard. In contrast, its north section passes through upscale neighborhoods near the River Ridge Golf Club. From the smoothly paved eight-foot-wide path, a broad view extends across the fields toward the Channel Islands Harbor to the west and all the way to the mountain ranges to the north.

Follow the River Ridge trail north as it parallels Patterson Road. To the left, a large field is tilled or filled with whatever crop is in season; a row of tall eucalyptus at the far end serves as wind break. After one and a quarter miles, the path branches right at Vineyard Avenue (go straight and you'll hit a dead end) and passes the River Ridge Golf Club as it heads east, all the while delivering a fine view of Oxnard's two skyscrapers in the distance. A brick wall borders the housing development across the street on your right, and pleasant landscaping continues alongside the bike path, which is now a concrete sidewalk. Where the route meets Ventura Road halfway across this eastbound section, it is replaced by a bike lane painted on the street, but skaters can continue on four-foot-wide sidewalks all the way up to H Street. Turn around here, and you will have skated 4.5 miles by the time you're back at Doris Avenue.

Alternatively, if you're ready to make a 5.5-mile loop by skating on more bike lanes, turn right to cross Vineyard Avenue, and follow H Street south through a variety of neighborhood pavement surfaces, making your Oxnard skating experience all the more memorable. Eventually, this southbound course will also return you to Doris Avenue; turn right on Doris to get back to your car.

20. Channel Islands Harbor 2 miles

Reference: **On the Pacific Ocean west of Oxnard; see number ㉑ on page 282.**

Ideal for: Beginners—Touring

Directions: From U.S. 101 in Oxnard, take the Victoria Avenue South exit. Proceed about five miles south to Channel Island Boulevard and follow it to the Harbor Boulevard intersection. Turn right and proceed one block on Harbor Boulevard, then make a left on Mandalay Beach Road. Park on the curb or in the free public lot; you're at the south end of Oxnard State Beach Park.

Map: Bikeways Map, A Guide to Biking in Ventura County, published by the Ventura County Transportation Commission; (805) 642-1591.

Local shop: Sports Mart, 230 North Rose Avenue, Oxnard, CA 93030; (805) 988-5000.

Tour notes: The Channel Islands Harbor is bordered by a delightful concrete promenade that follows closely along the marina's edge. Nearby Harbor Boulevard has wide sidewalks on both sides, plus spacious bike lanes, and when you combine the promenade with the boulevard, you've got a great little loop route.

Skate toward the harbor from the south end of Oxnard State Beach Park (described on page 299). The path veers inland next to a row of trees that don't quite hide a mobile home park, to meet the intersection where Channel Island Boulevard becomes Harbor Boulevard. Turn right at this intersection and skate south on the sidewalk for one block to reach the pedestrian crosswalk. Cross the street to reach the Channel Islands Harbor.

Enjoy the waterfront view here, but take care not to get your wheels caught in the cracks of the decorative brick or you might find yourself plunging into the harbor waters. The promenade sidewalk ends at Mariner's Emporium. Turn right if you want to skate out to Harbor Boulevard's sidewalks or bike lanes to return to the north end of the harbor. Otherwise, reverse directions on the promenade.

When you're ready for a break, you can stop at one of the lively eateries at the harbor's edge. If you time your visit right, you'll be treated to some live music while you get a good look at the vessels moored on the marina waters, and get to know some of the friendly folks who live in Ventura County.

21. Bubbling Springs Greenbelt   4.5 miles

Reference: A creekside path in the town of Port Hueneme; see number **21** on page 282.

Ideal for: Touring

Directions: From U.S. 101 in Oxnard, take the State Highway 1 exit south and pass through town. At the intersection with Wooley Road, go straight to remain on what has now become Saviers Road. Follow Saviers to its end at Port Hueneme Road and turn right. Turn left at Surfside Drive. Just down the street on the right, a big sign announces the Evergreen Springs Recreation Greenbelt and Park. Turn in at the parking-lot entrance and park.

Map: Bikeways Map, A Guide to Biking in Ventura County, published by the Ventura County Transportation Commission; (805) 642-1591.

Local shop: Sport Chalet, 1885 East Ventura Boulevard, Oxnard, CA 93030-1823; (805) 485-5222.

Tour notes: The Bubbling Springs Greenbelt starts out as a richly landscaped bike path that connects the lovely grounds of the Port Hueneme Cultural Center to wide-open Bubbling Springs Community

Park. Although the landscaping quality slips somewhat as you proceed north and the concrete starts showing signs of wear, the grass is just as green wherever you go.

To do the southern leg first, start from your parking spot at Evergreen Springs and skate south on the greenbelt trail. Be careful when you pass under the quaint wooden footbridge just before leaving the Evergreen Springs recreation area; the trail is very narrow and there's a blind curve. The landscape en route to the Cultural Center looks almost tropical, with mossy grass carpeting the banks of the little creek and leafy trees forming an arching tunnel of shade overhead. Beyond the foliage along the banks are some attractive small homes, with street lamps lining the path. Turn back where the path meets Surfside Drive at the Cultural Center. (See the next listing for details on Hueneme Beach Park, just across the street.)

After you return to Evergreen Springs, continue north to where the greenbelt trail crosses Port Hueneme Road. Try to avoid skating on the lumpy decorative bricks of the pedestrian crossing. The trail now enters another, less moneyed neighborhood; watch out for patchy concrete quality through here. When you reach the seeming end of the trail at Joyce Drive, look for the distinctive decorative bricks on the street that mark the route: they'll lead you to an apartment-complex driveway that's barricaded by posts. On the other side, the greenbelt path resumes, with the creek on the left and eucalyptus for shade.

Soon the trail meets Pleasant Valley Road. Turn left to follow the sidewalk up to the interminable light at Ventura Road. After you cross, turn right, back down Pleasant Valley, to enter the edge of a parking lot next to the greenbelt trail sign. Forget the trail and skate across the much smoother asphalt of the parking lot to where the trail exits the lot as a proper bike lane. Follow it as it curves to the right to pass through another neighborhood. The last section of the Bubbling Springs Greenbelt delivers you to sunny Bubbling Springs Community Park, just south of Bard Road.

22. Hueneme Beach Park   3 miles ⑧ 🧍 🚶

Reference: **On the Pacific Ocean near Port Hueneme; see number ㉒ on page 282.**
Ideal for: Beginners—Touring
Directions: From U.S. 101 in Oxnard, take the State Highway 1 exit south and pass through Oxnard. At the intersection with Wooley Road, go straight to remain on what has now become Saviers Road. Follow Saviers to its end at Port Hueneme Road and turn right. Turn left at Surfside Drive. Just down the street on the right, a big sign announces the Evergreen Springs Recreation Greenbelt and Park. Turn into the parking lot here and park.

Map: Bikeways Map, A Guide to Biking in Ventura County, published by the Ventura County Transportation Commission; (805) 642-1591.

Local shop: Sport Chalet, 1885 East Ventura Boulevard, Oxnard, CA 93030-1823; (805) 485-5222.

Tour notes: This tour follows a lush, beautifully landscaped greenbelt path to reach the elegant Port Hueneme Cultural Center located just across the street from the Pacific surf at Hueneme Beach Park.

Leave Evergreen Springs Park, heading south. Be careful on the steep, narrow little dip under the low footbridge as you exit the park and enter the Bubbling Springs Greenbelt—there's a blind curve blocking your view of oncoming traffic. After the footbridge, follow the gorgeous little creekside corridor (for details, see the previous listing) until you reach Surfside Drive at the Cultural Center. Here you'll find a ramp and some wide sidewalks near the main building, but you'll exhaust those opportunities in no time. Next, cross Surfside Drive to get to the waterfront walkways of Hueneme Beach Park, just across the street. There, six- and eight-foot-wide concrete sidewalks curve next to a well-tended lawn that runs along a wide beach. Near the main entrance to the pay parking lots, a 10-foot path encircles a trio of high flagpoles with brightly colored banners that snap in the breeze. Dwellers in the multistory apartment buildings across the way have a broad view of the beach, the white-capped surf, and the stacks of a power plant up the coast. The wind is a constant companion on this beach, a fact confirmed by the wooden windbreaks set up near the picnic tables.

You may be tempted to skate on the narrow sidewalk that extends up the coast from the parking area, but be forewarned: it terminates quite suddenly and unceremoniously in the middle of the sand, leaving you no choice but to skate back the way you came. When it isn't crowded, Surfside Drive next to Hueneme Beach Park is wide enough for skating, even with cars parked at the curb.

Heading down the coast from the park entrance near the Cultural Center, the sidewalk broadens to eight feet, curving lazily through the palms, ice plants, and street lamps for a very pleasant promenade. The walkway ends at a bridge that crosses the creek to some gated apartment buildings. Turn left at the foot of the bridge to follow a short path that returns you to Surfside Drive. From here, cross the street to regain the Bubbling Springs Greenbelt, and head back to Evergreen Springs.

If you're ready for another two-mile trip once you're back at Evergreen Springs, continue up the Bubbling Springs Greenbelt to its northern end on Bard Road; see the previous lisitng for details.

23. Moorpark College   3 miles

Reference: A college campus in the hills of Moorpark; see number ㉓ on page 282.

Ideal for: Figure/Stunts—Fitness—Hills/Slalom—Road/Street

Directions: From U.S. 101 in Thousand Oaks, exit onto State Highway 23 north. About 9.5 miles up, follow the signs to State Highway 118 east. Exit on Collins Drive, marked as the Moorpark College exit. Turn right on Campus Park Drive and follow the road around the east end of the campus and up the hill to park in one of the big lots on the north side, close to the main entrance.

Map: Bikeways Map, A Guide to Biking in Ventura County, published by the Ventura County Transportation Commission; (805) 642-1591.

Local shop: Val Surf & Sport, 3055 East Thousand Oaks Boulevard, Thousand Oaks, CA 91362; (805) 497-1166.

Tour notes: If you're lucky enough to be in town when Moorpark College is not in session, grab your skates and drive up to this hilly campus for a few hours of fun. You may even be serenaded by the coyotes living in the nearby hills.

Streetwise and hill-proficient fitness skaters will want to go back out to Campus Park Drive from the parking lot, turn left out of the lot, and make a counterclockwise loop to complete the 2.5-mile circumnavigation of the campus. As you might expect, the big hill you drove in on turns this loop into a real workout. Make a left to follow the bike lane on the north edge of campus, then go left again on Collins Drive to enjoy the downward slope on an eight-foot-wide concrete path. After turning left one last time onto Campus Park Drive, you'll skate back up the hill the way you drove in, on a four-lane road with no marked shoulders. Make sure traffic is sparse enough for you to occupy the right lane to climb the hill.

Skaters of other persuasions will be interested in the on-campus opportunities. Before you get rolling in earnest, take a look at the two interesting eight-foot-high computer-chip monoliths at the steps above the campus entrance. Literally falling away from here toward the administration buildings is a profusion of ramps, stairs, and rails. Good luck, kids. Behind the same clump of buildings, broad concrete avenues cross a sloped, grassy quad, making a small but ideal loop for practicing hill skating. To the east and just above the quad, Parking lot F, repaved during the summer of 1995, offers a generous expanse of smooth pavement with dynamite views to the south across Simi Valley.

24. Arroyo Simi Bikeway

11 miles ⑦ 🛹 🏃

Reference: **A creekside trail in the town of Simi Valley; see number ㉔ on page 282.**

Ideal for: Touring

Directions: From State Highway 118, the Simi Valley-San Fernando Valley Freeway, take the Tapo Canyon Road exit. Follow Tapo Canyon Road south until you reach the railroad tracks. Turn left onto Los Angeles Avenue immediately after crossing the tracks, and follow it east for four blocks to Tapo Street. Turn right, and park three blocks down at the curb where Tapo meets Ish Drive.

Map: Rancho Simi Recreation and Park District Street Map of Simi Valley.

Local shop: Val Surf & Sport, 3055 East Thousand Oaks Boulevard, Thousand Oaks, CA 91362; (805) 497-1166.

Tour notes: The scenery along Arroyo Simi Creek is a breath of fresh air for anyone accustomed to skating next to rivers that are more like concrete-walled canyons. Since Simi Valley is only a short drive from the San Fernando Valley, Los Angeles skaters should make it a point to schedule a spring visit when the wildflowers are at their most colorful and the hillsides their greenest.

Now for the bad news. The Arroyo Simi Bikeway wins the prize in this book for having the widest variety of pavement surfaces within the shortest distance: its quality ranges from prime number-one asphalt to the roughest, barely skateable aggregate. There are several street crossings with wooden gates on either side, often followed by a steep slope. Confusingly, at each intersection's pair of gates, the first posts a "trail end" sign and the second a sign that says "trail begin."

From your starting at Ish and Tapo, the path extends east for a third of a mile behind the Santa Susana Business Center, then curves up a slight hill to end at Los Angeles Avenue close to the Metro Link. Turn around and skate west to enjoy the best of the Arroyo Simi Bikeway. Grassy hills are close to the creek's south side, and soon the slab concrete of the easternmost creek bed gives way to more natural-looking rocky banks and patches of moss. Some of the creek bed in summer is as sandy as a beach, and little dams add interest. At this end, the bikeway is as clean as the creek and in mint condition. Its location on Simi Valley's outskirts is quiet enough to attract wildlife, including preening egrets, scampering squirrels, and even the occasional roadrunner.

Continuing west past business parks and across two intersections, the pavement quality drops, and patches of sand and gravel make things pretty slippery. A sharp curve up and away from the side of the creek requires some fancy footwork and leads to yet another "trail end" sign. Skate left for a block on the rough sidewalk to the point where the trail resumes a block away. Here the pavement grows smoother and passes behind some residential backyard fences until, just beyond the Royal Avenue crossing, it comes to a fork. (Ignore the hard-right branch in the trail that leads half a mile up to Los Angeles Street; the pavement is rough and narrow, with frequent dips to catch the rain runoff.)

The one-mile stretch after the Sycamore Drive intersection has some interesting park and backyard scenery, including human-sized (and slightly frightening) clumps of dead cactus—but unfortunately, this is also where the roughest pavement is. If you can endure a mile of unsettling vibrations, there are two more miles of good pavement ahead after the trail meets Erringer Road. The scenery between Erringer and First Street is also nice, but past First the trail runs behind industrial warehouses and shops until it finally ends at Madera Road and Easy Street. On the return trip, the views of the Santa Susana Mountains to the north and east make a great backdrop. Hint: Go very fast across the bad mile, and it will seem much smoother.

25. Wood Ranch Parkway   3.5 miles

Reference: **In the hills southwest of Simi Valley; see number ㉕ on page 282.**

Ideal for: Fitness—Hills/Slalom—Touring

Directions: From State Highway 118, the Simi Valley-San Fernando Valley Freeway, take the Madera Road South exit, also marked as the Ronald Reagan Library exit. Follow Madera 1.5 miles to Country Club Drive. Turn left on Country Club Drive and follow it to Wood Ranch Parkway. Turn left and then left again at Lake Park Drive to deposit your car at Rancho Madera Community Park, hopefully in the shade. The sidewalks bordering Wood Ranch Parkway are your trail.

Map: Bikeways Map, A Guide to Biking in Ventura County, published by the Ventura County Transportation Commission; (805) 642-1591.

Local shop: Val Surf & Sport, 3055 East Thousand Oaks Boulevard, Thousand Oaks, CA 91362; (805) 497-1166.

Tour notes: Experienced hill skaters will relish the delicious descent on beautiful Wood Ranch Parkway's superwide sidewalks, located in a country-club development no more than half a mile south of the Ronald Reagan Presidential Library. The nearby divided four-lane street services a series of expensive housing developments that line the cleft of Sycamore Canyon. Both sides of the road are bordered with prime-condition, landscaped concrete, in some places at least 12 feet across. If you want to make even wider slalom turns, the dual lanes on upper Wood Ranch Parkway itself are virtually empty during working hours and weekends.

What comes down, of course, must first go up. Wood Ranch Parkway makes a gradual climb, curving through the wide canyon, and past homes set far enough back enough from the street that you can enjoy their view of the surrounding hills. As you climb, you'll pass an intersection for Morrison Drive on the right; that route curves even more steeply up the side of the canyon, tempting those who brought their ski poles to skate its steep, black-diamond pitches. Continue up Wood Ranch beyond the last driveway to a pair of grand gates where the road ends in a cul-de-sac at the base of a high, grassy hill. Beware of the big longitudinal crack bisecting the last few slabs of sidewalk near the top; it's a real wheel-trap.

As you catch your breath from the almost-two-mile climb, turn around and enjoy the view that's accrued behind you. From this height, the northern panorama of the Santa Susana Mountains is deeply satisfying to the nature-loving soul.

And now the real fun begins!

---

26. Medea Creek Trail   3 miles 🌀 ♿ 🏃

Reference: **Southeast of Thousand Oaks, alongside a creek in Oak Park; see number ㉖ on page 282.**

Ideal for: Fitness—Hills/Slalom—Touring

Directions: From U.S. 101, the Ventura Freeway, near Agoura Hills, take the Kanan Road exit north. After 1.5 miles, turn left/east onto Conifer Street. After five blocks, Conifer intersects with Medea Creek Lane. Park at the curb on Conifer where it crosses the creek. The trail parallels the overgrown creek banks on both sides of Conifer.

Map: Bikeways Map, A Guide to Biking in Ventura County, published by the Ventura County Transportation Commission; (805) 642-1591.

Local shop: Athletes Sports Center, 5885 Kanan Road, Agoura Hills, CA 91301; (818) 889-1664.

Tour notes: The Medea Creek Trail starts out in a natural setting and ends on a tidy sidewalk of California suburbia. Along the way, it passes through a shady oak grove, winds through a quiet neighborhood, and then climbs a hill that promises a fast cruise back down.

Standing at the trail entrance on Conifer Street, look across the road to see a continuation of the trail disappearing into the dense brush and trees. Don't feel bad about passing it up (it's only a block long, and the pavement is very beat up); instead, skate into the oak grove along the east side of Medea Creek. A post-and-cable fence protects you from slipping down the bank into the creek bed. After a few curves and some little hills in the shade above the overgrown creek, the trail emerges from the woods onto a cul-de-sac below the backside of Oak Park High School. Look to the left to find the continuation where the trail leads out to Oak Hills Drive. Turn right to follow this street north half a mile. Where it meets busy Kanan Road, turn left to begin an easy climb up to Kanan Road.

On Kanan, the path is a meandering eight-foot-wide sidewalk featuring painted bike lanes. The landscaped route also provides a separate pedestrian walkway off to the side. As you skate up the hill, pay attention to wet patches from the watering system, which can lead to slippery uphill strokes and disastrous downhill skids. A brief downhill pitch rewards your first climb, and then you must climb again, this time for half a mile. You might as well spend a few of those moments admiring the community of Oak Park. On both sides of the trail, attractive housing developments proliferate. The ritziest ones are hidden in the high hills to the north.

The Kanan Road sidewalk ends where Kanan meets Lindero Canyon Road. Continuing any farther requires that you skate on the street's bike lanes, but if you're of that mind, you could skate a full eight-mile loop: To do that, you'd turn left where Kanan meets Westlake Boulevard, turn left again at Thousand Oaks Boulevard, and make the final left onto Kanan to follow it north to Conifer, where you left your car.

---

27. Oak Canyon Park   4 miles 🎖️ 🐾 🏃

Reference: **A community park in the hills of Oak Park; see number ② on page 282.**

Ideal for: Hills/Slalom—Historic—Touring

Directions: From U.S. 101 in Agoura Hills, take the Kanan Road exit north and proceed 2.5 miles. Turn right at Hollytree Drive and then take a left into the Oak Park entrance. Look to the right as you turn in and you'll see the nature trail entrance; parking is up the road on the left.

Map: Bikeways Map, A Guide to Biking in Ventura County, published by the Ventura County Transportation Commission; (805) 642-1591.

Local shop: Val Surf & Sport, 3055 East Thousand Oaks Boulevard, Thousand Oaks, CA 91362; (805) 497-1166.

Tour notes: Come and soak up the sights and sounds of nature in beautiful Oak Park on a weekday afternoon or evening when nobody's around. Oak Canyon is nestled among the rolling hills that were once home to the Chumash Indians. Note the word *hills*: skiers, bring your rubber-tipped poles for some excellent cross-training opportunities when there's no traffic. Even the parking lots are great for practicing tricks and artistic skating while enjoying the beautiful natural setting.

The park has a 1.5-mile paved nature trail marked with numbered stakes for those interested in a guided historical tour of the Medea Creek area (you'll need a park brochure for the interpretations, though, which won't be available if it's during off-hours). The northern asphalt

---

portion of the nature trail leaves the developed park and passes for half a mile through a cleft next to sandstone cliffs where winter rains are likely to leave a slippery deposit. Watch out for the little mounds of raised asphalt on the last climb to where the trail meets Bromely Drive; these will surely catch the inattentive on the way back down. A few strokes up and around the corner from the Bromely intersection, the trail ends at a wooden bridge. Advanced hill skaters will want to tackle the hills of Napoleon Avenue and Bromely, both leading up to the homes with the best views.

Within the park itself, the nature trail is paved in concrete and winds through the manicured grassy knolls among the picnic areas, play lot, and amphitheater. This section is also hilly, but the slopes are by no means as severe as the upper portion of the trail. Beginning skaters will find the grass-bordered knolls a safe spot for learning how to use the heel brake so that someday they might be up to the trail's steeper asphalt grades.

Besides the nature trail, the park's entrance road forms a smooth, three-quarter-mile slope that's perfect for linked slalom turns all the way from the circle at its northern end to the entrance at Hollytree. What a luxury it is to skate downhill on a full-width street when you're used to contending with eight- and 10-foot-wide bike paths. Ski poles make the climb back up a cinch. On a slow day at Oak Park, you can cross-train to your heart's content.

Los Angeles County

23 Great Places to Skate

Los Angeles County

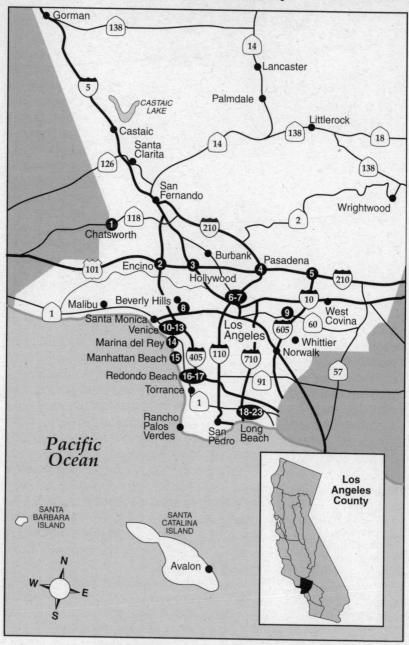

Skating Regions Beyond Los Angeles County

North .... Central Coast South, p. 281   South .... Orange County, p. 361; and
East .... Deserts, p. 339   Inland Empire, p. 353

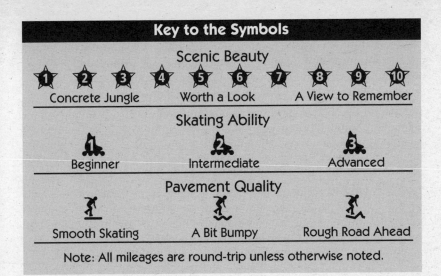

Key to the Symbols

Scenic Beauty

1 **2** **3** **4** **5** **6** **7** **8** **9** **10**

Concrete Jungle   Worth a Look   A View to Remember

Skating Ability

1   **2**   **3**

Beginner   Intermediate   Advanced

Pavement Quality

Smooth Skating   A Bit Bumpy   Rough Road Ahead

Note: All mileages are round-trip unless otherwise noted.

Ask a resident of Los Angeles County where you should skate, and you will most likely be directed to the Strand or one of its beach boardwalks. No wonder it's so crowded on the beaches that some areas have flashing yellow caution signals! On the other hand, in the sweltering days of summer—and temperatures regularly hit three-digit readings in the San Fernando and San Gabriel Valleys—why skate in the heat and smog when the cool scene (literally and figuratively) is on the coast?

Combine the length of the boardwalk trails between Pacific Palisades and Manhattan Beach, the Strand, and the Long Beach Shoreline, and the result is nearly 30 miles of coast with delicious ocean breezes, bright sun, and wide, sandy beaches. Throw in a diverse mix of cultures—an array of nationalities and skating styles—and you begin to get a picture of Los Angeles skating.

Venice Beach rules the heart of the skate scene, as it has since the roller skating craze took off in the 1970s. All of the locales along the South Bay Trail vary slightly in character, ranging from upscale Marina del Rey, Manhattan Beach, and Hermosa Beach to laid-back Redondo and Torrance Beaches, where you'll find relaxing skates and terrific views. If hockey is your preference, Santa Monica is billed as the ultimate in-line hockey pickup scene.

There are plenty of great places to skate inland, and they are rarely crowded. If you love skating fast, look at some of the river trails listed in this chapter and consider taking an early morning session in which you can get the desire for speed out of your system before you head to the beach.

Visitors who will be in the Los Angeles area for a week or more should keep tabs on the local entertainment guides. Almost any time of the year, listings include an in-line show at Magic Mountain, Knott's Berry Farm, or Disneyland.

---

1. Brown's Creek Trail

2.5 miles

Reference: **Running through Chatsworth in the San Fernando Valley; see number ❶ on page 312.**

Ideal for: Fitness

Directions: From Highway 118, the Simi Valley–San Fernando Freeway, exit south on Highway 27, Topanga Canyon Boulevard. A mile and a half south of the freeway, turn left onto Lassen Street and park at the Amtrak station on the right a block and a half up the street.

Map: Los Angeles County Bike Map, available for free by calling (213) 244-6539.

Local shop: Lake Balboa Skates & Kites, 16105 Victory Boulevard, Van Nuys, CA 91406; (818) 782-1234.

Tour notes: This trail is a short path that runs through the community of Chatsworth on the banks of Brown's Creek. It is located at the north end of Brown's Canyon Wash and connects the wash with a signed bike route heading east on Lassen Street.

Skating north from Lassen, the block up to Devonshire Street is an unlovely concrete canyon path bordered by twin chain-link fences. Catty-corner across the Devonshire and Canoga Avenue intersection, the trail gains in beauty and character, however, and becomes a standard asphalt path on the banks of a natural creek bed. The trail sports a full-on bridle trail on one side, but how a horse can get any exercise on such a short route is anyone's guess. Across the creek a pleasant concrete path for humans passes through a backyard corridor and terminates abruptly just short of Interstate 118.

---

2. Sepulveda Dam Recreation Complex

7.5 miles

Reference: **West of Encino in a park and flood control basin; see number ❷ on page 312.**

Ideal for: Fitness—Touring

Directions: On U.S. 101 approaching the interchange with Interstate 405, exit on Balboa Boulevard heading north. After you cross the first intersection, Burbank Boulevard, turn left into the Balboa Park parking lot. From Interstate 405 just after the U.S. 101 interchange, take the Burbank Boulevard exit and go left (west) past the golf course to the intersection with Balboa Boulevard. Turn right and park at Balboa Park and Sports Center on your left.

Map: Los Angeles County Bike Map, available for free by calling (213) 244-6539.

Local shop: Lake Balboa Skates & Kites, 16105 Victory Boulevard, Van Nuys, CA 91406; (818) 782-1234.

Tour notes: The Sepulveda Dam in the San Fernando Valley's huge Sepulveda flood control basin is tucked right up against the busiest freeway intersection in the whole world, where U.S. 101 meets Interstate 405. When not holding back floodwaters, the basin does double duty as the Sepulveda Dam Recreation Area, complete with the clean and attractive Lake Balboa. Other recreational facilities here include Woodley Avenue Park, a wildlife preserve, and on the west side of Balboa Boulevard, the Balboa Park and Sports Center.

People come here to skate the concrete bike path that makes a big loop around the developed part of the recreation area. In addition to the wide greens you would expect to see with two golf courses, the trailside scenery also features fields, trees, and natural grasses. On a clear day, the surrounding mountains add depth to the vista.

The big loop around the golf courses and Lake Balboa is the best for lap workouts. To start, skate up Balboa Boulevard to Victory Boulevard. On the way, pass the entrance to Lake Balboa, which will later be the endpoint of this tour. Turn right on six-lane Victory and skate on the concrete sidewalk. An open field is to the right, looking like nothing more than a patch of weeds in the dry heat of late summer. Turn right at Woodley Avenue and enjoy a long stretch of trail next to the Woodley Lakes Golf Course and the model airplane airport. At Burbank Boulevard, turn right to skate alongside the shady edge of Encino Golf Course. A short distance past the clubhouse, you will reach the street where you started, Balboa Boulevard. Turn right and soon you will be back where you began. Watch out for raised edges on the sidewalk, unrepaired damage from recent earthquakes.

At this point you will have completed the more scenic loop. To continue on the second half of the 7.5-mile loop, skate west on the concrete bike path that crosses the north end of the Balboa Sports Center where you parked. This takes you to the residential area on the other side. Veer right to follow the trail to Oxnard Street, on which the concrete bike lane continues west to White Oak Avenue. Skate across the Los Angeles River and turn right on Victory Boulevard. Follow Victory back to Balboa Boulevard a mile east, and cross at the light to its east side before you turn right. Skate south to the entrance road to Lake Balboa.

Now it's time for the promised dessert. Follow the mile-long entrance road over the bridge and around the perimeter of the lake.

Leaving the lake area, the road goes past the Woodley Lakes Golf Course clubhouse and an office of the Los Angeles Parks and Recreation Department, extending to end at Woodley Avenue. No bike lanes are provided near the lake, but traffic is light and drivers expect to see skaters and cyclists on the street. You can skate on the fine asphalt of the parking lots, but bikes and skates are not allowed on the lake's concrete sidewalks. Enjoy the view, and rest a while on the grass.

---

3. Hollywood Boulevard Walk of Fame

2 miles

Reference: **On the infamous sidewalks of Hollywood; see number ❸ on page 312.**

Ideal for: Touring

Directions: From U.S. 101 in Hollywood, take the Hollywood Boulevard exit west. Pay parking is available on the boulevard within a block, or you can drive a couple of blocks farther to look for public parking after you pass Gower Street (the 6100 block). The Walk of Fame starts at Cahuenga Boulevard (the 6300 block) and extends several blocks west.

Local shop: Venice Roller Works, 7 Westminster Avenue, Venice, CA 90291; (310) 450-0669.

Tour notes: Hollywood Boulevard, which is crowded with tourists and a tough crowd of street people, will not be every skater's cup of tea. However, adventurous skaters who want to be able to put another notch in their wheel frames should roll up the 10-foot-wide sidewalks of the boulevard to straddle the marble-embedded stars. Skate during daylight hours to reduce (but not eliminate) the chance of unwanted encounters with unstable street characters and drug dealers.

Skate up the street in front of such famous (but for the most part tacky) attractions as the Pantages Theater, the Hollywood Wax Museum, Ripley's Believe It or Not, and Mann's Chinese Theater, in that order. The most impressive building is the Hollywood Galaxy Theater, still new enough to be attractive. The Walk of Fame ends at La Brea Avenue, 13 blocks from the start.

Special note: The projected completion date for the Los Angeles Metro project had yet to be determined at the time this book was published. Therefore, parts of the street may be in a state of disrepair, and stars may have been removed temporarily for safekeeping until the street and sidewalk are restored.

---

4. Rose Bowl

4 miles ❼ 🛼 🏃

Reference: **In the park and parking lots surrounding a sports stadium in Pasadena; see number ❹ on page 312.**

Ideal for: Beginners—Figure/Stunts—Fitness—Hills/Slalom—In-Line Hockey—Touring

---

Directions: About a mile north of the Highway 134 interchange on Interstate 210 (Foothill Freeway) in Pasadena, exit at Mountain Street and drive west to where Mountain becomes Seco Street. After about three-quarters of a mile, Seco Street enters Brookside Park, where you will find ample parking south of the Rose Bowl.

Local shop: Lake Balboa Skates & Kites, 16105 Victory Boulevard, Van Nuys, CA 91406; (818) 782-1234.

Tour notes: When you think about it, it's not hard to figure out why the Rose Bowl is a favorite Sunday destination for hockey players, figure and fitness skaters, and even slalom enthusiasts. There are huge parking lots, it's surrounded by a ring of tree-covered hills, and a variety of pitches in the pavement invite every sort of in-line play. There's even a pedestrian path next to a road that loops around the lush greens of a golf course, providing great terrain for building up that all-important training heart rate. While Pasadena is far enough inland to be hit with hot weather during summertime, getting an early morning start helps with that problem. Besides, if you do work up a sweat, you can always cool off afterward with a dip in the Rose Bowl Aquatics Center's Olympic-size swimming pool. Look for the Aquatics Center down Arroyo Road at the south end of Brookside Park.

Explore all of the parking lots to find the one best suited to your style of skating. If you like slalom, there are some gentle slalom runs in the handicapped parking lot. If you are just getting started on in-lines, find the flattest place that isn't bustling with other activity (although that may be difficult on a beautiful Sunday). Hockey players will have no trouble finding a pickup game on most weekends. Even figure skaters should be able to find their own corner to practice leaps and spins. Keep your eyes open for smooth new pavement.

After you've checked out the opportunities and challenges offered by the parking lots, take the 3.4-mile tour around the bowl and Brookside Golf Course. Use a counterclockwise route to follow Seco Street, on the south edge of the parking lots, east to its intersection with Rosemont Avenue. Turn left and stick to the inside track as the route turns left twice more at Washington Boulevard and West Drive. As you pass the pretty golf course and take comfort in the shade of eucalyptus and pepper trees, it really doesn't seem like exercise. If you're a real hill addict, go straight instead of turning left at Washington Boulevard. A steep and curvy hill with no bike lane climbs out of the park into a neighborhood a quarter of a mile up. Don't attempt this unless you have the skills to handle downhill speed and know how to share the road with cars.

The locals caution that you should look out for student drivers, who value the spacious parking lots of the bowl as much as you will.

5. Santa Fe Dam Recreation Area 2 miles ⑧ 🚶🏃

Reference: **East of Pasadena at a recreation area and dam outside of Irwindale; see number ❺ on page 312.**

Ideal for: Beginners—Fitness—Touring

Directions: From Interstate 210 east of Pasadena, exit to the south on Interstate 605, the San Gabriel River Freeway. Take the first exit, Arrow Highway, and head east to cross the San Gabriel River. Turn left to enter the park on Orange Avenue (the right turn is Azusa Canyon Road). Approaching from the east on Interstate 210, take the Irwindale Avenue exit heading south, turn right on Arrow Highway and right again on Orange Avenue. The entrance fee at the gatehouse is $6, and you can come and go all day as long as you show your receipt at the gate. There is plenty of parking.

Map: Santa Fe Dam Recreation Area Map, available from the park office near the entrance or by calling (818) 334-1065.

Local shop: Bishops Skate Shop, 1024 North Citrus Avenue, Covina, CA 91722; (818) 966-1300.

Tour notes: Besides being an ideal parking and starting point for a skate on the northern San Gabriel River Bike Trail, Santa Fe Dam is a beautiful location for novice skaters to learn the basics of gliding, turning, and stopping. The concrete sidewalks are wide and smooth, and are bordered by thick lawns that make the occasional bout of klutziness more bearable. Behind the rocky levee that surrounds the park, the San Gabriel Mountains tower in all their majesty, adding drama and elegance to the pretty lakeside scene. On weekdays, the place is nearly deserted, leaving all of that prime pavement to the lucky visitor on wheels.

At off-peak hours, the sidewalks running next to the reservoir and through the shady park are a welcome respite to those who are used to the crowded skating locations near the ocean, often overpopulated by a wide variety of wheeled and nonwheeled users. It can get very hot this far inland, however, so plan to visit in springtime or on a cooler summer day. A park map plus a variety of other L.A. County trail maps can be picked up at the park office near the entrance at the east end of the lake.

To access the San Gabriel River Bike Trail, park in the first lot you see after descending the levee from the gatehouse. Driving in past the gatehouse, you will see the trail next to the road. To get to the river trail, skate back up toward the gatehouse on the trail near the entrance road and follow the levee to the west side, where the path goes back down the rocky bank on the other side to cross Arrow Highway and join the river trail. Although its northern section is not described in this edition of *California In-Line Skating*, the San Gabriel River Bike

Trail serves as an excellent fitness and speed skating route, and also as a connection to the Rio Honda via the Whittier Narrows Recreation Area seven miles southwest.

6. Griffith Park
6.5 miles

Reference: **A park in the hills northwest of downtown Los Angeles; see number ❻ on page 312.**

Ideal for: Hills/Slalom—Road/Street—Speed—Touring

Directions: Heading north out of Los Angeles on Interstate 5 (known here as the Golden State Freeway), exit at Zoo Drive and loop over the freeway to get to the park and the zoo parking lot.

Local shop: Sport Chalet, 100 North La Cienega Boulevard, Los Angeles, CA 90048-1938; (310) 657-3210.

Tour notes: In Los Angeles' vast Griffith Park, a shady asphalt bike path (about five feet wide) and fine bike lanes follow Zoo and Crystal Springs Drives, taking you on a somewhat hilly route through tall stands of eucalyptus and past the emerald green lawns of a golf course. Hit this trail early in the day before the weather heats up and traffic gets heavy. That way, you can appreciate the 6.5-mile end-to-end round-trip, a popular training route for local speed skaters. The bike lanes on the street are a clean and smooth alternative to the designated asphalt bike path.

The path passes the western edge of the parking lot on Zoo Drive. Start by skating to the south on the small hills that pass the zoo and golf course, a good warm-up for the big hill at the far end. Just before you reach the ranger station, the road splits in two, and soon you begin to climb the half-mile-long hill to the south end of the park. Turn around at the Interstate 5–Los Feliz Boulevard ramp. The southbound lane is less steep than the northbound lane, so if you don't feel quite up to descending the big hill and if you don't mind skating against the traffic, you might consider coming back down the same lane you climbed.

Heading north from the Zoo Drive parking lot, the bike lane follows Zoo Drive between Highway 134 and a forested hillside, leading eventually to Griffith Park's northwest entrance at Forest Lawn Drive. This curvy stretch makes a long and gradual climb to the northwest end of the park. Basically the path here resembles a hillside country road, except that the roar of the nearby freeway can be heard through the trees, pretty much ruining that whimsy. A tiny skate rental shop is located just off the road at the end of the park.

7. Downtown Los Angeles

4 miles

Reference: **In the heart of Los Angeles; see number ❼ on page 312.**

Ideal for: Hills/Slalom—Historic—Road/Street—Touring

Directions: From U.S. 101 in Hollywood, take the Temple Street exit just after the Interstate 5/Highway 110/Highway 2 interchange. Go straight to cross Temple and follow Hope Street down Bunker hill and through the Financial District to Sixth Street. Keep your eyes open for curbside parking or turn left on Sixth Street and go two block to Pershing Square, an outdoor mall area with underground parking.

Map: Downtown Los Angeles Map available from the Downtown Marketing Council and Community Redevelopment Agency; (213) 624-2146.

Local shop: Sport Chalet, 100 North La Cienega Boulevard, Los Angeles, CA 90048-1938; (310) 657-3210.

Tour notes: Intermediate and advanced street skaters in Southern California love downtown Los Angeles during the weekend when, in some districts, it is virtually deserted. These are skaters to whom "street" means challenging urban terrain, not busy downtown roads. You know what you're looking for, and you will find it here. For the rest of us, there are plenty of wide sidewalks for touring through this famous city. There are also some big, long hills, so this location is not appropriate for lower level skaters.

After you warm up on the concrete plaza and steps of Pershing Square, it's pretty much skater's choice as far as touring the nearby urban terrain. For starters, the Financial District, located three blocks west of Pershing Square, is most likely to be quiet. Grand and Hope Streets offer exciting opportunities to skate among the biggest skyscrapers there. If you're into hills, make the big climb up Bunker Hill to visit the Dorothy Chandler Pavilion and the Mark Taper Forum. From there, roll east on First Street and you'll pass the civic center. Main Street is on the far side of city hall. History buffs should go north on Main from here and pass under the Santa Ana Freeway to reach Olvera Street. On the right, a gazebo marks the site where the city of Los Angeles was founded.

Skating south from the Olvera Street historic district on Main Street, you can also visit Little Tokyo, the toy district, the flower markets, and the garment district (in that order) as well as the Los Angeles Convention Center in the southwest corner of downtown. Make sure you bring along a map so you won't get lost. To explore the main shopping district, skate up Broadway, one block east of Pershing Square.

8. UCLA Campus
2 miles **6 1**

Reference: **University of California at Los Angeles; see number
8 on page 312.**

Ideal for: Historic—Road/Street—Scene—Touring

Directions: On Interstate 405 (the San Diego Freeway) outside of Westwood, take the Wilshire Boulevard exit heading northeast. After three
blocks, turn left on Westwood Boulevard and follow it one block to
take the first right onto Lindbrook Drive. Again after only one block,
angle off Lindbrook to the left to get onto Hilgard Avenue. Look
for parking on Hilgard, which borders the east side of the UCLA
campus, or go to one of the streets close by on the blocks just east
of Hilgard.

Local shop: Sport Chalet, 100 North La Cienega Boulevard, Los
Angeles, CA 90048-1938; (310) 657-3210.

Tour notes: The UCLA campus offers an attractive setting with lots of
paved walkways for cruising and some long, steep hills for road-savvy
skaters. For a fun hour or two of exploration, plan to visit during a time
when classes are not in session. Better yet, skate here after dark, when
the whole campus is lit up, setting the beautiful structures aglow.

UCLA was once known as a hot spot for expert street skaters and
hockey players, but the academic playground is now experiencing a
crackdown by security staff. This is a trend emerging on campuses
across the state, most likely due to liability and property damage
concerns. While campus cops still allow students to commute on
in-lines between classes (barring excessive speed), they have started
enforcing rules against skating in parking lots and parking structures.
Street skaters can receive fines of $100 if caught grinding or jumping
UCLA stairs, planters, or curbs.

9. Whittier Narrows
Recreation Area
2 miles **7**

Reference: **Near Whittier in a park between the Rio Honda and the
San Gabriel River; see number 9 on page 312.**

Ideal for: Beginners—Fitness—Touring

Directions: From Interstate 605 north of Whittier, exit west on Highway
60, the Pomona Freeway. Take the first exit, Peck Avenue, and turn
left at the bottom of the ramp to cross under the freeway. Take the
first right onto Durfee Avenue, the Whittier Narrows entrance road.
(Make note of the entrance to the Nature Center on the left; if you
decide to skate the San Gabriel River Bike Trail, stop by for a free
local map.) After you pass Santa Anita Avenue, look to the right for
the parking lot off of Velsir Street. The bike path runs right by the
north edge of the lot.

Map: Whittier Narrows Nature Center and Wildlife Sanctuary brochure, 1000 North Durfee Avenue, South El Monte, CA 91733; (818) 444-1872.

Local shop: Bishops Skate Shop, 1024 North Citrus Avenue, Covina, CA 91722; (818) 966-1300.

Tour notes: If you want to get in a good session of roll-aerobics, visit the Whittier Narrows Recreation Area, where a network of bike paths loops around the three lobes of the centrally located Legg Lake. Folks in these parts are lucky to have such a nice place to skate a few laps and burn off some calories while enjoying the scenery and watching the ducks. Several miles in from the coast, Whittier Narrows is one of those skating destinations that is great in the spring-time, before the summer heat drives everyone out to the crowded beach boardwalks.

For beginning skaters, this quiet park, with its tree-shaded lakes and wide concrete bicycle paths, has all the qualities that make it an ideal spot for some early in-line skill building. Low mounds in the grassy landscaping supply the necessary terrain for learning how to deal with that helpless feeling of rolling when you aren't ready to roll. You can step off onto the lawn here, but on the beach, you'd better be prepared to use your heel brake to stop or slow down. There's nothing worse for your skates than sand and water in the bearings, a combination that can cause the urethane wheel to separate from the hub. The result? A dead wheel.

Whittier Narrows is a main connection point for access to the San Gabriel River Bike Trail to the west (28 miles long) and the Los Angeles River bikeway via Rio Honda to the east (29 miles long). Right across Durfee Avenue from where you parked, an access bike trail on the edge of the wildlife sanctuary takes you past the nature area to the intersection of the river bike paths. A free map put out by the Nature Center (a few too many photocopies away from the original) shows where to turn depending on which way you want to go.

Special note: Do not leave valuables unattended in your car here. If you have any removable electronics, hide them. Better yet, don't even bring them.

---

10. Parking Lot Pickup Hockey   .5 miles 🏵 🏃 🏊

Reference: In the seaside parking lots of Santa Monica; see number ❿ on page 312.

Ideal for: Beginners—Figure/Stunts—In-Line Hockey—Scene

Directions: From Interstate 405 (the San Diego Freeway) in West Los Angeles, exit onto Interstate 10 (the Santa Monica Freeway) and head west. Near the road's end at the beach, follow the signs exiting to Fourth Street. Follow Fourth Street south to Ocean Park Boulevard where you will turn right to get to the beach and the wide parking lots.

Local shop: Venice Roller Works, 7 Westminster Avenue, Venice, CA 90291; (310) 450-0669.

Tour notes: Santa Monica is the undisputed capital of in-line hockey in Southern California. Its vast seaside parking lots are perfectly situated alongside the sandy beaches just a short distance from the water's edge, and the ocean breezes help keep the players cool. Part of what makes this such a prime place for pickup games is the high level of hockey skills displayed by those who frequent the spot. Elite players from organized hockey leagues—and even some pros—populate the impromptu teams. Players show up in such great numbers that the games can span six parking lots. The lots are loosely organized according to skill level, with the most experienced players tearing it up on Court A, leaving Court B to the less competitive or skilled skaters. After a particularly good maneuver, cheers can be heard from passing spectators on the bike path that runs between the beach and the lots.

---

11. South Bay Trail: Santa Monica to Marina del Rey
8.5 miles

Reference: **Along the Pacific Ocean between Santa Monica and Marina del Rey; see number ⑪ on page 312.**

Ideal for: Beginners—Scene—Touring

Directions: From Interstate 405 (the San Diego Freeway) in West Los Angeles, exit onto Interstate 10 (the Santa Monica Freeway) and head west. Follow the signs to the Highway 1 junction and turn right, heading toward Malibu and Oxnard. Turn left into the first beach parking lot just north of the pier (you can expect to pay $6, but the skating here is well worth it). Skate north on the sidewalk that runs along the sand at the west edge of the lot.

Map: Los Angeles County Bike Map, available for free by calling (213) 244-6539.

Local shop: Venice Roller Works, 7 Westminster Avenue, Venice, CA 90291; (310) 450-0669.

Tour notes: Start your day at the Santa Monica Pier, one of the most popular skating sites in Southern California. Not only is it a great skate destination in and of itself, it is the second city along the northern section of the nearly 20-mile-long Strand bikeway. A gigantic parking lot at the shore end of the pier usually has a few parking spaces open at the far corner. During peak summer months, this is also a regular location for the popular Blade School clinics. More parking lots farther south are famous for attracting hockey enthusiasts looking for fast-paced pickup games. The bike path south of here runs through Ocean Park and then enters the wild and woolly domain of Venice Beach, a scene every visiting skater has got to be a part of at least once in a lifetime (see page 326.)

Skate under the pier and cross the rough bridge (watch out for the raised patches) to access the smooth 20-foot-wide concrete bike path that has made the Strand such a famous destination. To add to the luxury, there's a separate asphalt path that keeps pedestrians off the trail. Palm trees, street lamps, and a lawn border the trail through South Beach Park, where a concrete plaza inspires show-offs to perform a few tricks before moving on. A short asphalt stretch connects to a 12-foot-wide concrete path that runs right out on the beach. To the left are the parking lots that lure pickup roller hockey enthusiasts of the highest caliber. Ocean Front Walk—a shop-lined pedestrian promenade that is also a fun skating route—begins here but will likely be jammed with tourists. On the promenade route, you might get a glimpse of the oiled muscles of the bodybuilders who work out in the gym on the sand.

In the heart of Venice Beach, the bike path passes through the Pavilion, where another grassy park sports a ramp that is popular with skaters and skateboarders who dare to air. Wide walks that lead up to the boardwalk attract performers of all persuasions, in-line and otherwise. You'll recognize this de facto stage by the large crowd gathered around to watch.

Continuing south from the Pavilion, pass behind one of the most impressive displays of graffiti in the state, a defunct snack bar that has been taken over by equally colorful characters. The beach down here is still sandy and the water is blue, but the parking lots and old apartment buildings to your left are none too pretty. A rough quarter-mile-long stretch of asphalt doesn't enhance the experience. Continuing south, the trail and scenery improve on a route that ends at the entrance channel of Marina del Rey.

To continue skating south down the Strand, go back up to Washington Street at the end of the Venice Pier and follow it inland on its very nice bike lane (after you suffer through the first block on sidewalks). Watch out for the downslope, which is fun for experienced street skaters but highly dangerous for folks who don't have the skills or experience to skate safely next to fast-moving cars. Turn right on Palawan Way and then left on Admiralty Way, which leads to a bike path along a greenbelt that circles around the marina. After it takes you through a parking lot you will find yourself on Fiji Way, which curves around and dead-ends in a loop at Fisherman's Village. The bike path resumes at the south of the loop and takes you to the channel. Turn right onto the levee and cross the bridge a short way down. A bike path resumes at Playa del Rey's Dockweiler Beach (see South Bay Trail: Manhattan Beach to Playa del Rey, page 328). Follow the levee inland to skate the Ballona Creek Trail (see page 327).

12. South Bay Trail: Santa Monica to Pacific Palisades

7 miles

Reference: Along the Pacific Ocean between Santa Monica and Pacific Palisades; see number ⑫ on page 312.

Ideal for: Beginners—Scene—Touring

Directions: From Interstate 405 (the San Diego Freeway) in West Los Angeles, exit onto Interstate 10 (the Santa Monica Freeway) and head west. Follow the signs to the Highway 1 junction and turn right, heading toward Malibu and Oxnard. Turn left into the first beach parking lot just north of the pier (you can expect to pay $6, but the skating here is well worth it). Skate north on the sidewalk that runs along the sand at the west edge of the lot.

Map: Los Angeles County Bike Map, available for free by calling (213) 244-6539.

Local shop: Venice Roller Works, 7 Westminster Avenue, Venice, CA 90291; (310) 450-0669.

Tour notes: Meet your friends at the Santa Monica Pier and spend the day exploring the Strand bikeway, participating in a Blade School clinic, testing your stair jumping abilities, or watching the hockey skaters. Santa Monica is a major element in Southern California's in-line culture and offers the chance to have a memorable skating experience that must not be missed.

If you get an early start, you can beat the crowds and have this northernmost section of the Strand almost to yourself. The slopes of Topanga State Park and the ridge of the Santa Monica Mountains dominate the scenery to the north, making the view much more attractive than some seen from the beaches farther south. Painted every few hundred feet on the trail's concrete are the words "Bikes Only." This does not mean that you cannot skate on the path, only that pedestrians aren't welcome; don't worry, they have all of that sand to walk on! In any case, nobody is enforcing the rule, nor is there any speed limit on this section of the Strand.

In the first mile, the trail's sandy route passes near a row of older seaside homes sporting spiral staircases. Hotels and the requisite volleyball courts dot the inland side of the 10-foot-wide concrete path. Beyond that is the Pacific Coast Highway and its backdrop of sandy bluffs.

At the two-mile point, the path climbs a low hill and continues northward just below a shrub-covered bank close to the highway's edge. Through Will Rogers State Beach the concrete gives way to an asphalt path that has a separate lane for pedestrians. If the parking lots are empty enough, the pavement there is better than the trail farther north. Just beyond a little patch of grass and some rest rooms, the illustrious Strand dead-ends quite suddenly at a culvert after nearly 20 miles, humbly terminating as a beat-up six-foot-wide asphalt trail.

For some crowded trails and the hottest in-line scene on the Strand, continue south from the Santa Monica Pier to Venice Beach (see the next listing).

13. Venice Beach   2 miles

Reference: **The Marina Bay beach town of Venice; see number ⓭ on page 312.**

Ideal for: Scene—Touring

Directions: From Interstate 405 (the San Diego Freeway) in Culver City, take the Washington Boulevard exit and follow Washington to the beach. Park in a lot near the pier if possible. Locals give this advice: "Don't let the meter run out, and don't leave anything in your car."

Map: Los Angeles County Bike Map, available for free by calling (213) 244-6539.

Local shop: Venice Roller Works, 7 Westminster Avenue, Venice, CA 90291; (310) 450-0669.

Tour notes: Known for the wild variety of personalities (from kooks to street musicians to muscle heads) who congregate here, the Venice Beach boardwalk is *the* place to go when you're in the neighborhood. It is probably the biggest skating scene in the state, and even some Northern Californians are willing to admit that they come here to see and be seen. If you can find your own tiny patch of pavement in the midst of the dense crowds on a fine weekend day (get an early start), this is the perfect setting for strutting your stuff on skates. But you won't be the only hot wheeler around, because this place has been growing as a skate destination ever since it became known as the unofficial world capital of roller disco. And it's no wonder—with ocean breezes lifting the smog and keeping the inland heat at bay, it is possible to enjoy perfect weather on any day of the year.

Skate north from the Venice Pier at Washington Street on the bike trail next to the parking lots until it crosses the sand to pass behind a graffiti-covered snack bar. Just around the corner, you will come upon Windward Court, also known as the Pavilion. Because there is a large paved area, a long ramp, wide sidewalks, and garbage cans to jump over, this is where all the action is—where the hotshot skaters, skate dancers, and skateboarders assemble. It is also where the bike path splits off to a wide pedestrian promenade next to an array of shops.

Skate up the promenade to get a real feel for Venice, no matter how crowded it is. Be courteous, and plan to skate back on the curving concrete of the smooth beach bikeway. Fresh air, scents from the many food stands, and the sound of boom boxes waft around you, and performers and wild characters complete the scene.

14. Ballona Creek Trail

8 miles 🌟**4** 🏊**2** 🏃

Reference: **Along the flood control canal running inland from Marina del Rey; see number ⓮ on page 312.**

Ideal for: Fitness—Speed—Touring

Directions: From Interstate 405 (the San Diego Freeway) in Culver City, exit onto the Marina Freeway (Highway 90) and follow it toward Marina del Rey. Turn left on Culver Boulevard and then right on Highway 1/Lincoln Boulevard. One block down, turn left onto Fiji Way and follow it as it curves around to Fisherman's Village in Marina del Rey. Parking fees are charged by the half hour, but it's free if you get your ticket validated at a shop.

Map: Los Angeles County Bike Map, available for free by calling (213) 244-6539.

Local shop: Venice Roller Works, 7 Westminster Avenue, Venice, CA 90291; (310) 450-0669.

Tour notes: The Ballona Creek Trail runs along the banks of one of the nicer flood control canals in Los Angeles. Starting where the creek meets the Pacific at the mouth of the Marina del Rey harbor, the beachside portion of the trail extends southwest nearly half a mile on the top of the breakwater, delivering great views of the harbor to the north and of colorful multistory dwellings across the channel's rocky banks. From the coast, the trail takes you inland toward Culver City on a 10-foot-wide asphalt path that provides many thrilling dips under overpasses.

Except for a few serious cyclists, the Ballona Creek Trail receives little traffic, making it a great location to bring along your ski poles for an allover workout on the flats using cross-country skiing techniques. And of course, the underpass dips (usually paved in smooth concrete) are a delight, allowing skaters to switch to downhill slaloms.

Starting from the Fisherman's Village area, look for the trail entrance near the terminating loop of Fiji Way, south of the village. A few strokes brings you to the intersection at Ballona Creek. Turn right to skate out on the breakwater. The section of trail from here to the bridge across the channel is part of the route connecting the shoreline bikeway in Venice Beach (see South Bay Trail: Santa Monica to Marina del Rey, page 323) to the bikeway at Playa del Rey (see the next listing). At the bridge, continue skating on the breakwater to the end of the pavement, about a third of a mile out. It's a fine spot to stop for a moment to enjoy the cool breezes and watch the gulls and pelicans. Unfortunately, another breakwater protecting the entrance channel blocks a view out to sea.

Back at the intersection near Fisherman's Village, continue inland on an eight-foot-wide asphalt trail on the rockbound levee above

Ballona Creek, at this point full of water. For the first mile, a wide, grassy floodplain is beyond the chain-link fence to your left. After the initial chain-link section, the post and cable fence to your right is attractive and unobtrusive. After the canal passes under the Marina Freeway, the scenery changes to residential, ranging from modest homes to tenement housing. Ballona Creek is reduced to a mere trickle here, but the trail's pavement quality actually improves. Near the Marina del Rey Middle School, the trail crosses a wood-surfaced bridge to continue inland another couple of miles through Culver City neighborhoods.

15. South Bay Trail: Manhattan Beach to Playa del Rey

13.5 miles

Reference: Along the Pacific Ocean between Playa del Rey and Manhattan Beach; see number **⑮** on page 312.

Ideal for: Fitness—Scene—Speed—Touring

Directions: From Interstate 405 (the San Diego Freeway) just north of Torrance, exit at Hawthorne Boulevard (Highway 107) heading north. After 1.5 blocks, turn left onto Manhattan Beach Boulevard and drive west all the way to the beach. Park in the lot on Manhattan Beach Boulevard (be prepared to pay) or on a residential street off Palm Avenue or Hermosa Avenue. The trail can be found where it passes the end of the pier.

Map: Los Angeles County Bike Map, available for free by calling (213) 244-6539.

Local shop: Venice Roller Works, 7 Westminster Avenue, Venice, CA 90291; (310) 450-0669.

Tour notes: Enjoy the scene on the north section of the popular Strand trail and then continue up the coast through El Segundo and Dockweiler Beaches to Playa del Rey. The bikeway north of El Porto is sometimes known as a no-man's-land because its passage next to the Los Angeles International Airport limits access and renders it relatively (and to some, blessedly) desolate. On Dockweiler's broad beach, the giant shadows of airplanes taking off from the busy airport are outlined briefly on the sand as they head out over the ocean. Such attributes make this section of the bikeway especially appealing to fitness and speed skaters, as well as adventurers who are fed up with fighting the crowds farther south.

The attractive Manhattan Beach Pier is decorated with street lamps and railings painted a fresh sea blue. Better yet, it is skater-friendly and paved in concrete. You can skate to the end and take in the view, have a snack, or peek into the doorway of the Roundhouse Marine Studies Lab and Aquarium. You can't miss the great view looking back toward the shore.

Skating from the Manhattan Beach Pier, the Strand bikeway extends up the coast for 1.75 miles on a 12-foot-wide concrete sidewalk next to an ice plant–covered bank at the edge of the beach. Atop the bank, oceanfront homes and apartments with a view line the street. All the way to El Porto at the border of El Segundo Beach, skaters, pedestrians, and bicyclists crowd onto the popular bikeway, making fast skating pretty much out of the question during peak hours.

Continuing beyond El Porto, though, traffic on the trail diminishes dramatically, to just a few bicyclists and hardier skaters. The pavement quality takes a turn for the worse and rudely presents skaters with rough asphalt. However, along this narrow section of beach the trail is closer to the crashing waves, which partially makes up for the roughness. Fortunately, the surface improves as you approach the sewage treatment plants. The plant grounds close to the trail are enclosed by chain-link fences, but they include a pretty, grassy strip where employees gather to eat lunch.

Two miles north of El Porto, the bikeway's wide concrete paving resumes. After it passes Dockweiler Beach RV Park, it once again supplies necessary trailside amenities such as benches, rest rooms, and water fountains. For another three miles, the trail curves serenely along Dockweiler Beach, past a rest room/snack bar "oasis" of grass and palms, and next to a forest of tall wood posts (perhaps forgotten volleyball courts?). At Playa del Rey, it curves inland where the beach ends and takes you to the wide pedestrian bridge that crosses Ballona Creek and leads to Marina del Rey.

To continue north, follow the trail across the bridge over the creek to the breakwater. (Turn left to skate out to the mouth of the bay, where you can savor the view.) Turn right and skate inland to where the bike path makes a left turn at the intersection with the Ballona Creek Trail (see the previous listing). The bike path ends at Fiji Way, but you can skate on the sidewalk or bike lanes heading north on Fiji Way. A block or two after Fiji veers inland, the bike path resumes. Look to your left for a painted bike path that takes you into the parking lots of the harbor area. Follow the path through the unlovely harbor parking lots to where it crosses Admiralty Way and then passes through a greenbelt alongside Admiralty Way. At the Washington Boulevard intersection, turn left and skate three-quarters of a mile up the gradual ascent on the bike lane. Washington Boulevard ends at the Venice Pier and beach boardwalk.

16. South Bay Trail:
Redondo Beach to Palos Verdes

6 miles

Reference: **Along the Pacific Ocean between Redondo Beach and Palos Verdes; see number ⑯ on page 312.**

Ideal for: Scene—Touring

Directions: Approaching Torrance southbound on Interstate 405 (the San Diego Freeway), take the Crenshaw Boulevard exit and turn right to head south. After two miles, turn right onto Torrance Boulevard and proceed 3.5 miles to the beach. Torrance Boulevard terminates at the end of the Redondo Beach Pier in a parking structure that the Strand trail actually passes right through. Approaching northbound on Interstate 405 near the town of Carson, take the Sepulveda Boulevard exit and turn left to cross under the freeway. Head west for 5.5 miles to where Sepulveda meets Torrance Boulevard. Turn left onto Torrance and go five blocks to the parking structure. Approaching on Interstate 110 (the Harbor Freeway), take the Gardena Freeway (Highway 91) exit west and follow it two miles to Crenshaw Boulevard. Turn left and proceed two miles south until you reach Torrance Boulevard. Turn right onto Torrance and proceed to the parking structure.

Map: Los Angeles County Bike Map, available for free by calling (213) 244-6539.

Local shop: Roller Skates of America, 1312 Hermosa Avenue, Hermosa Beach, CA 90254; (310) 372-8812.

Tour notes: Embellished with teal accents and street lamps, the upscale shopping area and Redondo Beach Pier are very pretty, although no skating is allowed. As you head down the bikeway from Redondo Beach, the hills of Palos Verdes Point rise in an almost Mediterranean vision above the south end of the beach, the cheery red tile roofs of the buildings catching the sunlight. The view gets better and better as you continue skating.

Starting where the parking structure bike path emerges into the sunlight south of the pier, the asphalt trail widens to 12 feet, allowing pedestrians to use it, too. The sand next to the inland side of the trail is held in place by ice plant, with Esplanade Street just above. Down a short, sandy slope lies the beach, and rest rooms and other structures are accessible here and there next to the bikeway. Watch out for pedestrians and bicyclists during peak hours. The trail ends at one of the ubiquitous Alfredo's snack bars.

Nearby, a steep slope provides access up to Paseo de la Playa. If you skated the entire Strand all the way from Pacific Palisades, 22 miles north, congratulations. Now you can call a taxi from the nearby phone booth.

17. The Strand: 4 miles 🔟 🏃 🛹
Manhattan Beach to Redondo Beach

Reference: On the Santa Monica Bay shore between Manhattan Beach and Redondo Beach; see number ⑰ on page 312.

Ideal for: Beginners—Scene—Touring

Directions: From Interstate 405 (the San Diego Freeway) just north of Torrance, exit at Hawthorne Boulevard (Highway 107) heading north. After 1.5 blocks, turn left onto Manhattan Beach Boulevard and head west all the way to the beach. Park in the lot on Manhattan Beach Boulevard (be prepared to pay) or on a residential street off Palm Avenue or Hermosa Avenue. The trail can be found where it passes the end of the pier.

Map: Los Angeles County Bike Map, available for free by calling (213) 244-6539.

Local shop: Roll It, 1114 Manhattan Avenue, Manhattan Beach, CA 90266; (310) 372-2050.

Tour notes: South of the Manhattan Beach Pier, a smooth concrete bikeway stretches two miles down the beach known as the Strand, a major player in the Los Angeles-area in-line scene. Where the bikeway enters pretty Hermosa Beach, the attractive shoreline development there draws so much activity that flashing yellow caution lights are turned on during peak hours to control crowds. Bicyclists and skateboarders must dismount when the lights are on; fortunately, skaters aren't required to remove their wheels, yet.

You'll notice that, starting from the Manhattan Beach Pier, the trail has fewer pedestrians than you'd expect; they have their own walkway next to the homes on the street to the left. The trail jogs inland at the Hermosa Beach city limits and follows Hermosa Avenue for a few blocks on an asphalt bike lane. Take this route back to the beach at 26th Street. A 20-foot-wide concrete promenade greets you on the beach, with a low wall on the ocean side and views of the streets and fancy brick promenades on the left. A 10 mph speed limit is posted, and within half a mile, you reach the yellow light area. Embedded every few yards in the trail's concrete are yard-wide sections of brickwork with grooves that vibrate your skates. This may be a strategic design feature to remind trail users to keep their speed down. On skates, though, the faster you cross the bricks, the less annoying the vibration.

At Herondo Street, the northern city limit of Redondo Beach, the bikeway turns inland for a full mile to follow city streets around the back side of King Harbor.

To skate the inland connection to the Redondo Beach bikeway, take either the sidewalks or the bike lane on Harbor Drive, depending on your skills. After passing a brick plaza, you will find the bike path that passes through the marina and into the parking structure at the end of the Redondo Beach Pier. On the other side of the parking structure and its little plaza, the bikeway resumes its southward beach-side route. From here you can skate all the way to Palos Verdes (see the previous listing, South Bay Trail: Redondo Beach to Palos Verdes).

18. Los Angeles River Bikeway (LARIO)   29.1 miles one-way ⭐ 🛼 🏃

Reference: **Along the flood control canal running inland from Long Beach; see number ⑱ on page 312.**

Ideal for: Fitness

Directions: From the Long Beach Freeway (Interstate 710) heading south, follow the signs to downtown Long Beach. After you cross the Los Angeles River, proceed to Shoreline Drive. Look for free parking in the Aquatic Park area.

Map: Los Angeles County Bike Map, available for free by calling (213) 244-6539.

Local shop: Alfredo's, 700 East Ocean Boulevard, Long Beach, CA 90802; (310) 434-6121.

Tour notes: One official mileage count for the Los Angeles River bikeway (known locally as LARIO) cites a total of 29.1 miles. Now that's an endurance skate, especially if you don't have a ride back to your car at the end!

To access the LARIO from the Aquatic Park bike path, skate west toward the Los Angeles River mouth. The trail curves inland when it meets the bank of the river. The beautiful scenery of the Long Beach harbor is left far behind on this flood control canal, so a good strategy would be to skate inland up the river trail until you're half tired or hungry (remember, you still have to skate back against the wind) and then return to the harbor area to recuperate and congratulate yourself on a great workout. Skate across to the other end of Aquatic Park to replace worn skate parts at Alfredo's, then sit under an umbrella and eat a taco while you wait.

The eight-foot-wide asphalt trail parallels Interstate 710 and the Los Angeles River flood control channel inland from the Long Beach harbor area. The bikeway's first 10 miles pass through Deforest and Coolidge Parks in Long Beach, and then Hollydale Park in South Gate. A mile beyond Hollydale Park, just north of the Imperial High-way, the trail branches off to follow the Rio Honda to the Whittier Narrows Recreation Area, a good 20 miles from Long Beach. Here, a connecting trail to the east accesses the San Gabriel River route.

Sticking with the Rio Honda River Trail at the Whittier Narrows, the next major destination is the Peck Road Water Conservation Park another nine miles up. This northern leg is a favorite among Los Angeles bicyclists. If you make it this far, you really should pat yourself on the back!

Special note: The Los Angeles River is a popular hangout for drug dealers and homeless people. Do not skate alone here, or at any time other than under the bright light of day.

---

19. Downtown Long Beach 2 miles 9 3

Reference: In Long Beach; see number 19 on page 312.

Ideal for: Hills/Slalom—Historic—Road/Street

Directions: From the Long Beach Freeway (Interstate 710) heading south, follow the signs to downtown. After you cross the Los Angeles River, proceed to Shoreline Drive. Make note of Pine Avenue where the divided highway terminates. You will skate on Pine Avenue past the convention center to get to downtown. Look for free parking in the Aquatic Park area.

Local shop: Alfredo's, 700 East Ocean Boulevard, Long Beach, CA 90802; (310) 434-6121.

Tour notes: The city of Long Beach has a gorgeous metropolitan center close to one of the most beautiful harbors in the state. Highlights include a unique convention center and exciting urban terrain. The waterfront area provides access to the Long Beach Shoreline Bicycle and Pedestrian Path (see Long Beach Shoreline Trail, page 335), which connects the San Gabriel River Bike Trail with the nearby Los Angeles River bikeway (LARIO).

If you can't resist the stunning whale mural that adorns the outside of the cylindrical building at the convention center, skate from Aquatic Park back to Shoreline Drive and turn right up Pine Avenue. A bike lane on the street takes you past the entrance to the grounds of the convention center. From here, it's just another block or two up Pine until you reach Ocean Boulevard and can explore downtown Long Beach. Palm fronds fluttering in the breeze in the median divider give Ocean Boulevard that refreshing seaside touch as it passes the library and city hall, the courthouse, and the World Trade Center, all offering wonderful skating and sight-seeing opportunities. Map out your own route amid the high-rises lining the wide sidewalks on both sides of the boulevard, which has been refurbished with fresh-looking brickwork, promenades, and plazas. There are slopes throughout downtown, so watch your speed and be aware of the pedestrians and traffic around you.

Closer to the harbor, less street-oriented skaters might enjoy a flat roll and the chance to window-shop at Shoreline Village near the west end of the Downtown Shoreline Marina. Or, to get the most spectacular view of the harbor and of the *Queen Mary*, which is docked

---

across the channel, skate out to the end of the marina's breakwater. That geodesic dome near the *Queen Mary* is the hangar where Howard Hughes used to store his *Spruce Goose* airplane years ago. Local park rangers say that there is no speed limit here and that the "No Roller Skating" message painted on the sidewalk is not enforced due to public request.

20. Veteran's Building   1 mile ⭐ ⚫ 🏃

Reference: **The grounds of a medical center complex in Long Beach; see number ⑳ on page 312.**

Ideal for: Road/Street

Directions: From Interstate 405 (the San Diego Freeway) in Long Beach, exit south on Bellflower Boulevard. After about 1.5 miles, look to your left for Sam Johnson Drive, which enters the Veteran's Administration Medical Center complex at 5901 East Seventh Street. There are ample parking lots in the area. Park nearest to the terrain that tickles your fancy the most.

Local shop: Alfredo's, 700 East Ocean Boulevard, Long Beach, CA 90802; (310) 434-6121.

Tour notes: The Long Beach Veteran's Building is popular with street skaters because it has three sets of short flights of stairs (three or four steps each) connected by flat sections of concrete 20 to 30 feet long. A set of "S" curves ascends the handicapped ramp allowing you to get back up and try them all over again. The trick is, you've got to skate the grounds to find the 30-by-80-foot area where this sweet spot is located, because you will most likely miss it in a car. There are parking lots galore, so even searching for the treasured stairs can be fun.

When you skate in this area, please be respectful of the veterans who are rehabilitating here. If you are asked to leave, do so. You can always come back some other time, unless, of course, you raise such a ruckus about getting kicked out that stricter enforcement becomes necessary and ruins the setup for everybody.

Two miles away on a street route is another favored destination of street skaters in these parts: the small grounds of the Long Beach Olympic Plaza Natatorium (described in the next listing). Skate west on Seventh Street, on which the formal entrance to the Vet's Hall is located. Cross Highway 1, pass the golf course and, at Woodrow Wilson High, turn left onto Ximeno Avenue. Follow Ximeno for 1.25 miles, all the way to Ocean Boulevard and turn right at Ocean. Get onto the beach boardwalk at 54th Street and continue up the coast a quarter mile to the pier and the Natatorium.

21. Long Beach Shoreline Trail 10 miles 🏆🐾🎿

Reference: **Within the harbor and on the shoreline of Long Beach;
see number ㉑ on page 312.**

Ideal for: Beginners—Fitness—Historic—Scene—Speed—Touring

Directions: From Interstate 405 (the San Diego Freeway) in Long Beach,
exit on Studebaker Road heading south. Two miles down, turn right
on Westminster Avenue. After half a mile Westminster becomes Second Street. Follow the signs pointing to Belmont Shore, crossing the
island of Naples. Enter the seaside neighborhood at the first left turn
allowed and park on the street as close to the beach as possible. Skate
to Ocean Boulevard and cross it to take one of the path access trails.
The trail actually starts at Ocean and 54th Place, across the street from
an outdoor in-line hockey arena at the Bayshore Playground. (You can
also park in Long Beach and skate this trail in the other direction. See
Downtown Long Beach, page 333.)

Map: Los Angeles County Bike Map, available for free by calling
(213) 244-6539.

Local shop: Alfredo's, 700 East Ocean Boulevard, Long Beach, CA 90802;
(310) 434-6121.

Tour notes: Your skate will be enhanced by terrific harbor and city skyline views as you head up the middle of the sandy beach on the
17-foot-wide Long Beach Shoreline Bicycle and Pedestrian Path. The
12-foot-wide concrete bikeway, plus a generous five-foot pedestrian
lane, connects Belmont Shore to the Long Beach Convention and
Civic Center and the Downtown Shoreline Marina. Unlike the busier
Strand paths farther north, here there is no speed limit, and in spite
of the gorgeous vistas, the trail is a lot less crowded. In other words,
there are plenty of opportunities to go really fast!

Starting at the 54th Street entrance, skate out onto the trail and
relish the sandy roll up the coast (in this case, you're heading west
rather than north). Several access paths connect the main trail with the
streets along Ocean Boulevard. If it's windy out, you'll most likely be
fighting a head wind in this direction. An early morning start helps
alleviate the problem.

After a mile, you'll reach the Belmont Pier, worth checking out
with a quick roll. The pavement is smooth enough, but when it's busy,
all of those flying hooks and lines are rather unnerving. Curb grinders
will want to hang out at the Natatorium, site of the swimming events
for the 1988 Olympics. Up a short ramp, the shiny edges of the tree
planters seem to have been prewaxed for your grinding enjoyment.
You can skate right into one entrance of the Natatorium and view the
aquatic activities inside from behind a barrier next to the bleachers.
Leaving the Natatorium, the trail follows a grassy area out of sight

from the beach and then crosses behind a parking lot to climb a short but delicious 30-foot-wide concrete promenade. In spite of the raised cracks in the surface, it's fun to go up and down, up and down . . .

Another ramp on the other side of the building with the promenade brings the trail back down to more expanses of beach. As you skate on the curving path toward the forest of masts in the Shoreline Marina, the view just gets better and better. Islands out in the San Pedro Bay are spiked with iron towers and palm trees, creating a weird sort of tropical effect. Near the marina, there's a large and mysterious white bubble—the hangar used by Howard Hughes to house his *Spruce Goose*. The downtown Long Beach high-rises loom ahead on the horizon, and to the right, a few ritzy homes perch atop sandy bluffs that are protected from erosion by thick ground cover. Ahead lies the best stretch of trail for speed work.

At Bluff Park, veer right to skate around the parking lot and continue up the path. After another freewheeling stretch on the beach, you will reach Alfredo's, a trailside snack bar and skate specialty shop. Beyond Alfredo's you will be skating on the Shoreline Aquatic Park Bike Trail on the Downtown Shoreline Marina. Don't miss out on the breathtaking view from the end of the breakwater of the harbor area and downtown Long Beach. (Lucky for you, those "No Roller Skating" notices that are painted all over are not enforced, according to a local ranger.)

---

22. San Gabriel River Bike Trail   10 miles 🏴 4 🛼 🏃

Reference: **Along the flood control canal running inland from Long Beach; see number ㉒ on page 312.**

Ideal for: Fitness—Road/Street—Speed—Touring

Directions: From Interstate 405 (the San Diego Freeway) in Seal Beach, exit south at Seal Beach Boulevard and go 2.5 miles south to the intersection with Highway 1/Pacific Coast Highway. Turn right and enter central Seal Beach. After the 12th Street stoplight, watch for Main Street and Eighth Street. A tiny sign just after Eighth marks the left turn onto Marina Drive. Turn left (if you miss it, there's a light at Fifth Street where you can turn left to rejoin Marina Drive). Follow Marina Drive across the bridge over the San Gabriel River. There is plenty of parking on the other side at the marina and the Seaport Village Shopping Center. The trail is on the Seal Beach side of the river.

Map: Los Angeles County Bike Map, available for free by calling (213) 244-6539.

Local shop: Alfredo's, 700 East Ocean Boulevard, Long Beach, CA 90802; (310) 434-6121.

Tour notes: The San Gabriel River Bike Trail just keeps going, and going, and going. Speed, fitness, and endurance skaters will learn just how far they can keep going when they hop on the path, perhaps with a pair of ski poles for a full-body workout, cross-country style.

Along this relatively short sampling of the river's 28-mile-long route, the scenery delivers a study in contrasts. It is really quite pleasant near the marina, as far as concrete flood control canals go, with an attempt at landscaping evident next to the trail. But within a mile, you will be staring up at the towering smokestacks of three humongous power plants. Force yourself to skate the rough pavement through here, for you will be rewarded with three much more pleasant miles next to a canalside flower nursery. Cross the bridge to the other side of the river when you reach mile marker 4.0. The right fork is Coyote Creek, described in the Orange County chapter. Continuing northeast on the San Gabriel River, you will skate by the wild lands of the nature study area at El Dorado Park East. Before the Spring Street underpass, an obvious exit ramp allows you to leave the river trail and skate within the immaculate surroundings of El Dorado Park East (see the following listing). Farther up the trail, wildlife sightings in the thickly covered riverbed will add that natural touch to any serious endurance workout.

Fitness nuts, if you're ready for more skating after you return to the Long Beach Marina (and you don't mind skating on the street in bike lanes), consider taking the mile-long route across Alamitos Bay to roll on some of the smooth concrete of the beautiful Long Beach Shoreline Trail. You could also drive this connector route, but with the wheels already on your feet and a spirit of adventure in your heart, why not skate it? From your parking spot on Marina Drive, follow the bike lanes on Marina inland up to Second Street. Turn left to skate on Second Street's bike lanes and go across the island of Naples, passing over two bridges, then cross Alamitos Bay heading northwest. Once you reach Alamitos Bay Beach (after the second bridge), take the first left down Shore Avenue to get to Ocean Boulevard. Cross Ocean and turn right to meet one of the wide concrete access paths that head out across the sand to the Shoreline Trail.

---

23. El Dorado Park East — 5.5 miles

Reference: In north Long Beach; see number ❷❸ on page 312.
Ideal for: Beginners—Fitness—Speed—Touring
Directions: From Interstate 605 in Long Beach, exit at Spring Street and turn west. A park entrance is located off Spring Street. (If the westbound gate is closed, make a U-turn at the next light to enter at Spring Street's eastbound gate.) The entrance fee is $3 on weekdays and $5 on weekends. To park for free, continue west on Spring Street and turn right on Studebaker Road. Turn right again on Wardlow Road and then, just before you reach the river, turn right onto Stevely Avenue

and park at the corner of Wardlow and Stevely. Skate across the bridge and enter the park halfway down on the north side of Wardlow at the bicycle and pedestrian gate near the fire station. (You must skate across the four-lane street without a crosswalk to do this.)

Map: Los Angeles County Bike Map, available for free by calling (213) 244-6539.

Local shop: Alfredo's, 700 East Ocean Boulevard, Long Beach, CA 90802; (310) 434-6121.

Tour notes: There are three reasons why people come to El Dorado Park East to skate, and they appeal to skaters displaying a wide range of styles and skill levels.

For recreational skaters and beginners, the Billie Boswell bike path delivers four miles of smooth concrete throughout Areas II and III in El Dorado Park East. Groves of mature, loosely spaced trees provide shade over the spacious lawns where the six-foot-wide path wends its way among the various picnic areas. Tiny hills add some thrills. Two lakes attract ducks and other waterfowl, and make inviting picnic spots. This clean and well-maintained park is an excellent site for a morning's workout or a leisurely roll with friends. Whether you pay for your parking or skate in from Stevely, be sure to pick up a map at one of the entrance stations on Spring Street so you can get the lay of the land.

Eschewing the smooth bike paths, speed skaters have learned to value the loop around Area III, where Dovey Road offers some fine terrain for serious training. Actual competitions are occasionally held there, too. The asphalt on the road is rough, but with the speed and stability gained from five-wheel skates, it's not terribly noticeable. The one-way Dovey Road loop is 1.7 miles long, and traffic there is almost nonexistent during off-hours.

The third reason skaters come to El Dorado Park East is to use it as a convenient entry point for the San Gabriel River and Coyote Creek bike paths. The San Gabriel River Bike Trail runs a total of 28 miles on varying paved surfaces ranging from sublime to awful (just like the scenery). Access to the trail is at the southwest corner of Area III. About a mile south down the San Gabriel River Bike Trail, a bridge marks the branch to the northeast that is the Coyote Creek Trail. These are routes for adventurers and endurance skaters who want to skate long distances without battling crowds or stopping for intersections. Here, you'll be much more impressed with the colorful jerseys worn by the cyclists who share the trail with you than by the smoothness of the pavement or the quality of the canal scenery. The San Gabriel River Bike Trail is described in this chapter (see the previous listing). For a description of the Coyote Creek Trail, see page 368 in the Orange County chapter.

Deserts

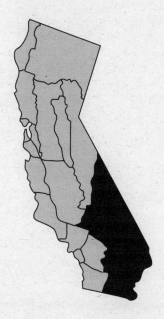

10 Great Places to Skate

Deserts

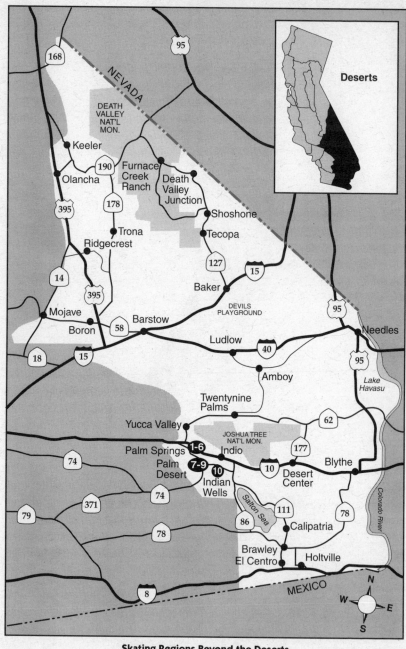

Skating Regions Beyond the Deserts

North .... Sierra Nevada, p. 243 West .... Central Valley South, p. 225; L.A. County, p. 311; and Inland Empire, p. 353

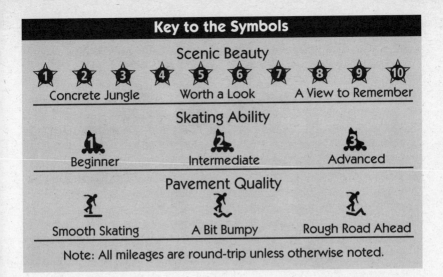

Key to the Symbols

Scenic Beauty

⭐1 ⭐2 ⭐3 ⭐4 ⭐5 ⭐6 ⭐7 ⭐8 ⭐9 ⭐10

Concrete Jungle — Worth a Look — A View to Remember

Skating Ability

Beginner — Intermediate — Advanced

Pavement Quality

Smooth Skating — A Bit Bumpy — Rough Road Ahead

Note: All mileages are round-trip unless otherwise noted.

The entrance from the northwest end of the Coachella Valley on Interstate 10 sets the stage for a visit to desert country. As you descend the barely perceptible but considerable grade from San Gorgonio Pass, your field of vision is filled with incredibly dry valley terrain that is ringed by mountain ranges. Joshua Tree National Monument is visible in the Little San Bernardino Mountains to the east, while the San Jacinto Mountains border the valley on the west. At the north end of the valley floor, fields of windmills sprout up like groves of some strange bionic palm tree.

Of course, the desert is infamous for its blazing heat. Death Valley, at 282 feet below sea level, gets hit with the most notoriously high temperatures, often in the 130s. The trick to skating in this region is to schedule your trip for the wintertime, because although the sun shines brightly over the valley an average of 330 days every year, the temperatures are much cooler in winter. Unfortunately, that is the region's prime tourist season and you will have to pay big bucks for lodging.

Be forewarned that the smooth concrete that makes skating in Palm Springs and Palm Desert so great is very slick when it gets wet. You'll have to be very careful because the lawns here must be watered constantly in order to retain their brilliant shades of green.

1. Tramway Road

2 miles 🎱 🐾 ⛷

Reference: At the base of Mount San Jacinto in Palm Springs; see number ❶ on page 340.

Ideal for: Hills/Slalom—Road/Street

Directions: Approaching Palm Springs from the north on Interstate 10, take the Highway 111 exit just past San Gorgonio Pass. Follow Highway 111 about eight miles to the north edge of Palm Springs, where you will see Tramway Road heading up into a mountain canyon on the right. Turn right and park on the gravel shoulder before the gate. Approaching from the south on Interstate 10, exit at Date Palm Road about three miles north of the Ramon Road exit. Drive west for almost five miles to Palm Canyon Drive, then turn right. After driving one mile north you will see Tramway Road on the left.

Local shop: Sports Fever, 73-360 Highway 111, Palm Desert, CA 92260; (619) 340-0252. Other contact: Palm Springs Information, 3200 East Tahquitz Canyon Way, Palm Springs, CA 92262; (619) 323-8299.

Tour notes: Are you the kind of person who has to experience new things if only to say you did? If so, and if you have good heel braking and hill skills you may be a candidate for Tramway Road. This two-laner climbs nearly two thousand vertical feet in 4.5 miles to provide access to the Palm Springs Aerial Tramway. Since 1963, the tramway has carried hikers, skiers, and tourists up another 12,800 vertical feet to an altitude of 8,516 in San Jacinto Wilderness State Park.

In spite of the fact that Tramway Road is very steep (you'll see signs that recommend turning off the air conditioner in your car), the first mile is a feasible skate. It is less steep and is straight enough to allow you to see almost everything, both ahead and behind. This is important because there are no paved shoulders, meaning you must skate on the street, possibly taking up both lanes in order to control your speed with slalom turns. Before you start, make sure you have a lot of rubber on your heel brake and know your abilities and limitations. Stop climbing at the 1,000-foot-altitude sign just before the road begins curving into the canyon. You don't want to be in the middle of the road when cars come barreling down the hill around a blind corner. Now turn around and claim your reward: a breathtaking view of the Coachella Valley and the Salton Sea beyond Palm Springs. Before heading down, watch the dip near the parking area for several seconds to make sure no car is emerging, and listen for cars approaching from behind. Unless you schuss most of the way down (bless your immortal soul), check the condition of your wheels once you reach the bottom. They'll lose some urethane with every carve on the asphalt road.

2. Canyon Country Club Route   4.5 miles 🌟6 🔱 🏃

Reference: **Southern urban Palm Springs; see number ❷ on page 340.**

Ideal for: Beginners—Road/Street—Touring

Directions: Approaching Palm Springs from the north on Interstate 10, take the Highway 111 exit just past San Gorgonio Pass. Follow Highway 111 for nearly 10 miles to Palm Springs and down Palm Canyon Drive through downtown. When Highway 111 curves to the left (becoming East Palm Canyon Drive), continue straight on South Palm Canyon for another half mile. Turn left at La Verne Way and park at the curb just after La Verne crosses Camino Real. Approaching from the south on Interstate 10, exit at Ramon Road in Thousand Palms and drive west for approximately 6.5 miles (passing through Cathedral City) to Sunrise Way. Turn left onto Sunrise and drive another 1.5 miles, past East Palm Canyon Drive, where Sunrise becomes La Verne and curves around to the right. Park just before the Camino Real intersection. Start skating south on Camino Real.

Map: Palm Springs Bicycle Touring Guide, available from the Community Recreational Services, 401 South Pavilion Way, Palm Springs, CA 92262; or by calling (619) 323-8272.

Local shop: Sports Fever, 73-360 Highway 111, Palm Desert, CA 92260; (619) 340-0252. Other contact: Palm Springs Information, 3200 East Tahquitz Canyon Way, Palm Springs, CA 92262; (619) 323-8299.

Tour notes: The south town country club neighborhood near Camino Real was built long before the city planners started putting in the wide, pink sidewalks you see elsewhere. Here you will be skating on the very smooth asphalt of the street itself. This area is quiet enough traffic-wise that residents feel comfortable pushing baby carriages along the road, and it is also part of the city bike route system. Many of the bike routes in town are designated both for bicycles and golf carts, so watch for the "Cart Xing" signs. Along the way you'll see homes that, although older, are quite elegant and uniquely designed, ranging from California Ranch style to art deco, all with modest one-story layouts. The landscaping is impeccable, and even some of the mailboxes are fascinating.

Camino Real meets Murray Canyon Drive after about 1.25 miles. Murray Canyon does have sidewalks, but they are of poor quality. You'll probably be tempted to stick to the street anyway, because the traffic is so light. If you do, cross to the south side and turn left on this four-lane road. Three-quarters of a mile east, head north on what has now become Toledo, another wide residential street with no bike lane. Skate in the street or on the sidewalks on the left (west) side to avoid the irritating double driveways that interrupt the sidewalks on the right. Toledo will take you back up to La Verne where you can turn left to return to your car.

An early diversion off Toledo is Via Estrella, a street on the left that turns north and becomes Caliente, which leads back up to La Verne. This route sticks close to the west border of the country club. Farther up Toledo and also on the left, Canyon Estates, with its new black pavement, is a loop worth exploring. Inside, Madrona Circle has a north outlet leading to La Verne.

---

3. Golf Course Bikeway   8 miles 🏅 🚲 🧍

Reference: **Eastern Palm Springs; see number ❸ on page 340.**

Ideal for: Beginners—Touring

Directions: Approaching Palm Springs from the north on Interstate 10, take the Gene Autry Trail exit heading south to Palm Springs. After seven miles, turn right onto Ramon Road and watch for the sign for Demuth Park. Turn left (south) and park at the mouth of the western-most parking lot off of Mesquite Avenue. Approaching from the south on Interstate 10, exit at Ramon Road in Thousand Palms and drive west for approximately five miles. Turn left at the sign for Demuth Park and follow the directions above.

Map: Palm Springs Bicycle Touring Guide, available from the Community Recreational Services, 401 South Pavilion Way, Palm Springs, CA 92262; or by calling (619) 323-8272.

Local shop: Sports Fever, 73-360 Highway 111, Palm Desert, CA 92260; (619) 340-0252. Other contact: Palm Springs Information, 3200 East Tahquitz Canyon Way, Palm Springs, CA 92262; (619) 323-8299.

Tour notes: The Golf Course Bikeway allows visitors to get a glimpse of the fountains and ponds and gorgeous greens that make Palm Springs appealing to so many golfers. From this central point in the Coachella Valley, the distant views in all directions are fantastic, too. To the west you can easily spot Mount San Jacinto. At 10,804 feet, it is the second highest point around, rivaled only by San Gorgonio Mountain, which rises 11,499 feet on the north horizon. In the clear desert air, these snow-covered peaks stand in brilliant contrast against the blue sky.

Starting from the baseball fields of Demuth Park, leave the gritty park sidewalk behind by skating west toward the lawns of Fairchild's Bel-Air Greens and Mesquite Golf and Country Club, both just across El Cielo Road. The bikeway passes through the Mesquite Golf Course, following along its north border. Here's a compelling reason to wear a helmet: one bad slice, and POW! The bikeway is well marked with signs at all entrances and intersections. As usual, you need to watch for wet patches caused by the constant watering necessary to ensure that the vast lawns will stay green in the hot climate of the Coachella Valley.

Farrell Road bisects the Mesquite Golf Course, and at Farrell, you have to roll down a short slope to the left before reaching the street-level sidewalk. Traffic here is usually light enough that you can "jay-roll" across to the bikeway entrance on the other side. Otherwise, go north to the stoplight intersection at Ramon Road to cross and then come back down. More landscaped terrain follows on the west section of the golf course as you pass by a series of two-story condominiums.

Just before exiting the golf course, you must cross a narrow old wooden bridge with big gaps and loose boards. Take it with some speed, keep your wheels lined up perpendicular to the gaps, and try to ignore the unsettling noise and vibration of the rattling wooden slats. You exit the golf course onto a street that takes you one block west to Sunrise Way. Turn left on Sunrise and proceed one block south to a bridge. You will see the trail between the river (or riverbed, depending on the time of year) and North Riverside Drive. Cross Sunrise Way (there is no pedestrian crosswalk or stoplight) to continue skating on a landscaped sidewalk path toward the west. The view of the San Jacinto range from North Riverside Drive is quite nice, and the street is quiet. The trail ends just short of Palm Canyon Drive and immediately beyond the pedestrian/bikeway bridge that crosses to Camino Real.

After returning to Demuth Park, intrepid explorers may want to climb the short sidewalk path on its south border to get to the ridge-top bike path that continues east toward Rancho Mirage. Along here, stunning views of the mountain ranges across the green valley are sometimes marred by the presence of chain-link fences. The quality of the pavement on this trail varies, from poor to fair asphalt road for the most part, to a nasty section of concrete on the underpass for the Gene Autry Trail, which is textured with ridges to aid in golf cart traction. The trail begins alongside the golf courses occupying the Tahquitz Creek and Palm Canyon Channel and eventually brings you to the local water slides. Turn right at the water slide trail junction to continue on your way to Rancho Mirage and the Tahquitz Creek Golf Course.

4. Ruth Hardy Park   .75 miles 🟊 🛼 🏃

Reference: **Palm Springs city center; see number ❹ on page 340.**

Ideal for: Beginners—Fitness

Directions: Approaching Palm Springs from the north on Interstate 10, take the Highway 111 exit just past San Gorgonio Pass. Follow Highway 111 nearly 10 miles to Palm Springs and down Palm Canyon Drive toward downtown. About three-quarters of a mile past Vista Chino Road (where Highway 111 makes a turn to the left), turn left on Tamarisk Road and drive six blocks to Ruth Hardy Park on the left. Turn in and park at the first lot. Approaching from the south on Interstate 10, exit at Ramon Road in Thousand Palms and drive west for about seven miles (passing through Cathedral City) to Indian Canyon Drive. Turn right and proceed north for three-quarters of a mile to Tamarisk Road. Turn right and drive to the park six blocks up.

Map: Palm Springs Bicycle Touring Guide, available from the Community Recreational Services, 401 South Pavilion Way, Palm Springs, CA 92262; or by calling (619) 323-8272.

Local shop: Sports Fever, 73-360 Highway 111, Palm Desert, CA 92260; (619) 340-0252. Other contact: Palm Springs Information, 3200 East Tahquitz Canyon Way, Palm Springs, CA 92262; (619) 323-8299.

Tour notes: Although small, Ruth Hardy Park is a perfect spot for first-time skaters. It's totally flat, and the sidewalks are a generous eight-foot-wide swath bordered by lawn. Leafy shade trees have grown quite tall here; however, the park is new enough to have sidewalks paved with the perfect pink concrete that is now standard in the Palm Springs area. At the west end of the park, the sidewalk makes a complete loop that is big enough to accommodate lap skaters looking for an aerobic workout. At the east end, it borders both Tamarisk Road and Caballeros Avenue but doesn't make a loop. This is good for beginners because faster skaters will most likely be on the other side of the park or, for that matter, skating elsewhere in the city. Picnic spots, rest rooms, tennis courts, and playgrounds are provided.

---

5. Pink Sidewalks

8 miles ⭐ 🐜 🏃

Reference: **Downtown Palm Springs;**
see number ❺ on page 340.

Ideal for: Beginners—Touring

Directions: Approaching Palm Springs from the north on Interstate 10, take the Highway 111 exit just past San Gorgonio Pass. Follow Highway 111 nearly 10 miles to Palm Springs, down Palm Canyon Drive, and through downtown to Ramon Road. Turn left and follow Ramon to Sunrise Way. Park in the lot at Sunrise Park on the left. Approaching from the south on Interstate 10, exit at Ramon Road in Thousand Palms and drive west for approximately 6.5 miles (passing through Cathedral City) to Sunrise Way. Turn right and park in the lot.

Map: Palm Springs Bicycle Touring Guide, available from the Community Recreational Services, 401 South Pavilion Way, Palm Springs, CA 92262; or by calling (619) 323-8272.

Local shop: Sports Fever, 73-360 Highway 111, Palm Desert, CA 92260; (619) 340-0252. Other contact: Palm Springs Information, 3200 East Tahquitz Canyon Way, Palm Springs, CA 92262; (619) 323-8299.

Tour notes: Palm Springs is a great destination for in-line skaters, who can appreciate the fact that many of the major streets have eight-foot-wide landscaped sidewalks on one or both sides. Sometimes the trademark pink paths are flat and straight and devoid of landscaping. But in many cases, the shoulders of the roads they line have been built up with grassy humps or decorated with cactus or palms and other trees to make the landscaping more inviting. Here the sidewalks roll gently up, down, and around the terrain.

Sunrise Park is a good central location from which to explore the most accessible sidewalks all at once. Follow the Ramon Road shoulders east and west from here, or skate north and south on Sunrise Way. Half a mile north up Sunrise, you will encounter Tahquitz Canyon Way, which runs parallel to Ramon Road. These sidewalks are generally contiguous, but at times you may need to cross to the other side of the street and skate a block or two between missing sections.

---

6. Bogert Trail
3 miles

Reference: **In a canyon south of Palm Springs; see number ❻ on page 340.**

Ideal for: Beginners—Figure/Stunts—Hills/Slalom—Historic—Touring

Directions: Approaching Palm Springs from the north on Interstate 10, take the Highway 111 exit just past San Gorgonio Pass. Follow Highway 111 nearly 10 miles to Palm Springs and down Palm Canyon Drive through downtown. When Highway 111 curves to the left (becoming East Palm Canyon Drive), continue going straight on South Palm Canyon for another 1.5 miles. Turn left when you reach Bogert Trail and follow it through a golf course, across the bridge over Palm Canyon Wash, and around the corner to the foot of the housing development on the hillside. Park on the gravel pad that used to be a sales office parking lot on the left. Approaching from the south on Interstate 10, exit at Ramon Road in Thousand Palms and drive west for approximately 7.5 miles (passing through Cathedral City) until you reach Palm Canyon Drive just south of downtown Palm Springs. Turn south and follow the directions above starting from South Palm Canyon Drive.

Local shop: Sports Fever, 73-360 Highway 111, Palm Desert, CA 92260; (619) 340-0252.

Tour notes: Offering one of the grandest views to be had in these parts without taking the Aerial Tramway, Bogert Trail is also a wonderful skating site for beginners and expert downhillers alike, at least as long as the lots in the failed lower phase of the Andreas Point housing development remain unsold. Looking north from the low table at the canyon's mouth, you can see the high ridges of the San Bernardino Mountains, with Palm Springs and the Coachella Valley in the foreground. The rocky walls rising behind you are starkly beautiful and very close, sheltering the palm canyons belonging to the reservation of the Agua Caliente band of Cahuilla Indians. The reservation's entrance gate is farther down Palm Canyon Drive, just around the corner.

A car may pass by every five minutes or so, but it is usually very quiet on Bogert Trail, with only the occasional buzz of a desert beetle or the song of a bird to disturb the silence. Skate first among the dry and empty lots of the lower Andreas Point housing development, following Sevilla Avenue either on the four-foot-wide sidewalks or on the street. Watch for sand here and there on the pavement. After admiring the view from lot number two, go back to Bogert Trail, turn left, and make your way up to Barona Road and its four big dead-end signs to get the widest view of the Coachella Valley below. Barona is just long and wide enough to provide very scenic grounds for figure skating practice and general play.

Expert hill skaters will want to test their skills at the other end of Bogert Trail behind the sales office parking lot, where it enters a palm-filled hillside housing development. There are two hills to choose from. Stick to Bogert Trail for a longer and more gradual climb that only becomes threatening on the last quarter mile. Turn back where the road makes its second curve to the left near the peppertree at 3750 A; if you proceed any farther, you will encounter a high-speed blind curve. For an alternate route, take the first left off Bogert just after you enter the neighborhood to ascend Andreas Hills Drive, which starts out gently enough but becomes very steep just before it meets Bogert at the top of the hill. The two streets actually make a loop, but the last section is so steep (both for uphill and downhill skating) that you really should avoid it if you want to save your skin. The brown pueblo- and adobe-style home on the left is a good landmark for turning back. No matter which road you choose, you want to be very careful in your descent, because halfway down there is likely to be a river of sprinkler runoff crossing both roads in the shallow culvert that runs down the middle of Hillview Cove.

7. Palm Desert Civic Center Park

1.5 miles

Reference: Downtown Palm Desert; see number ⑦ on page 340.
Ideal for: Beginners—Historic—Touring
Directions: From Interstate 10 at Thousand Palms, take the Monterey Avenue exit and head south for five miles to Fred Waring Drive, just past the College of the Desert. Turn left on Waring and then left again at San Pablo Avenue, next to the civic center. Turn right halfway up the block and park at the Community Center parking lot.
Local shop: Sports Fever, 73-360 Highway 111, Palm Desert, CA 92260; (619) 340-0252.

Tour notes: You won't find many community parks that are as beautiful (or as well funded) as Palm Desert Civic Center Park. To make up for the necessary functional design of the north side's many tennis, basketball, and volleyball courts and four well-appointed baseball diamonds (what happens when the kids all take up roller hockey?), the park's planners embellished it with a pond—complete with lily pads and two bridges—a variety of large sculptures, two colorful children's sandlots, a Holocaust memorial, and an impressive amphitheater that almost reflects in shape the silhouette of Mount San Jacinto, visible in the distance. This park even has a "Canine Common," a fenced-in area (supplied with ample tennis balls) where dogs are allowed to roam off leash. Unruly pooches and female dogs in heat are specifically forbidden according to the rules posted outside. All of this civic bounty is spread out in an oasis of diverse and interesting trees, shrubs, cactus, and lawns. The more exotic floral varieties are labeled with small descriptive signs.

When you add in the extra-wide version of those ubiquitous perfect Palm Springs sidewalks and good nighttime lighting, Civic Center Park becomes a skater's dream. But, just like the dogs, skaters must obey certain restrictions: make sure you stay off the ramps of the amphitheater and don't go out on the basketball and tennis courts, where a clearly posted sign states that skates are not allowed. As you roll along the sidewalks, at every intersection you will see directions that are well marked on large chunks of rock that are decorated with renderings of ancient Indian paintings. Beware of slippery concrete—there is always a sprinkler turned on somewhere. Take the sidewalk on the east border of the park north to the edge of the date palm grove. The trees here are oddly short compared to most that you see in the Coachella Valley.

After your tour of the park, if you feel a need to stretch out on the open space of wide asphalt streets, skate on Magnesia Falls Drive next to the date palm grove or take a few laps around the median divider strip on San Pablo Avenue; traffic is light there when the College of the Desert is not in session.

---

8. Marriott's Desert Springs Resort

3.5 miles **7** 👟 🏃

Reference: In Palm Desert; see number **8** on page 340.
Ideal for: Fitness—Hills/Slalom—Touring
Directions: From Interstate 10 at Thousand Palms, take the Monterey Avenue exit and head south. Three miles down, turn left onto Country Club Drive and proceed 2.25 miles east until you see the Manor Care Nursing Center on the left, across the street from The Estates, a gated community. Make a U-turn at the next light and come back to

park on the curb outside the nursing center. (Don't open your driver-side door too wide here, or an oncoming vehicle might hit it.) Carefully cross the street to get to the wide sidewalk encircling Marriott's. Skate around the resort in a counterclockwise direction.

Local shop: Sports Fever, 73-360 Highway 111, Palm Desert, CA 92260; (619) 340-0252.

Tour notes: Like so many of the resort oases in this desert, Desert Springs, the crown jewel of the Marriott chain, has a wide concrete sidewalk encircling its grounds. What makes the Marriott path so fun is the slope on Portola Avenue, a shaded section of sidewalk that forms an irresistible slalom course. As you start out, follow Country Club Drive west through the pine trees and past the Silver Sands Racquet Club until you reach the corner where Portola Avenue awaits. The half-mile downhill cruise, which is actually on Silver Sands property, ends at Silver Sands Parkway. Unfortunately, so does the shade.

Cross Silver Sands Parkway to continue heading south on a short stretch of as-yet unadorned sidewalk until you reach the Marriott property line. A typical resort wall will border the path on your left for the rest of the loop. It does have barred gaps every 16 or so strokes, so as you skate you can peer inside and see the oasis of green. Passing Park Palms and Lago de Las Palmas on the right, you may find it hard not to chuckle at the local tendency to slip the word "palm" into so many of the names.

Where Portola Avenue meets Hovley Lane, turn left. Try to concentrate your attention on the voluptuous silhouette of 1,952-foot-high Eisenhower Mountain, not on the post office and shopping centers on Hovley Lane. Turn left at Cook Street and skate up the east side of the Desert Springs Resort. The shade trees are decorated with violet blossoms in late spring; they are pretty but messy, leaving the sidewalk strewn with small twigs. Turn left at the Country Club Drive intersection to complete the last leg of the loop. Crossing the main entrance of Desert Springs is rather skater-unfriendly. The sidewalks curve in a few yards up the lane and then dump out onto the lane itself. Watch for cars and do your best.

---

9. El Paseo   5 miles

Reference: Downtown Palm Desert;
  see number **9** on page 340.

Ideal for: Road/Street—Scene—Touring

Directions: From Interstate 10 at Thousand Palms, take the Monterey Avenue exit and head south for just over five miles to one block south of the junction of Highways 74 and 111. Turn right on El Paseo Street and park in the corner shopping center parking lot. Skate back across Highway 74 to the sidewalks bordering either side of El Paseo.

Local shop: Sports Fever, 73-360 Highway 111, Palm Desert, CA 92260; (619) 340-0252.

Tour notes: In the relative cool of the evening, skating along El Paseo Street, where the trunks of the palm trees lining the road are wrapped in tiny white lights, can be a delightful experience. The pedestrian traffic is lighter then, so you can relax and enjoy window shopping on this commercial street, where vendors of paintings and sculpture, jewelry, clothing, and fingernail maintenance seem to have a monopoly on the local commerce. There are several eating establishments, and at least three of them offer outdoor seating. (The Daily Grill has the best location and the best food.) Sculptures are mounted along the street's center divider; they are better appreciated during daylight hours. You will cross several intersections, but at night there isn't much traffic to worry about. Just keep your eyes open for the big drainage crack (two inches wide) in the San Pablo Avenue intersection.

The downtown section of El Paseo may be only one mile long, but all up and down the street there are little tiled or bricked breezeways leading to more shops. On the north side, most of them draw you in with the inviting sounds of a splashing water fountain. On the south side, they lead to larger shopping grottoes with pools, but the bricks here are difficult to skate on. Pass through the breezeways to get behind the shops on both sides of El Paseo, and you will find two miles of parking lot playlands. The lots on the south side are concrete and compact, with curbs. At night, one or two of these lots are lit well enough to inspire thoughts of roller hockey, a sports craze just waiting to happen in Palm Desert. The big lots behind the shops on the north side of El Paseo belong to a shopping center and face Highway 111. Nighttime skating is really fun here because of the long, gentle slopes, good lighting and pavement, and few cars.

10. Indian Wells Tour   8 miles

Reference: The Coachella Valley town of Indian Wells; see number ❿ on page 340.

Ideal for: Historic—Road/Street—Touring

Directions: From Interstate 10 at Thousand Palms, take the Monterey Avenue exit and head south for 5.5 miles to the junction with Highway 111 (it looks like a standard downtown intersection). Turn left and head east for two miles until you reach the light at Cook Street. Make a U-turn to park in the shopping center on the northwest corner of the intersection. This trip continues following Highway 111 on sidewalks starting from the southeast corner.

Local shop: Sports Fever, 73-360 Highway 111, Palm Desert, CA 92260; (619) 340-0252.

Tour notes: It's not often that you get to skate on a state highway, and rarely are they as well landscaped as Highway 111 is where it passes through Indian Wells close to the base of Eisenhower Mountain. A lot of money went into installing the fine concrete sidewalks and trees that border the road, but then, this seems to be the standard for the perimeters of the resorts and country clubs in these parts.

Start out on the south side of the road, where the sidewalk is contiguous for the entire 2.5 miles. The beautiful grounds of the Stoffer's Esmerelda and Hyatt Grand Champion resorts are across the street as you head east. This is the Hyatt that hosts the famous Lipton Tennis Tournament. You are supposed to be able to see the mound of some old Native American burial grounds near the Indian Wells Country Club as you approach the end of the second mile. If you're really interested in this, ask someone to point it out, because it isn't immediately obvious.

Cross to the north side of the highway to start back alongside the Indian Wells Golf Resort. That way you can read the very interesting plaques on the historic monuments located next to the sidewalk at the Indian Wells civic center near the intersection of El Dorado Drive. You will learn about the history of the desert wells and the date palms, among other local attractions.

If you're still feeling fresh after your return to Cook Street, skate south on its roomy bike lane for half a mile to Fairway Drive, a low-traffic residential street that is wide enough for skating but has no bike lanes. Hidden behind the trees to the south is a very exclusive gated community, The Vintage Club. Follow quiet Fairway Drive a mile to the east and then turn left at El Dorado to skate back up to Highway 111. For another diversion on the way up El Dorado, explore The Estates, a neighborhood of fine homes (and equally fine asphalt pavement) on the left.

Note: The manager of the Foot Locker in Indio is a dedicated inliner who provides instruction and leads guided skates in the Palm Desert area. (Call Tom Huna at 619-342-3146 for information.)

Inland Empire

6 Great Places to Skate

Inland Empire

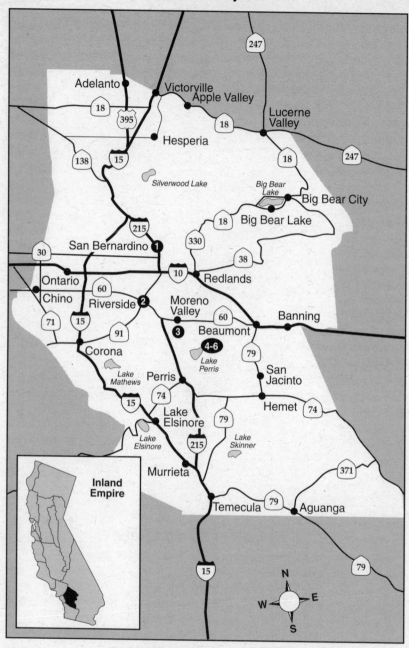

Skating Regions Beyond the Inland Empire

North .... Deserts, p. 339
East .... Deserts, p. 339
South .... San Diego County, p. 399
West .... Los Angeles County, p. 311

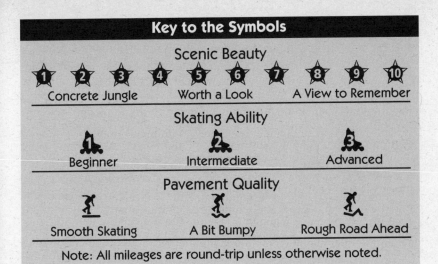

Key to the Symbols

Scenic Beauty

1 **2** **3** **4** **5** **6** **7** **8** **9** **10**

Concrete Jungle   Worth a Look   A View to Remember

Skating Ability

1   **2**   **3**

Beginner   Intermediate   Advanced

Pavement Quality

Smooth Skating   A Bit Bumpy   Rough Road Ahead

Note: All mileages are round-trip unless otherwise noted.

The Inland Empire is a land of peaks and valleys, a place where you can ski in the morning and skate in the afternoon. Yet when asked where they like to skate, local in-liners invariably cite the beach boardwalks of San Diego, Orange, and Los Angeles counties. Why? Heat and smog, for one: the urge to escape to the cooler coast could explain why this region has so few dedicated pathways for humans on wheels.

The best Inland in-lining can be found in the Moreno Valley and up at Lake Perris, especially on a clear spring day when the view and the wildflowers are at their finest. The small mountain ranges have a rocky beauty that hints at what you'll see when you visit the San Bernardino and San Jacinto ranges—their bigger brothers beyond.

For the determined street and hill skater, a few bike routes are worth considering: Lytle Creek Road, about eight miles northeast of downtown San Bernardino; San Timoteo Canyon Road, bordering the southwest edge of Redlands; and the Lake Gregory loop up in Crestline. But since their pavement and road-shoulder space are too dicey for enjoyable and safe skating, they aren't described in this book.

1. Seccombe Lake

3 miles **6** 🏃

Reference: **Near downtown San Bernardino; see number ❶ on page 354.**

Ideal for: Beginners—Touring

Directions: From Interstate 215 in San Bernardino, take the Fifth Street exit, which actually takes you first to a one-way section of Sixth Street. Just keep following Sixth to the east and you'll find yourself at the west entrance of Seccombe Lake.

Local shop: Big 5 Sporting Goods, 245 North E Street, San Bernardino, CA 92401; (909) 885-4006. Other contact: Visitors Bureau, 201 North E Street, Suite 103, San Bernardino, CA 92401; (909) 889-3980.

Tour notes: Almost every city has at least one small park with decent pavement where beginners can go to learn how to skate. In San Bernardino, that park is the one that rings pretty Seccombe Lake, and it's also just about the only place you'll be allowed to skate in town. The paved downtown looks appealing by day, but after dark it's just as well you aren't welcome on your wheels, since the neighborhood becomes unsafe. A hint of this roughness is represented by the profusion of trash floating on the waters at Seccombe Lake's eastern edge. The park itself is well-shaded, with an ample supply of eight-foot-wide concrete sidewalks bordered by lawn. The stairs and other concrete near the YWCA at the park's southwest corner are fun for learning beginning street-skating skills.

2. Bordwell Park

1 mile **5** 🏃

Reference: **A park in the city of Riverside; see number ❷ on page 354.**

Ideal for: Beginners

Directions: From State Highway 91 in Riverside, take the 14th Street exit east and follow it for one mile. After 14th becomes Martin Luther King Boulevard, it intersects with Kansas Avenue; there, you'll see the park just ahead on the right. Pull in and park in the lot.

Local shop: Cal Stores, 1263 Galleria, Riverside, CA 92503; (909) 353-1186.

Tour notes: Bordwell Park is by no means a destination skate, but for residents of this quiet neighborhood in Riverside, it offers excellent lawn-bordered sidewalks just right for learning how to skate. The low grassy hills are a good place for beginners to get the feel of managing speed and using their heel brakes. Watch out for slick sandy patches when skating near the kids' play area. Since the park is fairly new, the trees are still too small to offer much shade.

3. Iris Street and Moreno Beach Drive

10 miles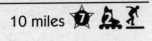

Reference: **In the Moreno Valley south of Moreno Valley; see number ❸ on page 354.**

Ideal for: Fitness—Hills/Slalom—Touring

Directions: From State Highway 60 at Moreno Valley east of Riverside, take the Moreno Beach Drive exit, south. This is also the exit for Lake Perris State Recreational Area. Proceed across the valley and climb the hill through the relatively new Moreno Valley Ranch Golf Club housing development. Almost three miles from Highway 60, Moreno Beach Drive turns left to go over the hill to Lake Perris; instead, go straight and you'll be on Iris Street. Just a block up on the right, park in the hospital parking lot.

Local shop: Cal Stores, 1263 Galleria, Riverside, CA 92503; (909) 353-1186.

Tour notes: The sidewalks bordering Moreno Beach Drive and Iris Street are 10 feet wide and smooth enough for some sublime hill skating. Both streets are four-lane roads with meridian strips and wide, clearly marked bike lanes. Flowing down the long hill on Iris Street from the Perris Lake turnoff, the sidewalk curves and undulates in a regular rhythm for nearly two miles through the grassy landscaping at the side of the road. When you get back to the hospital, follow Moreno Beach Drive back north toward Highway 60 to enjoy its long decline. After your hilly workout, check out the homes in the Moreno Valley Ranch Golf Club housing development on both sides of Moreno Beach Drive. The Moreno Valley itself is very pretty, with wide-open views of rolling hills, best appreciated in winter and early spring.

4. Lake Perris West

6 miles ❽

Reference: **South of Moreno Valley; see number ❹ on page 354.**

Ideal for: Fitness—Touring

Directions: From State Highway 60 at Moreno Valley east of Riverside, take the Moreno Beach Drive exit, south. This is also the exit for Lake Perris State Recreational Area. Proceed across the valley and climb the hill. Almost three miles from Highway 60, Moreno Beach Drive turns left to go over the hill to Lake Perris. The day-use fee is $6 per car at the entry kiosk. Head toward the lake and take the most westerly driveway into parking lots 1 and 2. You will drive past the trail as you enter the lot.

Local shop: Cal Stores, 1263 Galleria, Riverside, CA 92503; (909) 353-1186. Other contact: Lake Perris State Recreational Area; (909) 657-0676.

Tour notes: When you skate at the west end of Lake Perris, you can look forward to a refreshing dip at Sail Cove, the only spot on the lake where no powerboats are allowed. The trip is entirely flat where you cross the entire length of the dam. However, if you love the roller-coaster effect of little hills and dips, you won't want to miss the short section of trail that runs from the parking lot to the north end of the dam.

Leave the parking lots behind as you start skating west and enjoy a view of a rocky ridge on the right. (Who lives in that nice home on the hillside? It looks too nice to be park-ranger lodging.) Skate the whoop-de-do's through tough-looking desert scrub, then swoop down to the edge of the soft sand beach of Sail Cove. Round a corner and climb slightly to the northwest, and you've reached the crest of the Lake Perris dam. The crest-top path continues for two miles in a generally north-south direction, approaching the slab granite walls of the Bernasconi Hills on the other side of the lake, where rock climbers practice. From up on the crest you can survey the goings-on at the two fishing piers and compare the wind-sailors' skills with the Jet Skiers'. To the right is a broad view of Perris Valley's green- and brown-gridded fields, with more hills fading into the haze to the west. Two pit-stop areas offer a toilet and partial shade on the trek across this high sunny dam, but no water is available. The trail finally fades to gravel next to the rocky wall near the barricaded waterworks area.

---

5. Lake Perris East   11.5 miles 🌟 🏃 🏊

Reference: **South of Moreno Valley; see number ❺ on page 354.**

Ideal for: Fitness—Hills/Slalom—Touring

Directions: From State Highway 60 at Moreno east of Riverside, take the Moreno Beach Drive exit, south. This is also the Lake Perris State Recreational Area exit. Proceed across the valley and climb the hill. Almost three miles from Highway 60, Moreno Beach Drive turns left to go over the hill to Lake Perris. The day-use fee is $6 per car. Head toward the lake and take the second parkinglot driveway for lots 11 and 12. You'll drive past the trail as you enter the lot.

Local shop: Cal Stores, 1263 Galleria, Riverside, CA 92503; (909) 353-1186.

Tour notes: The path through the wild side of Lake Perris State Recreational Area is a real gem. At least half the trail is out in the middle of nature and also out of earshot from the shriek of the ubiquitous Jet Skis. Better yet, there are no pesky intersections! And in spite of these sterling qualities, it is highly possible that you will have this skate all to yourself. It might be due to the $6 Lake Perris entrance fee, or the one or two steep hills on the back stretch; the more likely reason, though, is that most people come here to play in the cool water.

The Lake Perris Recreational Area is set in exceptionally beautiful country and is especially pretty in spring, when wild grasses and blossoms serve as colorful foreground to the rugged Bernasconi Hills

---

and Lakeview Mountains to the south and the Badlands to the north-east (whose dry, craggy ridges may evoke memories of old Hollywood westerns in more imaginative folks).

Start by skating east from the trail as it passes above the parking lot, and roll down your first warm-up hill. As you pass the last beach, the eight-foot-wide asphalt takes you away from the shady parking lot and group picnic area, and into the waving grasses of a big open area. San Gorgonio Mountain, sometimes topped with snow, peeks out between the hills of the Badlands ahead, and a wide field hides a flurry of small furry critters to the left. As you round the bend to skate along the east side of the lake, the obnoxious hubbub of human activity is almost entirely muted by the thick trees along the shore. At the same time, you also lose sight of the lake itself. The first little pit stop soon appears, a portable toilet and a picnic table under a semishaded wooden structure. Similar pit stops are placed at miles two, three, and four, but none of them have drinking fountains, so if it's a hot day make sure to bring your own water. At pit stop number four the pavement is particularly rough with some surprise sunken spots, so keep your eyes on the trail as you pass.

At about mile 3.5, the trail climbs the first hill, and on the right you can get a glimpse of the lake. Coast down close to the water, and climb another hill in a narrow section between the lake and the base of the high ridge to your left. One last fairly steep climb brings you in view of a half-mile-long beach that's less developed than the ones across the water. More important, there's a plenitude of rest rooms, picnic areas, water fountains, and shade. Enjoy the fast sprint down-hill, and then take a right fork just before the trail ends at a road next to the parking lot.

Skate through the picnic area on the sandy asphalt path to reach the far side of the beach/picnic area. Now the trail gives way to a limited access road leading to the lake's powerhouse. Skaters, hikers, and mountain bikers share this road with rock climbers, who bring in ropes and other gear to ascend the granite slab wall just ahead on the side of the Bernasconi Hills. Just around the corner from the climbers you meet the state's chain-link fence, through which you can see the three-quarter-mile section of shore occupied by the lake's power-generating facilities—the only obstacle to entirely circumnavigating the lake on your skates.

6. Lake Perris Sidewalks

5 miles

Reference: **South of Moreno Valley; see number ❻ on page 354.**

Ideal for: Beginners—Hills/Slalom—Touring

Directions: From State Highway 60 at Moreno Valley east of Riverside, take the Moreno Beach Drive exit, south. This is also the Lake Perris State Recreational Area exit. Proceed across the valley and climb the hill. Almost three miles from Highway 60, Moreno Beach turns left to go over the hill to Lake Perris. The day-use fee is $6 per car at the entry kiosk. Head toward the lake and park in any lot.

Local shop: Cal Stores, 1263 Galleria, Riverside, CA 92503; (909) 353-1186.

Tour notes: There are so many wide, prime-quality sidewalks on the north shore of Lake Perris, you can almost get lost traversing them from parking lot to picnic area to marina to beach. The place could be a fantastic playland on a clear winter or spring day without the crowds and their various motorized modes of transportation to deal with. In-lines are ideal for getting around, and it's surprising how few people you'll be sharing the sidewalks with. Even at peak summer hours they're relatively empty, because the real action most people come here for is either at their picnic tables, on the beach, or in and on the water.

Most of the sidewalks border the parking lots, criss-crossing both lengthwise and up and down from the lots to the picnic and beach areas. In the up/down directions, a slight slope brings up adrenaline levels, and at the east edge of lot 12, another long, gently sloped section bordered by lawn attracts fledgling speed demons. Since this is a very popular family destination, please stay on the alert for children darting across your path, no matter where you skate. On a slow day, you should be able to cruise around some of the concrete picnic areas prevalent at the west end and frolic in the parking lots themselves.

Orange County

31 Great Places to Skate

Orange County

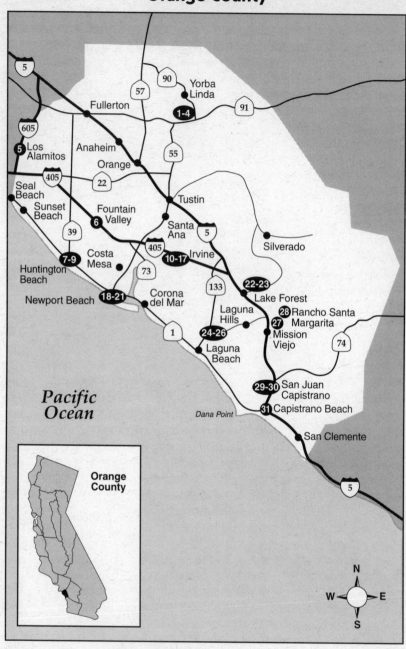

Skating Regions Beyond Orange County

North .... Los Angeles County, p. 311   South .... San Diego County, p. 399
East .... Inland Empire, p. 353

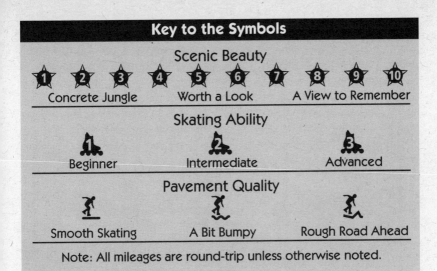

Although Orange County has more than 30 miles of coastline, the seaside bike paths are broken up more than those found farther down the coast. An eight-mile dedicated bikeway connects Sunset Beach to Huntington Beach State Park. Newport has a peninsula boardwalk, plus a fine trail through Upper Newport Bay Regional Park. For adventurous spirits, Balboa Island is a unique place to have fun on skates. And just up the San Diego Creek from Newport, the town of Irvine offers an amazing number of great skates.

Some of the most scenic touring in the county is available along the banks of Aliso Creek. A 12-mile trail connects the Aliso/Wood Canyons Regional Park to Whiting Ranch Wilderness Park, and every bit is skateworthy. For miles on this canyon route, skaters are treated to views of relatively untouched terrain. Even the neighborhood sections are landscaped or remain natural enough to make for a pretty tour. At its wild northern end, the Aliso Creek Trail terminates in mountain lion country, just south of the Cleveland National Forest. Fine skating is also found along the San Juan Creek, and pending improvements will result someday in a contiguous route.

Orange County's longest trail spans the county for nearly 30 miles, paralleling the Santa Ana River. The center sections aren't as interesting as either end, but the pavement is good and underpasses eliminate the need to interrupt your skate by stopping at street crossings. The section of trail where the river flows through Yorba Linda's Featherly Park is definitely a must-skate, featuring great scenery both up close and across the river valley.

1. Yorba Regional Park

2.5 miles

Reference: In Yorba Linda; see number **1** on page 362.

Ideal for: Beginners—Fitness—Figure/Stunts—Touring

Directions: Heading north in northeast Anaheim on Highway 55 (the Costa Mesa Freeway), veer east on Highway 91 (the Riverside Freeway). Proceed for two miles, then exit north on Highway 90 (the Imperial Highway). Cross the Santa Ana River, take the first right, and follow La Palma Avenue for 1.5 miles to Huxford Lane, the first entrance into Yorba Regional Park. You will find free parking near the baseball diamonds. The trails begin east of the playing fields.

Local shop: Sport Chalet, 2500 East Imperial Highway, Brea, CA 92621; (714) 255-0132.

Tour notes: Yorba Regional Park is a wonderful place to spend an entire day. Skaters of all levels and persuasions will find a favorite spot in or near the great terrain found in this lovely setting. The park borders the banks of the Santa Ana River for a mile, and there are multiple access points onto the long river trail. High, rugged hills rise across the valley of the river to the south and northeast, making the skyline visually appealing for 360 degrees around the horizon.

Start skating on the sidewalks near the baseball diamonds to enter the shady park grounds where eight-foot-wide concrete sidewalks pass through well-appointed picnic areas. Beginning skaters can usually stake out some uncrowded ground on these walkways so they can get rolling, especially during off-peak park hours. As skills improve, they can try the five-foot-wide asphalt path near the southwest end of the park for more of a challenge. This nature trail slips among duck ponds and tall marsh grasses, delivering a taste of what it is like to skate near the untouched scenery that more skilled skaters have access to all the time. Some low hills are just steep enough to present another kind of challenge, but with the grass to fall back on (literally) there is less threat of serious injury. In addition to the sidewalks and nature trail, the park roads are also smooth enough for in-lines. When empty, parking lots turn into figure skating rinks or places to practice simple stunts.

Skaters who are interested in an aerobic workout or who want to build up their distance or speed skills can use Yorba Regional Park as home base for a day of training and exploration on one of the most beautiful sections of the Santa Ana River Trail.

2. Santa Ana River to Featherly Park

9 miles

Reference: **Alongside the Santa Ana River near Yorba Linda; see number ❷ on page 362.**

Ideal for: Hills/Slalom—Touring

Directions: Heading north in northeast Anaheim on Highway 55 (the Costa Mesa Freeway), veer east on Highway 91 (the Riverside Freeway). Proceed for two miles, then exit north on Highway 90 (the Imperial Highway). Cross the Santa Ana River, take the first right, and follow La Palma Avenue for 1.5 miles to Huxford Lane, the first entrance into Yorba Regional Park. You will find free parking near the baseball diamonds. The trail is east of the playing fields.

Map: Orange County Bikeway Map, available free by calling the County of Orange, EMA/Transportation Planning office at (714) 834-3111.

Local shop: Sport Chalet, 2500 East Imperial Highway, Brea, CA 92621; (714) 255-0132. Other contact: County of Orange, EMA/Transportation Planning, P.O. Box 4048, Santa Ana, CA 92702-4048; (714) 834-3137.

Tour notes: Without a doubt, the best way to really appreciate the wild section of the Santa Ana River through the regional parks in Anaheim Hills and Yorba Linda is by skating it. Take this tour in the early morning or late evening hours to catch the best light for dramatic views of the Santa Ana Mountains across the riverbed to the south and the Chino Hills to the north.

Starting from the west end of Yorba Regional Park, skate to its south border, where several access points lead through the trees to the river and trail. This far inland, the Santa Ana resembles a real river, not a concrete canyon. Tall patches of tule and other marsh grasses are rooted in the sand of the wide, weedy riverbed. The only characteristics this stretch shares with its southern counterpart are the jumbo-sized mileage numbers on the 10-foot-wide divided asphalt trail, and perhaps the drone of the not-too-distant freeway.

At the boundary of Yorba Regional Park, the trail temporarily runs alongside busy La Palma Avenue. After crossing Yorba Linda Boulevard, it enters Anaheim Wetlands Park, where two steep dips traverse a brush-covered hill. The path then passes a shopping center and finally enters Featherly Park. A jungle of tall bamboo thrives in the Santa Ana River below an asphalt path that at this point is flat and 12 feet wide. A few rough patches on the surface seem to be the result of water damage.

The next mile takes you by one of the most beautiful riverscapes along the entire length of the Santa Ana River. Beyond the Gypsum Canyon Road underpass, the scenery just keeps improving, as you are presented with statuesque views of the hills and mountain ridges on both sides of the river valley. Here, too, the bed of the river is filled with 20-foot-high bamboo and marsh grasses. The trail ends at a gate below a neighborhood at the east end of town. After returning to Yorba Regional Park, take a cooldown cruise on the sidewalks and nature trail (see the previous listing).

3. Yorba Linda Trail

7 miles

Reference: **Near the Imperial Highway in Yorba Linda; see number ❸ on page 362.**

Ideal for: Hills/Slalom—Historic—Touring

Directions: From Highway 57, take the Highway 90/Imperial Highway East exit and follow it to Rose Drive. Turn right onto Rose and cross Bastanchury Road. Take the next three right turns: Loie Street, Prentiss Drive, and Prentiss Place. Park in the cul-de-sac at the end of Prentiss Place next to the asphalt ramp up to the trail.

Map: Orange County Bikeway Map, available free by calling the County of Orange, EMA/Transportation Planning office at (714) 834-3111.

Local shop: Sport Chalet, 2500 East Imperial Highway, Brea, CA 92621; (714) 255-0132. Other contact: County of Orange, EMA/Transportation Planning, P.O. Box 4048, Santa Ana, CA 92702-4048; (714) 834-3137.

Tour notes: Skate the Yorba Linda Trail's crooked route through the open space between several of the town's quiet neighborhoods. The fairly large lots along the way sport the trappings of country living, with the occasional rooster crow adding to the impression. Horses occupy small corrals in many of the backyards. Citrus, eucalyptus, and palm trees border the trail, and during the summer months, fences covered with bright oleander blossoms enhance the color scheme. Mileage posts help you track how far you've gone.

A jog left at the Yorba Linda Community Center brings the trail close to the Imperial Highway. It soon veers away to enter another neighborhood, where a horseback riding/pedestrian bridge provides access across a small creek. A block farther the surrounding landscaping becomes noticeably elegant. Round the corner and you'll find out why: the building next to the path is the Richard M. Nixon Library and Birthplace. The smooth, sloping asphalt of the parking lot is wonderful for carving slalom turns, and close to the library entrance, a large fountain splashes invitingly.

The asphalt trail continues on the other side of Yorba Linda Boulevard at the Mountain View crossing. After passing behind a school, it enters a tunnel under Lakeview Avenue, with a hard right on the other side. Climb up to the sidewalk to cross Lakeview and the Imperial Highway. The trail resumes to the right with a long, curving slope next to a grassy hillside. Be sure to take in the panoramic view to the south. Smooth asphalt and low-traffic street crossings characterize the rest of the neighborhood route until the trail ends at the intersection of Grand View and Buena Vista Streets.

4. Santa Ana River: Yorba Linda to Riverdale Park   6 miles ⭐ 🚴 🏃

Reference: **On the Santa Ana River levee between Orange and Anaheim Hills; see number ❹ on page 362.**

Ideal for: Touring

Directions: Heading north in northeast Anaheim on Highway 55 (the Costa Mesa Freeway), veer east on Highway 91 (the Riverside Freeway). Proceed for two miles, then exit north on Highway 90 (the Imperial Highway). Cross the Santa Ana River, take the first right, and follow La Palma Avenue for 1.5 miles to Huxford Lane, the first entrance into Yorba Regional Park. You will find free parking near the baseball diamonds. The trail is east of the playing fields.

Map: Orange County Bikeway Map, available free by calling the County of Orange, EMA/Transportation Planning office at (714) 834-3111.

Local shop: Sport Chalet, 2500 East Imperial Highway, Brea, CA 92621; (714) 255-0132. Other contact: County of Orange, EMA/Transportation Planning, P.O. Box 4048, Santa Ana, CA 92702-4048; (714) 834-3137.

Tour notes: The Santa Ana River is surprisingly beautiful where it passes through the town of Anaheim Hills. Craggy peaks of the Santa Ana Mountains dominate the horizon across the river corridor to the south. As gorgeous and green as they are in the springtime, the peaks retain a certain golden elegance even in the dog days of summer.

Yorba Regional Park borders the banks of the Santa Ana River for a mile, with multiple access points onto the long river path. Skate on the sidewalk near the baseball diamonds to reach the back side of the park and the connection paths. Turn right on the river trail. This route travels only three miles down the river, but the jumbo-sized mileage numbers painted on the 10-foot-wide asphalt path tell the true story of the Santa Ana's epic possibilities. Just beyond the lower end of Yorba Regional Park, the marker indicates mile 21.0 (for info on touring the river in the opposite direction, see the listing for Santa Ana River to Featherly Park, page 365).

Continue next to the wide riverbed on a route that delivers a great view of the southern mountains, almost making up for the presence of the noisy Riverside Freeway beyond the far bank. In the riverbed, dense grasses and bamboo grow 15 to 20 feet high between 20-foot-wide channels of water. A mile beyond the end of Yorba Regional Park the trail meets the Imperial Highway. Turn left and cross the river on the bridge. On the other side, skate through the underpass, making sure to keep up enough speed to roll easily across the six deeply grooved drainage slots slicing across the pavement.

A sign next to the trail lets you know that this section is called the Imperial Woods Trail. There's a nursery to the left on the riverbank, so the scenery is more or less natural. Soon the trail enters Riverdale Park, which is landscaped with lawns and shade trees.

Although this short tour of the northern portion of the Santa Ana River Trail ends here, the big mileage markers offer regular and, to some people, irresistible temptations to continue exploring the trail. Farther south, where it passes through more densely populated or industrial areas, the scenery tends to be dull. Still, this route is ideal for certain types of skating, such as speed work and endurance training, because it continues for mile after uninterrupted mile.

---

5. Coyote Creek Trail   11 miles ⭐ 🏃

Reference: **A canal trail starting in El Dorado Park, east of Los Alamitos; see number ❺ on page 362.**

Ideal for: Fitness

Directions: From Interstate 605 in Long Beach, exit at Spring Street and turn west. A park entrance is located off Spring Street. (If the westbound gate is closed, make a U-turn at the next light to enter at Spring Street's eastbound gate.) The entrance fee is $3 on weekdays and $5 on weekends. To park for free, continue west on Spring Street and turn right on Studebaker Road. Turn right again on Wardlow Road and then, just before you reach the river, turn right onto Stevely Avenue and park at the corner of Wardlow and Stevely. Skate across the bridge and enter the park halfway down on the north side of Wardlow at the bicycle and pedestrian gate near the fire station. (To do this, you must skate across the four-lane street without a crosswalk.)

Map: Orange County Bikeway Map, available free by calling the County of Orange, EMA/Transportation Planning office at (714) 834-3111.

Local shop: Shore Sport Inc., 5209 East Second Street, Long Beach, CA 90803; (310) 439-7250. Other contact: County of Orange, EMA/Transportation Planning, P.O. Box 4048, Santa Ana, CA 92702-4048; (714) 834-3137.

Tour notes: There are no two ways about it: the route of the Coyote Creek Trail, which follows the concrete canyon walls of a flood control canal, is strictly for training, not for sight-seeing. To speed skating and endurance enthusiasts, however, the opportunity to skate hard and fast for more than five miles without having to deal with crowds or stop at intersections is charm enough.

The Coyote Creek Trail is accessible from El Dorado Park's bike path, at the southwest corner of Area III. Start out by skating to the south on the San Gabriel River Trail. Along this first mile, the scenery is quite pleasing where the path passes El Dorado Park and its nature study area. Beyond that, a commercial nursery on the riverside supplies bright dashes of color where rows of blossoming potted plants are germinated. A bridge across the river marks the branch to the northeast that is the Coyote Creek Trail.

Cross the bridge and turn left to follow the Coyote Creek where it splits off to the northeast from the San Gabriel River. The creek marks one border of the dividing line between Los Angeles and Orange Counties. The Long Beach Parks Department tree farm can be seen across the canal to the left when the path dips for the underpasses of Katella Avenue and Interstate 605. To successfully coast across the seemingly gigantic grooves molded into the dips (presumably to keep water off the trail during the rainy season), keep your speed up and, with knees bent, push one skate slightly ahead to lengthen your wheel base and improve your fore-and-aft balance abilities.

Except for a brief break in the urban scenery where Lee Ware Park is in view, wall surfaces and a series of underpasses add the only visual variations to this concrete tour. The route runs slightly below and behind mature neighborhoods and past fences that are either wood, brick, or shrub-covered chain link. Graffiti colors several walls. The bike path ends at Cerritos Regional County Park near an intersection where two counties and four towns meet: the towns of La Palma and Cypress in Orange, and Cerritos and Lakewood in Los Angeles.

On the return trip, the bridge across the San Gabriel River marks the juncture where you can take a diversion down the San Gabriel River Bike Trail, described on page 336.

---

6. Mile Square Regional Park   4 miles

Reference: **West of the Santa Ana River in Fountain Valley; see number ❻ on page 362.**

Ideal for: Beginners—Touring

Directions: From Interstate 405 in Fountain Valley, take the Brookhurst Street exit and head north. Mile Square Golf Course begins at Warner Avenue. Keep going north and turn right at Edinger Avenue. Enter the park at Ward Avenue and find a place to park.

Map: Orange County Bikeway Map, available free by calling the County of Orange, EMA/Transportation Planning office at (714) 834-3111.

Local shop: Roller Skates of America, 1644 Superior Avenue, Costa Mesa, CA 92627; (714) 574-9966. Other contact: County of Orange, EMA/Transportation Planning, P.O. Box 4048, Santa Ana, CA 92702-4048; (714) 834-3137.

Tour notes: Beginning and first-time skaters can get a safe start on the smooth, shady sidewalks in and around Mile Square Regional Park.

Low knolls throughout the grassy park offer a chance to experience the thrill of speed without risking devastating consequences.

Picnic tables and water fountains allow struggling novices to take refreshing breaks so that they can get back out on the pavement to work on making effective strokes, turning corners and, of course, applying the heel brake. A couple of little bridges over a creek provide good practice for traversing the bumpy wood-slat bridges that cross rivers and creeks throughout the region.

Confidence and skills permitting, skate out to Edinger Avenue and follow its fine sidewalk up to Euclid Street. Turn right onto Euclid Street and continue south until you reach Warner Avenue. A small pond graces this corner, and more sidewalks extend into the central park area. Beginners should avoid continuing up the path on Warner Avenue, because it is paved with rough, pitted asphalt along the edge of Mile Square Golf Course. Faster, stronger skaters can skate the asphalt or take to the street close to the curb to continue around the loop, making another right at Brookhurst Street.

Next to Brookhurst, a six-foot-wide sidewalk meanders north to the intersection with Edinger Avenue. Eucalyptus and maple trees decorate the corner that the park shares with the David L. Baker Memorial Golf Course. At the right edge of the sidewalk, a low but unobtrusive fence allows a good view of the golf course.

7. South Huntington Beach   3 miles

Reference: On the Pacific coast between Newport Beach and Huntington Beach; see number **7** on page 362.

Ideal for: Beginners—Fitness—Scene—Touring

Directions: From Interstate 405 in Costa Mesa, exit at Brookhurst Street heading south. About 2.5 miles down, Brookhurst meets the Coast Highway at an entrance to a Huntington State Beach parking lot. If you get there early enough on the weekend while it's still foggy, free parking can be found at the curbside on Brookhurst near the intersection. You may have to make a U-turn. Otherwise, go straight across the highway to enter the Huntington Beach parking lot and drive to the southernmost lot. The $5 fee is well spent because you can skate in three directions from this spot near the Santa Ana River, on this route plus two others described in this chapter.

Map: Orange County Bikeway Map, available free by calling the County of Orange, EMA/Transportation Planning office at (714) 834-3111.

Local shop: Bud's Pro Skate & Surf, 16895 Beach Boulevard, Huntington Beach, CA 92647; (714) 843-6922. Other contact: County of Orange, EMA/Transportation Planning, P.O. Box 4048, Santa Ana, CA 92702-4048; (714) 834-3137.

Tour notes: The South Huntington Beach boardwalk is about as close as you can get to in-line heaven. A smooth swath of 20-foot-wide asphalt, it spans three miles between the Huntington Beach Pier and the Santa Ana River. This is a major part of the Orange County in-line scene and is definitely a must-skate destination, either as described here or as part of a seven-mile-long Huntington/Newport pier-to-pier route.

Crowds on the Huntington Beach boardwalk become problematic during peak times for the first mile south of the pier, where it is lined with food stands and other shops. A series of flashing yellow lights has been installed in an attempt to control traffic. Rather than fight the crowds, relax and enjoy a social cruise, complying with the speed limit of 10 miles per hour, which is reduced to five miles per hour around pedestrians. (Unlimited opportunities for faster and less crowded skating are found on the Santa Ana River Trail starting at the south end of Huntington Beach; see the next listing.)

Near the end of the high-traffic strip, skate rentals and supplies can be found at a friendly shop called Zack's Too. Continuing south for the next two miles, the crowds thin out. The inland side of the boardwalk is lined with wide parking lots; toward the ocean, however, there is an uninterrupted view of the activity on the wide sands of the beach. The boardwalk is amply outfitted with snack bars, showers, rest rooms, and drinking fountains. Be on the lookout for beachgoers who don't check for oncoming boardwalk traffic before crossing to and from these amenities.

Two more great skates are available at the south end of the Huntington Beach boardwalk. To access them, take the rough connection path up a low slope at the south edge of the parking lot. Turn left to skate across the Santa Ana River on the Coast Highway bridge, then follow the sidewalk a quarter mile to Orange Avenue and the Balboa Peninsula Trail. For speed and distance opportunities, turn right to take the underpass east to the Santa Ana River Trail. Both routes are described in this chapter.

---

8. Santa Ana River: Huntington Beach to Centennial Regional Park   14 miles

Reference: **Heading inland on the Santa Ana River from Huntington Beach; see number ❽ on page 362.**

Ideal for: Fitness—Speed—Touring

Directions: From Interstate 405 in Costa Mesa, exit at Brookhurst Street heading south. About 2.5 miles down, Brookhurst meets the Pacific Coast Highway at an entrance to a Huntington State Beach parking lot. If you get there early enough on the weekend while it's still foggy, free parking can be found at the curbside on Brookhurst near the

---

intersection. You may have to make a U-turn. Otherwise, go straight across the highway to enter the Huntington Beach parking lot and drive to the southernmost lot. The $5 fee is well spent because you can skate in three directions from this spot near the Santa Ana River, on this route plus two others described in this chapter.

Map: Orange County Bikeway Map, available free by calling the County of Orange, EMA/Transportation Planning office at (714) 834-3111.

Local shop: Bud's Pro Skate & Surf, 16895 Beach Boulevard, Huntington Beach, CA 92647; (714) 843-6922. Other contact: County of Orange, EMA/Transportation Planning, P.O. Box 4048, Santa Ana, CA 92702-4048; (714) 834-3137.

Tour notes: The Santa Ana River Trail is the ideal training ground for speed and fitness skaters, or for those who are tired of battling the crowds on the beach trails. Street underpasses add to the fun by allowing short, fast downhill runs. The early morning is the best time to get in a long speed workout here, because as a high sun warms up the inland, the resulting head wind will require you to assume a dedicated tuck position on the return trip.

Skate from the south end of the parking lot on a rough path that connects to the river trail. Head inland at the river's outlet into the Pacific Ocean, where on most summer mornings, the beach is shrouded in coastal fog. At first, seawater and the tide fill the mouth of the river from bank to bank, the gray waters reflecting a gray sky. A brightly colored mural featuring a giant in-line skate decorates the first underpass, part of Operation Clean Slate. The concrete walls all along the trailside are surprisingly free of graffiti in this area, possibly due to such projects.

About a mile and a half up the river, a rough and seemingly endless wood-slat bridge will have beginners grasping at the rail. It's easiest to cross at high speeds. At this point the riverbed has become sandy, interspersed with strips of marsh grasses and narrow rivulets that attract strolling egrets and hungry sandpipers.

Past the wooden bridge, another canal runs alongside the river. To the right is Fairview Regional Park and its connecting path. Soon the Santa Ana's high levee trail drops down to join the canal trail, and the river view is lost. After running for half a mile under buzzing power lines, the path passes a tiny park with one picnic table, some shade trees, and a drinking fountain. Situated about four miles up from the beach, this makes a welcome rest stop.

A few yards beyond the little park, the trail climbs back to the levee top. Here is the famous all-concrete Santa Ana riverbed prominently featured in a chase scene from the movie *Terminator II*. You may be tempted to slip down the banks and skate, but beware: massive semi trucks frequently scream by at 80-plus miles an hour, carrying dirt out of the mouth of the river. The setting on the right riverbank at this point is heavily industrial, but at the south edge of Centennial Regional Park, lawns, trees, and a little lake deliver more appealing views. Stop at the park for a rest in the shade before continuing up the river through Santa Ana (not described in this book) or turning back.

From the mouth of the Santa Ana River on the coast, two very popular skates await: head south down the Coast Highway to Orange Avenue, where the Balboa Peninsula Trail starts (see page 383), or go north to skate up South Huntington Beach to the pier (see page 370).

9. Bolsa Chica State Beach Trail   10 miles 🎱 ⚓ 🏃

Reference: **On the Pacific coast between Seal Beach and Huntington Beach; see number ❾ on page 362.**

Ideal for: Touring

Directions: From Interstate 405, take the Valley View Street/Bolsa Chica Road exit and go south to get onto Bolsa Chica Road. Four miles south, turn right at the "T" intersection on Warner Avenue. After 1.25 miles, Warner meets the Pacific Coast Highway (Highway 1). Cross the highway and turn right on Pacific Avenue, then left at Second Street, and park in the tiny free lot. (Get there early, or you will have to drive south down the Pacific Coast Highway and pay $5 to park at one of the big lots next to the beach.) To park at Huntington Beach, exit Interstate 405 at Highway 39 (Beach Boulevard) and head south. Two and a half miles down at the Ellis/Main Street intersection, turn right onto Main Street, which takes you the remaining three miles down to the coast. Park at the beach near the Huntington Pier. Head north to skate the Bolsa Chica State Beach Trail.

Map: Orange County Bikeway Map, available free by calling the County of Orange, EMA/Transportation Planning office at (714) 834-3111.

Local shop: Bud's Pro Skate & Surf, 16895 Beach Boulevard, Huntington Beach, CA 92647; (714) 843-6922. Other contact: County of Orange, EMA/Transportation Planning, P.O. Box 4048, Santa Ana, CA 92702-4048; (714) 834-3137.

Tour notes: The Bolsa Chica State Beach Trail connects Huntington Harbor with the Huntington Pier, five miles down the coast. The uncrowded path borders the Bolsa Chica Ecological Preserve just across the coastal highway, where the sight of boundless acres of marshland and dunes create a slightly isolated atmosphere. A generous 17-foot-wide asphalt avenue is dedicated to bicyclists, skaters, and pedestrians. It is not unusual to see young families taking advantage of the trail for a healthy outing, with dad jogging, mom on in-lines pushing a baby stroller, and junior riding a mini mountain bike.

From the Second Street parking lot, skate south to the cul-de-sac behind the Jack-In-The-Box, where the beach trail starts. With an early start on a foggy morn, you can enjoy the two miles of bikeway at your desired pace without having to navigate through crowds. Signs warn, "10 mph maximum, 5 mph when pedestrians present." The path extends down the edge of the parking lots, sheltered from blowing sand on the beach side by a low wall. Rest room facilities, showers, and snack bars are plentiful.

Approaching the camping and RV area, the pavement gets noticeably rougher, and at the end of Bolsa Chica State Beach, a quarter-mile stretch of six-foot-wide rough asphalt seems to go on forever where it crosses through low dunes just below the coastal highway. The Pacific Ocean surf crashes far across the sands of the wide beach, while surfers ride the waves and swells.

The trail passes through a grassy knoll where split pedestrian and bicycle paths offer an improved skating surface, as well as overlook views of the ocean. Approaching popular Huntington Beach, activity begins to pick up, and the trail passes through a narrow, grassy park decorated with tall palm trees and positioned on a low cliff above the beach. Across the street, beachside buildings replace the ecological preserve, and on the horizon to the south, the Huntington Pier comes into your sight line. The trail soon drops down to beach level and embarks on a rough route to the pier, where a 20-foot-wide asphalt boardwalk awaits. The Huntington Beach scene attracts such high-density crowds that flashing yellow lights are turned on as a traffic control measure. The trip from here to the Santa Ana River is detailed in the South Huntington Beach listing, page 370.

---

10. Yale Loop   5 miles 🌟 🛼 🏄

Reference: **Residential streets in the town of Irvine; see number ❿ on page 362.**

Ideal for: Fitness—Road/Street—Speed

Directions: From Interstate 5 in Irvine, exit south on Culver Drive. From Interstate 405 (the San Diego Freeway), exit on the same road heading north. At Barranca Road turn west and enter the Woodbridge Shopping Center. Turn right on Lake Road and enter the parking lots to the right. You will see the trail on either side of Lake Road's sidewalks just before it crosses a bridge over the river. Park nearby.

Local shop: Roller Skates of America, 1644 Superior Avenue, Costa Mesa, CA 92627; (714) 574-9966.

Tour notes: Like many college towns, Irvine is laced by a network of interconnecting bike lanes that traverse all of the major streets. The striped bike lanes on Yale Loop will appeal to street-ready skaters looking for a long, no-nonsense fitness route.

Starting from the Woodbridge Shopping Center, skate south of the parking lot to the San Diego Creek Trail (see page 381). Turn right

---

and follow the grassy banks of the river to West Yale Loop, the first underpass after Lake Road. Stay to the right to avoid going down the slope of the underpass unless you prefer to skate the outside bike lanes of the loop.

Turn right to follow West Yale Loop in a clockwise direction on the wide street's bike lanes. The route passes through the attractive neighborhoods surrounding the Woodbridge Shopping Center and the two Woodbridge Lakes. Where Yale Loop crosses Yale Avenue on both the north and south ends, the Yale Loop street name changes from West to East and back again. Access to the pretty North Woodbridge Lake and South Woodbridge Lake bike paths is available at both Yale Avenue intersections, from which you can catch a glimpse of the lakes. (See page 378.)

11. William R. Mason Regional Park

1.5 miles

Reference: **Near the University of California at Irvine; see number ⑪ on page 362.**

Ideal for: Beginners—Touring

Directions: From Interstate 405 (the San Diego Freeway) in Irvine, take the Culver Drive exit heading south. At University Drive, turn right, and then turn in at the park entrance on the left. The parking fee is $2 per vehicle. A map of the park is available at the entrance station, and it includes the bike paths in the wilderness area to the east.

Map: William R. Mason Regional Park Map, available at the park entrance station.

Local shop: Roller Skates of America, 1644 Superior Avenue, Costa Mesa, CA 92627; (714) 574-9966. Other contact: William R. Mason Regional Park, 18712 University Drive, Irvine, CA 92715; (714) 854-2491.

Tour notes: Nestled at the foot of the UC Irvine campus, William R. Mason Regional Park was originally part of the Rancho San Joaquin land grant. Today it is a pleasant and clean place to spend an afternoon building essential in-line skills. Smooth concrete sidewalks meander through the grassy park grounds past several picnic and tot play areas, three volleyball courts, and a unique Frisbee golf course. A little bridge crosses a narrow channel connecting Overlook Lake with Fountain Lake. Unfortunately, no swimming is allowed in these reclaimed waters.

Access to the park's wilderness area bike trails can be found across from the maintenance yard driveway at the east end of the park. Skate across Culver Drive and follow the sidewalk a few yards to the right, where the bike path enters the tule grasses. The wilderness trails are described on page 377.

12. Turtle Rock Greenbelt Bike Path

3 miles ⑧ 🛼 🎿

Reference: **In a neighborhood near the University of California at Irvine; see number ⑫ on page 362.**

Ideal for: Hills/Slalom—Touring

Directions: From Interstate 405 (the San Diego Freeway) in Irvine, take the Culver Drive exit heading south. Cross University Drive and pass Harvard Avenue. Turn left on Campus Drive and then left again one block up at Turtle Rock Drive. Climb the hill and turn in at the second left, Concordia. Park at the curb. The trail starts down the hill at the intersection of Turtle Rock and Campus Drives.

Map: William R. Mason Regional Park Map, available at the park entrance station.

Local shop: Roller Skates of America, 1644 Superior Avenue, Costa Mesa, CA 92627; (714) 574-9966. Other contact: William R. Mason Regional Park, 18712 University Drive, Irvine, CA 92715; (714) 854-2491.

Tour notes: The Turtle Rock Greenbelt bike path is a beautiful, though short roll up a gardenlike bikeway that passes behind attractive homes situated at the base of the San Joaquin Hills. User traffic is light enough here at midday hours during the week that skaters can indulge in some ski-specific cross training.

Skate south to enter the path above the tunnel under Turtle Rock. Here, the greenbelt's lush foliage is complemented by long, deep green grass and plenty of leafy trees. Although the shade is welcome on a hot day, the leaves tend to blanket the pavement below. As long as the ground underneath is dry, they aren't dangerous. When wet, however, the slippery leaves will hamper the long climb up to the summit of the hill at Starcrest and will present a hazard to skaters who brake or make slalom turns on the trip back down.

The dedicated greenbelt path ends temporarily at Starcrest, but it resumes farther up the street. Turn left to skate on the sidewalk to Ridgeline Drive. The trail branches off to the right to follow another back-neighborhood corridor, continuing to Turtle Rock Drive and, across the street, Turtle Rock Community Park.

Returning to the tunnel under Turtle Rock Drive, continue through it to follow the grass-bordered path near a street in front of the nearby dwellings. At Hillgate, the trail veers away from the street and passes between apartment buildings. Around the bend, it connects up with the William R. Mason Regional Park Wilderness (see the next listing).

13. William R. Mason Regional Park Wilderness

3 miles ⑥ 🏃 🎿

Reference: **Near and within a park in Irvine; see number ⑬ on page 362.**

Ideal for: Touring

Directions: From Interstate 405 (the San Diego Freeway) in Irvine, take the Culver Drive exit heading south. Cross University Drive and pass Harvard Avenue. Turn left on Campus Drive and then left again one block up at Turtle Rock Drive. Climb the hill and turn in at the first left, Hillgate. Park against the curb near where Hillgate meets Rockview. Look for the bike path on the north side of Rockview, where it crosses the lawn heading north between some apartments.

Map: William R. Mason Regional Park Map, available at the park entrance station.

Local shop: Roller Skates of America, 1644 Superior Avenue, Costa Mesa, CA 92627; (714) 574-9966. Other contact: William R. Mason Regional Park, 18712 University Drive, Irvine, CA 92715; (714) 854-2491.

Tour notes: Opened in 1988, the newest addition to the William R. Mason Regional Park is abundant with plant life that has been left for the most part in its pristine, natural state. Nestled at the base of the San Joaquin Hills, the sun-drenched, marshy lowlands harbor a variety of critters that live in the tall tule grasses.

Development in the wilderness portion of Mason Regional Park has been limited to three miles of flat, 10-foot-wide concrete hiking and biking trails and, where necessary to protect the habitat, a few chain-link fences. In some of the dense growth areas, the fences seem barely able to contain the tall grasses and cattails. When both sides of the smooth trail are behind barriers, you find yourself passing down interesting green corridors, unlike any other place you've ever skated. Watch out for wet patches where the marsh waters cross low points in the trail. The more open spaces of the wilderness area feature wild mustard, poppies, and small trees. Future plans include acquisition of Sand Canyon Reservoir, which should also result in trail expansion.

14. UC Irvine Campus

3 miles ⑥ 🏃 🎿

Reference: **The University of California at Irvine; see number ⑭ on page 362.**

Ideal for: Hills/Slalom—Road/Street—Touring

Directions: From Interstate 405 (the San Diego Freeway) in Irvine, take the Culver Drive exit heading south. Cross University Drive and pass Harvard Avenue. Turn right on Campus Drive and then right again at Berkeley Avenue. Park in the neighborhood across the street from the campus entrance.

Local shop: Roller Skates of America, 1644 Superior Avenue, Costa Mesa, CA 92627; (714) 574-9966.

Tour notes: UC Irvine features rolling terrain that provides great fun for hill and thrill seekers. As with any college campus tour, make sure you visit at a time when classes are not in session. There will be fewer people around, and you will enjoy better access to all that the grounds have to offer.

A bike path starts one block up Berkeley Avenue on the right, next to a big parking lot behind the Engineering Gateway building. In addition to that path, the bike lanes that line the Berkeley entrance road are quite decent for skating. For those who don't feel comfortable sharing the street with automobiles, a four-foot-wide sidewalk is available. Off to the left of Berkeley Avenue, a grass-bordered sidewalk enters a small grassy canyon that is worthy of exploration. Farther up the avenue, big sloping parking lots beckon with temptations of additional diversions. Make your own route.

Access to the San Diego Creek Trail (see page 381) can be found at the intersections of University and Campus Drives.

---

15. Woodbridge Lakes Trail   3 miles 🕖 🛼 🎿

Reference: A pair of lake loops in Irvine; see number ⑮ on page 362.

Ideal for: Road/Street—Touring

Directions: From Interstate 5 in Irvine, exit at Culver Drive and head south. From Interstate 405 (the San Diego Freeway), exit north on the same road. At Barranca Road, turn west and enter the Woodbridge Shopping Center. Turn right on Lake Road and enter the parking lots to the right. You will see the trail on either side of Lake Road's sidewalks just before it crosses a bridge over the river. Park nearby.

Local shop: Roller Skates of America, 1644 Superior Avenue, Costa Mesa, CA 92627; (714) 574-9966.

Tour notes: In east Irvine, pretty North and South Lakes enhance the neighborhoods on either side of the Woodbridge Shopping Center, and have come to be known by area visitors as the Woodbridge Lakes. Because private shoreline property is closed off, skating a contiguous loop around either lake is a navigational chore, and only half of each route is near the water. However, what remains still allows for a few excellent skating opportunities.

Near Lake Road, skate west on the San Diego Creek Trail (see page 381) to reach the concrete footbridge on the south side of the shopping center. At the other side, follow the path through a surprisingly barren field behind the Senior Center and then cross Alton Parkway on a wide concrete bridge. Turn left where the smooth, landscaped sidewalk branches and follow a shady corridor away from the water's edge. Make a right at the next intersection and skate next to a street named Springbrook South. Turn right at the tennis courts to return to the lakeshore. From this section of the gently rolling, grass-bordered sidewalk there is a fine view across the lake.

Cross the pebbled sidewalk at the far end of South Lake and then reenter the development at the Woodbridge Shore cul-de-sac. Turn left on Quiet Moon, and at the end of the street, enter the trail at the edge of school property. If nobody is around, take rink-style advantage of the row of perfectly paved multiple basketball courts. Farther up, the path passes another school and then hits the street at Blue Lake South. Turn right to get back to the lakeside sidewalks. Cross the wooden bridge that arches ever so prettily over the water. The arch and the rough, loose-fitting wooden slats present a real challenge to skaters. At the far end, turn left to return to the shopping center.

To explore North Lake, skate north from Lake Road to Barranca Parkway. Turn right and follow the sidewalk to the footbridge that crosses over Barranca to the south tip of the lake. Work your way up the great sidewalk that follows the lake's east shore until the barricades of a gated community prevent progress. The sidewalk turns away from the water to connect with bike lanes on the streets in the neighborhood. On the way back to Barranca don't bother crossing the wooden bridge: it will be too bumpy and steep for lower-level skaters, and the pavement on the other side is rough.

16. Atchison-Topeka Trail   8 miles 🌀 👥 ⛸

Reference: **A converted rail-trail on the outskirts of Irvine; see number ⑯ on page 362.**

Ideal for: Beginners—Fitness—Touring

Directions: From Interstate 5 in Irvine, take the Culver Drive exit at Sand Canyon Avenue and head south. Just beyond the railroad crossing a block away from the freeway, you will see the trail next to the trees on the right. Turn right into the gravel lane a few yards up and park in the sandy lot located right next to the trail.

Map: Orange County Bikeway Map, available free by calling the County of Orange, EMA/Transportation Planning office at (714) 834-3111.

Local shop: Roller Skates of America, 1644 Superior Avenue, Costa Mesa, CA 92627; (714) 574-9966. Other contact: County of Orange, EMA/Transportation Planning, P.O. Box 4048, Santa Ana, CA 92702-4048; (714) 834-3137.

Tour notes: Just by looking at a map, it is impossible to know that the arrow-straight Atchison-Topeka Trail is actually quite pretty, including a park and a two-mile stretch of greenbelt. The southeast extension passes through an agricultural area that's blanketed with fields of pungent, bright green basil.

Leaving the parking lot as you head west, the converted rail-trail parallels a still-active railroad line. Because of this, the scenery along the first quarter mile has an industrial flavor. Before long, the chain-link fences and train yards give way to wide vistas of burgeoning crops to the south, and the scenery is further improved by the tall eucalyptus and pepper trees that shade the path. Be on the alert for the big acorns that speckle the otherwise very smooth asphalt trail.

Giant dirt movers have been busy in the distance just south of Jeffrey Road, so it is possible that a new housing or shopping development has replaced the wide field that now borders the trail on the left. The trail crosses four-lane Jeffrey Road without benefit of a pedestrian crosswalk or a light, but the road is straight so you can see traffic approaching from several blocks away. On the other side of Jeffrey, a small neighborhood greenbelt welcomes you with a short patch of rough asphalt that soon gives way to prime pavement once again. Off the trail to the left, the concrete sidewalks at Hoeptner Park invite an exploratory side trip, or at least a visit to one of the drinking fountains. The wide railroad/power line easement running behind the neighborhoods allows the well-tended path to continue through fairly natural scenery for another two miles, all the way to Peters Canyon Channel near Jamboree Road. The greenbelt is so young that the trees are too small to offer much in the way of shade. Return the way you came.

Heading south from the parking lot, the Sand Canyon Avenue extension of the Atchison-Topeka Trail also kicks off with unappealing industrial scenery, but soon it, too, is surrounded by agricultural fields. If you're lucky, the wonderful scent of fresh basil will perfume the air as you skate this one-mile stretch of asphalt. When the bike path terminates, street skaters can continue on the road up to Alton Parkway. To connect to the Woodbridge Lakes Trail (see page 378) and San Diego Creek Trail (see page 381), turn right at Alton to reach the shopping center a mile and a half away.

17. Irvine Civic Center .5 miles 🌟 🛼 🧍

Reference: **In Irvine; see number 🔟 on page 362.**

Ideal for: Beginners—Touring

Directions: From Interstate 405 in Irvine, exit at Jamboree Road and proceed north a third of a mile to Main Street. Turn left and cross the San Diego Creek. The civic center is on the left, but you need to make a U-turn at the next light to get back to the main entrance. There is no curbside parking in the complex, so if the parking garage charges a fee during off-hours, park outside in a nearby business park and skate in.

Local shop: Roller Skates of America, 1644 Superior Avenue, Costa Mesa, CA 92627; (714) 574-9966.

Tour notes: The Irvine Civic Center displays an impressive set of matching high-rises in a circular setting. The buildings resemble nothing else as much as they do gigantic honeycombs. (Don't even try to imagine the size of the bees!)

The attractive landscaping and well-trimmed shrubs make the civic center an inviting locale for a relaxed exploratory cruise or for working on skating techniques. The pavement of the roundabouts that lead up to each building is smooth, and the sidewalks are clean and flat. Make sure you visit the Irvine Civic Center when the activity level is lowest. It won't be at all fun during business hours, and besides, you would probably be chased away.

From the grounds of the civic center, you have access to the San Diego Creek Trail just across the river on Main Street. Take the sidewalk across, where access paths dip down the underpass to join the trail. (See the next listing.)

---

18. San Diego Creek Trail   15 miles 🌀 👍 🏄

Reference: **Alongside San Diego Creek near Newport Beach; see number ⑱ on page 362.**

Ideal for: Fitness—Hills/Slalom—Speed—Touring

Directions: From Interstate 5 in Irvine, exit at Culver Drive and head south. From Interstate 405 (the San Diego Freeway), exit on the same road heading north. At Barranca Parkway turn west and enter the Woodbridge Shopping Center. Turn right on Lake Road and enter the parking lots to the right. You will see the trail on either side of Lake Road's sidewalks just before it crosses a bridge over the river. Park nearby.

Map: Orange County Bikeway Map, available free by calling the County of Orange, EMA/Transportation Planning office at (714) 834-3111.

Local shop: Roller Skates of America, 1644 Superior Avenue, Costa Mesa, CA 92627; (714) 574-9966. Other contact: County of Orange, EMA/Transportation Planning, P.O. Box 4048, Santa Ana, CA 92702-4048; (714) 834-3137.

Tour notes: This epic tour on the San Diego Creek Trail starts out in an overdeveloped shopping center, rounds a bend to deliver sensational panoramas of Irvine's classic downtown skyline, and finally rewards the persistent skater by traversing a marshy shore of the Upper Newport Bay Ecological Reserve. The route is paved with a smooth, 10-foot-wide mix of either asphalt or concrete, has no interruptions for stoplights, and is enlivened by several thrilling underpass slopes. The full round-trip of 15-plus miles will satisfy even the most demanding endurance or speed skating athlete.

Leaving Woodbridge Shopping Center, the trail starts on the grassy banks of San Diego Creek. As it passes behind Mervyn's, though, those lawns are replaced by concrete walls and then rocks. Skaters can avoid the slope of the Yale Loop underpass by taking the upper trail to cross the street at the light, an option that is available at nearly all of the overpasses along the way. When waters are high, this may be the only way to skate the full length of the trail.

Where the San Diego Creek turns toward the bay, a starkly empty field forebodes still more development. Business parks appear soon after on the left bank. The pavement is smooth and clean here, but on hot days you should keep an eye out for tar patches, which can become grabby. Ducks forage for food in the creek bed below, and on the other side there's a scenic view of Irvine's high-rise business and civic center. Take the Main Street overpass across the creek for a tour (see the previous listing).

After passing under Interstate 405, the trail parallels Harvard Avenue next to the Rancho San Joaquin Golf Course. The dramatic cityscapes slip deeper into the background across a wide field, and the creek environs are in a more natural state. The Campus Drive underpass marks the boundary of the UC Irvine campus, and now the route runs parallel to University Drive. The path tends to be a bit patchy through the state wildlife preserve across the creek from the campus.

Just before MacArthur Boulevard, a drinking fountain makes a good spot to take a welcome break about five miles southwest of the Woodbridge Shopping Center. When you reach busy MacArthur, the first sighting of the Upper Newport Bay is almost as gratifying as a long drink. Follow the nearby signs to Bristol Street. You will cross San Diego Creek on a barricaded path alongside MacArthur, then turn left to find the asphalt path known as the Back Bay Trail. At only 1.4 miles long, the nature skate feels far too short, but it offers a gratifying contrast to the cityscapes. Cross the long wood and asphalt boardwalk over the marshes, which will take you to the end of the trail at the far end of the reserve. To finish this tour with a kick (literally), make the long climb up Irvine Avenue for a fast skate all the way back down the hill.

19. Buffalo Hills Greenbelt   2 miles 🏅 🛼 🎿

Reference: **A community greenbelt trail in the hills of Newport Beach; see number ⑲ on page 362.**

Ideal for: Fitness—Road/Street—Touring

Directions: From Interstate 405 in Irvine, take the Jamboree Road exit heading south. Proceed about four miles to Ford Road and turn left. Follow Ford Road one mile and turn right at Old Ford Road West Connection. Just off Old Ford Road near this intersection, you will see the entrance sign for Buffalo Hills Park. There should be room to park at the curb.

Map: Orange County Bikeway Map, available free by calling the County of Orange, EMA/Transportation Planning office at (714) 834-3111.

Local shop: Roller Skates of America, 1644 Superior Avenue, Costa Mesa, CA 92627; (714) 574-9966. Other contact: County of Orange, EMA/Transportation Planning, P.O. Box 4048, Santa Ana, CA 92702-4048; (714) 834-3137.

Tour notes: The Buffalo Hills Greenbelt will never be called an in-line scene, in any sense of the term. But it does provide safe and un-crowded terrain on which lower level skaters can sharpen crucial stopping and hill skills that will expand their skating opportunities beyond the flat (and crowded) beach boardwalks. At the other end of the skill spectrum, experienced hill skaters can come to the greenbelt for a quick warm-up before tackling the hills of Newport Beach in the Fashion Island area. The dedicated bike paths shown on the Orange County Bikeway Map are actually wide sidewalks that parallel the busy parkways in the area: San Joaquin Hills Road, Spy Glass Hill Road, and Ford Road. A painted bike lane is provided on San Miguel between San Joaquin Hills Road and Ford Road.

Follow the Buffalo Hills Greenbelt south through a park that has picnic tables, trimmed lawns, and a variety of trees. Look closely at the pavement surface and you will see the telltale hash marks of skate tracks. A slight pitch to the path makes northbound skaters go fast enough that they may be inspired to get in a little stopping practice, secure in the knowledge that the lawn offers an emergency cushion to soften a fall. The greenbelt ends at San Miguel Road. Skate one block south (to the right) on San Miguel's bike lane to get to the bikeway on San Joaquin Hills Road, where you can explore the Newport hills on wide concrete sidewalks with few other users.

---

20. Balboa Peninsula Trail 8 miles ❼ 🛼 🏃

Reference: **The Balboa Peninsula in Newport Beach; see number ⓴ on page 362.**

Ideal for: Beginners—Scene—Touring

Directions: From Interstate 405 in Costa Mesa, exit at Harbor Boulevard heading south. Three miles down, Harbor Boulevard merges into Newport Boulevard. Proceed another two miles and cross the bridge at the intersection with the Pacific Coast Highway to get onto the Balboa Peninsula. Near the Newport Pier, Newport Boulevard be-comes Balboa Boulevard. Proceed all the way to the Balboa Pier. A parking lot with meters can be found on the north side. The board-walk passes through on the northward direction of the one-way park-ing lot road.

Map: Orange County Bikeway Map, available free by calling the County of Orange, EMA/Transportation Planning office at (714) 834-3111.

Local shop: Roller Skates of America, 1644 Superior Avenue, Costa Mesa, CA 92627; (714) 574-9966. Other contact: County of Orange, EMA/Transportation Planning, P.O. Box 4048, Santa Ana, CA 92702-4048; (714) 834-3137.

Tour notes: Whether you feel like showing off at the end of the pier or taking a cruise along the edge of the sand, the boardwalk trail at Newport Beach is the place to be. Skaters come from miles around to check out the Balboa Peninsula scene and to bask bare-skinned in the California sun, cooled by offshore breezes. The pier itself is off-limits to skaters, but the brick plaza where it meets the boardwalk is an ideal location for meeting and making friends or just tooling around. A favorite tour among local skaters is the seven-mile round-trip run up the coast to Huntington Pier and back.

There is an eight-mile-per-hour speed limit, and it's painted on the sidewalk. If you are inclined to keep a faster pace, go early (before 9 A.M. is best) to skate the beachside portion of the trail when there is less chance of getting issued a speeding ticket. As the crowds grow denser, skating fast is less fun and speeds are harder to maintain.

South of the pier, passage in front of the strip of beachfront shops can get pretty congested, and some of the characters who hang out there are pretty interesting. Heading north, the 10-foot-wide, divided route passes through a wide parking lot bordered by a short row of skate-up shops that supply food and drink and other seaside essentials. Emerging from the parking lot as a sandy, concrete boardwalk, the path then passes next to beachfront homes that line the edge of the sand, looking as though they have been around for years.

Starting at 36th Street just over two miles north of the Balboa Pier, the route moves one block inland to share a one-way street with automobile traffic. One lane is for northbound cars only, but the other is a continuation of the dedicated path, which is set apart from traffic with lines painted on the street. It isn't particularly scenic here, but no speed limit warnings are posted on the trail. When it is clear, you can skate as fast as you like in the traffic lane, as long as you don't get in the way of the automobiles. At the many minor intersections, keep on the alert for the occasional oncoming car. The trail seems to end at Orange Street, but by taking Orange one block east to the Pacific Coast Highway, you can skate on the wide pedestrian path to cross the bridge over the Santa Ana River. This brings you to the south end of the trail that continues up to Huntington Beach, mentioned in the first paragraph of this listing.

21. Balboa Island

2 miles 🏵 🕴

Reference: **Off the shores of Newport Beach; see number ㉑ on page 362.**

Ideal for: Touring

Directions: From Interstate 405 (the San Diego Freeway) in Irvine, take the Jamboree Road exit south. Proceed 5.5 miles and cross Highway 1 (the Pacific Coast Highway). To avoid Balboa Island's continual traffic jams, turn left on Bayside Drive and enter Bayside Square, a small business mall on the mainland next to the bridge to Balboa. Park here and you can easily skate across the bridge to get on the island.

Local shop: Roller Skates of America, 1644 Superior Avenue, Costa Mesa, CA 92627; (714) 574-9966.

Tour notes: The same qualities that attract carloads of tourists to Balboa Island at all times of the day appeal to the adventurous in-line skater. The island is packed as tight as a sardine can with shops, homes, and a ferry terminal. A wealth of enticing little alleyways and other nooks and crannies can be found in between. Cars are at a real disadvantage on these narrow two-lane streets, and that is probably the reason at least one vendor rents golf carts to visitors. Surefooted skaters can feel smug as they roll effortlessly from one street or shop to the next, because they really have the best and most convenient means of getting around and seeing the sights that Balboa Island has to offer. And on skates, if the crowds start to get a bit overwhelming, you are always just a short roll away from the less crowded end of the island.

Starting out, skate from the Bayside Square mall and over the bridge, which is paved with eight-foot-wide concrete sidewalks that make the crossing a breeze. At the far side, watch out for the rocks waiting to trip you at the bottom. Even on a pair of in-lines, you'll find the first block of Marine Avenue is usually quite congested. Luckily, the sidewalks on either side of the street are wide enough to accommodate the crowds of strolling window-shoppers as well as the occasional visitor on skates. To prevent conflicts with ferry traffic, Agate Avenue on South Bay Front is off-limits to skaters, but otherwise, the island is all yours. Whatever your route, be sure not to miss out on the three Bay Front streets, where a shoreline sidewalk gives the best vantage point for spectacular views of Newport Bay; look for South, East, and North Bay Front. Take some time to explore the inland streets and alleys that crisscross the island. Most of the residential streets are paved in concrete, but for people who prefer to stay out of traffic, these, too, are bordered by fairly decent sidewalks.

22. Aliso Creek Trail North   11 miles 🎗️ 🛼 🏊

Reference: **Alongside the Aliso Creek in Lake Forest; see number ㉒ on page 362.**

Ideal for: Fitness—Speed—Touring

Directions: From Interstate 5 in Laguna Hills, take the El Toro exit and drive a mile and a half northeast to Jeronimo Road. Turn right at Jeronimo and after you pass the Cherry Avenue intersection, enter El Toro Community Park on the right side of Jeronimo. Free parking is available down the driveway to the left. The creek trail can be seen to the right as you enter the driveway.

Map: Orange County Bikeway Map, available free by calling the County of Orange, EMA/Transportation Planning office at (714) 834-3111.

Local shop: Oshman's, 28331 Marguerite Parkway, Mission Viejo, CA 92692; (714) 364-3893. Other contact: County of Orange, EMA/Transportation Planning, P.O. Box 4048, Santa Ana, CA 92702-4048; (714) 834-3137.

Tour notes: The Aliso Creek Trail is a wonderful nature roll that flows more than five miles northwest through a wide creekside easement, with only one very minor street crossing! Starting from El Toro Community Park, the trail is enveloped in the sights and sounds of urban life: a golf course, ranch-style homes, noisy multilane expressways, and power lines. Just up the way, however, where the trail passes through acres of hilly grassland, one starts to heed the posted warnings of recent rattlesnake and mountain lion sightings.

Depart from El Toro Park on the steep dip that crosses under Jeronimo Road. Stay to the right to leave room for those who may be approaching from the other side. A wooden bridge with loose boards crosses the creek after the first block. Skate assertively and the boards won't rattle quite so much. As you start out, you may think that you need to clean your bearings, but this is only an effect caused by the constant, though gentle, upward climb of the Aliso Creek Trail.

The eight-foot-wide asphalt trail meanders quietly along the overgrown creek bed, passing homes that are set back behind trees on either side of the wide easement. Nearly a mile up the creek, it makes another dip under Trabuco Road, though this one is not quite as steep as the first. After another pleasant mile in dappled sun alternating with shade, the trail passes under and then parallels six-lane El Toro Road, a constant companion for the next four miles. Homes are perched on an overlook above the creek, visible from the concrete sidewalk next to the grassy easement. Surprisingly, the path transforms into a smooth, full-width service road that continues for a mile or more up to Santa Margarita Parkway.

Here, a stand of eucalyptus trees makes a good spot to rest a while and admire the view of the grassy hills all around. Gradually, the neighborhoods drop behind as the creek trail continues up into the north county countryside. The last 2.5 miles on the route pass through such wildly natural surroundings that some folks might feel compelled to whisper, "Lions and tigers and bears—oh my!"

The trail ends a quarter mile beyond the headquarters of Whiting Ranch Wilderness Park, which is located off to the left and up a steep side trail. If you have the energy, climb up to the well-preserved white ranch house, where you can get a drink of cold water and relax in the shade before turning back. Free copies of the Orange County Bikeway Map are given away there, too. Once you feel refreshed, return to the path and polish off the north portion of the Aliso Creek Trail by skating that last quarter mile up to Ridgeline Road. Congratulate yourself, and then turn around and get ready for a swift cruise all the way down to El Toro Park. The path may not be steep, but the pitch is just enough to make the trip back virtually effortless.

23. Aliso Creek: El Toro to Sheep Hills Park

6 miles

Reference: **Alongside the Aliso Creek in Lake Forest; see number ㉓ on page 362.**

Ideal for: Hills/Slalom—Touring

Directions: From Interstate 5 in Laguna Hills, take the El Toro exit and drive a mile and a half northeast to Jeronimo Road. Turn right at Jeronimo and after you pass the Cherry Avenue intersection, enter El Toro Community Park on the right side of Jeronimo. Free parking is available down the driveway to the left. The creek trail can be seen to the right as you enter the driveway.

Map: Orange County Bikeway Map, available free by calling the County of Orange, EMA/Transportation Planning office at (714) 834-3111.

Local shop: Oshman's, 28331 Marguerite Parkway, Mission Viejo, CA 92692; (714) 364-3893. Other contact: County of Orange, EMA/Transportation Planning, P.O. Box 4048, Santa Ana, CA 92702-4048; (714) 834-3137.

Tour notes: The hilly route between El Toro Community Park and Sheep Hills Park delivers such a mix of scenery that, when you look back on your trip, it is hard to believe all of those images were actually strung together within the same three-mile stretch.

Start skating south through El Toro Community Park II (that's what the sign calls it), past the sporting fields at the park and the driving range of the community golf center. Emerging from behind the huge green net of the driving range, the trail meets the north side of Los Alisos Boulevard and turns south between it and an arroyo full of brush that conceals Aliso Creek. Soon you reach El Toro Community Park I, and the route passes through on a sidewalk sprinkled with leaves from the eucalyptus trees that provide shade. Skate with caution when you see warning signs suggesting that bicyclists walk down the steep underpasses.

At the west end of El Toro Park I, the Aliso Creek Trail enters a concrete canyon where it curves under Los Alisos Boulevard and into the city limits of Laguna Hills. Just around the bend, the trail makes its way into a small and more natural, willow-filled canyon that continues for a mile and passes under Interstate 5 behind an otherwise quiet neighborhood. When you reach a four-way intersection in the heart of the canyon, continue straight ahead; the two side trails are access paths serving the residents of the neighborhood. At the end of the little backyard canyon, turn left to follow a landscaped asphalt trail alongside busy Paseo de Valencia, which requires a climb of nearly half a mile. At the Stockport stoplight, the trail cuts diagonally across Paseo de Valencia to follow the path on the south side of Laguna Hills Road. A forest of trees at the roadside adds a rural touch to the urban landscape as you descend to the next corner at Indian Hill Lane. Turn left and climb steeply up Indian Hill until you reach the entrance sign for Sheep Hills Park.

At both ends of the Aliso Creek route you just toured, more skating awaits. If you'd like to continue heading southwest, a fast descent down the sidewalk near the Sheep Hills Park sign takes you across the grass to the Sheep Hills-to-Wood Canyon leg of the Aliso Creek Trail (see the next listing). The Aliso Creek Trail North tour begins at El Toro Community Park II (see page 386).

---

24. Aliso/Wood Canyons Trail   7 miles 🟢 🚴 🏊

Reference: In Aliso/Wood Canyons Regional Park, south of Laguna Hills; see number ㉔ on page 362.

Ideal for: Touring

Directions: From Interstate 5 in Laguna Hills, exit on Alicia Parkway heading south. Turn right onto Paseo de Valencia and turn left one block up onto Laguna Hills Road. Turn left again at Indian Hill Lane and climb the hill. You will see the sign for Sheep Hills Park on the right once you reach the top of the hill. Park at the curb next to the steep sidewalk that descends into the park.

Map: Orange County Bikeway Map, available free by calling the County of Orange, EMA/Transportation Planning office at (714) 834-3111.

Local shop: Sport Chalet, 27551 Puerta Real, Mission Viejo, CA 92691-6381; (714) 582-3363. Other contact: County of Orange, EMA/Transportation Planning, P.O. Box 4048, Santa Ana, CA 92702-4048; (714) 834-3137.

Tour notes: The southernmost leg of the Aliso Creek Trail is wild and untamed along much of its route through Aliso/Wood Canyons Regional Park. More likely than not, you will spot a cottontail rabbit or two by the time you have completed the round-trip. With acres and acres of open space, Aliso/Wood Canyons Regional Park is sure to impress nature lovers who come in the full bloom of spring. By the time August rolls around, the dry grasses of the low hills that line both sides of the canyon have taken on the color of distressed gold. Dense brush grows close to the trail, a standard eight-foot-wide asphalt path with a dividing line.

Starting from Sheep Hills Park, down the canyon you roll, communing with nature tucked into a cleft below the urban development on the surrounding hills. When you reach the bridge that crosses over the creek to the left, stop and take a look at the pretty little scene as the water dances over the rocks below before whirling away to disappear underneath a patch of bamboo. Do not cross—unless you'd like to explore the well-kept grounds and sidewalks of the apartment complex just beyond the row of eucalyptus trees.

As you continue due south past a school, terraces climbing the ridge above sport block after block of tan houses topped with red tiled roofs. After the trail passes under an expressway, watch out for an asphalt detour around a washed-out section of what would have been a great 12-foot-wide concrete path, which may or may not have been repaired since this trip was researched. On the right side of the trail, a little park makes a nice spot to take a break, either now or on your way back.

Around a bend three miles south of Sheep Hills Park, a pair of schools is nestled in the long, narrow canyon. The now-landscaped path curves around the edge of the schools, close to Aliso Creek, which is filled with large stones and waist-high brush. Along the trail, poppies add a welcome dash of bright orange. Beyond the end of the school yards, the final underpass (decorated with a mural that depicts, among other things, a pair of in-line skates) signals the start of some rough pavement that continues another quarter of a mile. The official end of this trail is at the entrance to Wood Canyon near the intersection of Aliso Creek and Awma Roads.

Unofficially, it is possible to skate another mile or two into the most beautiful part of Wood Canyon, where Aliso Creek flows quietly through the lovely riparian scenery at the foot of the Sheep Hills. Although there is a smooth, wide road behind the closed entrance gate, only water district vehicles (including fast-moving water trucks) are allowed to use it. The approved public access is on a dirt trail that runs alongside. However, please note that trespassers who cannot resist the paved road are rarely bothered.

25. Chapparosa Park and Expressway Sidewalks

6 miles 🔵9 🐾3 🏃

Reference: A park and neighboring streets in Laguna Niguel; see number ㉕ on page 362.

Ideal for: Figure/Stunts—Hills/Slalom—Touring

Directions: From Interstate 5 in Mission Viejo, take the Crown Valley Parkway exit and proceed southwest for 1.5 miles. Turn left at Street of the Golden Lantern and drive another 1.5 miles to Chapparosa Park Road. Turn right to follow the lane down to Chapparosa Park. Parking is free.

Local shop: Sport Chalet, 27551 Puerta Real, Mission Viejo, CA 92691-6381; (714) 582-3363.

Tour notes: Laguna Niguel is a beautiful town located in the hills north of Dana Point. Residents and visitors who love to skate are lucky to have Chapparosa Park nearby. In and around the park, there are many opportunities for in-line skating, including large flat areas for free-style skating, access to nearby expressway sidewalks, and easy entry to the rolling expert run down the Salt Creek Trail.

Chapparosa Park is new enough that the parking lots and sidewalks are still in perfect condition. It is situated at the northern end of the canyon of Salt Creek Regional Park and is bordered by tree- and shrub-covered hills that rise steeply on both sides, preventing heavy development. The park's most tempting pavement is on the three basketball courts and on the sidewalk that borders the parking lot, which in itself is excellent terrain for freestyle practice. Picnic tables, water fountains, and shady patches of lawn make for a comfortable post-skate rest.

Ready to explore the easy section of Salt Creek Canyon and sample the slopes on the 10-foot-wide sidewalks just west of Chapparosa Park? Start at the southwest end of the parking lot, where you will see the sign marking the beginning of the Laguna Niguel Hike/Bike Nature Trail. The smooth asphalt is 10 feet wide, and mileage is painted on the pavement every one-tenth mile. (Ignore the numbered posts, which are there to be used with a nature trail brochure.)

Enter the Salt Creek Canyon between shrub-covered hills. Up on the ridges, the rooftops of homes on view lots are just visible. Follow the path past the seemingly misplaced street sign in the middle of nowhere that says "Anderson," and through the tunnel under Niguel Road. The trail branches at the other side. The right fork takes you to the Salt Creek Trail (for experts only!), described on page 391. Take the left fork to follow the concrete sidewalk that runs along the south side of the canyon, creeping up until it reaches Beacon Hill Way at Niguel Road to a landscaped sidewalk that continues south above the deep, dry gorge. Across from the Beacon Hill entrance, the sidewalk leaves the canyon and descends in a thrilling half-mile roll down to the intersection with Camino Del Avion. We leave you here to retrace your steps back to Chapparosa Park.

More diversions: The 10-foot-wide sidewalks on two other nearby expressways are worth exploring. Marina Drive, north of Chapparosa Park, is just over a mile long and has gentler slopes than those on Niguel Road. Street of the Golden Lantern connects the Chapparosa Park entrance road with Camino Del Avion two miles south. Its slopes are long and steep, and you must skate next to fast-moving cars. You should determine which route is best suited to your skills by driving them both beforehand.

---

26. Salt Creek Trail   8 miles 🔟 🎿 🚶

Reference: **Through the canyons of Salt Creek Regional Park in Laguna Niguel; see number ㉖ on page 362.**

Ideal for: Fitness—Hills/Slalom—Touring

Directions: From Interstate 5 in Mission Viejo, take the Crown Valley Parkway exit and proceed southwest for 1.5 miles. Turn left at Street of the Golden Lantern and drive another 1.5 miles to Chapparosa Park Road. Turn right and follow the lane down to Chapparosa Park. Parking is free.

Map: Orange County Bikeway Map, available free by calling the County of Orange, EMA/Transportation Planning office at (714) 834-3111.

Local shop: Sport Chalet, 27551 Puerta Real, Mission Viejo, CA 92691-6381; (714) 582-3363. Other contact: County of Orange, EMA/Transportation Planning, P.O. Box 4048, Santa Ana, CA 92702-4048; (714) 834-3137.

Tour notes: The untamed canyon of Salt Creek Regional Park will have expert hill skaters wondering if they've found heaven. A superb, smooth trail takes visitors over hills that are challenging, steep, curvy, long, fun, and difficult to ascend. And as icing on the cake, each passing mile on the way to the coast brings even better ocean views and canyon scenery.

The asphalt path is only 10 feet across, the standard width. Still, this is a great place for skaters who like to use rubber-tipped ski poles, which really make climbing much easier. Expert ski skaters will find that using poles on the downhills is wonderfully akin to snow skiing (but considerably less expensive).

Start from Chapparosa Park at the southwest end of the parking lot, where a sign marks the beginning of the Laguna Niguel Hike/Bike Nature Trail. The trail's mileage is painted on the pavement at every one-tenth mile. (Ignore the numbered posts, unless you have a copy of the nature trail brochure.) Enter the Salt Creek Canyon and

---

follow it for the first mile between shrub-covered hills, until you pass through the tunnel under Niguel Road. Where the trail branches, take the right fork to begin a steep climb on the Salt Creek Trail.

The trail follows the western edge of the deep canyon on the side of a high ridge. Succeed with the first climb and you will be rewarded with a wondrous view, including the first glimpse of the Pacific Ocean. An attractive barrier borders the trail, offering some assurance that you won't drop over the edge should you lose control. Make it a point to prevent that possibility by applying your heel brake as necessary for speed control.

After several curvy hills on the edge of the canyon, the path meets Camino Del Avion at the two-mile mark. This is the end of Salt Creek Regional Park but not the end of the trail. Go left to take the underpass to the other side and continue on a path through The Links, a ritzy neighborhood overlooking the Monarch Beach Golf Course. Now our canyon skate reveals a verdant scene of putting greens with the Pacific Ocean sparkling in the distance. As you pass the homes next to the trail, there may be mud slide damage that hasn't yet been repaired. Watch out for shifting asphalt patches covering the soft soil at the base of the hillside.

The golf course gives way to marshy grasses and sand dunes just before the trail turns a sharp corner and enters the dark tunnel of the Coast Highway underpass. On the other side, follow the signs to the public access beach. At the top of the rise, the immense Pacific reveals itself in all its glory below the cliffs. Skate through exquisite Bluff Park, where sloping lawns and benches next to the trail invite you to rest awhile and take in the view. The trail ends at a steep drop down the entrance road to Salt Creek Beach Park.

---

27. Lake Mission Viejo   3.2 miles 🎱 🏃

Reference: **A lake within a gated community in Mission Viejo; see number ㉗ on page 362.**

Ideal for: Fitness—Hills/Slalom—Touring

Directions: From Interstate 5 in Laguna Hills, exit at Alicia Parkway heading northeast and follow the signs to Lake Mission Viejo. Proceed three miles to Marguerite Parkway and turn left. At the first light, Vista del Lago, turn right and park in the shopping center as close as possible to the sidewalks on Marguerite Parkway.

Local shop: Oshman's, 28331 Marguerite Parkway, Mission Viejo, CA 92692; (714) 364-3893.

Tour notes: Located in a well-to-do area of Mission Viejo, Lake Mission Viejo is nestled in an intimate little basin surrounded by attractive homes with private docks. In this setting, the blue waters and brightly colored umbrellas on the white sand beach give it a Mediterranean

---

feel. Although the shorefront home owners dominate the gated property next to the water, you can enjoy two good views of the lake from a sidewalk loop around its perimeter. Catch a close-up of the sandy beach from Olympiad Road, and a broader, end-to-end view of the whole lake from the sidewalk next to Alicia Parkway.

The wonderfully paved sidewalks deliver some fun hill skating in a loop that measures exactly 3.2 miles. (Serious-looking walkers and joggers on any given route can always be depended on to know the exact mileage.) The trail includes long uphills and, of course, long downhills. There are a few driveway intersections to watch out for, but there's no need to wait at an intersection for the light to change, since the route loops around the lake without crossing any major streets.

One would expect the neighborhood scenery to be the same on all sides of the lake, but each landscaped four-lane expressway has its own character. Start skating on Marguerite Parkway, which climbs a long hill bordered by trees. The corridor of shade is very pretty but offers no view of the lake. Turn right onto Olympiad Road, where one short stretch of the loop allows the best overlook of the beach at the north end of the lake. Do pay some attention to the sidewalk surface here, though, because shifting slabs can trip the unwary. Neon yellow paint highlights the worst raised edges. Climb Olympiad to San Marcos Street, past new housing developments that are beginning to take over the grassy hilltop to the left. Turn right onto busy Alicia Parkway and skate a couple more hills through the neighborhood. Soon you will arrive at a nice spot on the right to enjoy a view of Lake Mission Viejo. A block up, follow a path that cuts the corner at Marguerite Parkway through some trees and grass near a marina. The short path returns to the sidewalk that takes you back to the start of the loop.

28. Santa Margarita Lake   1 mile 🛡️ 🏖️ 🏊

Reference: **In unincorporated Rancho Santa Margarita; see number ㉘ on page 362.**

Ideal for: Beginners—Fitness—Touring

Directions: From Interstate 5 in Laguna Hills, exit at Alicia Parkway heading northeast and follow it five miles up to Santa Margarita Parkway. Turn right and cross the Arroyo Trabuco canyon, following the parkway two miles to Fundadores Lane, which delivers you to the club parking lot in front of the lake.

Local shop: Oshman's, 28331 Marguerite Parkway, Mission Viejo, CA 92692; (714) 364-3893.

Tour notes: Rancho Santa Margarita is an unincorporated town on the northeastern reaches of Orange County. The community is fortunate to have a very pretty little man-made lake with a delicious one-mile loop that passes through attractive landscaping at the edge of the shoreline. Everyone in this community has access to Santa Margarita Lake's waters, not just a few lucky lakefront property owners.

Starting out in a clockwise direction on the west side of the lake, it is hard not to gape at the spectacular sight of nearby Saddleback Mountain. Benches are provided at the side of the trail so visitors can ponder the drama of the view without blocking the path. Continuing on, make a full circuit on the flat lake loop, sharing the way with others who are skating, biking, and fitness walking. Richly dense lawns and strategically placed shade trees are spaced along a route so well designed that the distance seems inconsequential. That makes it all the better for fitness-oriented skaters who can more easily enjoy time spent maintaining a calorie-burning heart rate. After doing a few laps to work up a sweat, you might want to head to the sandy beach, a good place to relax and soak up some sun.

For restless types, the Rancho Santa Margarita neighborhoods bordering the lake are smoothly paved. These make excellent destinations for further exploration while you wait for a friend to awaken from a nap on the beach.

---

29. San Juan Creek Trail   6 miles ⭐**5** 🛼**2** 🏃

Reference: **Alongside the San Juan Creek in San Juan Capistrano; see number ㉙ on page 362.**

Ideal for: Speed—Touring

Directions: From Interstate 5 in San Juan Capistrano, exit at Camino Las Ramblas and take the expressway southwest. Follow the signs to the Coast Highway (Highway 1) and head north. At the second stoplight, turn left at Harbor Drive (the left is Del Obispo Street). Park at Doheny State Beach.

Map: Orange County Bikeway Map, available free by calling the County of Orange, EMA/Transportation Planning office at (714) 834-3111.

Local shop: The Hockey Stop, 31931 Del Obispo Street #22, San Juan Capistrano, CA 92675; (714) 443-2781. Other contact: County of Orange, EMA/Transportation Planning, P.O. Box 4048, Santa Ana, CA 92702-4048; (714) 834-3137.

Tour notes: Disguised as a common creekside bike path, the San Juan Creek Trail comes with more than the usual serving of skating challenges. A loose, wood-slat bridge and deep grooves lurking at the bottom of the Coast Highway underpass will excite the nerves of all but the most expert skaters. Along the last mile, enchanting views of the high hills to the north are offset by a vibrating roll on rough pavement.

The trail starts at the mouth of the San Juan Creek on the south end of the Doheny State Beach parking lot. Skate inland on the left side of the creek for about a third of a mile. Just before the steep Highway 1 underpass, work with gravity to prepare for a fast coast. At the low part of the dip, two-inch-wide drainage grooves are cut out of the concrete every five inches, stretched out over the next four yards. Four-wheel in-lines will roll right across the deep grooves as long as they are kept perpendicular. In wet seasons, beware of standing water at the bottom of the underpass.

Continuing up San Juan Creek, the trail passes a smelly treatment plant, a baseball park, and then the narrow entrance through the chain-link fence to Del Obispo Park, where a tennis court has been converted into an outdoor roller hockey rink. Along the second mile, apartment complexes, the Stonehill Drive underpass, and mobile home parks don't provide much in the way of scenery, but the pavement is wide, smooth, and allows for fast skating. It's perfect for speed work, especially against the head wind on the way back.

After almost two miles, the creek branches to the left and the trail crosses San Juan Creek on an old iron and wood-slat bridge. (As of this writing, construction and a washout prevented further skating north on the San Juan Creek Trail.) Take a left at the end of the bridge to branch off onto the rough pavement of the Robert McCollum Memorial Bike Trail. Enjoy the pretty views of the high hills ahead after the trail passes under Del Obispo Street. A sudden jog into a neighborhood to the right announces the trail's termination in a cul-de-sac at Avenida de la Vista. On the trip back, a stop in shady Descanso Park near the trail's fork at the bridge will give you a welcome rest in preparation for skating against offshore breezes.

---

30. San Juan Creek Trail Northeast

2.6 miles

Reference: A rural route on the northeast outskirts of San Juan Capistrano; see number **30** on page 362.

Ideal for: Beginners—Touring

Directions: From Interstate 5 in San Juan Capistrano, exit at San Juan Creek Road heading northeast. Proceed one mile and turn left onto La Novia Avenue, then park on the dirt. The path starts at this intersection on the north side of San Juan Creek Road.

Map: Orange County Bikeway Map, available free by calling the County of Orange, EMA/Transportation Planning office at (714) 834-3111.

Local shop: The Hockey Stop, 31931 Del Obispo Street #22, San Juan Capistrano, CA 92675; (714) 443-2781. Other contact: County of Orange, EMA/Transportation Planning, P.O. Box 4048, Santa Ana, CA 92702-4048; (714) 834-3137.

Tour notes: Less than four miles up from its Pacific outlet on the coast at Doheny State Beach, this short inland extension of the San Juan

Creek Trail makes a pastoral contrast to its seaside portion. The homespun smell of horse stables replaces the salty sea air, and picket fences line a rural route next to the low hills that shadow the overgrown creek.

Starting at La Novia, skate northeast on the left side of San Juan Creek Road to follow the seemingly forsaken four-foot-wide asphalt path. Have heart, for the pavement soon improves, and by the time it reaches the shady grounds of the elementary school, it is upgraded to a concrete sidewalk. Beyond the school, a pair of white fences adds a charming country touch, and near the trail, a sign advertises horse boarding services. Across the street, grassy hills are awash in the green of spring or the straw gold of summer, depending on the season of your visit. As the route becomes rural, trees and brush across the field to the left are evidence that San Juan Creek is not far away. For the last half mile, a 10-foot-wide asphalt surface is enhanced by natural landscaping, street lamps, and a double wood fence. Soon after showing off its best, the trail stops at a dead-end gate at the termination of San Juan Creek Road.

---

31. Coast Highway Bike Route   8 miles 🟡 🛹 🛼

Reference: **Alongside the Coast Highway in Capistrano Beach; see number ❸❶ on page 362.**

Ideal for: Touring

Directions: From Interstate 5 at Capistrano Beach, exit onto Camino Las Ramblas and head toward the beach. Follow signs to the Coast Highway and turn left. Park at the curb on the west side of the street.

Map: Orange County Bikeway Map, available free by calling the County of Orange, EMA/Transportation Planning office at (714) 834-3111.

Local shop: The Hockey Stop, 31931 Del Obispo Street #22, San Juan Capistrano, CA 92675; (714) 443-2781. Other contact: County of Orange, EMA/Transportation Planning, P.O. Box 4048, Santa Ana, CA 92702-4048; (714) 834-3137.

Tour notes: Intermediate-level skaters with an urge to skate on the Coast Highway can take the flat sidewalks and bike lanes that connect Capistrano Beach with the town of San Clemente. Sandy bluffs line the route on the inland side, but the Atchison-Topeka railroad tracks between the highway and the ocean balance out the beauty factor.

Skate south next to Doheny State Beach on the wide sidewalks that connect it with Capistrano Beach Regional Park. During the summer, the sun isn't likely to warm your way unless you start skating after noon. Until then, the region's morning coastal fog is a familiar and expected companion.

When the sidewalks end, take to the bike lanes that run all the way to Avenida Pico in San Clemente, a straight shot. The ocean view is blocked for the south half of this route by the beachfront homes located at the side of the smoothly paved road. The route ends at San Clemente, an unassuming but rather charming little surfer town.

Upon your return to Doheny State Beach, another great skating route can be accessed less than half a mile north. Going north up the Coast Highway, cross the San Juan River and turn left to follow the signs to Doheny State Beach. The entrance to the San Juan River Trail is at the south end of the parking lots.

San Diego County

22 Great Places to Skate

San Diego County

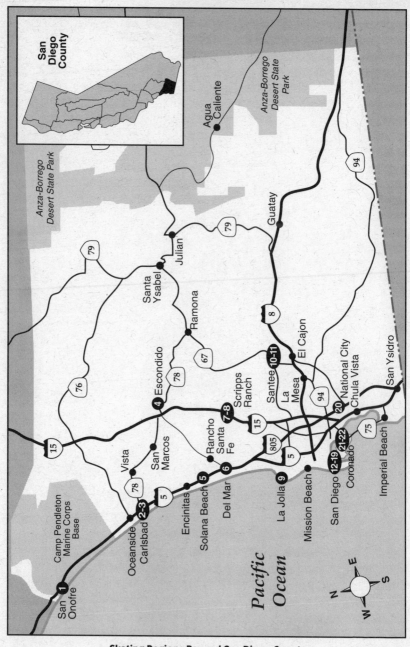

Skating Regions Beyond San Diego County

North .... Orange County, p. 361; and East .... Deserts, p. 339
Inland Empire, p. 353

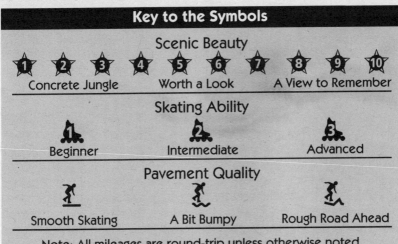

Key to the Symbols

Scenic Beauty

1 **2** **3** **4** **5** **6** **7** **8** **9** **10**

Concrete Jungle   Worth a Look   A View to Remember

Skating Ability

1 Beginner   **2** Intermediate   **3** Advanced

Pavement Quality

Smooth Skating   A Bit Bumpy   Rough Road Ahead

Note: All mileages are round-trip unless otherwise noted.

San Diego County offers the perfect climate for year-round skating. For the area's in-line community, that is both a blessing and a curse. As big and beautiful as Mission Bay is, so many people crowd onto the boardwalks that conflicts among trail users are beginning to result in speed limits, restricted areas, and other impositions curbing the freedom that personifies outdoor skating.

Fortunately, the entire west county is laced with miles of dedicated bikeways, and they are all identified on San Diego's excellent bicycle commuter map. The routes most suited to skating are detailed in this chapter, including an interesting range of river and lake trails waiting to be explored. You will be introduced to some truly unique skates that you are likely to have all to yourself.

To avoid the bottlenecks at the bay, some of the area's more experienced skaters have been redefining the notion of skateable terrain. They are learning to appreciate (and in some cases, relish) the seemingly boundless opportunities available in San Diego streets with and without bike lanes. The San Diego Skate Coalition is the heart of this movement. Their athletic tours of the city streets are building a strong corps of street-savvy skaters who are gearing up both literally and figuratively for a broader vision of the future of San Diego in-line skating. (See the Resource Guide on page 431.)

1. San Onofre Coast Route   21 miles 🏅 🛼 🏃

Reference: **An abandoned highway on the coast near San Onofre; see number ❶ on page 400.**

Ideal for: Fitness—Speed—Touring

Directions: From Interstate 5 at the north end of Camp Pendleton, take the Basilone Road/San Onofre exit to San Onofre Beach Road on the west side of the freeway. Proceed south past the entrance to the San Onofre power plant until you reach the San Onofre State Beach entrance gate. The day-use fee is $6. Drive three miles past the camping area and park at the end of the road near the gate that blocks vehicular entry to the bike path. Other entrance points are from the Las Pulgas Road exit and at the northern end of the Oceanside Marina. Important note: you will need to show your driver's license or other photo ID to pass through the Camp Pendleton gates.

Local shop: The Hockey Stop, 31931 Del Obispo Street #22, San Juan Capistrano, CA 92675; (714) 443-2781.

Tour notes: The remote stretch of abandoned highway that runs along the San Onofre coast lures competent skaters who are into fitness or speed training, as well as romantic diehards who can't resist the notion of skating it just to say they did. (You know who you are!) If you fit either profile, pack a lunch and a bottle of water and be prepared for an adventure. Try to schedule your trip around the wind: if it is hot inland, the breezes off the ocean will batter you the whole way. Starting early in the morning is best during the hot season, even though you will most likely be skating in the fog.

The San Onofre Coast Route includes all types of pavement. On this portion of the old coast highway, the quality ranges from the best (well, almost) to the worst. For a preliminary taste of the worst, you could have skated the three miles through the San Onofre State Beach campgrounds (and saved yourself $6). It's worth the money to drive beyond those long parking lots, where the terrible pavement is unavoidable.

Slipping through the gate at the end of the campgrounds, head south on the west edge of the old highway, where the painted-on bike lane occupies a relatively smooth concrete shoulder. On each side of the road, the earth is covered with low shrubs. The Pacific Ocean, of course, is to the right. The hills of the marine base are to the left, and across Interstate 5, they rise to join the coast range, close enough to present a formidable wall to the east. A mile and a half from the start, Horno Canyon opens up to the left, the first in a series of canyons that make interesting scenic diversions along the way.

Three miles of steady skating brings you to a Camp Pendleton gate, where you will be asked to show your ID before being allowed to continue. At this point you are at the Las Pulgas Road exit off Interstate 5. Take a break and check out the ocean view from the nearby vista point. Continuing from here, the route passes under the freeway and runs parallel on its east side for the remaining 7.5 miles of the tour. The old highway now passes Las Pulgas, Aliso, and French Canyons, in that order. Shortly after it crosses the Santa Margarita River, the San Onofre Coast Route terminates at the Oceanside Marina.

---

2. Carlsbad Walkway   5 miles 🎱 🐾 🏃

Reference: **Alongside the Pacific coast in Carlsbad; see number ❷ on page 400.**

Ideal for: Road/Street—Scene—Touring

Directions: From Interstate 5 in Carlsbad, exit at Tamarack Avenue and head west. Turn right onto Carlsbad Boulevard. One block north of Pine Street, as you enter a downtown area, turn left onto Oak Avenue, a side street dipping to the west toward the ocean. Turn left again where Oak meets Ocean Street, into a free (but frequently full) parking lot.

Map: The San Diego County Bike Map is available free by calling (619) 231-2453.

Local shop: Cal Stores, 1380 East Valley Parkway, Escondido, CA 92027-2312; (619) 489-1114. Other contact: Michael Jackson, City of San Diego Bicycle Coordinator, 1222 First Avenue, MS 503, San Diego, CA 92101; (619) 533-3110.

Tour notes: For north San Diego County residents, the Carlsbad Walkway is the place to skate. The beautifully designed promenade follows the cliffs above Carlsbad's Pacific Ocean Strand. Decorated with pretty blue handrails, the spiral access stairways that connect the walkway with the pedestrians-only sidewalk at the beach level are especially attractive. A low metal railing protects users from falling down the sandy cliffs to the beach below, and benches invite a rest and a survey of the ocean before you.

Besides the great view, beginning skaters will appreciate the perfectly smooth eight-foot-wide concrete path that starts at a small plaza near Pine Street. (A controversial sculpture featuring a series of barred gates decorates the plaza; some locals object to the resemblance to prison bars.) The nearby lawn is very handy for emergency landings. After half a mile, however, the path narrows down to an asphalt strip about six feet wide, with a slightly rougher surface. This continues the rest of the way down the Carlsbad Walkway to where it ends in front of the Carlsbad State Beach sign and the public showers. The grassy borders remain at the trailside, however, and in many places, the path splits into pullouts that help to equalize the traffic.

(In other words, you can pass slower folks.) Beginners should turn back at the Carlsbad State Beach sign.

For those skaters ready to explore farther south, the conditions continue getting rougher and steeper. More advanced skaters will want to step off the sidewalk and skate on the bike lane to cross the bridge where the sidewalk is narrow. This is the beginning of a mile-long downhill roll to Tamarack Avenue. After you cross the bridge, you might want to continue skating on the wide bike lane, because the sidewalks at the edge of the beach next to the road are covered with sand that was deposited by the wind and by beachgoers. On the bike lane, you can skate as fast as you want without worrying about pedestrians. Just watch out for car doors opening when you pass vehicles parked at the curb.

The sidewalks end at the electric plant, about a mile and a half south of Pine Street.

If you continue skating south on the bike lane, after a temporary break in the lane, you will reach another beach less than a mile away. Stay to the right when you come to the branch in the road at Cerezo Drive. Turn around when you reach the pullout parking lot on the left side of the road. The pavement gets too rough for skating beyond this point.

---

3. Urban Carlsbad   3 miles 🎱 🛼 🧍

Reference: **On the Pacific coast in Carlsbad; see number ❸ on page 400.**

Ideal for: Touring

Directions: From Interstate 5 in Carlsbad, exit at Tamarack Avenue and head west. Turn right on Carlsbad Boulevard. One block north of Pine Street, as you enter a downtown area, turn left onto Oak Avenue, a side street dipping to the west toward the ocean. Turn left again where Oak meets Ocean Street, into a free (but frequently full) parking lot.

Map: The San Diego County Bike Map is available free by calling (619) 231-2453.

Local shop: Cal Stores, 1380 East Valley Parkway, Escondido, CA 92027-2312; (619) 489-1114. Other contact: Michael Jackson, City of San Diego Bicycle Coordinator, 1222 First Avenue, MS 503, San Diego, CA 92101; (619) 533-3110.

Tour notes: The town of Carlsbad is skater-friendly, and its main street, Carlsbad Boulevard, makes for a fun little cruise on in-lines.

From the parking lot at Oak and Ocean Streets, go back up Oak and turn left onto Carlsbad Boulevard. Here, you will find a variety of quaint beach town "shoppes" that invite further investigation. If you have already skated the Carlsbad Walkway (see the previous listing), you may have worked up quite an appetite. If so, there are sidewalk cafes where you can indulge in a well-deserved meal. Even though Carlsbad Boulevard has inlaid decorative brickwork, the sidewalks are smooth enough for skating. Where the street traverses downtown Carlsbad, it is a four-laner with a landscaped meridian strip and wide, well-marked bike lanes on both sides.

Pausing at Carlsbad Village Drive, you can admire a beautifully restored Victorian home. At the north end of town where Carlsbad Boulevard meets Beech Avenue, the bike lanes become narrower, although the sidewalk continues. The pretty little downtown scenery comes to an unmistakable end with a view of a train yard from an overpass sidewalk. On the way back through town, explore the side streets according to your own inquisitive whims.

4. Bear Valley Parkway — 3 miles

Reference: **A neighborhood bikeway in Escondido; see number ❹ on page 400.**

Ideal for: Beginners—Hills/Slalom—Road/Street—Touring

Directions: From Interstate 15 in Escondido, exit at Bear Valley Parkway and follow it northeast to San Pasqual Valley Road. Park on the shoulder or on a side street near this intersection, where the asphalt bike path starts on the right side of Bear Valley Parkway.

Map: The San Diego County Bike Map is available free by calling (619) 231-2453.

Local shop: Cal Stores, 1380 East Valley Parkway, Escondido, CA 92027-2312; (619) 489-1114. Other contact: Michael Jackson, City of San Diego Bicycle Coordinator, 1222 First Avenue, MS 503, San Diego, CA 92101; (619) 533-3110.

Tour notes: Escondido and its southern neighbor, Rancho Bernardo, are growing bedroom communities where new housing developments are blooming on every ridge top. Bear Valley Parkway has the only dedicated bike path shown on the San Diego County Bike Map for these parts, although striped bike lanes and other bike routes can be found along almost every major road in the area.

Starting off your inland in-line exploration with a tour on the Bear Valley Parkway will give you a feel for this part of San Diego County. The path itself is flat enough for beginners, but this route also offers a delightful excursion off a side street up to the smooth streets of a hilly neighborhood.

From the corner of Bear Valley and San Pasqual Valley Parkways, skate north on the dedicated bike path on the east side of Bear Valley. The rural setting along this first block includes picket fences and blossoming oleanders against a backdrop of low, close hills. The six-foot-wide asphalt strip runs alongside the parkway past a few empty lots after Idaho Avenue, allowing a fine view of the hills on the right. At the end of a block of homes between Boyle Avenue and Hinrichs Way, the path crosses Glenridge Road. The branch to the right is just an access path to Orange Glen High School, and its pavement is narrow and rough. Pass a stand of tall eucalyptus trees as you skate on sidewalks in front of the school's sports field and then continue on the asphalt path. Watch for gravel spattered on its surface at entrances to driveways. At Citrus Avenue you could turn left and skate the final block on smooth concrete, or stay on Bear Valley Parkway to continue up a slightly longer block to the trail's end at the intersection with Valley Parkway.

Return the way you came. After passing the school, hill skaters will want to turn up Boyle Avenue to explore the neighborhood on the hill. The streets are wide and smooth, and the traffic is light enough that you can practice slalom turns or pick up eye-watering speed. Back at the San Pasqual Valley Parkway intersection, street-savvy skaters can continue south on bicycle lanes for another mile and a half.

If you like skating hills, whether it's for the thrill of speed or for getting in some ski cross training, cruise in your car through the newer ridge-top neighborhoods that are visible from Interstate 15 until you find slopes that suit your style.

---

5. Solana Beach Tour
3 miles

Reference: **In Solana Beach; see number ❺ on page 400.**
Ideal for: Touring
Directions: From Interstate 5 in Solana Beach, take the Del Mar Racetrack exit, Via de la Valle, and turn west. You will see the Welcome to Del Mar sign across the intersection with Old Highway 101 one block west of the Amtrak railroad overpass. After crossing 101, park at the curb next to the city building. The dedicated bike path starts at the northwest corner of this intersection, so you will need to return to the west side of Camino del Mar at the crosswalk.
Map: The San Diego County Bike Map is available free by calling (619) 231-2453.
Local shop: Cal Stores, 4030 Sports Arena Boulevard, San Diego, CA 92110; (619) 223-2325. Other contact: Michael Jackson, City of San Diego Bicycle Coordinator, 1222 First Avenue, MS 503, San Diego, CA 92101; (619) 533-3110.
Tour notes: You are likely to witness the workouts of some of the world's most serious triathletes in tiny Solana Beach, an unpretentious little coastal town located between Del Mar and Encinitas. Many of these competitors reside just up the road in Encinitas, where the region's mild climate allows for year-round training. It is awesome to watch them jogging and bicycling their way to Iron Man/Woman fame. On

weekends, get an early start to minimize encounters with large packs of jersey-clad bicyclists who train on the long coastal route between La Jolla and Oceanside.

This tour of Solana Beach follows what would have been referred to as "the main drag" in years past, then loops back on a quiet street one block to the west. Start skating north on the dedicated bike path that runs through town on the east side of Old Highway 101. To your right, the Amtrak train tracks vibrate with the approach of the next coast route train, known appropriately enough by the name "Coaster." On your left side, a striped asphalt dividing curb separates the bike lane from 101.

At Lomas Santa Fe Street, the bike path is temporarily replaced by a right-turn lane leading across the tracks to the Solana Beach Amtrak station. Free parking and the smooth parking lot pavement are also worth noting. Continuing north, the road is lined with buildings that show Solana Beach's age. For the last block, oleanders and some long-needle pines decorate the right side of the road and almost hide the Amtrak rail line. The dedicated bike lane ends at Ocean Boulevard, just as a view of the Pacific opens up to the northwest. Turn around and return to the stoplight at Lomas Santa Fe Street.

Turn right to cross the four lanes of the highway and skate up Plaza Street. One block west, Plaza meets Sierra Avenue at a beach access parking lot. Hill skaters won't be able to resist a quick run up Pacific Avenue, which branches off at a 45 degree angle across the street. To complete this loop, continue skating south three-quarters of a mile on Sierra Avenue, where light traffic makes up for the lack of bike lanes. At Border Avenue, turn left to return to your car.

6. Camino del Mar Bike Route   7.5 miles **7** 🐾🏊

Reference: **On the coastal highway near Del Mar; see number ❻ on page 400.**

Ideal for: Fitness—Hills/Slalom—Road/Street—Touring

Directions: From Interstate 5 in Solana Beach, take the Del Mar Race-track exit, Via de la Valle, and turn west. After passing the racetrack, turn left onto Camino del Mar and drive down the hill to park on the shoulder. The coastal bike lane beckons.

Map: The San Diego County Bike Map is available free by calling (619) 231-2453.

Local shop: Hamel's Action Sports Center, 704 Ventura Place, San Diego, CA 92109; (619) 488-5050. Other contact: Michael Jackson, City of San Diego Bicycle Coordinator, 1222 First Avenue, MS 503, San Diego, CA 92101; (619) 533-3110.

Tour notes: In northern San Diego County, a contiguous 40-mile bicycle route follows the course of Old Highway 101 close to classic Pacific coast beaches and cliffs, connecting San Onofre with UC San Diego. Much of the highway is embellished with adequate and sometimes excellent bike lanes. Several towns offer separate, dedicated bike paths or sidewalks (see the Solana Beach Tour on page 406). The challenge of conquering such a route will prove irresistible to the ambitious and physically fit skater.

This tour offers a taste of what the on-street skating is like along the section of Old Highway 101 that is now called Camino del Mar. At the north end of the town of Del Mar, wide, meticulously designed bike lanes border both sides of the road. Camino del Mar passes through downtown as a divided four-lane street and follows a route that offers little in the way of ocean views for the next three or so miles. Sidewalk skating is also an option through here.

Beyond the Del Mar town limits, the bike lane descends a long hill to the Penasquitos Lagoon. The bridge over the lagoon has raised seams, so if you descend with your heel brake engaged, raise it as necessary to accommodate the bumps without tripping. (You could also jump them.)

For the next half mile, enjoy great views of the Pacific Ocean, with Torrey Pines State Beach to the west, and the green marshland of Penasquitos Lagoon to the east. Beyond the lagoon, the Carmel Valley opens up the scenery below Carmel Mountain ("towering" 427 feet over the valley floor). Keep your eyes open as you skate next to shoulder areas where cars are allowed to park. Automobiles may be pulling in and out in front of you, and there is a chance that driver-side doors might open in your face.

At the turnoff for Torrey Pines Park Road, Camino del Mar becomes North Torrey Road, and starts a long, hard climb that reduces some cyclists to pushing their bikes. Unless you are making an "epic skate" on Old Highway 101, it's time to turn back.

7. Penasquitos Creek Bike Route   4 miles 🌟 🐕 🛼

Reference: **A connection bike route through the hills of Scripps Ranch; see number ❼ on page 400.**

Ideal for: Fitness—Hills/Slalom

Directions: From Interstate 15 northeast of San Diego, exit onto Mira Mesa Boulevard heading east. Turn left at the intersection with Scripps Ranch Boulevard, and then left again on Erma Road. Follow Erma around the corner and park across the street from the Scripps Town Home Tennis Courts. The trail begins between the courts and the freeway.

Map: The San Diego County Bike Map is available free by calling (619) 231-2453.

Local shop: Cal Stores, 4030 Sports Arena Boulevard, San Diego, CA 92110; (619) 223-2325. Other contact: Michael Jackson, City of San Diego Bicycle Coordinator, 1222 First Avenue, MS 503, San Diego, CA 92101; (619) 533-3110.

Tour notes: The Penasquitos Creek Bike Route makes a long and exciting dip down into the Cypress and Penasquitos Canyons and then climbs back up on the other side. When you turn around to come back, the excitement begins anew. The route is a connecting trail that follows the course of an old, now-closed frontage road between Scripps Ranch Boulevard and Rancho Penasquitos Boulevard.

Starting out next to Interstate 15, don't be alarmed by the quality of the pavement and the roar of the freeway, where cars are screaming by at 80 miles per hour just a couple of yards away. Take comfort in knowing that the missing protective chain-link fence resumes not far ahead. The path climbs a slight rise on rough asphalt that starts out 10 feet wide. Where it passes under the freeway exit sign for Mercy Road the pavement begins to improve. As the trail begins the first descent down the long slope into Cypress Canyon, it sinks below the freeway. Suddenly, the din of the cars subsides, and you can smell the aroma of wild anise growing in the fields of the canyon. The rugged scenery is very fitting as you joyously descend the slope either with slalom turns or in a screaming tuck to just short of the freeway off-ramp stoplight at Scripps Poway Parkway. Make sure you can stop to wait for cars before entering the intersection.

Across the intersection, a short access trail drops down to the old frontage road, which is blocked off to automobiles a quarter mile down. On the frontage road, you will enjoy an even steeper drop on wide, smooth asphalt to the roadblock, without an intersection to disrupt the fun. From here on, repaving has transformed a narrower section of the road into something more like a bikeway, and it descends much more gently to the concrete bridge that crosses Penasquitos Creek. On the wall at the far end of the bridge an elegant relief sculpture of speed cyclists honors the users for whom this path was developed. A concrete path now climbs up to Rancho Penasquitos Boulevard. If you're hot to conquer a few more hills, you can skate to the right up the sidewalk to Sabre Springs Parkway. Turn right on Sabre Springs to cruise a quiet neighborhood on smooth pavement and enjoy a terrific view out over the valley you just crossed.

8. Miramar Reservoir

4.9 miles

Reference: **A lake near the town of Scripps Ranch; see number ❽ on page 400.**

Ideal for: Beginners—Fitness—Hills/Slalom—Speed—Touring

Directions: From Interstate 15 northeast of San Diego, exit onto Mira Mesa Boulevard heading east. Turn right at the intersection with Scripps Ranch Boulevard, and then take a left onto Scripps Lake Drive. The entrance to the Miramar Reservoir is just up the hill on the left. At the top of the hump where the entrance road reveals a view of the lake, turn right and park in the free lots there.

Local shop: Cal Stores, 4030 Sports Arena Boulevard, San Diego, CA 92110; (619) 223-2325. Other contact: Michael Jackson, City of San Diego Bicycle Coordinator, 1222 First Avenue, MS 503, San Diego, CA 92101; (619) 533-3110.

Tour notes: Is this place a gift from the skating gods? For all but one mile, Miramar Reservoir is encircled by a smooth two-lane road that has rolling humps, swooping curves, and almost no cars. Autos are allowed as far as tiny Natalie Park four miles in, but since the road is blocked off to through traffic just around the corner from there, you are likely to see only one or two cars per lap. There are even signs warning drivers to "Watch for skaters." That's proper respect! Another sign nearby reads, "Watch for rattlesnakes." Do both.

Ducks, geese, and trout populate the rush-filled waters of this clean, man-made lake, and the scenery is naturally adorned with a few eucalyptus saplings, wild sagebrush, and other shrubs on the surrounding hillsides, with no signs of fussy, manicured landscaping. For most of the route, evidence of development is limited to the homes perched high on the surrounding ridges.

Most people skate the loop in a counterclockwise course, probably for the same reason that skaters at indoor rinks favor that direction: the predominantly stronger right leg. If you skate fast and don't want to have to wait for a clear view around the corner to pass people, consider skating in the opposite direction; no rules regarding the subject have been posted. Even with all of the hills and curves, lower level skaters can have fun here, too, because the road is wide enough to allow room for navigational corrections, no matter how wild they might be.

Beyond the roadblock, the last mile of the loop (when skated counterclockwise) is a standard asphalt trail with a few raised cracks. There is a broad view to the west where the trail crosses the dam at the end of the reservoir. Be sure to watch for automobiles as you skate back across the entrance road and through the parking lot to your car.

9. Downtown La Jolla
6 miles 🚲 ⛷ 🏊

Reference: **Exploring the downtown streets of La Jolla; see number ❾ on page 400.**

Ideal for: Hills/Slalom—Historic—Road/Street—Touring

Directions: Approaching La Jolla southbound on Interstate 5, exit at La Jolla Village Drive and turn right. After three-quarters of a mile, turn left onto Torrey Pines Road and proceed about 2.5 miles to Prospect Street. Turn right onto Prospect and follow it around the north curve of the peninsula for another mile until you reach Draper Street. Turn left at Draper to park at the La Jolla Recreation Center. Approaching northbound on Interstate 5, take the Ardath Road exit at the Interstate 5/Highway 52 interchange. After one northwesterly mile, Ardath merges onto Torrey Pines Road. Turn left and follow the directions above when you reach Prospect Street.

Map: The San Diego County Bike Map is available free by calling (619) 231-2453.

Local shop: Mike's Bikes N Blades, 756 A Ventura Place, San Diego, CA 92109-7751; (619) 488-1444. Other contact: Michael Jackson, City of San Diego Bicycle Coordinator, 1222 First Avenue, MS 503, San Diego, CA 92101; (619) 533-3110.

Tour notes: Downtown La Jolla has wide sidewalks that host sidewalk cafes, interesting shops, and some promenade-style walkways. The community is perched on a hilly peninsula that is bordered by steep drops down to the Pacific Ocean. For the intermediate to advanced skater, the opportunities in this area are rich and plentiful.

From the Recreation Center, skate northeast up the sidewalk on Prospect, the main shopping street of downtown La Jolla. You may find yourself avoiding the many pedestrians on the sidewalk during prime business hours or on a sunny weekend afternoon, but that's all part of the scene. Pass the La Jolla Museum of Contemporary Art on the left, at the Girard Boulevard intersection. After another block of window shopping on Prospect, cross the street to turn left at the Silverado Street/Coast Boulevard intersection and take Coast, a one-way street, down the hill to La Jolla Cove, making judicious use of your heel brake. Boomer Beach is just around the corner.

From this point, you can continue skating south and hugging the coast for another three miles to connect up with the Mission Beach Boardwalk (see page 415). To do so, take Coast Boulevard past Marine Street Beach, then work your way down three or four blocks on coastal streets to Neptune Place to skate next to Windansea Beach. Jog one block east on Palomar Avenue to reach Camino de la Costa and follow this all the way to Bird Rock. Take Chelsea Avenue until it makes a 90 degree turn inland (the shortcut across is Crystal Drive).

Turn right on La Jolla Boulevard and right again at Loring Street to reach the southern section of Crystal Drive, which leads to the entrance of the north end of the Mission Beach Boardwalk at the end of Law Street.

Back at Boomer Beach, take Girard Boulevard off of Coast Boulevard to return to Prospect. Cross Prospect and skate south on Girard's shopping blocks. At Pearl Street, turn right and skate one block to Fay Avenue. (For another diversion on this trip, you could continue on Pearl to explore La Jolla Boulevard, but it doesn't have the same downtown flavor as Prospect. What it does have, though, is more outdoor eateries where skaters are welcome.) Follow Fay Avenue south, either on the street, if the traffic is light enough, or on the historic sidewalks. Every few yards on the three-panel concrete sidewalk, you will see the dated signature of the paver. You are skating on a surface that was put down in 1914! Considering how long ago it was built, you have to admit that this sidewalk is aging rather well.

Skate all the way to the southern end of Fay Avenue where it meets Nautilus Street (some street skating is required). Across the intersection you can see a little-known connection path that used to be a railroad line. Cross Nautilus to enter the asphalt path and enjoy its interesting views, rolling terrain, and trailside foliage. Unfortunately, it is only three-quarters of a mile long; otherwise, it would merit its own listing in this book. On your way back up the short asphalt path, look for a branch to the left halfway up near a wood fence. Exit the trail here onto the cul-de-sac at the end of Draper Avenue. From here, savor the thrill of the hill while skating back down Draper to the Recreation Center. The pavement between Prospect and Pearl is especially smooth, and traffic along the whole hill is low enough that you can relax in the roll.

10. Father Junipero Serra Trail   2.5 miles 🔟 🧍 🏃

Reference: **A nature tour outside the town of Santee; see number ❿ on page 400.**

Ideal for: Hills/Slalom—Historic—Touring

Directions: From Interstate 5 in La Jolla, exit east on Highway 52 (the Soledad Freeway). About six miles past the Interstate 15 interchange, follow the exit signs for Mission Trails Regional Park (the freeway comes to an end here). Turn right at the stoplight at Big Rock Road and head west. After passing Mast Boulevard, stay to the right when the main road curves left uphill as Mission Gorge Road. Continue straight beyond two gated and signed trail entrances on the right (these trails are not paved). A half mile down the gorge, there is a parking lot for Mission Trails Regional Park on the right, next to the trailhead.

Map: The San Diego County Bike Map is available free by calling
  (619) 231-2453.

Local shop: Cal Stores, 4030 Sports Arena Boulevard, San Diego, CA
  92110; (619) 223-2325. Other contact: Michael Jackson, City of San
  Diego Bicycle Coordinator, 1222 First Avenue, MS 503, San Diego,
  CA 92101; (619) 533-3110.

Tour notes: The Father Junipero Serra Trail passes through a rugged
  gorge of the San Diego River in the ancestral homelands of the
  Kumeyaay Indians. Fortunately, city planners left the 5,700 acres of
  Mission Trails Regional Park through which it passes in a natural
  state "to preserve the true nature of San Diego." The views of the
  rocky peaks on both sides of the San Diego River are wild and beautiful, especially when spring is abloom.

  At the trail's entrance, a gate and a large Do Not Enter sign ensure
that the trail is open to cars in only one direction, leaving an entire
lane free for pedestrians, skaters, and bicyclists. The pavement is in
prime condition and is a full 10 feet wide. The converted road has a
big raised curb painted with yellow stripes to protect trail users from
the cars that pass infrequently on the other side.

  If you can visit the park on a weekday when it is less crowded and
if you know how to skate with ski poles, this is an ideal place to use
them, because there are three fairly substantial hills along the route.
Starting out from the gate, the first hill delivers the steepest descent
as you enter the canyon, making the first quarter mile a real thrill. If
you survive that one, you'll be fine from here on. (Remember, you can
always ride your heel brake.) You will face climbs in both directions,
but uphills are a cinch when you use ski poles, either double-poling or
skating cross-country style.

  As you round a corner near the far end of the trail, an impressive
building is perched on the ridge ahead. Is it some rich person's osten-
tatious mansion? No, it is the Mission Trails Regional Park Visitors
and Interpretive Center, a gorgeous structure. The dedicated Father
Junipero Serra Trail ends at the entrance gate to its deliciously paved
concrete driveway. Climb up the driveway to read a plaque describing
the history of the park, then sip from the drinking fountain just behind it. If you simply cannot resist and nobody is around, climb the
driveway to the top of the slope so you can slalom back down.

---

11. Mast Park Loop   2.5 miles

Reference: A suburban tour of Santee; see number
  ⓫ on page 400.

Ideal for: Beginners—Fitness—Touring

Directions: From Interstate 5 in La Jolla, exit east on Highway 52 (the
  Soledad Freeway). About six miles past the Interstate 15 interchange,

---

follow the exit signs for Mission Trails Regional Park. Turn left at the stoplight at Big Rock Road and head east for two miles. Turn left at Carlton Hills Boulevard, cross the bridge over the river, and immediately after the crossing, turn right at the sign for Mast Park. You can park in the lot.

Map: The San Diego County Bike Map is available free by calling (619) 231-2453.

Local shop: Cal Stores, 4030 Sports Arena Boulevard, San Diego, CA 92110; (619) 223-2325. Other contact: Michael Jackson, City of San Diego Bicycle Coordinator, 1222 First Avenue, MS 503, San Diego, CA 92101; (619) 533-3110.

Tour notes: Mast Park is a shady little community park with excellent paved sidewalks, an irresistible (but officially off-limits) basketball court, and some delectably laid out concrete, including a low set of stairs just right for budding aggressive skaters. The center rail shows signs of rail grinding, but you'd better not get caught. Nearby, smooth concrete sidewalks make an inviting fitness loop through the still-new neighborhoods.

Starting near the parking lot, an asphalt nature trail winds through the south side of Mast Park, where interpretive signs, shady rest areas, and exercise stations appeal to nature lovers and fitness nuts alike. (The fitness stations have even been set up with instructions for wheelchair-bound exercisers.) Although this tour starts in entirely natural surroundings, be prepared for a sharp contrast with the very human habitats you will encounter just a mile to the east.

Skate along the south edge of the park next to the river. If you avoid the one or two diversions to the left as you skate through the east end of the park, the asphalt trail will take you to the southwest corner of a new housing development. At this intersection, a pink concrete sidewalk branches to the north. A left turn takes you one-tenth of a mile slightly uphill to a street where the landscaped trail ends. Take a quick look-see if you so desire; when you get back to the trail intersection, continue on the asphalt trail on a grassy bank above the San Diego River. To the right, tules and willows keep the scenery green even in early August. A chain-link fence on the left separates you from a big field that will probably be developed within the next few years. The trail veers up a slope where it meets Cuyamaca Road. Turn left to skate past a small mall. (You can cross the bridge over the river on the right, but the pavement ends at an empty dirt lot just short of the massive Santee Town Center mall.)

Cross to the far side of the mall and turn left onto Mission Street. Here, the dual-purpose pink sidewalk is divided into a three-foot-wide pedestrian side made of pebbled aggregate and a five-foot-wide smooth concrete side for folks on wheels. If you're hot, stop at the fountain behind a building at the edge of the mall for a refreshing face rinse. Continue heading west to follow the route into a neighborhood that is still so new there are no shade trees. A block after you cross Whispering Willow Street, follow the wide trail as it veers to the left past several cul-de-sacs and a private tennis court. Cross to the right side of the street at the Silvercreek Drive and River Park intersection and follow the trail back to the Cuyamaca intersection. Turn right to return to the trail back to Mast Park.

12. Mission Beach Boardwalk   8 miles 🌟 🏔 🏃

Reference: **A beach boardwalk in San Diego; see number ⑫ on page 400.**

Ideal for: Beginners—Scene—Touring

Directions: In San Diego, take Interstate 5 and follow the signs to Interstate 8 west. Exit immediately onto Ingraham Street to cross the San Diego River Floodway. Pass the Sea World Drive/Sunset Cliffs off-ramp and take the next exit onto West Mission Bay Drive. As soon as you cross the Mission Bay Channel, you will find free parking lots to the right. Start skating south on the paved path at the southeast corner of the parking lot to cross under Mission Bay Drive into the Mariner's Basin area.

Map: The San Diego County Bike Map is available free by calling (619) 231-2453.

Local shop: Mike's Bikes N Blades, 756 A Ventura Place, San Diego, CA 92109-7751; (619) 488-1444. Other contact: Michael Jackson, City of San Diego Bicycle Coordinator, 1222 First Avenue, MS 503, San Diego, CA 92101; (619) 533-3110.

Tour notes: With its perfect weather, proximity to the beach, and fun trailside scenery and eateries, the Mission Beach Boardwalk has become one of the most popular places to skate in all of California. Too bad that it is also one of the most popular places to be, regardless of whether you are on in-lines. In the spring of 1995, an 8 mph speed limit was enacted in an attempt to manage the growing use of the boardwalk by skaters, bicyclists, joggers, and pedestrians. Tickets for exceeding the limit are $27, and people who are cited for "reckless behavior" are fined $127.

Starting from the north end of Mariner's Basin, begin your cruise with a relaxing roll south on the clean concrete that borders the basin's west shore. You are skating so close to the upscale bayfront homes, you might feel as though you are almost in the owners' backyards. It's very tempting to stop and ask if you can join parties in progress or sample what's cooking on the grill. This is the case along most of the boardwalk route. When you reach the south end of Mariner's Basin, follow the path to the right to skate through a little park and go west around the bend to the parking lot of South Mission Beach Park. The oceanfront boardwalk picks up on your right next to the sandy volleyball courts.

From here on, the boardwalk follows a smooth and flat three-mile route up the Pacific coast. This stretch is where it is most likely to be crowded. Forget about skating in a tuck position—just relax and enjoy the scene. Be prepared to slow down enough to weave among the bodies in front of the most popular food places. Watch out for pedestrians, bicyclists, patches of sand, and wet pavement. Near Mission Beach Park, you will pass The Plunge, an indoor swimming pool with a fun concrete exterior. Explore the small paved mall behind it and the carnival nearby, where a roller coaster sparks memories of how it felt the first time you tried on a pair of in-line skates.

Continuing north, the pavement gets a little sandy on the cliffs after Pacific Beach Drive. The boardwalk finally ends at Law Street, but with good navigational skills, the ambitious skater can continue north up the coast. To do so, skate up Crystal Drive for three blocks. Make a short jog to the east on Loring Street so you can go north on La Jolla Boulevard to Chelsea Avenue. The rest of the connection route is detailed (in reverse) in the write-up on Downtown La Jolla (see page 411).

---

13. San Diego Night Skate   15 miles 🌀 🧴 🧍

Reference: **Guided evening cruising in San Diego; see number ⓭ on page 400.**

Ideal for: Road/Street—Touring

Directions: In San Diego, take Interstate 5 and follow the signs to Interstate 8 west. Exit immediately onto Ingraham Street to cross the San Diego River Floodway. Pass the Sea World Drive/Sunset Cliffs offramp and take the next exit onto West Mission Bay Drive. Look for parking next to Belmont Park near the roller coaster.

Map: The San Diego County Bike Map is available free by calling (619) 231-2453.

Local shop: Hamel's Action Sports Center, 704 Ventura Place, San Diego, CA 92109; (619) 488-5050. Other contact: Michael Jackson, City of San Diego Bicycle Coordinator, 1222 First Avenue, MS 503, San Diego, CA 92101; (619) 533-3110.

Tour notes: The San Diego Night Skate features weekly recreational, social, and training-oriented skate sessions for people of all ability levels and skating styles. It is sponsored by the San Diego Skate Coalition, which promotes safe skating over a broad spectrum of paved surfaces, night or day. Perhaps the best service the group offers to visitors and locals alike is its campaign to get skaters off the overused Mission Beach boardwalks and onto alternative routes.

Whether skating on city streets or on the flat, sheltered board-walks, the Coalition actively promotes the wearing of full protective gear and the proper use of the heel brake. Both safety measures are necessary and required for anybody who wants to skate with this group and progress to higher skill levels.

Night skaters meet every Friday at 6:30 P.M. on the boardwalk at the end of Ventura Place. Look for a group of eight to 10 skaters wearing helmets outside of Hamel's Action Sports Center or Mike's Cafe, both on Ventura Place near the Belmont Park roller coaster. The typical evening revolves around choosing a place to eat, often in La Jolla, and then skating there and back. The trip covers a distance of anywhere from 10 to 20 miles.

Call Mac McCarthy, the heart and soul of the Skate Coalition, at (619) 294-2528 for details. He can also fill you in on issues ranging from Coalition or skate patrol membership to boardwalk and bike lane access to safety gear for night skating.

14. Vacation Island 1.5 miles 🟠 🔥 🏃

Reference: **An island in the middle of Mission Bay; see number ⑭ on page 400.**

Ideal for: Beginners—Fitness—Touring

Directions: In San Diego, take Interstate 5 and follow the signs to Interstate 8 west. Exit immediately onto Ingraham Street and drive across the channel to Vacation Island. Parking lots are available on both sides of Ingraham where it passes through the island. Bike paths connect the two sides on the south end of the island via underpasses under Ingraham.

Map: The San Diego County Bike Map is available free by calling (619) 231-2453.

Local shop: Mike's Bikes N Blades, 756 A Ventura Place, San Diego, CA 92109-7751; (619) 488-1444. Other contact: Michael Jackson, City of San Diego Bicycle Coordinator, 1222 First Avenue, MS 503, San Diego, CA 92101; (619) 533-3110.

Tour notes: Wide sidewalks, a grove of palm trees, fine views across the bay, and lots of picnic facilities—these are just some of the charms of Vacation Island. Best of all for beginning skaters, the location is far enough away from the crowded Mission Beach scene that sidewalk traffic is about 80 percent lower. That makes Vacation Island a safe and appealing place for novices to get a feel for their wheels on their maiden voyages.

Ten-foot-wide pink concrete sidewalks encircle Vacation Island and wind through the park on both sides of Ingraham Street. Throughout, the pavement is bordered by a soft cushion of thick lawn. Some very gentle slopes and curves near the man-made pond on the west side will challenge beginners, who will appreciate having the lawn nearby in case they need to make emergency stops.

More advanced skaters might want to come to Vacation Island for a laid-back roll or to skate laps around it for a nonimpact aerobic workout. In the summertime, cool breezes off the bay will keep even the most devoted fitness nut cool.

---

15. Sail Bay Loop
5 miles

Reference: **Circumnavigating the west lobe of Mission Bay; see number ⑮ on page 400.**

Ideal for: Fitness—Touring

Directions: In San Diego, take Interstate 5 and follow the signs to Interstate 8 west. Exit immediately onto Ingraham Street and drive across the channel to Vacation Island. Parking lots are available on both sides of Ingraham where it passes through the island. Bike paths connect the two sides on the south end of the island via underpasses under Ingraham.

Map: The San Diego County Bike Map is available free by calling (619) 231-2453.

Local shop: Mike's Bikes N Blades, 756 A Ventura Place, San Diego, CA 92109-7751; (619) 488-1444. Other contact: Michael Jackson, City of San Diego Bicycle Coordinator, 1222 First Avenue, MS 503, San Diego, CA 92101; (619) 533-3110.

Tour notes: An excellent paved route follows the shores of the northwest lobe of Mission Bay, making a fine in-line touring loop that offers some minor challenges for intermediate-level skaters. This tour of Mission Bay features the wide beaches of Riviera Shores, great views from the north perimeter of Sail Bay, a glimpse of the Mission Bay Yacht Club, and at least five named coves, big and small.

Leave Vacation Island heading north on the west-side Ingraham Street sidewalk, then cross the bridge over Fisherman's Channel to Crown Point. Turn left where the sidewalk meets Riviera Drive and skate alongside the Riviera Shores. Here, the route follows the eastern perimeter of Sail Bay on a sandy concrete sidewalk across the street from apartments with a beach and a view. The easy-to-follow walkway curves up and around the north end of Sail Bay to begin its course down the west shore. On this side of Sail Bay, there is more lawn and less sand, and you will skate past the Santa Clara Cove and Recreation Center and San Juan Cove. The Mission Bay Yacht Club is located at the end of El Carmel Point, which forms the south border of San Juan Cove.

Below Santa Barbara Cove, the path veers toward the sea near West Mission Bay Drive. (From here, you could easily skate west to find the Mission Beach Boardwalk, described on page 415.) At the

Gleason Road stoplight, stay on the left side of the road to cross the bridge on the sidewalk. Don't gain too much speed as the bridge begins to arc down on the other side, because you want to take the first left to descend the wooden stairs to Dana Landing Road. Follow Dana Landing Road toward the northwest to get back on the smooth pink sidewalk that passes through the little shoreline park there. The ubiquitous lawns and palm trees give the park that San Diego flavor, but the crowds are less dense than in other Mission Bay locales.

Be very careful when you cross the Dana Landing boat launch ramp. It is purposely paved with an extra-rough surface so that automobile tires can get good traction on the wet pavement when boats are being loaded and unloaded. Exit Dana Landing onto Ingraham Street at the first driveway you see after the boat launch. Cross back to Vacation Island on the sidewalk. Make sure you enjoy the view.

You can wind down from your tour with a relaxing loop around the perimeter of Vacation Island (see the previous listing).

---

16. Fiesta Island
2.75 miles

Reference: **An island in Mission Bay; see number 16 on page 400.**

Ideal for: Fitness—Speed—Touring

Directions: In San Diego, take Interstate 5 and follow the signs to Interstate 8 west. Exit immediately onto Ingraham Street and cross the San Diego River Floodway. Take the Sea World Drive exit and follow it east and then north until you reach Fiesta Island Road. Turn left and cross over to the island. Park for free wherever you find a spot.

Map: The San Diego County Bike Map is available free by calling (619) 231-2453.

Local shop: Performance Bicycle Shop, 3619 Midway Drive, San Diego, CA 92110-5252; (619) 223-5415. Other contact: Michael Jackson, City of San Diego Bicycle Coordinator, 1222 First Avenue, MS 503, San Diego, CA 92101; (619) 533-3110.

Tour notes: Unlike the highly developed shores that surround it, Fiesta Island, situated within the east lobe of Mission Bay, has retained much of the natural habitat that once was common to the region. As such, it has its own unique seaside character. There are no palm trees and no wide lawns with sidewalks. In fact, with just a few acres of sand and brush, the island has no shade, either. But there are trade-offs: no crowds competing for the same bit of eight-foot-wide pavement and no speed limits imposed on skaters.

Start by skating to the north on the rough asphalt of the one-way loop road, following the direction of traffic to circumnavigate the island in a counterclockwise direction. Automobile drivers usually obey the 25-mile-per-hour speed limit, so even though you must skate on the edge of a street that has no bike lanes, the situation is safe for competent skaters. Feel free to take advantage of the light traffic and spend some time sharpening your speed skating technique or maintaining an aerobic heart rate. The views across the waters of Mission Bay are interesting from all shores of the island as you skate the loop.

Just a word of warning to people with sensitive ears: on weekends and summer afternoons, the island's south and east side beaches are very popular with the Jet Ski crowd. The loud screams of the full-throttled engines are about as melodious as a chain saw. Fortunately, the noise is blocked somewhat on the west side shore.

17. East Mission Bay   9.5 miles

Reference: **Circumnavigating the east lobe of Mission Bay; see number ⑰ on page 400.**

Ideal for: Scene—Touring

Directions: In San Diego, take Interstate 5 and follow the signs to Interstate 8 west. Exit immediately onto Ingraham Street and cross the San Diego River Floodway. Take the Sea World Drive exit and follow it east and then north to cross Fiesta Island Road, where it becomes East Mission Bay Drive. Park in the first public lot you see on the left. The path runs through the grassy parks lining the bay next to East Mission Bay Drive.

Map: The San Diego County Bike Map is available free by calling (619) 231-2453.

Local shop: Performance Bicycle Shop, 3619 Midway Drive, San Diego, CA 92110-5252; (619) 223-5415. Other contact: Michael Jackson, City of San Diego Bicycle Coordinator, 1222 First Avenue, MS 503, San Diego, CA 92101; (619) 533-3110.

Tour notes: The sidewalks of Playa Pacifica on East Mission Bay Drive have become one of the most popular San Diego in-line scenes. The long, grassy bayside beach is dotted with palm trees and cooled by ocean breezes, attracting families from miles around for picnicking, sunbathing, Jet Skiing, and of course, skating. If mingling with hundreds of tanned in-liners, joggers, bicyclists, and pedestrians makes you happy, be sure to plan your visit for a sunny weekend when sidewalk traffic is at its highest. A word of caution, though: in order to control the crowds, the city has set an eight-mile-per-hour speed limit that is sporadically enforced. Tickets for exceeding the limit are $27, and people cited for "reckless behavior" are fined $127.

The East Mission Bay sidewalks get so crowded during peak times that skating is often reduced to slow-and-go. In this type of situation, it is very important to have impeccable trail etiquette: stay on the right side of the path and notify folks up ahead when you are about to pass on the left. Skate defensively and be especially careful around older pedestrians and little kids. You don't want to give our favorite sport a dose of bad press by getting into the news as the big, bad skater who knocked down a helpless victim.

The most dedicated in-line enthusiasts can still manage a relatively unhindered skate on these walkways by arriving early in the morning and/or skating in the fog. Start this tour by skating north to follow the sidewalk up to the San Diego Hilton, where an elongated outdoor patio with a smooth concrete deck is the one place you will want to visit during peak Sunday hours. A local DJ brings an assortment of music to accompany professional and amateur skaters (on both quads and in-lines) who practice spins, stops, and dance steps. The best performers are from the "Skate This" dance crew, and they enjoy showing off the results of hours of hard work. Because the Hilton patio is simply a wide spot in the trail, traffic continues to parade by, making for a pretty stimulating scene for the spectators sitting on the wall near the beach.

The Playa Pacifica sidewalk continues north past Leisure Lagoon and some boat launch ramps, passing wide lawns serving happy sunbathers and picnickers. The sidewalk finally ends at De Anza Cove, a swimming and volleyball area.

From the end of the sidewalk at De Anza Road, intermediate-level skaters can continue north to complete the full 9.5-mile East Mission Bay loop. To do so, skate up De Anza Road to North Mission Bay Drive and turn left to follow very rough pavement to the west. A proposed bridge across the Rose Inlet is shown on maps, but if it doesn't yet exist, turn right to follow the old bike route between the chain-link fences (watch for raised roots). A blind left curve at the end brings you to a steep climb up to Grand Avenue. Turn left on Grand and follow the sidewalk on the south side of the street past the high school. Turn left onto Olney Street and follow Olney to Pacific Beach Drive. Turn right and go one block, then head south on either the sidewalks or the street of Crown Point Drive past the wildlife refuge. Bike lanes, sidewalks along the street, and a concrete park sidewalk pass through Crown Point Shores; take your pick and make your way down to the Ingraham Street bridge to Vacation Island.

Skate on the sidewalk next to Ingraham, across the island and over the second bridge. (See the Vacation Island description on page 417.) Branch off Ingraham and proceed east along Sea World Drive (you must skate without bike lanes for about 500 feet) until it curves north past the Fiesta Island intersection, where it becomes East Mission Bay Drive. You are now a few blocks south of where you parked your car. Got all that? If not, take along your favorite San Diego/Mission Bay map.

18. The Embarcadero 　　　　 7 miles 🟡 🔅 🏊

Reference: **A harborside cruise in San Diego; see number
⓭ on page 400.**

Ideal for: Figure/Stunts—Touring

Directions: From Interstate 5 southbound, follow the signs to the San
Diego Airport exit. Take the one-way street below the freeway for a
mile and a half. Turn right onto North Harbor Drive, still following
the signs for the airport. After you pass the airport interchange, look
to the left for entrances to Spanish Landing Park, where there is
plenty of free parking. The trail begins under the bridge at the far
west end of the park.

Map: The San Diego County Bike Map is available free by calling
(619) 231-2453.

Local shop: Hamel's Action Sports Center, 704 Ventura Place, San
Diego, CA 92109; (619) 488-5050. Other contact: Michael Jackson,
City of San Diego Bicycle Coordinator, 1222 First Avenue, MS 503,
San Diego, CA 92101; (619) 533-3110.

Tour notes: Skate the Embarcadero to saturate your senses with the
seaside ambience at the heart of beautiful San Diego. This tour starts
at Spanish Landing Park, a pretty stretch of landscaped lawns and
trees with 10-foot-wide pink sidewalks right on the water's edge.
From this northern vantage point, you can fully relish the fantastic
views of Coronado Island behind a row of spiky masts and the downtown San Diego skyscrapers just across the channel. Colorful maps
posted at intervals along the trailside describe what you will see in
the harbor.

　　　The Spanish Landing sidewalks follow North Harbor Drive east
for one mile. At every main parking lot entrance, they detour onto
the smooth asphalt pavement, offering an irresistible opportunity to
stop and play when cars are few and far between. At the Harbor
Island Drive/Airlane intersection, turn right and skate down the
sidewalk a short way to cross near the Sheraton (watch for cars) and
continue on the bike route. A diversion presents itself here. If you
don't mind skating on a three-foot-wide sidewalk (or in the street),
you can tour the length of Harbor Island Drive. The reward is 1.4
miles of tidy landscaping and great views. Skating is only allowed on
the sidewalk on the north side.

　　　Continuing on the Embarcadero path next to North Harbor
Drive's noisy airport traffic, the next mile is virtually pedestrian-free
and great for fast skating. The wide concrete path is graced with trees
and street lamps, and the only interruptions are raised cracks and
rough asphalt where it crosses two or three Coast Guard driveways.
After passing the grounds of the U.S. Coast Guard station, the route

curves to the south toward downtown San Diego, offering another opportunity for taking some photographs. This is the official start of the Embarcadero.

Slow down to enjoy the cruise past the tuna fleet docks and up to the Maritime Museum with its Star of India and America's Cup display. From here on, crowds of tourists congest the Embarcadero, especially on weekends. The Coronado ferry departs on the hour from between the B Street and Broadway Piers. (Round-trip fare is $4. Remove your skates to board.) The Navy Pier is paved in concrete, which makes for a fun diversion. Oftentimes, a ship will be docked there for close inspection. The Tuna Harbor and commercial fishing pier are next on the route. Here the skating surface becomes unpleasant, forcing you to negotiate pebbled aggregate, lumpy brickwork, pitted asphalt, and even a set of railroad tracks. Grin and bear it. The brick and aggregate promenade takes you into Seaport Village, where skating is not allowed; you're better off avoiding it anyway, due to the aggregate. Turn left to stick with Harbor Drive, then take the first right into the parking lots behind the San Diego Convention Center, where you can make your way back to the Embarcadero along the south side of Seaport Village.

The Marriott Hotel looms above the shoreline as you pass the convention area and skate to the end of the Embarcadero path. One last diversion awaits up Marina Parkway to the right. Follow the street to the park on the peninsula where concrete sidewalks and fitness stations encircle the lawns and reveal yet another harbor view. During the summertime, outdoor concerts are held here, but at the other end of the social spectrum, this is also a daytime hangout for local homeless people.

---

19. San Diego River Channel   10 miles 🌀🏃‍♀️

Reference: **Along the San Diego River Floodway in San Diego; see number ⑲ on page 400.**

Ideal for: Fitness—Speed

Directions: In San Diego, take Interstate 5 and follow the signs to Interstate 8 west. Exit immediately onto Ingraham Street and cross the San Diego River Floodway. Pass the Sea World Drive/Sunset Cliffs offramp and take the next exit onto West Mission Bay Drive. Turn left at the stoplight next to the marina, then left again to follow Quivira Road around the Quivira Basin marina. Travel halfway around the marina and then pull into the free parking lots on the right next to the Marina Village and office. The river channel and its trail start across Quivira Road to the south.

Map: The San Diego County Bike Map is available free by calling (619) 231-2453.

Local shop: Hamel's Action Sports Center, 704 Ventura Place, San Diego, CA 92109; (619) 488-5050. Other contact: Michael Jackson, City of San Diego Bicycle Coordinator, 1222 First Avenue, MS 503, San Diego, CA 92101; (619) 533-3110.

Tour notes: The San Diego River has one of the most visually appealing river outlets to the Pacific Ocean in Southern California. Its bike path starts out on a lawn just across Quivira Road from the pretty Marina Village, where wide sidewalks line the edge of the Quivira Basin. (Skating is not allowed in the mall area.)

The first portion of the river route parallels Sea World Drive heading east. The tropical effect of the shrubs and palm trees used for the street's landscaping spills over to enhance the river trail. Unfortunately, the farther inland you skate, the more the channel's pavement deteriorates, and eventually the river and its channel disappear from view. For this reason, after the first mile, the San Diego River tour is best suited as a commuter route or fitness skate.

The 10-foot-wide asphalt path extends inland alongside the river and within half a mile passes under the Sunset Cliffs overpass. Skaters who are comfortable on the street can exit the river trail here to cross the bridge and skate west through Ocean Beach to reach Dog Beach on the South Jetty. The next underpass, the Sports Arena Boulevard Bridge, also supplies an access path that you can take to leave the river trail.

The bicycle path on top of the levee is replaced by a rarely used, rough service road, but the scenery along the next half mile is more natural and can be very pretty in the late afternoon light. The call of seagulls adds nautical sound effects to the sunny view of the wetland foliage in the riverbed. Palm-lined Sea World Drive is close by on the left, and at one point a rough driveway provides access to and from the four-lane road. (You can reach Fiesta Island and East Mission Bay by taking the driveway up to Sea World Drive and skating another half mile up the street; see pages 419 and 420.) A sign says "End" where Sea World Drive meets Friars Road, about 1.25 miles from the start. Most skaters will be happy to turn back here.

For the diehards eager to continue, turn right to follow the poorly maintained sidewalk or skate on a lumpy curb-separated bike lane at the south edge of Friars Road for another 1.3 miles. As you begin to climb slightly uphill, trees, fences, and buildings on the right block most of the views of the Stardust Country Club in the riverbed below. The dedicated bike path ends just short of the Fashion Valley intersection. Again, ambitious skaters can continue beyond this point by skating the bike lanes and routes. Cross to the south side of the river at the Mission Center overpass and follow Camino de la Reina east to Stadium Way/Texas Street, where another bike path takes you the rest of the way to the south edge of Jack Murphy Stadium. The stadium is reported to have fantastic parking lots.

20. Sweetwater Trail   5 miles 🌟 🐾 ⛸

Reference: **Following Sweetwater River through National City;**
   see number ⓴ on page 400.
Ideal for: Fitness—Speed
Directions: From Interstate 5 south in National City, exit east on Highway 54 (the South Bay Freeway). Immediately move over to the right
   lane to take the Highland Avenue/Fourth Avenue exit. Turn left to get
   onto Highland and cross the overpass, continuing up to 30th Street.
   Turn left again and follow 30th about a mile west to Hoover Street.
   Turn left one more time, and one block up, where Hoover makes a
   90 degree curve, you will see the trail entrance sloping up the bank
   to the right. Park at the curb.
Map: The San Diego County Bike Map is available free by calling
   (619) 231-2453.
Local shop: Hamel's Action Sports Center, 704 Ventura Place, San
   Diego, CA 92109; (619) 488-5050. Other contact: Michael Jackson,
   City of San Diego Bicycle Coordinator, 1222 First Avenue, MS 503,
   San Diego, CA 92101; (619) 533-3110.
Tour notes: Skating on the Sweetwater Trail, you will probably see 20
   squirrels for every human. How's that for uncrowded? The tour may
   not be pretty yet (the saplings are still too small), but this route has
   great merit for two in-line disciplines. Speed skaters will find the
   uninterrupted riverbed path an excellent place to work on technique.
   It is also a great place to work up a quality (nonimpact) aerobic heart
   rate, far from the hordes that make such athletic skating impossible
   elsewhere. There are no amenities in the way of rest rooms, water
   fountains, or food along the route, although there is a shopping
   center at the inland end of the trail.
      The eight-foot-wide asphalt path heads east from the wide, watery
   outlet where the Sweetwater River enters the San Diego Bay. While
   there is no need to worry about dodging through crowds or getting
   arrested for speeding here, you do have to watch out for the kamikaze
   squirrels. The furry little rodents are constantly darting out of the
   weeds on the north side of the trail and across the path to the safety
   of their rocky homes on the riverbanks.
      During the first mile, the traffic noise on nearby Highway 54 is
   hard to ignore, but as the trail dips, the volume becomes lower. After
   that first mile, in which the waters fill the entire width of the riverbed, marshy grasses begin to appear between the banks until, finally,
   no water can be seen at all. The last tenth of a mile passes over a
   raised concrete path that serves as a low bridge over the now-empty

riverbed, delivering you to the posts that mark the end of the path. To do it justice, with the tall tule grasses close by, this little crossing is actually quite pretty.

You should be prepared for a steady head wind on the return trip. Accept the challenge and use its force to improve the power and efficiency of your strokes. Put your chest low over well-bent knees and drive your heels straight out to the sides, engaging your thigh, hamstring, and gluteal muscles. Aerobic in-liners, envision yourselves as speed skaters.

21. Coronado Island   5 miles ⑧ 🐾 🏄

Reference: **Exploring the island of Coronado; see number ㉑ on page 400.**

Ideal for: Beginners—Hills/Slalom—Historic—Touring

Directions: From Interstate 5 south in San Diego, follow the signs to Highway 75 leading to the Coronado Bridge ($1 toll for westbound traffic only). Turn left on Orange Avenue and park downtown on a side street, or turn right at Orange and park near the little mall on 1st Street on the east shore of the island. Bike path routes on the island are posted on a sign at the mall's entrance.

Map: The San Diego County Bike Map is available free by calling (619) 231-2453.

Local shop: Cal Stores, 4030 Sports Arena Boulevard, San Diego, CA 92110; (619) 223-2325. Other contact: G. L. Andy Anderson, City of Coronado Public Services Department, 1300 First Street, Coronado, CA 92118-1595; (619) 522-7380.

Tour notes: It is easy to get a very civilized (okay, make that pampered) start for a day's tour on Coronado Island. Arrive early enough to park downtown, where you can skate to one of the many sidewalk cafes to have espresso and a croissant for breakfast.

Warm up in the residential areas just northwest of downtown by exploring the extremely fine pavement on wide, sloped streets with little traffic. It would be easy to spend an hour on this part of the island. As you skate the roads that gently descend toward the east, don't get too caught up in your speed skating or slaloms, because there are stop signs at some intersections. At the bottom of the hill (and the eastern edge of the island), turn right onto 1st Street, which leads to the little shopping mall with a nautical theme mentioned in the directions above.

Follow the bike path that continues south from the mall. The trail passes through a bayfront park on its way to a golf course at the southern tip of the island. This section of the path is flat and bordered by lawn, making it an ideal spot for first-time skaters to get a feel for their wheels. The concrete is in excellent condition, and a water fountain and rest rooms are located nearby. The view across the San Diego Bay is pretty spectacular from here, too.

Continue skating west around the perimeter of the island and the golf course. Glorietta Boulevard takes you to the intersection with Highway 75. Turn left and skate south on the left (inland) side of Highway 75 to reach small Glorietta Bay Park next to the Coronado Plunge. Here is another good beginners' practice area with a view, and you can have it pretty much all to yourself. This location also marks the north end of the Silver Strand Bikeway (see the next listing).

When you've exhausted the possibilities at Glorietta Bay, skate north up Highway 75 to the entrance to the Hotel del Coronado, a local landmark. The hotel grounds and parking lot are fun to explore on skates, although some places are off-limits. At the nearby beach-front sidewalk, you can sit on the wall and check out the action down on the sand.

Since downtown Coronado is just three blocks away, it must be time for a very civilized lunch.

22. Silver Strand Bikeway   14 miles ⑧ ♟ 🏊

Reference: **A converted railroad on the Silver Strand, south of Coronado; see number ㉒ on page 400.**

Ideal for: Fitness—Speed—Touring

Directions: Take Interstate 5 south past downtown San Diego and follow the signs to Highway 75 leading to the Coronado Bridge ($1 toll for westbound traffic only). Immediately after the bridge touches land, turn left onto Glorietta Boulevard and follow it alongside a coastal park to where it meets up with Highway 75 near the Coronado Yacht Club. Take the left fork and head a block south and then make another left to get off the Strand Highway and onto Strand Way. (The Strand Trail runs between the two.) From Strand Way you can park at Glorietta Bay Park next to the Coronado Plunge. To park on the south end of the Silver Strand Bikeway, exit Interstate 5 onto Highway 75 north and enter Imperial Beach. Near Seventh Street, the highway veers to the north and crosses the U.S. Naval Communication Station at the Coronado city limits. Park at the small roadside lot on the right, where a faded blue sign marks the South Bay Biological Study Area. The trail runs next to the bay.

Map: The San Diego County Bike Map is available free by calling (619) 231-2453.

Local shop: Cal Stores, 4030 Sports Arena Boulevard, San Diego, CA 92110; (619) 223-2325. Other contact: G. L. Andy Anderson, City of Coronado Public Services Department, 1300 First Street, Coronado, CA 92118-1595; (619) 522-7380.

Tour notes: The Silver Strand Bikeway can deliver a real workout, but hard skating somehow seems easier here because the bikeway also provides fantastic views across the San Diego Bay. The skyscapes range from the industrial silhouettes of Chula Vista and National City to the cosmopolitan skyscrapers of San Diego and Coronado Island. Natural, marshy wetlands border much of the bay side on the south end of the Silver Strand.

The best thing about this 10-foot-wide asphalt trail is that it seems to go on and on. In a busy port town such as San Diego, there is a relatively small price to pay for that length. Mostly on the north half, but also in a few places farther south, the bikeway is interrupted by intersections that serve beachgoers, the Naval Amphibious Base, and the homes in the Coronado Cays. Some of the crossings bear watching, where heavy use has caused lips of pavement to rise up high enough to catch a skate and where bits of gravel are scattered on the surface.

Unfortunately, glimpses of the Pacific Ocean are infrequent because of the low, sandy ridge that borders the west side of the highway. And of course, the highway is worth a moment's consideration. For the entire length of the strand trail, traffic on a four-lane divided road roars by constantly only a few yards away. The final warning is that you should be aware of the direction of the wind before you start your trip down this exposed strand. When skating a 14-mile round-trip such as this, it's better to plan ahead so that the wind is at your back speeding you along on the second half of your trip. There's nothing worse than battling a strong head wind when you're tired and ready to quit skating.

If you parked at Glorietta Bay Park and still have the energy, skate north to explore Coronado Island (see the previous listing).

Part Three
Best Skating Tours in the State

For Beginning Skaters

Fairway Road, Sierra Nevada, page 269.

Golf Course Bikeway, Deserts, page 344.

Monterey Peninsula Recreational Trail, Central Coast North, page 277.

Natural Bridges State Park Trail, San Francisco Bay Area: South Bay, page 155.

Sir Francis Drake Bikeway, Marin County, page 109.

The Strand: Manhattan Beach to Redondo Beach, Los Angeles County, page 331.

Yosemite Falls to Curry Village, Sierra Nevada, page 262.

For Intermediate Skaters

Father Junipero Serra Trail, San Diego County, page 412.

Nimitz Trail, San Francisco Bay Area: East Bay, page 170.

Ranchita Estates, Central Coast South, page 286.

Santa Ana River to Featherly Park, Orange County, page 365.

St. John's River Parkway, Central Valley South, page 235.

Sycamore Grove Park, San Francisco Bay Area: East Bay, page 198.

For Advanced Skaters

Jedediah Smith National Recreation Trail East, Gold Country, page 92.

Meridian Trail/Main Path Loop, Sierra Nevada, page 266.

Mirror Lake Road, Sierra Nevada, page 261.

Pozo Road, Central Coast South, page 287.

Sacramento River Trail, North Mountains, page 61.

Salt Creek Trail, Orange County, page 391.

Most Scenic Fitness Tours

Berkeley Marina, San Francisco Bay Area: East Bay, page 171.

Canada Road, San Francisco/The Peninsula, page 134.

Lake Merced, San Francisco/The Peninsula, page 127.

Lake Mission Viejo, Orange County, page 392.

Marina Green, San Francisco/The Peninsula, page 125.

Miramar Reservoir, San Diego County, page 410.

Russell Boulevard Bike Trail, Central Valley North, page 207.

South Huntington Beach, Orange County, page 370.

Truckee River Bike Trail, Sierra Nevada, page 249.

Vacation Island, San Diego County, page 417.

Most Scenic Speed-Training Tours

Canada Road, San Francisco/The Peninsula, page 134.

Contra Costa Canal East, San Francisco Bay Area: East Bay, page 164.

Lake Merced, San Francisco/The Peninsula, page 127.

Miramar Reservoir, San Diego County, page 410.

Part Four
Resource Guide
In-Line Clubs and Organizations

NATIONAL

Gravity Research, Inc., 9144 Exposition Drive, Los Angeles, CA 90034; (310) 280-2757. This Southern California in-line organization does sales marketing and promotions for Rollerblade Incorporated, including special events, fun rolls, and the ongoing Blade School program.

International In-Line Skating Association (IISA), 1077 Vistavia Circle, Decatur, GA 30033; Henry Zuver, executive director; (800) 367-4472 or (404) 728-9707. The IISA is a nonprofit organization formed to promote in-line skating as a recreational activity and competitive sport. Supported by the in-line industry's manufacturers, retailers, and skaters, the IISA develops safety and educational programs, works to protect and expand access to public skateways, sponsors the National Skate Patrol, and sanctions events and competitions. (See additional listings for IISA National Skate Patrol and IISA Government Relations Committee.)

IISA Government Relations Committee, 1135 North Denwood, Dearborn, MI 48128; Dave Cooper, chairman; (313) 594-2323. The purpose of the International In-Line Skating Association's Government Relations Committee is to protect skaters' rights and access to roads, paths, and trails nationwide. Skaters in communities that are threatening to ban skating in certain areas can contact the committee for information and advice.

IISA National Skate Patrol, 23970 Colehester, Farmington, MI 48336; (313) 337-2830. The National Skate Patrol grew out of a need to promote education, rather than legislation, in response to a more than 200 percent growth in in-line skating participation each year. Recognizing a need for park systems that would help skaters better coexist with cyclists, pedestrians, and other park users, the IISA established the Skate Patrol to monitor shared paths and help keep them safe for all users. Services include distribution of safety and trail etiquette information, instruction in stopping methods, and emergency assistance for injured skaters. For information on starting a local chapter, contact coordinator Vivian Walls at (810) 474-7225.

National In-Line Racing Association (NIRA), 4708 East Fourth Place, Tulsa, OK 74112; Joe Kotter, executive director; (800) SK8-NIRA (758-6472). Endorsed by the IISA, NIRA is a speed-skating governing body that organizes regional events and national competitions. Events include indoors short track races similar to the Olympic ice speed-skating format and outdoors long track and endurance events.

U.S. Amateur Confederation of Roller Skating (USAC/RS), 4730 South Street, Lincoln, NE, 68506-0578; George Pickard, executive director; (402) 483-7551. This is a well-established national governing body for competitive roller and in-line skating. Recognized by the U.S. Olympic Committee, USAC/RS promotes skating by preparing athletes and teams for international competition, and sanctions hundreds of professionally officiated programs each season for artistic skating, speed skating, and roller hockey events. Club membership is required for competition in its events.

REGIONAL

Adult Recreational Skating, Roseville/Rocklin, CA; contact Brian at (916) 784-7861 or Mark at (916) 783-4099 for information about weekend group outings in the Roseville and Rocklin area, located 15 miles northeast of downtown Sacramento. Skaters of all abilities are welcome; call ahead for schedules and meeting places.

California Outdoor Rollerskating Association (C.O.R.A.), 2549 Irving Avenue, San Francisco, CA 94122, David G. Miles, Jr., president; (415) 752-1967. A $30 annual membership in C.O.R.A. includes insurance, store discounts, race participation discounts, and participation in many annual San Francisco and statewide events, often promoting a worthy cause. Regular mailings keep members posted on doings that include speed skating, hockey, tours, and much more. Contact vice-president Glen Kirby for information on the Bay Area's Ridge Bay Trail project at (510) 581-8193.

Contact Sk8, Anaheim, CA; contact Nick or Arnold Vagts at (714) 535-5078. This is a club for aggressive, recreational, and speed skaters, although most members are avid street and stunt skaters. Informal get-togethers are organized by phone. Team Contact, the club's aggressive team, participates in National In-Line Skate Series events (see Other Organizations, page 435).

Golden Gate Skate Patrol, 2549 Irving Avenue, San Francisco, CA 94122; David Miles, founding member; (415) 752-1967. Members patrol at Golden Gate Park and the Midnight Rollers Friday Night Skate downtown. Duties include enforcing safe skating rules and providing skater assistance.

Humboldt In-Line Skate Club, Arcata, CA; contact Don Hoch at (707) 826-1769. The club offers skating clinics and an in-line hockey program.

Inline Rollerworks, 1630 Superior Avenue, Costa Mesa, CA 92627; contact Kon Ammosow, proprietor, at (714) 760-6955 or (714) 645-7655 (shop). This ramp, speed, and recreational skating club holds in-line events and has its own small ramp setup in the parking lot of a Costa Mesa skate shop.

Roller Divas, San Francisco, CA; contact Kelly McGown at (415) 665-0336; e-mail: sk8away@hooked.net. Founded by a pair of professional in-line speed skaters, Roller Divas is a not-for-profit, San Francisco-based female skating club aimed at creating a supportive network to empower women through athletics. The $25 membership fee includes a monthly newsletter plus eligibility for discounts on skates and accessories. Clinics, workshops, group skates, and other events are regularly scheduled. Meetings are held the second Wednesday of the month at the Park Branch Public Library, 1833 Page Street, San Francisco, from 7 to 9 P.M.

San Diego Skate Coalition, San Diego, CA; contact Mac McCarthy at (619) 223-5415. This community proactive skaters' advocacy organization promotes safe skating and use of protective gear, fights skate bans, and works to preserve access rights. Weekly guided tours introduce participants to street skating and urban tours that go beyond the boardwalks.

Santa Rosa In-Line Club, Santa Rosa, CA; contact Chartelle Tarrant, IISA-certified instructor, at (707) 538-2823. Sunday group skates are held twice a month, locally or farther afield. Occasionally groups go to San Francisco on Fridays for the Midnight Rollers skate. Call to ask when the next "full moon" skate is scheduled or to find out about local women's roller hockey activities.

Silver Streaks, Los Gatos, CA; contact Layne Hackett, founder, at (408) 354-5605. Club activities include skate trips, video analyses to check progress, and occasional social events. The Silver Streaks skate year-round, once or twice a week. In the early days, membership hinged on having at least one gray hair (thus the name).

AGGRESSIVE SKATING

Aggressive Skaters Association (ASA), 171 Pier Avenue, Suite 247, Santa Monica, CA 90405; contact Aaron Spohn, co-founder, at (310) 399-3436. This is a governing organization created to help promote the sport of aggressive skating worldwide and address issues confronting this fast-growing segment of in-line skating. ASA promotes amateur contests, standardizes judging rules, and provides competitors with insurance, a quarterly newsletter, the ASA annual directory, a T-shirt, stickers, a photo ID card, and discounts with preferred retailers (retailers should call (310) 399-3436 about enlisting in the ASA Preferred Retailer program).

Team Adventures, Salinas/Monterey, CA; (408) 646-5378. This aggressive stunt-skating team welcomes inquiries from interested applicants. Call for more informaion.

Team Contact of Contact Sk8, Anaheim, CA; (714) 535-5078. This aggressive team that participates in National In-Line Skate Series events (see Other Organizations on page 435).

Team NUVO, San Francisco and Oakland, CA; (800) SKATE BY (752-8329). This aggressive stunt-skating team welcomes inquiries from interested applicants. Call for more information.

HOCKEY

National In-Line Hockey Association (NIHA), 999 Brickell Avenue, Miami, FL 33131; (800) 358-NIHA (6442). The NIHA sanctions amateur hockey leagues nationwide, providing standardized rules and assistance with league management and organizing. Members receive league information, player insurance, equipment and apparel discounts, a membership card, and travel discounts, plus a subscription to the organization's magazine *Hockey Talk. The Hockey Resource Guidebook,* available to schools and retailers, describes NIHA programs. NIHA is recognized as the national organizing body of amateur in-line hockey by the USAC/RS and IISA.

North American Roller Hockey Championships (NaRch), San Diego, CA; contact Paul Chapey, organizer, at (619) 436-2901. NaRch organizes annual regional hockey tournaments in the United States and Canada for experienced players in all divisions including women, youth, and seniors.

Roller Hockey International, Professional League, 7780 Windcrest Rowe, Parker, CO 80134; (303) 840-0752. RHI sponsors state and national competitions for professional in-line hockey leagues. Starting with beginner-level enthusiasts, RHI development programs groom players for a future at Olympic or professional levels.

USA Hockey InLine, 4965 North 30th Street, Colorado Springs, CO 80919; contact Mark Rudolph, director, at (719) 599-5500. This organization offers guidelines for structured playing, coaching, and officiating. Its mission is to use its advancement and administrative efforts to promote the growth of in-line hockey, by providing the best possible experience for amateur players. Membership benefits include player insurance, event sanctioning, and a subscription to *USA Hockey InLine Magazine*.

SPEED SKATING

Bay Area In-Line Racers (BAIR), Menlo Park, CA; contact Lee Cole at (415) 244-9800. BAIR organizes and promotes two to four speedskating races per year.

Chico Skate Club, Chico, CA; contact D. McGee at (916) 672-3124 or (916) 633-5809.

El Dorado In-Line Skating Association, El Dorado, CA; contact Scott Johnson at (916) 672-3124 or (916) 622-5809.

Group 7 Rollerblade Association, San Diego/Mission Beach, CA; contact C. Woodruff at (619) 284-4666.

Nor-Cal Skeelers, Flying Wheels Speed Club, Modesto, CA; contact Rick Babington at (209) 521-6816 (work), (209) 524-7928 (home). An indoor and outdoor speed-skating club.

Sacramento In-Line Skate Association, Sacramento, CA; contact Mel Ryan-Roberts at (916) 443-2527.

Skatey's Skate Club, Los Angeles County, CA; contact Bob Lagunoff at (213) 823-7971.

Southern California Speedskaters, Manhattan Beach, CA; (213) 545-6969.

SRI Chinmoy Marathon Team, San Francisco, CA; contact Golapendu Ng at (415) 665-8626.

Team Karim, Berkeley, CA; contact Adlai Karim at (510) 849-4004. Speed teams for in-line and ice. Nonmembers are invited to come and work out during team practices.

TRAIL ADVOCATES

East Bay Regional Parks District, 2950 Peralta Oaks Court, Oakland, CA 94605-0381; contact Steve Fiala, trails coordinator, at (510) 635-0135. The East Bay Regional Parks District administers an extensive system of paved multiuse trails in Alameda and Contra Costa counties. Detailed maps with directions are available for each of the 20 regional trails. To order maps, call the Public Affairs Department at (510) 635-7275, extension 2200. To promote safety, the trails are served by a volunteer force of bicycle/skate/equestrian patrollers. Frequent in-line beginner clinics (taught by your humble author, Liz Miller) are offered through the district's "Regional in Nature" activities guide.

ISTEA, 1506 21st Street NW, Suite 200, Washington, D.C. 20036; (202) 463-8405. The U.S. Government's 1991 Intermodal Surface Transportation Efficiency Act (ISTEA) provides money for trail expansion, authorizing $3 billion for such transportation enhancements as bicycle and pedestrian facilities. The act requires all states to hire bicycle and pedestrian coordinators in charge of trails; since its inception in 1992, more than $560 million has been approved for construction of paths, trails, bike lanes, pedestrian bridges, sidewalks, and access to transit. Call the National Bicycle and Pedestrian Clearinghouse at the number listed above for more information.

Rails-to-Trails Conservancy, 1400 16th Street NW, Washington, D.C. 20036; (202) 797-5400. RTC is a nonprofit charitable organization devoted to enhancing America's communities and countryside by converting abandoned rail corridors into a nationwide network of public trails. A 1994 book, *500 Great Rail Trails*, is the conservancy's 164-page directory of all converted railroad beds nationwide and is available by credit-card order for $9.95 plus shipping; call (800) 888-7747, ext. 11.

San Francisco Bay Trail Project, P.O. Box 2050, Oakland, CA 94604-2050; contact Bill Bliss, Bay Trail co-chair of California Recreational Trails Committee, at (510) 464-7935. This project, administered by the Association of Bay Area Governments, aims to complete a 400-mile multiuse recreational trail to completely encircle the San Francisco and San Pablo Bays. Tax-deductible donations go fully into construction; administrative costs are covered by other funds.

OTHER ORGANIZATIONS

National In-Line Skate Series (NISS), Anywhere Sports Productions, 3101 Washington Boulevard, Marina del Rey, CA 90292; (310) 823-1826. NISS is an annual series of professional aggressive-skating competitions put on by Anywhere Sports Productions, featuring contests on a portable 11-by-24-foot vertical ramp and a street course in locations around the United States. Events are televised on Prime Sports and attract many of the world's top aggressive skaters, also giving amateurs a chance to begin a competitive career.

Roller Skating Associations (RSA), 7301 Georgetown Road, Suite 123, Indianapolis, NE 46268, contact Katherine McDonell at (317) 875-3390. RSA is a rink-owners' organization. A member list is not available to the public. See your local yellow pages.

Where to Get Lessons

Bauer Skate School, Northern California; contact Kelly Corliss, instructor, at (916) 729-5569. This school provides seasonal hockey instruction for all ages and abilities at selected retail locations in Sacramento Valley.

Blade School University, Los Angeles, CA; contact Ruth Goldammer, coordinator, at (310) 559-ROLL (7655). Presented by Gravity Research, Inc., Blade School is a Rollerblade-sponsored program that offers classes at various locations throughout Southern California in San Diego, Orange, Los Angeles, and Ventura counties. Enrollees gear up for free with Rollerblade-brand skates and protective gear. Rates are $15 for adults (a four-class discount rate is also available) and $12 for kids.

Camp Rollerblade, 1665 West Steele Lane, Santa Rosa, CA, 95403; contact Jill Schulz, director, at (707) 546-3385. Camp Rollerblade offers four-day workshop retreats with small classes. The specialized courses cover beginning basics, recreational, freestyle/artistic, speed skating, roller hockey, street/stunt and skate-to-ski. Participants can also attend one-, two-, and three-day versions. In addition to lots of goodies, breakfast, lunch, and evening activities round out each day's clinics. Full protective gear is required. Call for schedule and current rates.

IISA/ICP Instructor Certification Program, 3927 Meridian Avenue, Suite 7, Miami Beach, FL 33140; contact Kalinda Aaron, executive director, at (305) 672-6714. Sponsored by the International In-Line Skating Association, the ICP program publishes the free *Gear Up! Guide to In-line Skating*, with tips on in-line basics, plus national listings of IISA-certified instructors (to order, call 800-567-5283). The program also holds several certification clinics nationwide each year and certifies instructors at three levels; top-level certification covers such specialties as aggressive, skate-to-ski, and more. Call for the current certification schedule.

Rollerblade In-Line Skating Lessons, Northern California; contact Erin Bauer at (510) 273-9422 or (408) 374-0100. Rollerblade's Northern California school provides individual and organization-affiliated instruction at various locations throughout the region. Enrollees gear up for free with Rollerblade-brand skates and protective gear. Call (510) 273-9422 for a recorded list of upcoming lessons or (408) 374-0100 to discuss special needs.

Your World Sports, 437 South Highway 101, Suite 101, Solana Beach, CA 92075; (619) 755-7882. This shop provides certified instructors and protective gear for lessons on Wednesdays at Lake Miramar and Thursdays at the Solana Beach Boardwalk Shopping Center for $30/hour. Instruction is based on student needs. Staff also gives lessons on the premises to first-time buyers.

Great Skating Shops Across the State

To help make it easier to find a store in a particular area, the following shops within each region are alphabetized by city rather than name.

North Mountains

Alpine Outfitters Sports and Bikes, 950 Hilltop Drive, Redding, CA 96003-3812; (916) 221-7333.

Board Mart, 1261 Market Street, Redding, CA 96001; (916) 243-2323.

Play It Again Sports, 1619 Hilltop Drive, Redding, CA 96002-0253; (916) 223-2646.

North Coast

New Outdoor Store, 876 G Street, Arcata, CA 95521; (707) 822-0321.

Pro Sport Center, 508 Myrtle Avenue, Eureka, CA 95501; (707) 443-6328.

Skate City Roller Center, 2146 South State Street, Ukiah, CA 95482; (707) 468-8600.

Wine Country

C C Skates, 930 Coombs Street, Napa, CA 94559; (707) 253-2738.

Get In Line, 1150 Sebastapol Road, Santa Rosa, CA 95407-6833; (707) 542-7914.

Great Skates, 1208 Mendocino Avenue, Santa Rosa, CA 95401; (707) 546-0660.

Sonoma Outfitters, 145 Third Street, Santa Rosa, CA 95401; (707) 528-1920.

Gold Country

Sierra Skate, 365 Nevada Street, Auburn, CA 95603; (916) 823-2763.

Go Skate Surf & Sports, 7630 Fair Oaks Boulevard, Carmichael, CA 95608-1704; (916) 944-2753.

Surf & Skate, 12417 Fair Oaks Boulevard, Fair Oaks, CA 95628; (916) 721-5000.

Adventure Sports, 330 East Bidwell, Folsom, CA 95630; (916) 983-3900.

Play It Again Sports, 1016 Riley Street, Folsom, CA 95630-3269; (916) 983-6376.

Free Flight Sail & Skate, 11793 Nevada City Highway, Grass Valley, CA 95945; (916) 272-7790.

Mark Sports, 12105 Sutton Way, Grass Valley, CA 95945; (916) 272-8896.

Sports Fever, 736 Taylorville Road, Grass Valley, CA 95949; (916) 477-8006.

Marin County

Any Mountain, 71 Tamal Vista Boulevard, Corte Madera, CA 94925-1145; (415) 927-0172.

Achilles' Wheels, 167-A Throckmorton Avenue, Mill Valley, CA 94941; (415) 380-8333.

Old Town Sports, 871 Grant Avenue, Novato, CA 94949; (415) 892-0577.

Demo Ski, 509-B Francisco Boulevard, San Rafael, CA 94901; (415) 454-3500.

San Francisco/The Peninsula

A Skater's World, 856 Old County Road, Belmont, CA 94002; (415) 591-8739.

Foster City Cyclery and Sport, 999-B Edgewater Boulevard, Foster City, CA 94404; (415) 349-2010.

Any Mountain Ltd., 928 Whipple Avenue, Redwood City, CA 94063; (415) 361-1213.

B&D Sports, 137 Roosevelt Avenue, Redwood City, CA 94061; (415) 364-5995.

Achilles' Wheels, 2271 Chestnut Street, San Francisco, CA 94123-2637; (415) 567-8400.

Golden Gate Park Skates and Bikes, 3038 Fulton Street, San Francisco, CA 94118; (415) 668-1117.

Nuvo Colours, 3108 Fillmore Street, San Francisco, CA 94123; (415) 771-6886.

Skate Pro Sports, 2549 Irving Street, San Francisco, CA 94122; (415) 752-8776.

Skates on Haight, 1818 Haight Street, San Francisco, CA 94117; (415) 752-8375.

East–West Hockey, 2176 South El Camino Real, San Mateo, CA 94403; (415) 574-3022.

Nuvo Colours, 1600 South El Camino Real, San Mateo, CA 94402; (415) 571-1537.

Inline Skate Warehouse, 405 South Airport Boulevard, South San Francisco, CA 94087; (415) 588-1714.

Skates off Haight, 384 Oyster Point Boulevard, South San Francisco, CA 94080; (415) 873-0200.

San Francisco Bay Area: South Bay

Inline Sports, 19998 Homestead Road, Cupertino, CA 95014; (408) 252-5233.

Courtesy Sports, 4856 El Camino Real, Los Altos, CA 94022; (415) 968-7970.

Gremic Skates & Hockey, 15349 Los Gatos Boulevard, Los Gatos, CA 95032; (408) 358-1169.

Nuvo Colours, 145 North Santa Cruz Avenue, Los Gatos, CA 95030; (408) 395-6006.

Nuvo Colours, 162 University Avenue, Palo Alto, CA 94301; (415) 326-6886.

Palo Alto Sport Shop, 526 Waverly Street, Palo Alto, CA 94301-8555; (415) 328-8555.

Go Skate Surf & Sports, 2406 Almaden Road, San Jose, CA 95125; (408) 978-6487.

Go Skate Surf & Sports, 1554 Saratoga Avenue P-405, San Jose, CA 95129; (408) 378-1958.

Mel Cotton's Sporting Goods, 1266 West San Carlos, San Jose, CA 95126; (408) 287-5994.

Go Skate Surf & Sports, 601 Beach Street, Santa Cruz, CA 95060; (408) 425-8578.

Skateworks, 107 River Street, Santa Cruz, CA 95060; (408) 427-4292.

Play It Again Sports, 4770 Soquel Drive, Soquel, CA 95073-2450; (408) 475-1988.

Power-Play Hockey, 573 East El Camino Real, Sunnyvale, CA 94087; (408) 737-1362.

San Francisco Bay Area: East Bay

Alameda Sailboard Exchange, 2327 Blanding #C, Alameda, CA 94501; (510) 522-8966.

Willows Skate & Surf, 1431 Park Street, Alameda, CA 94501; (510) 523-5566.

California Bike & Snowboard, 1469 Danville Boulevard, Alamo, CA 94507; (510) 743-1249.

Champs Sports, County East Mall, Antioch, CA 94509; (510) 706-9553.

Wheels In Motion Skate Shop, 733 First Street, Benicia, CA 94510; (707) 746-8856.

Karim Cyclery, 2801 Telegraph Avenue, Berkeley, CA 94705-1118; (510) 841-2181.

Lax Sports, 2020 Center Street, Berkeley, CA 94704; (510) 843-5030.

Any Mountain Ltd., 1975 Diamond Boulevard, Concord, CA 94520; (510) 674-0174.

Dublin Surf & Skate, 7752 Dublin Boulevard, Dublin, CA 94568; (510) 828-8353.

Play It Again Sports, 4035 Mowry Avenue, Fremont, CA 94538; (510) 505-9696.

Tri-City Sporting Goods, 40900 Grimmer Boulevard, Fremont, CA 94538; (510) 651-9600.

Sunrise Mountain Sports, 2290 First Street, Livermore, CA 94550; (510) 447-8330.

Montclair Sports, 1970 Mountain Boulevard, Oakland, CA 94611; (510) 339-9313.

Marina Skate, 335 Central Avenue, Pittsburg, CA 94565; (510) 439-2341.

Surf & Skate, 655 Contra Costa Boulevard, Pleasant Hill, CA 94523-1514; (510) 798-4400.

INLINE, 3506 Old Santa Rita Road, Pleasanton, CA 94588; (510) 227-0750.

Nor Ski, 4855 Hopyard Road, Pleasanton, CA 94588-3224; (510) 460-0222.

Play It Again Sports, 5548 Springdale Avenue, Pleasanton, CA 94566; (510) 734-6750.

Sports Mart, 1933 Davis Street, San Leandro, CA 94577; (510) 632-6100.

Any Mountain Ltd., 490 Market Place, San Ramon, CA 94583; (510) 275-1010.

Bike & Snowboard, 490 Ygnacio Valley Boulevard, Walnut Creek, CA 94596; (510) 934-2453.

Nuvo Colours, 1602 North Main Street, Walnut Creek, CA 94596-4609; (510) 938-6886.

Sunrise Mountain Sports, 490 Ygnacio Valley Road, Walnut Creek, CA 94596; (510) 932-8779.

Central Valley North

Chico In-Line Sports, 336 Broadway, Chico, CA 95926; (916) 894-7528.

Chico Sports Ltd., 240 Main Street, Chico, CA 95828; (916) 894-1110.

Alpine West, 130 G Street, Davis, CA 95616; (916) 756-2241.

Sportlife, 514 Third Street, Davis, CA 95616; (916) 758-6000.

Play It Again Sports, 2743 Texas Street, Fairfield, CA 94533-1204; (707) 434-0123.

Big 5 Sporting Goods, 760 Merced Mall, Merced, CA 95348; (209) 723-8202.

McNamara's Sports, 3144 North G Street, Merced, CA 95340; (209) 722-3593.

City Skates, 136 East Granger Avenue, Modesto, CA 95350; (209) 575-2837.

Valley Sporting Goods, 1700 McHenry Avenue #D50, Modesto, CA 95350; (209) 523-5681.

The Shop, 306 North Sunrise Avenue, Roseville, CA 95661; (916) 773-2020.

Alpine West, 1021 R Street, Sacramento, CA 95814-6519; (916) 441-1627.

Play It Again Sports, 3176 Arden Way, Sacramento, CA 95825-3700; (916) 971-1269.

Surf & Skate, 2100 Arden Way, Sacramento, CA 95825; (916) 927-2005.

Hammer Skate, 3119 West Hammer Lane, Stockton, CA 95209; (209) 951-5873.

Sundance Sports, 3201 West Benjamin Holt Drive, Stockton, CA 95219; (209) 477-3754.

Surf & Skate, 6557 Pacific Avenue, Stockton, CA 95207; (209) 478-9890.

Pacific Underground, 894 11th Street, Tracy, CA 95376; (209) 836-9460.

Bilson's Sport Shop, 201 Lander Avenue, Turlock, CA 95380; (209) 634-4543.

Central Valley South

Action Sports, 8200 Stockdale Highway, Bakersfield, CA 93311; (805) 833-4000.

Big 5 Sporting Goods, 5488 North Blackstone Avenue, Fresno, CA 93710; (209) 439-3351.

Herb Bauer Sporting Goods, 6264 North Blackstone Avenue, Fresno, CA 93710; (209) 435-8600.

Valley Sports, 6511 North Blackstone Avenue, Fresno, CA 93710; (209) 432-4649.

Valley Sports, 2333 South Mooney Boulevard, Visalia, CA 93277; (209) 636-7050.

Sierra Nevada

Mountain Sports Chalet, 1771 Highway 4, Arnold, CA 95223; (209) 795-3885.

Footloose Ski Shop, 6175 Minaret Road, Mammoth Lakes, CA 93546; (619) 934-2400.

Oakdale Sports, 1275 East F Street, Oakdale, CA 95361-4140; (209) 847-0648.

Lakeview Sports, 3131 Highway 50, South Lake Tahoe, CA 96150; (916) 544-1083.

Vertical Sports Limited, 2318 South Lake Tahoe Boulevard #4, South Lake Tahoe, CA 96150; (916) 542-1411.

Alpenglow, 415 North Lake Boulevard, Tahoe City, CA 96145; (916) 583-6917.

Cycle Paths Mountain Bikes, 1785 West Lake Boulevard, Tahoe City, CA 96145; (916) 581-1171.

Porter's Ski & Sport, 501 North Lake Boulevard, Tahoe City, CA 96145; (916) 583-2314.

Dave's Summer Sports, 10200 Donner Pass Road, Truckee, CA 96160; (916) 582-0900.

Porter's Ski & Sport, Lucky/Longs Shopping Center, Truckee, CA 96161; (916) 587-1500.

Truckee Ski Works, 11400 Donner Pass Road, Truckee, CA 96162; (916) 582-1451.

Central Coast North

Play It Again Sports, 220 East 10th Street, Gilroy, CA 95020; (408) 847-7678.

Adventures by the Sea, Inc., 299 Cannery Row, Monterey, CA 93940; (408) 372-1807.

Sunshine Surf & Sport, 443 Lighthouse Avenue, Monterey, CA 93940; (408) 375-5015.

Play It Again Sports, 954 North Main Street, Salinas, CA 93906; (408) 443-9611.

Sunshine Surf & Sport, 1654 North Main Street, Salinas, CA 93906-5102; (408) 442-3033.

Central Coast South

Power Play In Line, 200 Traffic Way, Arroyo Grande, CA 93420-3335; (805) 473-0282.

Sport Chalet, 1885 East Ventura Boulevard, Oxnard, CA 93030-1823; (805) 485-5222.

Sports Mart, 230 North Rose Avenue, Oxnard, CA 93030; (805) 988-5000.

Sunstorm Skatery, 811 13th Street, Paso Robles, CA 93446; (805) 237-8766.

California Cheap Skates, 736 Higuera Street, San Luis Obispo, CA 93401; (805) 541-9284.

Central Coast Surfboards, 986 Monterey Street, San Luis Obispo, CA 93401; (805) 541-1129.

Copeland's Sports, 1144 Chorro Street, San Luis Obispo, CA 93401; (805) 543-3663.

A Skater's Paradise, 537 State Street, Santa Barbara, CA 93101; (805) 962-2526.

Morningstar Surf & Sport, 195 South Turnpike Road, Santa Barbara, CA 93111; (805) 967-8288.

Skates on State, 324 State Street, Santa Barbara, CA 93101; (805) 963-9008.

Encore Sports, 22715 Ventura Boulevard, Thousand Oaks, CA 91362; (818) 701-9205.

Resolution Skate Shop, 2955 East Thousand Oaks Boulevard, Thousand Oaks, CA 91362; (805) 494-3679.

Val Surf & Sport, 3055 East Thousand Oaks Boulevard, Thousand Oaks, CA 91362; (805) 497-1166.

Dave's Skateboards, 2098 East Main Street, Ventura, CA 93001-3543; (805) 656-7207.

Los Angeles County

Skate-N-Stuff, 2 South Garfield Avenue #6, Alhambra, CA 91801; (818) 300-8315.

Bishops Skate Shop, 1024 North Citrus Avenue, Covina, CA 91722; (818) 966-1300.

Golden Bear Skate Shop, 10712 Washington Boulevard, Culver City, CA 90232; (310) 838-6611.

Roller Skates of America, 1312 Hermosa Avenue, Hermosa Beach, CA 90254; (310) 372-8812.

Roller Skates of America, 16726 Hawthorne Boulevard, Lawndale, CA 90260; (310) 371-0770.

Golden Bear Skate Shop, 2383 West Lomita Boulevard, Lomita, CA 90717; (310) 534-3100.

Alfredo's, 5411 East Ocean Boulevard, Long Beach, CA 90802; (310) 930-0167.

Alfredo's, 700 East Ocean Boulevard, Long Beach, CA 90802; (310) 434-6121.

Shore Sport Inc., 5209 East Second Street, Long Beach, CA 90803; (310) 439-7250.

Golden Bear Skate Shop, 10712 Washington Boulevard, Los Angeles, CA 90232; (310) 838-6611.

Nuvo Colours, 1029 Westwood Boulevard, Los Angeles, CA 90024; (310) 208-5442.

Sport Chalet, 100 North La Cienega Boulevard, Los Angeles, CA 90048-1938; (310) 657-3210.

Roll It, 1114 Manhattan Avenue, Manhattan Beach, CA 90266; (310) 372-2050.

Skateys Sports Inc., 102 Washington Boulevard, Marina del Rey, CA 90292; (310) 823-7971.

Spokes 'N Stuff, 4175 Admiralty Way, Marina Del Rey, CA 90292-6206; (310) 306-3332.

LA Skate, 16161 Roscoe Boulevard, North Hills, CA 91343; (818) 895-6466.

Valley Skate and Surf, 16914 Parthenia Street, North Hills, CA 91343; (818) 892-5566.

Val Surf & Sport, 4810 Whitsett Avenue, North Hollywood, CA 91617; (818) 769-6977.

Valley Skating, 11410 Burbank Boulevard #1, North Hollywood, CA 91601; (818) 980-0414.

Marina Bike Rentals, Incorporated, 505 North Harbor Drive, Redondo Beach, CA 90277-2003; (310) 318-2453.

Shore Sport Inc., 550 Deep Valley Drive, Rolling Hills, CA 90274; (310) 439-7250.

Lake Balboa Skates & Kites, 16105 Victory Boulevard, Van Nuys, CA 91406; (818) 782-1234.

Valley Sports, 7100 Van Nuys Boulevard, Van Nuys, CA 91405; (213) 480-1200.

Venice Roller Works, 7 Westminster Avenue, Venice, CA 90291; (310) 450-0669.

Skate Junction, 901 West Service Avenue, West Covina, CA 91790; (818) 960-4402.

Val Surf & Sport, 22211 Ventura Boulevard, Woodland Hills, CA 91364; (818) 888-6488.

Deserts

Foot Locker, 82227 Highway 111, Indio, CA 92201; (619) 342-3146.

Sports Fever, 73-360 Highway 111, Palm Desert, CA 92260; (619) 340-0252.

Inland Empire

Extreme Boards Shop, 2771 Green River Road, Corona, CA 91720; (909) 270-0404.

Cal Stores, 1263 Galleria, Riverside, CA 92503; (909) 353-1186.

Sportmart, 3380 Tyler Street, Riverside, CA 92503-5356; (909) 352-0896.

Big 5 Sporting Goods, 245 North E Street, San Bernardino, CA 92401; (909) 885-4006.

Sportmart, 897 Harriman Place, San Bernardino, CA 92408-3594; (909) 884-7200.

Orange County

Skate Depot, 11113 183rd Street, Artesia, CA 90701; (310) 924-0911.

Sport Chalet, 2500 East Imperial Highway, Brea, CA 92621; (714) 255-0132.

Roller Skates of America, 1644 Superior Avenue, Costa Mesa, CA 92627; (714) 574-9966.

Bud's Pro Skate & Surf, 16895 Beach Boulevard, Huntington Beach, CA 92647; (714) 843-6922.

Oshman's, 28331 Marguerite Parkway, Mission Viejo, CA 92692; (714) 364-3893.

Saddleback Recreation, 25631 Diseno, Mission Viejo, CA 92691; (714) 768-0981.

Sport Chalet, 27551 Puerta Real, Mission Viejo, CA 92691-6381; (714) 582-3363.

The Puck Stops Here, 27001 La Paz #190, Mission Viejo, CA 92691; (714) 859-9604.

Xanadu Skate Rentals, 106 22nd Street, Newport Beach, CA 92663; (714) 675-3026.

The Hockey Stop, 31931, Del Obispo Street #22, San Juan Capistrano, CA 92675; (714) 443-2781.

San Diego County

Cal Stores, 1380 East Valley Parkway, Escondido, CA 92027-2312; (619) 489-1114.

Play It Again Sports, 1348 West Valley Parkway #E, Escondido, CA 92029-2137; (619) 489-1644.

Cal Stores, 4030 Sports Arena Boulevard, San Diego, CA 92110; (619) 223-2325.

Hamel's Action Sports Center, 704 Ventura Place, San Diego, CA 92109; (619) 488-5050.

Mike's Bikes N Blades, 756-A Ventura Place, San Diego, CA 92109-7751; (619) 488-1444.

National Skate Locker Inc., 4545 La Jolla Village Drive, San Diego, CA 92122; (619) 558-2203.

Performance Bicycle Shop, 3619 Midway Drive, San Diego, CA 92110-5252; (619) 223-5415.

Skates Plus Inc., 3830 Mission Boulevard, San Diego, CA 92109; (619) 488-7587.

Sport Chalet, 4405 La Jolla Village Drive, San Diego, CA 92122-1210; (619) 453-5656.

The Puck Fan, 2720 Howard Avenue, San Diego, CA 92104; (619) 280-5448.

Your World Sports, 437 South Highway 101, Suite 101, Solana Beach, CA 92075; (619) 755-7882.

Rinks, Arenas, and Parks

Without a doubt, the two fastest-growing in-line disciplines are roller hockey and aggressive skating, and new hockey arenas and skate parks appear on the scene so often, it's impossible to maintain an up-to-date list in print. Still, this book wouldn't be complete without a directory of these facilities, so below you'll find the names of 67 California hockey arenas, 38 indoor skating rinks, and 23 skate parks, listed alphabetically by city within each region.

The hockey listings refer to locations used as arenas by teams or leagues, and also include indoor skating rinks that actively promote the sport. To find other arenas in towns not listed, try calling the city recreation department, the YMCA or YWCA, local in-line and hockey specialty shops, and skating rinks.

Skating parks that serve both in-liners and skateboarders may have separate hours for each, so call first. For outdoor skating parks with no phone, the number of the nearest shop is provided.

Indoor roller rinks are also listed because they offer great rainy-day skating and in many cases offer lessons, hockey clinics, or court time.

HOCKEY ARENAS AND RINKS

North Mountains
Redding Indoor Hockey Arena, 1515 Charles Drive, Redding, CA 96003; (916) 223-2646.

Viking Skate Country, 735 Auditorium Drive, Redding, CA 96001; (916) 246-3901.

North Coast
Roller City, Del Norte Fairgrounds, Crescent City, CA 95531; (707) 464-7149.

Redwood Acres, Eureka Fairgrounds, Eureka, CA 95501; (707) 839-0743.

Wine Country
California Skate and Roller Park, 6100 Commerce Boulevard, Rohnert Park, CA 94928; (707) 585-0500.

Black Top Hockey, 630 Russell Avenue, Santa Rosa, CA 95403; (707) 579-0671.

Gold Country
Sierra Skate, 365 Nevada Street, Auburn, CA 95603; (916) 823-5070.

Natomas Station Park Hockey, Natomas Station Road at Blue Ravine, Folsom, CA 95630; (916) 355-7285.

American Hockey Arena, 1960 Railroad Drive, Sacramento, CA 95815; (916) 641-7361.

Sacramento Inline Hockey Arena, 8174 Berry Avenue, Sacramento, CA 95828; (916) 387-5080.

Woodland Indoor Hockey Arena, 519 Bush Street, Woodland, CA 95695; (916) 668-5678.

San Francisco/The Peninsula
Redwood Roller Rink, 1303 Main Street, Redwood City, CA 94063; (415) 369-5559.

Bladium, 1050 Third Street, San Francisco, CA 94107; (415) 442-5060.

San Francisco Bay Area: South Bay

Golden State Roller Palace, 397 Blossom Hill Road, San Jose, CA 95123; (408) 226-1156.

Gremic Roller Hockey, 401 East Jackson Street, San Jose, CA 95112; (408) 971-2200.

Roller Hockey Rink, 99 North 21st Street, San Jose, CA 95116; (408) 286-0195.

Skate & Splash, 3635 Pearl Avenue, San Jose, CA 95136; (408) 267-7834.

World Roller Rink, 3667 Stevens Creek Boulevard, Santa Clara, CA 95051; (408) 247-7773.

The Rink and Hat Trick Hockey Pro Shop, 251 Kings Village Road, Scotts Valley, CA 95066; (408) 438-2233.

San Francisco Bay Area: East Bay

Roller Haven Skating Center, West 10th Street, Antioch, CA 94509; (510) 779-0200.

Cal Skate, 980 Los Coches Street, Milpitas, CA 95035; (510) 946-1366.

The Dry Ice Inline Hockey Arena, 210 Hegenberger Loop, Oakland, CA 94621; (510) 562-9499.

Marina Skate, 335 Central Avenue, Pittsburg, CA 94565; (510) 439-2341.

Central Valley North

Cal Skate, 2465 Carmichael Drive, Chico, CA 95928; (916) 343-1601.

Coyote Roller Rink, 1000 South Third Street, Chowchilla, CA 93610; (209) 665-4011.

University of California at Davis, Sports Camp Hockey Arena, Davis, CA 95616; (916) 752-5444.

Skateland Roller Rink, 2250 North Texas Street, Fairfield, CA 94533; (707) 425-0667.

RPM Hockey, Fresno Fairgrounds, Fresno, CA 93702; (209) 251-3736.

Roller Land, 1445 West 18th Street, Merced, CA 95340; (209) 723-1282.

Modesto In-Line Hockey Arena, 631 Kearney Avenue, Modesto, CA 95350; (209) 578-9818.

Central Valley South

Standard Park Rink, East Minner Street, Bakersfield, CA 93308; (805) 833-4000.

Valley Hockey Supply, 1312 Canyon Court, Bakersfield, CA 93307; (805) 831-1004.

Central Coast North

Flippo's Skate Harbor, 220 Atascadero Road, Morro Bay, CA 93442; (805) 772-7851.

Central Coast South

Santa Barbara Hockey Center, 30 South La Patera Lane, Goleta, CA 93117; (805) 681-0413.

Village Skate Center, 176 Vulcan Drive, Lompoc, CA 93436; (805) 733-3036.

Hockey: The Lot, 18 East Haley Street, Santa Barbara, CA 93101; (805) 564-0833.

Roller Dome, 950 Avenida de los Arboles, Thousand Oaks, CA 91360; (805) 493-8800.

Los Angeles County

Lakewood YMCA, 5835 East Carson Street, Lakewood, CA 90713; (310) 425-7431.

Holiday Skating Center, 45431 North 23rd Street West, Lancaster, CA 93536; (805) 945-4543.

City of Long Beach Roller Hockey, 54th Place at Ocean Boulevard, Long Beach, CA 90802; (310) 570-1715.

Rollerplex, 8345 Hayvenhurst Place, North Hills, CA 91343; (818) 893-3424.

Sherman Square Roller Rink, 18430 Sherman Way, Reseda, CA 91335; (818) 344-0866.

West Valley YMCA, 18810 Vanowen Street, Reseda, CA 91335; (818) 345-7393.

California Street Hockey Association, 1837 Raleo, Rowland Heights, CA 91748; (818) 964-0590.

Torrance Skate Association, 2200 Crenshaw Boulevard, Torrance, CA 90503; (310) 320-9529.

Wilson Hockey Park, 2200 Crenshaw Boulevard, Torrance, CA 90501-3322; (310) 320-9529.

Whittier Skate Land, 12520 Whittier Boulevard, Whittier, CA 90602; (310) 696-6779.

Inland Empire

City of Claremont Roller Hockey, 840 North Indian Hill Boulevard, Claremont, CA 91711; (909) 399-5495.

Inland Empire Roller Hockey, 11530 Sixth Street, Cucamonga, CA 91730; (909) 980-6621.

Inland Empire Roller Hockey, 14561 Hawthorne Avenue, Fontana, CA 92335-2508; (909) 355-7878.

California Skate, 12710 Magnolia Avenue, Riverside, CA 92503; (909) 354-7060.

Roller City 2001, 10765 Magnolia Avenue, Riverside, CA 92505-3057; (909) 688-4121.

Orange County

The Park Skating Center, 7951 Commonwealth Avenue, Buena Park, CA 90621; (714) 521-0453.

Costa Mesa Roller Hockey League, 2131 Tustin Avenue, Costa Mesa, CA 92627; (714) 642-8372.

Golden West Roller Hockey, 6533 Teakwood Street, Cypress, CA 90630; (714) 827-3480.

Del Obispo Park Roller Hockey, Del Obispo Street, Dana Point, CA 92629; (714) 443-2781.

Stuart's Rollerworld, 464 West Commonwealth, Fullerton, CA 92632; (714) 871-8761.

Irvine Boys and Girls Club, 295 East Yale Loop, Irvine, CA 92714; (714) 551-8214.

Irvine Roller Hockey Club, 17421 Murphy Avenue, Irvine, CA 92714; (714) 222-2219.

Saddleback School District Recreation Department, 25631 Diseno Drive, Mission Viejo, CA 92690; (714) 768-0981.

Holiday Skating Center, 175 North Wayfield Street, Orange, CA 92667; (714) 997-5515.

Stuart's Rollerworld II, 2190 North Canal Street, Orange, CA 92665; (714) 283-4778.

Shore Sport Inc., 550 Deep Valley Drive, Palos Verdes Peninsula, CA 90274; (310) 439-7250.

San Juan Capistrano Roller Hockey, 31421 La Matanza, San Juan Capistrano, CA 92675; (714) 493-5911.

San Diego County

Escondido Roller Hockey, 1106 Second Street, Encinitas, CA 92024; (619) 436-2901.

La Mesa Roller Hockey, 9586 Murray Drive, La Mesa, CA 91942; (619) 460-0684.

RHI Skate Center, 5130 Kearny Mesa Road, San Diego, CA 92111; (800) 204-6253.

INDOOR SKATING RINKS
Wine Country

Star Skate World, 2075 Occidental Road, Santa Rosa, CA 95401; (707) 544-7000.

Gold Country

Sunrise Rollerland, 6001 Sunrise Vista Drive, Citrus Heights, CA 95628; (916) 961-3339.

Roller King, 889 Riverside Avenue, Roseville, CA 95678; (916) 782-7781.

Foothill Skate Inn Inc., 4700 Auburn Boulevard, Sacramento, CA 95841; (916) 488-4700.

Kings Skate Country, 2900 Bradshaw Road, Sacramento, CA 95827; (916) 363-2643.

San Francisco/The Peninsula

San Mateo Rolladium, 363 North Amphlett Boulevard, San Mateo, CA 94401; (415) 342-2711.

San Francisco Bay Area: East Bay

The Golden Skate, 2701 Hooper Drive, San Ramon, CA 94583; (510) 820-2525.

Central Valley North

Cal Skate, 2881 Peach Avenue, Clovis, CA 93611; (209) 291-0242.

Cal Skate of Lodi, 512 North Cherokee Lane, Lodi, CA 95240; (209) 334-0332.

Madera Skate, 1850 West Cleveland Avenue, Madera, CA 93637; (209) 674-7655.

Roller King, 2000 West Briggsmore Avenue, Modesto, CA 95350; (209) 521-6816.

Central Valley South

Rollerama, 1004 34th Street, Bakersfield, CA 93301; (805) 327-7589.

Skateland, 415 Ming Avenue, Bakersfield, CA 93307; (805) 831-5567.

Roller Towne, 520 South Linwood, Visalia, CA 93277; (209) 733-7474.

Central Coast North

Gilroy Skate Arena, 10th Street and Monterey Street, Gilroy, CA 95023; (408) 847-5283.

Del Monte Gardens Skating Arena, 2020 Del Monte Avenue, Monterey, CA 93940-3710; (408) 375-3202.

Skate Mor, 2198 Riverside Avenue, Paso Robles, CA 93446; (805) 237-9702.

Los Angeles County

Skate Depot, 11113 East 183rd Street, Artesia, CA 90701; (310) 924-0911.

Downey Skate, 11947 Paramount Boulevard, Downey, CA 90242; (310) 869-5245.

Skate O Rama Roller Rink, 12310 Woodruff Avenue, Downey, CA 90241; (310) 803-1446.

Roller City, 945 Bonita Avenue, Glendora, CA 91740; (818) 339-8453.

Hot Skates, 2411 Hyperion Avenue, Los Angeles, CA 90027; (213) 669-8429.

World On Wheels, 4645 1/2 Venice Boulevard, Los Angeles, CA 90019; (213) 933-3333.

Sherman Square Roller Rink, 18430 Sherman Way, Reseda, CA 91335; (818) 344-0866.

Fiesta Roller Rink, 136 South San Gabriel Boulevard, San Gabriel, CA 91776; (818) 287-6669.

Skate Junction, 901 West Service Avenue, West Covina, CA 91790; (818) 960-4402.

Inland Empire

Skate Express, 12356 Central Avenue, Chino, CA 91710; (909) 465-1383.

California Skate Grand Terrace, 22080 Commerce Way, Grand Terrace, CA 92313-5401; (909) 824-8114.

Holiday Roller Rink, 805 East Foothill Boulevard, Rialto, CA 92376; (909) 875-4233.

Holiday Skating Center, 14950 Palmdale Road, Victorville, CA 92392-2506; (619) 241-6813.

Orange County

Fountain Valley Skating Center, 9105 Recreation Circle, Fountain Valley, CA 92708; (714) 847-6300.

San Diego County

Rollerskateland, 626-L Chula Vista Street, Chula Vista, CA 91911; (619) 420-4761.

Ups-N-Downs Roller Rink, 862 North Broadway, Escondido, CA 92025-1820; (619) 745-5966.

Side By Side, 16091 Gothard Street, Huntington Beach, CA 92747-3608; (714) 847-8333.

Aquarius Roll A Rena, 8992 La Mesa Boulevard, La Mesa, CA 91941-4089; (619) 462-2778.

Skate San Diego at Sweetwater, 700 East 24th Street, National City, CA 91950; (619) 474-1000.

Skateworld Roller Rink, 6907 Linda Vista Road, San Diego, CA 92111; (619) 560-9349.

Rollerskateland, 9365 Mission Gorge Road, Santee, CA 92071; (619) 562-3790.

SKATING PARKS
North Mountains

Redding Indoor Hockey Arena, 1515 Charles Drive, Redding, CA 96001; (916) 223-2646.

Wine Country

Napa Community Skate Park, Pearl Street and Yajome, Napa, CA 94559; (707) 257-9529.

Santa Rosa Skate Park, 1700 Fulton Road, Santa Rosa, CA 95403; (707) 543-3737.

Gold Country

Ramps at The Shop, 306 North Sunrise Avenue, Roseville, CA 95661; (916) 773-2020.

The Grind, 2709 Del Monte Boulevard, Sacramento, CA 95691; (916) 372-7655.

San Francisco Bay Area: South Bay

Pali in Greer Park, East Colorado Street, Palo Alto, CA 94303; (415) 328-8555.

Derby Skate Park, Woodland Street, Santa Cruz, CA 93455; (408) 425-8578.

San Francisco Bay Area: East Bay

Benicia Skate Park, Willow Park at Seventh and West K, Benicia, CA 94510; (707) 746-4285.

Central Valley North

Davis Skateboard Park, Community Park at Covell Road, Davis, CA 95616; (916) 757-5626.

Central Valley South

RCI: Red Curbs Iron Lion Skateboard Park, 3164 North Marks #101 (near Shaw Street), Fresno, CA 93722; (209) 497-5466.

The Ark, West side of Fowler Avenue, three-quarters of a mile north of Herndon Avenue, Fresno, CA 93727; (209) 437-1630.

Visalia YMCA, 49716 Highway 180, Mira Monte, CA 93641; (209) 627-0700.

Sierra Nevada

Bijou Park, Al Tahoe Boulevard, South Lake Tahoe, CA 96156.

Central Coast North

Las Animas Park, Wayland Street, Gilroy, CA 95020.

Monterey Bay Sk8 Station, 1855 East Street, Sand City, CA 93955; (408) 646-5378.

Central Coast South

Atascadero Skate Park, 6351 Olmeda, Atascadero, CA 93422; (805) 461-4148.

Los Angeles County

UCLA Campus, 5151 Paseo Rancho Castillal, Los Angeles, CA 90032; (213) 343-3000.

Venice Beach, Windward Court Beachfront, Venice, CA 90291; (310) 450-0669.

Inland Empire

Sports Spectrum, 11530 Sixth Street, Cucamonga, CA 91730; (909) 980-6621.

Sk8 Underground, 24550 Sunnmead Boulevard, Moreno Valley, CA 92388; (909) 924-4573.

Orange County

Roller Skates of America, 1644 Superior Avenue, Costa Mesa, CA 92627; (714) 574-9966 (shop), (714) 760-6955.

San Diego County

Magdelena YMCA Skate Park, 200 Saxony Road, Encinitas, CA 92923; (619) 942-9622.

Mission Valley YMCA, 5505 Friars Road, San Diego, CA 92110; (619) 298-3576.

Index